ZHANG

Expanding Visions of a Shrinking World

HONGTU

ZHANG HONGTU: Expanding Visions of a Shrinking World

Editors:
Luchia Meihua Lee
Jerome Silbergeld

With Contributions by
Julia F. Andrews and Kuiyi Shen
Alexandra Chang
Tom Finkelpearl
Michael FitzGerald
Wu Hung
Luchia Meihua Lee
Morgan Perkins
Jerome Silbergeld
Eugenie Tsai
Thuy Linh Nguyen Tu
Lilly Wei

Queens Museum, New York, 2015
Duke University Press, Durham and London, 2015

Table of Contents

ACKNOWLEDGEMENTS

Luchia Meihua Lee and Jerome Silbergeld

To overcome many impediments and actually bring to fruition this book and exhibition about the art of Zhang Hongtu has involved a great effort on the part of many people and organizations. This project could not have been conceived of without the artist himself, Zhang Hongtu, and his wife, Miaoling Huang, an essential supporter of her husband, and also an artist herself. In his unceasing creation of a multifaceted art in an intercontinental career, Hongtu has always sought to expand the way in which viewers of his art perceive the world, and to draw connections between different cultures — hence the title of this book. Additional thanks are due to him for his two years of thoughtful and enthusiastic answers to our endless questions. Our special thanks are also due to an inspiring leader, the former executive director of the Queens Museum and now the New York City Commissioner of Cultural Affairs, Tom Finkelpearl, who has made this unique retrospective exhibition at the Queens Museum possible. It was Tom's vision to design this exhibition on a grand scale and give viewers an appreciation of the full scope of Zhang Hongtu's expansive career. This contrasts with many past exhibitions and publications, where we have glimpsed only parts of his work. Both this book and the associated exhibition offer wider and deeper coverage of this exceptional career than ever before.

Abundant gratitude is due to Tina Keng and Shelly Wu of TKG Foundation for Arts & Culture; without their support, neither the book nor the exhibition would have been possible. TKG Foundation for Arts & Culture has very keenly supported artists in Taipei and all over the world. The careful attention from Shelly and her team is reflected on every page of the book. In particular, Catherine Y. Hsieh has worked both on the book design and on the accompanying exhibition.

Manjari Sihare, former curatorial manager of the Queens Museum, has provided invaluable assistance and support throughout the various stages of development, and has stood beside Hongtu and us from the first day of the whole procedure. Also, our deep thanks go to the current Queens Museum director, Laura Raicovich, with her global and open-minded view; to Jodi Hanel, director of development, for supervising this book and exhibition project during her time at the Queens Museum; to Hitomi Iwasaki, director of exhibitions, for overseeing the whole; and to Louise Weinberg, registrar, who effectively facilitated the loans of art from various museums and collectors. The staff at the Queens Museum — including John Wanzel, exhibition production manager; and Sophia Marisa Lucas, curatorial assistant — has provided immeasurable administrative assistance.

We both have had many occasions — at exhibitions, lectures, and in classes — to meet and work with Hongtu. For example, the exhibition entitled "Infinity/Unknown: Culture and Identity in the Digital Age" at the Taipei Gallery of the Taipei Cultural Center of TECO (Taipei Economic and Cultural Office) in New York. Mounted in the Rockefeller Center McGraw-Hill Building, this exhibition contained several pieces that impressed Luchia and intrigued her with Hongtu's creative and advanced ideas in 2001. Numerous other exhibitions to display Hongtu's different artistic series, such as "Shuffling the Deck" at the Princeton University Museum, and "Reason's Clue" at the Queens Museum of Art in 2008, confirmed and strengthened this feeling for both co-editors of this book. For us, Zhang Hongtu is one of the artists we most respect and with whom we feel most comfortable among all the many Chinese artists in New York. With his free mind, his true genius, and his generous wit, Hongtu is simultaneously a traditional artist and a very modern character.

This book starts with an essay of introduction providing a full view of Hongtu's life and oeuvre. It closes by treating the environmental concerns that have marked the artist's recent development. In between, many distinguished authors provided admirable breadth. Wu Hung, from the University of Chicago, has a background similar to Hongtu's, and has contributed a superb in-depth essay on Hongtu's new work, *Great Wall with Gates*, and Hongtu's "Door" series. It is interesting to read in Thuy Linh Nguyen Tu's essay how the world of fashion design has been impacted by Hongtu's interpretation of Mao's image. Eugenie Tsai conducted an interview with Hongtu of more than 30,000 words covering the dialogue between Western and Eastern aesthetics, which she reduced to a size that could be accommodated in this book and gave the beautiful and mythical title of "The Man in the Moon." Michael FitzGerald, an expert in Cubism, presents an elegant analysis from Hongtu's Picasso pieces to the Cubist influence in his oeuvre. Also, our thanks to Alexandra Chang, who considers Hongtu's art in the context of the Chinese diaspora, and to Kuiyi Shen and Julia F. Andrews who joined forces for an essay about Hongtu's "Van Gogh" and "Buddha" series that presents them from a fresh perspective. Lilly Wei contributes an overview of the nexus between New York artists—and in particular, Hongtu—and popular culture. Morgan Perkins contributes an astute essay about the relationship between the artist and his oeuvre and its place in the world. Tom Finkelpearl reminds us of Hongtu's status as a member of the Queens art community.

Nell McClister was strongly recommended by Tom Finkelpearl as our copy editor, and she has provided us with attentive reading and perceptive editing. Tom also brought us to Duke University Press, where editorial director Ken Wissoker graciously accepted this project. Michael McCullough, sales manager, and Christopher Robinson, copy writer, brought their professionalism to publicizing and marketing this book. We would like to extend a heartfelt thanks to the Taiwanese American Arts Council founders, who allowed Luchia to take time that she would otherwise have contributed to the Taiwanese American community; they are Thomas Chen, Lung Fong Chun, and Patrick Huang. Also Crystal Window and Door Systems helped with the manufacture of exhibit vitrines. Many individuals, such as Kenneth Howell and Edward C. Hsu, helped to make this project run smoothly.

A panoply of collectors and organizations have facilitated this exhibition with generous loans of private and institutionally owned artworks. The Art Students League of New York curator Jillian Russo and Princeton University Art Museum Asian art curator Cary Y. Liu were especially helpful in arranging loans from their institutions. Tina Keng Gallery, Lin & Lin Gallery, and Ethan Cohen Fine Arts generously lent works for the exhibit. Sumiko Roberts from Christie's Japan provided help, as did Sotheby's. Other collectors, including Leo Shih, Andrew Cohen, Jeff Wimmer, Miani Johnson, and many private collectors also provided invaluable assistance in this regard.

Working with designer Lin Xiao-Yi of Atom No Color Design, and Shelly Wu and Catherine Y. Hsieh of TKG Foundation for Arts & Culture to see this book design take shape has been a great experience. You now hold in your hands the fruits of the extraordinary creativity and talent of their design.

FOREWORD: "DARING TO BREED THE HORSE WITH THE COW"

Laura Raicovich

If we believe that art and culture have the power to shift the ways in which we see the world around us, then Zhang Hongtu's work certainly provides an engaging example. Consistently willing to defy expectations by, in his own words, "daring to breed the horse with the cow," Hongtu performs mash-ups of icons and common objects, traditional forms and contemporary ideas, East and West, big philosophical questions and humor, the culturally specific and the universal. He pokes holes in (and fun at) what we might think we know, sometimes literally.

It has been a great pleasure to get to know Hongtu in my early days at the helm of the Queens Museum. Hongtu embodies the Queens ethos of hybridity through his life and art. Having emigrated from China in 1982, Hongtu hails from a particular generation of Chinese artists in America. Born to a devout Muslim Chinese family, he went to art school in China in 1964, lived through the vicissitudes and brutality of the Cultural Revolution, got married and had a son, came to the United States, bore outraged witness from afar to the tragedy of 1989's Tiananmen Square student protests, and has seen the impact of transformation in China via expanding migrations in his home borough of Queens—all throughout, working as a uniquely observant artist.

Looking backward and forward simultaneously is a great talent of Hongtu's. The exhibition on the occasion of which this book is published bears witness to his ability to shift among styles and iconographies, media, and cultural signs to create his signature hybrid paintings, objects, and installations. Taken together, this is a celebration of an artist's daily practice of thinking and making and thinking again. Thank you, Hongtu, for entrusting the Queens Museum with presenting such an expansive exhibition of your work. We are truly proud.

The Queens Museum is grateful to Luchia Meihua Lee for working so diligently and passionately as curator of the exhibition. Her dedication to the artist's vision is singular. We are also indebted to Tina Keng and TKG Foundation for Arts & Culture, without whose extraordinary support this exhibition would not be possible. Shelly Wu has been invaluable at every step of the way.

The lenders to the exhibition—including the Princeton University Art Museum, the Art Students League of New York, Jeff Wimmer, Miani Johnson, Ethan Cohen Fine Arts, Benito Sim, Lybess Sweeey and Ken Miller, The Contemporary Chinese Art Fund, Zhang Hongtu Studio, Lin & Lin Gallery, Leo Shih, and Tina Keng Gallery, Taipei—have made it a reality. It is a sheer delight to see Hongtu's works gathered so beautifully.

Sincere thanks also go to Jerome Silbergeld of Princeton University for serving with Luchia as co-editor of this publication and supporting Hongtu's work so enthusiastically. Further, each of the contributors to this book has added nuance and depth to our understanding of Hongtu's practice. And Duke University Press has been an ideal partner in the distribution of this tome.

At the Queens Museum, the show would not have been possible without curatorial manager Manjari Sihare's unrelenting dedication and thoughtfulness. Thanks also go to director of exhibitions and curator Hitomi Iwasaki, registrar and archives manager Louise Weinberg, and exhibition production manager John Wanzel, who, along with our entire installation crew, played crucial roles in mounting the exhibition.

It is an aim of the Queens Museum to show the work of artists whose visions reveal something about the ways in which our daily lives are constructed. Through "Zhang Hongtu: Expanding Visions of a Shrinking World" we are invited into his world, and as a result, we see ours in a new light.

*THE DISPLACED ARTIST SEES
THINGS FOR US:
ZHANG HONGTU AND THE ART OF
CONVERGENCE*

Jerome Silbergeld

The back of the Peng-bird measures I don't know how many thousand *li* across, and when he rises up and flies off, his wings are like
clouds all over the sky. When the Peng rises ninety thousand *li*, he
must have the wind under him. Only then can he mount on the back
of the wind, shoulder the blue sky, and nothing can hinder or block
him.

—Zhuangzi[1]

We live in an age of geographical compression, when technology has conspicuously
made the world "smaller" and brought all its parts into much closer communication.
No one needs to be told this; it is articulated by media and events throughout our daily lives. But what does it mean? What is its impact? Technologically induced compression is by no means new, but only within the past few generations has the pace of
compression increased to the point of making it readily visible within some fraction of

a human lifespan. In earlier times, it was the visionary or the transcendent being alone who could attain the overarching perspective, or "grand view" (*da guan* 大觀) as the Chinese called it, to adduce the changing nature of things and convey its meaning to those being changed. Metaphorically, to attain this view one had first to become displaced, transported from the normal to the extraordinary, to be like Zhuangzi's ascendant Peng-bird or to climb the Great Mountain. No better description of the human visionary exists than what Mencius wrote of the Master:

> Confucius ascended the Eastern Hill, and Lu appeared to him small. He ascended the Great Mountain, and all beneath the heavens appeared to him small. So he who has contemplated the sea, finds it difficult to think anything of other waters, and he who has wandered in the gate of the sage, finds it difficult to think anything of the words of others.
> 孔子登東山而小魯 , 登泰山而小天下 . 故觀於海者難為水 , 遊於聖人之門者難為言 .[2]

The lesser artist only has to draw well what the eye can see, to transfer things from one medium to another. The "real" artist must be transcendent, one who transmits his insight into something visible so that others can learn from this transcendent vision. His artistic impulse, which he must trust fearlessly, is the mighty wind that will bear him aloft. If displacement is the price of insight, then the life of Zhang Hongtu—punctuated by displacement in his family experience, in his relationship to China and its arts, in his place among the community of artists—should have more than its share of insight by which to fashion his art. Informed by cultural distance, he has (and not without some irony) focused his art on the major cultural characteristic of our time, namely, the expansion of cultures with the compression and convergence of geographies. The purpose of his art has been to liberate his viewers from those local values and outdated views bred into them by a world in which cultures that once seemed to exist as stable entities in isolation from one another now no longer do.[3]

A DISPLACED LIFE

Zhang Hongtu was born into a Muslim family that was regularly on the move and never quite belonged to any of the places it moved to. The family's ancestral home was Luoning, in Henan Province. But Hongtu's grandfather Zhang Wenzheng, who ran a fur and leather business—a common Muslim trade in China—kept a store in Xi'an while maintaining the family residence in Pingliang, a hundred miles northwest of Xi'an, in the northeast corner of the northwestern province of Gansu. Pingliang was deep in Muslim territory, and Hongtu's father, Zhang Bingduo, like many in his family, was devout (*Fig. 1*). In 1932 Zhang Bingduo was sent to Cairo for six years to study the Qur'an. On his return, he joined with other Muslim students in Chongqing, where he

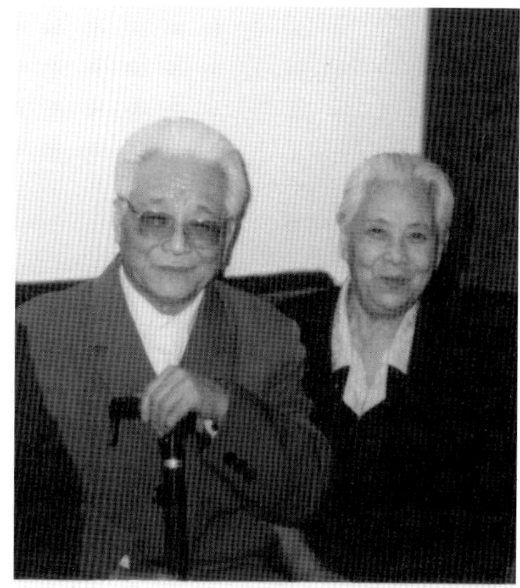

Fig. 1

broadcast in Arabic about the Japanese invasion. At the outset of the war, the young man was introduced as an Islamic scholar to the Nationalist government's minister of education, Zhu Jiahua, in Chongqing and refused, as a strict Muslim, to bow with him to a portrait of Sun Yat-sen. The incident drew considerable attention and was brought to the attention of Chiang Kai-shek, but Chiang excused Zhang Bingduo's behavior and even appreciated it for its religiosity. Later at an Islamic gathering, Zhang Bing-duo shocked even his fellow Muslims by demolishing a clay statue of the Prophet.

Zhang Bingduo soon moved back to Pingliang. Hongtu was born there in 1943 (he would be the second of four sons with one younger sister). Deeply involved in Islamic education, Zhang Bingduo traveled widely, founding schools to teach the Arabic language. Teaching, translating, producing a book on the sayings of the Prophet, and helping to establish Arabic-speaking religious schools kept him traveling constantly, north to Ningxia, south to Guilin. Then, with the war against Japan over but the Chinese Civil War raging, from 1947 to 1950 the entire family was mobilized. The Zhangs moved from Pingliang in the northwest to Shanghai, Suzhou, and Nanjing in the southeast, and back north to Zhengzhou. During this turbulent period, Zhang Bing-duo managed twice to go to Mecca on Haj. When the Communist victory seemed imminent, Zhang Bingduo acquired tickets for the entire family to depart for British-held Hong Kong, but a Muslim professor of history convinced him to remain in China, and the family moved instead to Beijing just as it became the new stronghold of Communist Party politics.

Unlike Pingliang, where Muslims were numerous, in Beijing the Zhangs were cultural outsiders. But Zhang Bingduo took advantage of the situation, and with his linguistic skills he worked for the new government's Minority Affairs Association, where he served as chief editor and translator for a government-run Arabic-language propaganda magazine, *Chinese Muslim*. He also worked with the government-regulated National Muslim Association and rose to become its vice president. But the family's religious and economic background increasingly became a serious political burden in a state where officially all religions were "tolerated" but the state itself was officially atheist. In practice, says Zhang Hongtu, state policy "mentally, psychologically destroys your beliefs. If the discrimination were physical, you'd be set back but you'd recover, you'd be even stronger. But this way the state destroyed Muslim people's identity." As the political rectification movements of the 1950s gathered momentum, Zhang Bingduo's "revolutionary inheritance" and Islamic activities finally caught up with him: for his father's "capitalist" background and pre-1949 association with the Nationalists ("basically, just making the payoffs required to protect his business," says Zhang Hongtu), for the family's religious activity, and for his public support of a multi-party system for China, Zhang Bingduo was branded a rightist in the Anti-Rightist Campaign of 1957. Hongtu's mother, Zheng Shouzheng, lost her job. His father avoided being sent down for political reeducation; despite his "rightist" label, his language skills were unusual and much needed and eventually he was sent to work with the Arabic languages department of the Xinhua News Agency.

During the Great Leap Forward, beginning in 1958, things got worse. Famine set in as a result of economic mismanagement, and recriminations were directed against the peasantry itself, ultimately resulting in the loss of thirty or more million lives through starvation and mass executions. Zhang Hongtu recollects:

> We discovered all the hungry people, beggars from the country so skinny, with no clothes. Every single day, and you're so hungry yourself that you just couldn't sleep but so tired you can't wake up. We heard one thing from school and the newspapers but we saw something else from reality and we felt betrayed. You needed a scale to weigh out food to make sure there'd be some at the end of the month. I'd go with my father to the park to pick plants to eat.

By 1963, Zhang Bingduo was working for the Central Broadcasting Administration. But learning Arabic was no longer welcome around the house. One could no longer pray five times daily, and talk of religion disappeared. A strict fundamentalist whose ideals combined Confucian and Islamic discipline, Zhang Bingduo afterwards became bad-tempered, "angry all the time, even worse than most Chinese fathers." In 1966, at the outset of the Cultural Revolution, the National Muslim Association was disbanded. After the Cultural Revolution ended in 1976, it was reestablished and Zhang Bingduo was invited back to his old position, but, deeply disillusioned, he refused. The government's disingenuousness, he said, was just like the old Chinese idiom, "hanging out a sheep's head [advertising lamb] but only selling dog meat" (*gua yang tou mai gou rou* 掛羊頭賣狗肉).

A LIFE IN ART

The Muslim proscription against representational art was not widely adhered to among Chinese believers, but the strict Zhang Bingduo was not a father who wanted his son to become an artist. Hongtu inherited his father's iconoclastic views of art, but Zhang Bingduo was no icon to his son. Given the official intolerance of religion in the 1960s, the father resisted Hongtu's artistic ambitions, but he could hardly enforce his own religious objections to Hongtu's study of art. At the age of sixteen, in 1960, Hongtu enrolled in the high school attached to Beijing's prestigious Central Academy of Fine Arts. There he studied Western painting and drawing, as well as some Chinese ink painting. The training was designed to produce "one more screw in the Great Revolutionary Machine." From 1954 to 1957, the academy students were offered training in Socialist Realist–style oil painting by the Soviet advisor Konstantin Maksimov. By the time Hongtu arrived, China's relationship with the Soviet Union had turned hostile, and all the advisors had been sent home. In 1960, Mao's Anti-Rightist Campaign and his disastrous Great Leap Forward obliged the party chairman to cede his position as head of state to Liu Shaoqi. In an attempt to win the educated class back into the fold, discriminatory policies toward China's cultural past were relaxed and ink painting made something of a comeback. But in art education, European history still stopped just before Impressionism, and everything from there onward was dismissed as "corrupt, reactionary, decadent, and declining bourgeois arts." In the 1960s and '70s, bad art and artists were not just shunned, they were displayed in "black arts" exhibitions, paraded in public, and denounced. Hongtu's class was taken to an exhibition of "negative examples" at the National Gallery of Art in 1963. Still, he remembers, "It afforded me the opportunity to see the art of Georges Rouault, which I have loved ever since."

In 1964, Hongtu's graduation year, the Socialist Education Movement was launched as a prelude to the Cultural Revolution and Mao's return to power. Mao's wife, Jiang Qing, began her own rise to cultural hegemony with an attack on the Central Academy, with the result that the academy was closed to new admissions. So Hongtu began his professional art studies instead, at Beijing's Central Academy of Arts and Crafts, the nation's leading institution for training commercial artists. While still oriented toward painting, he chose to study in the ceramics department "because Picasso also did ceramics." One year ahead of him in the department was the student Huang Miaoling, with whom he began a shy courtship and who later became his wife (*Fig. 2*).

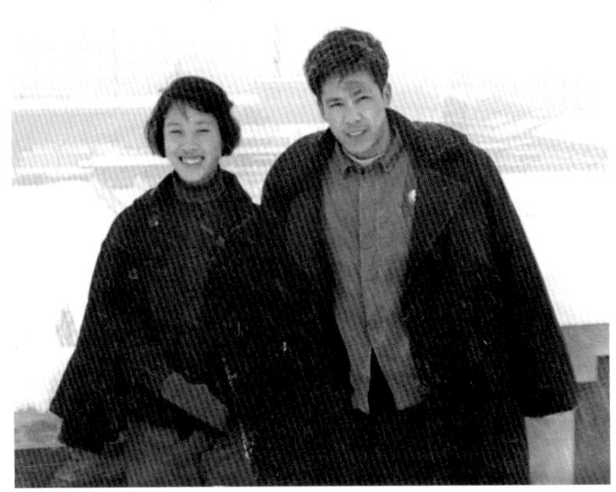

Fig. 2

Two years afterward, in 1966, the outbreak of the Cultural Revolution put an end to Hongtu's art studies, and political activities took center stage.

At the outset of the Cultural Revolution, Chinese trains were made available for free student travel throughout the country under the policy of "linking up" with the people. This served the dual function of bringing the revolution "down" to the masses and educating the educated about the lives of the common people. The well-traveled Zhang Hongtu became a traveler again, first taking the train west to Xinjiang (to Urumqi and Wusu, in Muslim territory, where all of the mosques had been closed down in the cultural "cleansing"), then from there to Guangzhou in the far southeast. In Guangzhou, however, Zhang was stranded: the "linking up" program had become unmanageable, and the free-travel campaign was suddenly ended by the government. With the famous Long March in mind as a model, Zhang and his friends decided on a "long march" of their own across the countryside, using their art in the service of the current political movement. As a "test march," Zhang and one friend first walked southward overland "toward the sea," a goal they never quite reached. Then, a group of five, including Yu Youhan, who was a year behind Zhang at the Central Academy and later would become a prominent painter, marched north over rugged mountain terrain to the Jinggang Mountains in Jiangxi Province, the scene of Mao's earliest organizational activities on behalf of the young Chinese Communist Party. From there, walking week after week, Zhang and one friend headed westward to Mao's birthplace at Shaoshan. Along the way, they bore flags and a portrait of Chairman Mao, held high at all times, and bore on their backs a heavy set of wooden printing blocks they had carved. At each of the villages they passed through, they printed and distributed sets of propaganda leaflets on three political themes: "The Foolish Old Man Removes the Mountains" (Mao's propaganda tale about removing the dual burdens of feudalism and imperialism); the "barefoot doctor" Norman Bethune (a Canadian who rose above nationalism to serve the medical needs of rural peasants); and illustrations to a text

entitled "Serve the People." After their stay at Shaoshan, the two young revolution-
aries returned by train to Beijing.

By the time of Zhang's return, the Cultural Revolution had begun to take its ven-
geance on the Zhang family. The young artist found himself being criticized as a "black
sprout of revisionism" for his family's political background and for his strong interest
in Western art. As a result, he was proscribed from painting Mao's portrait. But his
"linking up" travels, by contrast, had been "so happy," Zhang remembers. "Nobody
bothered me at that time about my family background. It was nice to see the landscape, so nice for a city boy. But after this trip, I changed a lot. The bad part is, I saw
people kill each other, literally." He remembers a middle-aged man beaten to death
by a group of kids with a belt "for being a capitalist." "I began to ask, 'Is this really the
"Cultural Revolution"?' I saw people put so many books all together like a hill and then
burn them. I saw so many poor people, it was beyond my imagination. The reality of
it didn't fit my imagination of the Cultural Revolution. I got back and instead of being
a participant, I became an 'escapist' (*xiaoyao pai* 逍遙派)." In Beijing, the family home
was searched by Red Guards for counter-revolutionary materials, and although none
were found, Hongtu was obliged to criticize his father "again and again, deeper and
deeper." He recalls, "At first, I trusted everything Mao wrote. I found Mao's writings so
idealistic that I followed him." But all this turned into a sense of betrayal.

> I had to criticize my own painting. I was denounced by my own friends with "big
> character posters." After that, you lose all your trust in people. One friend, who
> was so good toward me but really was just spying, checked out my diary without
> telling me, to see how badly I hated the Communist Party. He found nothing and
> said so, but I was so hurt. After that, I couldn't write anything. That was the worst
> result of the Cultural Revolution. To this day, people don't trust each other, don't
> think about the future, they just think about themselves and find security only in
> making money. That's hard to change now, and most people in my generation
> just don't want to talk about the Cultural Revolution. But at least people afterward
> had to reconsider the Communist Party, to re-examine Mao, and maybe if not for
> that, China today would be another North Korea.

Except for ongoing political routines, criticism and self-criticism, education came to
an end at the Central Academy of Arts and Crafts in 1966. The entire school was then
sent down to the countryside, to Huolu near Shijiazhuang, the capital of Hebei Province, to work for three years in the rice fields there. The last two years there, they were
permitted to make artwork on Sundays, storing their painting equipment in the same
baskets they used for collecting cow pies, so that they became known as the "Dung
Basket School of Painting" (*fen kuang huapai* 糞筐畫派). In 1972, at the end of their

rustication period, to conclude their five-year term-to-degree, the class was assembled and belatedly given their diplomas—minus an education.

One year later, Zhang was assigned to work with the Beijing Jewelry Import-Export Company, organized under the Second Ministry of Light Industry, producing items to be sold abroad as part of the government's capital-raising campaign. "I never saw my mother wear jewelry," Zhang wondered, "so how could I design anything?" The answer to that question was, their designs were all based on photographs from imported fashion magazines. "In an era where wearing jewelry was condemned as 'bourgeois lifestyle,' what an absurdity!" During his nine years of producing professional jewelry designs, Zhang made his own artwork only on evenings and Sundays, mostly still-life drawings, landscapes, and paintings from models. Toward the end, from 1979 to 1981, he joined an unofficial art group, which was then very daring in China, both politically and artistically. In June 1980, his "Contemporaries" group (*Tong Dai Ren* 同代人) became the first unofficial art group to exhibit their work at the National Art Gallery, two months before the better-known "Stars" Group (or "Sparks," *Xingxing Hua Pai* 星星畫派) exhibition there, with works consisting mostly of landscapes and portraits. Zhang exhibited his painting of an anonymous Han dynasty artisan sculpting the now-famous funerary statue of a tiger at the first-century BCE tomb of Huo Qubing, Han emperor Wudi's favorite general. This was the first of Zhang's paintings to attract major attention and was collected by the National Art Gallery. Zhang's idea for the painting was simple but not intended to be apparent to most people: "Everybody says 'Mao Zedong *wansui*, Long live to Chairman Mao.' I just wanted to ask, Which will live longer, Mao or art?" Even the artist himself is shown as tired, short-lived. Thus the title of the work, *Eternal Life*, applies to the art itself (*Plate 1*).[4]

After nearly a decade of uninspiring work as a commercial designer, in 1981, Zhang suggested to his supervisors that they send him to study the early Buddhist cave paintings at Dunhuang in Gansu Province, from the fourth through fourteenth centuries, to gather ideas for his jewelry design.

> I found a way to go there, which is the bad part of myself: I cheated my company. I used nationalism to encourage them. We had these magazines from Japan and from Hong Kong and Italy. I said, "Our own jewelry design cannot only follow Japanese and Hong Kong style. We have our own style." I could have done the same study from photographs of Dunhuang, but that idea got me there. I spent two days there making jewelry drawings from the painted Bodhisattvas—when I got back, everybody said "Good! You've made so many sketches!"—and twenty-nine days on my own making copies of the murals, which became very important for my later paintings.

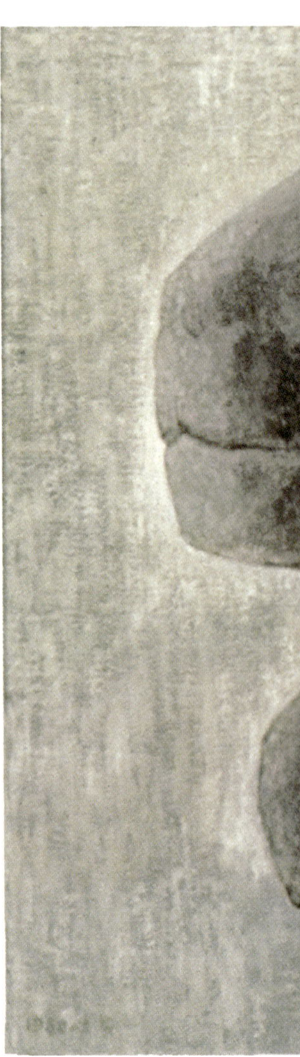

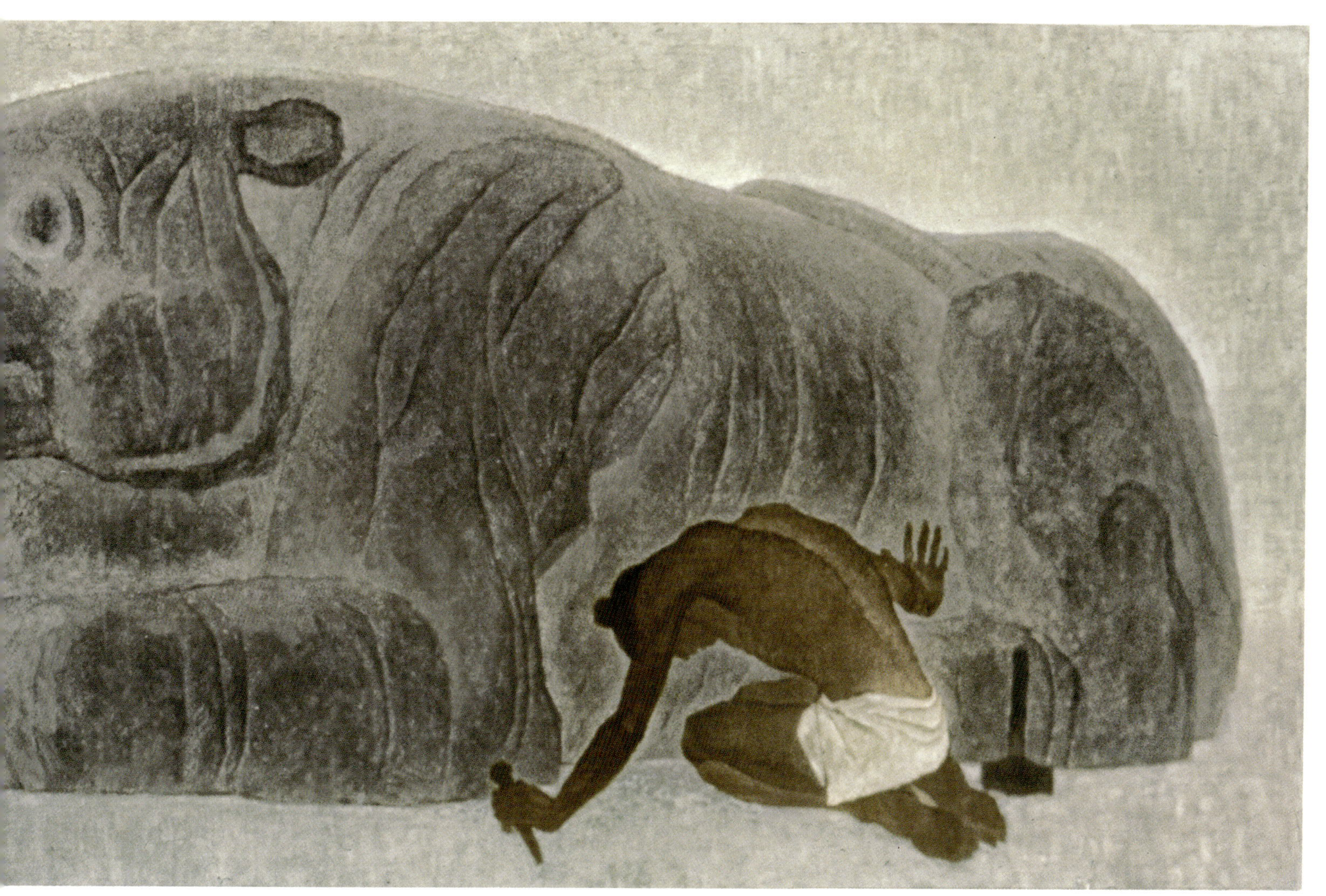

Eternal Life, 1980. Oil on canvas, 33 ½ x 63 ½ in.

What Zhang experienced and learned at Dunhuang changed his life. What it had to do with, most of all, was *freedom*. Contemplating the focused, mechanized, and limited nature of his education, he muses that in his student days, everyone made plaster portraits of classroom models, and after returning from lunch to work, you couldn't even tell whose work was whose. Dunhuang taught him, above all, about how much he had not been taught and barely even knew existed. He now recalls:

> To me, Dunhuang was new, not old. It was the start and the source to me, to learn something new, even though it goes back fifteen hundred, two thousand years . . . . After Dunhuang, there was a big difference in my work, for example in mixing and using colors. I just felt more freedom. Being an artist my whole life, most important is freedom, not only freedom from dictatorship, not only freedom from any pressure from society, but also being free from what you learned when you are young.

Zhang Hongtu found in the early Dunhuang artists' unconventional use of color, line, and narrative structure—which modern artists might either dismiss or embrace as "folk art"—a liberation from the confines of his Socialist Realist artistic training. He says of a copy that he made of one Buddhist mural (*Plate 8*), which today hangs prominently in his living room, "They're dancing on the mountains and the dancing actually has nothing to do with the story, but the mountains under their feet, or between their legs, and these eight people above the mountains—that made me just go crazy! I really, really liked it." And from all this, he draws a historical lesson:

> Among the literati painters [from China's past], really, nobody knew about Dunhuang, nobody even mentioned it. If we could have borrowed from Dunhuang five hundred years ago, Chinese painting would be different, Chinese art history would have been different. So I ask myself, with so many smart artists, why didn't they do that? When I was in art school, I hated Socialist Realism. I really hated it. You couldn't challenge Socialist Realism with Picasso or with Matisse during that period when I was a student, for they would just be called bourgeois, decadent artists. But I thought that if you opposed Socialist Realism with something from ancient China, it made more sense to the teacher, to other Chinese people. If you said, "Oh, this is Dunhuang influence," nobody would really bother you. Socialist "realism" was never really realistic. You always had a formula: Mao Zedong always had to be taller than everyone else, and soldiers, peasants, and workers always had to be red-cheeked with big muscles. Even the composition of the painting has nothing to do with being realistic. But in school, everything is just like copying a photo. If you're painting a model, you have to make it look as much like him as possible and don't put any personal feeling, don't put any

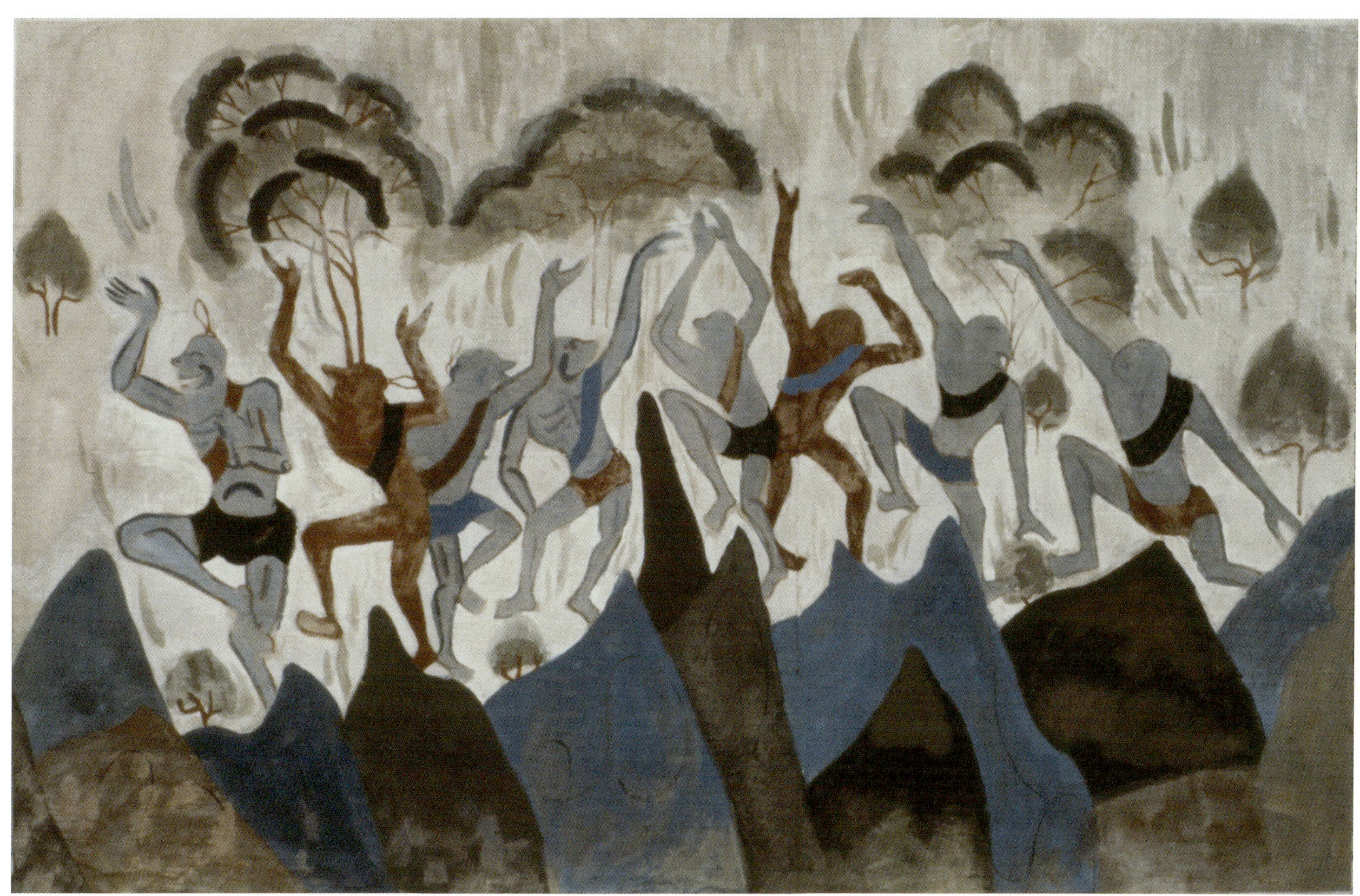

Plate 8

Dunhuang Study #7: Copy of Eight Beggars Who Went to See the Buddha, Dunhuang Cave 428, 1981. Ink and gouache on rice paper, 42 x 66 in.

personality or your own ideas into the painting. The painting is not about you. It's about the model. But Dunhuang lets you express *yourself*.

The attention given to Zhang's painting *Eternal Life* helped him win an unofficial invitation to join the faculty at his old institution, the Central Academy of Arts and Crafts. Similar offers came, for a drawing position in the architecture department at Tsinghua University and for an oil painting position at the Central Academy of Fine Arts. He requested permission to change jobs, but the jewelry company would not release his file. He argued, fought with them. "I said, 'I never studied jewelry and we should work at what we studied.' But nobody argues with you, and there was only one word in response: No." Conditioned by years of discrimination as a Muslim, politically alienated, inspired to seek new possibilities by his Dunhuang experience, and now frustrated as an artist with his creative future at stake, he determined at that moment to leave the country for the sake of his work. This well-traveled artist was set to go traveling once more. Zhang cited an opportunity to study at the Art Students League in New York as his excuse, and to his great surprise, the jewelry design company complied in great haste. In only three days he had their permission. The prestige of Zhang's Huo Qubing painting had helped him get his American visa.

A LIFE ABROAD

In 1972, Zhang had married his fellow ceramics student from the Central Academy of Arts and Crafts, Huang Miaoling—today a fine artist in her own right—and in 1976 they became parents to a son, Dasheng. A devoted family man, Zhang was obliged to leave his wife and son behind to come to the United States in 1982, not knowing what would come next. It was two years before his family was able to follow him. The economics of his move did not make things easy. For years to come, Zhang worked in construction, painting walls for $50 a day and cutting stone, as well as cutting mats for a fine-art framing company. Two years passed, and then he managed to sell two paintings. The second of these went for $1,800 to the World Bank in Washington, DC, which gave him some encouragement. Another early work, *Fish*, from 1985 (*Plate 11*), expressed his feeling of being a fish out of water, an ocean away from the world he knew and understood. Is it any wonder that his fish stare at us as consciously as we stare at them, both fish and audience uncertain about the "reality" of this coming ashore?

In 1987, Zhang had no idea of the significance when he took brush in hand and added a bit of paint to a cylindrical box of Quaker Oats cereal. Every day throughout his years in America he had been eating oatmeal, which came closest to the breakfast gruel he had been used to in China, and it occurred to him one morning that there

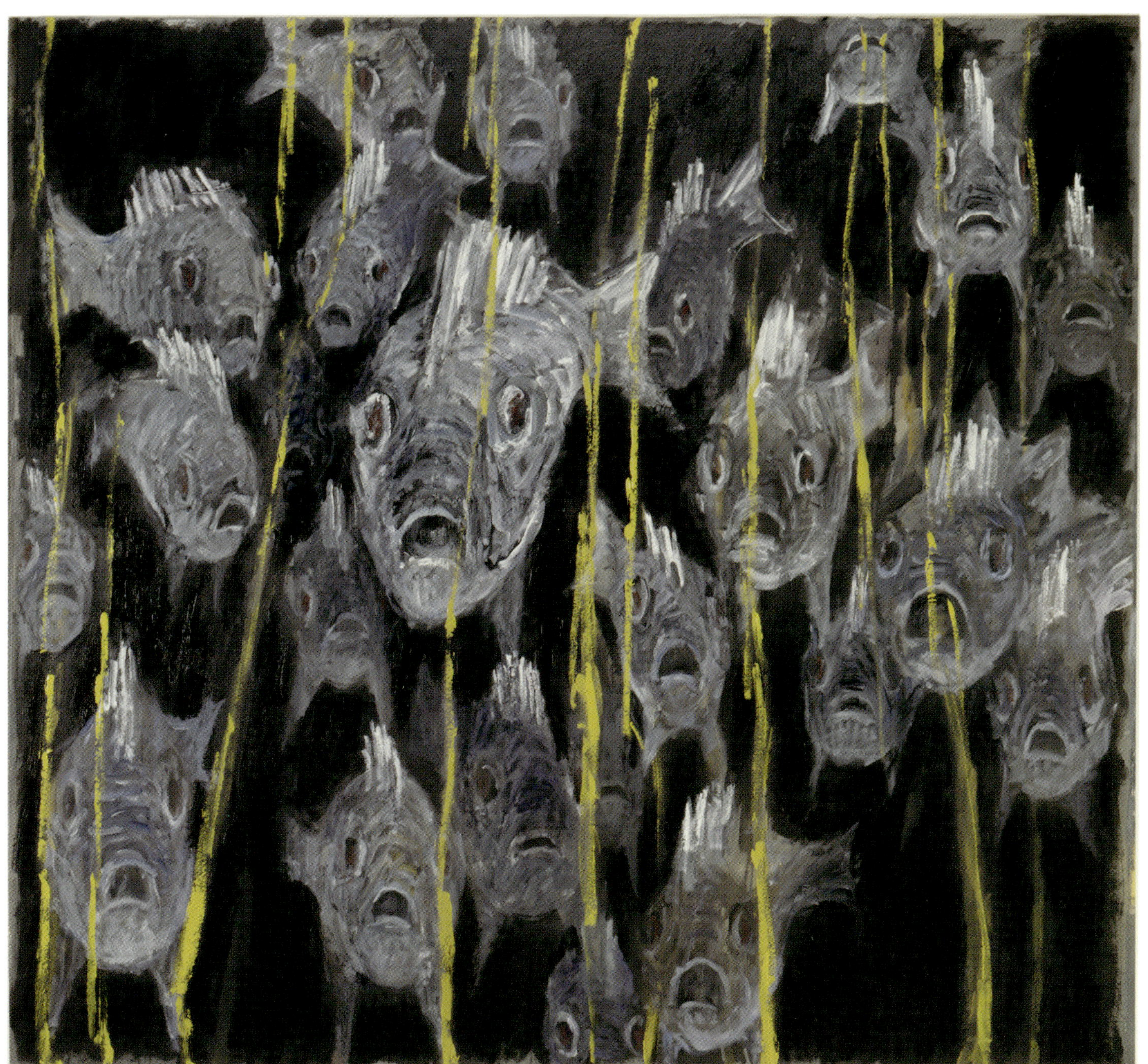

Plate 11

Fish, 1985. Acrylic on canvas, 65 x 72 in.

was more than a passing resemblance between the "Quaker Man" on his breakfast table and Chairman Mao back home. The idea that the chairman was ubiquitous—so hard to get away from, even here in America—and that just a few quick strokes of the brush could turn an American icon into a Chinese one, proved to be another turning point in Zhang's career. With those few strokes he possibly became the first exemplar of the "Political Pop" movement that helped launch contemporary Chinese painting on its current international trajectory.[5] He had no idea (until I told him, years later) that the Quaker Oats Company was a foremost corporate contributor to anti-Communist politics in America throughout the Cold War era, sending a living, dressed-up "Mr. Quaker" to schools across the country to lecture young students on the dangers of the "international Communist conspiracy."

Zhang's "experiment" was the beginning of a long romance between Chinese and Western icons. His *Quaker Oats Mao* boxes themselves became iconic of the experimental movement in contemporary Chinese art, but not before another work drew even greater attention. Painted shortly after the traumatic events surrounding Tiananmen Square in the spring of 1989, Zhang's *Last Banquet* satirized the Communist deification of Mao Zedong and the sanctity of Mao's ideological scriptures. The irony of Mao's ideological rigidity, centered on his published writings and his Little Red Book, was an "all Mao all the time" conformity in which Mao worshipped Mao and, in a self-initiated fall from grace, Mao betrayed Mao. In 1990, responding to the Tiananmen massacre, a senatorial group sponsored an exhibition in the Russell Rotunda of the United States Capitol, for which Zhang submitted this work. The irony of ironies, then, came when the liberal senior senator from Massachusetts, Edward Kennedy, barred the inclusion of this work as "sacrilegious." With this, Zhang had come full circle, censored on two continents, including an American exhibition protesting censorship in China. Rather than submitting a substitute piece as requested, Zhang pulled out of the exhibition and most of his fellow artists followed suit. When *Last Banquet*, originally priced at $4,000, was sold five years later for $50,000, Zhang was astounded and decided it was time at last to quit his construction work and become a full-time artist in America.

Zhang's *Quaker Oats Mao* boxes and his *Last Banquet* helped set the stage for his subsequent work, much of which drew on his uncomfortable experiences as a displaced observer, first as a Muslim outsider in China, next as a disenfranchised painter, and then as a Chinese exile in America. Reaching back into his personal history, he began to draw deeply on the contradictions of his own life. From his father, Zhang inherited an ironic attitude toward art, a belief that art is not meant for profit or personal reputation. "Art is art," his father had said, not for representation but for ethical instruction. At the same time, Zhang believes in the positive value of art: "I do not believe in the *authority* of the image," he emphasizes. "I do believe in the *power* of the image." Zhang's works are all about authority and belief, about the power that icons exercise over the audience. His iconoclasm is cross-cultural, designed to offend all audiences equally, and to have something positive left over in the form of "fun," a good laugh, a deeper political understanding, and, despite his father's fundamentalism, something beautiful.

> People try to understand each other across cultures, but there are walls there. In my art, I try to make a way through the wall, to put a door or a hole in the wall, by using Western art with my own art. There's a Chinese saying, "You can't breed a horse with a cow" (*feng ma niu bu xiangji* 風馬牛不相及). My work is the opposite, like "Daring to breed the horse with the cow" (*pianyao feng ma niu* 偏要風馬牛).

Combining the positive with the negative, Zhang's next major projects grew out of the pattern established by these two seminal works, *Quaker Oats Mao* and *Last Banquet*.

First came several series of Mao Zedong portrait projects—his *Chairmen Mao* (1989), his "Material Mao" series (done mostly in 1992–93), and his "Unity and Discord" series (nine works, from 1997). These were followed by "Repainted Shan Shui," a landscape series that is still ongoing in a revised format. These works, each in its own way, took on important aspects of traditions East and West. Zhang uses the term "hybrid" to describe this series, but in the sense of their being meta-hybrids:

> Because of the influence from my life experiences and my multicultural background, I have always been interested in different cultures and the relationship between them. My recent "hybrid" works don't give an answer to these current issues such as "globalization," "East and West," "high and low," elite culture from the museum and mass culture from the society. Rather, what I have been doing via my art is to question viewers' conventional taste, to evoke viewers' thinking on these issues from a different perspective.

Works in Zhang's *Chairmen Mao* piece represent this hybridity, like his portrait of the Chairman sporting a thick Stalinesque moustache, à la Duchamp's *Mona Lisa*, with the letters below, "H.I.A.C.S.," adapted from Duchamp and intended to mean "He is a Chinese Stalin."[6] His portrait of the Chairman in pigtails was made to illustrate Mao's adage "The Masses are the real heroes, while we ourselves are often childish and ignorant." Works in this series became so popular that they appeared on book covers, and international fashion designer Vivienne Tam used them in a "Fashion Mao" dress design series in 1994.

Zhang's *Mao* works feature Mao's presence-through-absence, appearing everywhere (in grass, in popcorn, in wire mesh) and nowhere at all.

> If you stare at a red shape for a long time, when you turn away, your retina will hold the image, but you will see a green version of the same shape. In the same way, when I lived in China, I saw the positive image of Mao so many times that my mind now holds a negative image of Mao. In my art I am transferring this psychological feeling to a physical object.

To this Zhang adds, "Sometimes the hole in my work might remind you of the Nothingness of Daoism or the negative space of traditional Chinese ink painting. But the visual inspiration of my work really comes directly from a bagel!" (Spoken like a real New Yorker.) What is left of Zhang's ping-pong table of 1995 once the holes have been cut (beyond recalling the sports exchange that accompanied America's adoption of the "One-China" policy in 1972, which Zhang says he did not have in mind at the time but was brought up by many early reviews) should remind his audience of the narrow line that one has to tread in Chinese politics, neither straying too far from Party dicta nor getting too close to the dangerous center of politics: a reminder of how Mao turned against most of his closest cohorts, one by one. Each of the *Mao* works leaves viewers with the opportunity to see Mao and Maoism in their own way, just as his diverse and often-divided followers did for themselves.

The figures in Zhang's "Unity and Discord" panels look back to a classic photograph of Mao at Tiananmen in 1966, reviewing Red Guards at the outset of the Cultural Revolution. Painted in the manner of various Western artists—Seurat, Picasso, Magritte, de Kooning, Roy Lichtenstein, Joseph Kosuth, and others—they mix East and West in composition and style, extending the hybridity in Zhang's *Quaker Oats Mao* and *Last Banquet* and forming a bridge to Zhang's "Repainted Shan Shui" landscape series.

AN ART OF CONVERGENCE

After arriving in New York on a student visa in 1982, Zhang studied for four years at the Art Students League, and he spent weeks and months in New York's museums studying and practicing the techniques of Cézanne, Monet, and Van Gogh. But his studies of these artists did not begin there. His affection for these three artists dates back to a Swedish-published book on world art that he saw in 1962, while still in high school. Not something one could buy in a store, not even in those slightly more liberal days under President Liu Shaoqi, this gift to his school was a book forbidden to students but showed to him by a teacher. Only a few years later, during the Cultural Revolution, Zhang would be publicly exposing his own paintings inspired by this vision and using them as the basis for his required self-criticisms. Going back to his last years in China, one sees in his luminous and skillfully arranged paintings of persimmon orchards and grazing cows his absorption of these artists' lessons, violating taboos and pushing against cultural barriers.[7] Decades later, from 1998 on, Zhang began to wed these famous European brush styles to equally famous Chinese painting compositions in his series "Repainted Shan Shui": Fan Kuan and Guo Xi painted in the manner of Van Gogh, Ni Zan meets Monet, Dong Qichang as seen by Cézanne, Shitao's studio shimmering beneath Van Gogh's starry sky, and so forth (*Plate 70*).

In New York, Zhang found himself even more dislocated than he had ever been as a Muslim and a cultural dissident in China. Chinese treated him as a New Yorker while New Yorkers still regard him as Chinese. Is it any wonder that this "outsider" art should seek to locate and blur the boundary between East and West? A lifetime of social peripheralization helped Zhang develop a philosophical perspective on the question of boundaries. Actually, while radical and irreverent, the hybridizing here goes only one step beyond the radicalism of Dong Qichang, who, in the seventeenth century, taught Chinese artists how to select the "best" artists from the past (his own favorites, only, and no others), extract the "essence" of each, and systematically blend them together in a "great synthesis" (*da cheng* 大成). Dong's once-radical teaching—with features that might strike today's viewers as foreshadowing Cubism or fractal structures—proved so successful that it ultimately became a new conservatism, the settled orthodoxy for generations to come. While Dong's strategy was geographically inward and culturally backward-looking, sometimes seen as extracting the last remaining ounce of life from the Chinese tradition, Zhang's step beyond Dong Qichang was to stretch the Chinese realm, drawing it into the context of a world of convergent arts and cultures. Zhang referenced this process in his inscription on a composition by Dong's follower Wang Hui, which he painted in the manner of Monet:

> Scholars consider Wang Hui's life work to have been based on the copying of ancient masters, in such a way that he learned to master the techniques of the many great artists since the Song and Yuan dynasties. Wang Hui himself said, "It would be a great accomplishment to have combined the lines of the Yuan, the composition of the Song, and the magnificence of the Tang." Is it not all the more marvelous to add to that the color of the famous Impressionists?[8]

Zhang understands that for Dong Qichang, as for the post-Impressionists who three centuries later drew inspiration from East Asia, painting was no longer a matter of just visually representing things but of establishing aesthetically conceptual structures, always with an eye toward history. And he understands, too, that there has to be more in such works than meets the eye. "It's no good just to surprise people, and for them

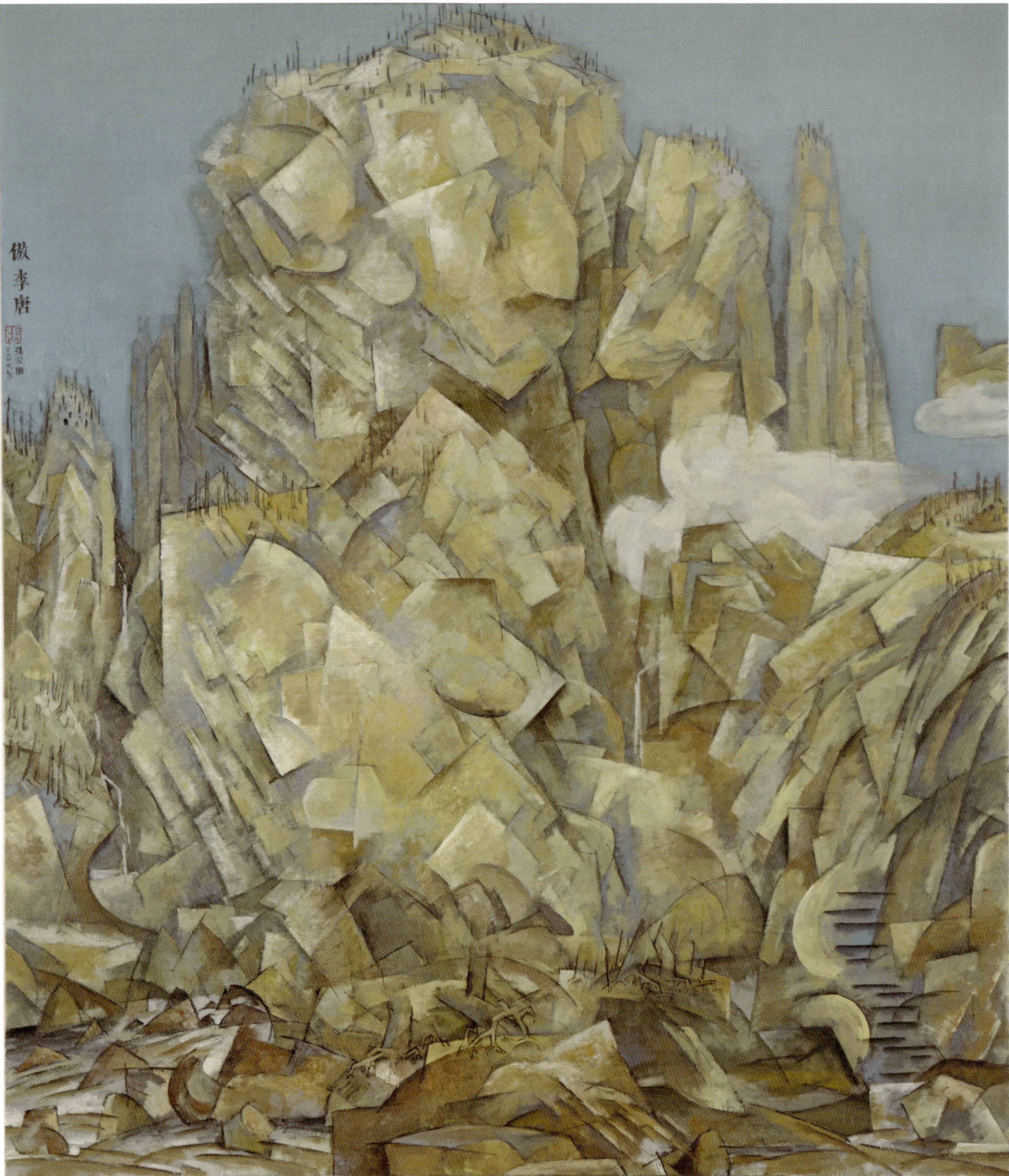

Plate 70

then to find that there's really nothing much there." Like Xu Bing's now-famous unreadable "Chinese characters" in his *Book from the Sky*, which aren't Chinese characters at all, Zhang's deconstructive mode is all about engaging viewers' expectations with the unanticipated aspects of his art and depends on their participation.

> Beauty attracts the audience, but then the audience has to go to the second level. If it is too easy, people won't appreciate your work. If it's too difficult, there's no room for them to finish their part. If you present your work to the public, people have the right to create your work in their own imagination, even to misunderstand it.

He appreciates that some in his audience have felt him to be sacrilegious, making a "plaything" out of "serious" art that ought to be seriously revered. "That's good," he asserts. He also sympathizes when the audience feels he hasn't fully mastered these master painters' styles, despite his best efforts to do so:

> Fortunately, I'm not trying to be them. Still, it's a very nice challenge. But the challenge depends on who you are in the audience, Chinese or Western. The Chinese part is easy. If it looked like Van Gogh came to Hongtu's studio and helped him finish this painting, then it wouldn't be Hongtu. Van Gogh's paintings were small, while mine are many times bigger. When I move my arm over a bigger painting than his, it *has to be* different. A smaller painting can look so fresh, since Van Gogh added wet oils to still-wet oils, but working on a bigger scale, the paint dries and when you go back to add more paint, it's not in time and the paint is more dull. But I'm getting better!

Little has escaped Zhang's attention, or the broad technical range of his training in the arts and crafts, as he extends the concepts of Dong Qichang and Andy Warhol into the three-dimensional realm with a repackaging of a McDonald's burger and fries like a Shang dynasty (ca. 1600–ca. 1046 BCE) bronze set, and a celebration of Coca-Cola's universal reach via Ming dynasty (1368–1644) blue-and-white ceramics, the latter done with the assistance of his talented wife, Huang Miaoling, and the technicians of Jingdezhen. A computer aficionado as well as a traditional calligrapher, Zhang has tied the fourth-century calligraphic style of Wang Xizhi to the modern exploitation of Chinese labor through mock help-wanted in Chinatown ads, written with soy sauce and then digitized in the style of a Christie's auction catalog, with an estimated sale price and all the trappings. One of Zhang's finest works in the computerized realm is his large-scale double hanging scroll of *Bikers*, the first edition of which was produced in 2001, with dozens of Chinese bikers whom Zhang photographed individually and in small groups from a Beijing overpass, then digitally collaged into two compositions, with painting and calligraphy in the distance. In the first scroll, the bikers are seen riding out of the past, with the upper portion of Shen Zhou's *Lofty Mount Lu* of 1467 behind them, suggesting their cultural past.[9] But then they turn around and head into the cultural grasp of Chairman Mao, represented in his own calligraphic script with his famous poem "Snow," of 1936, in which the chairman pauses to praise the Chinese landscape ("This land so rich in beauty") before strutting his ambition ("For truly great men / Look to this age alone").[10] The contrast, for Zhang, is wrapped in the irony that in its failure, Mao's Great Proletarian Cultural Revolution stripped China of great men and robbed most Chinese of any ambition loftier than to make a lot of money.

Ultimately, duality became Zhang's overarching mechanism. He spent years learning and using Western brush techniques, eventually applying them to Chinese compositions. Having achieved this, like the bikers coming and going in his double photomontage, he decided, "If I tried to reverse the situation and paint a Western composition in Chinese styles, that would be even more difficult," and set himself the goal of painting all thirty-nine extant Van Gogh self-portraits in a variety of traditional Chinese ink techniques, from Liang Kai and Muqi of the later thirteenth century through Bada Shanren of the seventeenth century. After studying these brush-and-ink techniques as rigorously as he did those of Van Gogh, Cézanne, and Monet, Zhang began painting the entire series of portraits in 2007 and eventually completed the cycle, including a depiction of Van Gogh as Bodhidharma, the first patriarch of Chan (Zen) Buddhism in China, in the style of a Chan ink painting (*Plate 119*). To strengthen his argument that he was but closing a historical circle, Zhang noted that Van Gogh once gave a self-portrait to Gauguin, about which he wrote that it was like a Buddhist monk, and that like a monk going to the desert (or "facing the wall," meditating in a cave, as Bodhidharma did), Van Gogh abandoned Paris for the South of France so that he could concentrate on his work.

Currently, no social issue concerns Zhang or China itself more than China's deteriorating ecological condition, and Zhang has engaged this issue through art in a second phase of his ongoing landscape series, entitled "Shan Shui Today" (*Plate 70 and Plate 75*). Emphasizing that his *shan shui* works are based not on real landscapes but on traditional paintings, he declares his genuine love for the landscape and laments that

> in today's *shan shui*, today's water is dirty, today's air is polluted. Today's mountains are too covered with polluted air to even see. I don't want to make propaganda, but I want to catch the artist's love of *shan shui*, to share the artist's hopes and his hopeless feelings about what has happened to the environment in China.

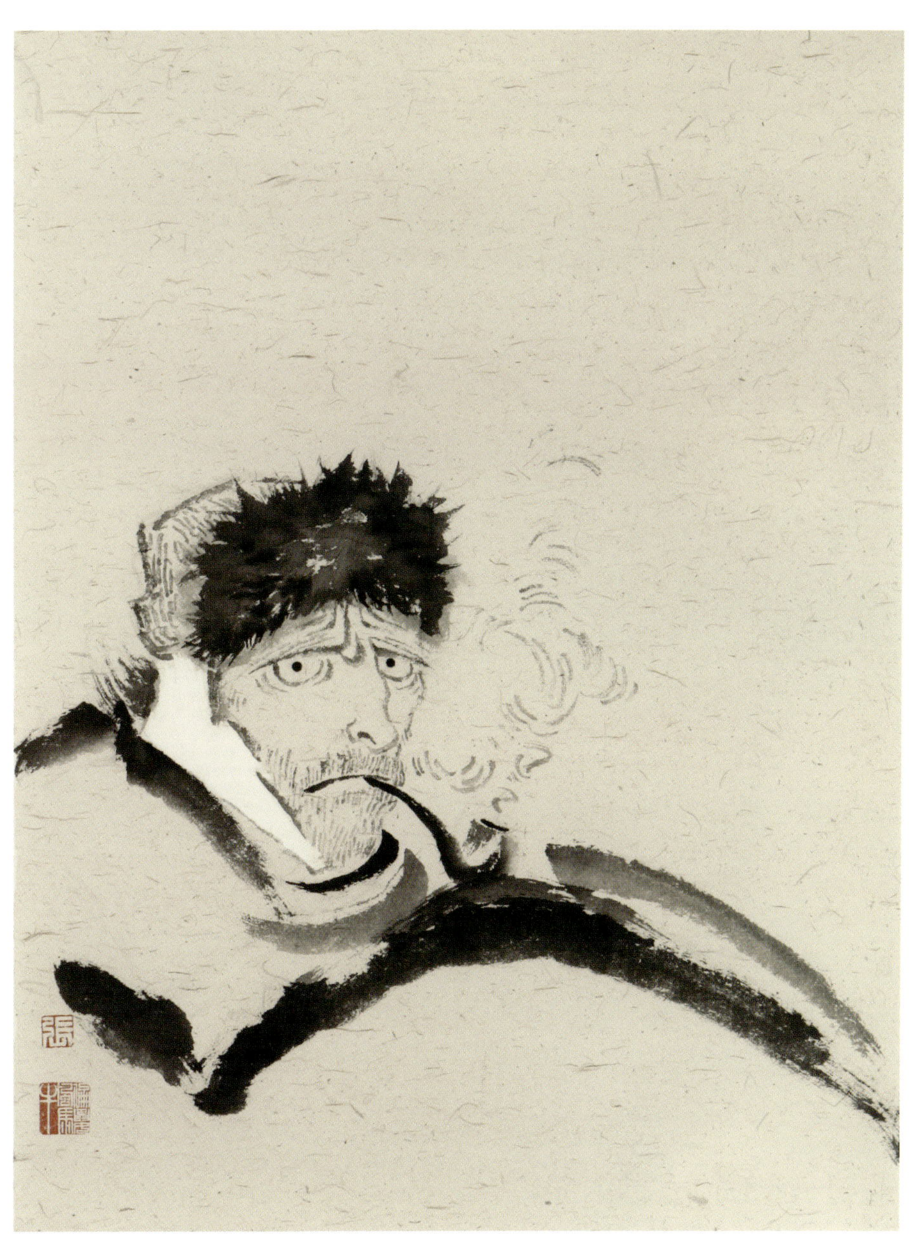

Van Gogh-Bodhidharma (QM), 2015. Ink on paper, 35 x 27 in.

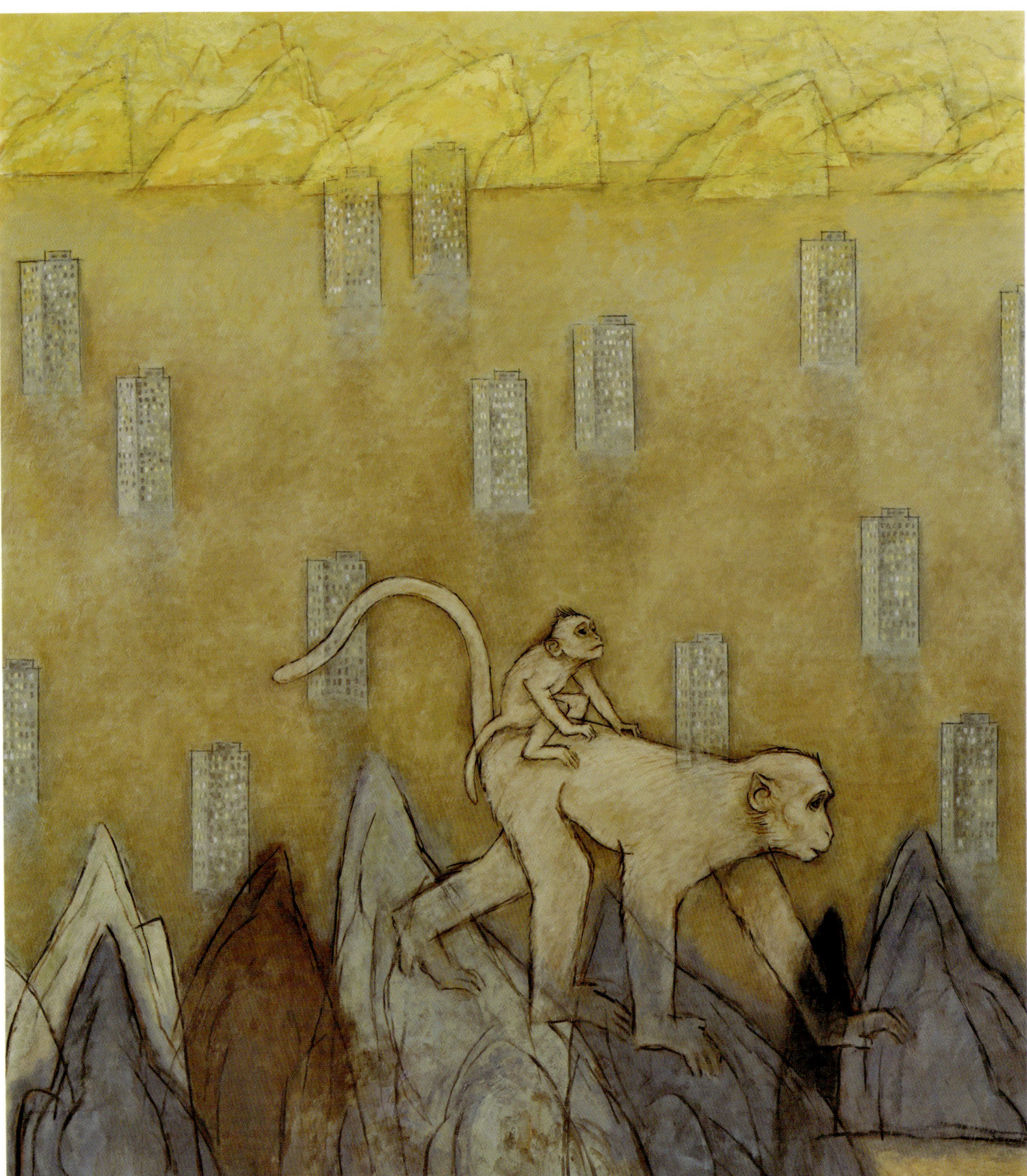

Plate 75

Untitled (Mother and Child), 2010. Mixed media and oil on canvas, 74 x 67 in.

He began the series by taking as his referent the famous twelve-leaf album of water studies made for the royal empress Yang Meizi (and inscribed by her) in the early thirteenth century by the court painter Ma Yuan. In oils on canvas and on a far larger scale than the originals, Zhang rephrased ("remade") the original, largely monochrome work in a freer, more colorful painting style. Its indication of the traumatic condition of China's drought-reduced and pollution-ridden waters remained subtle: only some sea-foam, the result of industrial waste, in one; rosy clouds, colored not by the setting sun but by gaseous pollution, in another, a reddish-tinged effluent, lovely yet poisonous; the parched and cracked bed of a dried-up Yellow River in summertime, in a third.

The pure waters like those Ma Yuan once painted so beautifully no longer exist in China, which leads Zhang to ponder:

> I tried to envision how the ancient Chinese *shan shui* painting masters would face today's mountains and water. For example, if Ma Yuan were to stand before today's rivers and lakes, fouled by chemical toxins and industrial waste, would he still be able to paint his twelve-part Water Album? This kind of consideration guided my new series.

In several of the more recent works in this series, Zhang has populated his landscapes with high-rise buildings that have led to the radical reconstruction of rural China and the displacement of its animal species. Monkeys are his current favorite animals to roam the landscape in search of the forests that once were their home.

Displaced many times over in his lifetime, Zhang has long led the life of an outsider. When art critic and historian Gao Minglu curated an exhibition in 1998 that initiated the rise of contemporary Chinese art collecting in America, Zhang was not included—displaced yet again for having arrived too early, in 1982, to be part of the social circle of Chinese artists who emigrated after the Tiananmen tragedy of 1989.[11] But today, this is no longer the case. Recognition of the centrality of his works to the contemporary Chinese art movement, beginning with his *Quaker Oats Mao*, and an appreciation of the unusually diverse and creative character of his many contributions, have made him a leading artist in the field. Now, like a monkey longing for its former wilderness—and a very philosophical monkey at that—Zhang concludes:

> I would like to go back to when nobody wanted my paintings but I was free. I have called all of my galleries and asked them not to bother me—"I'll call you, don't call me."

1   Burton Watson, trans., *The Complete Works of Chung Tzu* (New York: Columbia University Press, 1970), 29–30. Translation slightly modified.

2   James Legge, trans., *The Chinese Classics, II: The Works of Mencius* (Oxford: Hong Kong University Press, 1960), 463.

3   This essay draws upon interviews and information I have previously published, including "Zhang Hongtu's Alternative History of Painting," in *Zhang Hongtu: An On-Going Painting Project* (New York: On-going Publications, 2000); "Zhang Hongtu: The Art of Straddling Boundaries," in *Zhang Hongtu: The Art of Straddling Boundaries* (Taipei: Lin & Keng Gallery, 2007), vii–xxv; "Double-Vision: Art Out of Joint," in *Reason's Clue* (New York: Queens Museum of Art and Lin & Keng Gallery, 2008), xvii–xxxiii and *Asian Art News* 18.5 (September/October 2008); "An Outsider's Outsider Comes In: Zhang Hongtu," in *Outside In: Chinese x American x Contemporary x Art* (Princeton and New Haven: Princeton University Art Museum, Tang Center for East Asian Art, and Yale University Press, 2009), 257–69; and "Four Paths from Dunhuang: A Memorial and Three Interviews," in *Inspired by Dunhuang: Re-Creation in Contemporary Chinese Art* (New York: China Institute in America, 2013), 11–30.

4   See *Outside In*, 251, fig. 1.

5   Art historian Wu Hung once observed, "When [Zhang Hongtu] painted a Mao cap onto the Quaker Oats man on an oatmeal carton in 1987, he almost accidentally created perhaps the first work of Chinese political pop, which would become an extremely influential artistic genre in China in the early to mid-nineties." Wu Hung, *Transience: Chinese Experimental Art at the End of the Twentieth Century* (Chicago: The David and Alfred Smart Museum of Art, The University of Chicago, 1999), 45.

6   Like Duchamp, Zhang left it up to viewers to figure out what his letters mean. Duchamp's inscription "L.H.O.O.Q." has been presumed to pun (in French, of course) on the sexuality of the woman.

7   See *Outside In*, 263, figs. 6, 7.

8   For this work, see *Zhang Hongtu: An On-Going Painting Project*, 62.

9   For Shen Zhou's painting, see Yang Xin et al., *Three Thousand Years of Chinese Painting* (New Haven: Yale University Press and Foreign Languages Press, 1997), pl. 200.

10   For the text of "Snow," see *Mao Tse-tung Poems* (Beijing: Foreign Languages Press, 1976), 23.

11   See Gao Minglu, *Outside In: New Chinese Art* (San Francisco: San Francisco Museum of Contemporary Art; New York: Asia Society Galleries; and Berkeley: University of California Press, 1998). In 2000, Gao Minglu gave me the privilege of organizing the events that accompanied this exhibition on tour in Seattle and Tacoma and Zhang Hongtu was added to the artists participating in the lectures held there.

WALL, GATE, HOLE: THREE RECURRENT MOTIFS IN ZHANG HONGTU'S ART

Wu Hung

What kind of wall rejects doors and gates? Is there any door or gate not attached to a wall? Does a door or gate become a wall when it ceases to open? Can people dig big holes on a wall without causing it to collapse? Do such holes become gates that never close? These questions come to mind when we look at some works in this exhibition, from *The Great Wall With Gates* on the outside wall of the gallery, to *The Red Door* and *Front Door* in the gallery, and *The Big Red Door* in the sunken living room. Zhang Hongtu must have wrestled with similar questions while making these works.

THE WALL

Two actual walls have played pivotal roles in Zhang's conceptualization of these works: the Great Wall of China and the Berlin Wall that divided the East and West during the Cold War. He created one of his first "wall images" in late 1989 (*Fig. 1*). It is the design for a poster that features a sphere in the middle, whose identity as a globe is suggested by the text written in bold capital letters above and below: "CAN MAN SAVE THIS WORLD FROM POLLUTION BY WALLS?" The image reconfirms the

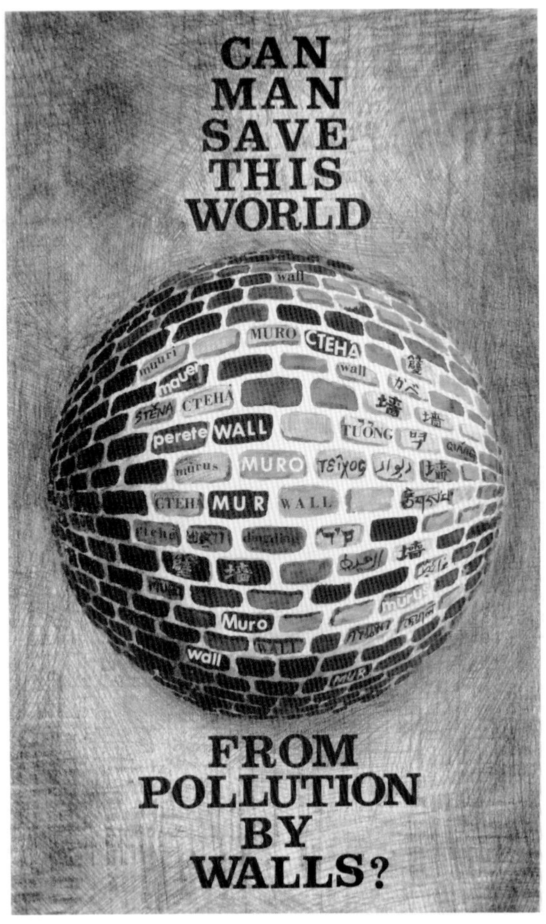

Fig. 1

question rather than responding to it: layers of solid bricks cover the entire sphere, turning it into a surreal, impenetrable "walled globe." Graffiti on the bricks repeats the single word "wall" in different languages, sealing off the globe with a linguistic and cultural barrier superimposed on a physical one. The gloominess of this Kafkaesque vision is enhanced by its colorlessness: drawn in shaded gray, the globe is suspended in a cavern carved out with sharp pencil marks.

The date of the image explains its grim pessimism: Zhang made it in the aftermath of the student demonstrations in Tiananmen Square, which ended in bloodshed on June 4, 1989. This event turned him into one of the most politically committed Chinese artists abroad (he had emigrated to America in 1982). Indeed, the June Fourth Movement, as the demonstrations are commonly called, marked a new stage in his art. Before this moment, he was a young, adventurous "modern painter" exploring new art styles and methods in a foreign environment. After this moment, his works acquired a distinct political dimension, responding to the June Fourth Movement and connecting

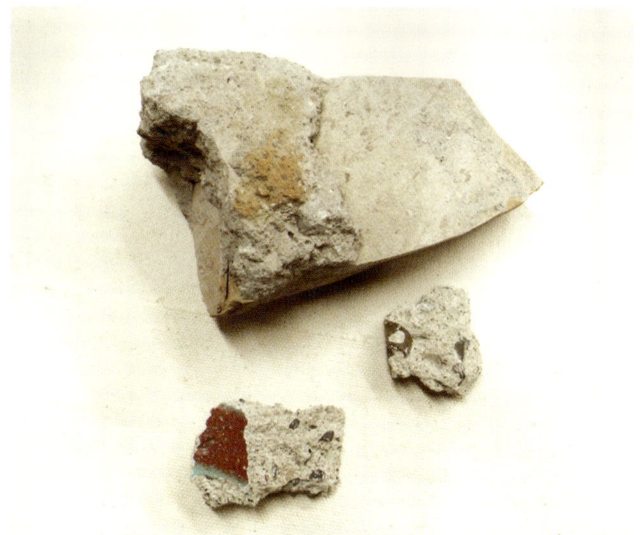

Fig. 2

this tragedy to his memory of the Cultural Revolution (1966–76), a disastrous period in China's modern history that he had himself lived through.[1] Immediately after the June Fourth Movement, he appropriated Leonardo da Vinci's *Last Supper*, replacing all the figures in the masterpiece with Mao in multiple guises, including a "Christ Mao" in the center speaking into a microphone and a "Judas Mao" holding the Little Red Book.

Understood in this context, the omnipresent walls in the 1989 poster design refer to three political/historical conditions: the failed June Fourth Movement, Zhang's memory of the Cultural Revolution, and international relations during the Cold War era. About this last condition, Zhang emphasized that he had made the design "before the crushing of the Berlin Wall."[2] Instead of drawing walls to surround a particular nation or region, he covered the entire globe with hard bricks, alluding to the general state of world politics at the time as dominated by hatred.

He was ecstatic when the Berlin Wall fell. Soon afterward he received a gift from a German friend: several pieces of the wall that the friend had personally broken off from it. Zhang still keeps them in his studio as memorabilia of a bygone era (*Fig. 2*). But he also knows that many other walls still stand, practically and symbolically blocking the flow of people and ideas. Among these walls, the one constantly on his mind is the Great Wall of China. Because of the importance of this particular wall in his art, a brief review of its history and symbolism is called for.

The Chinese name for the Great Wall is the "Long Wall" (*changcheng*). According to the author Arthur Waldron, the myth that a single Long Wall encircled China began to dominate the historical imagination after the First Qin Emperor unified China in the third century BCE.[3] The emperor, who only repaired and connected some existing "long walls" from earlier periods, was instantly credited with the establishment of a *Wanli Changcheng*, or a Ten-Thousand-Mile-Long Wall. The reason for this attribution to him seems transparent: prior to unification, various feudal lords built individual walls to defend themselves from their neighbors, yet only a single frontier wall was necessary to protect and spatially identify a unified Chinese empire. Consequently, the concept of a single, superior Long Wall appeared. The second-century BCE writer Jia Yi wrote that within this "wall of iron," the First Emperor "had established a rule that would be enjoyed by his descendants for ten thousand generations."[4]

It is ironic, however, that when the Long Wall became a national symbol, the Chinese people—those supposedly protected by the wall—sensed little benefit from its construction. Indeed, none of the emperors, generals, and historians actually built the wall; the Qin and the Han rulers dispatched several hundred thousand men to work on the frontier, and later still more people were conscripted to build the Ming dynasty Long Wall in the fifteenth century. In historical records these builders only formed an anonymous corvée labor force, but to individual laborers and their families the Long Wall was imbued with memories of endless suffering. Folk songs were created not long after the Long Wall myth began:

> If a son is born, mind you don't raise him!
> If a girl is born, feed her dried meat.
> Don't you see just below the Long Wall
> Dead men's skeletons prop each other up.[5]

A legend also circulated about an ordinary woman, Mengjiang, whose husband had been sent to the wall construction site. In winter, worrying about his welfare, she set out to take him warm clothes, only to learn after the long journey that she was too late: her husband had already perished and his body had been buried beneath the wall. Overcome, the woman knelt down and cried. Her grief miraculously caused the wall to break open and reveal her husband's bones (*Fig. 3*). As this story gradually developed into one of the country's most popular tales, a folk tradition was invented in opposition to the official glorification of the Long Wall. Whereas the government continued to extend and praise the wall, Mengjiang and millions of men and women cried out for the wall's destruction.

The Long Wall finally became a purely symbolic monument during the modern era, when it ceased to play any practical role. Its military significance vanished when bombers and battleships could cross the sky and oceans; its repair was intended to preserve the wall as a national treasure. From the early twentieth century on, the Long

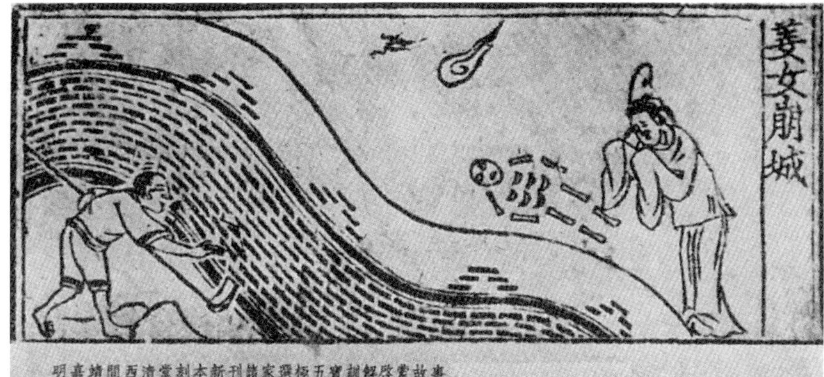

Fig. 3

Anonymous, *The Story of Mengjiang*, woodblock illustration, 16th century, Ming dynasty (1368–1644)

Wall was considered the prime symbol of China as an emerging modern nation-state. Sun Yat-sen (1866–1925), the so-called Father of Modern China, claimed that the wall was a mighty creation of his people and had protected the Chinese race since the third century BCE.[6] On the other hand, he also took the wall as the monument of a future new China, a modern nation freed from foreign invasions and internal turmoil. His rhetorical use of the wall became an important part of nationalist, and then Communist, propaganda. A song written during the Sino-Japanese War called upon all "who will not be slaves to take our own flesh and blood, to build a new Long Wall!" The song was adopted in 1949 as the national anthem of the People's Republic of China; the old myth of the Long Wall was thus sanctioned as an essential element of Chinese Communist ideology. The wall became a favorite motif of paintings, photos, and Chairman Mao buttons during the Cultural Revolution. Even today, every foreign leader who visits China is led to the wall to experience China's mighty power.

On the other hand, Mengjiang's legend never died; it was only updated. Even though Sun Yat-sen had affiliated the wall with a future new China, some critical writers, including the essayist Lu Xun (1881–1936), compared it to the enclosure of an enormous prison. The wall, he wrote in 1925, "surrounded and enclosed the living, and suffocated and killed them." It was composed of "both old and new bricks." It stood for the Chinese nation at the expense of individuals; it was, in his words, "the mighty and accursed Great Wall."[7]

Against this historical background we can understand a countermovement in China around the mid-1980s. In September of 1984 Deng Xiaoping (1904–1997), who became China's new leader after the Cultural Revolution, launched a campaign: "Let us love our country and restore our Long Wall." The campaign involved both restoring the wall's national symbolism and its physical presence. Books and articles were published to trace the wall's glorious history, and scientists and archaeologists were sent to survey its present condition and to excavate its buried foundations. Rebellious,

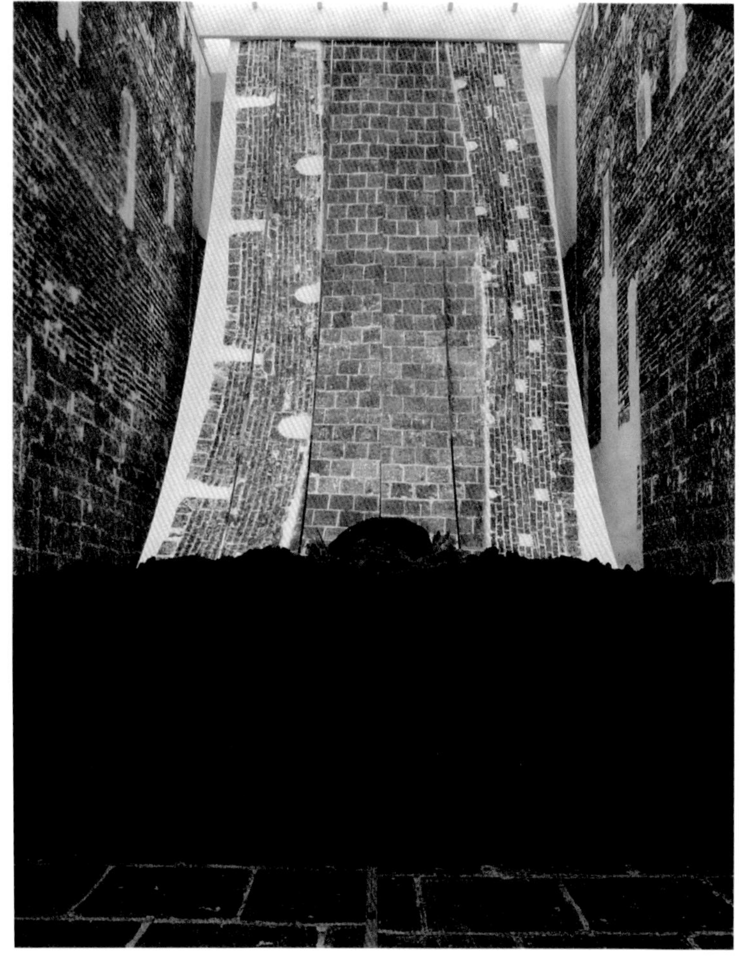

Xu Bing, *Ghosts Pounding the Wall*, 1990–91. Mixed-media installation/ transferred print from the Great Wall, ink on paper, 1260 x 591 in. Installation view, "Three Installations by Xu Bing," Elvehjem Museum of Art, Wisconsin, 1991. Courtesy Xu Bing Studio.

Fig. 4

experimental artists challenged this official effort, however. In 1988, they staged a series of large performances on the Long Wall, wrapping their bodies and a whole section of the wall in white bandages. A young man covering himself with bandages became a recurrent image in the '85 Art New Wave movement. "We are injured, tied up by tradition," an artist explained. "These are our true images."[8] The same movement also produced Xu Bing's *Ghosts Pounding the Wall* in 1990 (*Fig. 4*), Wang Youshen's "Newspaper" series and Zheng Lianjie's *Binding the Lost Souls: Huge Explosion* in 1993, Ma Liuming's *Fen-Ma Liuming on the Great Wall* in 1998, and He Chengyao's *Opening the Great Wall* in 2000.[9] Similar to these projects, Zhang's *A Section of the Wall* (*Fig. 5*) subverts the conventional monumentality of the Long Wall, but its visual logic differs from those more iconic works. I have suggested elsewhere that Xu Bing's *Ghosts Pounding the Wall*, for example, is a counter-monument that subverts traditional monumentality by transforming a conventional monument into something else; its violation of traditional monumentality results in a new monumental form.[10] By

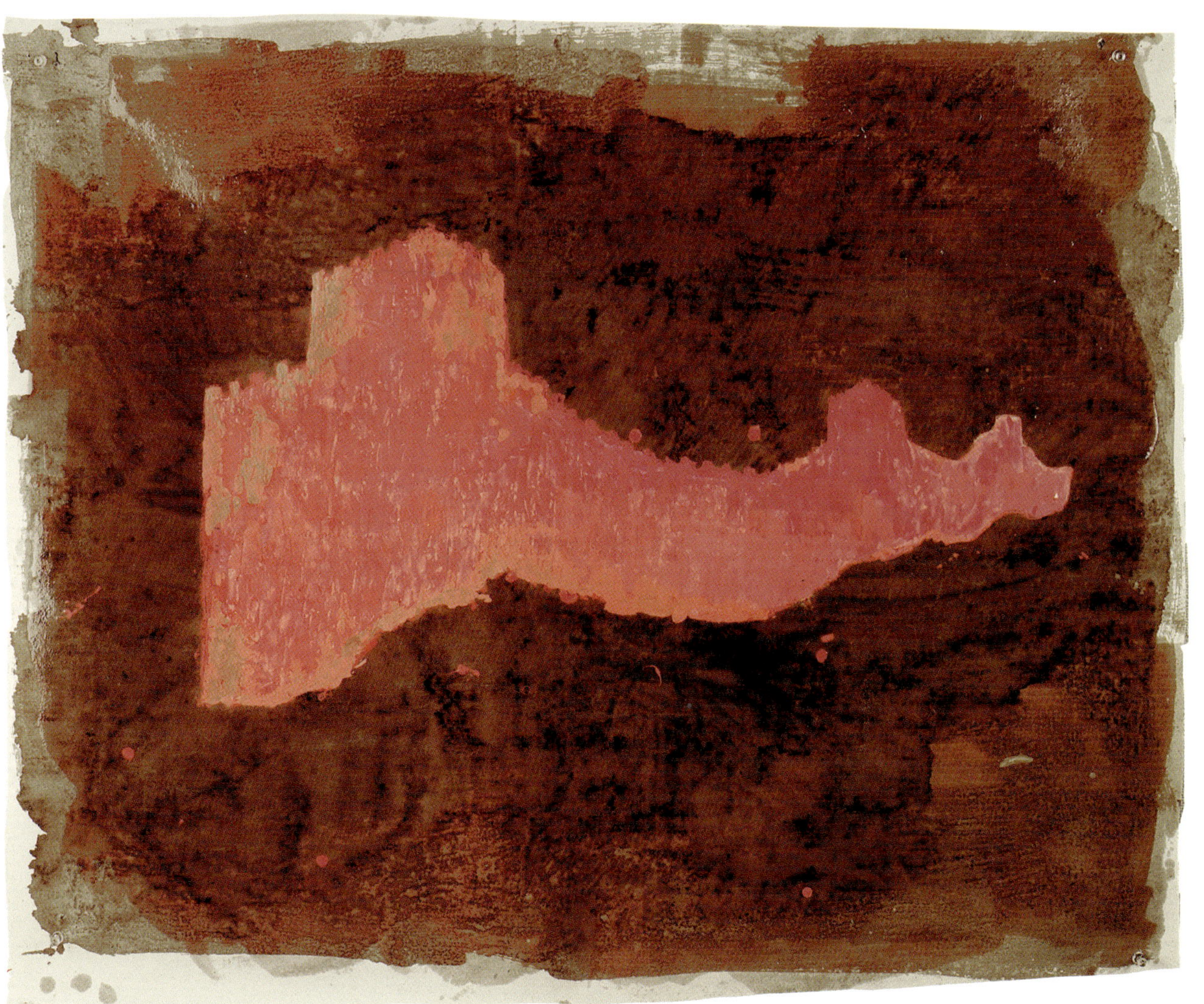

A Section of the Wall, 1996. Soy sauce and nail varnish on paper, 31 ½ x 40 in.

contrast, Zhang's *A Section of the Wall*, created in 1996, can best be described as an image of an anti-monument. It is a small drawing with a hollowed-out image of the Long Wall at the center, which vaguely shows the wall's silhouetted battlement. This image can be considered that of an anti-monument because it rejects any form of monumental expression. To reinforce the significance of such a rejection, Zhang also used Chinese soy sauce and nail varnish—non-art materials from the kitchen and bathroom—to make the image, simultaneously canceling the subject's sacredness and the work's artistic aura.

THE GATE

In a 1995 interview Zhang discussed the symbolism of the Chinese character *men* 門, which means both door and gate:

> The door/gate is a very meaningful object in China. You can tell people's position in society by the image of their doors. For example, only a door in the Forbidden City can have 162 decorative studs, which constitute a symbol of power, authority, and dictatorship. . . . The emperor lived behind the gates of the Forbidden City, but after 1949 Mao and his government also lived behind these big red gates with 162 studs. People feared these gates, but at the same time they desired to know what was going on behind the gates.[11]

The fear of and fascination with a closed gate—the chief significance of a door/gate Zhang describes here—is not new, but is rooted in traditional Chinese political philosophy. In a famous passage, the third-century-BCE writer Han Fei teaches kings and emperors that power must be generated by secrecy:

> The Way [of the ruler] lies in what cannot be seen, its function in what cannot be known. Be empty, still, and idle, and from your place of darkness observe the defects of others. See but do not appear to see; listen but do not seem to listen; know but do not let it be known that you know. . . . Hide your tracks, conceal your sources, so that your subordinates cannot trace the springs of your action. Discard wisdom, forswear ability, so that your subordinates cannot guess what you are about.[12]

Han Fei's teaching was faithfully practiced by the First Qin Emperor in the third century BC and again by Mao Zedong, an admirer of both Han Fei and the First Emperor, some 2,200 years later. Mao's growing mystique during the Cultural Revolution was closely related to his withdrawal from public view. From unknown places he issued endless "supreme orders" (*zuigao zhishi*) for political persecutions. The whole

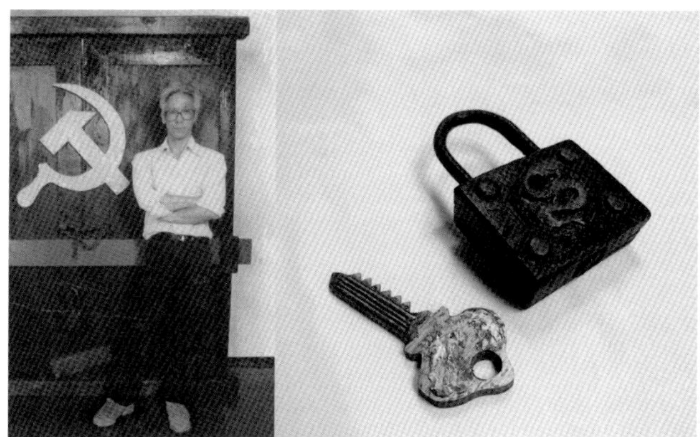

Fig. 6

population was increasingly controlled by fear, for anyone could be the next enemy of the people and be turned in by his closest friends or relatives. Although such fear subsided after the Cultural Revolution, especially after the new generation of Chinese leaders introduced "open door" policies in the late 1970s, it was resurrected by the government's heavy-handed suppression of the student demonstrations in 1989. For people like Zhang, it was as if they had to relive the nightmare of the Cultural Revolution a second time. He expressed this feeling of *déjà vu* with an installation that he made in September 1989 as a response to the Tiananmen massacre. It was a large wooden door painted entirely black. Tightly shut, locked, and further secured with a red bar, it bore the emblem of the Communist Party across the stiles. A photo shows that this work was displayed in the exhibition "CHINA June 4, 1989," organized by the Asian-American Arts Center in New York to protest the Chinese government's suppression of the peaceful student demonstrations (*Fig. 6*)[13]. Zhang later destroyed this work because of its overly forthright symbolism. He continued to employ the motif of a door, however, and used it to develop subtler and sometimes hilarious political images.

Two such later "door" works, one called *Front Door* and the other *The Red Door*, were both shown in "Material Mao," Zhang's solo exhibition at the Bronx Museum of the Arts in 1995. *Front Door* is equipped with multiple fake locks (cutout photographic images) and a real peephole. A hidden tape recorder repeats the sound of someone rhythmically knocking on the door. Responding to the knock, you look through the hole to see who is outside; confronting you are Mao Zedong's waiting eyes. Here the artist/viewer assumes an interior space. Although the peephole on this door is designed for us to look out, our view is deflected by a more powerful gaze from outside, which transforms us into a passive object of looking. While this installation clearly conveys Zhang's experience back in China, *The Red Door* in the same exhibition is more amusing. There is a gap between the front panels of this door. Peeking through the crack, one finds a TV screen playing a film clip of Mao

Zedong dancing with a young girl at a Communist Party gathering. (A later clip from this documentary shows the chairman sitting in an enormous armchair surrounded by a bevy of young women.)

Like *The Red Door*, Zhang's new version of *Studs 9 x 9 x 2* in this exhibition transforms a serious political symbol into a joke, but in a more succinct manner (*Plate 116*). The artist has retained (and to some extent exaggerated) the shining red door panels of an imperial gate in the Forbidden City, but has replaced its glamorous golden studs with ugly metal rivets, which look like rows of phalluses in various degrees of inadequate erection. The humorous effect of these "studs" cancels out the sense of secrecy. As mentioned earlier, the traditional symbolism of the gate is rooted in its separation of interior and exterior spaces, and its power lies in its concealment of the space behind it. In retrospect, we realize that Zhang's two earlier door installations (*Front Door* and *The Red Door*) still rely on this symbolism. Both works emphasize the interplay between the spaces and gazes divided by a gate; and both address issues of political dominance, the empowerment or disempowerment of the gaze, and the exercise of one subject's power onto another. These are not the purposes of *Studs 9 x 9 x 2*, which is a straightforward political satire. The phallus-like studs are the secret that the gate is supposed to hide. The gate's mystique vanishes when this (unimpressive) secret exposes itself to the outside.

THE HOLE

A third persistent element in Zhang's work is the empty space of a hole. He has employed this visual device in two types of representations, both political in nature but serving different purposes. The first type is iconoclastic, as he replaces a sacred icon with an empty, negative space. The second type is transformative, as he opens up large holes on a monumental wall to change its meaning and function.

We have discussed one example of the first type: the hollowed-out Great Wall drawn on a piece of wrinkled paper (*Fig. 5*). But most works in this category are designed to demystify Mao by "emptying" the iconic image of the great leader. "Material Mao" is a large group of negative images of Mao that Zhang created between 1991 and 1995. Using various materials ranging from brick, corn, fur, and metal to paper soaked in soy sauce, he made large and small frames to outline Mao's famous silhouette. In Jonathan Goodman's words, here "Mao, or rather his absence, becomes the means for an experiment in formal application. Through repetition, the content of Mao's form is rendered meaningless."[14]

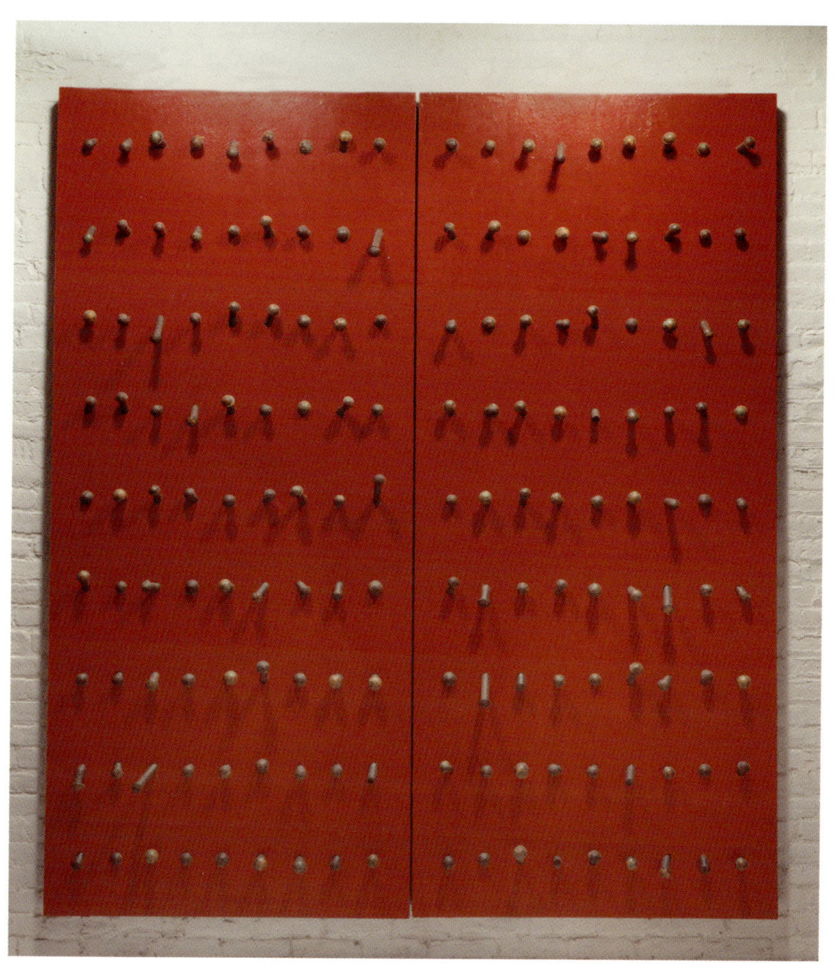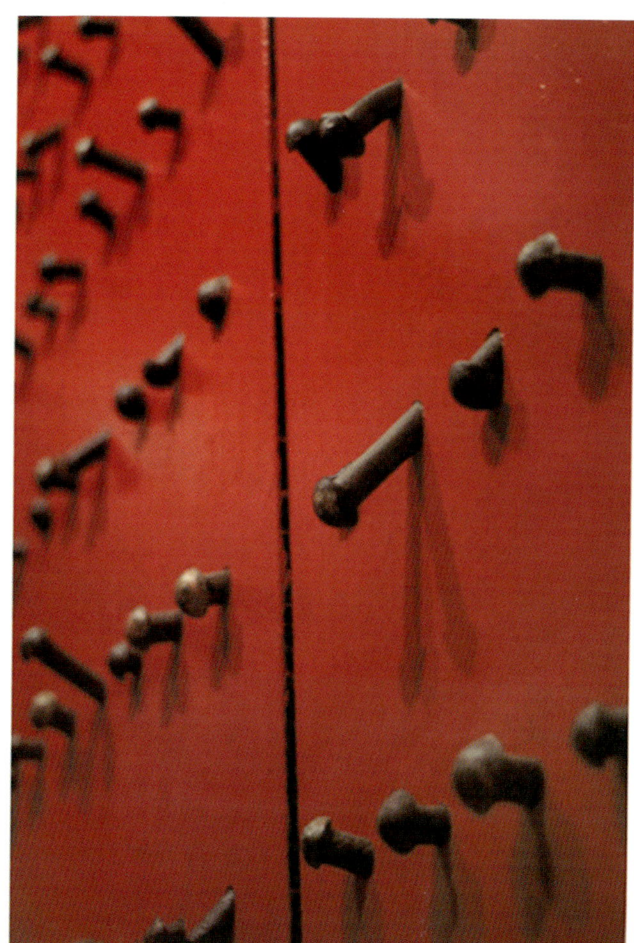

Plate 116

Studs 9 x 9 x 2, The Big Red Door, 1992. Metal, wood, and paint, 96 x 86 ½ x 6 in.

These iconoclastic images do not just destroy a political symbol, however; rather, the process of demystifying Mao also refreshes the artist's memory of a painful and confused period in his life. As Zhang recalls:

> At the beginning of the Cultural Revolution, like everyone of my generation, I completely trusted in Mao. Yet what Mao did during the Cultural Revolution changed my mind. I saw art and culture being destroyed by the Red Guards. I saw people dividing into different groups, fighting and killing each other, but everyone—killers and victims—declared they were on the side of Mao's revolution. I found that all the young people, including myself, were all fooled and used by Mao. . . . For me, Mao's image was god-like in China. What I have done is pull down this image from the pantheon to reality. Working on Mao is one way to extricate myself from the nightmare; first I felt sinful and fearful, now I feel nothing.[15]

Here Zhang reveals his fundamental technique to destroy the Mao myth: to turn a sacred icon into "nothing." It is his way to cure the historical trauma induced by the Cultural Revolution under Mao's rule. But in order to do so he must constantly revisit his traumatic experience and repudiate part of himself. The Political Pop artist Yu Youhan, for example, was quoted in the *New York Times* as saying, "If we reject Mao, we reject a part of ourselves." Zhang responded sharply, "So what if we [must] reject part of ourselves?"[16]

The second group of works in which Zhang likewise inserts empty holes is without exception linked to the Great Wall. Three untitled pencil drawings from 1992 are the earliest examples in this group (*Fig. 7, 8, 9*). These drawings were not made public until 2006; that year, several California artists, including Tomas J. Benitez and Shervin Shahbazi, formed a group called The Ministry of Culture and launched the online forum Great Wall of Chinga in response to the US government's decision to build a 700-mile barrier along the US–Mexico border. Zhang's friend Sonia Mak had seen his drawings and invited him to participate in the project; she turned the drawings into a slideshow and posted it on YouTube.[17] In one drawing, a section of the Great Wall stands in isolation on a steep mountaintop, with a big round hole opened up near the base of the central watchtower. Above this gate-like cavity, a smaller hole appears near the top of the watchtower like a fan-shaped window. Other holes of various shapes—vertical, oval, and semicircular—penetrate the flanking walls, turning the solid defense structure into a honeycomb. In another drawing, a hollowed-out section of the Great Wall is further twisted into a double curve like soft rubber. These and four other drawings were used to compose the video on YouTube; a text by Zhang runs along with the images to explicate their meaning:

Fig. 7
Drawing of Wall Project #2, 1992.
Pencil on paper, 15 ½ x 21 ½ in.

Fig. 8
Drawing of Wall Project #8, 1992.
Pencil on paper, 21 x 31 in.

Fig. 9
Drawing of Wall Project #3, 1992.
Pencil on paper, 15 ½ x 21 ½ in.

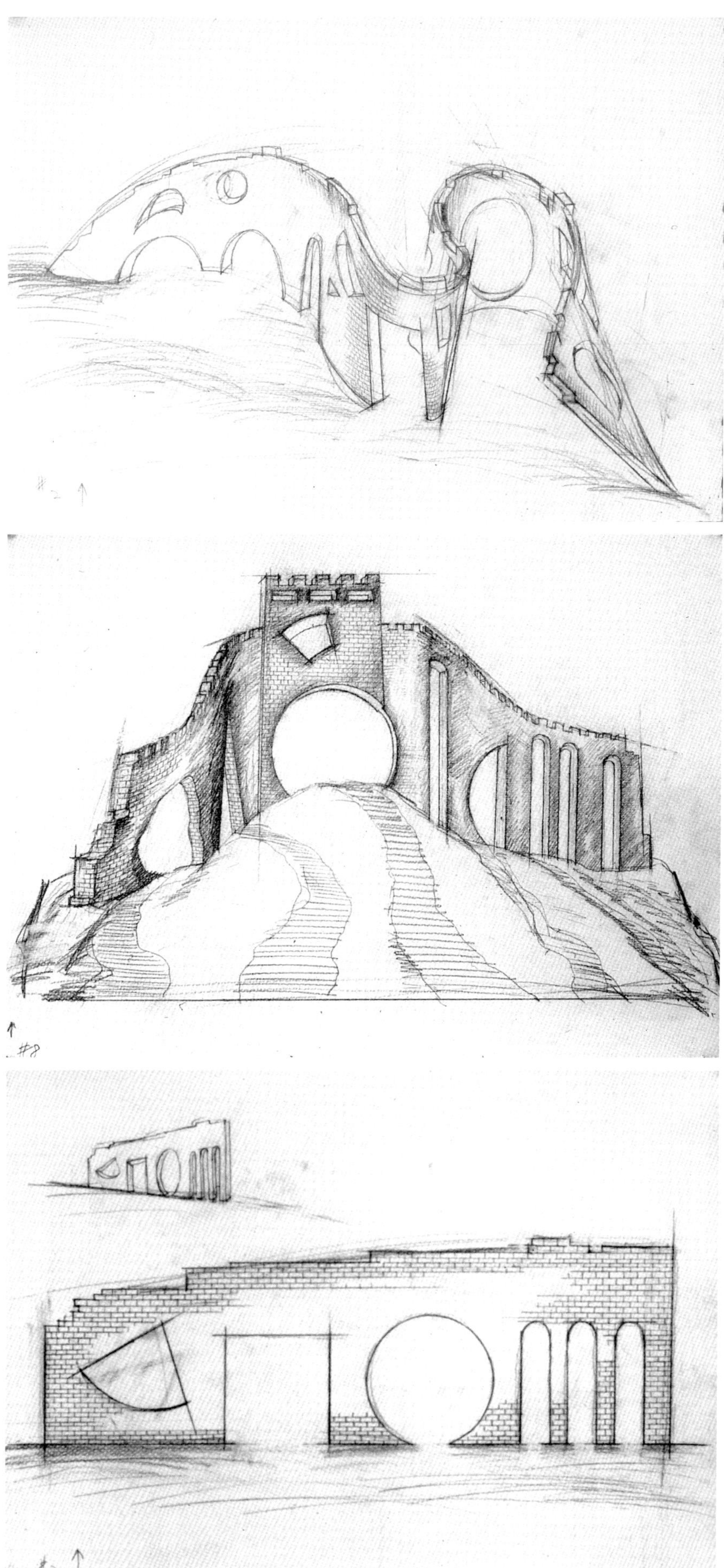

Walls . . . separate, divide, isolate, obstruct, and segregate. A wall is a boundary, a limitation, the cause for misunderstanding, the cause for distrust, the cause for alienation and hatred. If I make a hole in a wall . . . I can twist the wall, soften the wall, or lay down the wall, or . . . roll up the wall. People can . . . walk through. Kids can play on it.[18]

Since then Zhang has refined these drawings and has also developed them into the design of a large mural, which he conceived in 2009 on the twentieth anniversary of the fall of the Berlin Wall (*Plate 117*). His accompanying text starts with the paragraph cited above, and then proposes the construction of a new kind of wall that will fundamentally eliminate the structure's inherent restrictive nature. As he writes:

A physical wall can be destroyed by the changing of political situations, like the Berlin Wall, or can lose its function by the changing of time, like the Great Wall of China. But psychologically, the invisible walls between different people, different religions, and different cultures are difficult to remove. My project is to build a real wall but with holes in it to eliminate its function, from the visible object to the invisible walls in people's minds.[19]

The imagined mural illustrates this vision by presenting a panoramic view of a fictionalized Great Wall. Created with the help of Photoshop, the monument appears newly refurbished, with the surface freshly cleaned and chinks neatly filled in. Bathed in bright sunlight against the blue sky, the wall is shown from below, enhancing its monumentality; the tall mountain behind it further boosts its magnificence. But this is not the Great Wall in official propaganda posters or popular tourist postcards: a row of huge holes or arches penetrates the wall's thick body. These cavities are not the result of destruction, but must have been constructed together with the wall, since their surfaces join the wall's in a smooth, impeccable fashion. They form permanent openings that forever change the function and symbolism of the wall, from a divider of peoples and places to a linkage between them.

Comparing this design with Zhang's 1989 *A Section of the Wall* (*Fig. 5*), we find an interesting shift in the artist's conceptualization of the Great Wall. As discussed earlier, the "empty" Great Wall in the 1989 picture can be considered an anti-monument, which rejects the very notion of a monument as a supreme embodiment of history and memory. The 2009 design, however, reinvents the Great Wall as a new type of monument. It is optimistic instead of iconoclastic. And here we detect the fundamental idealism of the artist, who, even after having witnessed so many tragedies and experiencing so much disillusionment, still looks forward to the future.

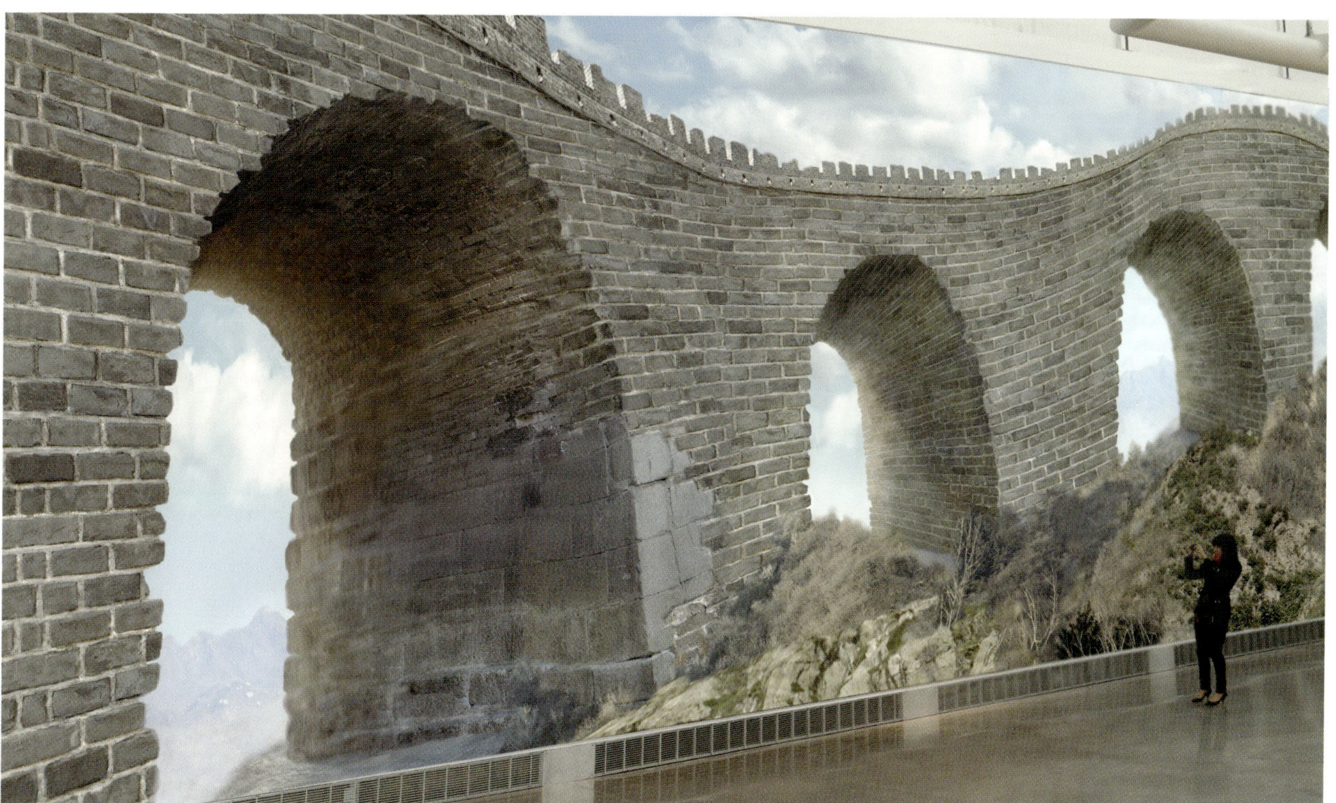

Great Wall with Gates II (detail), 2015. Installation view, Queens Museum.

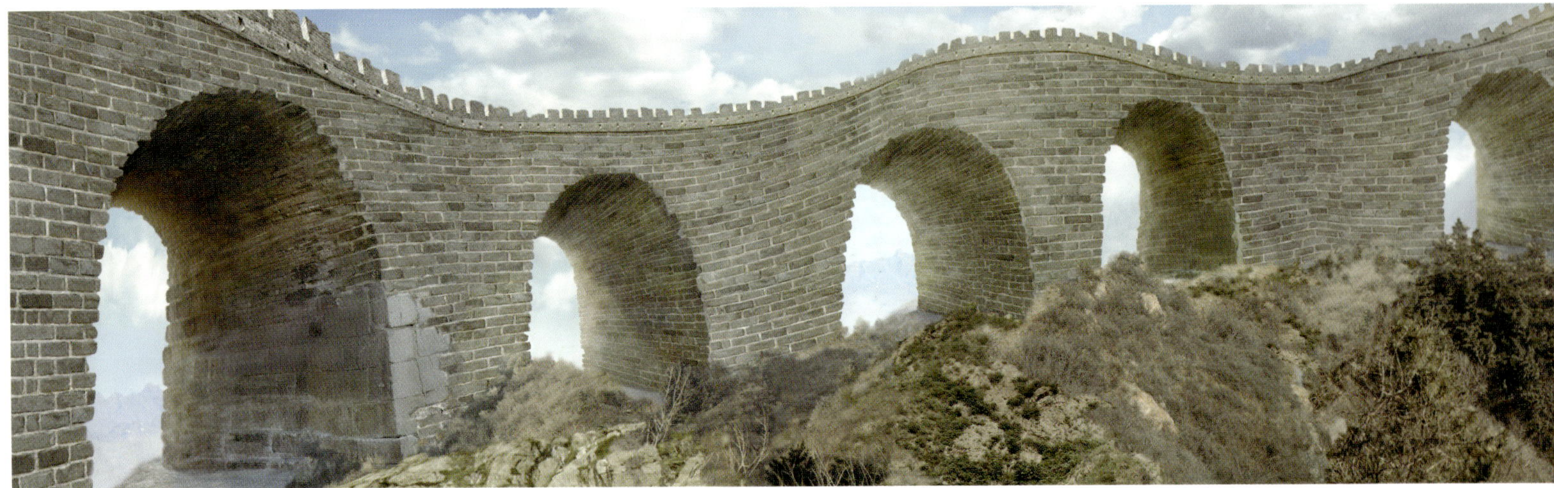

Plate 117

Great Wall with Gates II, 2015. Photographic wallpaper, 14 feet 9 inches x 98 feet.

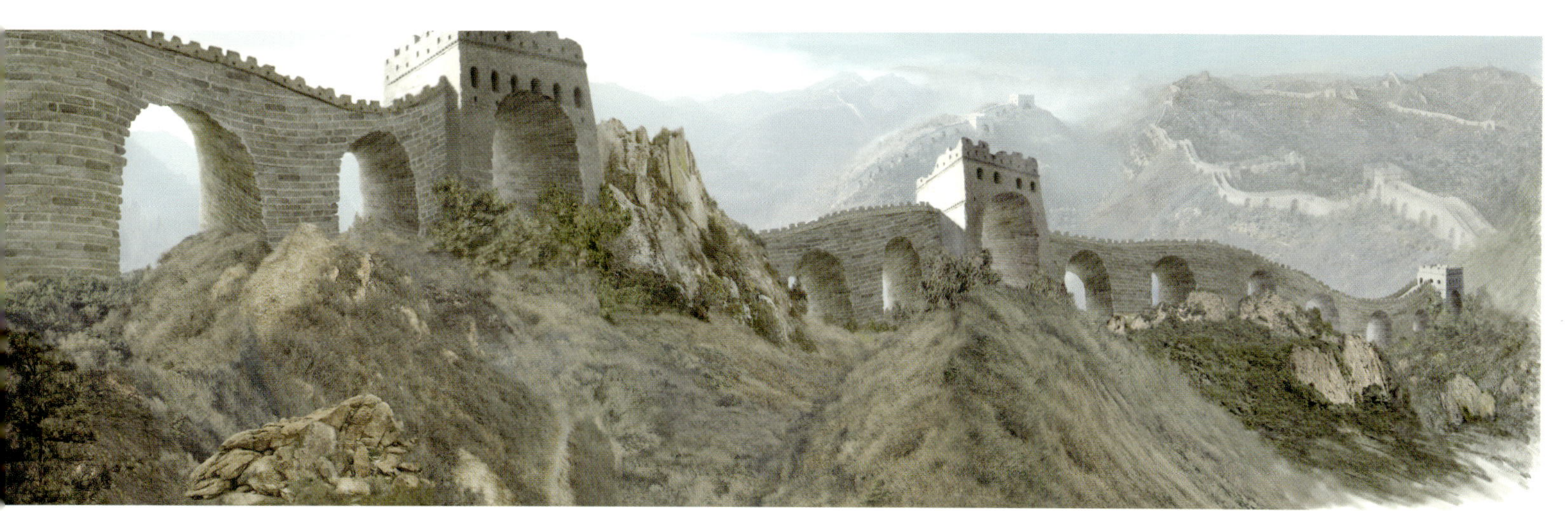

*	This essay incorporates interpretations developed in my book *Transience: Chinese Experimental Art at the End of the Twentieth Century* (Chicago: The David and Alfred Smart Museum of Art, The University of Chicago, 1999.)

1	For further information about Zhang Hongtu's work and ideas, see *Works by Zhang Hongtu* (Hong Kong: HKUST Center for the Arts, 1998); and "Zhang Hongtu/Hongtu Zhang: An Interview," by Jonathan Hay, in *Boundaries in China*, ed. Jonathan Hay (London: Reaktion Books, 1994), 280–98.

2	Zhang Hongtu, email to the author, December 3, 2014.

3	Arthur Waldron, *The Great Wall of China: From History to Myth* (Cambridge: Cambridge University Press, 1990), 6.

4	Translation from *Sources of Chinese Tradition*, ed. Wm. Theodore de Bary, vol. 1 (New York: Columbia University Press, 1960), 151–52.

5	This folk song was probably written in the second or first century BCE. Translation by Anne Birrell in *New Songs from a Jade Terrace: An Anthology of Early Chinese Love Poetry*, ed. J. H. Prynne (London: George Allen & Unwin, 1982), 49.

6	Sun Yat-sen, *Sun Wen Xueshuo* [Teachings by Sun Yat-sen] (Taipei: Yuantong, 1957), 38–39.

7	Lun Xun, "Changcheng" [The Long Wall], in *Lu Xun quanji* [The complete collection of writings by Lun Xun], vol. 3 (Shanghai: Xinhua, 1981), 58–59.

8	Interview by the author, Beijing, 1991.

9	For a description and discussion of these art projects, see Wu Hung, *Contemporary Chinese Art: A History* (London: Thames & Hudson, 2014), 210–14.

10	Wu Hung, *Transience: Chinese Experimental Art at the End of the Twentieth Century* (Chicago: The David and Alfred Smart Museum of Art, The University of Chicago, 1999), 340.

11	Lydia Yee, "An Interview with Zhang Hongtu," in *Zhang Hongtu: Material Mao* (New York: The Bronx Museum of the Arts, 1995), 6. Translation slightly modified.

12	*Basic Writings of Mo Tzu, Hsün Tzu, and Han Fei Tzu*, trans. Burton Watson (New York: Columbia University Press, 1963), 17–18.

13	This exhibition took place October 12–November 12, 1989, at the Blum Helman Warehouse in New York's SoHo district. It then traveled to Los Angeles and was restaged at Merging One Gallery, Santa Monica, as "Art and Democracy" (December 7, 1989–January 13, 1990).

14	Jonathan Goodman, "Zhang Hongtu at the Bronx Museum of the Arts," *Asia-Pacific Sculpture News* (Winter 1996): 58.

15	Lydia Yee, "An Interview with Zhang Hongtu," 2, 3.

16	Ibid., 5. Political Pop (*zhengzhi popu*) is a trend in contemporary Chinese art that emerged in the late 1980s and early 1990s. Inspired by Pop art of the 1960s, it mingles images from the Cultural Revolution and capitalist consumer culture. For a discussion of the relationship between Zhang Hongtu and Political Pop, see Geremie R. Barmé, *Shades of Mao: The Posthumous Cult of the Great Leader* (Armonk, NY: M. E. Sharpe, 1996), 46.

17   https://www.youtube.com/watch?v=93P_vdWh6-w&feature=emshare_video_user.

18   Ibid.

19   Information provided by Zhang Hongtu.

ZHANG'S CONTEMPORARY CUBISM

Michael FitzGerald

Although Zhang Hongtu is best known for an art of political critique, his densely layered work is as engaged with the history of art as with issues of free speech.[1] Among these dialogues with art, his involvement with Picasso's work most fully displays both his deep understanding of past achievements and his probing departure from historical models to create his own, original art.

Zhang's attention to Picasso places him among a diverse group of global artists who increasingly view Picasso as a paradigm of contemporary culture. This revival of interest in Picasso's art has occurred largely beyond the scope of critical attention and comes as a surprise to many art-world observers, who long ago proclaimed the irrelevance of his work to contemporary practice. Nonetheless, in the past year, three exhibitions (in Barcelona, Hamburg, and Paris) have showcased the breadth and depth of contemporary artists' responses to Picasso.[2] Zhang's work was featured in the Barcelona and Hamburg shows.

The range of contemporary artists' approaches to Picasso is extremely diverse, with artists addressing nearly every phase of his art, as well as his public personas and role in the art market. The Indian artists Maqboul Fida Husain and Atul Dodiya build on the precedent of *Guernica* to address humanitarian issues in the subcontinent; the Congolese Cherí Samba and South African Gavin Jantjes employ *Les Demoiselles d'Avignon* to plumb cultural conflicts between Africa and the West; and the Brazilian Vik Muniz creates exact reproduction of the labels on the backs of Picasso's masterpieces to address his fame.[3] These are only a few of the many choices artists have made in recent years to engage Picasso's precedents.

Zhang shares many of his contemporaries' concerns, yet his interest in Picasso stems from the internal development of Zhang's art. Indeed, the lack of attention to Picasso among contemporary critics has resulted in most artists being unaware that they share an involvement in his work. With the appearance of the recent exhibitions and accompanying catalogues, individual artists have become linked in a growing and vital community, one that Zhang eagerly joined during the symposium that marked the opening days of the Barcelona exhibition.[4]

In the 1980s, Zhang entered the critical debates that drive the art world with two works that respond to two radically different traditions in Western art. With only a few strokes of his brush, he transformed the image on the box of his accustomed cereal from a jolly Quaker gentleman to a forbidding Chairman Mao. This minimal gesture evokes the conceptual conceits and restrained interventions of Duchamp's assisted readymades, while eliding those cerebral works with the accessibility of Pop's engagement with consumer culture. By enlisting these two traditions of Western art, Zhang harnessed Duchamp's sly criticism with Pop's embrace of commercialism to ridicule heroic portrayals of Mao. This relatively simple gesture led to a much more laborious attack on the legendary Chinese leader. *Last Banquet* stretches across three panels (each nearly five feet wide) to mock the propaganda of Mao's omniscience and omnipresence by portraying him not only as Christ but also every one of the disciples, including Judas—thereby insinuating that Mao betrayed his own principles. Zhang's choice of Leonardo's *Last Supper* as the compositional precedent for his monumental painting engages yet another tradition in Western art, as embodied by one of the most iconic artists of the Renaissance, and a foundational image for what became the convention of Western academic art. Reduced to an academic model, Leonardo's *Last Supper*, with its monumentality and rhetorical display, is not far from Socialist Realism. Only its religious subject matter disqualifies it from this canon, a contradiction Zhang employs to ridicule Mao's virtual deification.

Picasso does not fit within the conventions of these traditions. His art is frequently defined in opposition to academic standards, and it is often characterized as lacking the intellectual basis of Duchamp's approach as well as the affirmation of consumer culture underlying Pop. Picasso's position at the head of a painterly tradition and his emphasis on self-expression would seem to offer little to Zhang.

Nonetheless, in 1997, Zhang explicitly used Picasso as a model for one panel of *Unity and Discord*. Consisting of nine canvases arranged in a three-by-three grid, this work again engaged Mao, this time based on a photograph of the chairman saluting ranks of Red Guards as they march past his reviewing platform. The array of nine paintings begins at the upper left with Zhang's rendering of this photo and then modulates through eight wildly varied transformations of the image. Each of these variations presents Mao in the style of a different artist, among them René Magritte, Willem de Kooning, Robert Ryman, Georg Baselitz, and a cartoon style related to Andy Warhol and Roy Lichtenstein (with a nod to Duchamp).

The most telling metamorphosis is arguably Zhang's appropriation of Picasso (*Plate 51*). Inspired by Picasso's portraits of the late 1930s, Zhang radically inverted the circumstances of the photo. Instead of commanding a vast assembly of troops marching across a sweeping landscape, Mao appears confined in a paneled room that barely contains his bulk. He still raises his right arm in salute, but in this room, his only audience is himself. This startling context severs Mao from his minions and suggests he is a prisoner, rather than a supreme leader. Moreover, it suggests that Mao's motivations are personal and deeply suspect. While he still wears his military uniform and holds his cap emblazoned with a red star, Mao's salute addresses himself. He raises his arm as he gazes at his reflection in a small mirror hanging from a nail in the wall. His motivation appears to be narcissistic, more about self-importance than societal betterment. Moreover, Zhang's resort to Picasso's Cubist technique of multiple profiles offers a visual counterpart to Mao's "two-faced" performance.

Zhang chose his source from the catalogue of "Picasso and Portraiture," an exhibition held at the Museum of Modern Art in 1996.[5] He selected *Dora Maar Seated* (1937), a brilliantly colored image of Picasso's lover set within a white cubicle, whose vertical and horizontal lines of paneling suggest a cage.[6] As Brigitte Léal wrote in the catalogue, the jauntily posed Maar seems "caged in a sort of barred cell."[7] Picasso explored this opposition between a monumental woman and the room's enclosing frame in a series of paintings during the late '30s and early '40s that culminates in *Woman Dressing Her Hair* (1940).[8] The claustrophobia of this situation (often enhanced by mirrors hanging on the walls) and the increasing anguish of the women are frequently interpreted as registering Picasso's response to the growing instability of European

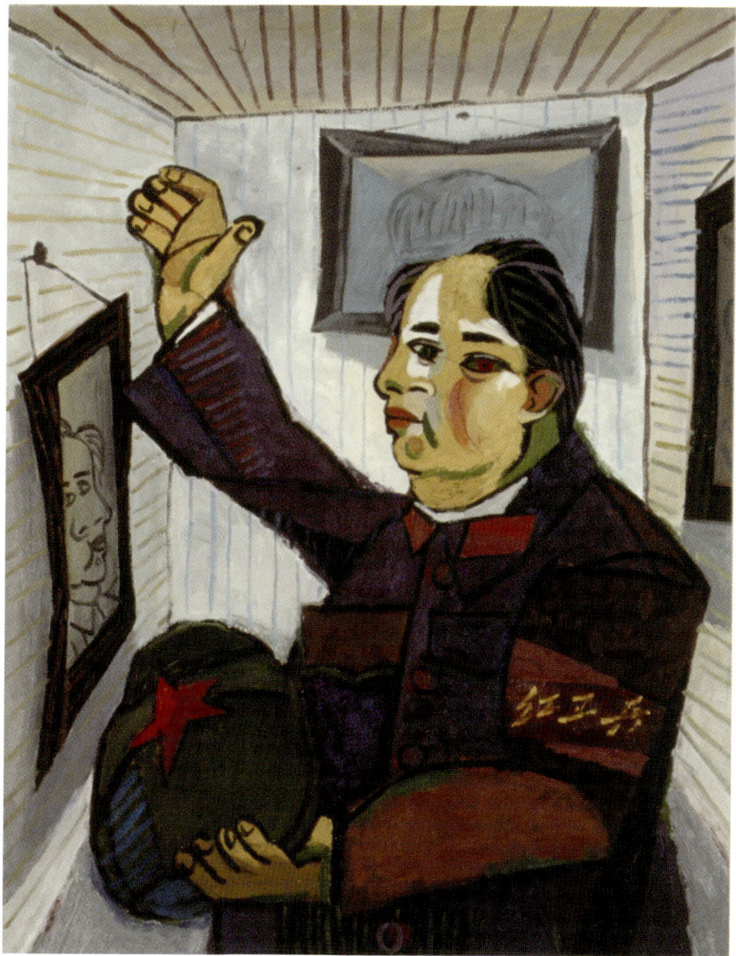

Plate 51

society in the late '30s and the Nazi occupation of France beginning in 1940. While Picasso's paintings are not overtly political, Zhang harnessed their underlying response to oppression as a constructive principle for his own satire of Mao and the Chinese Communist Party.

His resort to Picasso, however, is not limited to this selection of specific images. Although Zhang did not make explicit references to Picasso's work until 1987, he had become fascinated with it long before he came to the US in 1982. Many years earlier, Zhang had been introduced to Picasso's work through images of doves that Picasso had made in support of the Communist Party and were featured on posters and stamps to mark the Asia-Pacific Peace Conference in 1952.[9] These images reflect Picasso's membership in the French Communist Party, which he had formally joined at the end of World War II; he remained actively involved in Party activities until the mid-1950s.[10] In Zhang's youth, Picasso was officially hailed as a paragon of Communist ideology, even if much of his art obviously ignored the principles of Socialist Realism. Zhang recalls that Picasso was probably the first Western artist he learned about, and, in 1972, he made a remarkably precocious still life that explores the formal side of Picasso's art, combining the simplified form of his pre-Cubist paintings with his later innovation of collage through the inclusion of a real page of a newspaper (*Plate 3-a*).

As Picasso's involvement with the Party subsided (he never formally resigned), the obvious contradiction between Party ideology and his art came to dominate discussions of his work. Instead of a paradigm of the Communist artist, Picasso became, in the Party's view, a prime exemplar of the bourgeois Western artist.[11] Zhang observed this transformation in Picasso's reputation, yet his interest in Picasso's art grew, and he had the exceptional opportunity to see reproductions of his work, along with that of other Western artists, when a teacher allowed him to study the volumes of a history of Western art that were housed in his school library but were prohibited to students. His appreciation of Picasso's status as a "counter-revolutionary" heightened the satire in *Unity and Discord* as he presents Mao in this "decadent" style.

Rather than a new initiative, Zhang's selection of Picasso as a reference for his panel of *Unity and Discord* was steeped in his longstanding admiration for Picasso's work and his understanding of Picasso's deeply problematic reputation in relation to Communist ideology. Yet once Zhang explicitly introduced Picasso into his art, he found greater inspiration in Cubism than in Picasso's later Surrealist work. Indeed, during the first decade and a half of the twenty-first century, Cubism has become one of the primary tools of his art.

The growth of Cubism's importance for Zhang is evident by 2001, when he began a *Self-Portrait*, and it reached a new level of complexity in 2013, when he executed a new painting of Mao for an exhibition devoted to contemporary artists' responses to Picasso. Zhang had made previous self-portraits, including an image of himself seen from behind to emphasize his awareness of being a stranger in the US. The painting he began in 2001 and completed in 2004, however, moves beyond denying a coherent sense of self to exploring the multiple, contradictory directions that define Zhang's worldview (*Plate 103*).

To assemble this composition, he also adopted a new preparatory technique. Using a digital camera, Zhang took photographs and then manipulated them in Photoshop to construct an image of himself that uses the language of Analytic Cubism.[12] The result of this collage process is a self-image whose head reflects the multiple viewpoints of Picasso's *Dora Maar Seated* in the subdued tones of early Cubism. Moreover, the shifting planes of head and torso (complete with a disarticulated right arm) construct

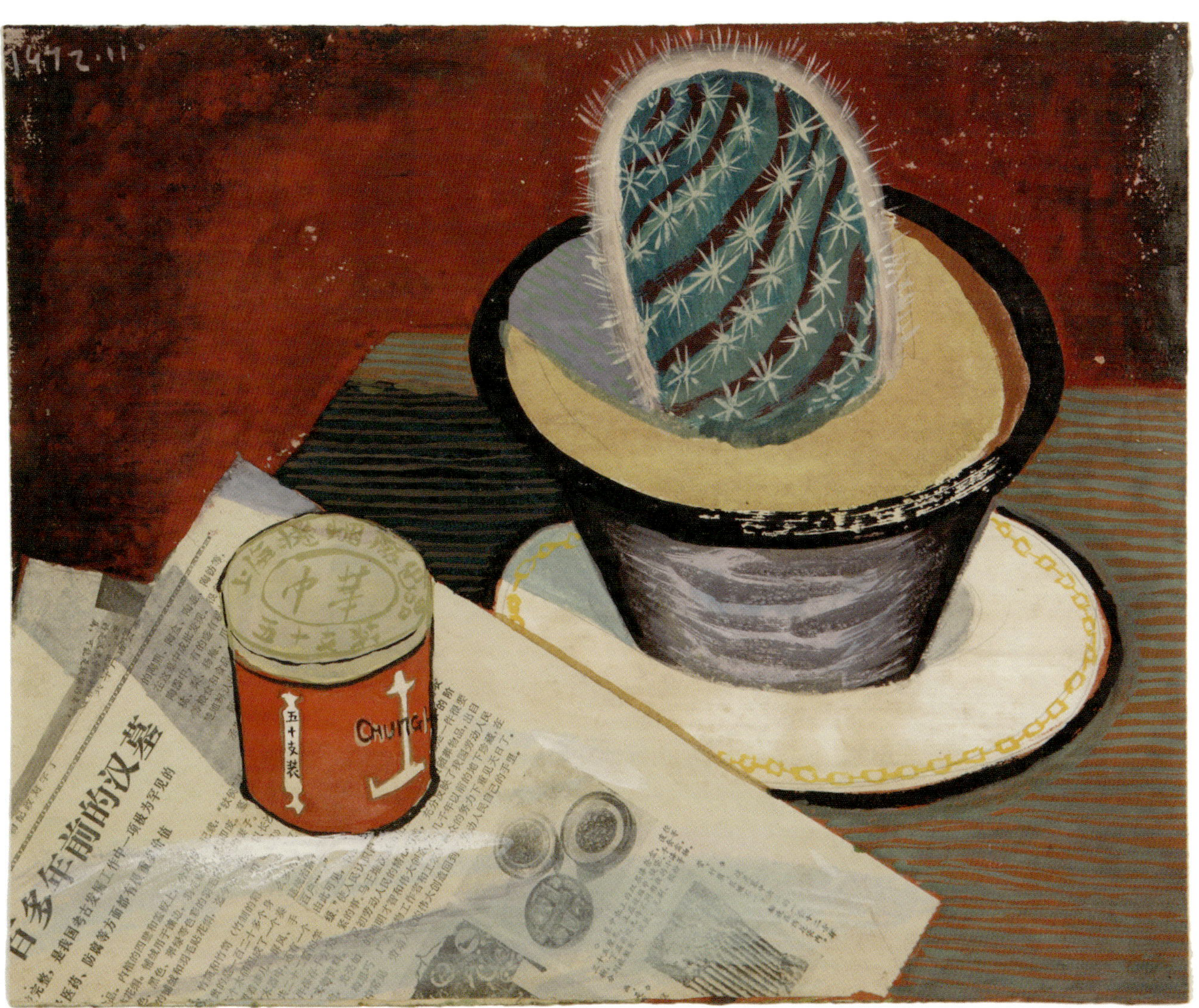

Plate 3-a

Still Life with Cactus, 1972. Watercolor on paper, 12 ¼ x 15 ⅜ in.

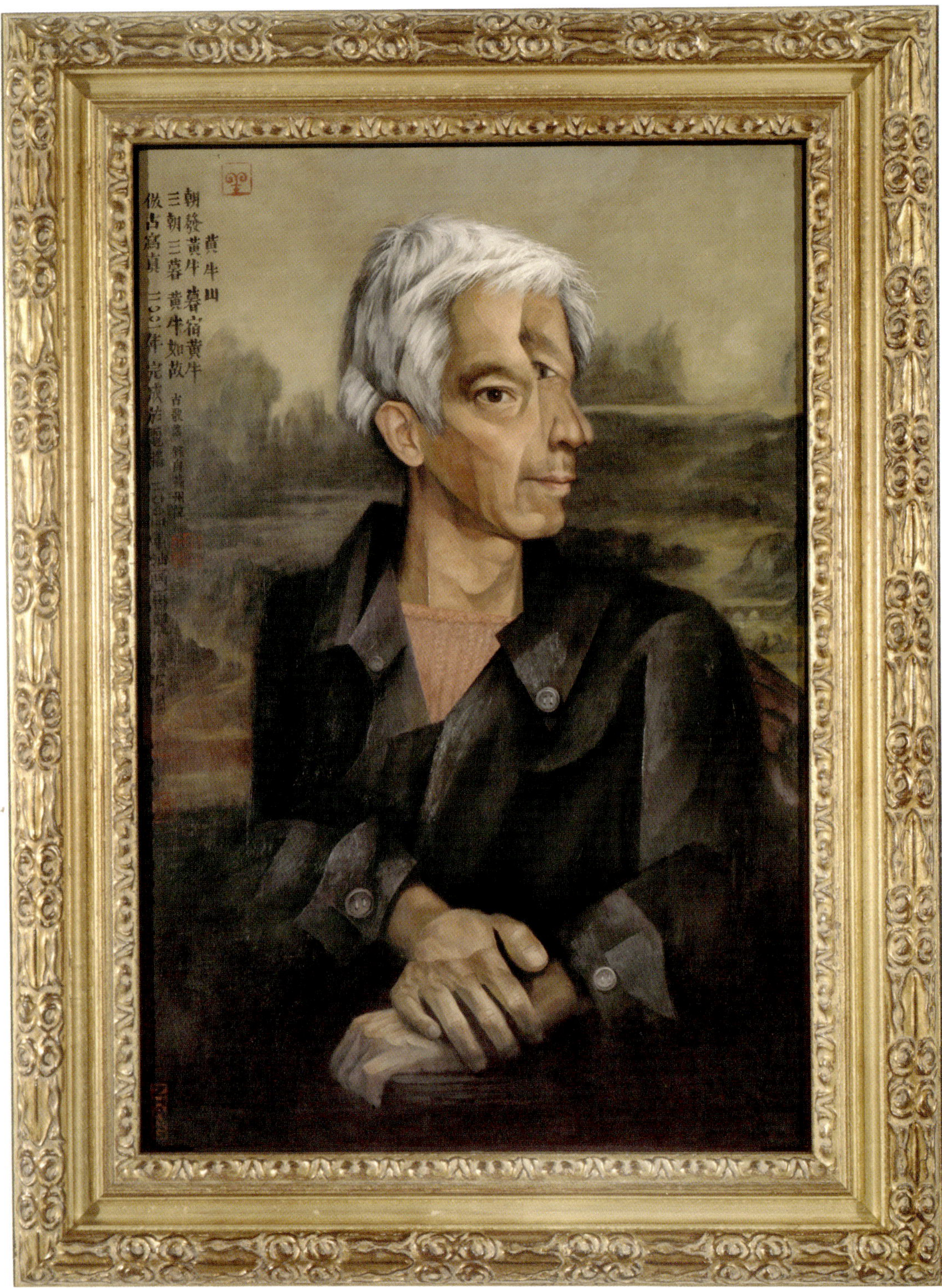

Plate 103

Self-Portrait in the Style of the Old Masters, 2004. Oil on wood panel, 38 x 29 in. Collection of Leo Shih, Taichung, Taiwan.

effects of two dimensions eliding into three, an interplay of volumes that was common in Picasso's early Cubism but no longer characterized his approach in the 1930s.

Zhang did not simply appropriate the stylistic elements of early Cubism, he integrated them into a much more varied composition and employed their discontinuities to signify his own wide-ranging values. The title of the painting is *Self-Portrait in the Style of the Old Masters*, and Zhang's references extend beyond the modern (himself and Cubism) to earlier masters of both Western and Chinese art and literature. While his fractured self-image wears contemporary studio dress, the remainder of the composition evokes deeper historical references. The Chinese characters along the upper left edge of the canvas transcribe an ancient ballad about endurance on the Yellow Ox Mountain, which Zhang sees as a metaphor of his long, episodic relationship with painting.[13] The landscape both contrasts with the geometric rendering of the figure and blends with its somber tonality and fluid shifts of plane. In its subtlety, the landscape evokes traditions of Chinese brush painting, yet it is constructed of passages from the background of Leonardo's *Mona Lisa*. The comparison reveals that Zhang partially modeled his self-image on that painting as well, particularly the placement of the figure in relation to the landscape and the position of his crossed hands.[14] Finally, the ornate gilt frame is integral to the work. It reinforces the "old master" quality of the composition, even as it contrasts with Zhang's image of himself. The painting consists of a series of juxtapositions, including the opposition of Leonardo's classic beauty and the confusing "ugliness" of Picasso's Cubism. The result is a kaleidoscopic passage through multiple chronological and cultural references that ultimately coalesce through Zhang's dusky tonality and modulated style.

Since the late 1990s, Zhang has been deeply involved with landscape painting, both the traditions of classical Chinese masters and those of Western modernists, such as Monet, Van Gogh, and Cézanne. Among the diversity of his work, these paintings are his most far-reaching embrace of the hybrid concepts that are at the center of his art. Although he creates an amalgam of Chinese and Western styles in these paintings, Zhang follows a foundational principle of late Ming and early Qing dynasty painters of the sixteenth, seventeenth, and eighteenth centuries: great art should not be based on the direct observation of nature, but rather on an imaginative interaction with past masterpieces. Zhang extends this tradition in unexpected ways by taking traditional Chinese landscape paintings as his point of departure and modifying them through the introduction of Western styles, particularly Impressionism and Post-Impressionism, styles closely associated with depicting nature.

His most challenging leaps across cultures are the paintings in the "Shan Shui Today" series that ally Chinese masterpieces with Cubism, a style that is far more associated with the figure or still life than landscape. As in all of his appropriations of Cubism, Zhang does not copy specific works but constructs his own variations.[15] Conceptually, Zhang links the traditional Chinese painting's emphasis on the imaginative transformation of nature with Cubism's extreme departure from representation, and he finds coherence in both approaches' tendency to build compositions through abstract patterns. His *After Wang Yuanqi* from the "Shan Shui Today" series (*Plate 71*) revisits a panel of the great Qing master's scroll *Wangchuan Villa* (*Fig. 1*) to explore the massive, layered structure of the mountainous landscape in the reductive geometry and merging planes of Cubism.

Zhang's resort to Cubism augments his serial exploration of Eastern and Western styles with a powerful subject that pervades his art: the state of contemporary China. He does not only assimilate the technique of Wang Yuanqi with Cubism but uses the formal features of Cubism to highlight changes in the modern era—"Shan Shui Today." The monochromatic palette of Cubism pervades the scene and eliminates the vibrant greens and reddish highlights of *Wangchuan Villa*. The angular facets of Cubism fill the canvas, eradicating the ample sky of Wang Yuanqi's composition and creating an oppressive space. These stylistic transformations match Zhang's depiction of the scene. The verdant pines in Wang Yuanqi's painting are now only stumps scattered across the landscape, streams have run dry, and the villa is abandoned and partially collapsed. This ruined landscape is Zhang's commentary on the government's policy of urban development and his lament at the loss of connection to nature in traditional Chinese culture. What began as a dialogue with past art expands to encompass a pointed critique of contemporary life in China.[16]

Along with Zhang's *Quaker Oats Mao*, his *Bird's Nest in the Style of Cubism* (*Plate 115*) has become a defining achievement of his career. Made to ridicule the Communist Party during the international showcase of the Olympic Games in Beijing, the painting is loaded with knife-edged attacks on the current and past positions of the Chinese government. While other essays in this book will no doubt explicate these diverse references, my analysis is focused more specifically on the means Zhang employed to array his multi-pronged attack. It constitutes a significant deepening of his ongoing engagement with Cubism.

When Zhang set out to deconstruct the Beijing Games' premier symbol of China's success, the purpose-built stadium called "The Bird's Nest," he turned to the fractured planes of Cubism as a visual metaphor of his ideological critique. In contrast to the process he used to compose his self-portrait, Zhang worked directly on the canvas and resorted to only a few pencil sketches to prepare his composition. Following a Cubist strategy, he fragmented the stadium's web into geometric shards. More

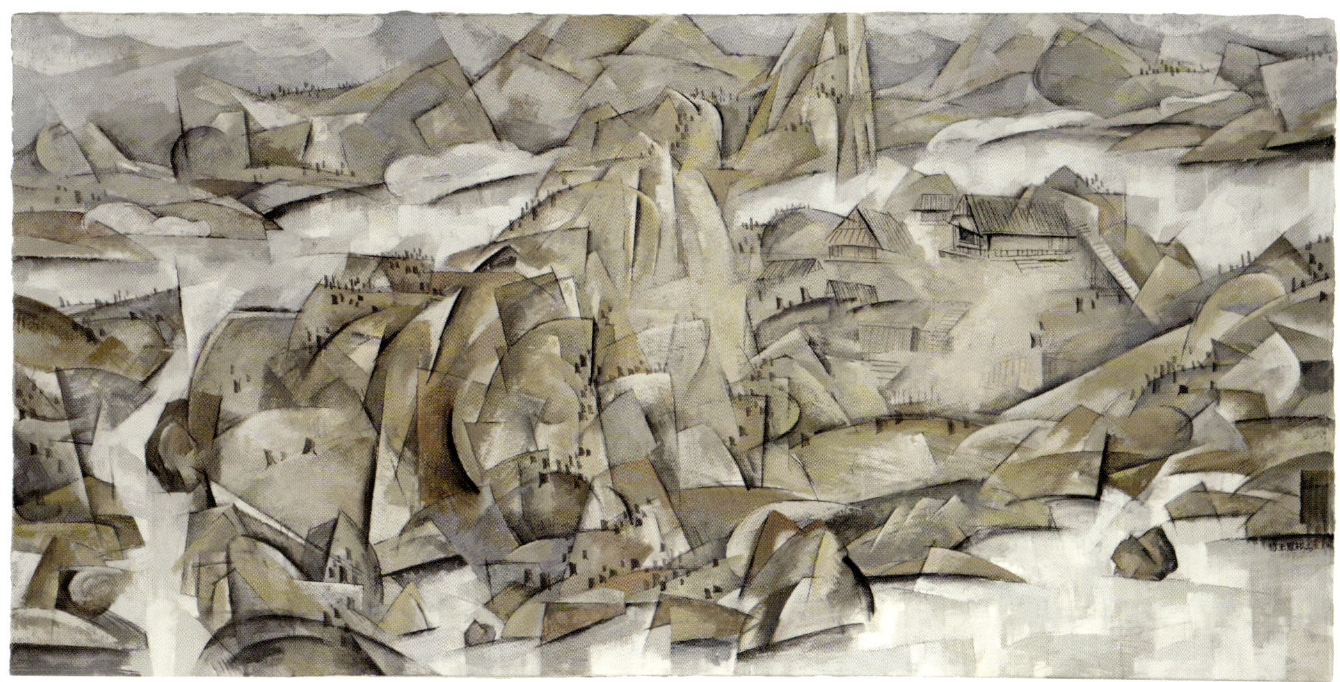

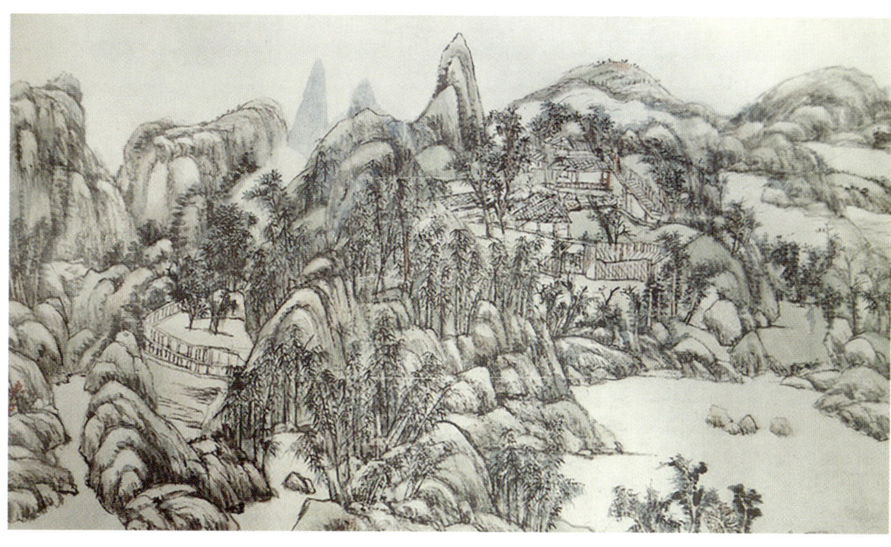

Plate 71
After Wang Yuanqi, 2009. Ink and mixed media on rice paper mounted on canvas, 40 x 82 in.

Fig. 1
Wang Yuanqi, *Wangchuan Villa* (detail), 1711. Handscroll ink and color on paper, 14 in. x 17 ft. Collection of the Metropolitan Museum of Art, New York, Ex. coll.: C. C. Wang Family, Purchase, Douglas Dillon Gift, 1977. Image © The Metropolitan Museum of Art

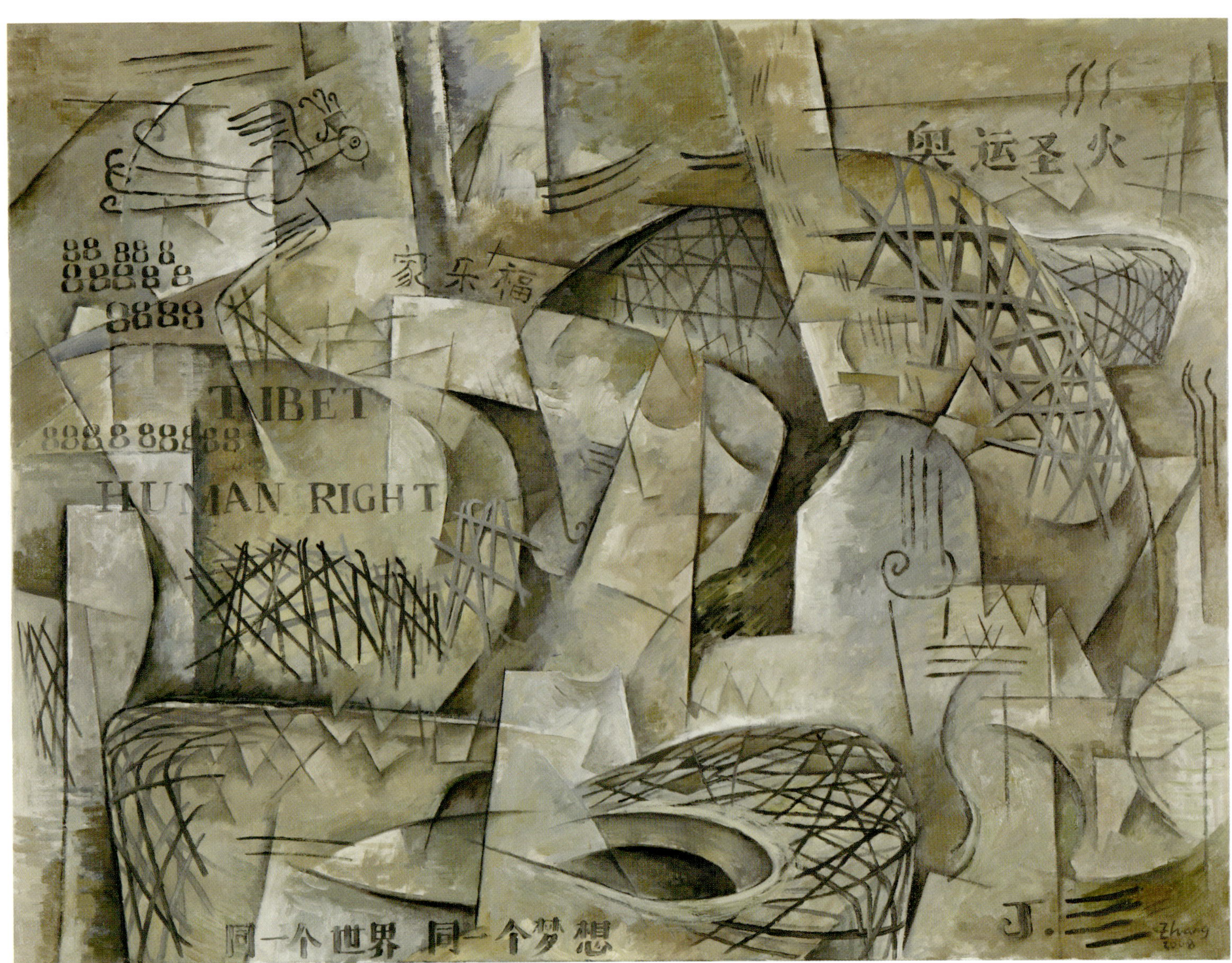

Plate 115

Bird's Nest in the Style of Cubism, 2008. Oil on canvas, 36 x 48 in.

importantly, he adopted the structural principles of Analytic Cubism to reconfigure these disparate parts and the other associations he chose to include. Analytic Cubism is not only an art of dissolution, fragmenting objects into separate planes, but also of reconstruction. Its virtual grid supplies an underlying pattern for integrating practically anything the artist wishes to include—not only snippets of objects but also words and visual signs of any sort. By not attempting to reproduce realistic space and instead providing a clearly artificial visual field, Analytic Cubism frees artists from representation and offers boundless opportunities to create independent, synthetic wholes constructed of fragments that overlap, abut at hard edges, and coalesce across blended boundaries.

In *Bird's Nest*, Zhang provocatively explored this conceptual space and, in the process, vigorously revived a century-old style. Zhang's resort to Analytic Cubism is not unique, even if it is startling. Among his contemporaries, Georg Baselitz, George Condo, and Sean Scully, to name a few, have renewed the style in their recent work. But Zhang's Cubism is exceptional for his use of the style to address political issues, an approach that figures only tangentially in the work of Picasso, although it is found in the work of Zhang's contemporary the Argentine artist Guillermo Kuitca.[17]

Zhang fully exploited Cubism's possibilities by deftly integrating fragments of the stadium among verbal references to his opposition to government policies ("TIBET," "HUMAN RIGHTS") and the Tiananmen protests (the date June 4 is referenced by "J." and four horizontal lines at the lower right corner of the composition). The result is one of the most imaginative and evocative reinvigorations of Cubism in our time, despite the government's notorious rejection of the painting for its explicit references and supposedly "dull" palette. Its remarkable synthesis of formal virtuosity and political subversion seamlessly mates Picasso's Cubism with the humanitarian themes of *Guernica*.

In 2012, Zhang returned to his pairing of Picasso and Mao for his contribution to an exhibition I curated for the Museu Picasso in Barcelona, "Post-Picasso: Contemporary Reactions" (March–June 2014). As he considered how to revisit the image he had created fifteen years earlier for *Unity and Discord*, Zhang had several additional Picassos in mind.[18] Although it does not feature in the final painting, *Guernica* remained an inspiration to create art with a potent political message. Zhang shared his belief in the mural's relevance to contemporary politics with a global span of artists, including his friend and fellow artist Lin Lin, who had painted his own version of the composition to commemorate the Tiananmen massacres, with a large portrait of Mao juxtaposed with Picasso's malevolent bull.[19] Zhang was reminded of the relevance of Picasso's work during the Spanish Civil War and World War II by an exhibition at the Guggenheim Museum during the fall of 2012, "Picasso: Black and White." The somber palette of the work included in the exhibition inspired his new painting's much more subdued tonality in comparison to *Unity and Discord.*

In *Unity and Discord,* Zhang critiqued Mao through two transformations: the portrayal of Mao in the vivid colors and multiple profiles of Picasso's Surrealist style and the rough room that isolates the figure's self-regard. In his revision, he not only muted his palette but also significantly enhanced the complexity and resolution of the work through his refined draftsmanship and newly added references to Chinese culture. *Mao, After Picasso* (Plate 52) is a painting of great sophistication and power, a composition that deserves its position as a stand-alone work, rather than as a part of the multi-panel design of *Unity and Discord.*

Working in ink and oil on rice paper, Zhang achieves a particularly precise rendering in his drawing. Whether he is describing the mirror's frame, the features of Mao's face (and reflection), or the Cubist faceting of figure and space, Zhang employs crisp lines to bound forms, articulate their shifting planes, and detail their features. The contrast with the broadly brushed first image is striking given that both stem from Picasso's *Dora Maar Seated.* Zhang's subtle drawing in *Mao, After Picasso* enables him to articulate Mao's double vision—contemplating both himself and the viewer—as well as the reflection of this dual regard in the mirror.

By compressing Mao's figure and his extended salute, Zhang gained the space to expand his critique of Mao beyond the confrontation with Picasso to encompass emblems of pre-Communist China. Using Photoshop, he reproduced a section of door of the Forbidden City, a massive slab studded with knobs and the head of an Imperial dragon. A palace lantern hangs above Mao's head. The result is a Mao who is not only cut off from the Chinese people but also immersed in the environment of Imperial China. Mao has become an Emperor.

Contemplating the process of creating *Mao, After Picasso* and the experience of seeing both the eighty-odd works in "Post-Picasso" and the Museu Picasso's collection of Picasso's art that surrounded the exhibition in Barcelona, Zhang stated, "I started to see Cubism in a more ideological way."[20] His respect for its formal principles has expanded to emphasize the imaginative freedom that underlies its departure from representation and the nearly unlimited range of associations it may encompass. This conceptual approach to Cubism perfectly matches Zhang's wide-ranging and anti-hierarchical art. It inspires much of his current art, whether or not these paintings explicitly resemble the Cubism of Picasso.[21]

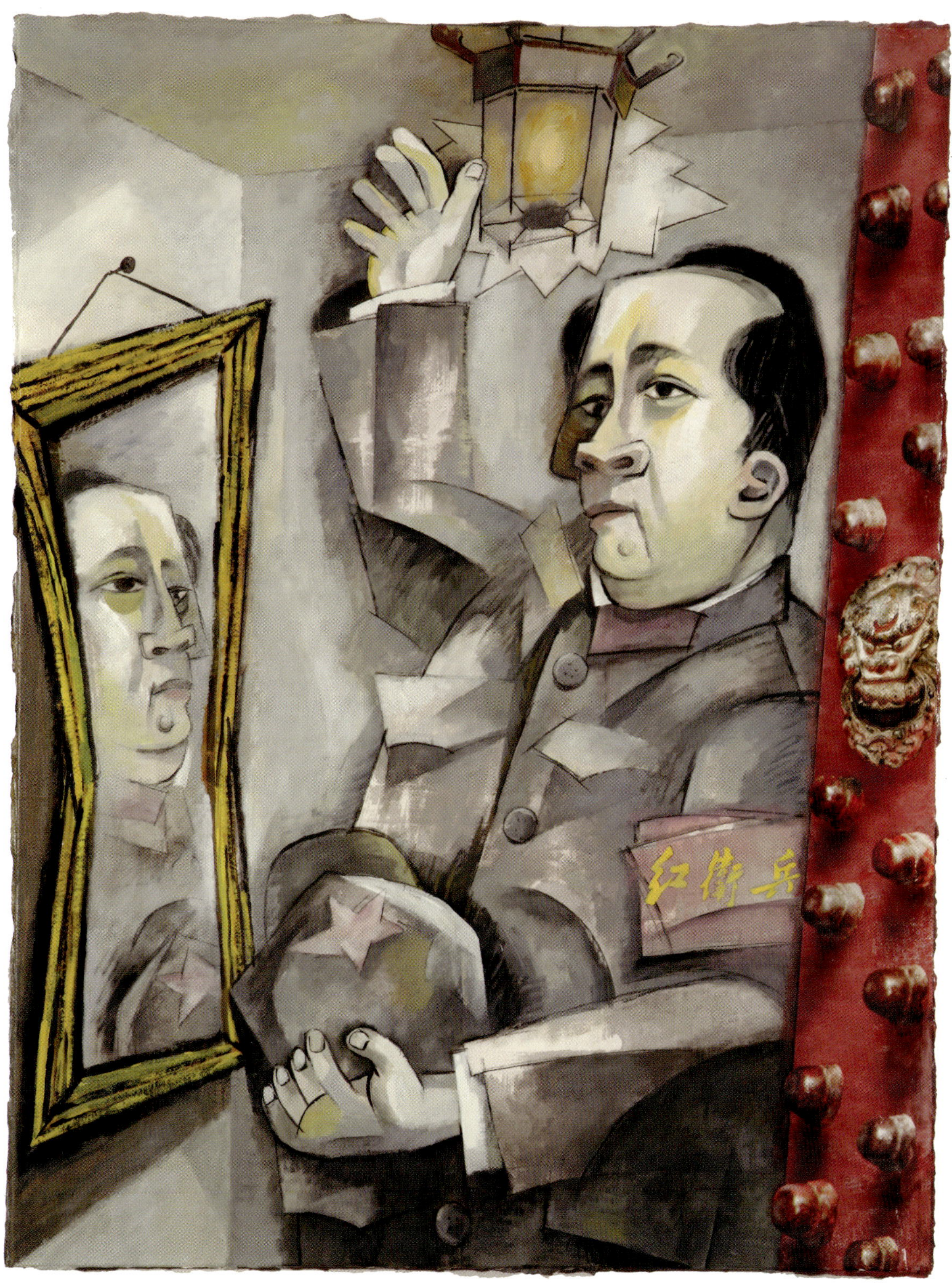

Plate 52

Mao, After Picasso, 2012. Ink and oil on rice paper and photo collage mounted on canvas, 44 ½ x 34 ½ in.

1   I would like to express my great appreciation to Zhang Hongtu for his patient answers to my many questions about his work in recent years. I would also like to acknowledge the important contributions that Jerome Silbergeld has made to the study of Zhang's work, especially his essay "Zhang Hongtu: The Art of Straddling Boundaries," in *Zhang Hongtu: The Art of Straddling Boundaries* (Taipei: Lin & Keng Gallery, 2007), vii–xxv.

2   The exhibitions were "Post-Picasso: Contemporary Reactions," Museu Picasso, Barcelona, March 5–June 29, 2014; "Picasso and Contemporary Art," Deichtorhallen, Hamburg, April 1–July 12, 2015; and "Picasso.mania," Grand Palais, Paris, October 7, 2015–February 29, 2016.

3   For a discussion of these artists, see Michael FitzGerald, *Post-Picasso: Contemporary Reactions* (Barcelona: Fundació Museu Picasso de Barcelona, 2014).

4   The symposium, organized by the author, and discussion among a number of the artists in the exhibition galleries took place on March 6, 2015.

5   Zhang Hongtu, conversation with the author, January 25, 2015. The exhibition was "Picasso and Portraiture: Representation and Transformation," Museum of Modern Art, New York, April 28–September 17, 1996.

6   The painting is in the collection of the Musée Picasso, Paris. It is reproduced in *Picasso and Portraiture*, ed. William Rubin, exh. cat. (New York: Museum of Modern Art, 1996), 391.

7   Brigitte Léal, " 'For Charming Dora': Portraits of Dora Maar," in Rubin, ed., *Picasso and Portraiture*, 392.

8   *Woman Dressing Her Hair* is in the collection of the Museum of Modern Art, New York, and reproduced in Rubin, ed., *Picasso and Portraiture*, 401.

9   Zhang Hongtu, email to the author, January 15, 2015.

10   For Picasso's involvement with the Communist Party, see Gertje Utley, *Pablo Picasso: The Communist Years* (New Haven: Yale University Press, 2000).

11   The opposition between Picasso's art and the Social Realist styles promoted by the Communist Party became a public controversy when Picasso's portrait of Stalin was published in the French newspaper *Les Lettres françaises* (March 12–19, 1953). See Michael FitzGerald, "A Triangle of Ambitions: Art, Politics, and Family During the Postwar Years with Françoise Gilot," in Rubin, ed, *Picasso and Portraiture*, 436–38.

12   Zhang Hongtu, conversation with the author, January 25, 2015.

13   Zhang has kindly transcribed the text: "Yellow Ox Mountain. Departing from the Yellow Ox Mountain in the morning, / resting at the Yellow Ox Mountain in the evening, / after three days and three nights / I am still here at the Yellow Ox Mountain."

14   Zhang also chose to paint his self-portrait on a wooden panel in emulation of

Leonardo's *Mona Lisa*.

15   Picasso painted a rare landscape series at Horta de Ebro in 1909; Zhang did not refer to them.

16   Zhang explained his goals in the "Shan Shui Today" series in a telephone conversation with the author, February 15, 2015.

17   For a discussion of these artists' work, see FitzGerald, *Post-Picasso: Contemporary Reactions*.

18   Zhang Hongtu, email to the author, August 29, 2013.

19   In an email dated October 8, 2012, Zhang sent the author an image of Lin Lin's painting. Tragically, Lin Lin was shot dead on August 18, 1991, while drawing a portrait near Times Square in New York. See Richard Bernstein, "For Chinese Artists, Shattered Dreams Despite Freedom," *New York Times*, August 28, 1991.

20   Zhang Hongtu, email to the author, January 15, 2015.

21   Ibid.

THE MAN IN THE MOON: A CONVERSATION WITH ZHANG HONGTU

Eugenie Tsai

Eugenie Tsai: One thing that's always impressed me about your practice is how open it's been to the work of many other artists. When you showed me some of the small paintings you made in the 1950s, before you went to art school, I thought they could have been the work of an American or a European artist. So I'm curious about your training.

Zhang Hongtu: I was interested in art when I was very young. In China in the '50s, government control over art and culture was not as strong as it became in the '60s, especially during the Cultural Revolution. In the '50s we could still learn something about, say, Renaissance art or even a modern artist like Picasso, whose image of a dove appeared on a poster and a stamp for the Asia-Pacific Peace Conference in 1952 (*Fig. 1*).

Fig. 1

Chinese stamp with Picasso's dove, 1950.

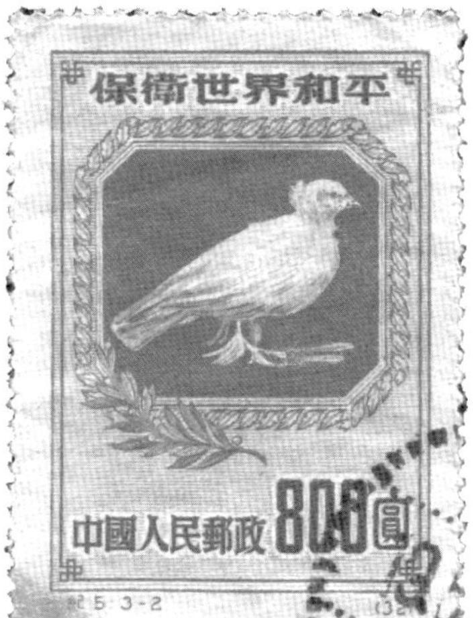

ET: A dove! That's surprising and perhaps a little ironic that an image by a European artist would be chosen for such a conference.

ZH: Although Picasso was considered a Western artist, he was known and promoted by the Chinese government for a few specific reasons: he had drawn a portrait of Stalin for Stalin's birthday, he was a member of the French Communist Party, and he was against the Korean War. He did a painting about that based, I believe, on a painting by Manet.

ET: It sounds as though the Chinese government's interest in Picasso had less to do with his role as an artistic innovator and more to do with his political point of view.

ZH: That's right.

ET: So initially, your take on Picasso was quite different from that of an artist who was trained in America or Europe. You were really looking at him through the lens of Chinese politics at that time and not as an avant-garde artist.

ZH: Yes. In the '50s I knew nothing about Picasso except for his image of the dove and his membership in the Communist Party. In the early '60s, when I was in middle school, I had an opportunity to learn more. The Department of Culture gave a gift to our school (which was attached to the Central Academy of Fine Arts), a set of books about world art history. The gift actually came from the Swedish government as a kind of cultural exchange. The set was kept in the library, where students were not allowed to look at any of the volumes or check them out. Only teachers could do this. So the only way we could see the books was by cultivating a good relationship with our teachers. They would bring books home, where we could then go to look at them. That's how I was able to see Picasso's abstract paintings, like *Three Musicians*, and some of his sculptures. Both were eye-opening. Before that, I knew a little bit about Impressionism from a book about the movement. That book was accessible only to those who were of a high enough rank in the government. Since the father of one of my classmates was a very famous professor who taught oil painting at the Central Academy of Fine Arts, my friend got the book from his father so that I could look at it. The reproductions were in black and white, which distorted one of the key concepts of Impressionism, which is all about color. But still, the story was very interesting. The book talked about the Impressionists' ways of looking at nature and the contemporary world, and the role these played in this new form of artistic expression. We also learned about Western art through reproductions in magazines from Russia, Poland, and Yugoslavia. Looking at these prompted some of us to try different things, like making the color in our paintings stronger, rather than just copying what we saw. I even tried pointillism.

ET: How did your teachers respond to this experimental approach?

ZH: When we looked at work in the classroom, what our teachers considered a good painting depended on their ideas. Works that received high scores looked like the teacher's work. At that time, Socialist Realism was the dominant style. If you did something different, you could be criticized for making work that looked like a Western style. The work would then be called decadent bourgeois (*Plate 2-b*). I remember that I once brought my work home. My mother looked at all of it and liked only the brightly colored pointillist painting. That made me think about standards and how they can differ from person to person.

ET: So, Socialist Realism and other European realist traditions—for example, the paintings of Courbet and Millet—were accepted by your teachers.

ZH: Yes, even David and Manet were fine. But not Monet.

ET: Manet was acceptable but not Monet. That's very interesting, especially considering the prominent role Monet's work later played in your "Repainted Shan Shui" series. You've often said that your work incorporates East and West. When I think about the West, I've noticed that you tend to be drawn to well-known, even iconic artists like Picasso, Van Gogh, Monet, and Cézanne. Since I'm not familiar with the Chinese artists you reference in that series, is that also the case with them?

ZH: Yes, the same thing.

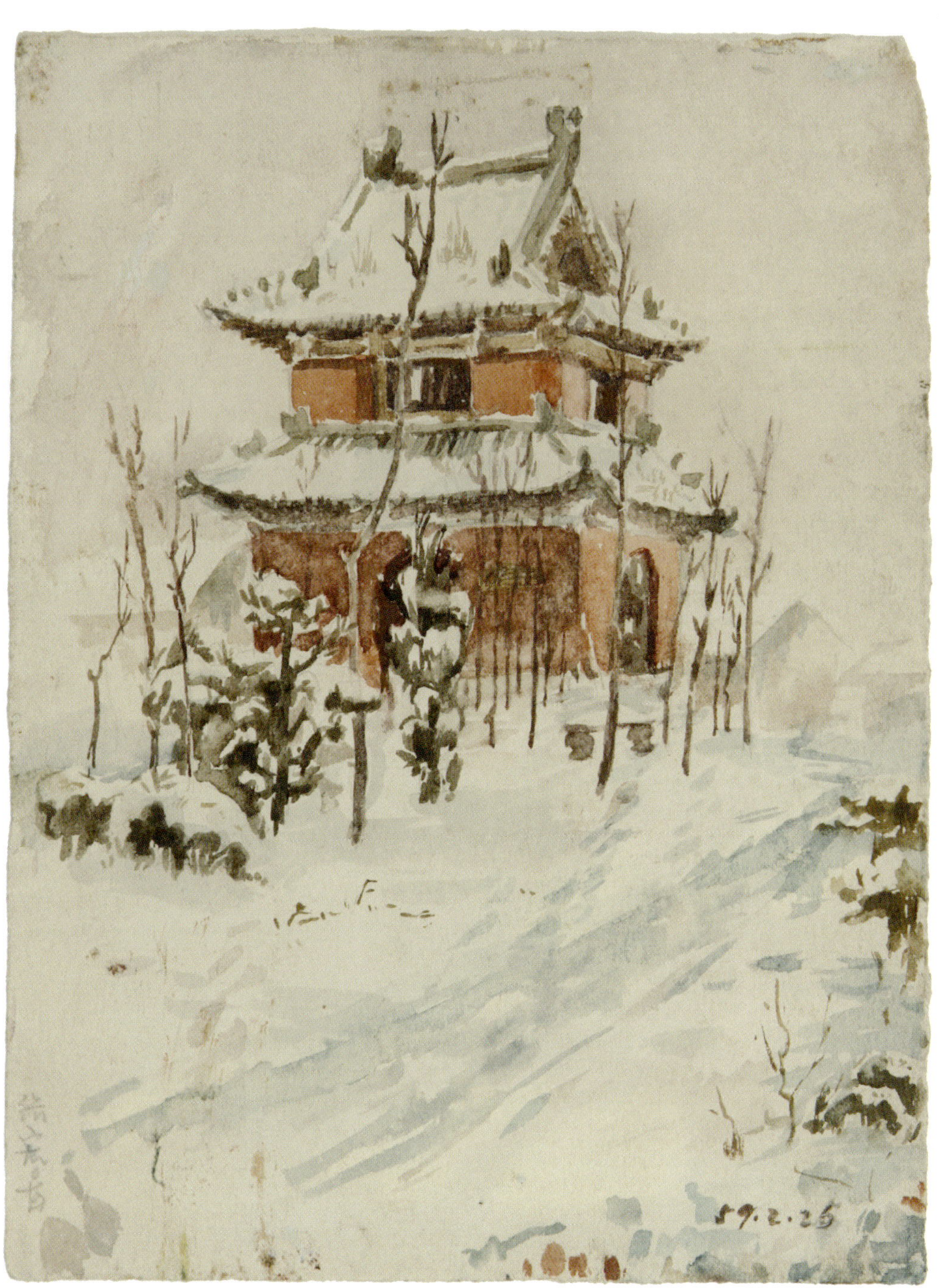

Plate 2-b

Snow in the Park, 1959. Watercolor on paper, 7 ½ x 5 ¾ in.

ET: So why are you attracted to their work?

ZH: That happened after I arrived in the US. From my studies, I knew a little bit about Pop art. After I came here, I learned about Andy Warhol. I saw his huge portrait of Chairman Mao in the Metropolitan Museum. I was puzzled by this. We had a large portrait of Mao at the Tiananmen gate. No one considered that fine art. It was just our great leader's portrait. But I wondered why Andy Warhol's portrait of Mao was in a museum. Warhol just added some brushwork. But that question opened up the opportunity to learn more about Warhol and Pop art. Since I was no longer in China, I could read and research these topics freely. I was very interested in the concept of icons, because in China during the Cultural Revolution, no one could compare with Chairman Mao as a popular image. People worshiped his image as though he was a god. During the Cultural Revolution, my original trust and belief in him turned to doubt. I wanted to challenge his status as an icon, challenge him as an iconic figure. When you blindly worship an iconic figure, you lose your sense of self. Everybody is an individual with an important inner self. Once you've lost that, you've lost too much. Warhol showed me a new way to treat icons. He utilized different kinds of icons drawn from politics, religion, and pop culture as a strategy to lessen or even eliminate their power. I saw Warhol's portrait of the Mona Lisa first as a print. It was different from Leonardo's painting *Mona Lisa* so I thought this might show Warhol's disrespect for the original. But then I realized that Warhol's transformation blurred the boundary between elite culture and popular or mass culture. I admired the way he made people get away from the limitations of the hierarchy of high culture found in museums, and popular or mass culture including street art, graffiti, and public art. So the way Warhol challenged the boundaries between high and low had a great influence on me.

ET: Did Warhol's influence become evident in your work at that time?

ZH: Yes. One thing I did was to use soy sauce to do calligraphy. The style of the calligraphy was from a thousand years ago, by Wang Xizhi (王羲之), one of the great Chinese masters. In China people consider this artist not just a master but a sage. I borrowed his style.

ET: So the calligraphy is from a tradition that's considered refined and scholarly.

ZH: Yes it is. I used his style of writing using soy sauce instead of ink. But the text, the content of the calligraphy was copied from a Chinese sweatshop help-wanted advertisement (*Fig. 2*). So it's a mix of something really high and something really low that visually has nothing to do with the work of Andy Warhol. But the work reflected his ideas.

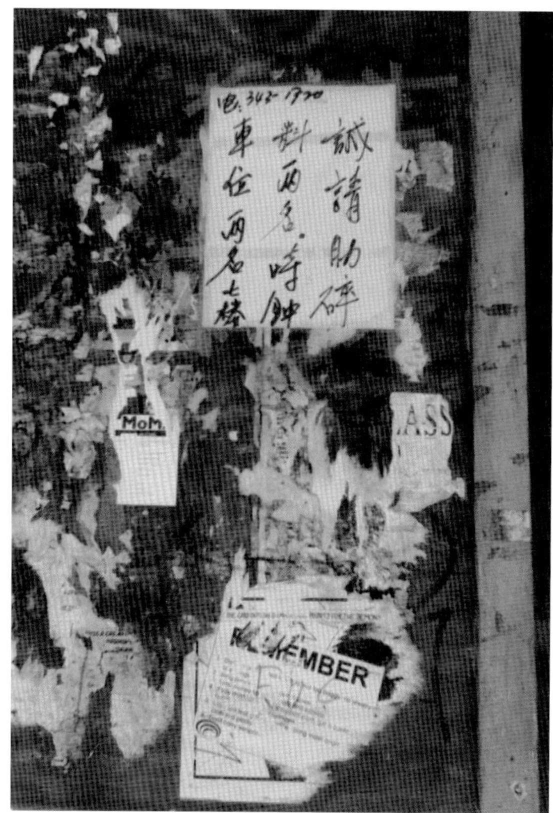

Fig. 2

ET: How does this relate to your "Repainted Shan Shui" paintings, which bring together the work of iconic European and iconic Chinese artists?

ZH: When I arrived in the United States, I found that the two cultures approach icons in different ways. Here in America and in Europe, people are more concerned with the present. In contrast, Chinese culture respects—perhaps even reveres—tradition and the past. In the Chinese artistic tradition, landscape painting rendered in black ink has always been the most significant kind of painting. Artists and connoisseurs are actually able to discern different colors in black ink painting, which is considered the highest form of art. This view has not changed for centuries.

ET: That's quite a contrast to Impressionist paintings, which are known for their vivid colors and lively brushwork, both made possible by oil paint.

ZH: Yes. I thought I would use oil paint to redo Chinese painting in color, with something in common: landscape. Although figurative painting exists in traditional Chinese art, it's not regarded as a significant subject in the way that landscape is. And there's no tradition of pure abstraction. My original idea was to challenge people's

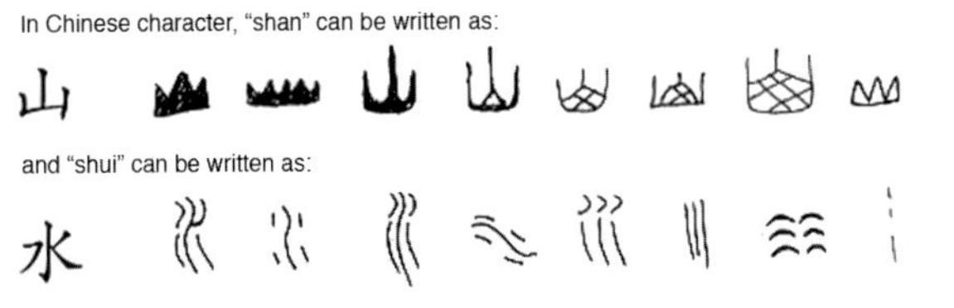

conventional view about what's West, what's East. Of course, I'm not the first artist to combine East and West; that started over a hundred years ago. Even Van Gogh was inspired by Japanese prints. The dialogue between East and West was evident when the Princeton University Art Museum acquired one of my landscape paintings inspired by a piece by Shitao in its collection, which I painted in the style of Van Gogh. The first question I asked the curator is whether the painting would go into the Asian or European collection. Of course, it could go into either, I didn't really care. It ended up going into Asian.

ET: When I first encountered the "Repainted Shan Shui" paintings I found them both beautiful and disconcerting. On the one hand I could tell they looked like a Van Gogh, or a Monet, maybe a Cézanne, but they were somehow different in a way I couldn't quite pin down. I wasn't quite sure where to situate the pieces. Now you have a new series called "Shan Shui Today." How are the two series related?

ZH: I stopped making the "Repainted Shan Shui" series about eight or nine years ago, even though the paintings were extremely well received. I began to feel that people were more focused on the aesthetic qualities of the paintings rather than the ideas behind the series. I felt it was important to continue making art that people would find provocative and challenging. I kept one painting from the series and called this last piece *Fang Wang Yuanqi* (2009). It's not pure Cézanne, but Cézanne-influenced. After I finished it, I copied the definitions of ink painting, *shan shui* painting, and Impressionism from the Chinese version of Wikipedia onto the painting. That way, I make the audience read it, though it's comprehensible only to those who read Chinese.

ET: You'll have to translate for me.

ZH: What is *shan shui*? In Chinese characters *shan* can be written as 山 and *shui* can be written as 水. Now, *shan* is translated as *hill* or *mountain* and *shui* is translated as *water* or *river* (*Fig. 3*). In the Chinese-English dictionary, *shan shui hua* (*hua* means *painting*) is translated as *Chinese landscape painting*, and for many English speakers, *Chinese landscape painting* means all ancient Chinese paintings with mountain and water images. I believe that all ancient Chinese paintings with mountain and water images should only be called *shan shui painting*. When Chinese painters work on *shan shui painting*, they do not try to present an image of what they have seen in nature, but what they have felt, thought, and imagined about nature. No one cares whether the painted colors and shapes look like the real object or not. So *shan shui painting* cannot be translated as *landscape painting*. I want everyone to call ancient Chinese paintings with the images of mountains and water *shan shui painting* instead of *Chinese landscape painting*. Besides, *shan shui* is not too difficult to pronounce, just follow me, loudly read this word three times, you will never forget it.

ET: Thanks. The distinction you make between the term "landscape painting" and "*shan shui*" is very nuanced.

ZH: I wanted my paintings to be not only about visually pleasing results but also what I consider the boundaries between West and East, the boundaries between painting a thousand years ago, the Chinese tradition, and then painting a hundred years ago, the Impressionists, and here's me myself, working today, in my way trying to create something new from two old traditions. Sometimes I compare my way of working to recycling, recycling old stuff, old fashions. Today, even Chinese painters who carry on the tradition of ink painting want to make something modern that can be sold at auction houses for sky-high prices. But that tradition is difficult to update because the resulting paintings still tend to look like they're a thousand years old. After I stopped making works for the "Repainted Shan Shui" series, I still wanted to do something related to the Chinese tradition: landscape with mountains and water. Basically, I learned my technique from Western artists. Although I learned ink painting, I'm more interested in oil painting. So I thought I'd try to bring older Chinese masterpieces to reality.

ET: That sounds interesting. What do you mean by that?

ZH: In traditional *shan shui* painting, people considered the beauty of nature and the very beautiful feelings about nature conveyed by the artists in their paintings. So these *shan shui* paintings are always peaceful and always beautiful. They are regarded as representing the height of culture. Brushwork is important. When I say "bring to reality", actually, it is literally a *shan shui* painting, but actually I'm more concerned about *shan*, mountain, and *shui*, water, which to me is the environment. So, in "Repainted Shan Shui," I'm referring to the older masterpieces by artists like Wang Yuanqi (王原祁). What I'm doing now is the mountain and water of *shan shui* viewed through my current experience of nature, which is of damaged mountains and polluted water. Sadly, this is our reality and something that's been on my mind for a long time. Of course, I admire the work Al Gore has done to draw attention to the environment. I saw the movie and, of course, bought his book.

ET: So you're talking about nature in broader sense of the word. Are you thinking about the degradation of the environment globally or are you referring specifically to China?

ZH: Globally. Since I use the format of traditional Chinese painting, people might think I'm speaking only of the situation in China. But I'm not. The paintings don't portray specific places, so no one can tell if a mountain is a Chinese mountain, or if the water is Chinese water. Perhaps the composition, motifs, and style of particular works lead people to believe the conversation is about what's taking place in China. China does have a big problem. Environmental pollution may be its biggest problem. But I've had visitors to my studio here in Queens who see my paintings and immediately begin to talk about what's happening in America, like the Colorado River catching fire. So people around the world are concerned about the destruction of the environment. My recent paintings sometimes include a tall residential building set in a natural setting. And sometimes monkeys.

ET: It's interesting because, of course, in China there's a long tradition of learning by copying old master paintings, and you've really done that. In the process, you've avoided blindly copying for the sake of copying. Instead, you've transformed your research into something that's distinctly your own. But since your days as a student, you've been extremely open to outside influences, and that's reflected in your art, which has a real spirit of generosity that cuts across cultures.

ZH: Although the turning point started long time ago, an experience I had shortly after I arrived here was extremely important. In 1983, there was a show about Scandinavian art at the Guggenheim Museum. I remember it clearly. At the time, I didn't read English well, but I do remember the wall text, which was taken from the catalogue. There were two sentences that read, "National art is bad. Good art is national." Before I came to the United States, I thought I had a mission to promote Chinese art. Do you want to know why?

ET: That's a surprising statement. What do you mean by that?

ZH: While growing up in China, I already had a strong sense of nationalism, which can lead to terrible situations, as we saw actually happened.

ET: But what traditions did you feel you had to promote?

ZH: What I knew about Western art and its concepts that I had learned in China by reading art history books. I also learned about Chinese art and its thousand-year-old tradition. It's a tradition I was proud of. I thought "you guys," meaning you Westerners, maybe your artistic tradition started with Cézanne, but in China we started with the Yin dynasty. Because I had learned about Western artistic traditions I felt that Western people should make more of an effort to learn more about Chinese art. We knew more about Western art than you knew about Chinese art. I felt I could do something to promote Chinese art so that Americans would know what real Chinese art was.

ET: What did you think you were going to do? Did you make some work that actually tried to do that?

ZH: I did, though when I look back I realize it was somewhat superficial. I made abstract paintings with acrylic on rice paper using a Chinese brush. I tried to do some line work differently with oil painting, light brushwork. Of course I see now that I didn't really understand either artistic tradition very well. I just had an attitude. To tell you the truth, I learned more about Chinese art after I started the "Repainted Shan Shui" series, when I was nearly sixty years old, here, not in China. Because when I started the "Repainted Shan Shui" works, at first I thought it was just kind of like making fun of both sides. Like Pop art. You have an icon, I have an icon. How could I put two icons together to say what's going on? I didn't expect a new concept to emerge. I thought from my life experience and from my knowledge of both traditions, I could put both sides together to make fun of them.

ET: You may have started with the intent to make fun of both traditions, but that's not what happened in the end.

ZH: It didn't happen. Do you know why? Because when I really wanted to do this, I realized I had to learn. In order to combine this one or that one and to put together something on your canvas, you actually have to know the technique of the artists. Take Van Gogh. You have to understand his painting deeply. So I started learning. I went to museums. I went to both the Metropolitan Museum and the Museum of Modern Art. I went to Van Gogh's place in Arles in Southern France, to experience the light, the wind, what Van Gogh looked at and felt. This helped me understand why he painted the way he did. And at the same time, I went to the two different Palace museums, one in Taipei, one in Beijing. So the whole process of doing the "Repainted Shan Shui" paintings became a process of learning.

ET: Which is exactly what the Chinese tradition advocates, learning from the masters. In your case, not only Chinese masters.

ZH: That's right. So out of my initial idea to poke fun at both traditions, a clearer idea emerged, which became the "Repainted Shan Shui" paintings. Once the idea crystallized, I could combine the two, resulting in work that had more layers of meaning than I had originally thought. The concept underlying the "Repainted Shan Shui" series made me think of a traditional story about an old man with a white beard who lives in the moon. He would use red string to tie two people together and those two people would get married. It was fate bringing them together; it was meant to be. So sometimes I think that I'm just like the man in the moon. I bring this one tradition from China, another from Europe. In my studio I tie them together. Soon after the marriage, they happily report the birth of a baby boy, which are my paintings.

ET: That's so beautiful, that's perfect! Your paintings were meant to be.

"A HUNDRED WAYS TO LEARN"
ABOUT ZHANG HONGTU

Morgan Perkins

The retrospective is a unique and honored occurrence in an artist's career for it allows viewers to see while not always a complete representation, at least an approximation of all that has been produced to that point. Certainly the scope of Zhang Hongtu's œuvre is such that only a retrospective of his wide range, in media and subject matter, can allow the viewer to gain insight into the consciousness that he has manifested into the material form of art objects over his distinctive career. If we are to understand the unique qualities of art as distinct from other forms of material culture, we must consider whether the consciousness and the subjective agency of the artist take on objective form through his art. To go one step further, does an artwork indeed have a life of its own? The anthropologist Alfred Gell suggests that art objects themselves have agency as they engage over time and space with other people as "distributed objects" that embody the "extended mind" of the artist.[1] In a recent conversation to discuss the ideas for this essay, Zhang Hongtu and I were exploring these concepts when he recalled an epiphany that arose from this retrospective moment in his career. This perspective allowed him to reunite with many artworks that he had not seen in person for decades, as they have been distributed in public and private collections throughout the world.

> I have a lot of work—many pieces I haven't seen after they left my studio, may-be [for] around even thirty years. . . . I thought, wow, I have so many different works, different periods—now it is all together, but when all the works get togeth-er, displayed on the wall, on the floor, I thought that actually all of the hundred pieces look like one work. That very, very strongly made me rethink how as an artist, your life and your personality is related to your art. . . . I always do art that reflects my life experience and how society and people surround me. . . . In this case when I look back at my work it's just like I am looking back at myself—with many pieces that I haven't seen for thirty years I feel like a stranger, but they are still part of me.[2]

The notion that all of his artwork is "like one work" implies that even very disparate works are interrelated, and even the artist himself, when confronted with the collected body of work, can respond in unanticipated ways. If we view each work as a part of one whole, what role does the retrospective then play in his, and our, understanding of his artwork as an extension of his mind? In Zhang's case a spatial and temporal division exists between the artwork that he created while still living in China and the works produced once he left for the United States in 1982. Although he exhibited his work in Taiwan and Hong Kong, he only began to exhibit his work in China again twenty years after his departure. The levels of knowledge that viewers in these dif-ferent cultural settings bring to bear on his work make the process of interpretation an increasingly complex one. When he speaks of his artworks as emerging from his experiences, he interestingly refers to some in terms of a social relationship, in the sense that their distribution over time and space can make him "feel like a stranger" to an older work.

It is here that we come to the two particular components of Gell's broader theory that have particular relevance to our understanding of a retrospective of Zhang's work. On the one hand, we have the question of how the disparate artworks, as representa-tions of Zhang's whole consciousness, relate to one another as parts of one work. On the other is the question of how those works created by one artist can relate to other people, how they may have agency themselves. These components are connected, as Gell explains: "The artist's œuvre externalizes or objectifies the same types of relations as exist between the artist's internal states of mind as a being endowed with consciousness. The artist's œuvre is artistic consciousness (personhood in the cognitive, temporal sense) writ large and rendered public and accessible."[3] In this regard, Zhang's artworks index his evolving consciousness; they relate to one another and, separate from the artist, may take on the qualities of a person with agency by provoking responses in the viewer and providing opportunities to engage with the mind of the artist. The relationship between art object and viewer is limited conversationally as artworks cannot (usually) talk back. Yet forms of mutual inspiration among artists that may have conversational qualities may often be more likely to develop through encounters with artworks than with the artists who made them. Two concepts, the relations between artworks and their relations to other people, warrant some further clarification before we turn to some of Zhang's bodies of work to explore their relevance.

When viewing the entirety of an artist's output, including preparatory sketches and even unfinished works, the relationships between artworks generally become clear through works that are connected to others to a greater or lesser extent, particularly in objects produced in a series, as so many of Zhang's have been. The retrospective inherently implies a moment in time, a perspective, generally late in an artist's career, from which artworks created up to that point can be viewed. Following Edmund Husserl's model of internal time-consciousness, Gell suggests that the artist's body of work comprises a network of relationships in which any work can be viewed through its references to past works (or *retentions*) and its projections toward future works (or *protentions*).[4] These relationships between works may exist to greater or lesser degrees based on style, concept, emotion, or other qualities that may then create similar or entirely different relationships with viewers. Viewed from different temporal perspectives—the moments in which it is conceived and developed, the moments in which it is created, and the moments in which it is referenced—no single work exists exclusive of other works or in one exclusive moment in time. Even when viewing one work we are not simply trying to interpret that one object, but rather engage with a part of an interconnected whole; just as a thought is not separate from the whole consciousness, an object is not separate from the œuvre. Each artwork thus represents moments when Zhang's inner thoughts and agency become manifest in external objects before moving on to new thoughts and objects.

If we then accept that there is a social relationship between the artwork and the viewer, then we also have to accept the interaction as one that inevitably generates misunderstanding. Zhang has remarkable insight into this dynamic. "I think when artists finish their work in the studio they only finish part of their work. When your work goes to the public you cannot control people's comments, you cannot even control how people feel. Sometimes I feel disappointed because people misunderstand my work, but you have to allow someone to misunderstand you."[5] As viewers with varying relationships

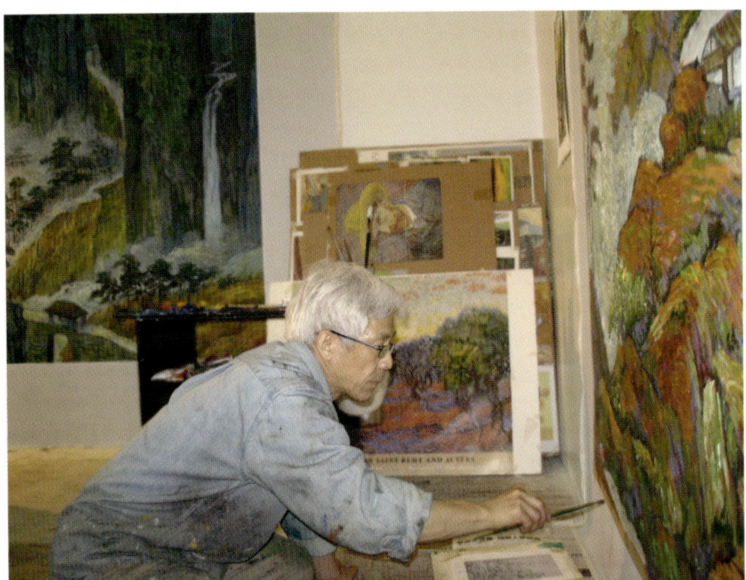

Fig. 1

with the artist and his work we can only respond and perhaps interpret from our own perspectives. To speak of consciousness in art is not simply to view art as a symbolic representation of ideas, with a correct or incorrect interpretation, but rather to engage with a complex stew of experiences, thoughts, emotions, memories, intentions, and so on, manifested over time—on the part of both the artist and the viewer.

The most intimate relationship between Zhang and his art is his and his alone. Yet the process of creating art, like the interpretation, can be imprecise even for the artist. "I try to show my mind through my art—to be sharp and clear—but sometimes it is still only at the *ge xue saoyang* level" (隔靴搔癢 , "like trying to scratch an itch through a boot").[6] The material forms of an artwork can never completely capture what is in the mind. The process of making art is akin to the thought process over time. Perhaps the clearest representation of the artist's thought process in material form is the working studio, in which reference materials, sketches, and preparatory studies as well as both finished and unfinished works coexist in relationships to one another (*Fig. 1*). When creating an artwork Zhang explains, "I have to think [about] it first and then I try to find the correct skill, the correct medium, the correct way to make my thinking become an object. . . . The process itself also can make my art idea clear—even sometimes a piece is already finished and still I cannot tell you one hundred percent clearly about what is in my mind. . . . This is a visual art; you can't do it in a scientific way."[7] I have known him personally for almost two decades, so my interpretations of his art may be as valid as any;[8] however, I can never, even if I discuss them with him before, during or after their creation, fully appreciate the thoughts embodied in each. Indeed I may add interpretations that, from his perspective, may or may not be valid. Zhang feels that some viewers interpreting his work often do the same. "When students write homework about my work they usually overanalyze my work, they describe my ideas more than I thought [about them] myself."[9] With such imprecision in mind, let us turn to some examples of how such anthropological approaches to art might be applied to Zhang's specific artworks that, though often produced in series that are quite distinct in form and media, may be considered, as Zhang asserts, one work.

Zhang's cultural transition influenced his consciousness in profound ways that emerge in his artwork. As we follow this process through a number of pieces, let us begin with his various Mao works as they are perhaps best known, and even notorious in some circles. This wide-ranging series is one that Zhang has discussed in many ways over the years, but it is arguably only when the series was complete that he could look back at it (with a retrospective viewpoint) and consider just what function it served in his mind. "I remember feeling so guilty when I first cut Mao's image for a collage, but then the creation of different images of Mao became a form of psychotherapy. The Mao series ended because Mao no longer had power over me."[10] As an assessment of the relationship between mind and art, this comment could hardly be more direct and insightful. The series began once Zhang had left China, but his cultural knowledge moved with him and the series evolved over time for deeply personal reasons. Yet the engagement with an icon that was imposed on artists during the Cultural Revolution—like the style of Socialist Realism reflected in many of Zhang's early works (*Plate 3-e*)—was psychologically very different from the efforts at catharsis that his Mao work reflects.[11] The iconic potency of the series is such that it has inevitably led to wide-ranging and often disparate interpretations when the audience views the images through their own personal and cultural lenses. Although the series continues to be banned from exhibition in China (even though reproductions readily circulate there along with artworks featuring Mao by many artists likely influenced by Zhang), consider the different interpretations by viewers in Hong Kong and America: "My Mao paintings shown over here [in America] and shown in Hong Kong get different reactions. Here people ask me, 'Why, if Andy Warhol did Mao in the 1970s and now it is the 1990s, do you still use Mao's image?' They are concerned from an art historical perspective. When I showed this work in Hong Kong, just one year before the 1997 Hong Kong handover, people were only concerned with the political issues."[12] These are questions of interpretation resulting from differences in cultural knowledge that, though relevant, only brush the surface of the position of the series in Zhang's consciousness.[13]

The potential for Zhang's work to inspire other artists is balanced by the many ways in which he is inspired by other art forms. As an immigrant himself, Zhang was deeply moved by the events surrounding the plight of the *Golden Venture*, a boat carrying refugees from the People's Republic of China that ran aground in New York Harbor

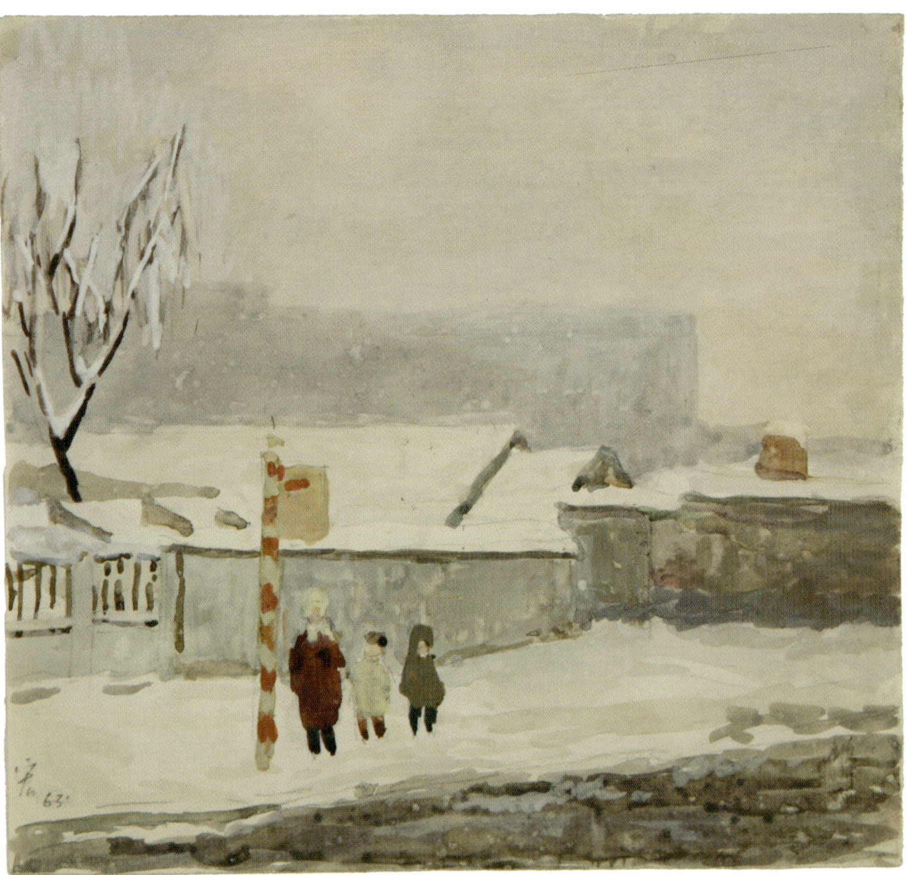

Plate 3-e

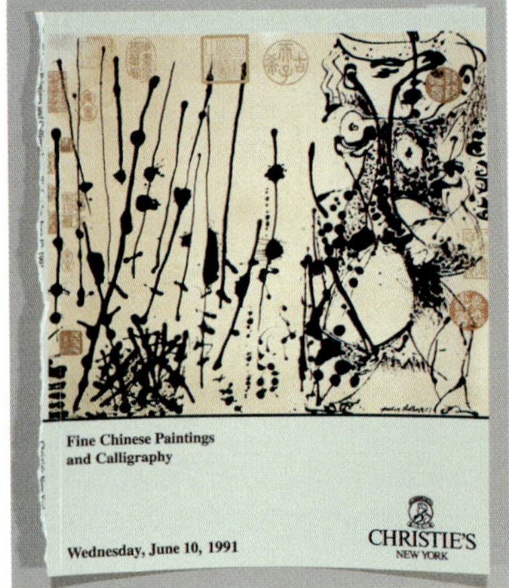

Plate 104

Plate 3-e

Waiting for the Bus, 1963.
Watercolor on paper. 7 ½ x 7 ⅝ in.

Plate 104

Christie's Catalog Project: The Cover, 1998.
Computer-generated image printed on paper,
10 x 8 in.

in 1993. Several drowned while trying to swim ashore and the survivors spent many years incarcerated in prisons and detention centers as illegal immigrants. They passed the time by making small birds and other figures using a variation of traditional Chinese paper folding. "The idea for *Flying Blues* (*Plate 101*) comes from the *Golden Venture* tragedy. . . . One of the birds [an eagle perched on a branch] made by jailed *Golden Venture* survivors had the Chinese words 'flying to freedom' [written] on the branch. It moved me terribly."[14] As a metaphor for freedom, Zhang chose to incorporate feathers into the centerpiece of the installation to represent the emotional and spiritual elements involved in the tragedy, as well as his own motivations to seek artistic freedom in America. The overall form of the beautiful and balanced piece comes from the ancient Chinese concept that Heaven is round and Earth is square (*tianyuan difang*, 天圓地方). Inverting earth and sky, the feathers—unable to achieve complete freedom from earthly connections—hang from a square canvas depicting the Chinese and Western compass points. Yet they stretch and float toward the round sky drawn with sand, reminiscent of the impermanent and meditative sand mandalas of Tibetan Buddhism. Inspired by the tragedy and by these different cultural art forms, Zhang created a moving and distinctly personal reflection "on the relationship between humankind's desire for freedom and the reality."[15]

Turning to the more humorous elements of cultural transition, the arrangements of objects on mock auction-catalog pages in Zhang's *Christie's Catalog Project* (*Plate 104*) satirize art-world conventions of language and photography used to create value and satisfy certain tastes in fine art and antiquities, while often obscuring original contexts and functions. Depending on their knowledge and cultural background, buyers may understand little about the complex meanings and functions of objects from China that are culturally and historically specific. Yet while the pages themselves are tangible objects, the items pictured are completely imaginary. They exist purely in Zhang's consciousness—or do they? Although originally conceived as objects he might create, they remained ephemeral until their digital form appeared in the interpretive and valuation framework that is the auction catalog page. Circumstance and expense limited his ability to realize the tangible objects until a 2003 exhibition opportunity at Princeton University allowed him to have produced several objects based on the digital forms originally appearing on the pages (*Fig. 2*). The subsequent display of these objects among the types of objects that inspired them serves, of course, as a satire of display practice and audience interpretation. The tangible objects are parodies of current art-world practices while also being retentions of past forms, both his own works (the pages) and the historical and cultural objects that inspired them. If we consider the evolution of the *Christie's Catalog Project* as a material representation of Zhang's experiences as a person who has been transported from one cultural context to another—like many objects from China—and often been misunderstood because

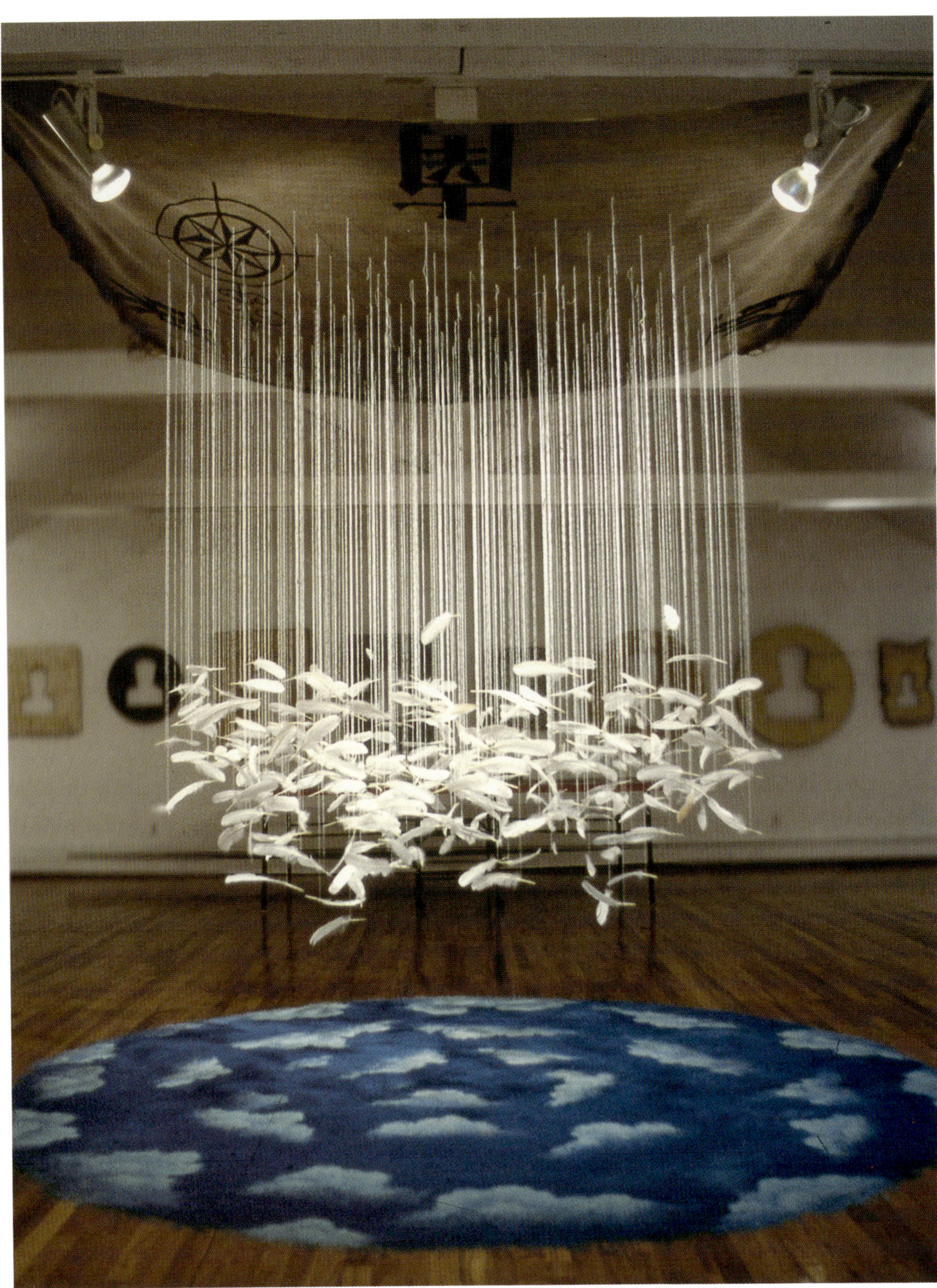

Plate 101

Flying Blues, 1996.
Sand, feather, and mixed-media installation. 96 x 96 x 118 in.

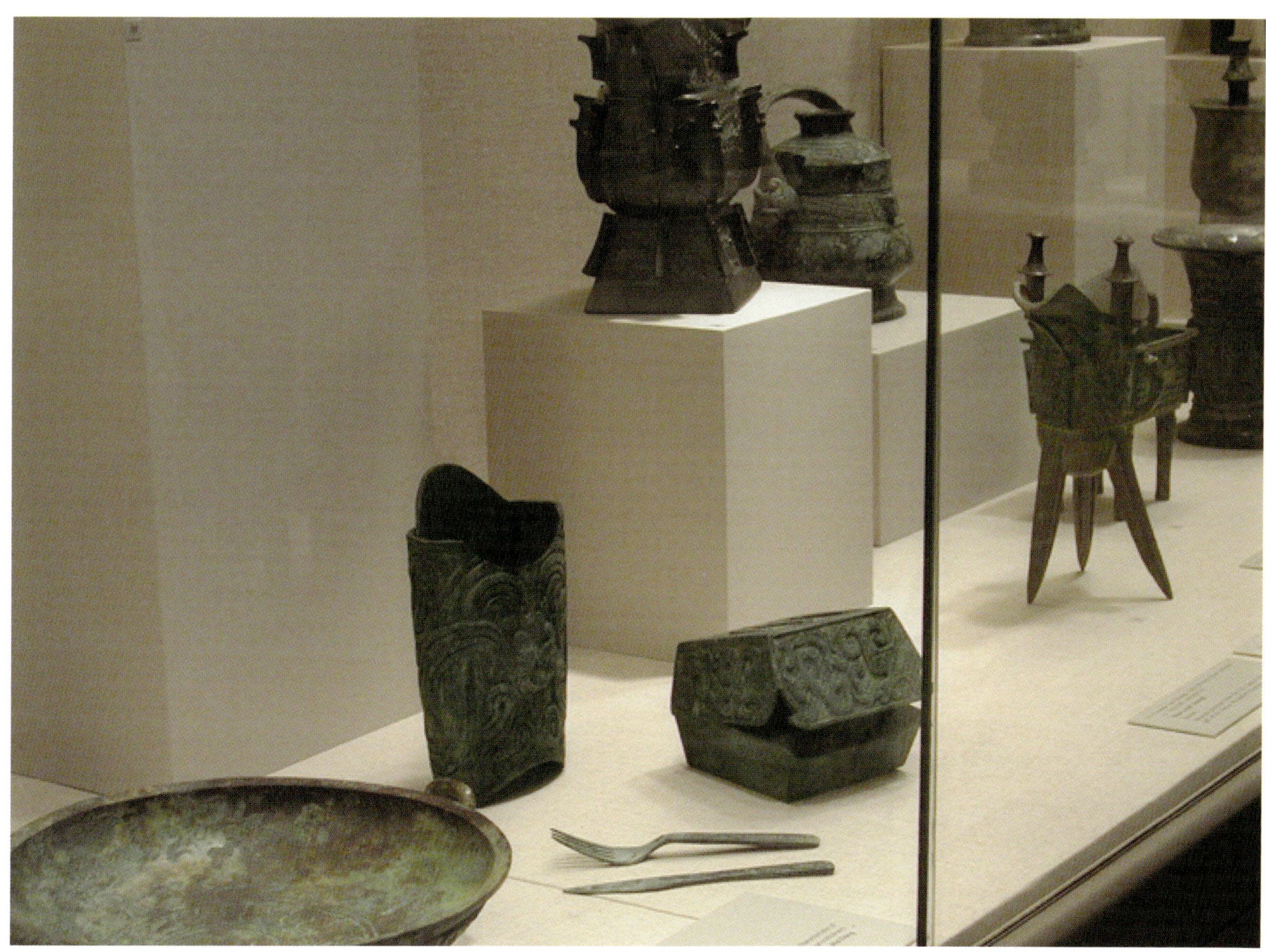

Fig. 2

Mai Dang Lao (McDonald's), 2002. Bronze tableware inspired by the *Christie's Catalog Project* installed among other bronze objects from China for the exhibition "Shuffling the Deck: The Collection Reconsidered" at the Princeton University Art Museum, 2003.

of that transition, then perhaps as viewers we can engage with the series as a manifestation of Zhang's consciousness—his process of working through his cross-cultural identity. He has gone on to further examine many cultural conventions of art practice and display—such as differing expectations on the materials and techniques to be used in painting, the use of frames or scrolls, restrictions on the handling of objects, and so on—in subsequent artworks.[16]

Zhang began his "Repainted Shan Shui" series in 1998, the same year as the Christie's project, by pairing compositions of historical Chinese *shan shui hua* (山水畫 , literally "mountain water painting") with European styles and materials—specifically those of Cézanne, Monet, and Van Gogh. This fusion of cultural forms is the most basic element in the paintings, but the evolution of the series also involves complex relationships among Zhang's paintings. When viewing each painting the audience is encountering an object that represents both a single painting and the totality of the series through which Zhang expresses his cross-cultural identity, and his ideas about the intersections of these two cultures through form, technique, and practice. Zhang has frequently mentioned the understandably different audience responses: "[Upon seeing] my *shan shui* paintings displayed in my studio, my Chinese friends who come will say as their first words, 'Oh, this is probably Shitao or Dong Qichang,' but my American friends who come will say as their first words, 'Wow, this looks like Van Gogh, this looks like Cézanne, like Monet,' so people have different entrances, different windows to look at the same painting, which is interesting, which I think is even good because this means my paintings reflect two different cultures."[17] If recognition of historical composition or style provides one entry point to the relationship between viewer and painting, I would argue that it is on the level of practice that the relationship becomes truly complex.

The practice of copying others' compositions and brushstroke techniques is, broadly speaking, "traditional" from a Chinese painting perspective. In this respect Zhang is most faithful to traditional practice even if his particular approaches and motives may vary. If we return again to the consciousness of the artist emerging over time in material forms to which viewers can respond, then the many multiple versions of paintings (*Fig. 3*, *Fig. 4*) and the extensive use of smaller studies provide unique insights into the complex web of relationships between the paintings and Zhang's thoughts over time. Gell observes, "We can easily see that 'remembering' something which has happened in the past is very like 'copying' a picture that one has painted in the past, or that 'making a preliminary sketch for a picture' is very like mentally anticipating some future happening or course of action."[18] In this regard, Zhang is not merely copying compositions and styles, or even emulating central elements of the practice of art education in Chinese ink painting, he is making tangible an intangible consciousness through the passage of time. Unlike the finished "Material Mao" series, his thoughts

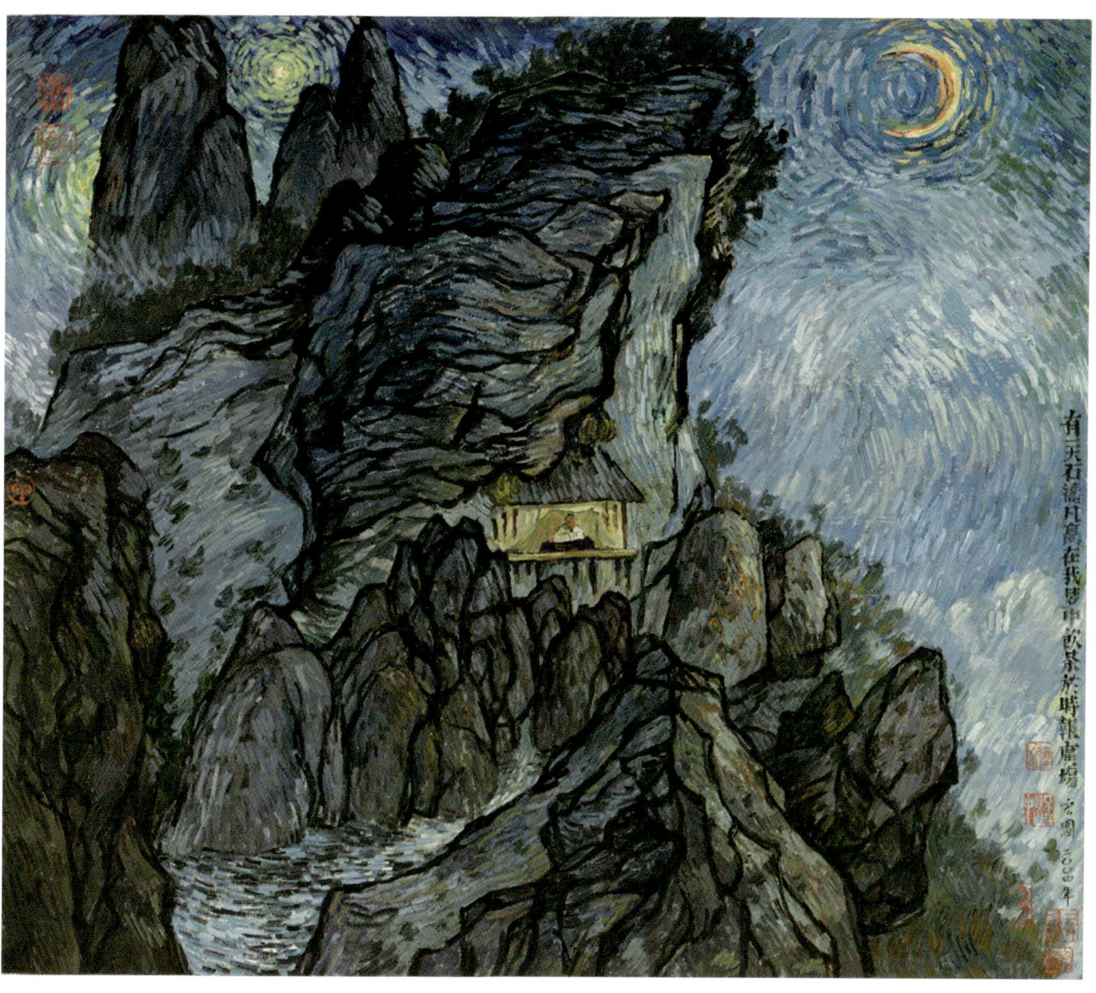

Fig. 3

Shitao—Van Gogh #3 SLS Green Night, 2004. Oil on canvas, 41 x 48 in. Private collection.

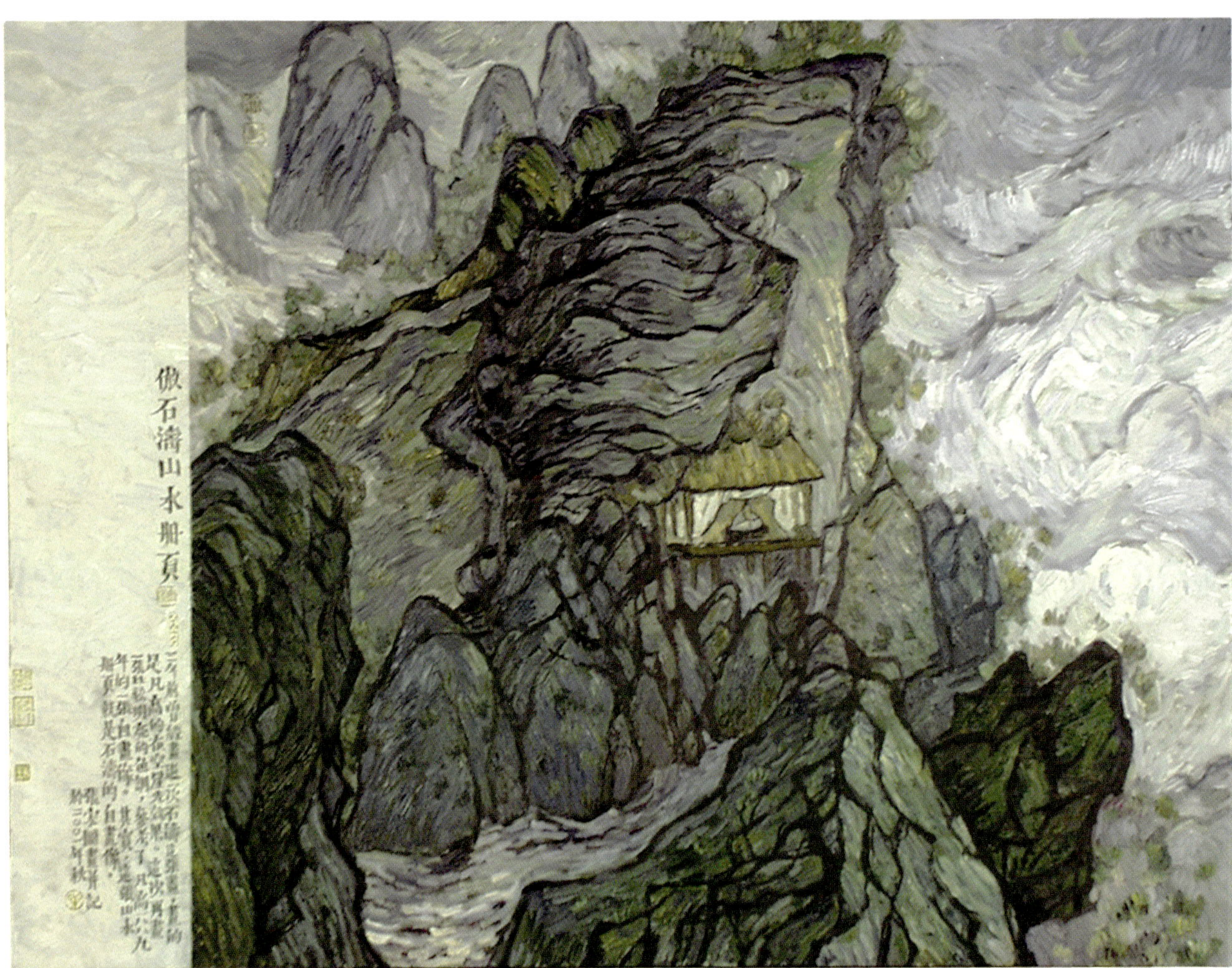

Fig. 4

Shitao—Van Gogh #4, 2001. Oil on canvas, 51 x 70 in. Private collection.

on these paintings still emerge over time so Zhang very intentionally termed his *shan shui* series as "ongoing," and it is still labeled as such on his website.[19]

Zhang's efforts at creating an intimate relationship between painting and viewer continue to delve deeper into artistic practice through the use of inscriptions. While providing further insight into the thought process behind the artworks, he again emulates an integral practice in Chinese ink painting—indeed he encourages collectors to add their own inscriptions. Not only does he often engage directly with the viewer through these, he sometimes provokes. In the inscription on the painting *Mu Xi—Monet*, 2006–7, for example, he questions the cross-cultural identity of the painting from the perspective of the viewer: "Is it Eastern, or is it Western? I can only answer this with laughter. It is just a painting!" Although such inscriptions reflect the particulars of Zhang's contemporary cross-cultural experience, the practice connects him, however delicate the thread, to the consciousness of Chinese painters in the past. Among other rituals, social relationships, and myriad practices, the use of inscriptions by painters, viewers, and collectors, which physically alter a painting, establish interpretations and forms of social relationships documented over time and space. The painter and those present at the moment of creation may have the most intimate relationship with the artwork, but inscriptions may allow later viewers to participate conceptually, even more so if they add their own inscriptions. The art historian Richard Vinograd explains how these inscriptions and the viewing and handling of objects can establish conceptual relationships between artists and viewers over centuries through a process referred to as *shen-hui*, or "spirit-communion."[20] In emulating practices such as inscriptions and copying, and by his deep engagement with historical paintings through reinterpretations and his own cultural background, we could consider that Zhang is responding in the present with a semblance of the same ritual knowledge.[21] If we follow this concept of a communion of artists across space and time, we are also moving very close to the "collective consciousness" envisioned by Émile Durkheim as a unified system of cultural beliefs and practices that often extend to objects.[22]

Can we in fact apply a concept of artistic consciousness in one artist's œuvre to the broader cultural "tradition" of Chinese ink painting? I highlight the term "tradition" because such a perspective may dismantle distinctions between tradition and innovation, perhaps allowing contemporary experiments such as Zhang's to appear less isolated in relation to historical forms. The validity of this approach may depend on the cohesiveness of the cultural tradition—so I limit myself to painting rather than to more diverse arts in China—and even if we specify literati (*wenren*, 文人, literally, "cultured person") painting as our example, perceptions of cohesiveness could still be challenged. If we set aside Zhang's affiliations with European paintings and concentrate here on Chinese artistic practice, we are still concerned with the role of the retrospective as a particular perspective on artistic consciousness that may allow us to see more completely the relationships between artworks and between artworks and their viewers.

As this is one of the goals of his theory, Gell can provide some assistance if we want to extend the notion of the distributed object beyond an individual artist to encompass a collective cultural tradition. Since Zhang is both drawing on traditions of painting and, like many of his predecessors, attempting to innovate with each new creation, each painting could be seen as a retention of past forms—his own and others'—as well as a protention toward future works. If we see each artwork produced from an individual or within a collective tradition in this respect, we might see that, as Gell suggests, "a continuously shifting perspective on tradition and innovation in an historical assemblage of artifacts means that the process of understanding art history is essentially akin to the process of consciousness itself, which is marked, likewise, by a continuous perspectival flux."[23] Each new painting that may have been inspired by another painting then becomes a potential reference or inspiration for new paintings—becoming part of the tradition that may attract, repel, or otherwise compel artists to innovate. Certainly many literati painters, for example, might create with the knowledge that any particular painting might refer back to paintings of their own or by others and might anticipate or inspire new paintings.[24] Such relations between paintings were part of the broader social relations between painters.

If we can see the relationships between artists and artworks back and forth through time—whether within the work of one artist or across a cultural art form—then divisions between tradition and innovation become more active, fluid, and interconnected. As Gell argues, "There is no absolute sense in which any given work can be seen, either as a recapitulation of a previous work, or as a precursor of a future one; the ensemble of an artist's works, strung out in time, constitutes a dynamic, unstable entity; not a mere accumulation of datable artifacts. We can only appreciate it by participating in its unfolding life."[25] This broad perspective then allows for the many ways that Zhang is inspired or influenced by past artists to intersect with his influence on artists who have or may yet emerge. I have of course oversimplified the complexities of Chinese ink painting for the sake of this brief argument; I would suggest, however, that a conception of Zhang's consciousness existing within his artworks can indeed be extended to a potential collective consciousness embodied in the artworks and relationships emerging from the Chinese cultural traditions with which he so closely engages.

In our efforts to learn about Zhang Hongtu through his artwork, this retrospective moment can only bring us closer to the artist as any gathering of parts brings one closer to the whole. If Zhang himself can view his many artworks "like one work," then to learn about the artist and his art we must consider the relationships between the individual and collective elements of his art. The enthusiasm for art from every conceivable culture by the so-called international contemporary art world means that viewers are constantly exposed to artworks that embody unfamiliar cultural forms. Even if an artwork is produced in what I would call a common artistic "language"—installation art, performance art, conceptual art, mixed media, and so on, in comparison to more "traditional" art forms generally excluded from the institutions of contemporary art—it still requires extensive effort to interpret the cultural specifics as well as the personal components. To learn, Zhang is willing to use a dictionary when viewing art that incorporates words in an unfamiliar language, or to learn about the artist and his cultural background through the countless forms of information at our disposal—often including direct conversation with the artist. While a global turn in contemporary art requires efforts that Zhang is willing to make himself in regard to others' artworks, he feels that many have criticized his work for being inaccessible because it is too Chinese or too personal, because he uses Chinese characters and so on. We should be willing to make the effort.

> You can find a way to make dialogue with other people, to make conversation with other people through your art, even if you have something too strong from your education, or your life experiences in China, or your cultural background that makes your art difficult for people to understand easily, but that is not important. I think that [for] anyone if they really want to learn something there are a hundred ways to learn.[26]

While he may hope that a viewer understands his intentions, the personal and cross-cultural natures of these viewings always guarantee some unique mixture of accurate and inaccurate interpretation. These distributed art objects form relationships with viewers—most of whom Zhang has never, nor will ever meet—often in ways that Zhang never anticipates. This retrospective moment, however, allows us a unique opportunity to learn about Zhang Hongtu in "a hundred ways" through an assemblage of the artworks that together provide a more complete understanding of his artistic consciousness in material forms.

1   Alfred Gell, *Art and Agency: An Anthropological Theory* (Oxford: Clarendon Press, 1998). Gell's theory remains controversial in the anthropology of art. For a relevant critique, see Howard Morphy, "Art as a Mode of Action: Some Problems with Gell's Art and Agency," *Journal of Material Culture* 14, no. 1 (2009): 5–27. For a review of the entire discipline, see Howard Morphy and Morgan Perkins, "The Anthropology of Art: A Reflection on Its History and Contemporary Practice," in *The Anthropology of Art*, ed. Howard Morphy and Morgan Perkins (Oxford: Blackwell Publishers, 2006), 1–32. David Freedberg has examined many aspects of the relationships between object and viewer that are relevant to anthropological approaches. See David Freedberg, *The Power of Images: Studies in the History and Theory of Response* (Chicago: University of Chicago Press, 1989); and David Freedberg, "Warburg's Mask: A Study in Idolatry," in *Anthropologies of Art*, ed. Mariët Westermann (Williamstown, MA: Sterling and Francine Clark Art Institute, 2005), 3–25. For perspectives on the intersections between art history and anthropology, see Ruth Phillips, "The Value of Disciplinary Difference: Reflections on Art History and Anthropology at the Beginning of the Twenty-First Century," in *Anthropologies of Art*, 242–59. For some particularly relevant studies of art in China that relate to anthropological approaches to social relations and culture, see James Cahill, *The Painter's Practice: How Artists Lived and Worked in Traditional China* (New York: Columbia University Press, 1994); Craig Clunas, *Elegant Debts: The Social Art of Wen Zhengming* (Honolulu: University of Hawai'i Press, 2004); Jonathan Hay, "The Functions of Chinese Paintings: Toward a Unified Field Theory," in *Anthropologies of Art*, 111–23; Jerome Silbergeld and Gong Jisui, *Contradictions: Artistic Life, the Socialist State, and the Chinese Painter Li Huasheng* (Seattle and London: University of Washington Press, 1993); Richard Vinograd, "Private Art and Public Knowledge in Later Chinese Painting," in *Images of Memory: On Remembering and Representation*, ed. Susanne Küchler and Walter Melion (Washington and London: Smithsonian Institution Press, 1991), 176–202; and Wu Hung, *The Double Screen: Medium and Representation in Chinese Painting* (Chicago: University of Chicago Press, 1996).

2   Zhang Hongtu, conversation with the author, January 21, 2015. Our conversations were conducted in English, and they have been edited slightly for grammatical clarity. Any significant editorial additions appear in brackets. Zhang's use of Chinese words in our conversations was based upon our common familiarity with particular terms, and translations are provided accordingly.

3   Gell, *Art and Agency*, 236.

4   Edmund Husserl, *The Phenomenology of Internal Time-Consciousness* (1887; Bloomington, IN: Midland Books, 1966).

5   Zhang Hongtu, conversation with the author, January 21, 2015.

6   Zhang Hongtu, conversation with the author, March 5, 2015.

7   Zhang Hongtu, conversation with the author, January 21, 2015.

8   I first met Zhang Hongtu in 1998 while conducting dissertation research on Chinese art education. See Morgan Perkins, "Reviewing Traditions: An Anthropological Examination of Contemporary Chinese Art Worlds" (doctoral dissertation, University of Oxford, 2001). I first visited his studio in 2002 in preparation for an exhibition. See Morgan Perkins, ed., *Icons and Innovations: The Cross-Cultural Art of Zhang Hongtu*, exh. cat. (Potsdam, NY: Roland Gibson Art Gallery, SUNY Potsdam, 2003).

9   Zhang Hongtu, conversation with the author, January 21, 2015.

10   Zhang Hongtu, conversation with the author, December 18, 2002.

11   Considering the notoriety the icon has brought him, it is ironic to consider that Zhang was banned from producing Mao images during the Cultural Revolution due to his family's class background.

12   Zhang Hongtu, conversation with the author, January 21, 2015.

13   For a detailed examination of the agency of Zhang's Mao series through particular audience responses, see Morgan Perkins, "Exhibition Cultures: Zhang Hongtu and Cultural Practices of Display," in *China on Display*, ed. F. Dal Lago (Leiden: Brill, forthcoming).

14   Zhang Hongtu, conversation with the author, February 26, 2015.

15   Ibid.

16   Elsewhere I have proposed that Zhang's critique of exhibition practice constitutes a form of artistic ethnography. See Perkins, "Cultural Knowledge on Display: Chinese and Haudenosaunee Fieldnotes," in *Between Art and Anthropology*, ed. Arnd Schneider and Christopher Wright (Oxford and New York: Berg, 2010), 135–46. For an effort to reconcile the "white box" of contemporary art practice with the needs of Chinese art, Chang Tsong-zung proposes intriguing adaptations through a metaphorical "yellow box." See Chang Tsong-zung, "The Yellow Box: Thoughts on Art before the Age of Exhibitions," *Yishu* 4, no. 1 (2005): 42–53. For a recent examination of relevant concerns in the field of museum anthropology, see Ivan Karp and Corinne Kratz, eds., *Museum Frictions: Public Cultures/Global Transformations* (Durham: Duke University Press, 2006).

17   Zhang Hongtu, conversation with the author, January 21, 2015. For extensive analysis of viewers' responses to Zhang's "Repainted Shan Shui" series, see Perkins, "Exhibition Cultures: Zhang Hongtu and Cultural Practices of Display."

18   Gell, *Art and Agency*, 236.

19   Zhang Hongtu, "Museum of My Art Only," www.MoMAO.com. It should be noted that Mao still makes an occasional appearance in new artworks, for

example, *Mao, After Picasso*, 2012.

20   Vinograd, "Private Art and Public Knowledge in Later Chinese Painting."

21   The intentional emulation of literati forms and practices by some contemporary
      ink painters in China has become quite elaborate. For one effort by a painter
      from Hangzhou, see Morgan Perkins, "Painting on Location: Lin Haizhong and
      Contemporary Chinese Ink Painting," in *Asia Through Art and Anthropology:
      Cultural Translation Across Borders*, ed. Fuyubi Nakamura, Morgan Perkins,
      and Olivier Krischer (London: Bloomsbury, 2013).

22   Émile Durkheim, *Division of Labour in Society* (New York: Palgrave Macmillan,
      2013).

23   Gell, *Art and Agency*, 256.

24   Such potential inspiration for other painters leaves aside inspiration for other
      types of artworks. The complex intersections between painting, poetry, and
      calligraphy, for example, are particularly relevant here as forms of artistic
      inspiration over time, as John Hay, among many others, has argued. See John
      Hay, "Poetic Space: Ch'ien Hsuan and the Association of Painting and Poetry,"
      in *Words and Images: Chinese Poetry, Calligraphy and Painting*, ed. Alfreda
      Murck and Wen Fong (New York and Princeton: The Metropolitan Museum of
      Art and Princeton University Press, 1991).

25   Gell, *Art and Agency*, 242.

26   Zhang Hongtu, conversation with the author, January 21, 2015.

RESTORING THE AURA

Julia F. Andrews and Kuiyi Shen

A provocative aspect of Zhang Hongtu's body of work is the way in which it deploys art history as a vehicle for artistic, social, institutional, economic, and political critique. Both playful and deadly serious, the artist often exploits the semiotic potential of style, shape, motif, or image to expose fissures between the ideal and the actual, the revered and the neglected. His "Soy Sauce Calligraphy" series, begun in 1995, is particularly sharp. One work from 1996, for example (*Fig. 1*), resembles in its general format a priceless fragment by Wang Xizhi (303–361 A.D.), China's most venerated calligrapher, a sage whose spirit and brush were emulated by writers for a millennium and a half. Carefully mounted for display, the work of semi-cursive calligraphy bears what appear to be collection seals of venerable men of history: the Yuan dynasty calligrapher-painter Zhao Mengfu (1254–1322), the Ming Suzhou patron and collector Xiang Yuanbian (1525–1590), and the eighteenth-century emperor Qianlong (1711–1799), among others. Zhang Hongtu presents each piece in the series as though it were a museum treasure. The viewer is thus set up to appreciate the formal

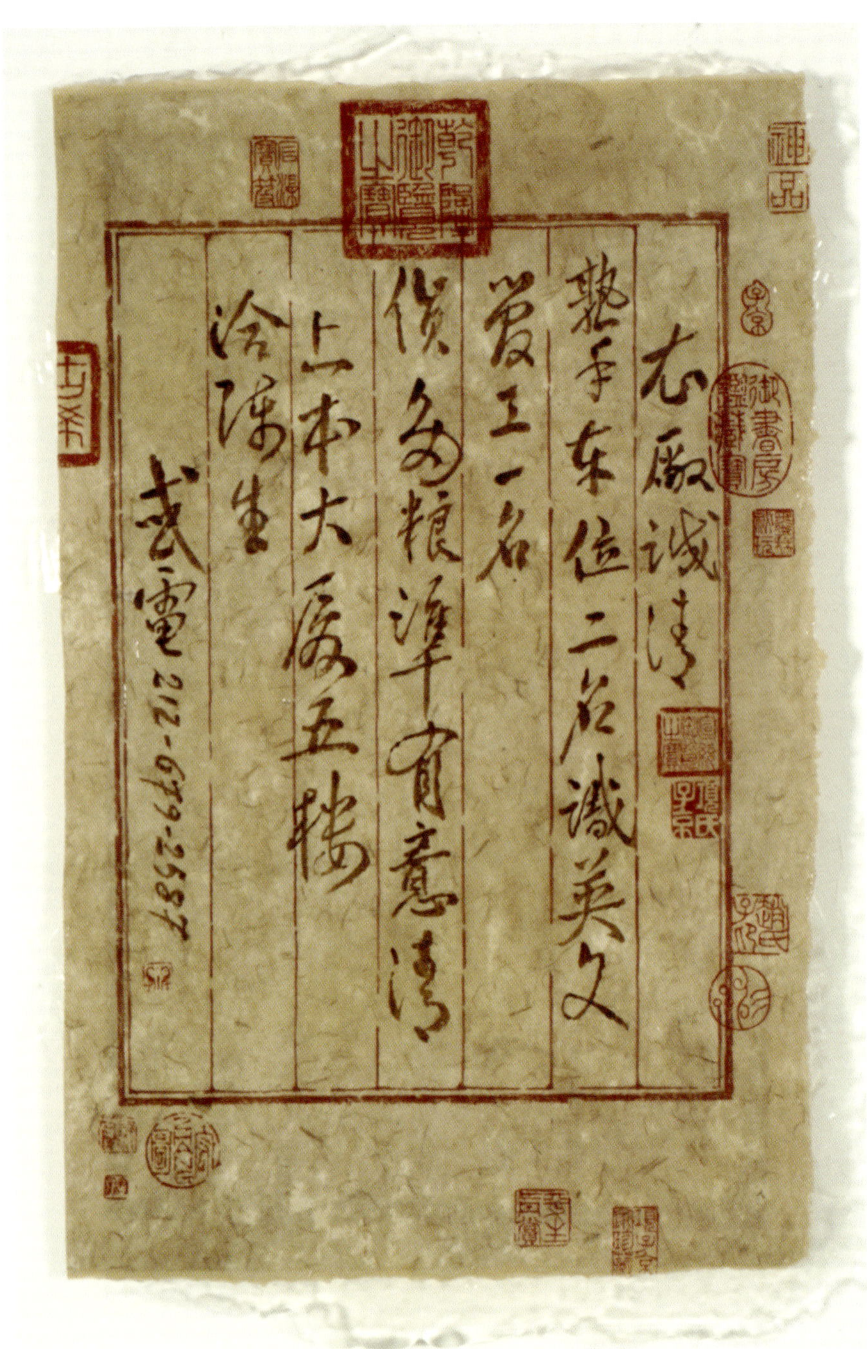

Fig. I

Chinatown Sweatshop Help Wanted Ad, Wang Xizhi (303–361 A.D.) Style, 1995.
From the series "Soy Sauce Calligraphy." Soy sauce on rice paper, sealed in epoxy
resin, 29 ½ x 19 in.

beauty of the calligraphy and the genius of the artist from whose hand it came, as did connoisseurs who treasured it in the past. In scrutinizing the object to find traces of the ancient master, however, one notices a few anomalies: the paper on which the text is written, with its handsome red border and column guidelines, is a kind of letter paper that, while quite out-of-date in the 1990s, could still be purchased in many stores in China (or Chinatown) that carried office supplies, from the corner grocery to a stationery shop. Its yellowed appearance is the result not of great age but of the rough quality of its inexpensive manufacture. Further, the calligraphy itself is brushed not with the expected black ink, but, as the series title announces, with the rich brown of soy sauce. When one actually reads the text, the elegant fiction is conclusively destroyed. The "calligraphy" is a Chinatown sweatshop ad:

> Our factory sincerely seeks [the services of] two skilled seamstresses and one supervisor who can read English. There is plenty of work and good pay. If interested, please come to the fifth floor of this building and contact Mr. Chen or call 212-679-2587.

Mundane materials, down-to-earth content, and exquisitely refined formal appearance bring forth a multitude of contradictions between high and low art, the elegant amusements of the elite and the economic lives of common people, the enjoyable outings of art-loving museum visitors and the job-seeking of new immigrants. These juxtapositions expose contradictions inherent in Chinese culture of the 1990s, particularly the enormous gaps between China's magnificent ancient heritage and the difficult experiences of real Chinese living in the present age. The possible interpretations are as open as the viewer might make them, but are pointed. The juxtaposition of ancient sage and modern seamstress, or writing brush and soy sauce, might suggest that American culture, at least in the period before China's economic boom, could appreciate China only through the sensory extremes of classical Chinese art, cheap apparel, and fast-food take-out. The project more certainly speaks to Zhang's own immigrant experience, in which famous professors and artists might become restaurant workers, losing their identities and agency after crossing the cultural and linguistic boundaries that rendered familiar systems of social value meaningless.

One might accurately say that Zhang's practice of creative appropriation in "Soy Sauce Calligraphy" is a postmodern approach, one in which Wang Xizhi is China's Mona Lisa or Marilyn. Based on his early work, however, such as *Eternal Life*, simple appreciation of the irony of Zhang's constructed encounters between past and present is insufficient to fully understand the depth of his questioning of art, history, and contemporary culture. Moreover, China's millennia-long history of painting presents many striking examples of artists who consciously referred to old painting, but transformed it, and even some who openly challenged its techniques, conventions, or theoretical foundations.

Does this pre-modern legacy have any meaning in understanding Zhang's postmodern art? Born in 1943, he is a member of the first generation of Chinese intellectuals to be educated almost entirely, from primary school through college, under the cultural and political policies of the People's Republic of China. That education, based in part on Mao Zedong's 1942 "Yan'an Talks on Literature and Art," taught that art was a weapon in the revolutionary struggle, that artists were cogs in the revolutionary machinery, and that art should serve the people, particularly the workers, peasants, and soldiers. These principles were fundamental to the elite artistic training that Zhang received in the four-year program at the Central Academy of Fine Arts attached high school, from which he graduated in 1964 (*Fig. 2*). Thus educated to possess perfect loyalty to Mao Zedong as founder of the new nation and as its most important thinker, Zhang passed his formative years in an era when many of China's people harbored idealism and optimism for the collective project of building a better future, despite the hardships and scarcities from which they all then suffered. Yet despite the people's faith, unintended consequences of Mao's policies opened gaps in the polished surface of the ideology he promoted.

At CAFA's Soviet-style preparatory school for artistically gifted young people, Zhang received a well-balanced technical education, with rigorous training in drawing modeled after the pedagogical methods of Russian art educator Pavel Chistyakov, but extending not only to oil painting but also to Chinese ink painting.[1] Zhang's matriculation in 1960 occurred immediately after the shocking break in relations between China and the USSR, which led to the withdrawal of Soviet experts from the nation and a dramatic ideological reconfiguration. Moreover, Mao's Great Leap Forward of 1958–59, an impractical program opposed by the Soviets, led to famines and starvation in the countryside and food shortages in the cities. Although the full extent of the disaster was hidden by the authorities, the existence of food shortages was seen or experienced by almost every urban Chinese. In response to the widespread anxiety caused by these catastrophes, the authorities briefly liberalized their control of cultural policy, providing spiritual solace by permitting exhibitions by elderly artists such as Lin Fengmian, whose work explored formal, aesthetic, and even emotional concerns, rather than political issues. Pushing away from Soviet Socialist Realism back to artistic instincts rooted in 1930s cultural nationalism, when renewal of the unique art of Chinese ink painting was seen as a point of pride in the competition among nations, the Chinese Communist Party sponsored newly invented forms of Socialist Realism in which lyrical ink and color landscapes on Chinese paper told stories of a nation burgeoning with factory chimneys, electric power lines, newly constructed reservoirs,

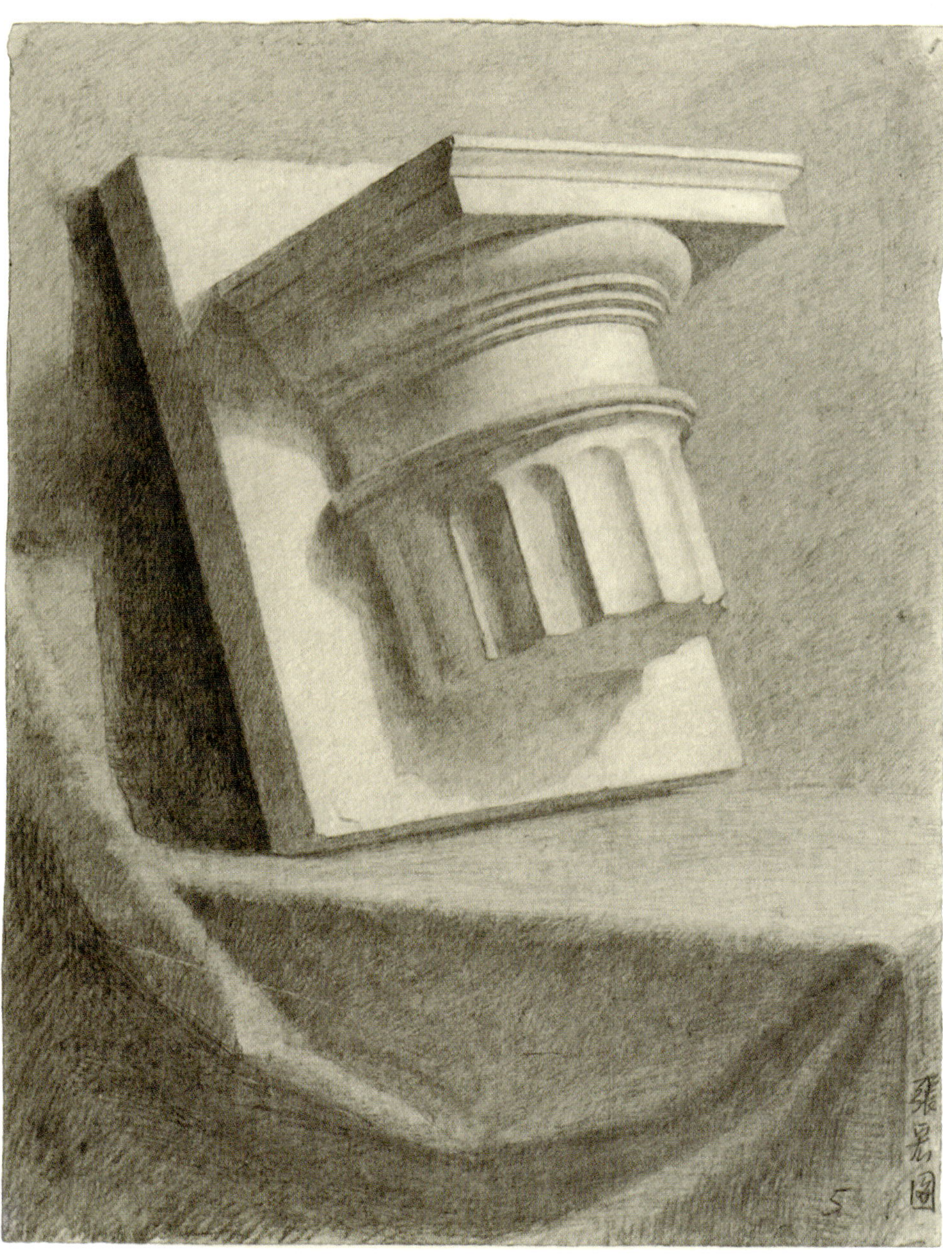

Fig. 2

Pencil study from freshman course at Central Academy of Fine Arts high school, 1961.

and strip mines, each more beautiful than the next.[2] Hailed as "revolutionary realism," it was only one of a number of artistic experiments that briefly saw the light of day in this desperate era.

Zhang recalls chafing under the restrictive guidelines of the art high school, but the cultural policies of the early 1960s presented possibilities for a resourceful young artist to expand his knowledge of foreign and Chinese art. Published records list an "internal" exhibition of abstract art (a form of art normally banned) that was held at the Central Academy of Fine Arts in the summer of 1960, the kind of show, under a didactic guise, only open to selected viewers, those with correct credentials or personal connections. A historical exhibition organized for political purposes by the Chinese People's Committee to Protect World Peace in September of 1960 brought forth stylistically diverse images of foreign art to celebrate "three famous men of world culture": namely the 600th anniversary of the birth of Russian icon painter Andrei Rublev (ca. 1360–ca.1430), the 300th anniversary of the death of Diego Velasquez (ca. 1559–1660), and the 200th anniversary of the birth of Katushika Hokusai (1760–1849). Ranging from a medieval master to a Japanese printmaker, this brief show brought attention to the same kind of artist who had inspired the European modernists, even though the latter were themselves banned. To inquisitive and rebellious art students like Zhang, such commemorations would have presented striking alternatives to the Socialist Realist mainstream of the day. Moreover, a range of relatively apolitical contemporary ink paintings, ranging from the aesthetically modern (if theoretically traditionalist) bird-and-flower ink paintings of Pan Tianshou, shown in 1962 at the Chinese Artists Association Exhibition Hall, and more classically oriented works by Xie Zhiliu and Hu Peiheng, to a range of new-style landscape paintings by Qian Songyan and other famous artists of the day, presented alternatives to both the idea that all art had to be political and to the hard-line concentration on Socialist Realist figure paintings that dominated the art-school curriculum.

Meanwhile, during the four years Zhang was in high school in central Beijing, the Palace Museum exhibited an extraordinary array of treasures: copies of the newly discovered Yonglegong mural paintings in the spring of 1960; in September copies of the Dunhuang murals; followed by a feast of original masterpieces, including calligraphy of Wang Xizhi; calligraphy and painting of Zhao Mengfu; the Ming Academy and the Zhe School; Shen Zhou; Chen Hongshou; Shitao and the Yangzhou Masters; The Four Wangs, Yun, and Wu Li; Portrait Paintings; Deng Shiru calligraphy, and so on.[3] Whether or not the young Zhang personally visited these exhibitions, the activities themselves, their publications, and the always crucial word-of-mouth brought the artworks into the common artistic consciousness of the day, demonstrating to the cultural world a new Chinese art-historical canon under formulation by leading museums and institutions. The art academy (and most of its students) privileged oil painting and drawing, and venerated the artists who had created the Western artistic canon. There is no reason to think that Zhang would be less *au courant* than his classmates—indeed his great technical mastery of oil painting suggests both excellent instruction and intensive practice. Nevertheless, the regularization of display of classics of Chinese art made awareness of the alternative, indigenous tradition almost unavoidable.

Moreover, following the Sino-Soviet split of 1960, as China turned inward, the official art press was filled with articles exhorting artists to find a way to develop a "national style" in oil painting, a topic that Zhang remembers as being on everyone's lips. Exploration of native art-historical sources for novel ideas, a practice that oil painters exiled inland had begun during World War II, resurfaced. Like CAFA professor Dong Xiwen, who began working in outline after visiting the early Buddhist murals in the Mogao caves at Dunhuang in 1943, oil painting teachers at the high school, such as Sun Zixi, similarly experimented two decades later. In Sun's well-known painting of 1964, *On Tiananmen*, he emphasized outlines and large areas of flat color, rather than the more textural applications of pigment characteristic of Russian painting.[4] Dong Xiwen would have been aware of European modernist precedents, although those remained unspoken after 1949. For Sun Zixi and those who followed, such sources would have been identified instead in Chinese pictorial art. Regardless of what they were called, various experiments, including some that revived efforts made under the preceding regime, were briefly encouraged as long as they contributed to the national narrative.

In short, despite the strictness (or even rigidity) of the high-school curriculum, ideas about alternatives to its strictures were swirling around the Beijing environment. Zhang's high school years, normally a time for developing independent thinking, if not outright rebellion, were thus passed during a brief period of ferment for the entire Chinese art world. By the time Zhang finished high school, however, China was already beginning a political and cultural tightening that would eventually lead to the Cultural Revolution. Although unseen to most Chinese, the ground was being prepared for a massive power struggle in which Mao would pit the power of his revolutionary mythology against the pragmatic administrators who had tried to rescue the nation from the economic and human catastrophe of the Great Leap Forward. When Mao launched the Cultural Revolution in the spring and summer of 1966, all schools enthusiastically responded to his call to participate in a new movement to root out counterrevolutionary forces in society.

A new phase in Zhang's social and political education began outside the classroom. Students from the Central Academy of Arts and Crafts, where he began college in

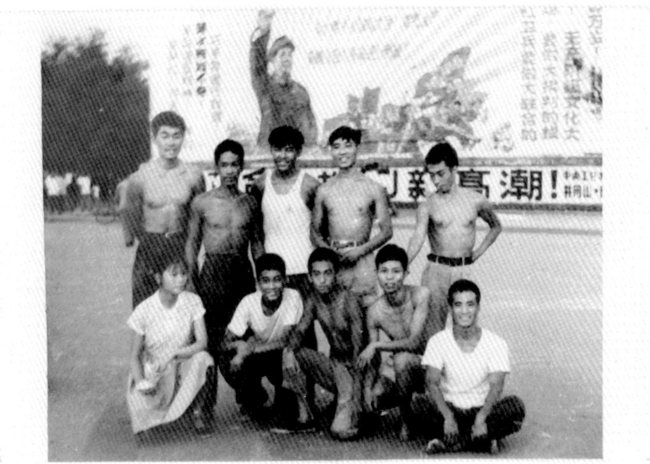

1964, seized control of a giant billboard at Tiananmen Square and covered it with visual interpretations of the ever-changing ideological statements that emerged from China's political center, the nearby Zhongnanhai complex where Mao Zedong and the central government lived and worked (*Fig. 3*). In the process, the young artists brought to a crescendo the imagery that would dominate China's visual world for the next decade. However exciting these brightly colored Maoist images were then, and whatever visual appeal such pictures may still have today, they were far from the real story. Some of the students mentally and physically abused innocent people in the name of eliminating enemies of the revolution. As student groups split into factions, each believing it was more loyal to Mao than the other, the Red Guard, as they called themselves, began to turn on one another. Even enthusiastic supporters of the patriotic ideals of the Cultural Revolution were sidelined when it was discovered that they came from "problematic" family backgrounds. Zhang recalls encountering a group of young students on the street who had just beaten to death a middle-aged man they thought was a capitalist. Humane people who witnessed such violence could not help but have doubts about the Red Guard movement. It was, however, not until the defection of Mao Zedong's chosen successor, Lin Biao, five years later that the high-minded slogans they had so urgently implemented were exposed to be no more than a rhetorical screen obscuring a personal struggle for power.

Zhang, whose devoutly religious Muslim father was attacked as one of society's enemies, and who was therefore considered the product of a bad seed, came of age in the midst of this chaos. Colleges and schools were closed and many of their professors incarcerated by the Red Guard in makeshift jails. Zhang found temporary solace during the Dachuanlian or "linkup" in the fall of 1966, when China's students were permitted to travel all over the nation at no cost. He and his friends hiked for three months from Guangzhou to the Jinggang Mountains and then on to Mao's birthplace

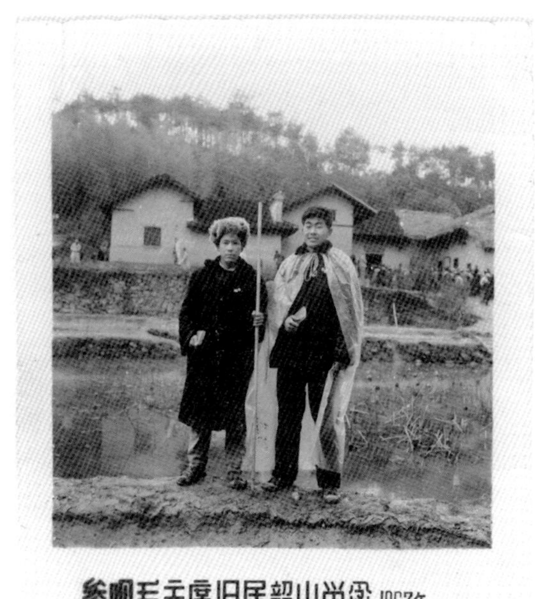

Fig. 4

at Shaoshan, performing their own version of the Red Army's legendary Long March (*Fig. 4*). From 1970 to 1972 he was sent down with everyone from the academy to labor under the supervision of the People's Liberation Army. In 1973, given a permanent job assignment, he was dispatched back to Beijing to work in a frustrating job as a designer in an export factory.

One might characterize Zhang as typical of his generation of artists. More than just typical, however, it might be more accurate to say that when China began to open up he was often a leader and outstanding practitioner of new artistic trends. As a member of the Contemporaries (Tong Dai Ren), a group of young artists in Beijing pushing the boundaries of established styles, Zhang was making work in the early post–Cultural Revolution period that suggested the subversive power of style and iconography even before there was much, if any, contact between Chinese artists and postmodernists abroad (*Fig. 5*). His early reputation in China was based to a large extent on his 1980 painting *Eternal Life*, now in the National Art Museum of China, which was painted as a statement against the state-mandated Socialist Realist style that had dominated the Chinese art world from the beginning of the Cultural Revolution. At face value, it may be taken as a paean to the sublime beauty of China's most ancient artworks. As though literally turning his back on Maoism, as well as on anyone who looked at his painting, whether critic, censor, party bureaucrat, or ordinary viewer, an exhausted craftsman seems to bow before the masterpiece he has created, a large, highly abstract sculpture of a tiger.

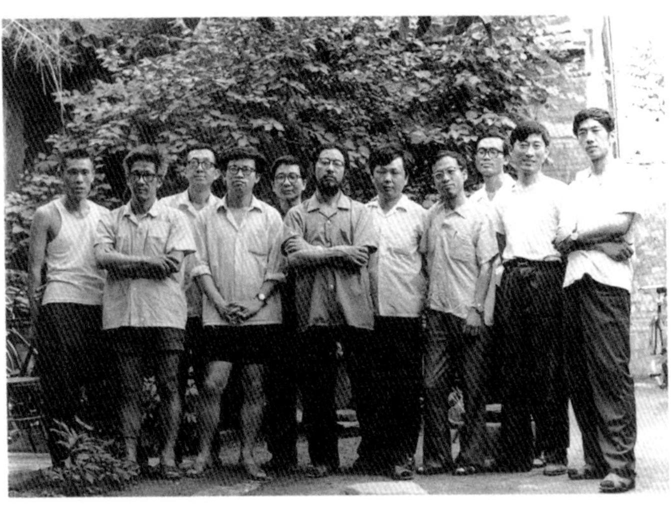
Fig. 5

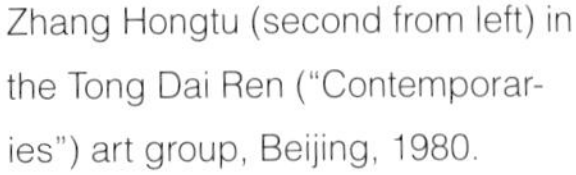

Zhang Hongtu (second from left) in the Tong Dai Ren ("Contemporaries") art group, Beijing, 1980.

The anonymous sculptor is depicted in outline mode, his well-muscled body radically foreshortened for dramatic effect, but perhaps in a style evoking Klimt rather than Chinese painting. The exaggerations of Socialist Realist perspective are here used to criticize the narrow artistic policies of the Cultural Revolution by pointing out the cultural glories of China's ancient past. The stone image the man has carved, somewhat anachronistically eroded into its twentieth-century appearance, is immediately recognizable as a sculpture that flanked the tomb mound of Han dynasty general Huo Qubing (140–117 BCE). Art historically, the subject Zhang chose represents one of China's oldest surviving monumental stone sculptures, a testament in its very medium to the cosmopolitan connections of the diplomat and military leader on whose tomb it was placed, and from a larger perspective, the internationalism of the entire epoch. During the previous Republican era (1911–37), nationalists had identified these works, made by the throne for a general who brilliantly established Han dominance in Central Asia, as particularly inspiring artifacts of China's cultural and military glory.[5] The narrative in Zhang's work, almost half a century later, however, removes such specific historical significance from the site and reinterprets it for his own generation. "Everybody says 'Long live Chairman Mao.' I just wanted to ask, 'Which will live longer, Mao or art?'"[6]

For Zhang in 1980, this primitive-looking object evoked pure art. In that role, its simplicity and abstraction of form are striking violations of the realism that undergirded art education in his day, and the dominating artistic practice of Socialist Realism. And, by challenging Socialist Realism, even this indirectly, the work became, in the context of its time, a political statement. Its main argument, running counter to hardline Maoist dogma, was that there was no single correct way to make art.

This painting also suggested an approach to the role of the artist that has remained key to Zhang's career. If the stone tiger represents all art, its maker, brilliant and highly skilled, represents all artists. In Zhang's painting, however, the artist is dwarfed by the object he has created—art is more important than its anonymous maker. Zhang, having himself studied at China's premier design academy, the Central Academy of Arts and Crafts, and worked for a decade as a designer, chooses to praise most highly the craftsman, and not the famous artist.

Before leaving China in 1982, Zhang undertook his own exploration of the liberating aesthetic possibilities of the Dunhuang caves in works that he exhibited in New York in 1984. Studying at the Art Students League, he experimented with a range of different modes of painting, and then moved into mixed media. The art of the found object found him in 1987, as the smiling man on the Quaker Oats box transformed into images of Mao Zedong ("Long Live Chairman Mao" series, 1987–95). The profoundly shocking Tiananmen Massacre of 1989, in which so many innocent lives were lost, forever changed his work. Following like a second attack came an official prohibition against acknowledging that the massacre had even occurred. This combination led to an almost obsessive concentration on *absence* that occupied Zhang's work for about a decade. Zhang mourned the death from AIDS in 1990 of his fellow artist Tseng Kwong Chi by excising Tseng's image from the photographic self-portraits that were his signature work, leaving only an empty silhouette cut out of Tseng's carefully staged settings. Then Zhang moved on to images of Mao, cutting them out of almost any material, including a ping-pong table. By 1995, Zhang had finally succeeded in exorcising Mao's image. Meanwhile, beginning in 1993, China ended the post–June Fourth freeze by reopening to international trade. The Chinese art market began to enjoy newfound visibility, initially in the Guangzhou–Hong Kong region.

In 1996, the year after Zhang initiated the "Soy Sauce Calligraphy" series, he was invited to Hong Kong University of Science and Technology as a visiting artist. In response to his experiences in this globalized metropolis, he launched a new series. Although based in a relatively new technology, and concerned with a different part of the economy, the project was conceptually related to the "Soy Sauce Calligraphy" series. He created a series of fake auction catalog pages that featured what appeared to be photographs of works of ancient Chinese art. Each page, including the "art object," was entirely simulated digitally. What appears to be a bold ink painting appears on the cover of a 1991 Christie's catalog of "Fine Chinese Paintings and Calligraphy." Covered with Ming and Qing collectors' seals as if it had come out of the palace collection, the painting also bears a barely legible signature at lower right: "Jackson Pollock 51." Lot number 25, described in English as a blue and white bottle, appears to be underglaze cobalt porcelainware from the Jingdezhen kilns, with painted floral arabesques, lotus motifs, and auspicious images of boys playing with hobby horses in the Ming dynasty style. The "reign mark" on the bottom reads "Coca Cola," and indeed the bottle is so shaped. The auction estimate is given as $4.99 for a six-pack. Lot 39, "Very rare set of complete zodiac figures (Tang dynasty, 618–907)," is estimated to sell at $1,200,000–2,000,000. It appears to consist of three-color low-fired ceramic funerary figures that represent the twelve animals of the Chinese cyclical calendar. The actual archaeological objects on which this image is modeled are strange enough—animal-headed beings wearing long court robes—but those in Zhang's version are wearing the Mao suits of a Communist cadre.[7] Lot 113, identified as Han dynasty bronze tableware, borrows the decorative motifs found on ritual bronze vessels of the mid-Zhou period, objects that were usually cast to celebrate the power of a king or feudal lord, to cover what appear to be containers for McDonald's French fries and a Big Mac. The Big Mac holder is decorated with a "clan sign" in the form of the double-arch company logo, and the French fries container is ornamented with a small inscription in archaic characters reading "*Mai Dang Lao*" (麥當勞), the brand name in China, which is carefully documented in the catalog. The two pieces are incongruously accompanied by a knife and fork, a method of eating adopted by some neophyte Chinese fast-food customers, and the estimated auction price is $3.99.

The intersection of globalized American fast food and the most rarefied objects on the auction market exposes the unequal position China still occupied in 1997 vis-à-vis the globalized economy—junk food coming in, priceless treasures going out—as well as challenging the priorities of its consuming public, economic hegemony, and governmental authorities. Zhang is not unique among contemporary artists in offering a critique of globalization and the art-world economy. Ai Weiwei has often smashed or permanently altered actual archaeological objects, thus combining his attack on the workings of a system that makes them into collectible objects with a seeming disdain for the objects themselves. Part of his project seems to be to destroy the sacred aura of antiquity. By contrast, Zhang's critique is never directed against the art itself but only calls into question the social and economic system in which it may be found today. As though to make his respect for the anonymous ancient makers completely visible, in 2002 he set about actually producing three-dimensional versions of the imaginary objects he had rendered in digital form. Patinated bronze, carefully painted porcelain bottles, and brightly glazed ceramic tomb figurines emerged as though to restore the lost antique aura. The economic commentary that is intrinsic to this hybridization project may be all the more vivid in 3-D; one can't help but laugh, or groan, as one considers exactly who might be the target of his irony. At the same time, one senses a subtle celebration of the marvels of pre-modern imagination and manufacture that cannot be fully recaptured in the present day.

1 Discussion of the goals and methods that underlie the system adopted in China may be found in Oksana Pivniouk, "Teaching Methods and Pedagogical Ideas of Pavel Petrovich Chistyakov—A Talented Russian Artist and Exceptional Art Educator," MA thesis, University of Arizona, 2013.

2 A range of such works by Fu Baoshi may be seen in *Chinese Art in the Age of Revolution, Fu Baoshi (1904–1965)* (Cleveland and New Haven: Cleveland Museum of Art and Yale University Press, 2012), 147–72.

3 See *Zhongguo meishu nianjian* [Annual of Chinese Art], *1949–1980*, ed. Zhongguo meishuguan [China Art Gallery] (Guilin: Guangxi meishu chubanshe, 1993): 1025–29; 1080–82. "Zhang Hongtu remembers a classroom assignment based on the exhibition of copies of Daoist mural paintings from Yonglegong (永 樂宮) but recalls not being particularly interested in Chinese painting (*guohua*, 國畫) at that time. He nevertheless recollects greatly liking an exhibition from about 1962 of paintings by guohua artist Lin Fengmian. —Eds."

4 Among other places, the painting is reproduced in Julia F. Andrews and Kuiyi Shen, *The Art of Modern China* (Berkeley: University of California Press, 2012), 159, and Andrews and Shen, *A Century in Crisis: Modernity and Tradition in the Art of Twentieth Century China* (New York: Guggenheim Museum, 1998), plate 137.

5 For discussion of a 1930s interpretation of the theme, see Joan Judge, "Ancient Ruins, Poetic Loss, and the Limits of Poetic Remediation: Zhang Mojun's Hymn to the Ancient Northwest," presented at the Association of Asian Studies annual meeting, Chicago, March 27, 2015, 27. A modern textbook version seems to echo this viewpoint. See Michael Sullivan, *Arts of China* (Berkeley: University of California Press, 2008), 75.

6 As cited by Jerome Silbergeld, "The Art of Straddling Boundaries," in *Zhang Hongtu: The Art of Straddling Boundaries* (Taipei and Beijing: Lin & Keng Gallery, 2007), xiv–xv.

7 See, for example, an unglazed Tang dynasty set excavated in Xi'an in 1955–56, in *The Quest for Eternity: Chinese Ceramic Sculptures from the People's Republic of China* (Los Angeles County Museum of Art, 1987), 86, 141–43, and plate 76.

ZHANG HONGTU: PLAYING WITH POWER

Alexandra Chang

In the 1990s, Zhang Hongtu could be found treading through the triangulated grid of lower Manhattan with his signature full head of silvering hair and a watch with no face strapped to his wrist (*Fig. 1*). He was a man obsessed with the cruel tricks of Time and still subject to the perpetual grasp of the melancholia of its felt loss or wasting away that he had experienced during the Cultural Revolution before his arrival in New York City the decade before.

Time for Zhang had been stunted, and he made up for this, generating in just one year in New York what he estimates might be a decade's worth of work while in China (*Plate 25*).

Zhang's early career in China as an art student was filled with endless verbal and psychological abuse by his schoolmates and teachers due to prejudice against his

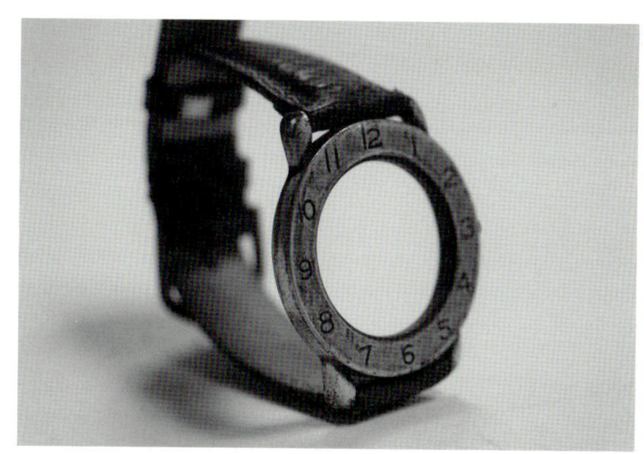

Fig. I

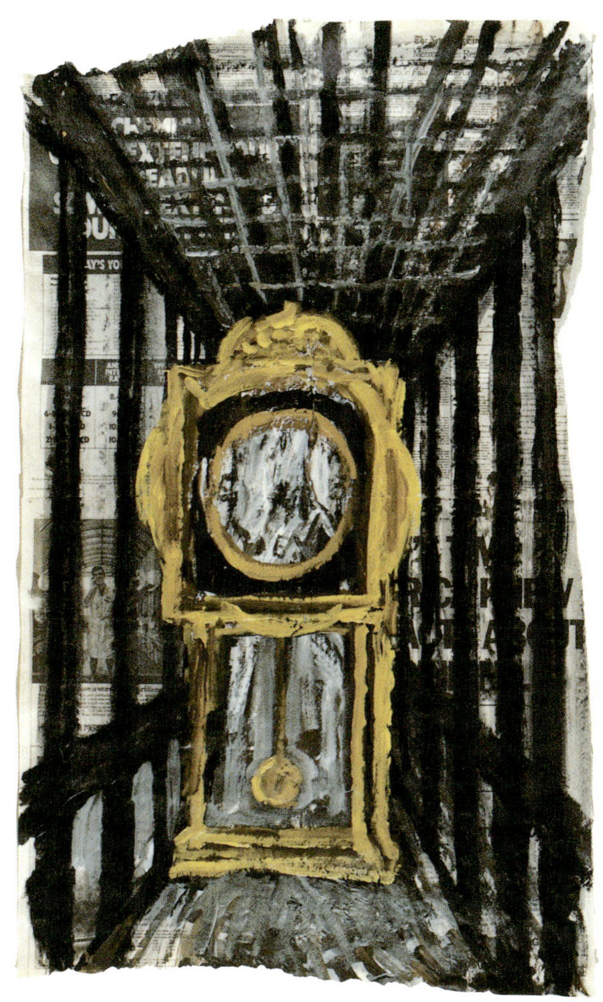

Plate 25

Fig. I
A watch with the face cut out, which the artist wore during the 1990s.

Plate 25
Untitled (Newspaper Series) #5, 1985. Ink and acrylic on newspaper, 42 x 27 in.

family's Muslim background and was cut short due to the Cultural Revolution. In 1960, he entered the Central Academy of Fine Arts high school, which was closed during the Cultural Revolution. He then attended the Central Institute of Arts and Crafts, leading him into his early career of jewelry design. With a desire to escape a forced profession, he found offers of employment to teach art, but his employers held onto his papers, compelling him to remain. After Deng Xiaoping's Open Door Policy began to take effect, the government's restrictions on art and culture were loosened and arts groups began to emerge, such as the Stars Group (Xingxing Hua Pai) and Beijing Oil Painting Research Association (Beijing youhua yanjiuhui). Zhang formed the Contemporaries (Tong Dai Ren) art group with artists he had gone to school with, and in 1980, the group showed at the National Art Museum of China. His work *Eternal Life* was collected by the museum. Soon after, with loosened travel restrictions, he found a chance to move to the US but had to leave his wife and child behind for the moment as he searched for a life outside China.[1]

Zhang arrived in New York City in 1982 with the determination to become the artist he could not be in China at the time (*Fig. 2*). While still in China, he had learned about the Art Students League in New York, which was popular with international students due to its reasonable tuition fees and the fact that the school did not require an English language test. Traveling to the US on a student visa, he arrived in New York and stayed with his wife's cousin from Tai Shan, Guangdong, who had launched a restaurant business and by 1982 had a house on Staten Island. Zhang lived there for a month and found work in temporary construction jobs that afforded him the time he required to attend classes and to produce work. By chance, his employer offered him an apartment near Madison Square Garden in the empty building he worked on during the day. In exchange for guarding against air-conditioner thieves, he lived alone in its cavernous quarters. The building owner decided to stage an exhibition in the empty building, and Zhang was approached by a real-estate agent who, unable to purchase his artwork, instead offered the artist free lodging in one of his buildings, at 71 Sullivan Street, placing Zhang in the middle of SoHo in the 1980s. Zhang recalled that during this time, his bank account always hovered around $600, providing him enough for the essentials of paying the bills, buying art materials, and purchasing food. When his bank balance dipped, it was time for him to take on another temporary construction job.[2]

At the Art Students League Zhang found that he could take classes from an array of teachers, rotating classes every few weeks and learning a different style from a different instructor in each room. He met Richard Pousette-Dart, who taught twice a week at the school. It was Pousette-Dart who made the artist profoundly rethink his approach to art. "He didn't really tell you how to make your painting. . . . He never [told]

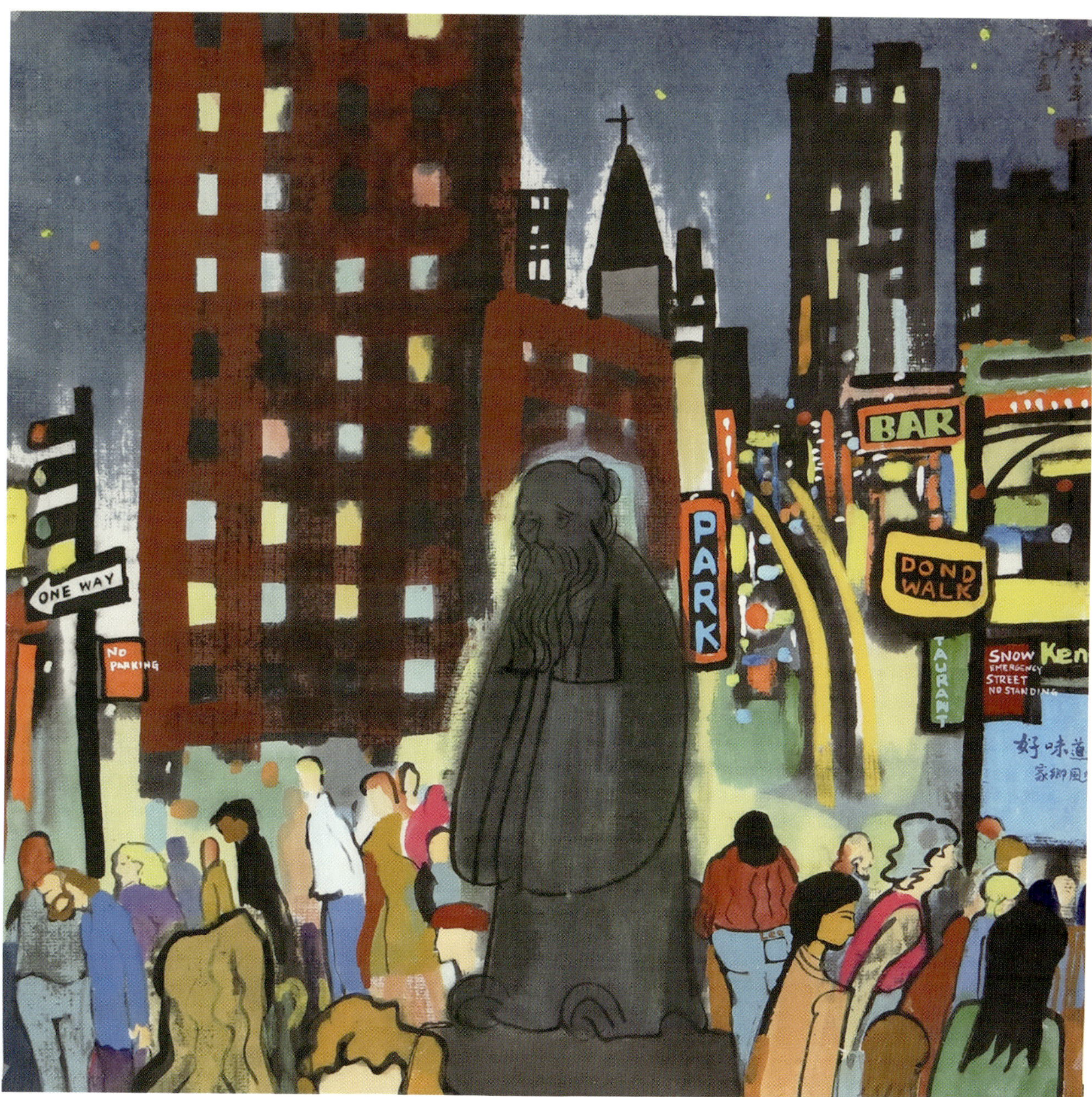

Fig. 2

The first painting Zhang Hongtu made in New York was *Tang Ren Jie*, a view of
Chinatown in September 1982.

me as a Chinese teacher look[ing] over your shoulder, oh this is wrong, you have to do this way or you have to do that way. He just gave you [a] general idea about your life, about how your work related to your life. Just very generally, but this was a big help to me to understand American culture, to understand myself." Zhang still remembers how Pousette-Dart invited the students to his country studio for his birthday, which the artist recalled as shifting his concept of the teacher-student relationship in the culture in which he was now creating. Zhang sought opportunities to exchange ideas. "I found it very interesting early for me because the Art Students League is like New York, at that time it [was]—what is the word? Hybrid. Many artists from different countries. For example, [in] only a few days, I had a friend from Colombia visit my studio. His English [was] better than my English, not that perfect, my English [was] still very bad, but we still talked in my studio for four hours!"[3]

The first works that appeared were purposely divorced from the color-laden figurative portraits and landscapes Zhang had painted while in China. Instead he implemented browns, blacks, grays, and found materials, including old newspapers and burlap that he would scavenge from the weekly remnants thrown out by the carpet stores nearby. He used plaster and wire, pushing his body and hands into the plaster, trying to bring about a personal closeness to the physicality of his sculptural relief work, his physical body pressing and shaping the work itself, as in *The Body* (1988). The portrait painting he had been engaged with in China seemed to fail him in his attempt to realize the subject beyond the singular moment of a captured facial expression. As a counter-reaction, he created *Self-Portrait (The Back)* (*Plate 13*) and *Back of Three Heads* (1987), casting the heads in plaster, face and countenance completely obscured. Instead of an outward manifestation or realist approach, his interest was the inner individual being, something more resolute and less fleeting.

Away from his family, in a city where he could not communicate well with the limited English he possessed, Zhang experienced a keen sense of isolation. His work from this period reflects a pervasive solitude and desire to move forward from the struggles of the past into the future, however unknown. During this time, he worked on his "Ox" series. Zhang notes, "I thought of myself, I'm strong, I have inner power. It's not a beautiful animal like a Dragon or a Lion or a Tiger. A useful animal." The abstract figurative series set the ox as a sole figure or in a small group in severe red and black color fields or ashen gray landscapes. The dark gray or black figure is portrayed as walking forward toward the viewer into an un-visualized present off the canvas or back into the painting beyond the horizon. *A Walking Man* (*Plate 10*) also poses a shadowy solitary figure, walking away from the background toward the viewer, into something new and unknown.

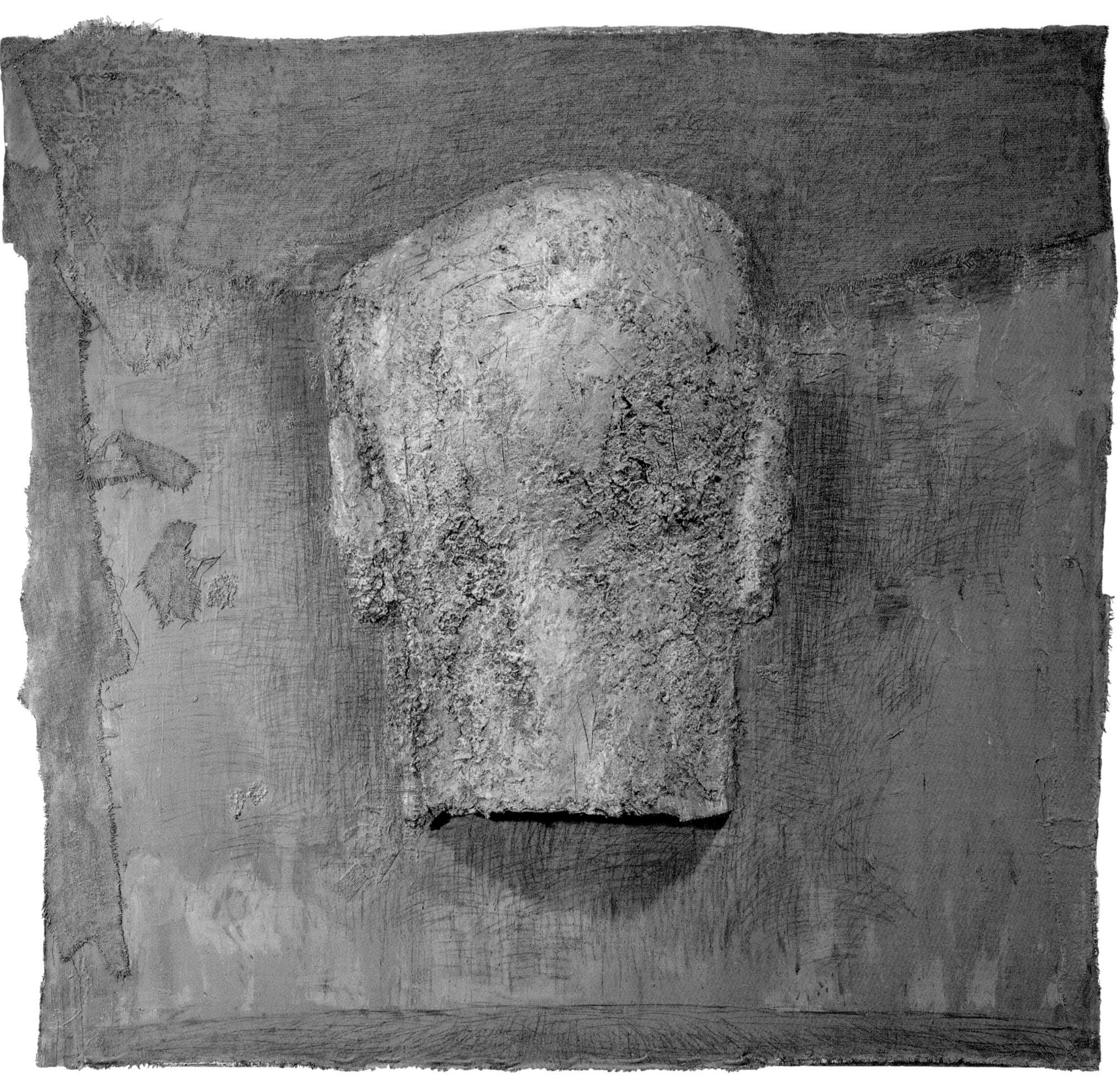

Plate 13

Self-Portrait (The Back), 1987. Mixed media on canvas, 73 x 81 in.

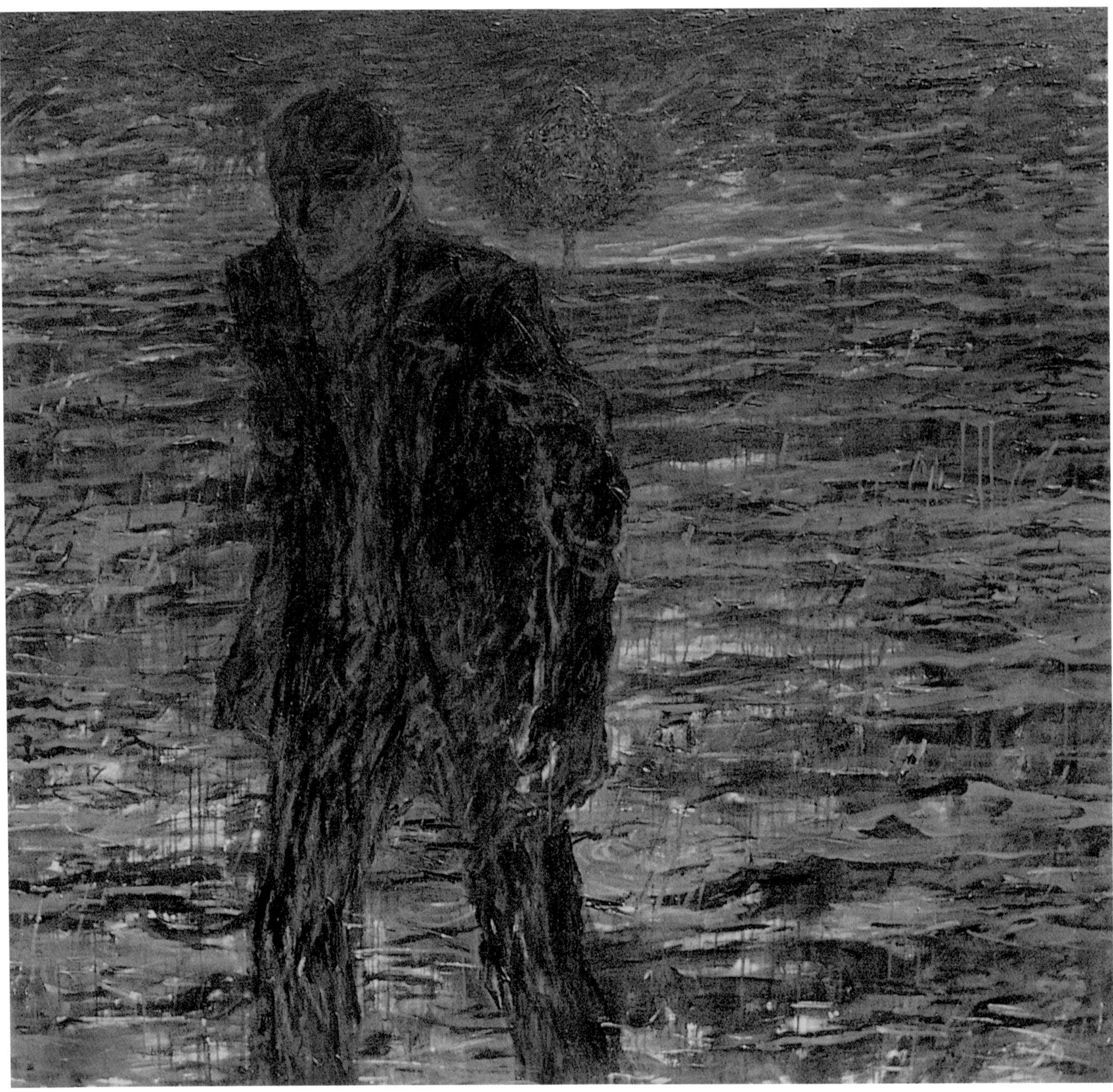

Plate 10

A Walking Man, 1985. Acrylic on canvas, 56 x 62 in. Collection of the Art Students
League of New York.

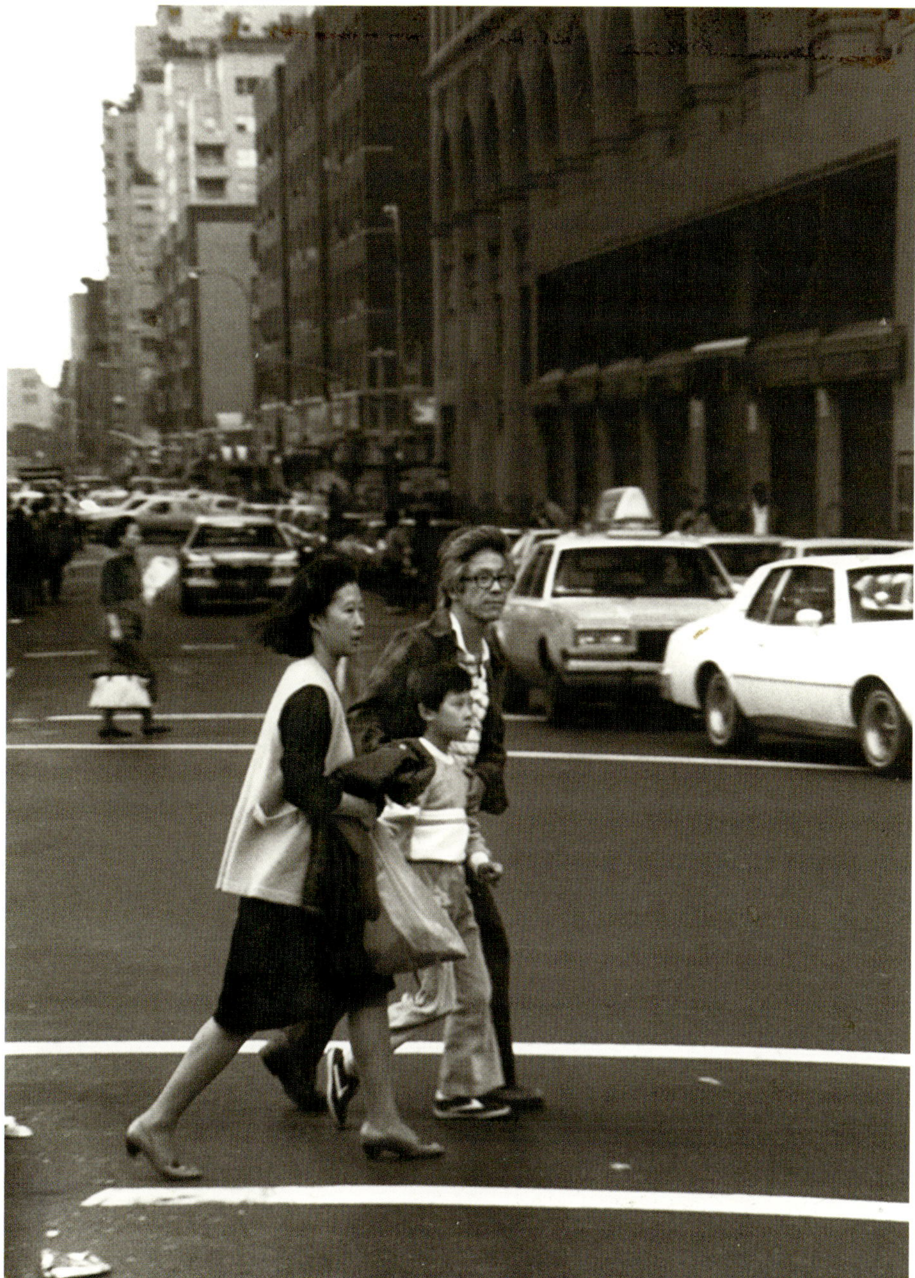

Fig. 3

In 1984, Zhang's wife Miaoling and eight-and-a-half-year-old son Dasheng arrived to live with him in the East Village between Avenues A and B, where other Chinese diasporic artists, such as Ai Weiwei, also gathered in the city (*Fig. 3*). Zhang's wife, herself a ceramicist, was working in textile design. At that time, Zhang was working at some of the most dangerous construction sites as a stone worker, hanging off the sides of many of the most famous landmark buildings in the city—including Brooklyn City Hall and Saint Thomas Church on Fifty-third Street across from the Museum of Modern Art—breathing in the thick dust as he worked suspended in mid-air rebuilding their ornaments and cement and rock walls. This dangerous trade paid more and it also taught the artist about the medium.

The artist's "Newspaper" series (*Plate 21, Plate 26*), painted on broadsheets of found newspapers from a single day, April 1, 1984, show the extraordinary contrast between the New York Zhang experienced and the New York he imagined through the media and the newspaper clippings. He found the ashen bodies of the tired day laborer, sweatshop worker, and his family acquaintances were in quiet opposition to the glamour in the daily pages. He painted these works in gray, black, and white acrylic and ink, presenting the tired bodies or the everyday tools of the trade, such as an iron, onto the newspaper broadsheets. The work often injected humor into an otherwise bleak subject with ironic headlines or images in contrast with the painted subject. His later "Soy Sauce Calligraphy" works, made in the mid-1990s, also speak to the immigrant experience with ads he would see posted in Chinatown, tacit evidence of a lifestyle beneath the surface of what is presented, as histories written in calligraphic texts in Chinese diasporic art history. What is brought forth is the perception of the immigrant's American dream, crumpled, but still intact on newsprint or in soy sauce on rice paper.

Zhang slowly gained acquaintances from among Chinese diasporic artists, some of whom had also left around the same time he had during the later 1970s and 1980s to the US, Europe, and Australia, whom he met or reconnected with while they passed through or were living in New York. These artists included Yuan Yunsheng and Wang Keping, who founded the Chinese United Overseas Artists Association in 1987. Other artists who were a part of this circle included Lin Lin, Bai Jingzhou, Yang Qian, Yan Li, Zhang Wei, and Ai Weiwei, who were included in the *Annual*, a publication that the association produced of their work in 1988. The group was also able to mount an exhibition of works at the popular Palladium nightclub, organized by Mark Moskin. It was there, amid the thousand pulsing club-goers each week, that Zhang's *Quaker Oats Mao* from the "Long Live Chairman Mao" series was first exhibited. The series was created as a way for the artist to counter the psychological imprinting of Mao's image in his mind that was demanded throughout his lifetime in China. Seeing the Quaker Oats box one morning, he wondered if anyone else saw how closely the Quaker resembled Mao, or if it was he who was seeing Mao at every turn. With a few brushstrokes, he turned the Quaker into Mao, defying the power of the eternal icon and bringing his image into play with the everyday, and into a pop cultural artifact.

While each of the participants in the group had different reasons for his membership, they coalesced around their shared experience in China. Some, including Yuan, had hoped to underline the work of contemporary Chinese artists in the field; however, a general overriding mission was to gain visibility and support each other's work. These differences were exacerbated after the Tiananmen Square tragedy in 1989, with conflicting political positions among the group. According to Zhang, some felt Deng

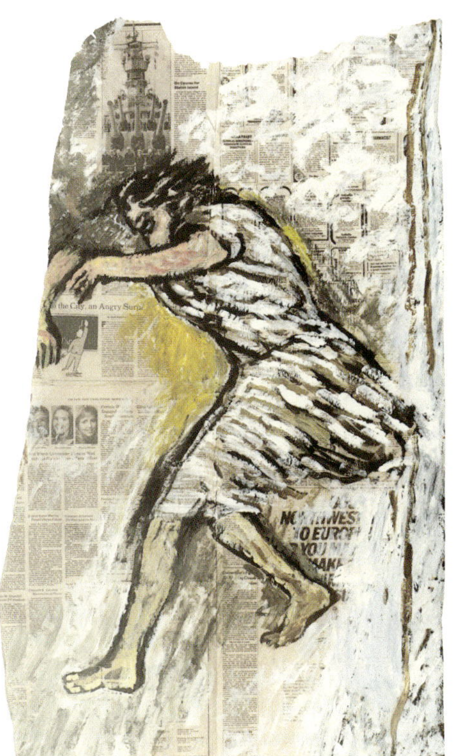

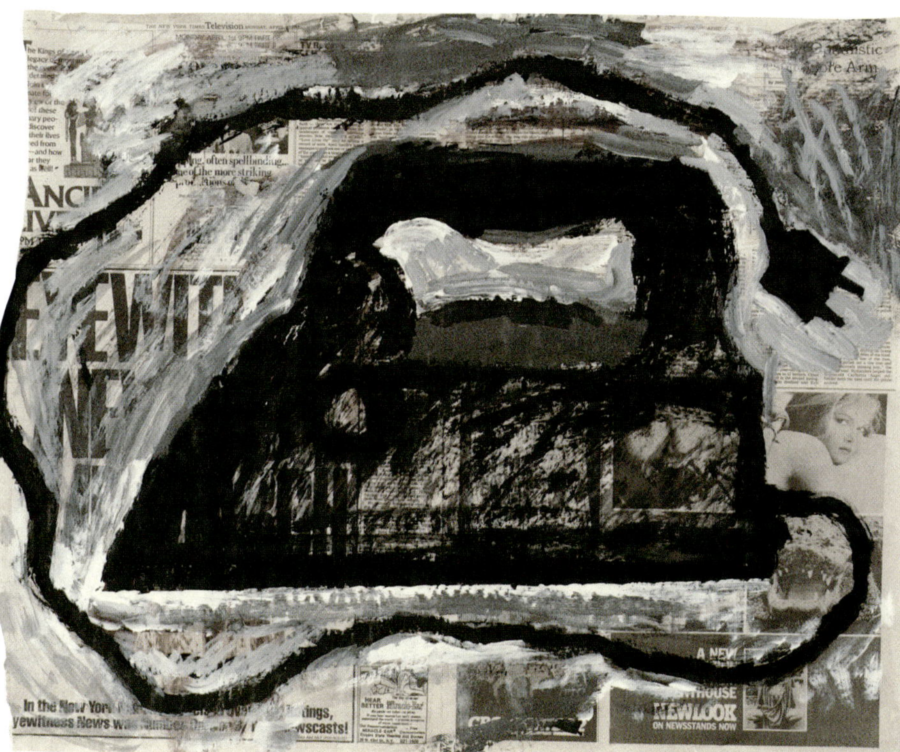

Plate 21

Plate 26

Plate 21

Untitled (Newspaper Series) #13, 1985. Ink and acrylic on newspaper, 43 x 27 in.

Plate 26

Untitled (Newspaper Series) #10, 1985. Ink and acrylic on newspaper, 23 x 27 in.

Xiaoping's past work to open up China shouldn't be forgotten, while he and others could not let that eclipse Deng's deadly suppression of the protest. When Yuan Zuo, the nephew of Yuan Yunsheng, suggested the space at the gallery where he was teaching at the Massachusetts College of Art for the group to show an exhibition reflecting on the events of Tiananmen, the group disbanded with differences of opinion.[4]

During and after the protest in 1989, Zhang was a vocal diasporic presence in New York. He participated in a roundtable discussion featured in *Art Spiral*, the publication of the Asian American Arts Centre in Chinatown, and also signed a statement with several artists in protest that was picked up by the *Village Voice*. He also joined the "June 4th" exhibition of 300 artists responding to the events at Tiananmen Square spearheaded by the Asian American Arts Centre's director Robert Lee and Bing Lee, who directed the programs at the Centre and had extensive contacts with the diasporic Chinese artist community. The exhibition was held at Blum Helman Warehouse, where Zhang showed his work *Last Banquet* and *Chairmen Mao*, and at PS 1, where Zhang participated with other artists in creating "doors" on long wood-panel slabs as responses to the deadly crackdown. The doors he contributed included a black door with the Communist symbol of the yellow hammer and sickle, barred and fastened by a chain with a key with six teeth and four notches and a lock with a dragon image. This piece was eventually destroyed by the artist, as he felt it was too illustrative.[5] He also created the work the *Bilingual Chart of Acupuncture Points and Meridians (Front & Back)* for the exhibition. In this work, Zhang again takes stabs at the image of Mao by charting the history of ideologies and movements impacting Chinese history onto the body of Mao as acupuncture meridians.

Last Banquet played on the famed last meal as painted by Leonardo da Vinci in *The Last Supper*, but with Mao's image in place of the disciples and Jesus and made of collaged pages torn from the Little Red Book. The *Chairmen Mao* installation similarly played with the image of Mao, caricaturizing his iconic portrait bust through pop renderings of his image and satirizing elements of the Little Red Book. Zhang was invited to participate in an exhibition at the Russell Senate Building Rotunda in Washington, DC, also organized by Bing Lee. Ironically, three of the exhibition's works were censored, including Zhang's work *Last Banquet*. Due to the censorship, the artists all pulled out of the show and the exhibition never took place.

Through his connection to the Asian American Arts Centre downtown, Zhang became acquainted with Bing Lee, Frog King Kwok, and Ming Fay, who were from Hong Kong. The three artists were a part of the artist group Epoxy, and Zhang was invited to join shortly after it was founded in 1983. The group chose the name Epoxy after the way the resin's bond is created when two separate components are joined to make something altogether new.[6] They thrived on the concept of collaborative practice in this way. Zhang recalls the group's installation *The 36 Tactics* that was a part of the New Museum's component of the seminal exhibition "The Decade Show: Frameworks of Identity in the 1980s" with the Studio Museum in Harlem and the Museum of Contemporary Hispanic Art in 1990. For this work, the group met at the New York Public Library and foraged through microfilm looking for material to create a Xerox collage and epoxy works based on a collection of Chinese proverbs outlining thirty-six stratagems of war and politics. It was here that Zhang learned the technique of using epoxy resin that he would use in his later work, including his cut-out icons.

The works that came after the pop Mao imagery in 1989, which slowly developed in his well-known "Material Mao" series, included cutout imagery as Zhang further explored and countered the aesthetics of power of the icon and ideology.[7] During the early 1990s, he created a series of works including *A Scroll Painting* (1990), *The Archangel Michael* (1991), *Trinity* (1991), *A Book* (1992), and *Soy Book* (1994–95) (*Fig. 4*, *Fig. 5*, *Fig. 6*). The pieces utilize mixed media from acrylic and burlap to books on sheet metal to soy sauce and rice paper. Each of these works brought with it the desire to negate the icon. For Zhang, the book, the scroll painting, the religious figure all speak to value systems. In these works, the artist plays with the abstract *yin* and the physical *yang* by disappearing the icon, creating a cutout of the shape of each subject, so that the viewer sees the materials around the empty space—the soy sauce, the sheet metal, the burlap, the everyday and found materials with no value. "The book, to me, it is spiritual, it is *yin*, it is abstract, but the soy sauce. . . you use every day and it is cheap and nobody pays attention [to it] for the color."[8]

Also during this time, another theme in Zhang's work revealed itself through his exploration of self, and that was his newfound identity as a diasporic Asian American artist. The artist found himself immersed in the conversation of a group of artists he also joined, Godzilla: Asian American Art Network, which grew to include more than 200 artists nationwide. The network was loose in mission, but many members hoped to create a movement of solidarity to support the visibility of diverse artists within the larger art-world institutions. The group is well known for its letter to David Ross, then director of the Whitney Museum of American Art. The letter was critical of the museum's "conspicuous absence of Asian American visual artists in the current Biennial" and called for increased diversity at the museum.[9] Zhang's main reason to become involved was his interest in the conversations the artists were having internally about identity, which helped him shape questions that manifest themselves with his practice through the questioning of the assumed and articulated notions of East and West in art and aesthetics, questioning art historicity. This questioning appears in his "Repainted Shan Shui" paintings, purposely hybrid paintings rendering classic Chinese shan shui

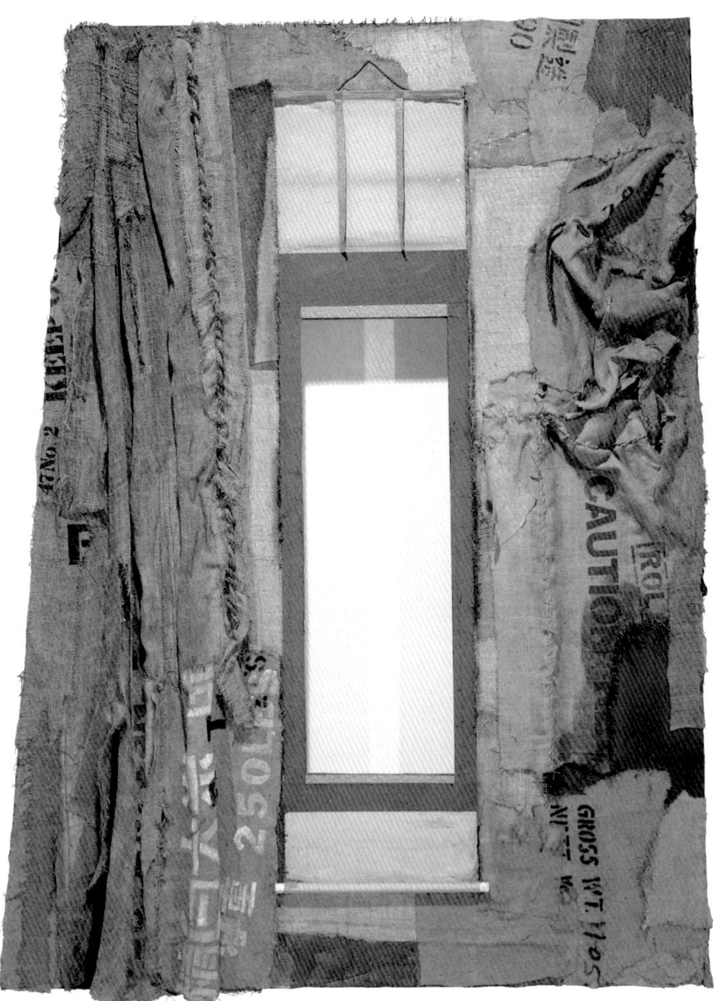 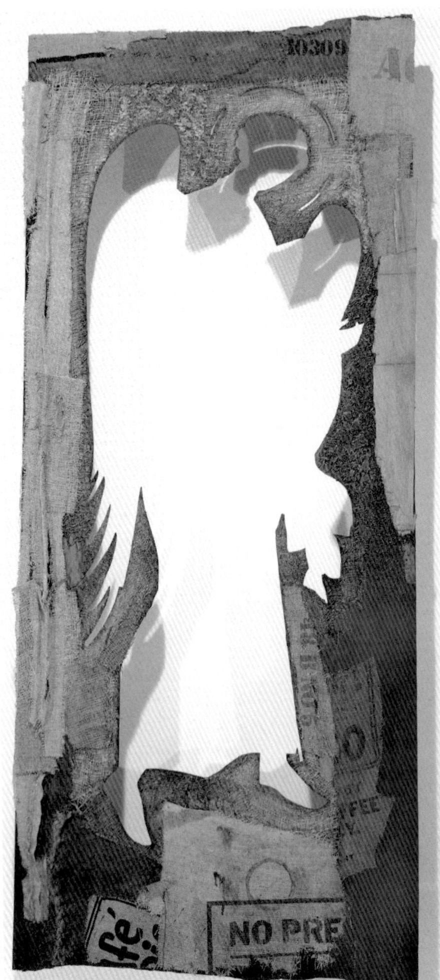

Fig. 4

Fig. 5

Fig. 4
A Scroll Painting, 1990. Burlap and acrylic on wood and canvas, 95 x 71 in.

Fig. 5
The Archangel Michael, 1991. Burlap, plywood, tar, and acrylic on wood, 87 x 35 in.

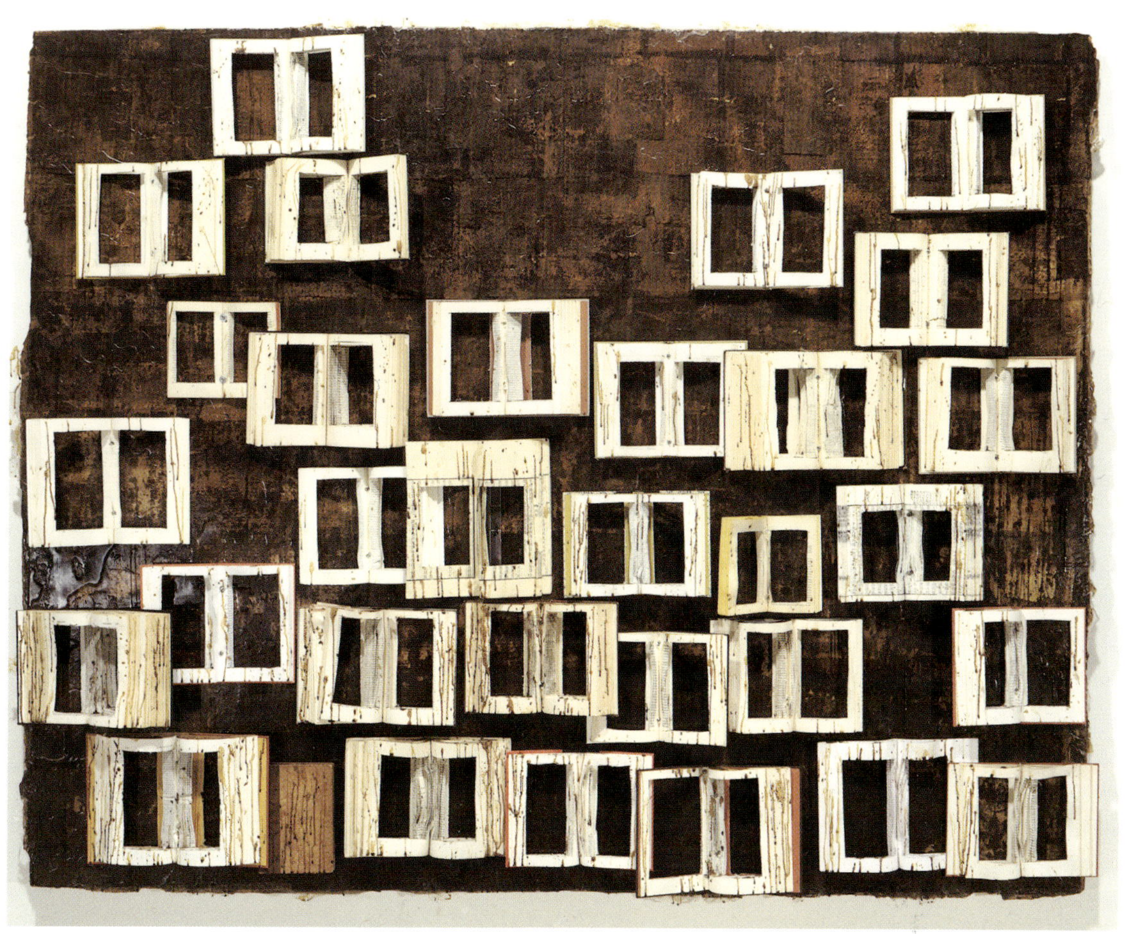

Fig. 6

Soy Book, 1994–95. Books, soy sauce, rice paper, and plywood, 66 x 84 x 3 in.

masterworks of Fan Kuan, Li Tang, and Shitao, among others, in European styles reminiscent of Monet, Cézanne, and Van Gogh.

The work that Zhang is best known for may be his pop Mao imagery, used on his cylindrical appropriation of the popular Quaker Oats boxes and in his "Material Mao" and "Repainted Shan Shui" series. However, the pathway to the creation of these works and the work that continues can find its roots in the artist's early work in newspaper, soy sauce, and cutouts that came before and were directly influenced by his early experiences in New York.

Zhang's diasporic placement overlaps legacies of power including that of Cultural Revolution and post–Cultural Revolution Mao and his subject position as the *other* and the residual elements of an aesthetics of power over his imaginary. Once Zhang enters the US in 1982, his body moves into the post-colonial power legacies of the US and its interrelated histories of the West and the *other*. These legacies are embedded within the tiers of the art circles in which Zhang travels, from his circle of recent post-1980s Chinese diasporic artists to New York (as well as in France and Australia), the Asian American art movement with an internal US politics stemming from the late 1960s and '70s civil rights and solidarity movements, and diffused into the '90s culture wars and his participation in groups such as Epoxy and Godzilla.

Zhang negotiates his position by interrupting the power economy of the image or icon through a play on its very foundational constructs, a totalitarian and colonial aesthetics of power, injecting humor and satire and tearing through power aesthetics by way of medium.

Zhang's works reveal themselves through the contexts surrounding and enveloping the artist, spun through influential elements of his daily and expanded accumulative life experiences—from small and of-the-moment and everyday to vast, spanning time, globally interconnected. In his most current works to date, one might see glimpses of his past as they accumulate to their manifestation in the present, with the depth of the layered histories of a life lived and the emotion and working-through injected into them that stands as something not quite present or past, yet also yielding to both.

1   Zhang Hongtu, interview with the author, New York, December 4, 2014.

2   Ibid.

3   Ibid.

4   Zhang Hongtu, Skype interview with the author, March 4, 2014.

5   Zhang Hongtu, email to the author, March 11, 2014.

6   Interview with Bing Lee, co-founder of Godzilla, interviewed by the author for Art Spaces Archives Project, September 10, 2009. "The meaning of epoxy is that [it's] a glue that uses two different kinds of chemicals, A and B, and we mix together and then it will be a very strong binding agent. So we used that as symbolic meaning of the group." http://www.as-ap.org/content/oral-history-bing-lee-0 accessed March 25, 2014.

7   Nicholas Mirzoeff, *The Right to Look: A Counterhistory of Visuality* (Durham, NC: Duke University Press, 2011), xv. Mirzoeff writes, "In this sense, I consider visuality to be both a medium for the transmission and dissemination of authority, and a means for the mediation of those subject to that authority." In this way, Zhang is taking on elements of authority and visuality through his work.

8   Zhang Hongtu, interview with the author, New York, December 4, 2014.

9   Letter from Godzilla: Asian American Art Network to David Ross, May 13, 1991. Author's personal papers.

ZHANG HONGTU'S FASHIONABLE TURN

Thuy Linh Nguyen Tu

The historian Eric Hobsbawm once wrote, "Why brilliant fashion-designers, a noto-riously non-analytic breed, sometimes succeed in anticipating the shape of things to come better than professional predictors, is one of the most obscure questions in history and, for the historian of culture, one of the most central."[1] Hobsbawm was no lover of fashion, but his comment revealed a grudging admission of how fashion—so accustomed to recycling and reinventing historical ideas and images—might actually be a useful form for narrating the past and envisioning the future. Fashion designers are constantly in the throes of history. If it is true that "to see the future," one must "look at the past," as Hobsbawm later wrote, this is precisely why they seem to always en-vision the "next thing" so clearly.[2]

Though his name rarely rolls off the lips of fashionistas, Zhang Hongtu has been one of the most adept users of this form, seizing its potential to convey historical per-spective. In 1994, he collaborated with the designer Vivienne Tam on a collection that featured images of Mao adapted from Zhang's artwork. Together they created eight images, including "Mao So Young" (Mao with pigtails), "Ow Mao" (being stung by a bee), "Psycho Mao" (with psychedelic glasses), "Holy Mao" (with a clerical collar), "Miss Mao" (with lipstick), and "Nice Day Mao" (Mao as a yellow smiley face). When Zhang painted Mao with pigtails, Tam added a Peter Pan collar and gingham dress;

when he put a bee on Mao's nose, she added stripes and colors to the background. Tam added a clerical collar to Mao's official portrait, Zhang smeared lipstick on the chairman's face, and so on. As Tam put it, "Zhang's art was political, but I thought I could loosen it up a bit with fashion, to represent the new openness of China. This would show its humor and warmth, and the growing freedom of its people from Mao's image."[3]

The results were indeed playful, but this "freedom from Mao's image" had been, for Zhang, hard-won. In the lexicon of Asian images, few are as prominent or as widespread as the image of Mao Zedong. During his term as chairman of the Communist Party of China (1943–76), images of Mao appeared on stamps, currency, and schoolbooks, in public spaces and private homes. These images proliferated during the late 1960s, at the height of the Cultural Revolution, when they were used to shore up support for Mao's most ambitious reforms. At a time when advancing age and flawed reform initiatives like the Great Leap Forward (1958) had tarnished his revolutionary sheen, Mao's pervasive images worked to emphasize his authority and to generate the spirit of affiliation that his movement to "revolutionize daily life" demanded.[4]

For years before working with Tam, Zhang had incorporated Mao's image into his art practice. Like many artists of his generation, Zhang lived through the social and political tumult of the Cultural Revolution, and understood well how Mao's image became a part of everyday life, framing what it meant to "feel Chinese," as Zhang put it. Mao's ubiquitous portraits fostered an imaginative closeness between the chairman and his subjects: he could not be everywhere, but his images certainly could. This enforced intimacy came at a cost, and taking on Mao's image became cathartic for the artist, a "psychic release," as he saw it.

Over the next decade, Zhang incorporated Mao's image in a variety of media. *Quaker Oats Mao* (1987), completed before the Tiananmen protests, was his first effort. In this work, Zhang painted a proletarian cap on the familiar Quaker, suggesting a family resemblance between these two icons. While other Chinese artists working in Political Pop also took up this image, they did so mainly to satirize a bygone political culture. Zhang, however, was primarily interested in the present, in how it is informed and shaped by the past. His art refused to accept any distance between personal history and political icon. It refused to see Mao as only an international symbol, detached from the lives of Chinese still affected by his legacy.

He made this most explicit in the "Material Mao" series (1991–95), sculptures he created by cutting Mao's famous silhouette into blocks of different material, including corn, rice, soy sauce, fur, brick, stone, and iron. The materials—basic and necessary—

highlight Mao's indelible stamp on everyday life. At times, as in *Mesh Mao* (1993), they depict the chairman as a ghostly specter in ways that recall the writing of Liu Xiaobo and other dissidents.[5] At a time when China was entering the Mao craze— whether out of nostalgia for Mao or as a satire on him—Zhang's work, like that of dissidents outside of China, urged a critical consideration of Mao's legacy.

These weighty concerns were, however, often taken up with great humor—a perspective that he shared with Vivienne Tam. Long before their collaboration, Zhang had been borrowing from popular culture to generate playful tongue-in-cheek critiques. In his "acupunctural art," Zhang reworked the traditional acupuncture chart by fitting it with Mao's corpulent body: press on Mao's left forehead to release "class struggle," his right cheek for "revolutions," his left foot for "democracy." Even more vivid was his remake of the McDonald's French fries case in Chinese bronze and the Coca-Cola bottle in blue-and-white porcelain. The recasting of these disposable objects in near-sacred materials—so valued as to have launched ships and caused wars—allowed Zhang to play with the very idea of value, of what and who is valuable.

Zhang's work with clothing was perhaps the most complex among his various engagements with popular forms. Clothing as a cultural medium lies at the intersection of the intimate and the public. "A part of the strangeness of dress," the scholar Elizabeth Wilson has said, "is that it links the biological body to the social being, and public to private."[6] In this linkage—this suturing of self to other—"clothing marks an unclear boundary ambiguously," making it difficult to distinguish between the individual and the collective, the profoundly intimate and the intensely public.[7] In this regard, clothing could potentially serve as the perfect medium for the types of personal struggles and public critiques that Zhang's art sought to enact.

But working in fashion, as many artists have discovered, can open up unexpected theoretical questions, political possibilities—and practical problems. Tam's Mao collection ultimately proved to be a hit, and Tam became a certified fashion star. The tops she created with Zhang were by far the most popular. Each of the eight designs got its own shirt, backed by decorative patterns and enhanced by several hundred sequins. In these pieces, Mao's already outrageous visage was made even more so by the embellishments; in a certain light, his face seemed to actually twinkle. Tam's designs took Zhang's subtle wit to an extreme, turning his politicized imagery into pop parodies. The sense of gravity that accompanied Zhang's paper collages, even in their humor, was now largely gone. What remained was fun, cute, whimsical Mao.

In investing Zhang's images with "a bit of fashion," had the collection simply popularized and depoliticized them? Perhaps, but if Zhang's work attempted to expose the ways that the presentation of Mao as authoritative and charismatic leader relied in large part on the presentation of him as a masculine, paternal, and powerful figure, then this collection undermined that image even more powerfully. Tam was able to feminize Mao and make explicit the sexual undertones to which Zhang's work gestured. Mao in these garments was absolutely and spectacularly unmasculine. Rather than detract from the critiques posed by Zhang, the shirts in some ways extended it.

With its absolute proximity to the body, Tam's clothing emphasized more assertively the concept of intimacy expressed in Zhang's work. To see Mao's image draped so closely, and in some cases so provocatively, on the wearer is to be struck by the way that it is made and remade by the human form precisely at the point of contact between the public and the private, between the exposed and the hidden. No longer just a symbol handed down from above to be embraced below, Mao's image is generated, accepted, embellished, or rejected at this point of connection.

"That was the thing that really hit me when I first saw the fashion show," Zhang recalled when seeing his images on Tam's dresses (*Plate 46*). "People who looked at the collection had different reactions to the images depending on where they were from and the bodies that wore them."[8] The consumption of clothing is an inherently open-ended process, one in which wearers perform and attach different meanings to these material objects based on their social contexts.[9] Certainly the significance of Mao's image also varies according to the context and viewer. But Zhang's comments reveal the ways in which bodies can enact—or generate—meaning at the point of aesthetic production. Fashion, as Anne Hollander observed decades ago, is a "form of visual art, a creation of images with the visible self as its medium."[10] Mao's image on these garments is not static, frozen, and framed like other works of art. It serves as prop, backdrop, and stage for the wearer's own performance. It shifts and changes with bodies and contexts. These images, in other words, are made and remade not just by Zhang and Tam, but by all who wear the garments.

Zhang seemed to have recognized the critical potential of this. The following year, inspired perhaps by this foray into fashion, he designed a series of T-shirts to commemorate Hong Kong's return to Chinese rule in 1997 (*Plate 99*). The series similarly employs iconic images in new ways. In "Hong Kong 1997" the artist juxtaposed the Great Wall and Hong Kong's skyline, with the wall positioned prominently behind, as if looming over the city. The closeness of the Great Wall to Hong Kong's cityscape suggests both intimacy and distance, both similarity and difference—they may appear to belong together (both are monumental in scale), but there is dissonance in the juxtaposition. The design seems to ask, how will these two entities really fit together in the "one country, two systems" plan? In "Good Luck for the Year of the Ox," Zhang paints

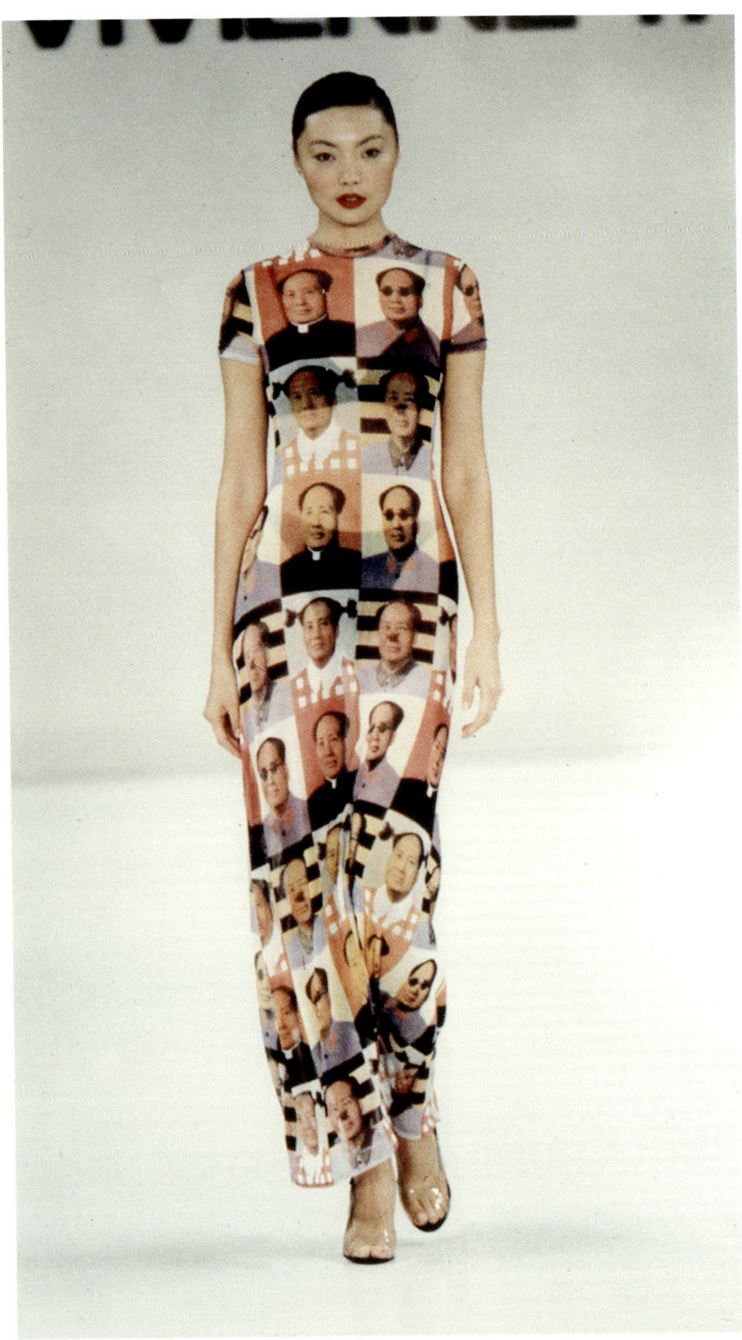

Plate 46

Collaboration between Zhang Hongtu and Vivienne Tam. *Fashion Mao*, 1994, still from collaborative video.

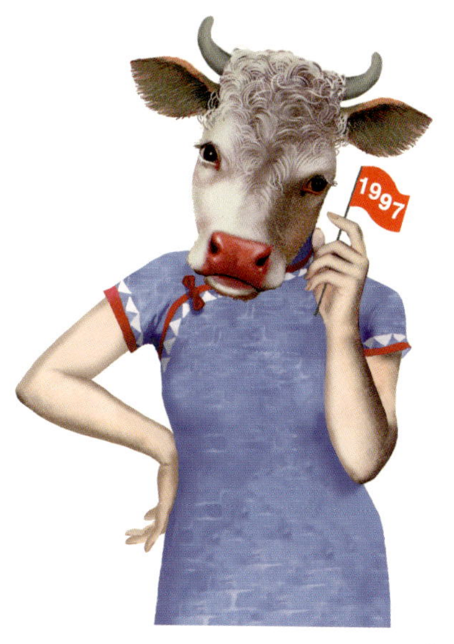

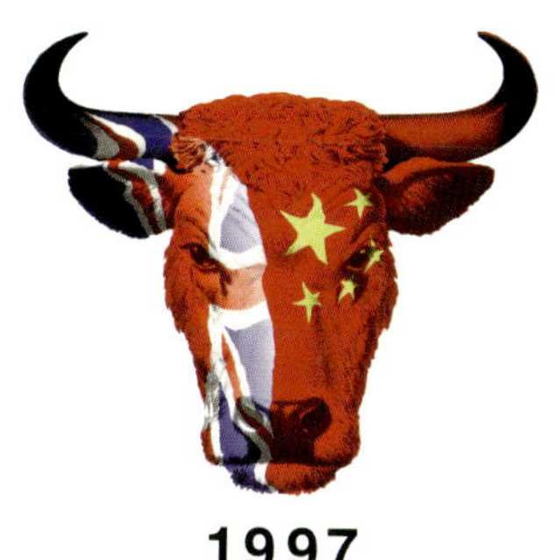

Plate 99
A, B, C, D:
Designs from the "Hong Kong 1997" T-shirt series:
A. *Transition/Translation*.
B. *Welcome!*
C. *Good Luck for the Year of the Ox.*
D. *Hong Kong 1997.*

the Chinese and British flags side by side over the face of an ox. In "Welcome!," he places an ox's head over a female body wearing a westernized *qipao*. The ox and the flag hint at the difficult internal history of Hong Kong. Enveloped by both Chinese and British flags, the ox shows its hybrid influence (this mixture is literally embodied in the ox-human hybrid in "Welcome!") as if to ask what exactly its own history is, and how this history will change once Hong Kong's political affiliations change.[11]

Though Zhang never worked with Tam again, he continues to use clothing as medium. Most recently, Zhang printed T-shirts in 2009 with a simple set of numbers—90 30 20 2009—across the chest. These numbers represent the 90th, 30th, and 20th anniversaries in 2009 of three crucial events in China's modern history—the May Fourth Movement (1919), the formation of the Democracy Wall (1979), and the Tiananmen Square protests (1989)—whose imprint, like Mao's image, lingers on in contemporary Chinese life. Despite their historical significance, popular discussions about these events remain largely proscribed. Sending these T-shirts far and wide, Zhang hopes to prompt a discussion—quiet but loudly visible—among those who will immediately recognize these numbers and those who will wonder, however briefly, about their meaning.

Like the Mao collection, Zhang's T-shirts similarly present history as a set of questions that bear repeating. Whether imprinted with images from a cognitive remove, or composed of very intimate portraits, Zhang uses fashion to bring to light historical events, figures, and ideas shaping Chinese collective memories. The use of Mao in Zhang and Tam's collection here doesn't just rescript him as a celebrity—on par with Marilyn Monroe and Elvis Presley, as Warhol's art might—but instead evokes the particular legacies of Chinese political history, even or especially for those who have emigrated elsewhere. Here we do not see Mao as a mass icon, as a reflection of what we know of him from a distance. We see instead an intimate figure that can still haunt the imagination of Chinese people and to excite in them deep emotions.

Zhang's fashionable turn was then not a departure from the goals of much Chinese avant-garde art, from which it clearly drew inspiration, but an extension of them. If avant-garde artists used the idiom of commercial culture to satirize Mao's legacy, Deng's reforms, and the creeping forces of capitalism, Zhang and Tam used commercial culture itself to participate in those conversations. Their collection must be understood within this broader context. Their use of Mao subjected him to the type of ridicule, adoration, and critique that was very much a part of Chinese visual culture at the time. Moreover, they announced loudly what avant-garde artists often only whispered: in repeating the images that haunt the present, they could "fail to repeat loyally," and in the interface between subject and society imagine a space for change.[12]

1 Eric Hobsbawm, *The Age of Extremes: The Short Twentieth Century, 1914–1991* (London: Joseph, 1994), 178.

2 Eric Hobsbawm, "To See the Future, Look at the Past," in *The Guardian* (London), June 7, 1997: 21.

3 Vivienne Tam, *China Chic* (New York: Regan Books, 2000), 88.

4 Melissa Schrift, *Biography of a Chairman Mao Badge* (New Brunswick, NJ: Rutgers University Press, 2001), 56.

5 Liu Xiaobo, "The Spectre of Mao Zedong," in Geremie R. Barmé, *Shades of Mao: The Posthumous Cult of the Great Leader* (Armonk, NY: M. E. Sharpe, 1996), 276.

6 Elizabeth Wilson, *Adorned in Dreams: Fashion and Modernity* (New Brunswick, NJ: Rutgers University Press, 2003), 2.

7 Ibid.

8 Quoted in Tam, *China Chic*, 94.

9 The classic example is Dick Hebdige, *Subculture: The Meaning of Style* (London: Routledge, 1979). See also F. Davis, *Fashion, Culture, Identity* (Chicago: University of Chicago Press, 1981); Shari Bernstock and Suzanne Ferriss, eds., *On Fashion* (New York: Routledge, 1994); Diana Crane, *Fashion and Its Social Agendas* (Chicago: University of Chicago Press, 2000); Malcolm Barnard, *Fashion as Communication* (New York: Routledge, 2002); and Joanne Entwistle, *The Fashioned Body: Fashion, Dress and Modern Social Theory* (Cambridge: Polity Press, 2002).

10 Anne Hollander, *Seeing Through Clothes* (New York: Avon, 1975), 311.

11 Wu Hung has suggested that Zhang's use of these images reveals his ambivalent relationship to Hong Kong. Looking at Hong Kong from across the Pacific Ocean, Zhang is an outsider whose visual vocabulary is informed by the stock images of the global media, which posit the handing over of Hong Kong as an already predetermined media spectacle. Projected from external locations, whether Britain or China, these images represent Hong Kong without an intrinsic history or an internal space—as a symbol of the tug of war between British colonialism and Chinese nationalism. At the same time that Zhang uses these tropes, he voices a deep skepticism about this published history. His T-shirts pose questions and highlight contradictions without resolving them. Wu Hung, "Afterword: Hong Kong 1997," in *Public Culture* 9, no. 3 (Spring 1997): 415–25.

12 Judith Butler, *Bodies That Matter* (New York: Routledge, 1990), 124.

POP, POLITICS, AND PAINTING

Lilly Wei

Zhang Hongtu left China in 1982 in search of the freedom of expression that is essential to an artist. He was thirty-eight years old at the time and had come of age during the tumult of the Chinese Civil War, the Great Leap Forward, and the Cultural Revolution, when Socialist Realism was the only means of artistic expression that was officially sanctioned.

Born in Gansu Province in 1943 of Muslim heritage (his father was a noted scholar who translated the Qur'an into Chinese), Zhang was aware of his family's intellectual, ethnic, and religious otherness from an early age. In reaction to that, he developed an independence of attitude and resiliency that resulted eventually in quitting a homeland that was not quite his homeland. Irony and objectivity also pervades his work, and must have sustained him during harsh times.

A talented artist trained in many disciplines, he began his art studies early, and as a teenager attended the high school affiliated with the Central Academy of Fine Arts in Beijing, one of the most prestigious art schools in China. It was closed down in 1964 for a time, Zhang said, charged with corruption by Jiang Qing, Mao's ruthless wife.[1] He then went to Beijing's Central Academy of Arts and Crafts, which itself closed in 1966, at the start of the Cultural Revolution's ten-year reign of terror.

Chinese Socialist Realism poster,
ca. 1960s.

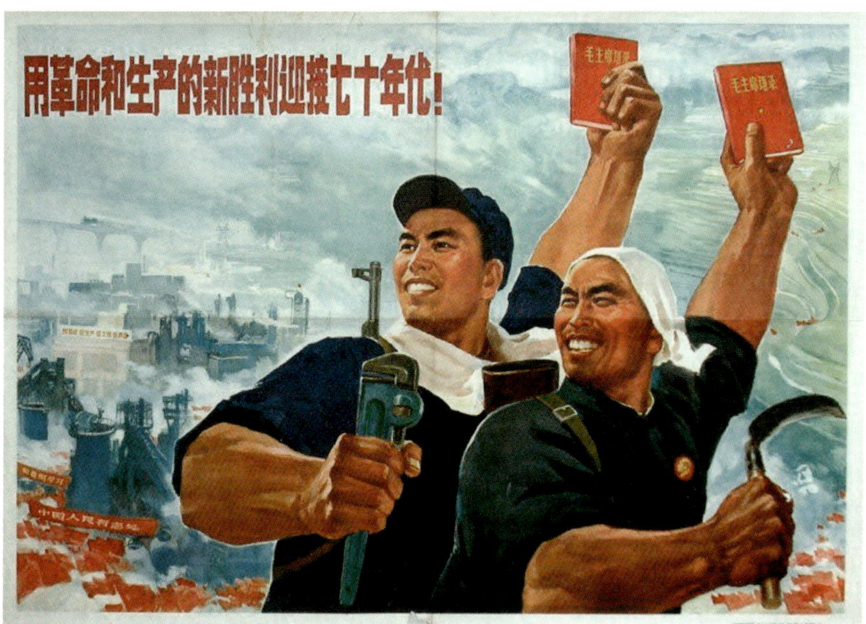

Fig. I

Zhang was deeply interested in Chinese ink paintings and Western oil painting, in the illustrious history of Chinese art as well as in Western modernism and contemporary art—in fact, in almost everything but Socialist Realism. He had always scorned the term as practiced in China, noting that it was grossly inaccurate since it was "neither social nor realistic"; its relentlessly upbeat propaganda constituted fantasies at odds with the disastrously real failures of Mao Zedong's ill-considered reforms (*Fig. 1*). It was his great desire from the beginning of his artistic life to synthesize all these disparate aesthetics and ideologies into something richer, more expansive, reflecting the scope and jumble of the modern world. Due to his family and its background, he had great-er access to information about countries and cultures outside China, he said, and chafed under an authoritarian regime that stifled experimentation and prevented the free exchange of knowledge, banning so much that interested him as "bourgeois, re-actionary, and corrupt."

When Zhang arrived in New York, it was a thriving, prosperous city, crackling with creative energy and promise, its bright lights not yet shadowed by the scourge of AIDS. Postmodernism was in full swing, powered by new interpretations of Marcel Duchamp's theories, an artist who exerted an enormous influence over Zhang (*Fig. 2*). Intrigued by modernism, by Warhol and Rauschenberg, by Pop art, by readymades and found objects, by art that incorporated newspapers, comic books, television images, consumer products, and celebrities, Zhang reveled in the city's exhilarat-ing contemporaneity and its immensity of choice. Its embrace of the novel, the idio-syncratic, and the transgressive must have been thrilling after the censorship and

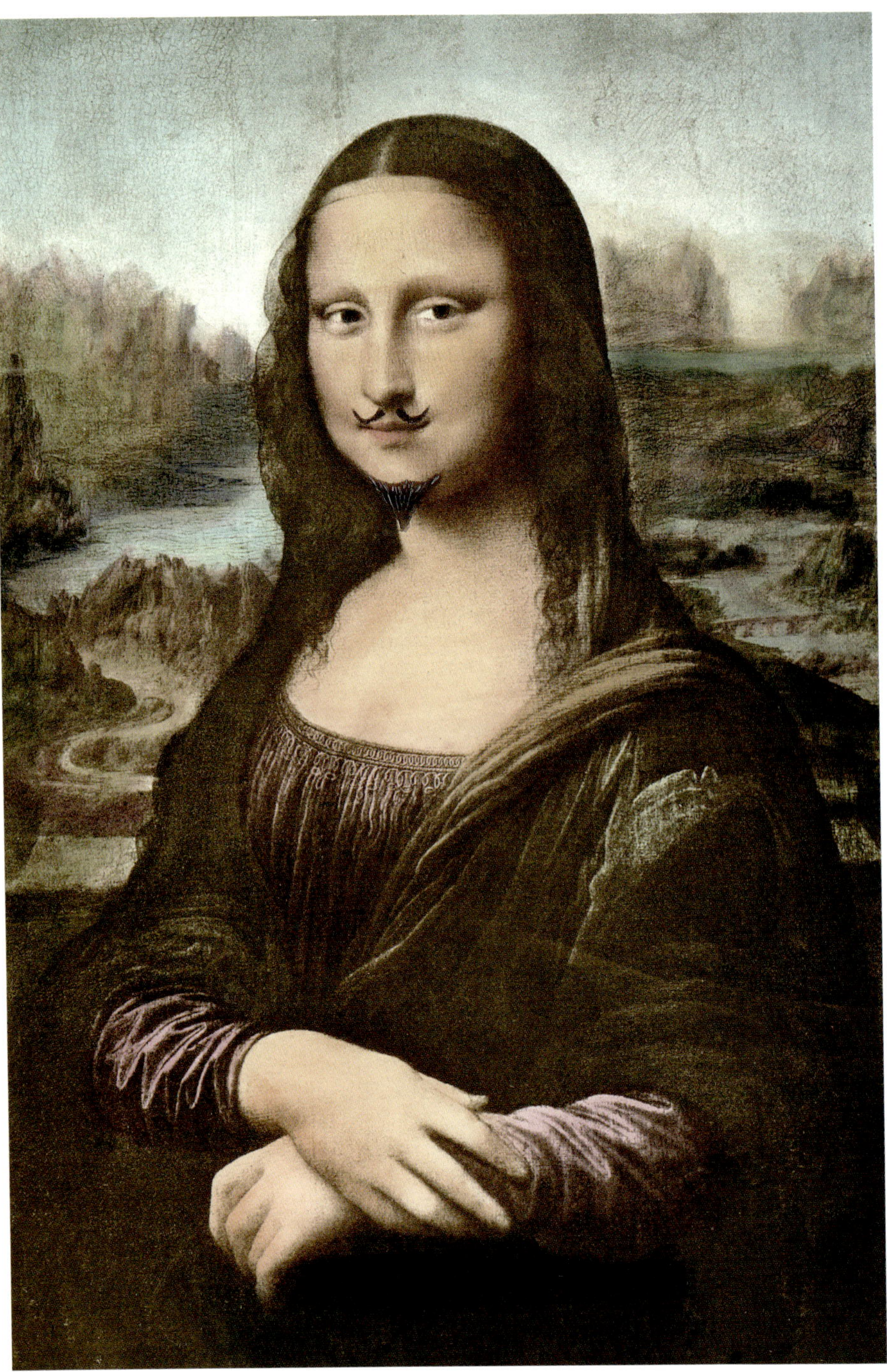

Fig. 2

Marcel Duchamp, *L.H.O.O.Q.*, 1919. Rectified readymade: pencil on reproduction of Leonardo da Vinci's *Mona Lisa*. 7 ¾ x 4 ⅞ in. © ARS, NY. Private collection. Photo: Scala/White Images / Art Resource, NY.

self-censorship that he had been subjected to. Cultural and ideological blendings of fine art and kitsch and all manner of media jostled each other in the galleries and streets of SoHo and the East Village, in downtown Manhattan, and, further removed, in Brooklyn, Queens, and the Bronx and proved to be generative as well as intoxicating.

A more truly international, cross-pollinated, decentered art world was coming into existence, a turning point in the history of contemporary art as Western European and North American dominance of the discourse and the market lessened. More and more art from previously unrepresented countries in Asia, Africa, and South America began to appear at important exhibitions such as Documenta and the Venice Biennale to enthusiastic acclaim. Perhaps the most exemplary, the most insistently international of these pioneering ventures was "Les Magiciens de la Terre," curated by Jean-Hubert Martin in Paris in 1989, coincidentally opening just two months after the June 4, 1989, student massacre at Tiananmen Square.[2] Also, it was during the early to mid-'90s that contemporary Chinese artists began to receive worldwide attention, followed not long after by a phenomenal rise in the market value of their work.

Zhang has often been associated with Political Pop. The term was coined by Beijing critic Li Xianting in a 1991 article, "Apathy and Deconstructive Consciousness in Post-1989 Art" to designate a group of Chinese contemporary artists whose ironic, mordantly humorous work addressed the swiftly changing political, social, and economic landscape of post–Tiananmen Square China.[3] Political Pop artists focused on the startling rise in Chinese consumerism that would soon make China the world's third-largest economy, mimicking the bold, eye-catching design of advertisements and adapting instantly recognizable American brands like Coca-Cola and Camel. As well, they honed in on superstars from the West, like Michael Jackson, and tirelessly caricatured Mao, whom Andy Warhol's silkscreened portraits had already transformed into a pop idol in 1973, inspiring many Chinese artists. As Warhol said, "Pop artists did images that anyone walking down the street would recognize in a split second."[4] Political Pop also satirized Socialist Realist paintings, and its artists worked in media and disciplines that were still a novelty, such as film, video, photography, found objects, performance, and installation, and some continue to do so (*Fig. 3*).

While Zhang, too, took his cue from mass culture, juxtaposing fine art with kitsch and the mass-produced, experimenting with what was once prohibited, he makes it clear that he was not a Political Pop artist, but an artist influenced by Pop art—and still is. He was a generation older and had left China a decade before Political Pop's inception, his ideas different since he had grown up in a China under Mao and the artists of Political Pop had not. They, on the other hand, had lived through the '89 Democracy Movement and he had not, although it has always been much on his mind. Every

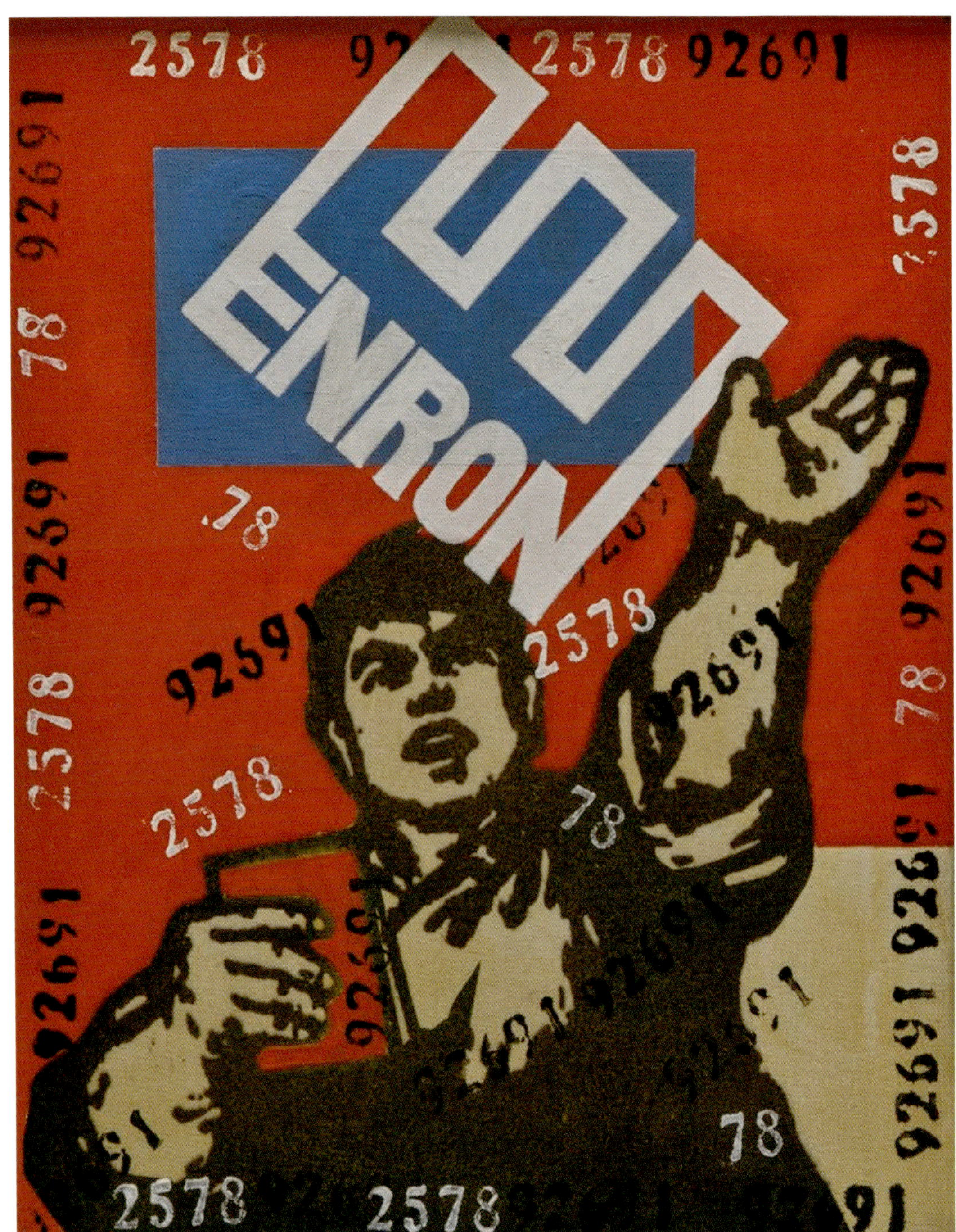

Fig. 3

Wang Guangyi, *Great Criticism—Enron*, 2003. 20 x 16 in. Courtesy Pékin Fine Arts, Beijing.

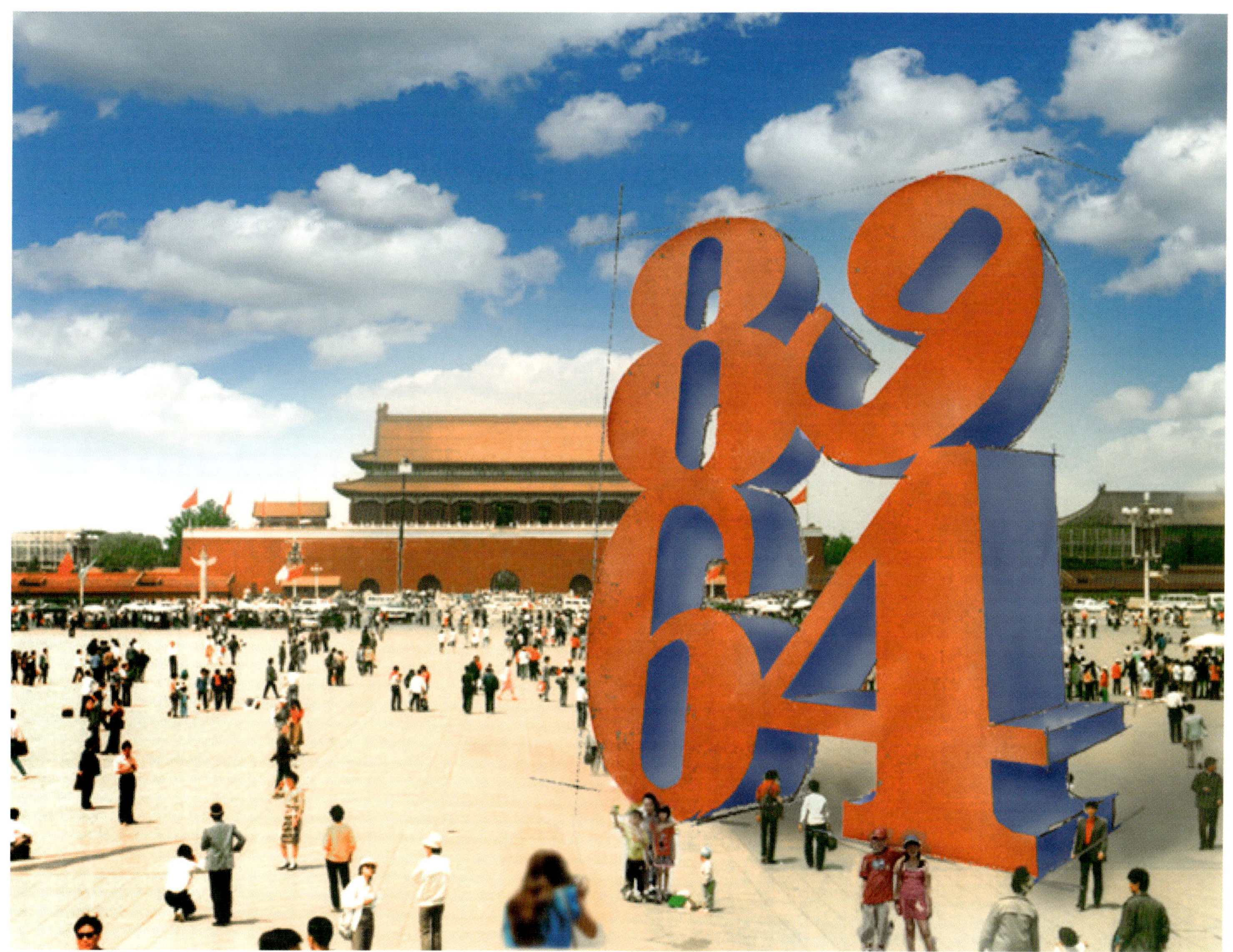

Fig. 4

Remember June 4, 1989, 2013.
Computer-generated image, dimensions variable.

June 4 from 2008 to 2013, he has made one or two computer-generated works, such as *Remember June 4, 1989,* 2013. (*Fig. 4*). It recalls a Socialist Realist poster, with the date, "8964," in Robert Indiana's famous LOVE formulation inserted among the visitors to Tiananmen Square, a word that subliminally underlies the numbers, as the lives lost there underlie the lives of those present.

Despite what must have been the difficulties of transition, of financial limitations and entering an alien culture and land in which customs and language were so radically different, Zhang was grateful to be in New York where he didn't feel that potential spies were everywhere, that "someone [was] always looking over my shoulder." He was "reborn," he said, when he arrived on July 14, 1982, liberated also from a millennia-old culture and its conservatism. In a city that was only a few hundred years old, in an open society that valued youthfulness, difference, and change, he felt unburdened and invigorated.

Zhang now had ready access to art that he had seen only in reproduction as well as much, much more, from the artists and movements then dominating the discussion, such as Neo-Abstraction, Neo-Geo, and appropriation and performance artists, to the masters of Pop and Minimalism, such as Jasper Johns, Claes Oldenburg, and Roy Lichtenstein, and of European and American 19th and 20th-century art. In New York, he was able to see the paintings of Van Gogh, Monet, and Cézanne, and the Abstract Expressionists—all artists whose work he eventually incorporated into his own vision. He was free to see the encyclopedic holdings of world-renowned institutions such as the Museum of Modern Art and the Metropolitan Museum of Art, where masterpieces of traditional Chinese culture, ironically, were more easily viewed than when he was in China.

Like his new peers, encouraged by discourses that questioned originality, authenticity, and authorship, Zhang felt free to borrow at will, to mix and match. His ideas were influenced by the conversations around him, but also by his formative experiences in Communist China and his layered heritage. Defiantly, because he was told it was corrupt and reactionary—and because it was magnificent—he had retained a love for China's ancient artistic traditions, seen more acutely from the vantage point of distance. Originality—so intrinsic to the American psyche—had become more complicated after Duchamp and his champions, as had the idea of the copy, with curious parallels to Chinese thought in which the act of copying was a form of homage, a synthesis of past and present.

Zhang, like the Chinese artists of Political Pop, became fixated on making images of Mao, the formerly revered, ubiquitous visage worshiped by tens of millions. Disillusioned, he felt that he, his family, and the Chinese people had been betrayed by Mao's unfulfilled promises to create a new, egalitarian, and better China. But because he had been taught to venerate it, because he had once believed in Mao, he felt a sense of sacrilege when he first began to use his image. From this body of work, which he concentrated on for eight years, came the "Long Live Chairman Mao" series—Zhang usually worked in series—and some of his best-known works. Unlike Westerners or a younger generation of Chinese artists for whom it had simply become a pop icon, that seemingly benevolent face signified much more for him, since he had lived under Mao's discredited and darkly erratic rule. Even before he used Mao's actual face, he had painted a number of sunrises in 1989, which were abstract, relatively spare, and symbolized Mao, who was considered the ascendant sun. Tentative at first, he called these gritty, somber paintings "Impression: Sunrise" after Monet's very different 1872 seascape as a way to avoid direct reference. A related series is "Back of the Head," which he worked on from 1985 to '89, in which his head, seen from the back, is the central motif. Zhang has discussed the composition as a rejection of the past, the head facing into the indeterminate space of the painting and an unknown future. It represents both a "presence and an absence," he said. It is finite, physical, occupies space, and is positive while consciousness and the mind inside it are not measurable, a void, a negative space within the head. Mao for him is an image that occupies both positive and negative space, a presence and an absence.

Zhang has said that he is not a Political Pop artist, but that does not mean his work is not political and Pop. His Mao works, which dominated the first fifteen years or so of his New York life, are the most representative of this aspect of his practice. After his hesitant start, his depictions of Mao became more direct, more assertive, imagined as both filled-in portraits and empty outlines. *Lipstick Mao* (1992) consists of multiple cutouts of Mao's head, each piece of paper smeared with a different shade of lipstick, suggesting a cosmetic-counter color chart. It alludes to the late chairman's widely quoted declaration that women hold up half of the sky, but the statement was empty, like Mao's cut-outs, Zhang points out, since, in reality, he had done nothing to promote women's equality or better their lives. With a different message, *Fashion Mao*, Zhang's 1994 collaboration with fashion designer Vivienne Tam, resulted in a line of striking apparel with Mao's image on it that seems humorously retributive, the once-powerful chairman's face reduced to a decorative motif for the adornment of stylish women.

Zhang's earliest work of Pop art was the *Quaker Oats Mao* from 1987, when he transformed the avuncular face of the "Quaker Man" displayed on the familiar cylindrical cereal container into the Chinese leader. Replacing the Quaker hat with a Mao cap was a gesture that was half Warholian, half Duchampian, like drawing a moustache on a reproduction of the *Mona Lisa*, something Zhang also did in a later picture,

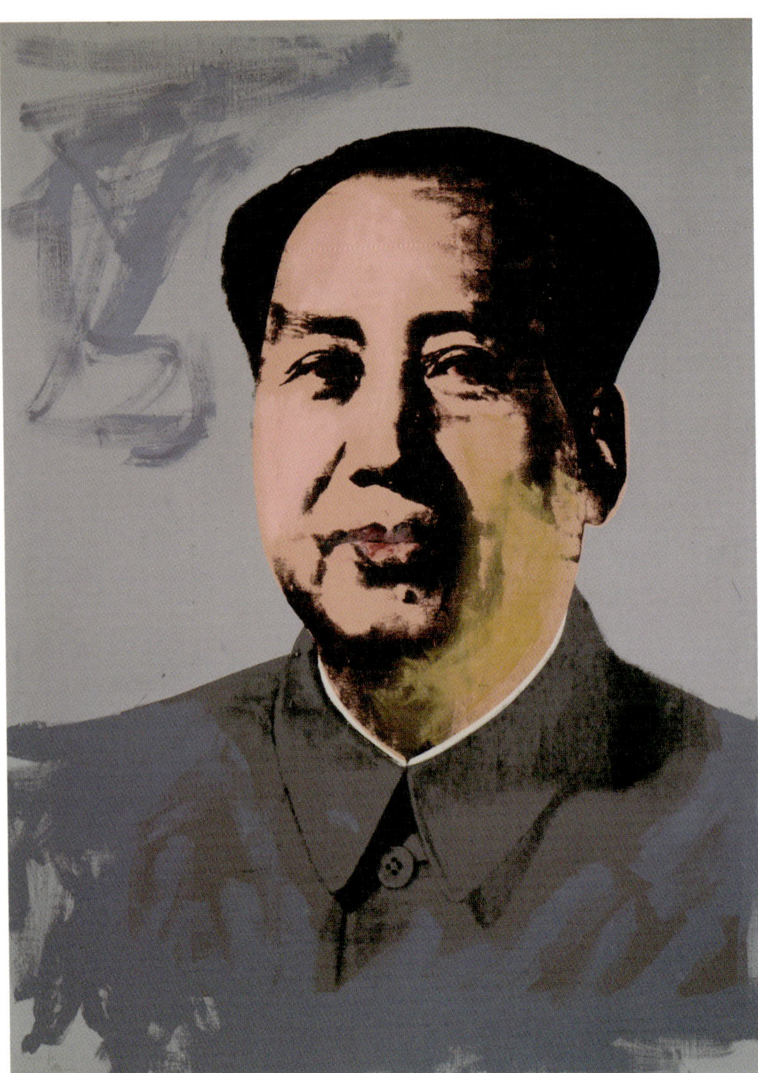

Fig. 5

Andy Warhol, *Mao*, 1972. Acrylic and silkscreen ink on linen, 82 x 61 in. The Andy Warhol Museum, Pittsburgh; Founding Collection, Contribution Dia Center.

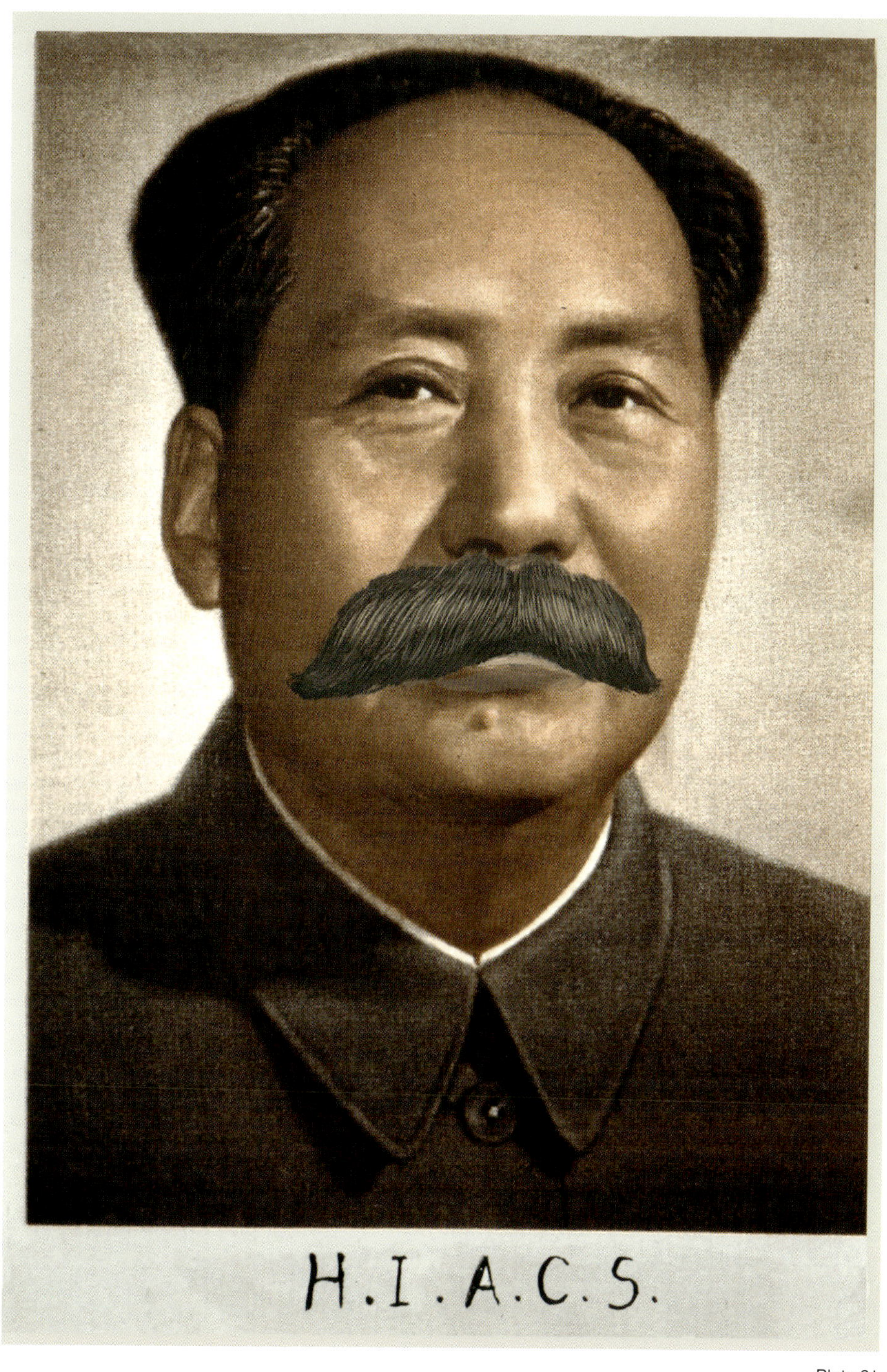

Plate 31

H. I. A. C. S. (He Is a Chinese Stalin) (detail from *Chairmen Mao*), 1989. Photo collage and acrylic on paper, 11 x 8 ½ in.

attaching a more luxuriant flourish of hair to Mao's upper lip (*Fig. 5, Plate 31*). Among his most popular works, *Quaker Oats Mao* resulted from months of idly staring at the face on the box of oatmeal at breakfast, says Zhang. One day he saw a similarity between the two faces. He first showed ten of the *Quaker Oats Mao* in 1988 at the Palladium in downtown Manhattan in a large exhibition of contemporary Chinese artists. Works that followed included *Chairmen Mao* (1989), a series of Mao's head shown in different guises arranged in a grid, the benevolent image reconfigured, androgenized, and otherwise ridiculed, presented in an array of "bourgeois" and "decadent" Western styles such as Cubism and Surrealism. *Last Banquet* (*Plate 29*), conceived in the aftermath of the Tiananmen Square tragedy, also depicts multiple Maos. Reprising the composition of Leonardo's *Last Supper* and the theme of betrayal as a high-powered Chinese state banquet, the painting casts Mao thirteen times, betraying his better selves, betraying his own legacy, in one reading. It is also a reminder of the deadly famines that occurred under Mao, part of the meaning of other Zhang portraits of him made from corn, rice, soy sauce, and MSG.

In the later work *Ping-Pong Mao* (1995), Zhang cut two silhouettes of Mao out of a ping-pong table to create a disruptive void on either side of the net, an amusing, but sharply critical pairing of one of China's most popular pastimes (an English invention that has curiously become a stereotype of Chineseness) with its once omnipotent ruler, a game and political gamester that have long conjured China for the outside world.

Other Pop works had other targets, once Zhang had exorcised Mao from his production—except for occasional reappearances, such as his *Mao, After Picasso* (2012)—and include examples of his urge to hybridize, to mischievously re-colonize the colonizers. Commenting on the flow of cultural (and economic) influence, he tells us that it is no longer a one-way street, if it ever was, and that appropriation across cultures is universal.

His Coca-Cola bottles are one instance of Zhang-style fusion. With *Kekou-Kele (Six Pack)* (*Plate 111*), Zhang has sinocized an unmistakably American object, turning it into a Chinese blue-and-white patterned porcelain vessel, scaled to actual size: the very delightful offspring of what might be called time travel and a mixed marriage. A similar cultural and consumerist mash-up are the cast bronze McDonald's take-out containers of *Mai Dang Lao* (*Plate 112*), also actual size, cunningly changed into Zhou dynasty ritual vessels, again representing two seemingly very different cultures and rituals, one contemporary, the other dated to the first millennium BCE, one the creation of popular culture, the other that of an elite. Another transposition of form and function is Zhang's version of the Chanel bottle, an emblem of costly elegance turned into a plastic kimchi container, much enlarged.

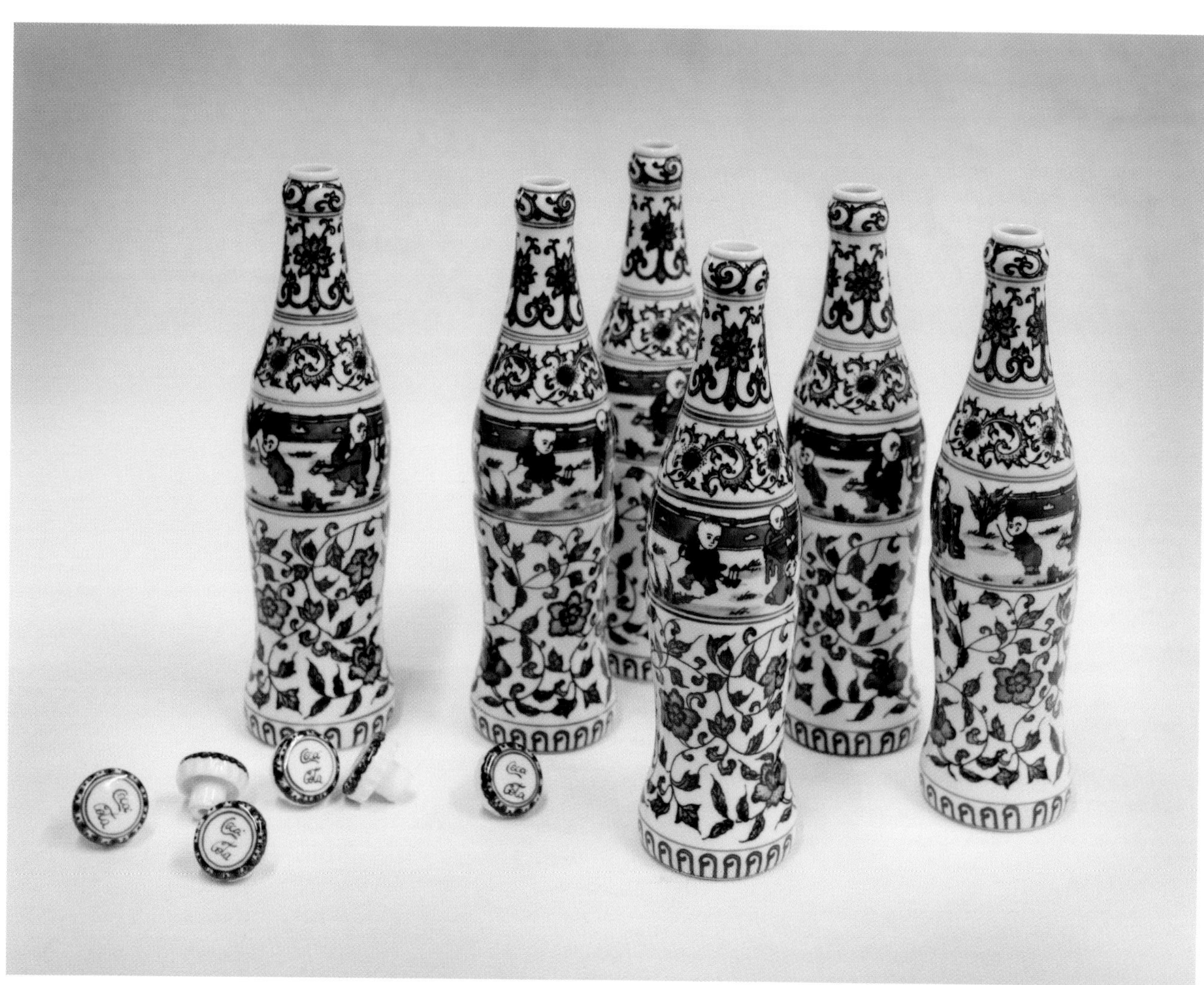

Plate 111

Kekou-Kele (Six Pack), 2002. Porcelain, actual size.

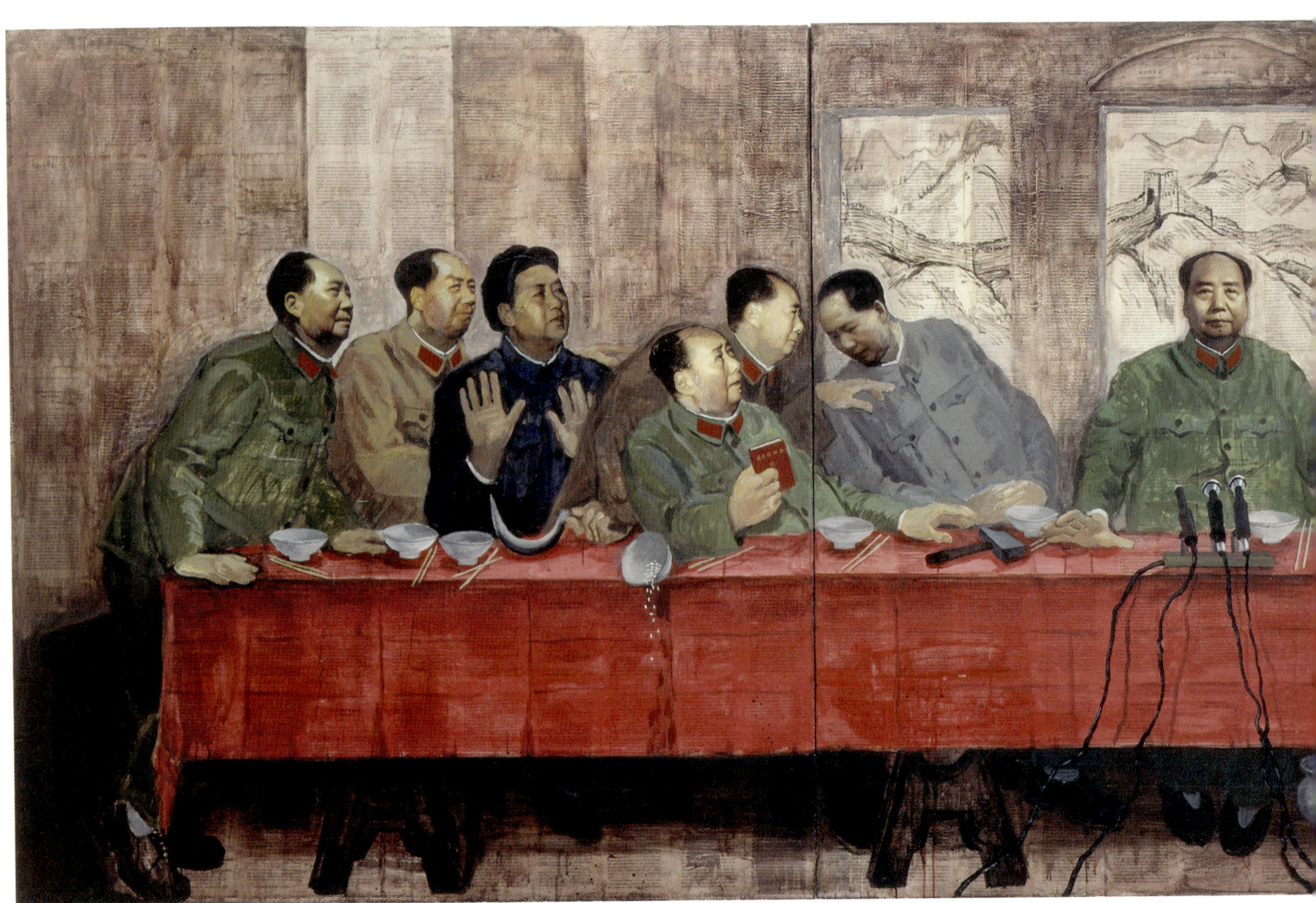

Plate 29

Last Banquet, 1989. Laser prints, pages from the Little Red Book,
and acrylic on canvas, 60 x 128 in.

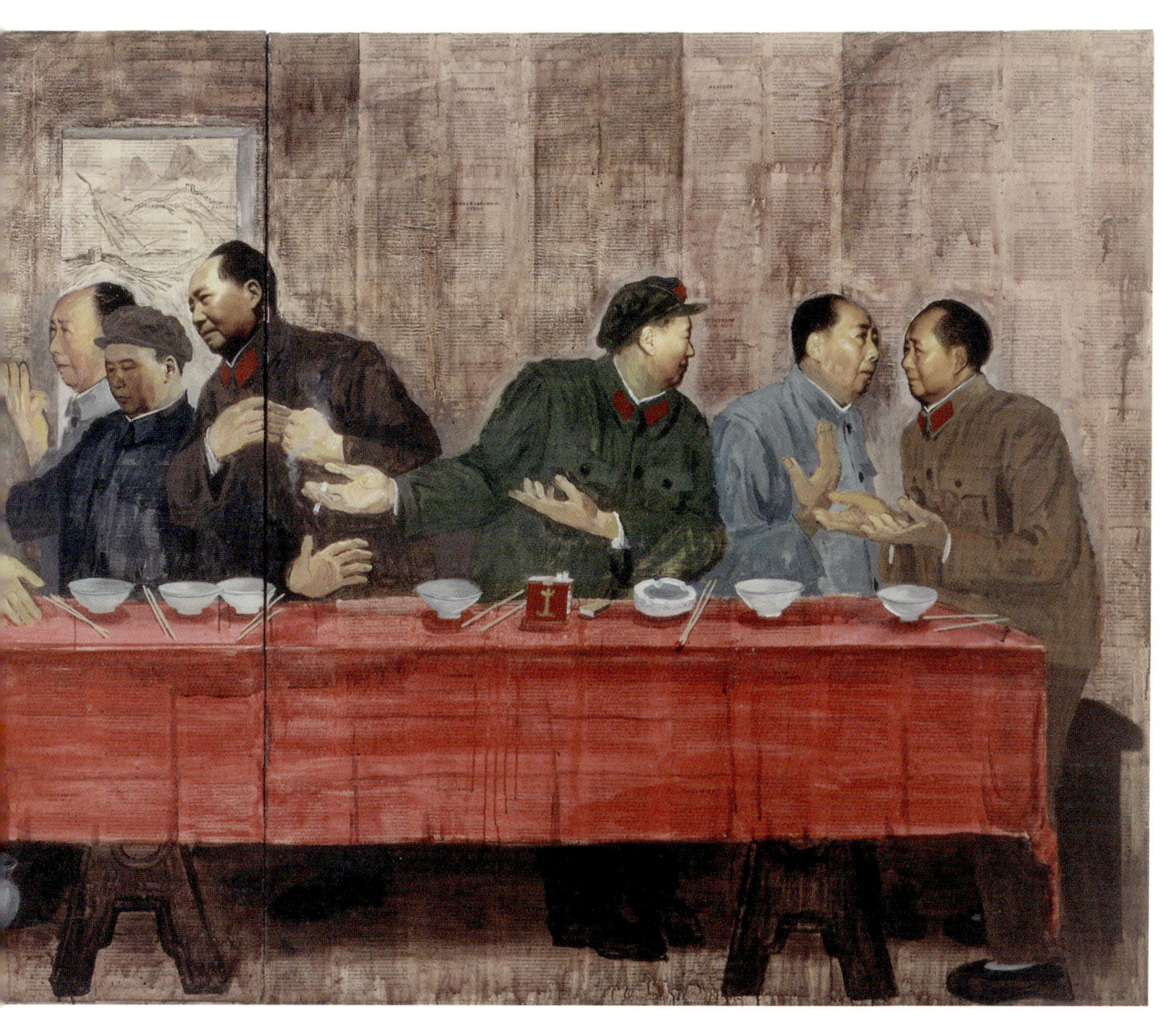

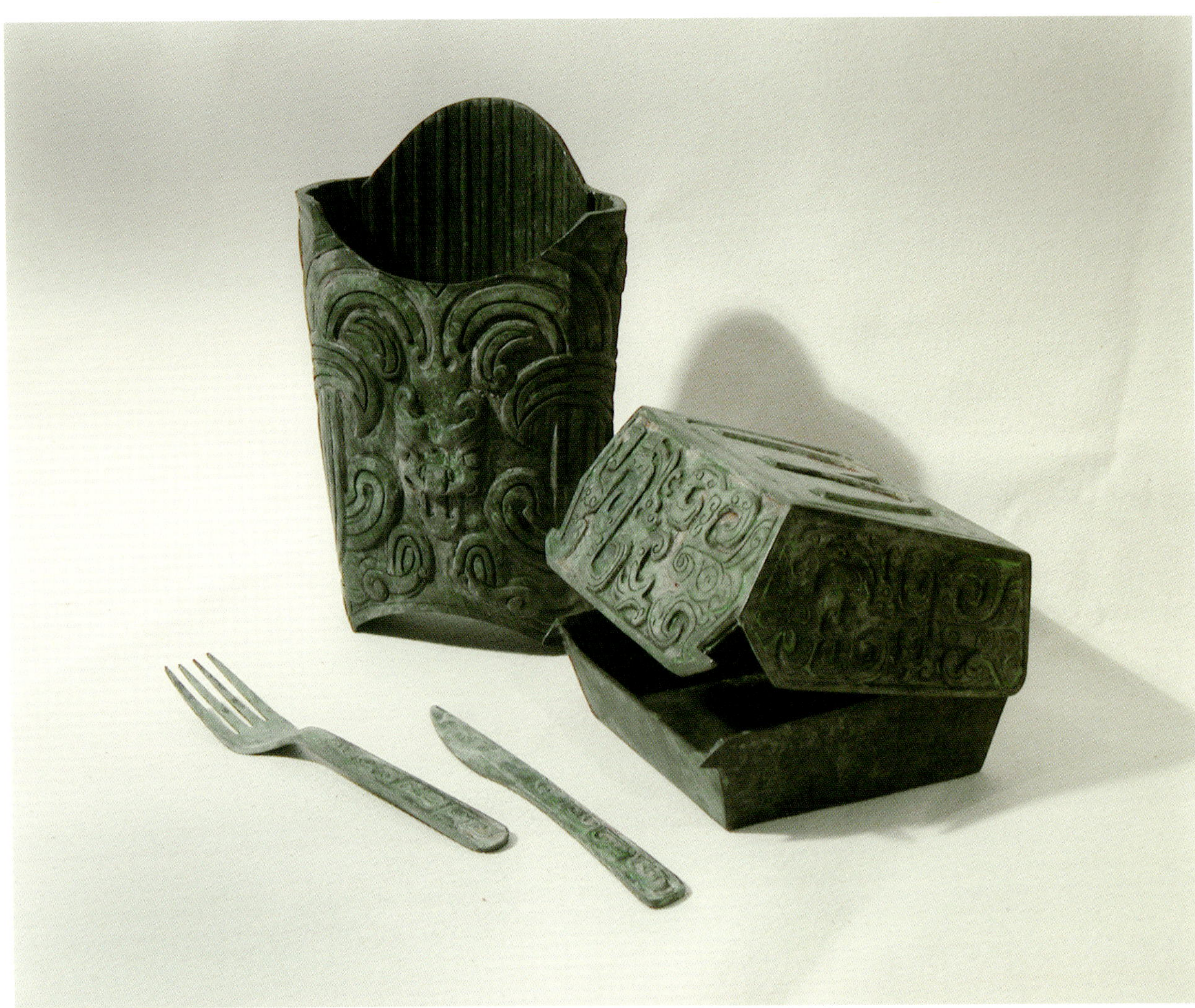

Plate 112

Mai Dang Lao, 2002. Cast bronze, actual size.

Zhang then concentrated more on his striking, beautifully painted *shan shui* (mountain and water) paintings, which are copied from Chinese masterpieces by artists such as Fan Kuan, Zhao Mengfu, Shitao, Ni Zan, and Ma Yuan. Zhang adds a further level of appropriation by re-interpreting them in the distinctive styles of Monet, Cézanne, Van Gogh, and others, tinged with the spirit of Daoism and Confucianism. He also reversed the strategy, beginning with celebrated works by Western modernists and executing them in a classic Chinese manner or with Chinese subjects, inflected in more recent work by environmental concerns. He says these paintings are also inspired by the concepts of Pop art, if not its style.

For Zhang, Pop has always been pivotal, giving him a key to unlock fetters of all kinds that characterized much of his former life in China. It "opened the window" to a refreshed world of unlimited possibilities and allowed him to build imaginative bridges between different cultures, fusion now being much more commonplace in a world where there are few locations more than twenty-four hours away. Always an outsider, he has been identified as Chinese, Chinese American, Chinese Muslim, and Muslim. He disregards all of these designations, ultimately, since he is all of them and none of them. Instead, he thinks of himself as an individual in a global world, an artist with his own distinctive visual philosophy, his own distinctive history, who cannot represent more than that even if he would like to do so.

1   All comments attributed to Zhang come from a conversation with the author on March 21, 2015.

2   "Magiciens de la Terre," presented at the Centre Pompidou and the Grande Halle de la Villette in 1989, has become legendary, a seminal exhibition in the globalization of contemporary art, highlighting areas of the world beyond Western Europe and America.

3   Cited in an article by Andrew Cohen in the November 2010 issue of *Art Asia Pacific*.

4   Cited in "Warhol in His Own Words," in *Andy Warhol: A Retrospective*. ed Kynaston McShine (New York and Boston: Museum of Modern Art and Bulfinch Press/Little Brown, 1989), 457–67.

ZHANG HONGTU'S QUEENS

Tom Finkelpearl

Like tens of thousands of his generation, Rogelio "Viko" Ortega made his way from Puebla, a province in southeast Mexico, to Queens in the 1990s. After an apprenticeship in a French pastry shop in Manhattan, Ortega opened his own restaurant, La Flor, on Roosevelt Avenue in Woodside, a working- and middle-class section of western Queens. Overhead the 7 train rumbles by, and the flow of humanity visible through the restaurant's generous windows reminds you that this borough is the most culturally diverse place in America. A woman sporting a headscarf walks past, followed by an elderly (perhaps Italian?) woman, then a couple of young Latinos. There is a certain Queens feel to La Flor—you might see the same marble tabletops in a nearby diner, but here they are juxtaposed with Gaudi-esque tilework on the walls and columns. At the center of the main wall on a high shelf sit twenty cookbooks, everything from Mario Batali to Mexican cuisine, from Italian to French. Likewise the menu is almost outrageously eclectic. Yes, there is typical fare that might cater to the locals from Puebla, but other dishes could be described as neo- or post-Mexican. And there is New American cuisine and fish prepared in a fashion that would feel at home in a French restaurant in Manhattan. One review framed and hanging on the wall calls the restaurant French, while another declares that it has the best Mexican brunch in the city.

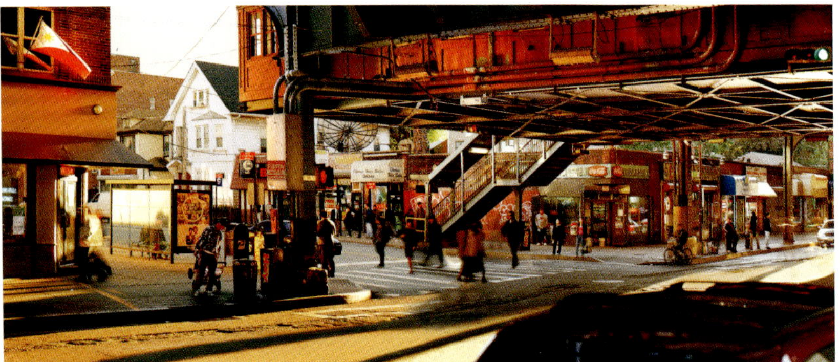

Fig. I

Viko Ortega is not only the executive chef but also the cook. As we finish our meal he asks eagerly how we found his place: "Are you from the neighborhood?" We let him know that a Chinese friend from around the corner has recommended the restaurant. When I ask him about the wide-ranging menu, he simply says that he likes to travel a lot. It is a casual eclecticism, completely unpretentious, but adventurous and creative. La Flor is one of Zhang Hongtu's favorite restaurants, just a short walk from his home. It is rivaled by another nearby—TJ Asian Bistro, just off Queens Boulevard—that mixes Chinese and Japanese fare. Both restaurants enact the diversity and hybridity of Queens. Woodside is the neighborhood where Zhang has settled in the last decade, a perfect place for an artist of mixture and hybridity to land.

The story of Queens is well known to any student of the modern American city. Like many communities, Queens was transformed drastically in the wake of the opening-up of immigration policies in the mid-1960s. When he signed the Hart-Celler Immigration Act in 1965, President Lyndon Johnson said, "This bill we sign today is not a revolutionary bill. It does not affect the lives of millions. It will not restructure the shape of our daily lives."[1] Rarely has a politician underestimated legislation so drastically. Across the land, the doors opened to immigrants excluded in the quota system that had been in place, particularly those from Latin America and Asia *(Fig. 1)*. The difference between Queens and other American urban areas is the sheer enormity of the transformation. Most New Yorkers have heard the statistics: somewhere between 138 and 160 languages are spoken in Queens.[2] Some of the borough's most interesting areas are "melting-pot communities" where there is no majority culture, where many languages are spoken, where cultural exchange happens on a daily basis in every bodega, deli, and restaurant. Queens was the driver as New York became the most diverse city in America. According to the 2010 census, the very most diverse place in New York was Queens Village—the second most diverse neighborhood in America, according to Forbes.[3] And the diversity continues to grow, driven by a steady inflow of Asian and Latino immigrants. Between 2002 and

2010, the white non-Hispanic population decreased by around 116,000 people, and the African-American population decreased by 27,000. But the Asian population increased by 119,000 and the Latino population increased by 57,000.[4] So if the emblematic artists from Queens at mid-twentieth century might be white or African American like Tony Bennett (born Anthony Dominick Benedetto) of Astoria or Louis Armstrong of Corona, the twenty-first century equivalents would be Latino or Asian, like John Leguizamo or Lucy Liu, both of Jackson Heights. La Flor and TJ Asian are indicative of that trend, and so is Zhang—but only to a degree.

It is tempting to think of Zhang in direct relationship to these immigration trends. After all, he and his wife are members of the Asian community that is flowing into the borough. But it is important to remember that they had been living in Manhattan for eighteen years before relocating to Queens. Their move from Manhattan mirrors another time-honored tradition—the economic and lifestyle decision to seek more space, less congestion. Ceding their Manhattan apartment to their son, they sought a place to live that had more trees and more air, away from the intensity and density of Manhattan. This reflects a flow of people that we see pressing across the East River from Manhattan, and up across the border from Brooklyn. It is often discussed in terms of gentrification, the flows of upper-middle-class residents into neighborhoods like Woodside—displacing the longtime working-class residents. These patterns are happening in parts of Queens, but their prevalence is diminished somewhat by the large percentage of homeownership across the economic spectrum. Like Zhang, many of his neighbors own their apartments or houses, slowing the pace of displacement.

Another way to look at Zhang's place in New York relates to the flows of a very specific demographic: artists. The way that Zhang narrates the story has anecdotal validity, though there are no hard numbers available: In the late 1970s and 1980s, a significant number of mainland Chinese artists came to live in New York. They were looking for a place with a vibrant art marketplace and also an environment where they could create their work without the sort of restrictions one experienced at home under the Communist Party. With the loosening of restrictions as well as the emergence of the burgeoning market in China, artists stopped coming to New York in the late 1990s and after the turn of the millennium, while some of the artists living in America (including Ai Weiwei and Xu Bing, for example) returned to China seeking a stronger art market for their work there. Others like Gu Wenda remained in New York, but opened studios in China as well. In the last ten years Zhang has seen a flow of mainland Chinese arts professionals back to New York, but this time it is students, young people seeking a college education at NYU, Columbia, and other schools. Some of these students have then stayed to work at New York City galleries and auction houses seeking the renewed Chinese market. During this time, Zhang stayed in New York, and perhaps because of the nature of the content of much of his work, he remained at some arms' length from the mainland market. So his place is a bit of an enigma—associated with his mainland roots, but actively interacting with the Asian-American scene.

Zhang's and his wife Miaoling's love of Queens was not immediate. After finding an apartment in a large building in Kew Gardens, where they felt a bit isolated, they moved to Woodside, a classic Queens community. Zhang tells me that on their block in Woodside, where they have lived for the past ten years, you can find neighbors from Singapore, Puerto Rico, and Italy; there are African Americans, Tibetans, Indians, and Chinese. For an outsider, perhaps it is easy to fit into a place where there is no single normal pattern. For an immigrant, it is certainly easier to find commonality with other immigrants, be they from the four corners of the world. Dense by American urban standards, their community seems to unfold at a slower pace, with a calmer lifestyle, a more humane streetscape than Manhattan. This is the semi-suburban vision of the borough as depicted in *The King of Queens*, or *Spiderman*, or even Archie Bunker's *All in the Family*. Of course, perceiving Queens as suburban is the observation of an artist who grew up in the density of Beijing only to move to the center of Manhattan, also the vision of a Chinese immigrant family living among an incredibly diverse group of other immigrants.

Zhang's vision of Queens reminds me of an afternoon when I was rushing off to a Mets game with a friend, the artist Ik Joong Kang. On the way there we stopped by a Korean bakery to pick up some goodies. In the third inning as we were eating the pasty, semi-sweet Songpyeon with chopsticks, Kang looked around the ballpark and commented, "This is so *American*!" Yes, in fact it was American, if we think of the American dream as open to the world, multicultural, the new city created (though not envisioned) by the legislators who opened our doors in 1965. If not the present of all of America, it is the likely future, and this future is often best experienced in Queens. Zhang fits perfectly into this place, a mix-artist like Viko Ortega.

1   Center for Immigration Studies, "Three Decades of Mass Immigration: The Legacy of the 1965 Immigration Act" (September 1995).

2   See, for example, About.com: Queens, NY; and Thomas M. Baker, "Queens Resident Wants to Inscribe Wall With All Languages Spoken in Borough," in *New York Daily News* (June 14, 2013).

3   Jed Kolko, "America's Most Diverse Neighborhoods And Metros" (November 13, 2012), Forbes.com.

4   Center for Urban Research, The Graduate Center, City University of New York, "New York City demographic shifts, 2000 to 2010" (2011).

WHAT'S NEXT FOR US? ZHANG HONGTU'S ENVIRONMENTAL SHAN SHUI

Luchia Meihua Lee

In his *Spheres* trilogy, Peter Sloterdijk describes the profound individual alienation within contemporary civilization and attributes such conditions broadly to modernity's disorientation.[1] Indeed, many of society's dilemmas, highlighted by an ambivalence toward rising sea levels, mass deforestation, predatory banking practices, and culturally destructive warfare, evoke images of a global village run amok. These images force us to confront the illusory beauty of landscape and our surroundings, what once was, and what is left to be. New York artist Zhang Hongtu reflects on this incommensurable subject in his paintings. He reveals the relationship between living organisms and their environment, and the partnership between human culture and the physical condition of life. While Zhang's work frequently quotes the past, it is entirely immersed in the present.

In 2008, Zhang began a significant body of work on landscapes, "Shan Shui Today." The earliest work in this series is a group of paintings collectively entitled *Re-make of Ma Yuan's Water Album* (*Fig. 1*). Nearly 800 years ago, Ma Yuan (1160–1225) created

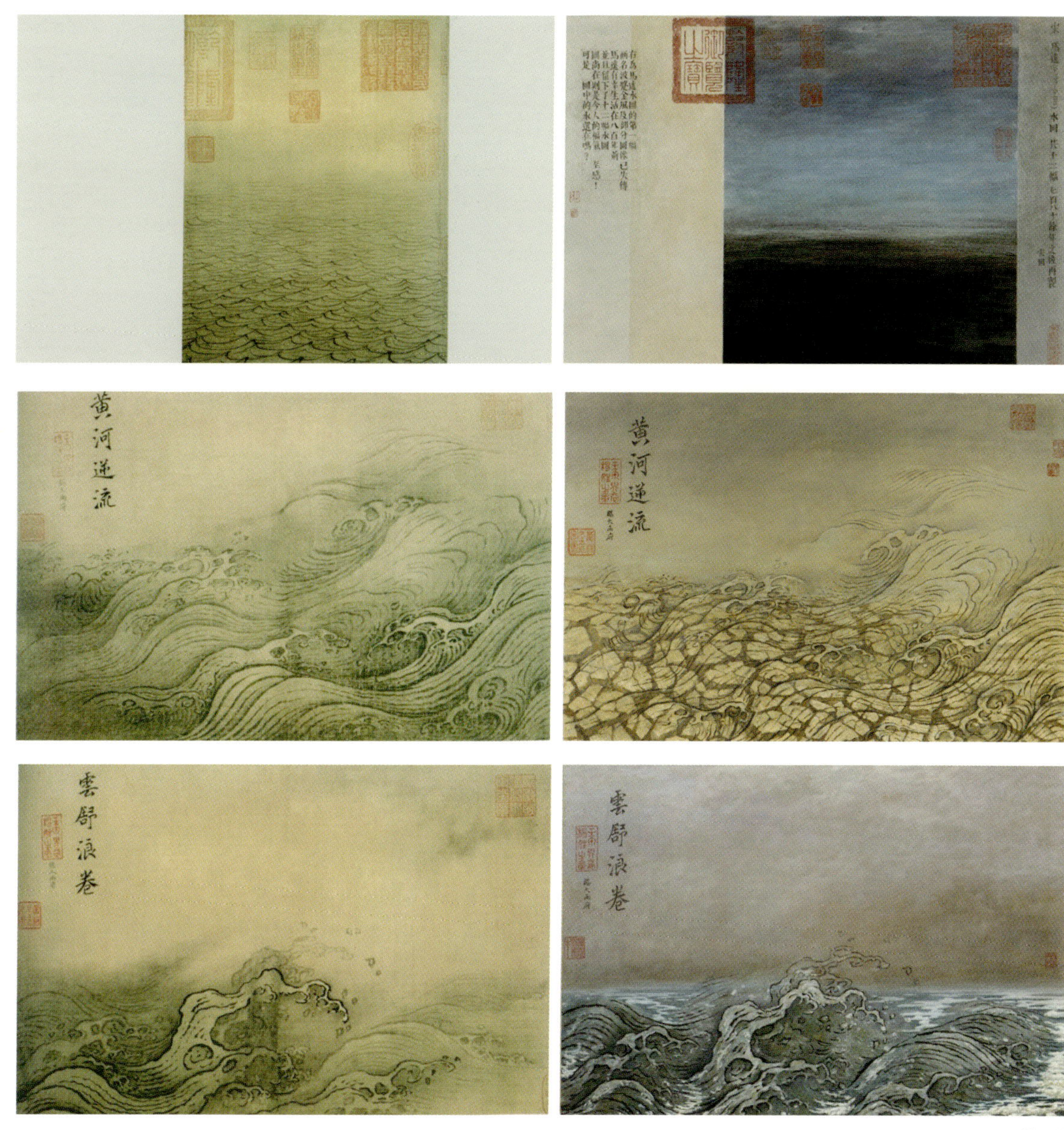

Fig. I

(Left)
Selections from Ma Yuan, Water Album, Southern Song Dynasty (1127–1279), 12 ink and
light color paintings on silk, 11 x 16 ½ in. each. Collection of the Palace Museum in Beijing.

(Right)
Selections from Zhang Hongtu, *Re-Make of Ma Yuan's Water Album (780 Years Later)*,
2008. 12 paintings in oil on canvas, 50 x 72 in. each.

an album of twelve paintings, rendered in ink and light color on silk, each depicting a different water scene.[2] Ma Yuan's original Water Album consists of splendidly vivid demonstrations of different views of water. Ma Yuan inherited and further developed the Northern Song style, and brought new ideas to painting. His brush is disciplined yet full of emotion. Although he rarely used color, Ma Yuan layered complex shades of gray to a similar effect. Large strokes depict cracked hard rocks. A few economical strokes running in a crosswise direction sufficed for more twisted structures; the viewpoint is natural and evocative. Given the emphasis on abstraction over pictorial representation in Chinese landscape, his water paintings offer a detailed observation of nature and paradoxically demonstrate his superb realistic ability.

Zhang retained Ma Yuan's different wave patterns in his *Re-make of Ma Yuan's Water Album*, while adding trash floating on the water or foam from chemical pollution, or making the formerly clear water green or soy-sauce colored. While the composition and essential elements of Ma Yuan's water paintings remain, Zhang transforms these pieces to reflect today's dire environmental conditions.

Even for the brush ink virtuoso, drawing water is the most difficult challenge. Like human thought, it is formless and ever-changing. Ma Yuan's original series has been esteemed as the best and the most expressive illustration of water in traditional Chinese painting. But Zhang once pointed out, "If Ma Yuan lived today and saw the polluted water, would he still paint his twelve paintings of water?" In a further editorial comment, calligraphy by Zhang appears in the upper right section of the first painting in *Re-make of Ma Yuan's Water Album*. The first of Ma Yuan's paintings is entitled *Waves Pushing the Golden Wind*, and Zhang's commentary on it reads, "Part of the painting is lost. Ma Yuan left this Earth almost 800 years ago. From his water album, only these 12 paintings remain. That the paintings are still with us is our fortune and deeply appreciated; but the water depicted in the painting, is it still there?"

The stark contrast of black and white, a common characteristic of traditional Chinese brush ink painting, and uncompromisingly apparent in Ma Yuan's work, is strikingly subverted by Zhang's addition of color. In the same vein, while Ma Yuan's water paintings have individual titles,[3] Zhang uses quasi-alphabetical captions of the form *Re-make of Ma Yuan's Water Album—A, Re-make of Ma Yuan's Water Album—D*, and so on. In each of the paintings, he tints the water or the sky green, purple, or red to emphasize its contaminated state. For example, Ma Yuan's *Stretch Clouds, Curb Waves* depicts a tumultuous scene. The artist has drawn waves that seem to be rearing up to the sky; the dark clouds rolling in over the water and covering the sky add to the menacing spirit of the painting. The tableau is small, yet the great boldness of vision spectacular. While Zhang has re-created the scene and the brushwork, his pink clouds suggest pollution, leading the viewer to question whether his angry waves are likewise tainted. In another painting in the series, Zhang shows cracked, sun-baked earth in spaces that Ma Yuan had filled with abundantly flowing water.

To fully appreciate Zhang's profound intent in "Shan Shui Today," one must grasp not only his fondness for Ma Yuan's water and unparalleled talent in depicting it, from the rippling lines to splashing torrents, but also a sense of awe and reverence toward nature's beauty that is at the heart of Chinese landscape paintings. In playing on such enduring themes, Zhang asks us to question the value of unbridled development and consider its threat to natural beauty.

Ma Yuan lived and painted during the Southern Song dynasty. The Chinese idiom "Residual Mountain, the Remaining Water"[4] (殘山剩水) reflects the change in traditional *shan shui* to include only partial elements—mountains that were merely half present and rivers that wandered into and out of the picture. This was an artistic response to a turbulent political situation—the defeat of the Song dynasty by Jurchen tribesmen, as a result of which the Song dynasty abandoned the northern part of the empire to their rivals and regrouped as the Southern Song dynasty south of the Huai River. Similarly, "Shan Shui Today" is an artistic response to our current environmental crisis. Water is no longer pure; the mountains are no longer carpeted with greenery.

Zhang's entire "Shan Shui Today" series questions the government slogan "Better City, Better Life."[5] Frequent elements in the series—contaminated air and water, expanding cities, and acres of tree stumps—intimate that "better cities" leads to worse quality of life. In fact, in many countries environmental damage continues, and pollution has been widely documented. Research published in the journal *Science* shows that approximately 8 million metric tons of plastic waste ends up in the world's oceans every year, with China leading the list of polluters by contributing as much as 3.5 million metric tons of marine debris each year.[6] A recent report by the US Environmental Protection Agency concluded that 55 percent of US rivers and streams are in poor condition.[7]

Chinese rivers are an assortment of colors—red, green, or black—but not clear. This appeared in the photos of the 2013 Prince Claus Award winner Lu Guang and others.[8] These photographs investigate the costs of depletion and pollution of natural resources caused by rapid industrialization in China today. Photographs of open-pit coal mining, air pollution, chemical waste, and contaminated water (*Fig. 2*) reveal the Earth's devastation and the pain inflicted upon the people, particularly China's working poor. Now, analyzing these photographs and Zhang's work, both are quite literal. However, while the photographs importantly document present conditions, Zhang

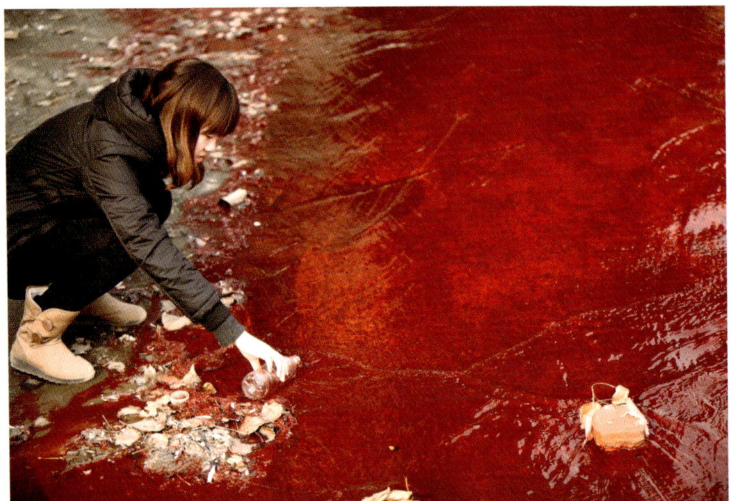

A journalist takes a sample of the red polluted water in the Jianhe River, Luoyang, Henan Province, China, December 2011. The sources of the pollution are two illegal chemical plants discharging their wastewater into sewer pipes. Photo: Zhang Xiaoli / China Foto Press

indirectly reflects on them by borrowing traditional motifs to place them in a larger cultural and historical context, and asks us to draw connections for ourselves. Zhang's more nuanced response is made possible by his self-imposed distance from current events.

Living in an unassuming house in Queens, with an exquisite studio built by a Japanese interior designer, Zhang watches Manhattan's skyscrapers and their contained wealth from the side, and observes Beijing's political manipulations from abroad. This is reminiscent of one of his "Shan Shui Today" paintings, which shows four monkeys seated and facing away from the viewer on a mountain rib watching China's CCTV (China Central TV) building. As detached as the monkeys, Zhang is able to paint the plain facts. His daily living style recalls the Chinese literati who separated themselves from the dusty world and thus from the fluctuating vagaries of political authority. While Southern Song painters were able to express their regret at the diminution of the empire only by quietly showing partial mountains and traces of rivers, Zhang more directly expresses his environmental concerns. Unlike some socially active artists, Zhang does not directly participate in criticism of the government or its policies.

Recalling the trajectory of Zhang's life both in China and in New York, we find many contradictions and hardships. His stint as a temporary construction worker was reflected in the bleak paintings *A Walking Man* (1985) and *Fish* (1985). The former shows a man in dark clothing stumbling along alone over a rugged, uneven surface, his face dim, possibly at sunset; and the latter shows a group of open-mouthed fish facing the viewer head-on, against a black background. The chilling atmosphere suggests an inability to breathe, a supreme alienation. Zhang himself says that the "fish out of water" theme in this painting refers to his own life at the time.

While the conditions of his material life then were hard, Zhang does not have the self-pity of the Chinese literati, instead placing his faith in artistic freedom. He has no bitterness in self-exile; he knows that there are bigger challenges calling him than the struggle to survive in China. He escaped the cultural wilderness of Mao's China, leaving close relatives and friends behind barbed wire. Only a high degree of optimism and personal spiritual wisdom allowed him to survive so successfully his outsider status in China and his early years in New York. Zhang's humor manifests itself in his art as mockery and a desire to mix everything up, making things upside down, inside out and outside in, and in seeming disorder, opening an art playground. His early work in New York dating from the early 1980s shows that Zhang intended to throw away political propaganda as a subject; his works from this time are quasi–Abstract Expressionist. But giving full rein to the sensitivities of his subconscious led the artist to the figurative work in the Mao series at the end of the decade, and later in the "Repainted Shan Shui" series.

Environmental relevancy first staked its claim in the late '60s through Land Art, or earthwork, followed by Ecological Art. Initially this took the form of art that either harmonized with the natural environment or presented as a stark intrusion into it. Examples range from Robert Smithson's *Spiral Jetty* (1970) to Spencer Tunick's *Aletsch Glacier* (2007),[9] to the 2014 exhibit "The Rubbish Collection" by British artist and curator Joshua Sofaer.[10] These trends are international; New York–based Taiwanese artists Lin ShihPao and Yang Chin Chih collect recycled material to use in their artworks and performances.[11] And many others use digital or new media to show their concern for the urgent environmental state of our world. This is a relatively new development both in social consciousness and in art history. For the majority of its history, landscape in Western painting has been a supporting character behind a protagonist, thus underlining human domination of the environment. With few exceptions, it was not until Impressionism stormed onto the art scene that Western artists began to focus on the changing effects of light on color analysis.

It is no coincidence, then, that when he looked to connect Western and Chinese landscape, Zhang chose Impressionism and *shan shui*. He is perhaps best known for merging masterpieces of Western Impressionism and Chinese *shan shui*. In preparation for the "Repainted Shan Shui" series, Zhang extensively studied the structure, stroke, color, light, and emotion of Impressionist masters and their techniques. The culmination of this scrutiny shines through the brilliant pieces of this series with a familiar yet strange aesthetic, of which Zhang's *Zhao Mengfu and Monet (Morning, Noon and Evening)* is an example. Even after the period 1987 to 1990, during which he created the "Repainted Shan Shui" series, Zhang continues to borrow from Western vocabulary. This is evident in his digital artworks, which began as early as 1998.

Zhang's proclivity for combining elements of traditional Chinese art practices with Western social phenomena has already appeared in his *Mai Dang Lao* and "Christie's Catalog" works. *The Bikers* is a digital photo piece that causes the viewer to clap and smile. It is so appealing because Zhang is sarcastic in a playful way. He uses the form of a Chinese long scroll painting and pictures of hundreds of bikers, in addition to a picture of a famous *shan shui* painting by Shen Zhou (1427–1509), and Mao's poem "Snow," which praises the beauty of the landscape. In these pieces, Zhang displayed his unique observation of the contemporary world in which he is situated.

After *Re-make of Ma Yuan's Water Album*, "Shan Shui Today" changed course, and is in fact still ongoing today. The remainder of the series presents much more of Zhang's personal elements and art language. While referring to the Dunhuang cave paintings, they are less obviously a marriage of Eastern and Western traditions. Commenting on today's environmental issues, these paintings reveal a melancholic nostalgia for times past. The works in the series typically feature the changing forests, mountains, and valleys, with monkeys standing on the peaks contemplating the skyscrapers and utility poles encroaching on the forest, crowding over the horizon, and invading their universe.

Shortly before he left China, Zhang spent an entire month studying and sketching the paintings of the Dunhuang grottoes. They are flat and ornate, with the mountains either cascading in saw-toothed profile with very abrupt brushstrokes or standing schematically with shading indicating folds and valleys. The somber colors of the mountains and plains contrast with the bright lights of the city. Allusions to the Dunhuang style abound in many of the "Shan Shui Today" paintings.

The Dunhuang portrayals of nature are often referred to as "boneless *shan shui*," with *shan shui*'s mountains reduced to outlines in an illustrative style. Formally, these paintings are composed of many independent units; the Dunhuang artists frequently dispensed with perspective. The most interesting part of the Dunhuang cave paintings is not the religious icons but the background murals, which may have been painted by Chinese artists and combined central Asian, Indian, and Chinese influences, and sprang to life because of their color and movement.

In *After Wang Yuanqi 0910* (2009–10) (*Fig. 3*), also from the "Shan Shui Today" series, Zhang has preserved a trace of the Dunhuang cave paintings in the shape of the mountains. Taking as his subject the famous Wanchuang Villa outside of Xi'an, once one of the most celebrated garden spots in China, and famously commemorated by Wang Yuanqi (1642–1715), Zhang as usual introduces some changes. Tree stumps punctuate the scene, the only remnant of a green forest that must have surrounded

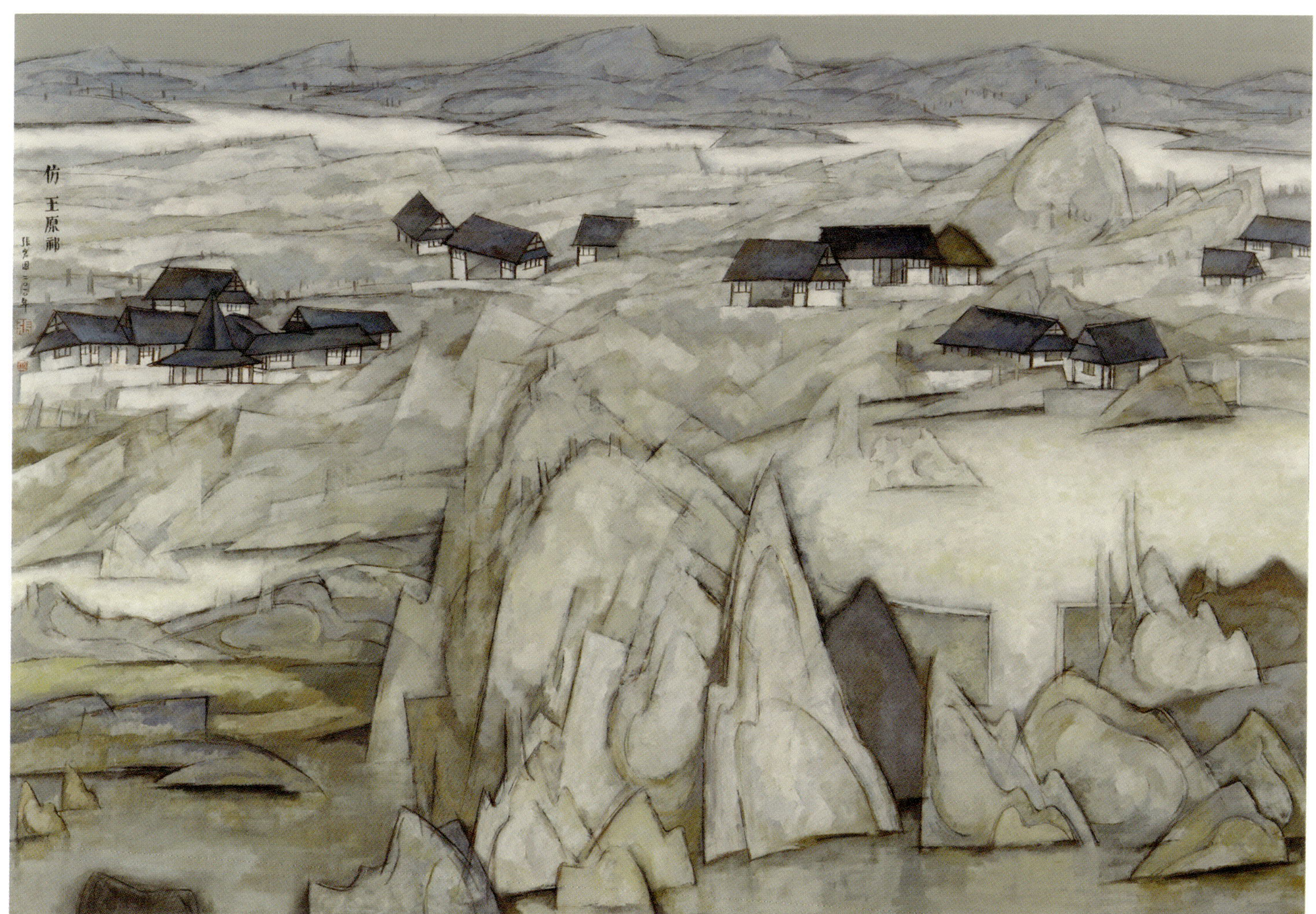

After Wang Yuanqi 0910, 2009–2010. Mixed media and oil on canvas, 64 x 96 in.

Fig. 3

Wanchuang Villa. White mountains bring to mind the arid countryside surrounding Xi'an. Zhang has transformed a Qing (1644–1912) masterpiece to reflect the environmental despoliation of the intervening centuries.

In a related painting, *After Wang Yuanqi, 287 Years Later* (2008), Wanchuang Villa is pictured in disarray. The villa is now missing its roof, trees are growing from what formerly was the interior of the villa, and the surrounding countryside is bleak and uninviting. In most of the "Shan Shui Today" series, the color blue is applied either to the mountains or to the monkeys, which recalls both mineral pigment effects and the blue clothing worn by the working class, with an added meaning in Western terms of sadness.

This series also includes *Ode to the Sound of Autumn* (Plate 78), painted in 2011, in which small buildings are huddled inside a forest of delicately intertwined trees blown by the autumn wind. This painting is one of exquisite classic beauty in medium color tones, and refers to a poem of the same title by Ouyang Xiu (1007–1072) that eulogizes the clear, empty autumn night.[12] The sadness traditionally associated with the season is made more poignant by the buildings crowding into the forest and littering the horizon. The scene's curiously modern, mysterious atmosphere is intensified by the contrast between the solidly unrelenting skyscrapers and the wind-blown trees.

The most curious feature of "Shan Shui Today" might be the monkeys. Sitting on or traveling over mountains in the foreground, they are clear references to the Monkey King (Sun Wu Kong) in the famous Ming dynasty novel *Journey to the West*. In Daoism, controlling the Mind Ape is an important goal for appropriate behavior, making it possible to achieve the heights of this mystic philosophy. The uncontrolled Mind Ape is an apt metaphor for our restless society, characterized as it is by incessant innovation and an inability to concentrate on long-term goals such as environmental propriety.

In his youth, Zhang was not interested in Chinese ink. He liked color and intense images, things that were loud and clear. At the time, he believed that Western expression had a greater capacity to convey human emotions. However, after further painting and studying, he arrived at a different understanding, namely that Western art could be used to reinterpret Chinese painting. To do this, he immersed himself in both realms. From not appreciating Chinese painting and criticizing it, he came to love and appreciate its artistic value. In particular, he came to understand that the technical challenges and unforgiving nature of brush ink painting make it the most difficult and personal test of the artist. Zhang's artistic reappraisal opened many opportunities to reinterpret the Chinese tradition using different tools and materials.

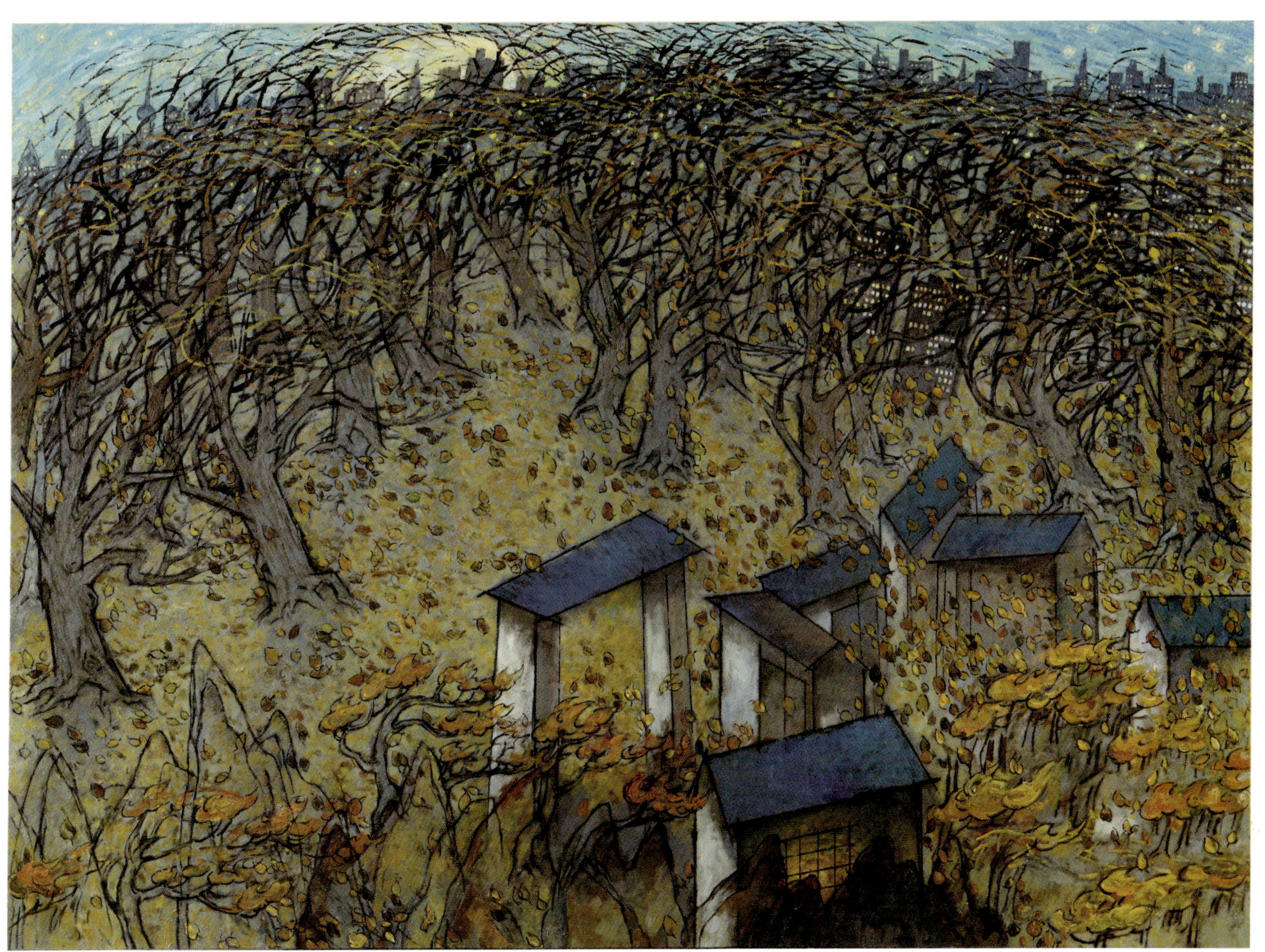

Plate 78

Ode to the Sound of Autumn, 2011. Mixed media and oil on canvas, 64 ½ x 89 in.

Chinese brush ink painting is a fusion of mind and matter. It is said that for the painter, images and feelings should coalesce. This is evident in Zhang's work. Early Western art, in comparison, deploys realistic images to express profound feelings. Conversely, direct representations of reality are not valued in Chinese brush ink painting, which eschews accurate perspectival details in pursuit of deliberate abstraction to reveal emotional and philosophical content. In traditional Chinese philosophy, harmony with nature, and therefore with heaven, gives humans the possibility to unite with oneness. Such is the Daoist sense of nature.[13] This philosophy permeated lyrics in seals and poems that were included in paintings and represented the mind of the painter. Traditional Chinese *shan shui* paintings showed the human figure fading into the landscape—drinking tea inside a pavilion, walking along a mountain trail, rowing a boat in the river, or sometimes only indirectly suggested by the presence of a hut. Humans were seen as a small and insignificant part of nature, and not depicted in precise proportion or perspective. In a way, we might name it as surrealism in its disregard of representation, while it is exact in its expression of the philosophy of harmony. Such nuances are evident in Zhang's work.

In the most recent "Shan Shui Today" paintings, *Shan Shui, Untitled* and *Little Monkey* (both 2013), there emerged a new technique. For these works, Zhang attached rice paper directly to a wooden panel rather than either attaching it to canvas or painting on canvas. Using brush ink methods, he painted some areas using a dry brush, some with a wet brush, and simply left other areas blank. The ink brush composition was overlaid on a grid of repeating squares. The layers of ink and the geometric pattern lent a new dimensionality to the painting and are an extension of Zhang's earlier studies on Cubism. (See Michael FitzGerald's essay in this book for more on Zhang's interest in Cubism.) Zhang laid down ink, which spread through the rice paper, then superimposed black skyscrapers. *Little Monkey* and *Shan Shui, Untitled* extend his continuing studies of Cubism. The result is a mingling of Western and Eastern techniques, materials, and concerns. A brush stroke can still be seen under a color. Zhang is comfortable with the result of this procedure, and will employ it more in the future.

To observe Zhang's merging of Western style and Eastern subject matter (as in "Repainted Shan Shui") or Western subject matter and Eastern style (as in Van Gogh's self-portraits in the style of Chinese brush ink painting) is to see the artist at his core. Likewise, to appreciate Ma Yuan's evocative ink brush paintings so subtly transformed, yet radically reconceptualized, is to witness Zhang in his native element. Indeed, the artist's creativity is that he does not just wipe the past out, but blends East and West, old and new. We find in his work a strong tie to the past that lacks neither audacity nor originality. His work gives a fresh sense to time and space. Duchamp once said, "I don't believe in the essential aspect of art. . . . Everything is tautology except black coffee, because the senses are in control!"[14] As we carefully investigate Zhang, we see that he makes art with a direction and a purpose. His direct presentations partake of Duchamp's "black coffee" sense, and he interprets Duchamp's radicalism as a complete denial of the notion of reverence for past masterworks in art. Paradoxically, however, Zhang's appreciation of the accomplishments of both Western and Eastern traditions has increased over time. Such disregard for convention coupled with re-spect is the foundation of his unlimited creative freedom.

Little Monkey not only presages a possible revolution in media, but also perhaps a subtle shift in message and content from those of an artist always ready to explore new frontiers. The eponymous little monkey, surrounded by endless clusters of sky-scrapers, gazes toward the starry sky with an isolated and helpless expression. At the center of the painting, detached from the surrounding visual noise, it reflects. Per-haps it is distressed by pollution; perhaps by the absence of trees; perhaps by all the paraphernalia of our all-too-technological society. Perhaps this blue baby represents the next generation and calls for our attention. In this interpretation, the malaise and alienation that Sloterdijk remarks on are contained in this baby monkey and its implied questions.

1   Peter Sloterdijk, *Spheres*, vol. 1, *Bubbles: Microspherology*, trans. Wieland Hoban (Los Angeles: Semiotext(e), 2011), 27.

2   Ma Yuan (ca. 1190–1224) is one of the most important painters of the Southern Song dynasty (1127–1279); his paintings won royal favor, and many bore inscriptions by Emperor Ning-Zong or his empress; Ma Yuan, Li Tang, Liu Song, and Xia Gui collectively were referred to as the "four Song masters," while Ma Yuan and Xia Gui gave their names to the innovative and evocative Ma-Xia school of painting.

3   The twelve Ma Yuan water paintings in this album were titled: 1. *Wave Pushing the Golden Wind*, 2. *Dongting Lake Breeze*, 3. *Waves Overlapping Waves*, 4. *Cold Pond*, 5. *Yangtze Hills*, 6. *Yellow River Reflux*, 7. *Autumn Water Echo Wave*, 8. *Cloud Generate Sea*, 9. *Splendid Lake Water*, 10. *Stretch Clouds, Curb Waves*, 11. *Dawn Breaking Over the Hill*, and 12. *Small Waves Floating* (波蹙金風、洞庭風細、層波疊浪、寒塘清淺、長江萬頃、黃河逆流、秋水回波、雲生滄海、湖光瀲 灩、雲舒浪卷、曉日烘山、細浪漂漂). The Water Album was formerly in the collection of the Taipei National Palace Museum and is now in the collection of the Palace Museum in Beijing.

4   The phrase referred to the loss of territory that was a central fact of life in the Song dynasty; it symbolized the incomplete country of the Southern Song, to which Ma Yuan belonged. The phrase itself came from a Tang dynasty poem (唐，杜甫《陪鄭廣文游何將軍山林》" 剩水滄江破，殘山碣石開 ").

5   Britta Erickson, "Zhang Hongtu's 'Shan Shui Today': A New Direction," in *Shan Shui Today* (Taipei: Tina Keng Gallery, 2011).

6   Jenna R. Jambeck et al., "Plastic Waste Inputs From Land Into the Ocean," *Science* 13 vol. 347, no. 6223 (February 2015): 768–71.

7   According to the EPA's National Rivers and Streams Assessment released February 28, 2013, only 21 percent of US rivers and streams are in good condition; 23 percent are in fair condition and 55 percent in poor condition.

8   Lu Guang (b. 1961, Yongkang) was honored for his moving photographic testimony of hidden human tragedies and devastated environments.

9   Luchia Meihua Lee, "Art in Environmental Reactions," in *Raising the Temperature* (Queens, NY: Queens Museum & Rainforest Art Foundation, 2014), 6.

10   Joshua Sofaer, "The Rubbish Collection," Science Museum, London, June–September 2014. The artist and the museum collaborated to display daily human garbage as exhibition objects in order to remind people of their attitude toward "material."

11   Yang Chin Chih's performance *Kill Me or Change* took place in July 2013. To raise awareness of consumerism, Yang collected more than 30,000 recycled cans, put them all in a net, suspended them 60 feet overhead from a crane,

then had the cans dropped on his head. Lin Shih Pao has fashioned sculpture from recycled bottles, pens, and pennies. Now he is collecting recycled cell phones. Both artists have shown their work in New York.

12 Ouyang Xiu, "Ode to the Sound of Autumn," in which the narrator is disturbed by strange sounds while reading at night. Britta Erickson, "Zhang Hongtu's 'Shan Shui Today': A New Direction."

13 As it is expressed in *Dao de jing*, Man follows earth, earth follows heaven, heaven follows Dao, and Dao follows nature.

14 "I Live the Life of a Waiter," in Pierre Cabanne, *Dialogues With Marcel Duchamp* (New York: Da Capo, 1987), 100 and 107. Cabanne asked Duchamp, "Do you believe in God?" Duchamp replies, "No, not at all. Don't ask that! For me, the question does not exist; God is a human invention. Why talk about a Utopia? When Man invents something, there's always someone for it and someone against it. It's mad foolishness to have made up the idea of God."

Plates

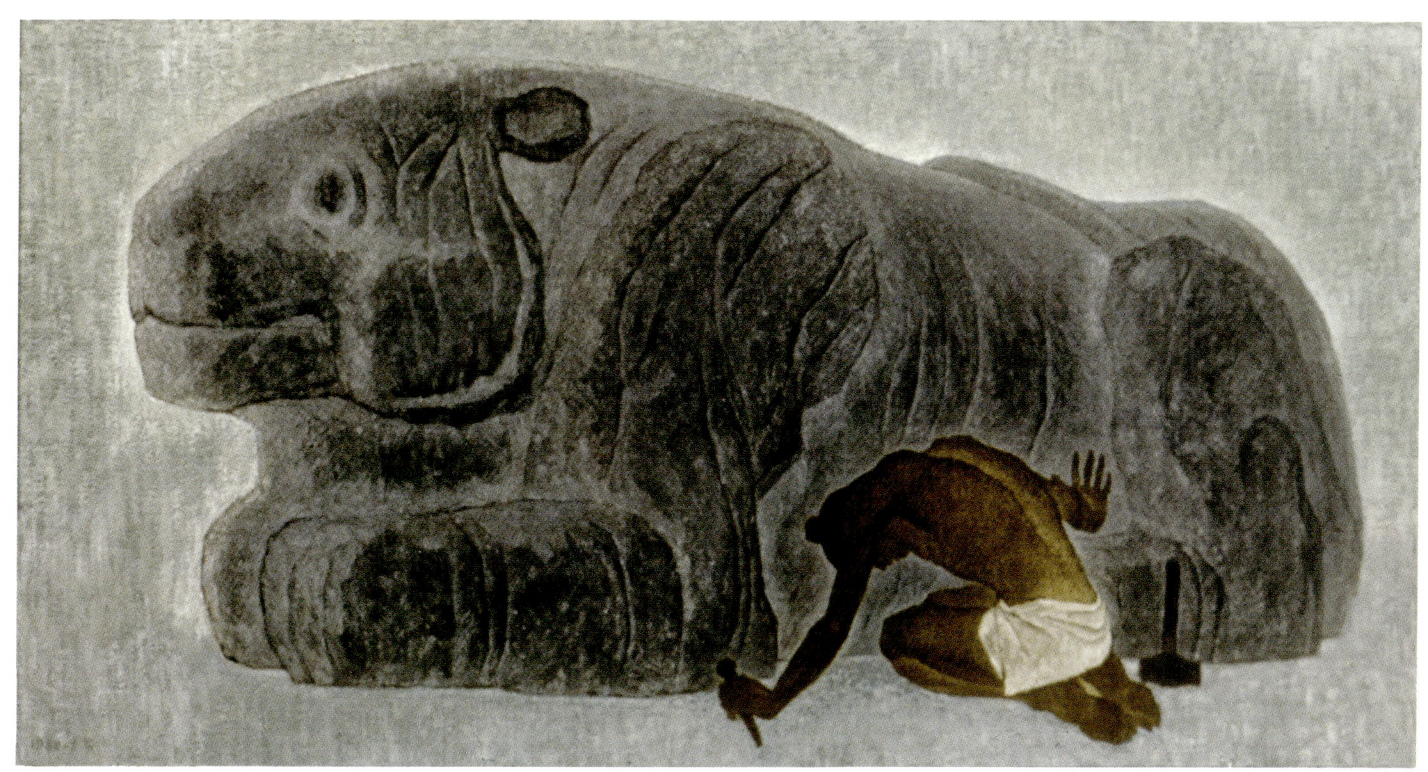

001
Eternal Life, 1980.
Oil on canvas,
33 ½ x 63 ½ in.

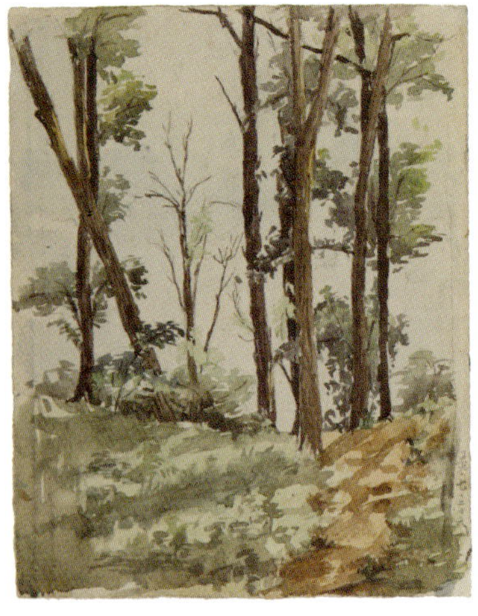

002-a

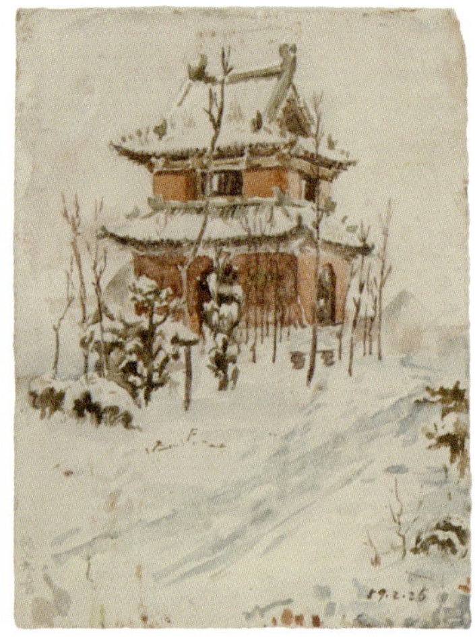

002-b

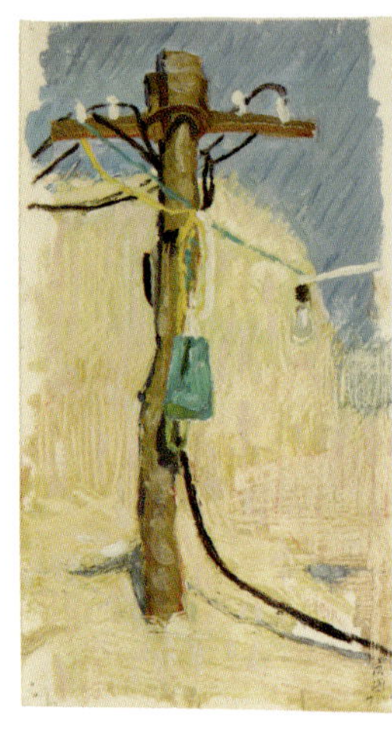

002-c

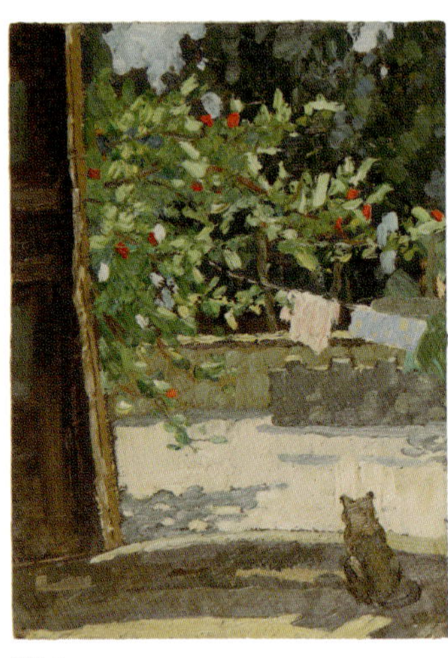

002-d

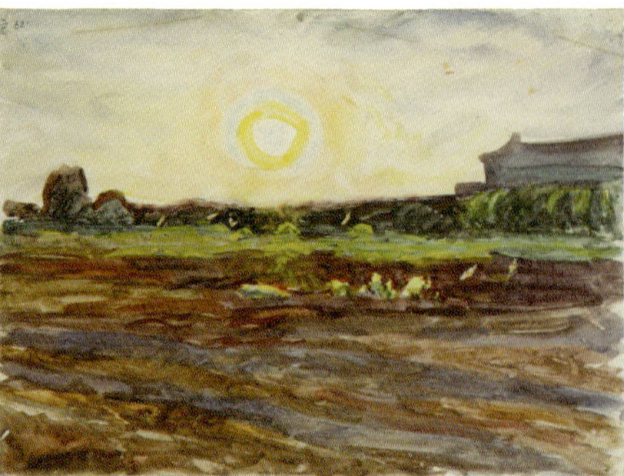

002-e

002-f

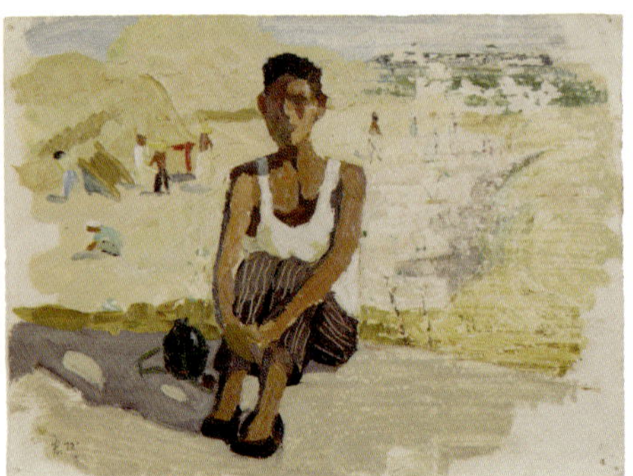

002-g

002-a
Trees, 1959.
Watercolor on paper,
7 ½ x 6 in.

002-b
Snow in the Park, 1959.
Watercolor on paper,
7 ½ x 5 ¾ in.

002-c
Electricity Pole, 1972.
Oil on paper,
10 ½ x 6 in.

002-d
Li Village, 1973.
Oil on paper,
10 ⅝ x 7 ⅝ in.

002-e
Black Horse, 1963.
Watercolor on paper,
7 ⅝ x 10 in.

002-f
Sunset, 1962.
Watercolor on paper,
7 ⅝ x 10 ¾ in.

002-g
Boy with Army Bottle, 1972.
Oil on paper,
7 ¾ x 11 ⅝ in.

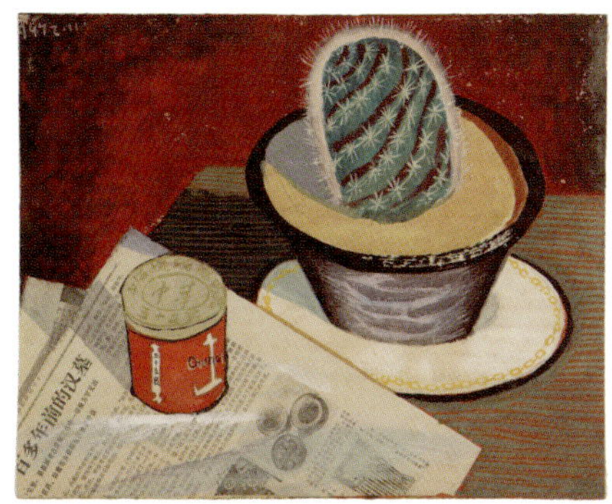

003-a

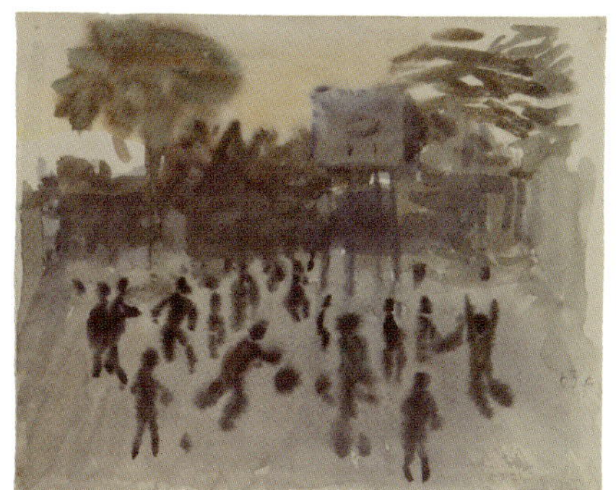

003-b

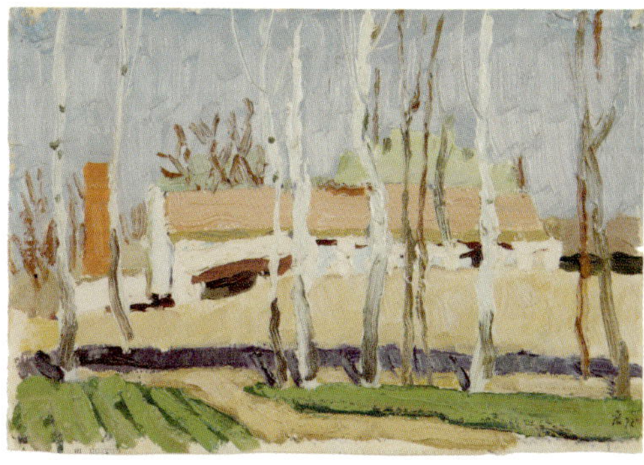

003-c

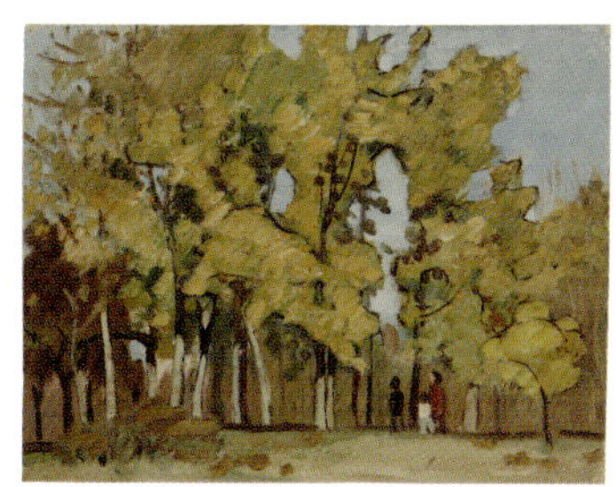

003-d

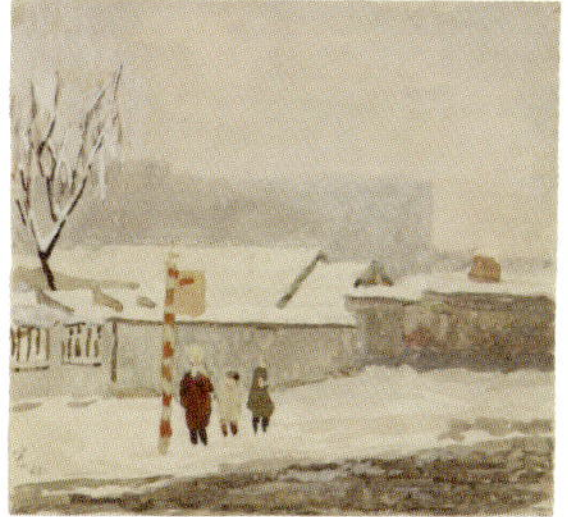

003-e

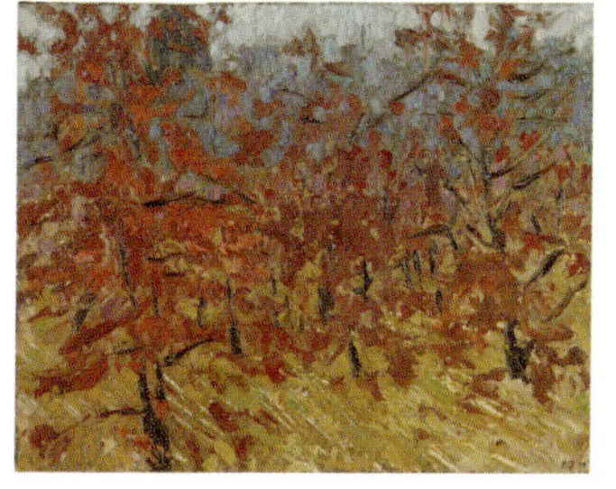

003-f

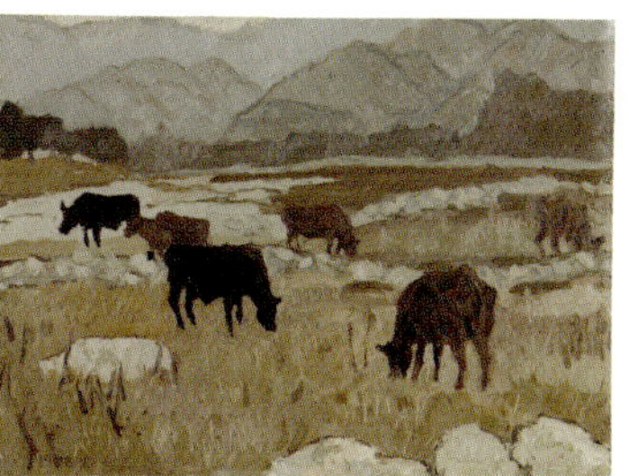

003-g

003-a
Still Life with Cactus, 1972.
Watercolor on paper,
12 ¼ x 15 ⅜ in.

003-b
Ball Game, 1963.
Watercolor on paper,
7 ⅝ x 9 ¾ in.

003-c
Early Spring, 1972.
Oil on paper,
6 x 9 ⅞ in.

003-d
Autumn in the Park, 1973.
Oil on paper,
12 x 15 ¾ in.

003-e
Waiting for the Bus, 1963.
Watercolor on paper,
7 ½ x 7 ⅝ in.

003-f
Autumn Trees, 1978.
Oil on paper,
10 ¾ x 13 ¾ in.

003-g
Cows in the Field, 1978.
Oil on paper,
11 ¾ x 14 ⅞ in.

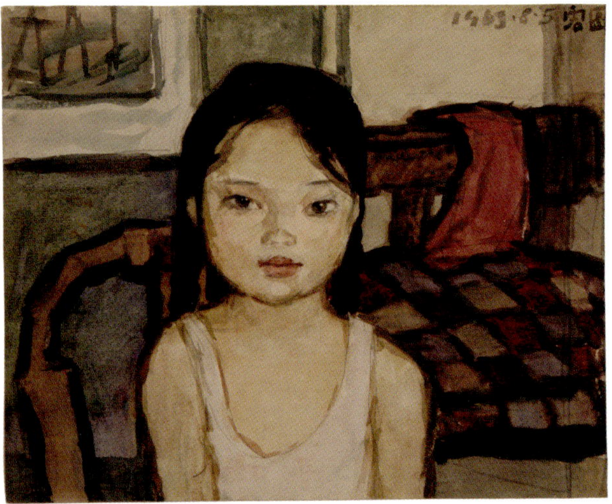

004-a

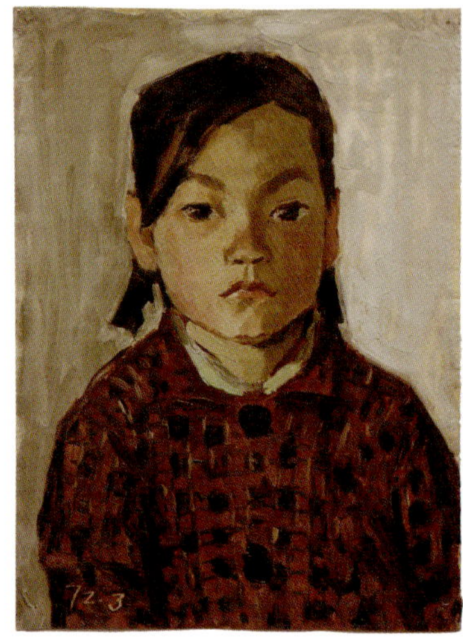

004-b

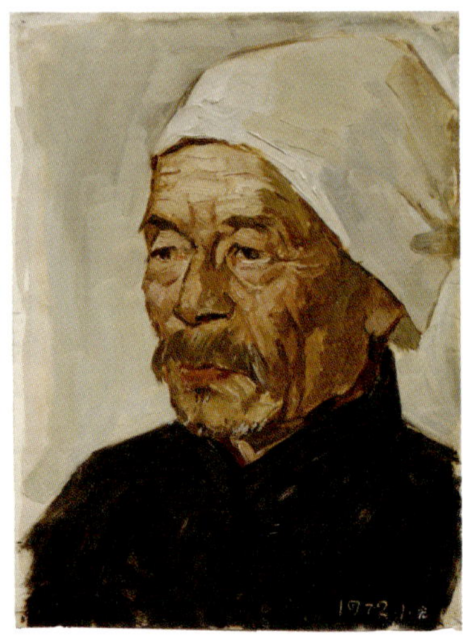

004-c

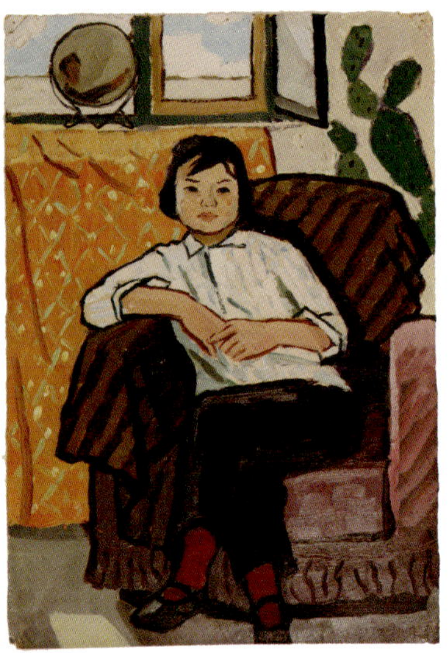

004-d

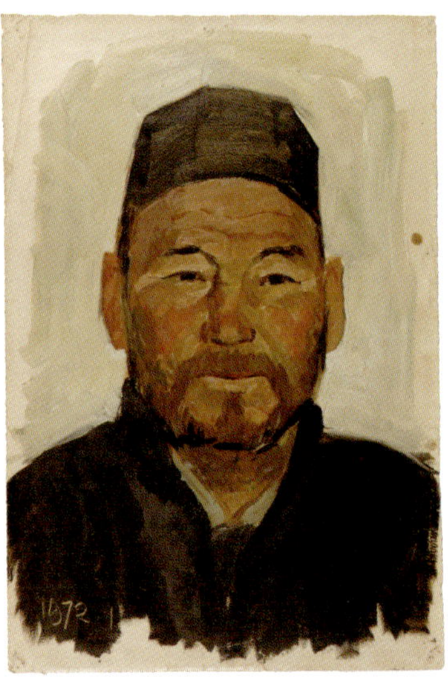

004-e

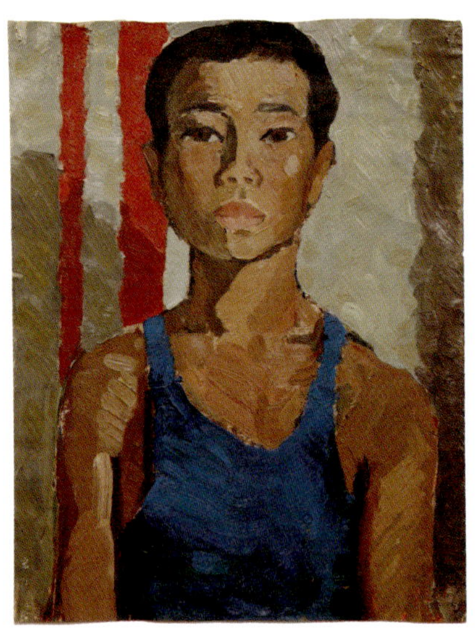

004-f

004-a
Girl at Home, 1963.
Watercolor on paper,
7 ⅝ x 9 ⅝ in.

004-b
Girl in Red, 1972.
Oil on paper,
11 ½ x 8 ¾ in.

004-c
Old Man with Turban, 1972.
Oil on paper,
12 x 9 in.

004-d
Portrait of the Artist's Sister, 1972.
Oil on paper,
15 ¼ x 10 ¾ in.

004-e
Old Man with Black Hat, 1972.
Oil on paper,
15 ⅝ x 11 ¾ in.

004-f
Boy, 1972.
Oil on paper,
11 x 8 ¾ in.

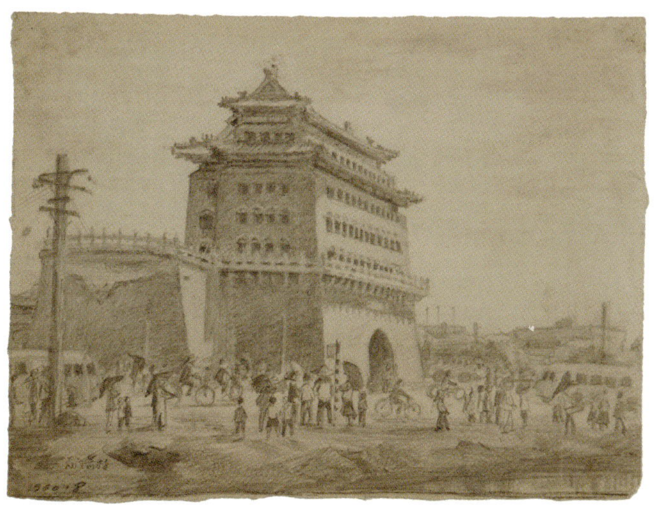

005-a

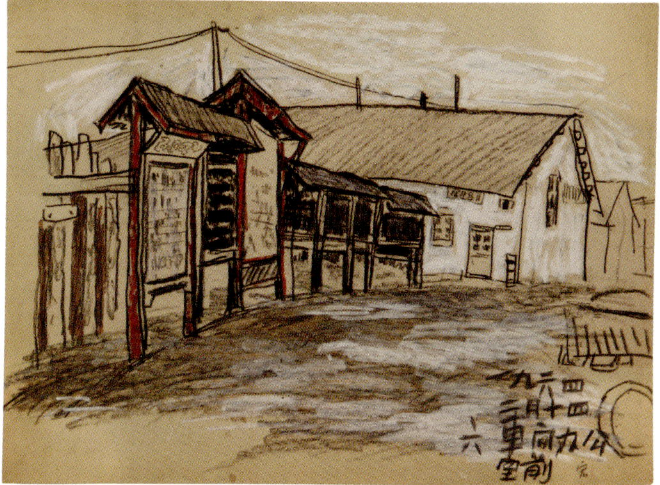

005-b

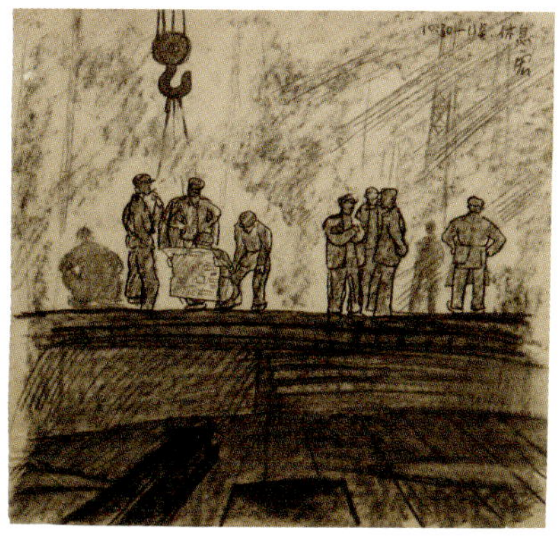

005-c

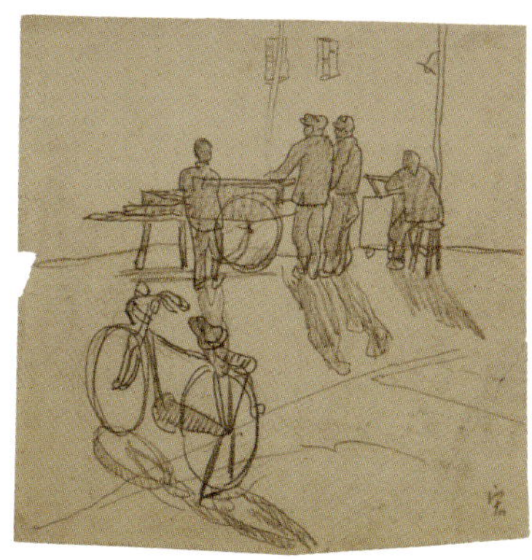

005-d

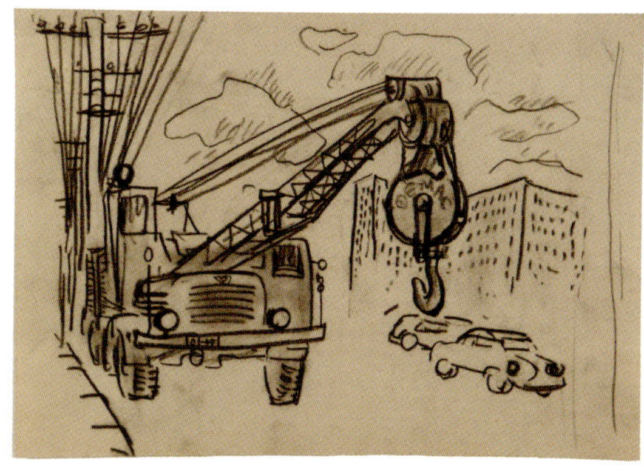

005-e

005-a
Zhengyang Gate with Watchtower, 1960.
Pencil on paper,
6 ¾ x 10 ¼ in.

005-b
Factory Notice Board, 1964.
Charcoal and pastel on paper,
10 ½ x 14 ¼ in.

005c
Break Time, 1963.
Charcoal on paper,
10 ½ x 11 in.

005-d
Street Vendor at Night, 1962.
Pencil on paper,
8 ¾ x 8 ¾ in.

005e
Crane Truck, 1963.
Charcoal on paper,
7 ¼ x 10 ⅜ in.

181

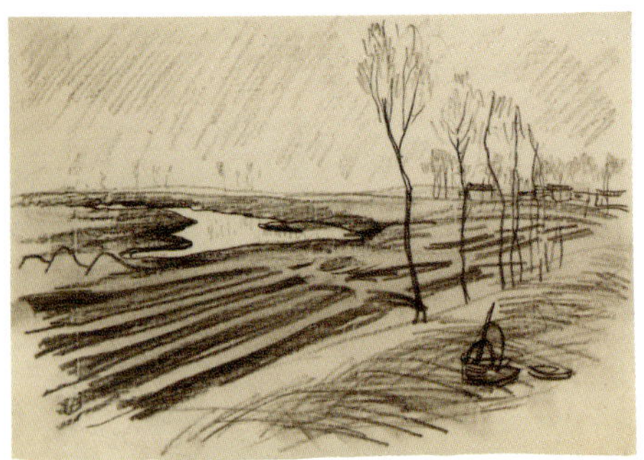

006-a

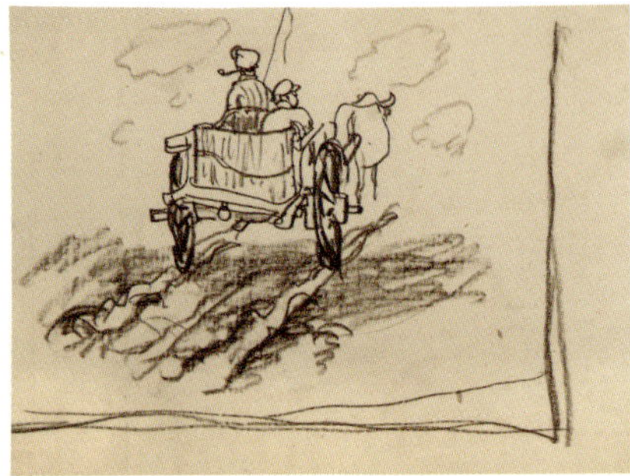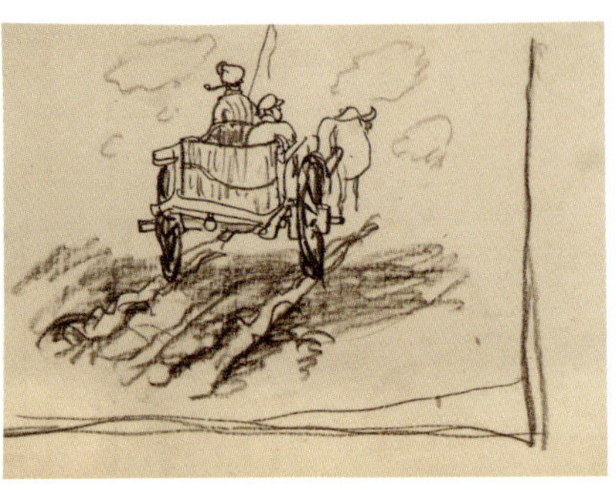

006-b

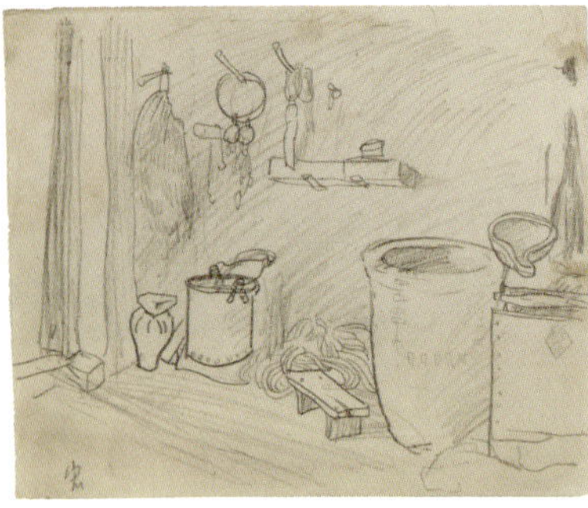

006-c

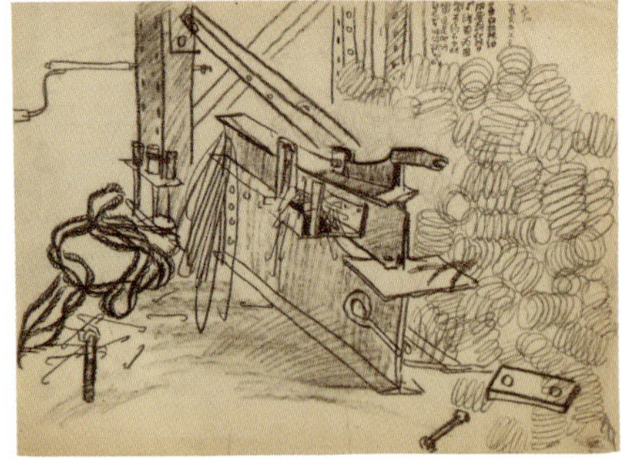

006-d

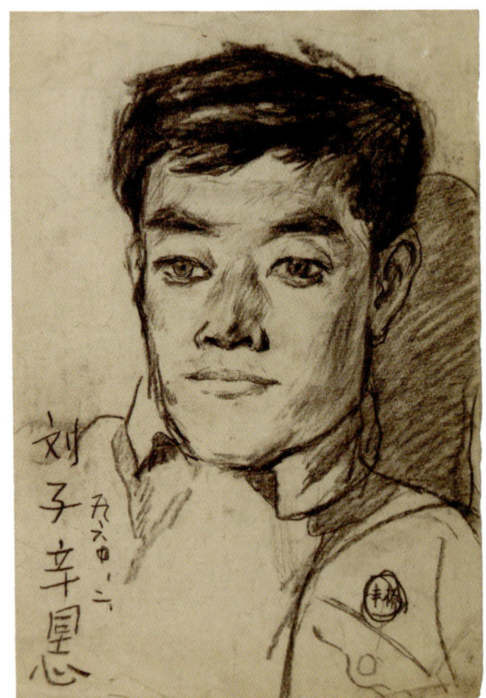

006-e

006-a
Spring, 1962.
Pencil on paper,
7 ½ x 10 ¾ in.

006-b
Ox-Cart, 1963.
Charcoal on paper,
7 ½ x 10 ⅝ in.

006-c
Peasant House with Water Barrel, 1962.
Pencil on paper,
10 ¾ x 13 ⅛ in.

006-d
Spring Factory, 1964.
Charcoal on paper,
10 ¼ x 14 ½ in.

006-e
Portrait of Liu Zixing with Model's Signature, 1964.
Charcoal on paper,
15 ½ x 10 ¾ in.

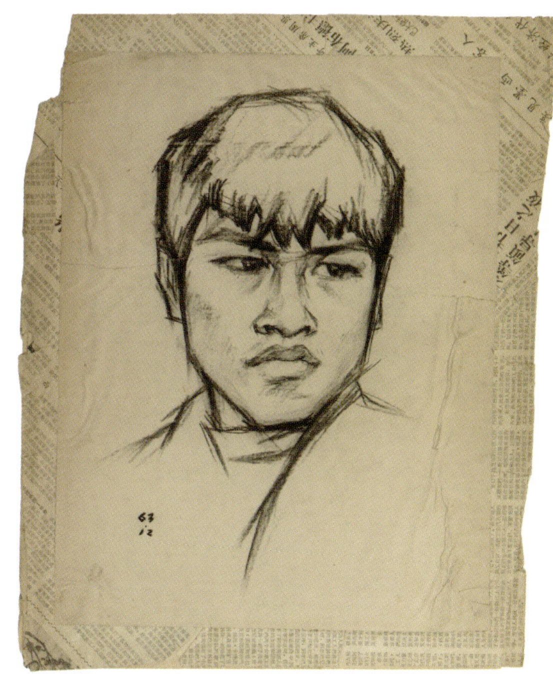

007-a

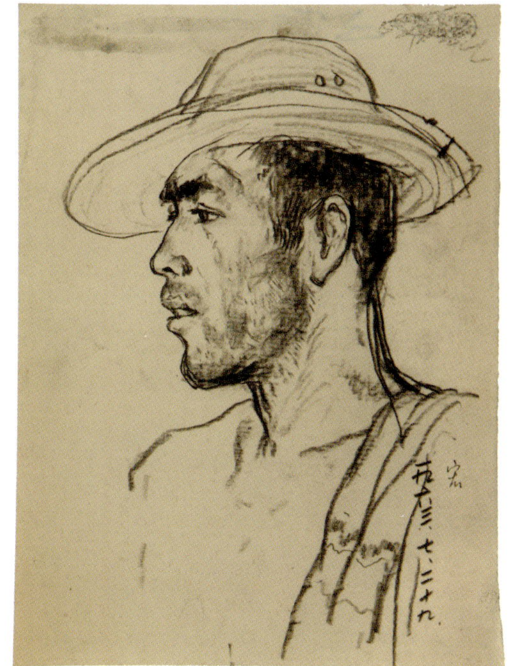

007-b

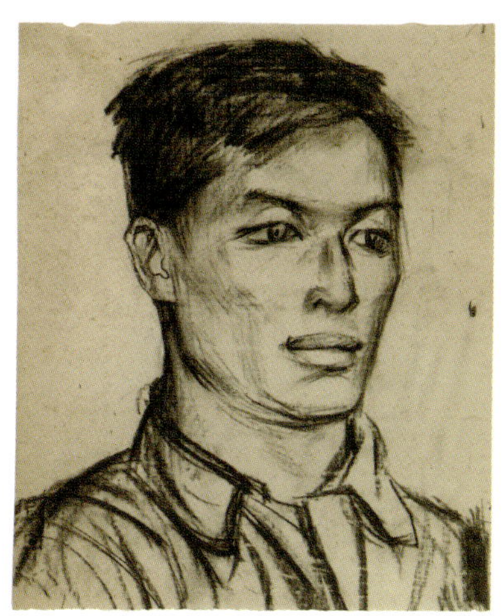

007-c

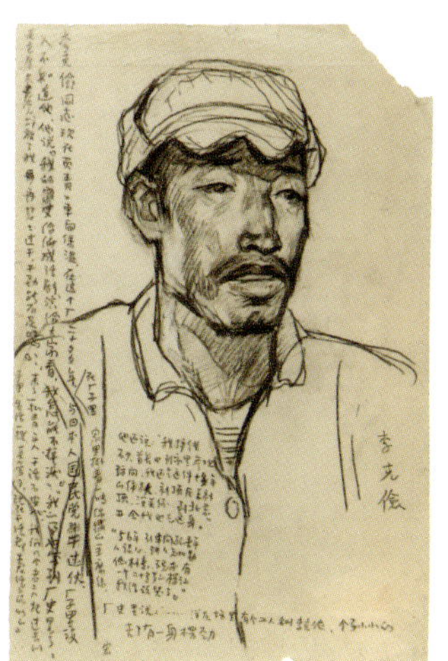

007-d

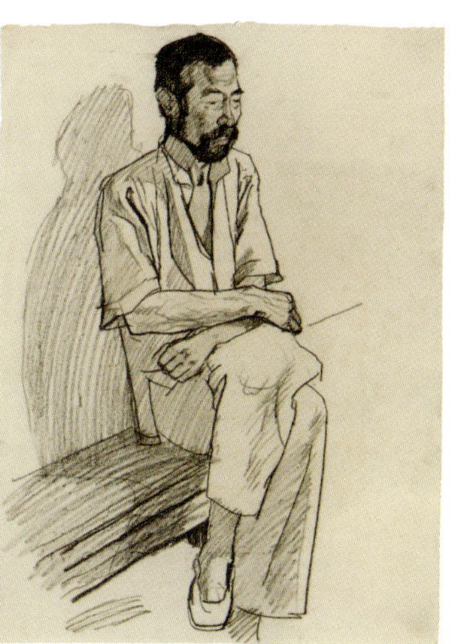

007-e

007-a
Portrait of Shupei, 1963.
Charcoal on paper mounted on newspaper,
15 ⅛ x 12 ¼ in.

007-b
Man with Beard, 1963.
Charcoal on paper,
10 ⅜ x 7 ⅞ in.

007-c
Qingli, 1963.
Charcoal on paper,
12 ¼ x 10 ¼ in.

007-d
Portrait of a Factory Worker, 1964.
Charcoal on paper,
16 ¾ x 11 ½ in.

007-e
Sitting Man, 1962.
Charcoal on paper,
15 ¼ x 11 ½ in.

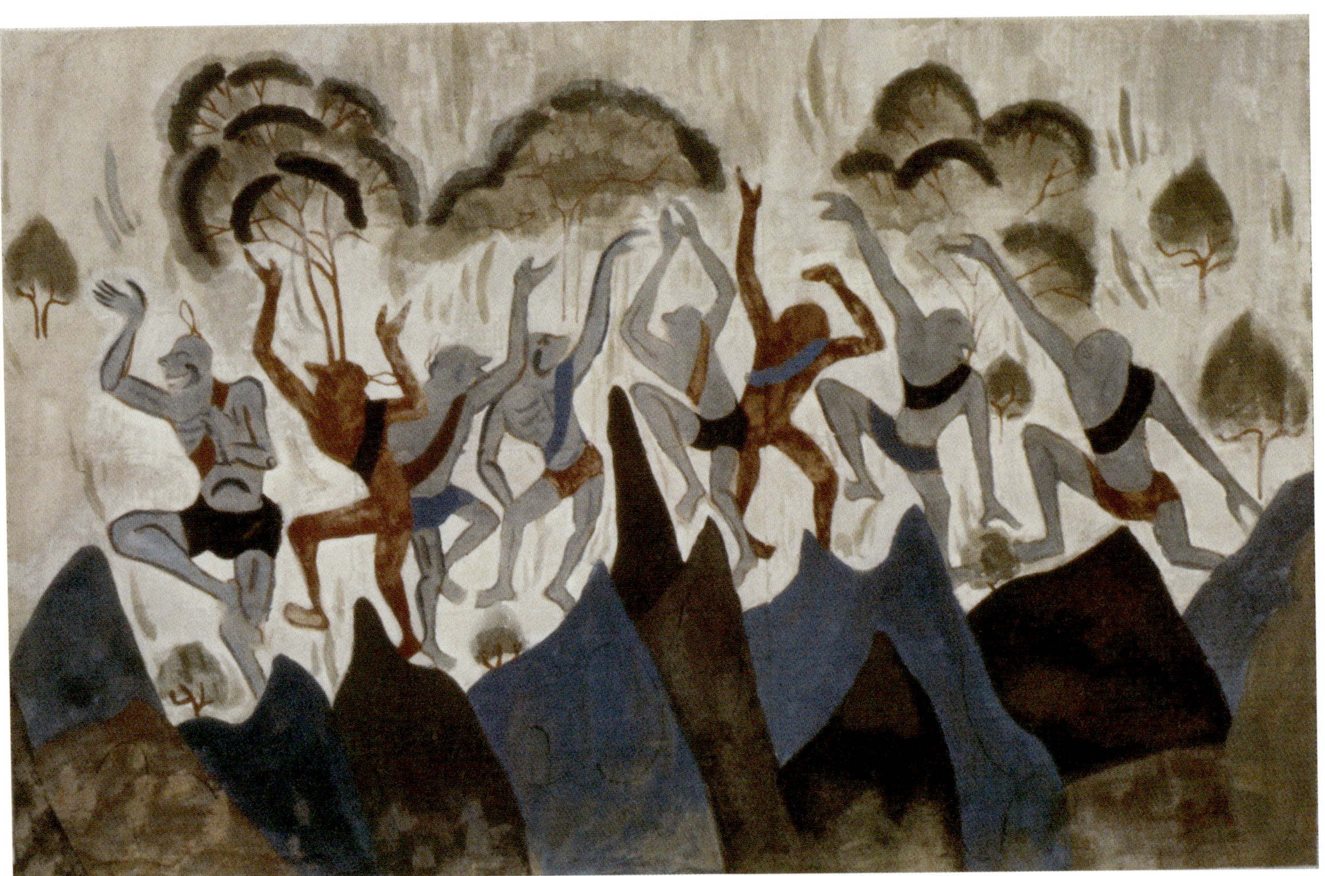

008
Dunhuang Study #7, 1981.
Copy of Eight Beggars Who Went to See the Buddha, Dunhuang Cave 428,
Ink and gouache on rice paper,
42 x 66 in.

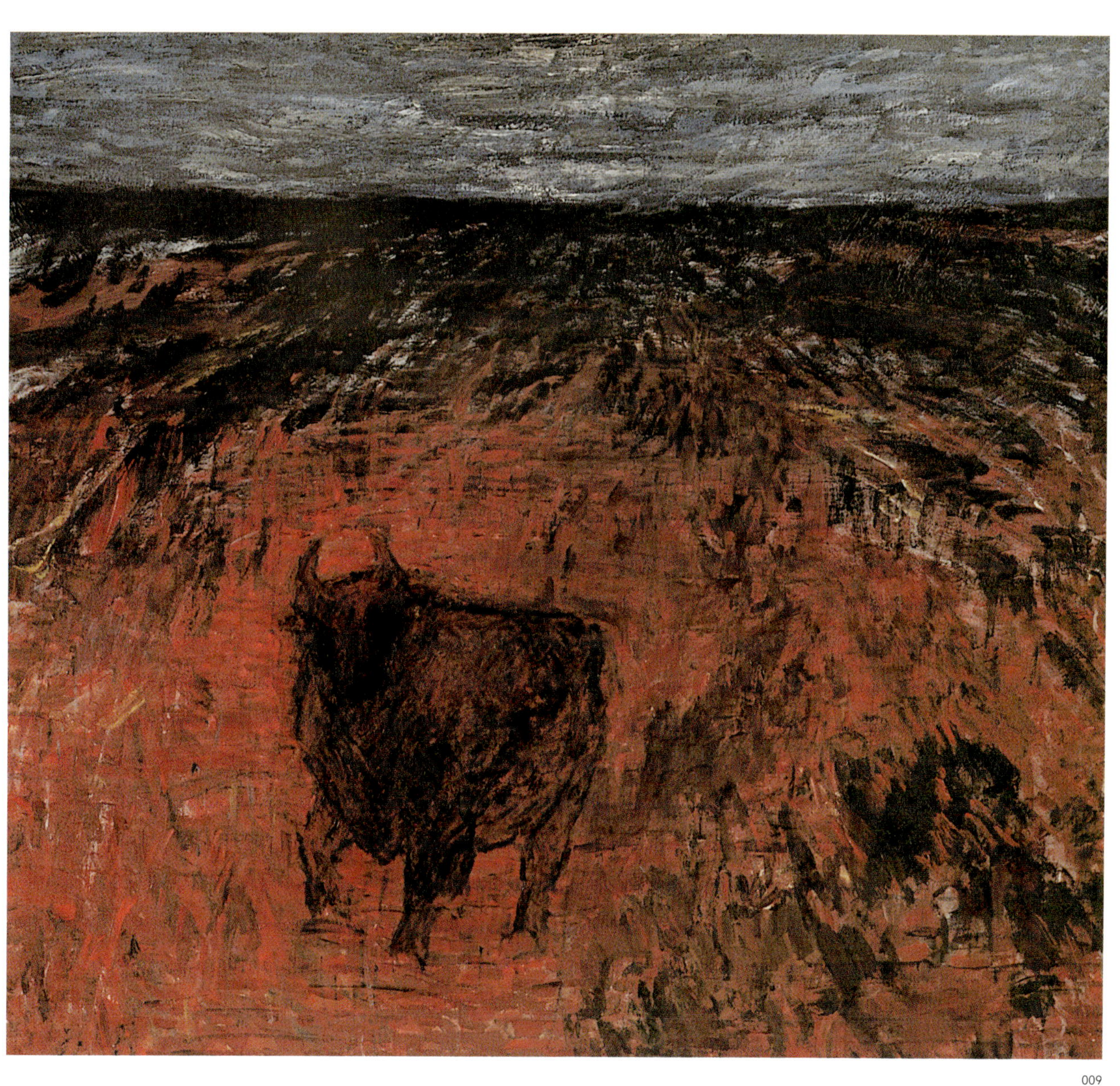

009
Ox Series #3—Red Land, 1983.
Acrylic on canvas,
52 x 62 in.

185

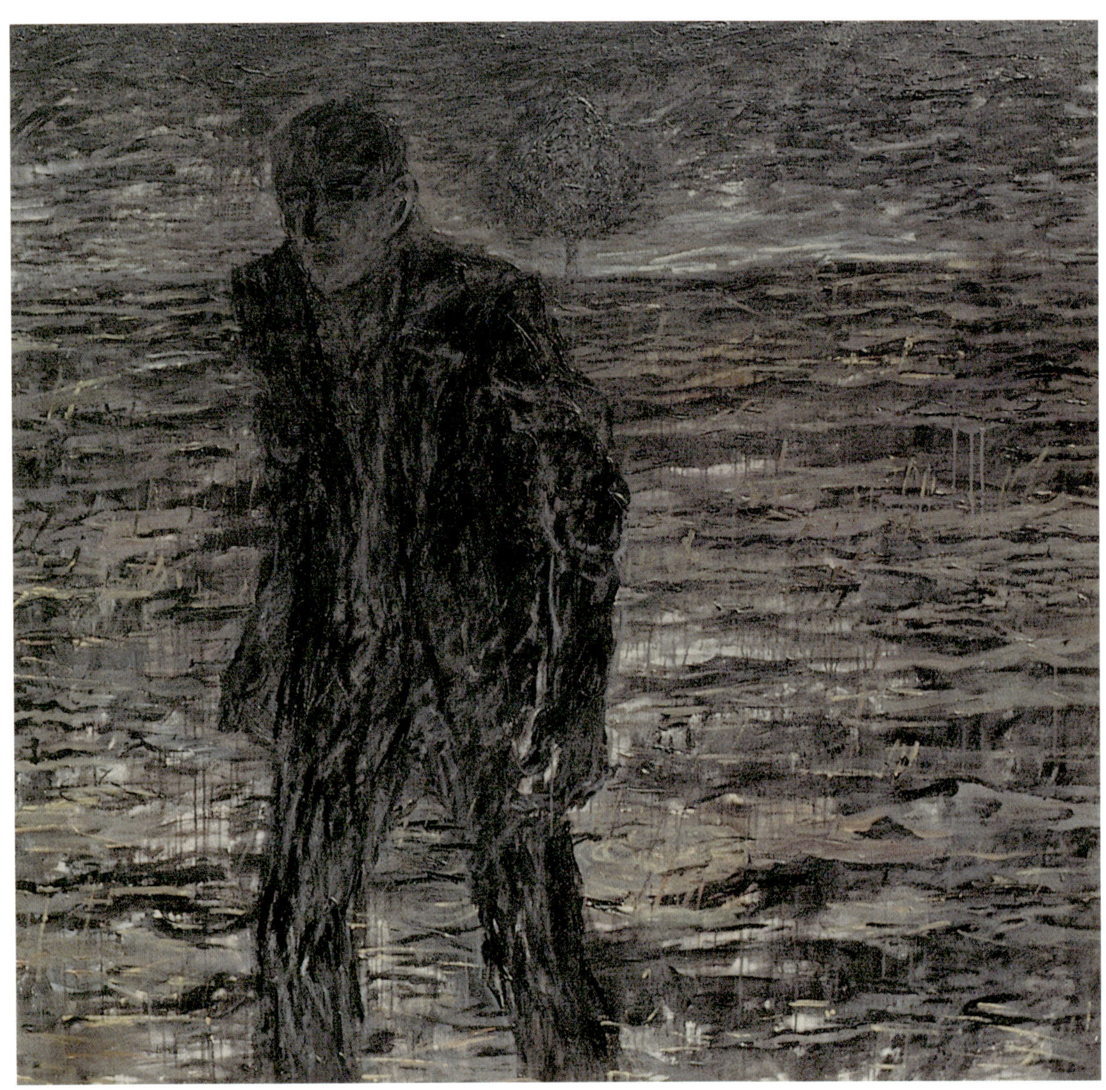

010

010
A Walking Man, 1985.
Acrylic on canvas,
56 x 62 in.

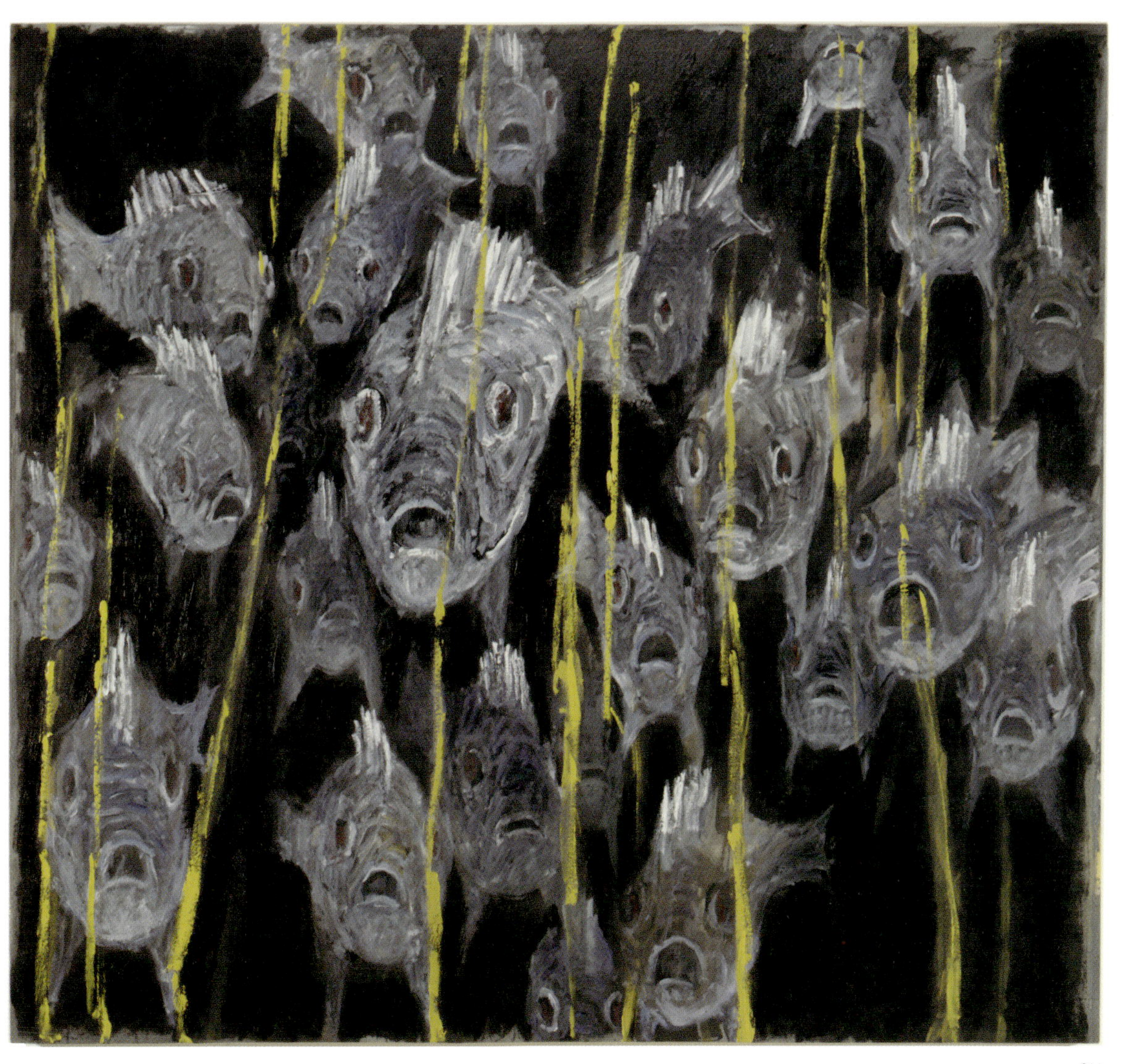

011

011
Fish, 1985.
Acrylic on canvas,
65 x 72 in.

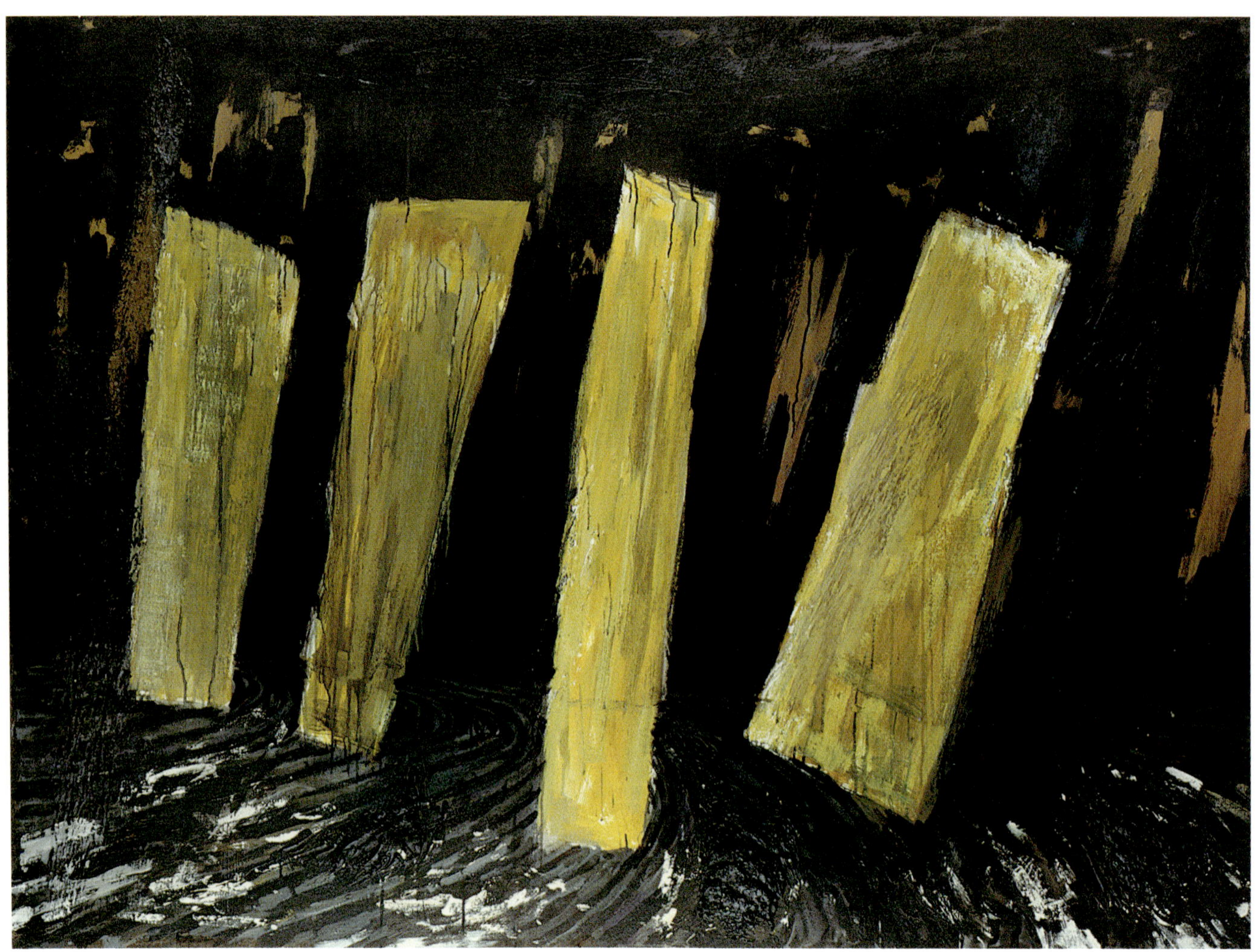

012
Falling—Yellow, 1985.
Acrylic on canvas,
52 x 70 in.

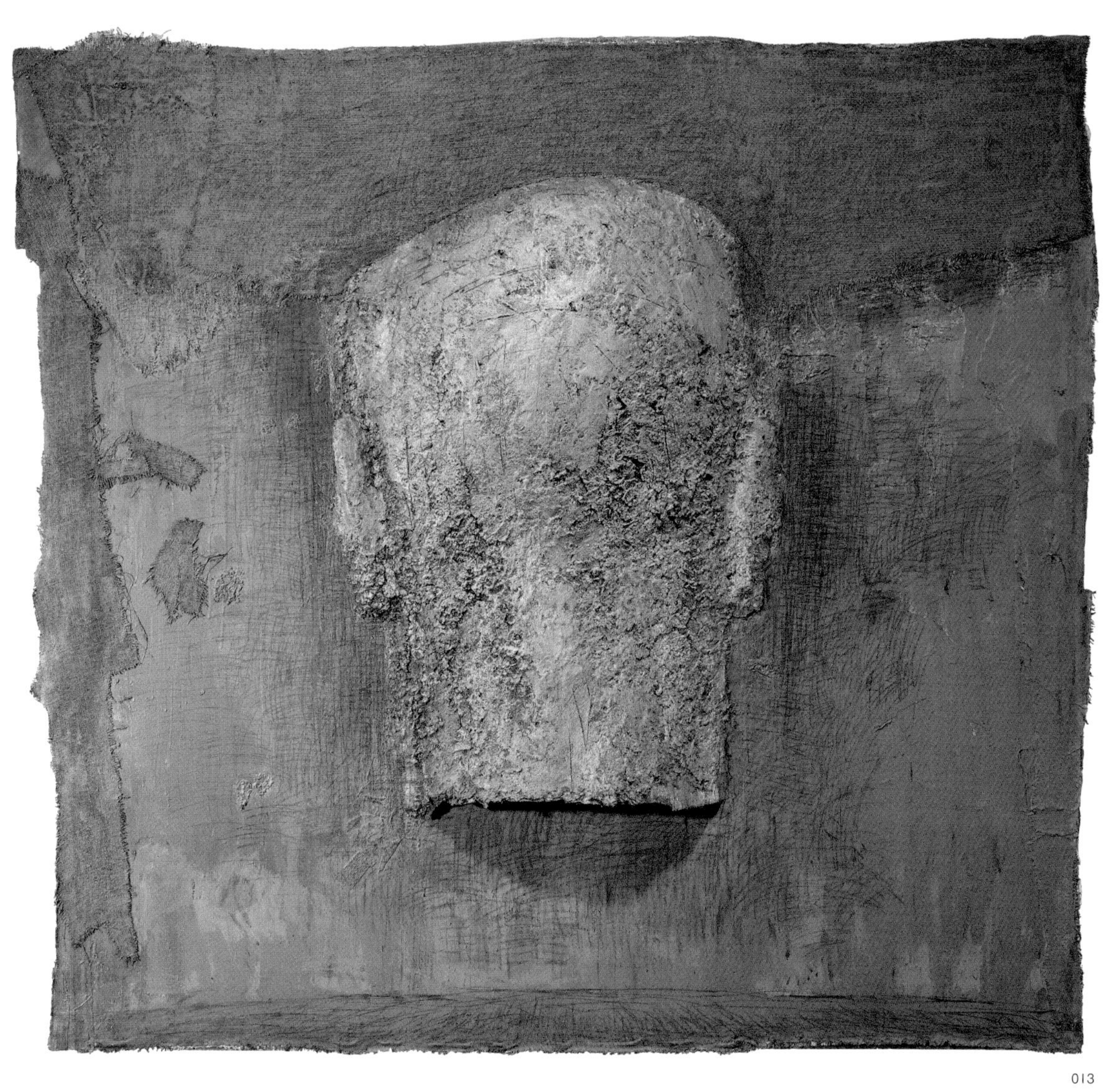

013

013
Self-Portrait (The Back), 1987.
Mixed media on canvas,
73 x 81 in.

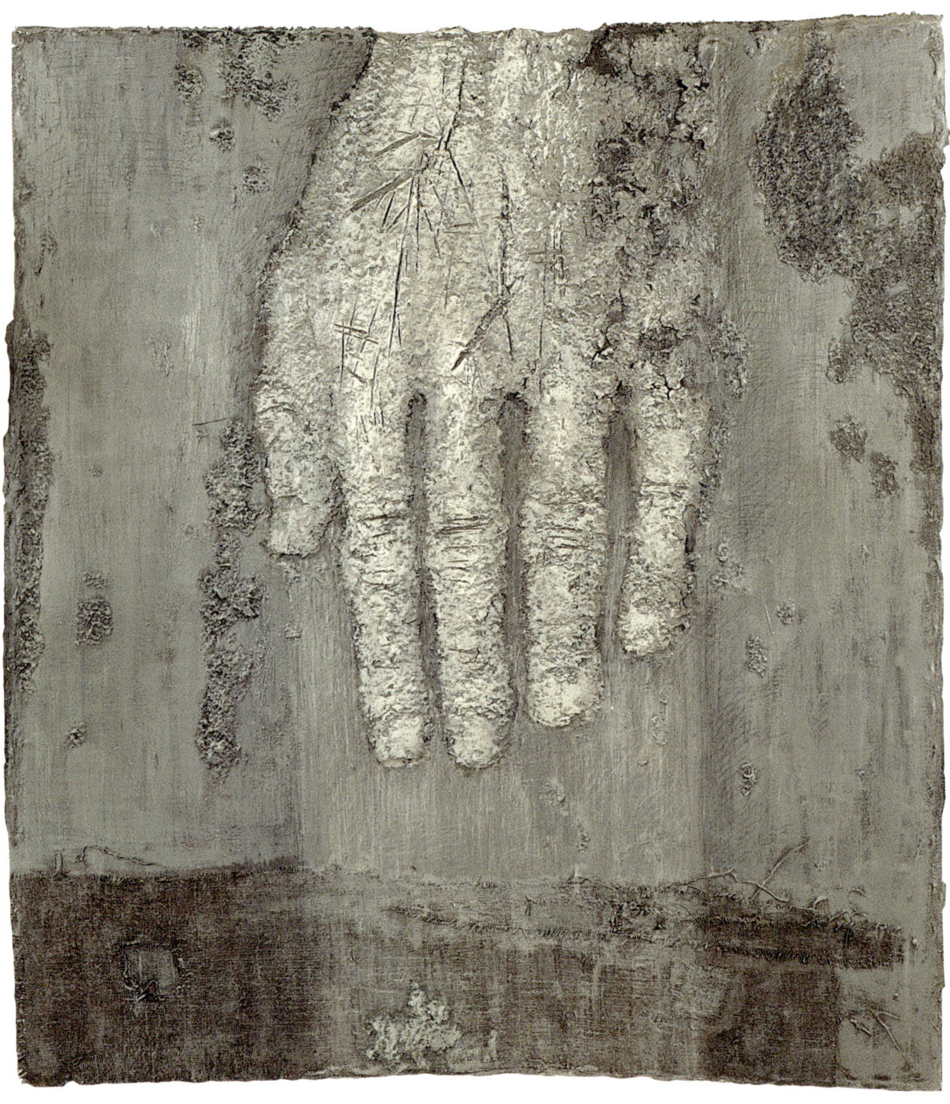

014

014
The Hand #2, 1988.
Acrylic and mixed media on canvas,
65 x 57 in.

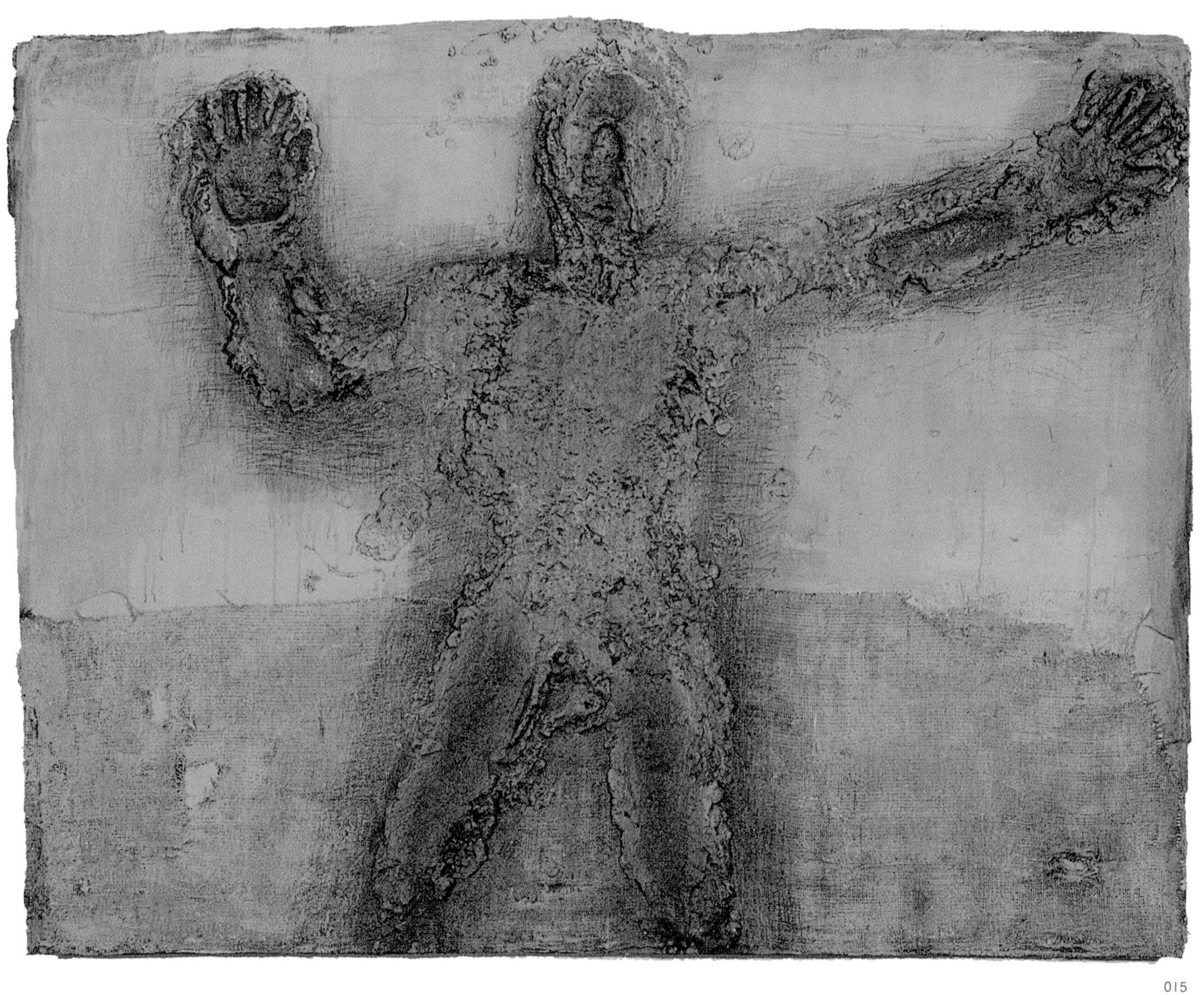

015
The Body, 1988.
Mixed media on canvas,
48 x 60 in.

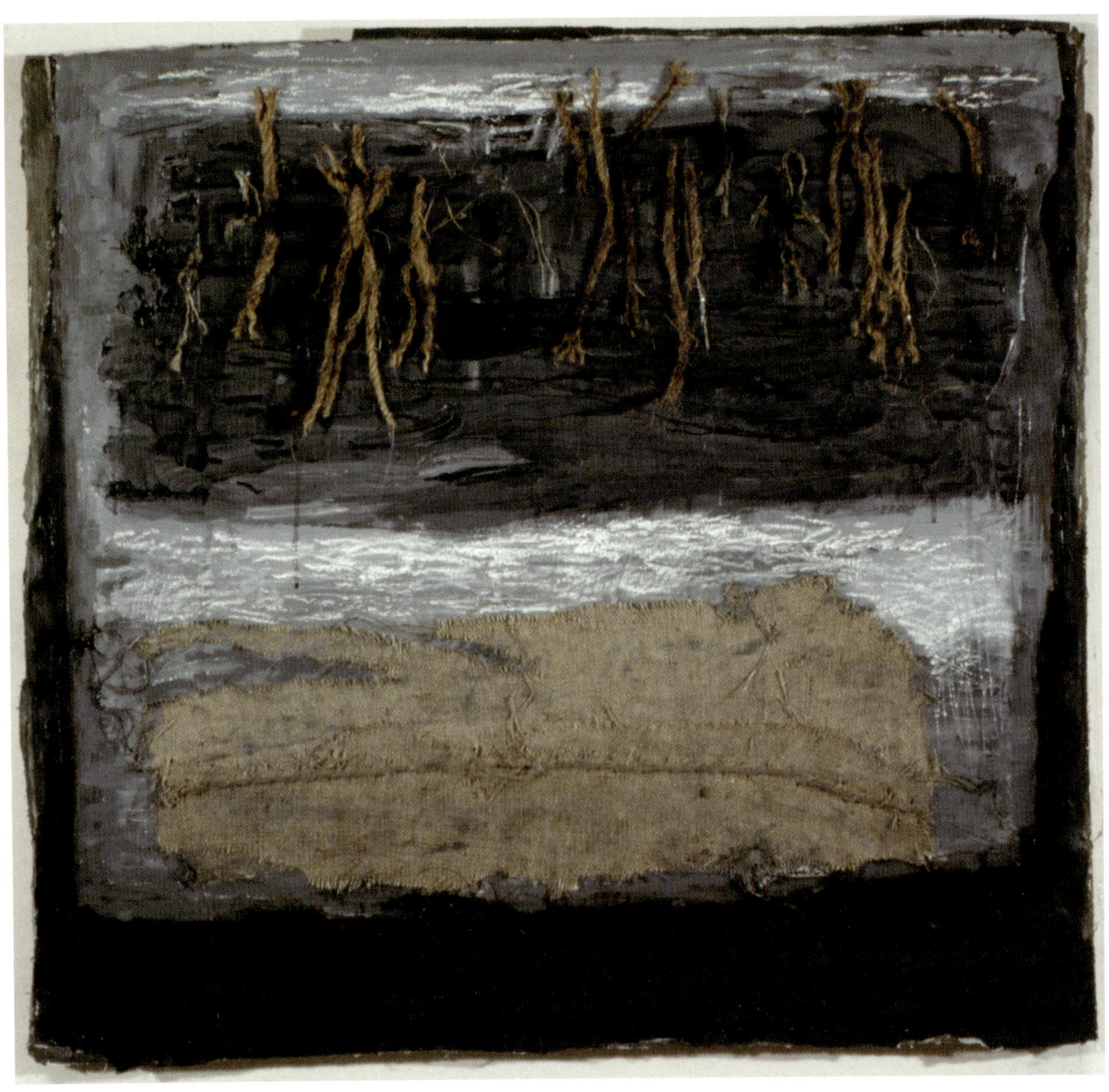

016

016
Sunrise Series #13, 1988.
Mixed media on paper mounted on canvas,
42 x 44 in.

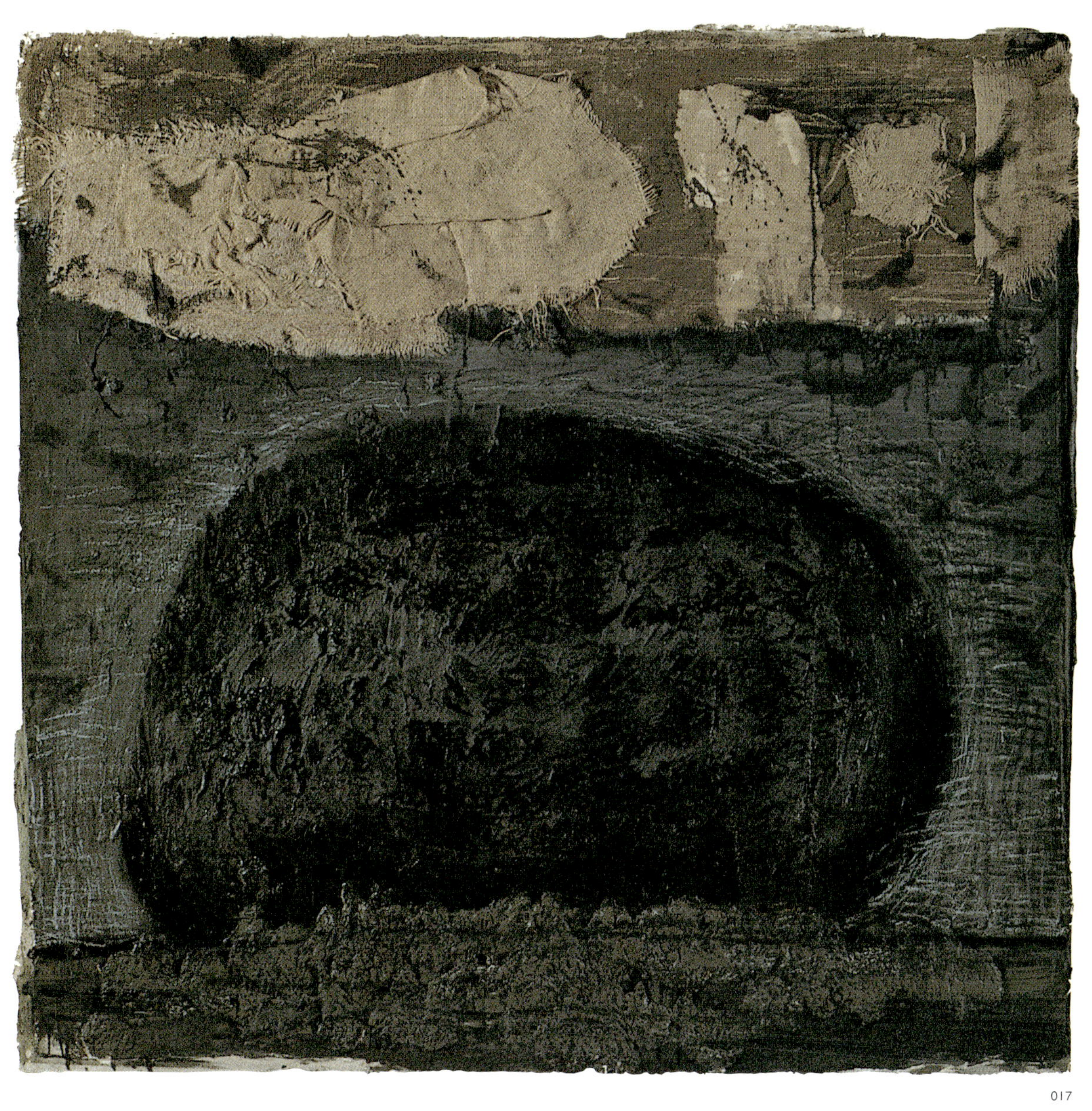

017

017
Sunrise Series #14, 1988.
Mixed media on paper mounted on canvas,
44 x 46 in.

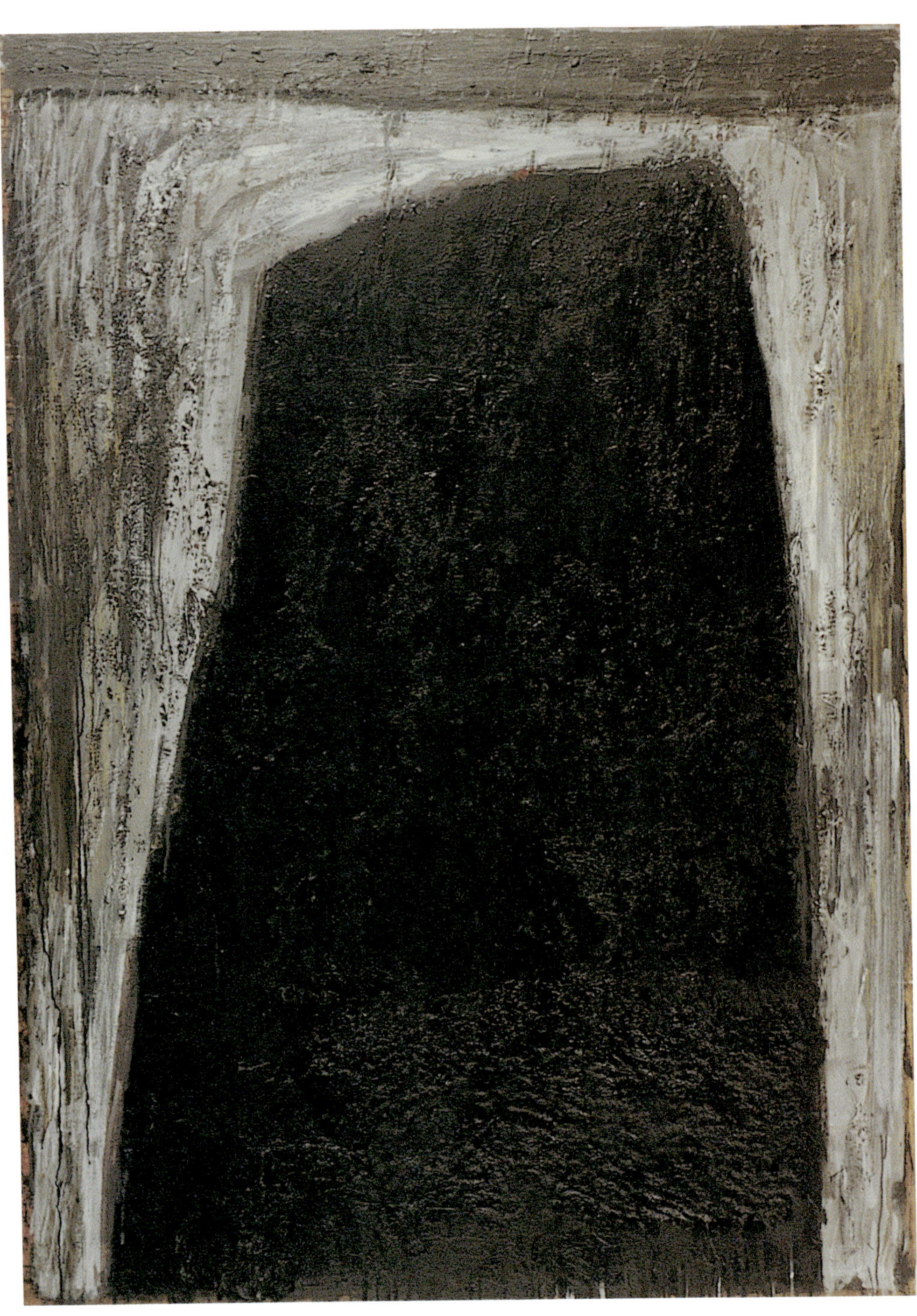

018

018
Shan Shui, 1987.
Acrylic and mixed media on canvas,
70 x 51 in.

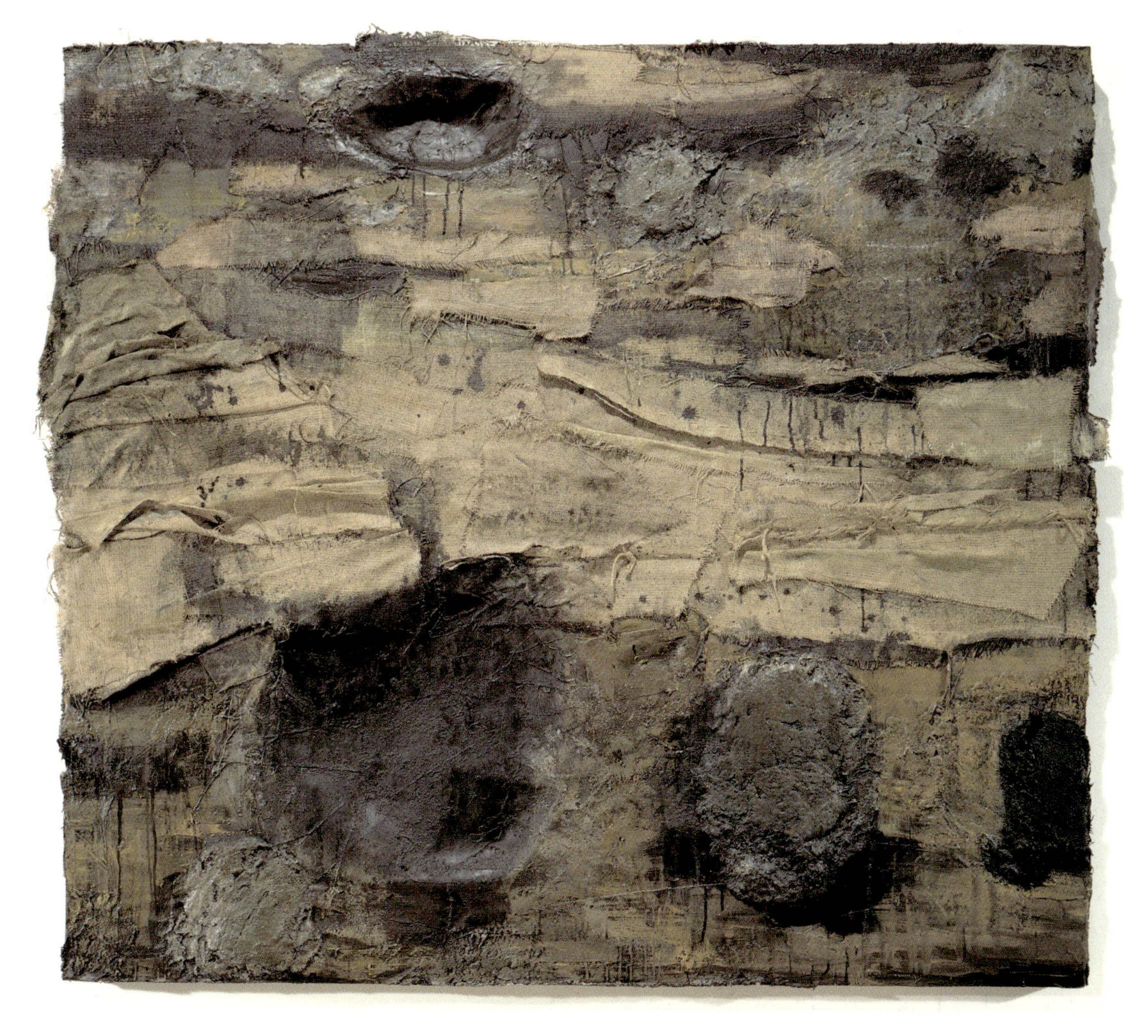

019

019
Landscape #5: Impression Sunrise 117 Years after Monet, 1989.
Mixed media on canvas,
60 x 67 in.

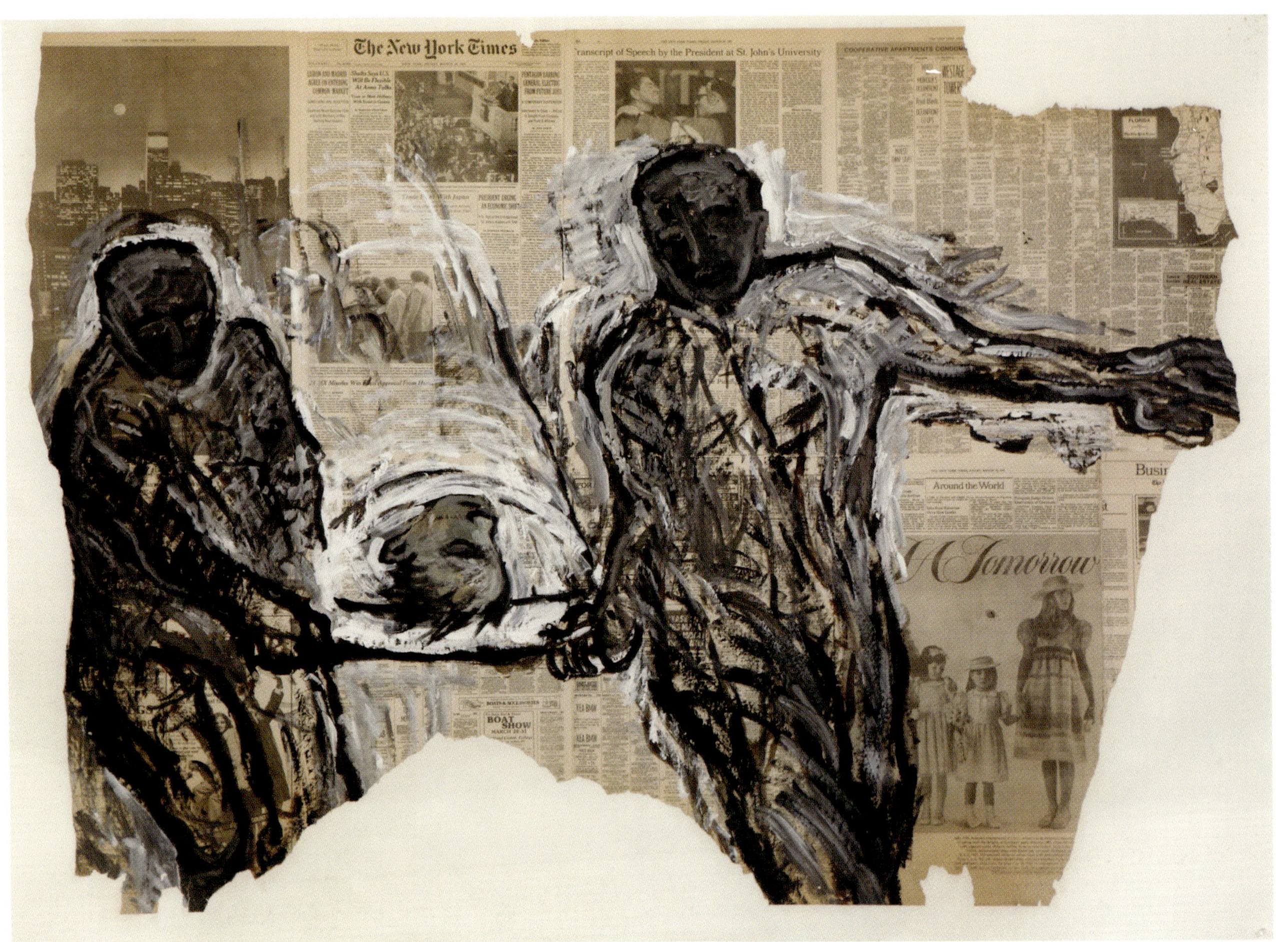

020

020
Untitled (Newspaper Series) #9B, 1985.
Ink and acrylic on newspaper,
43 ¾ x 61 in.

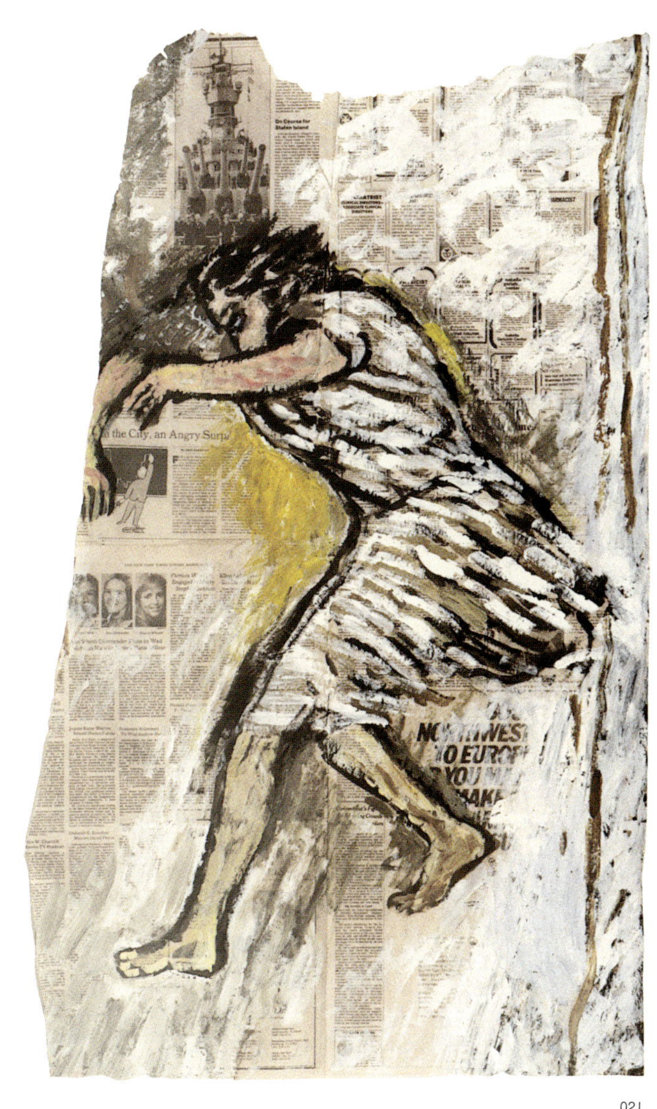

021

021
Untitled (Newspaper Series) #13, 1985.
Ink and acrylic on newspaper,
43 x 27 in.

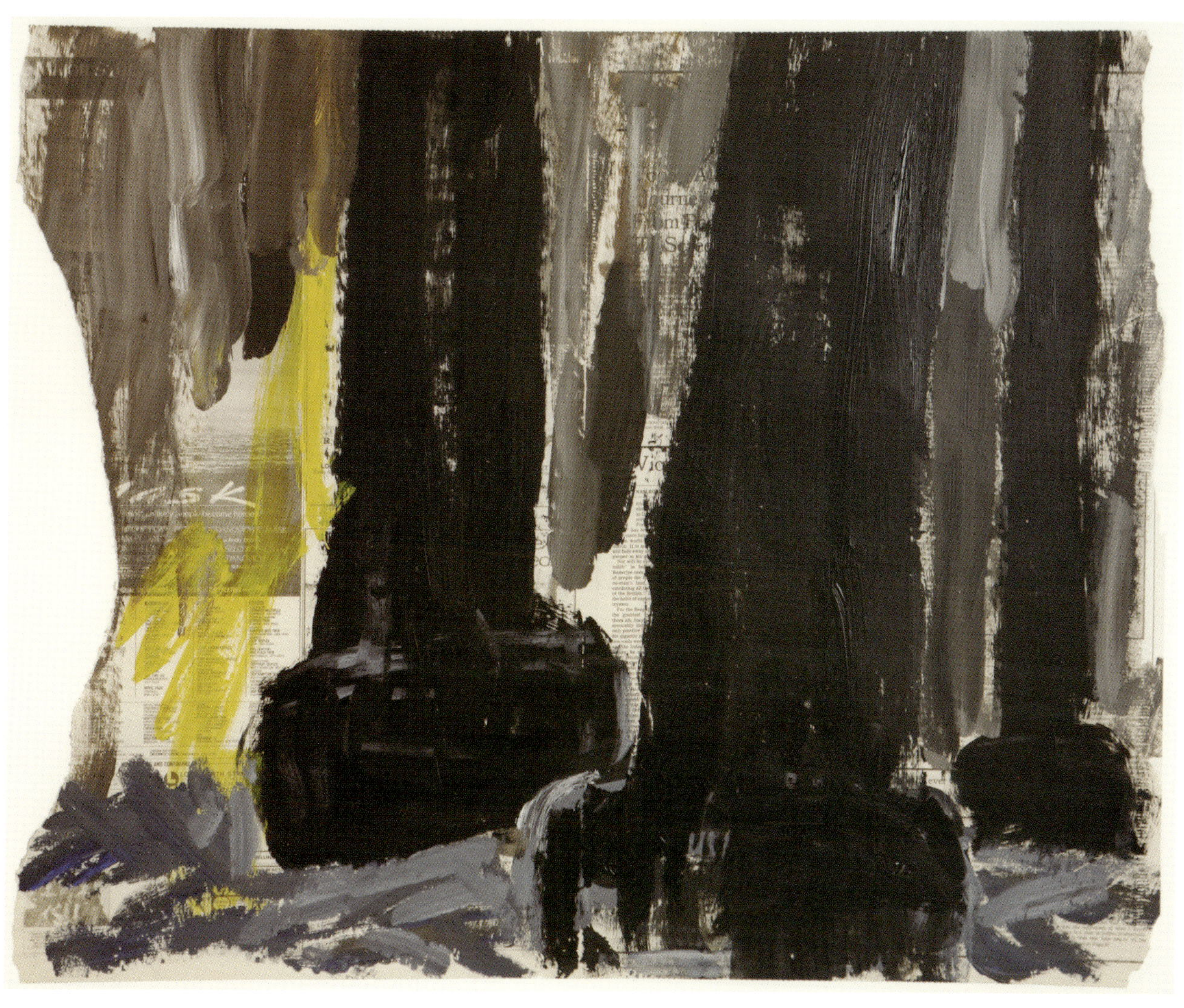

022

022
Untitled (Newspaper Series) #11, 1985.
Ink and acrylic on newspaper,
22 x 27 ½ in.

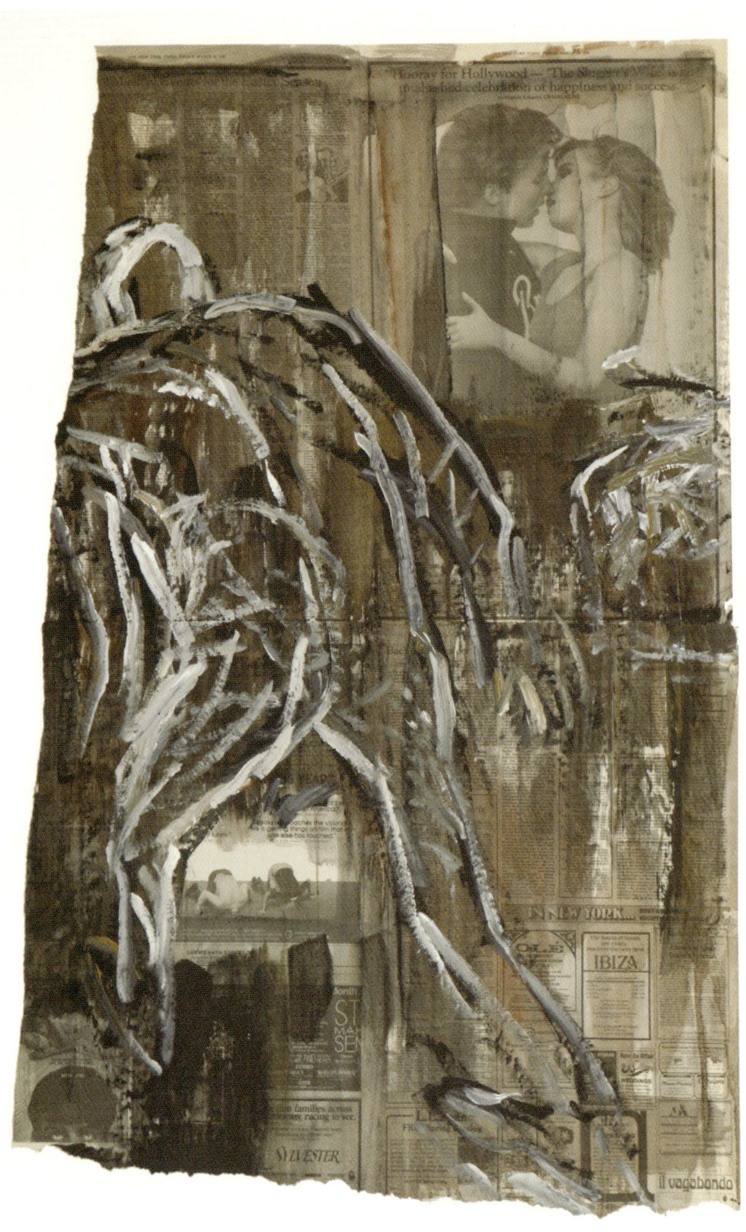

023
Untitled (Newspaper Series) #14, 1985.
Ink and acrylic on newspaper,
42 ½ x 27 in.

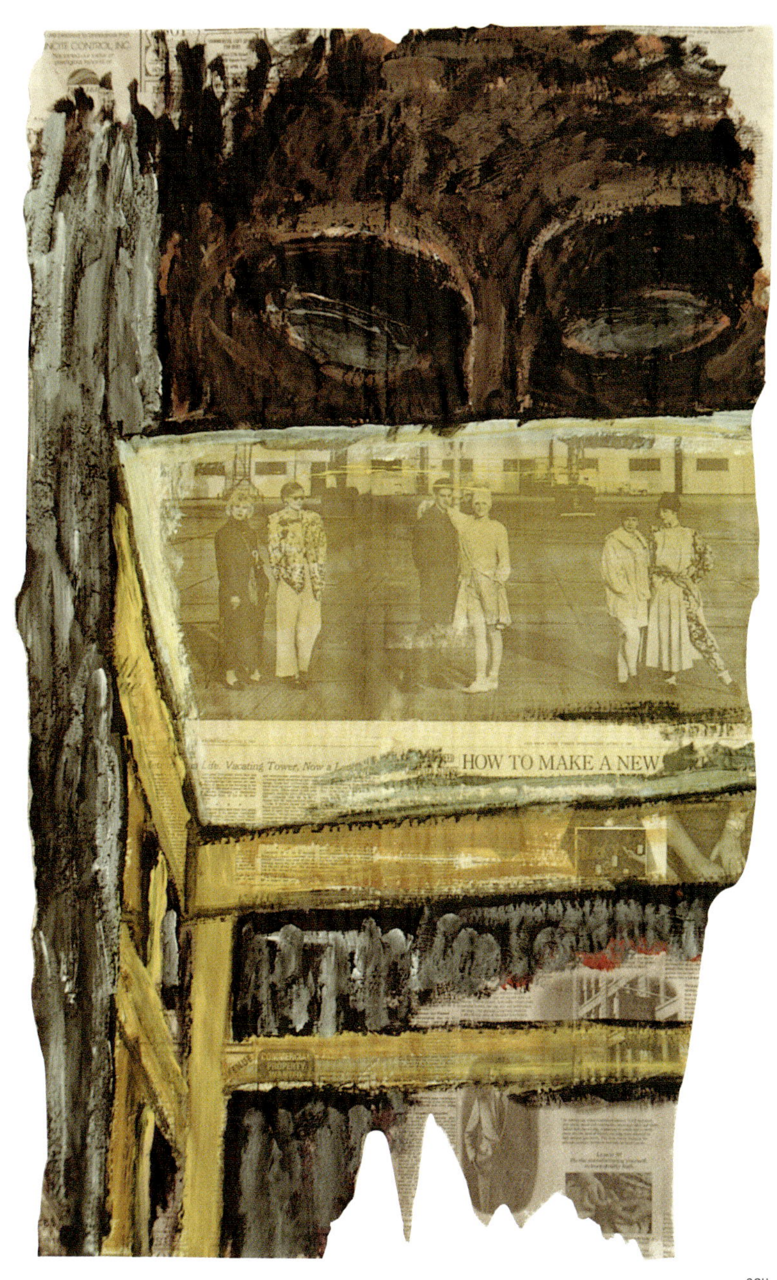

024

024
Untitled (Newspaper Series) #6, 1985.
Ink and acrylic on newspaper,
42 x 28 in.

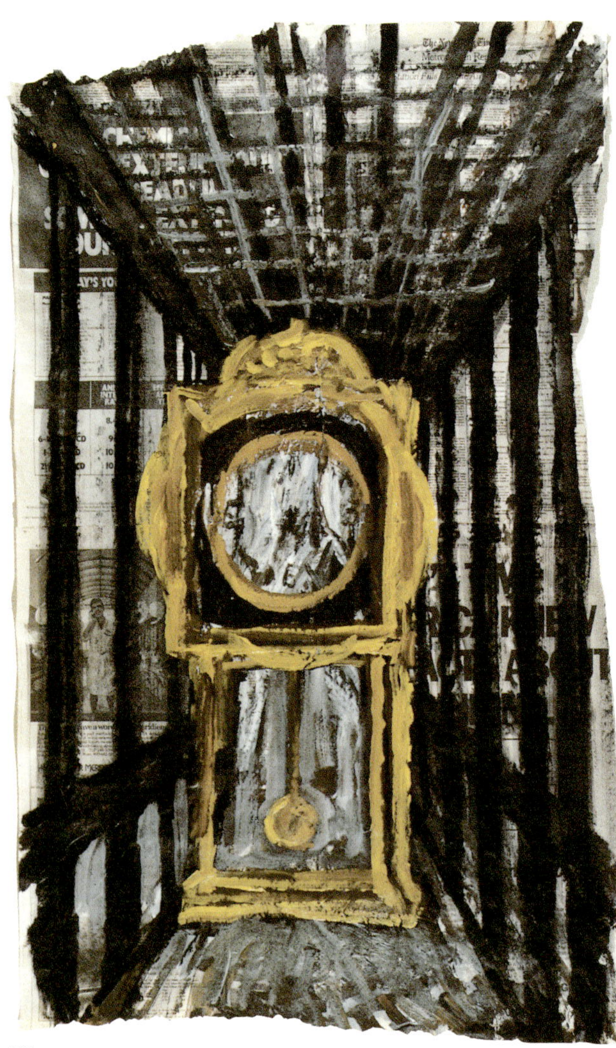

025
Untitled (Newspaper Series) #5, 1985.
Ink and acrylic on newspaper,
42 x 27 in.

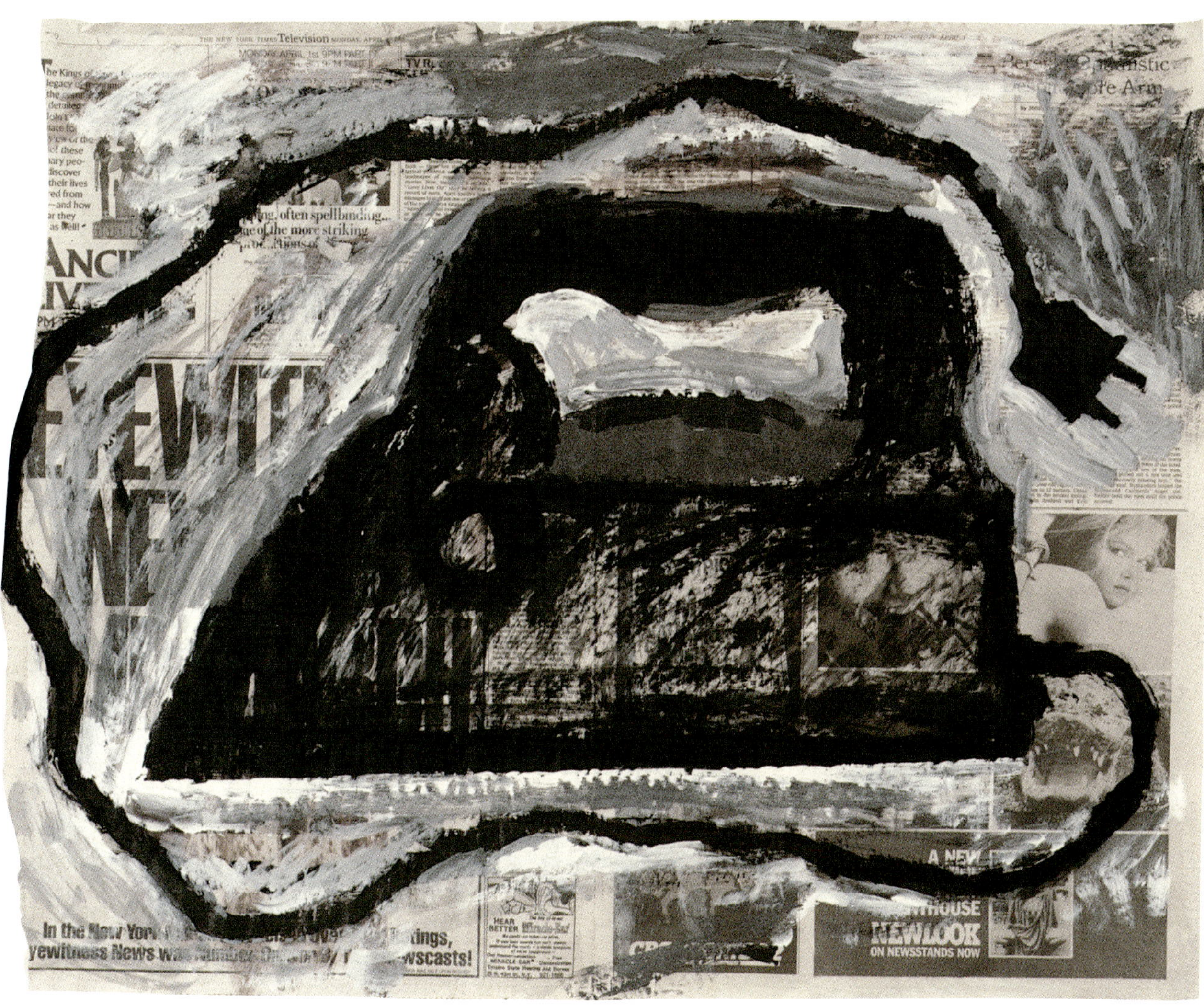

026
Untitled (Newspaper Series) #10, 1985.
Ink and acrylic on newspaper,
23 x 27 in.

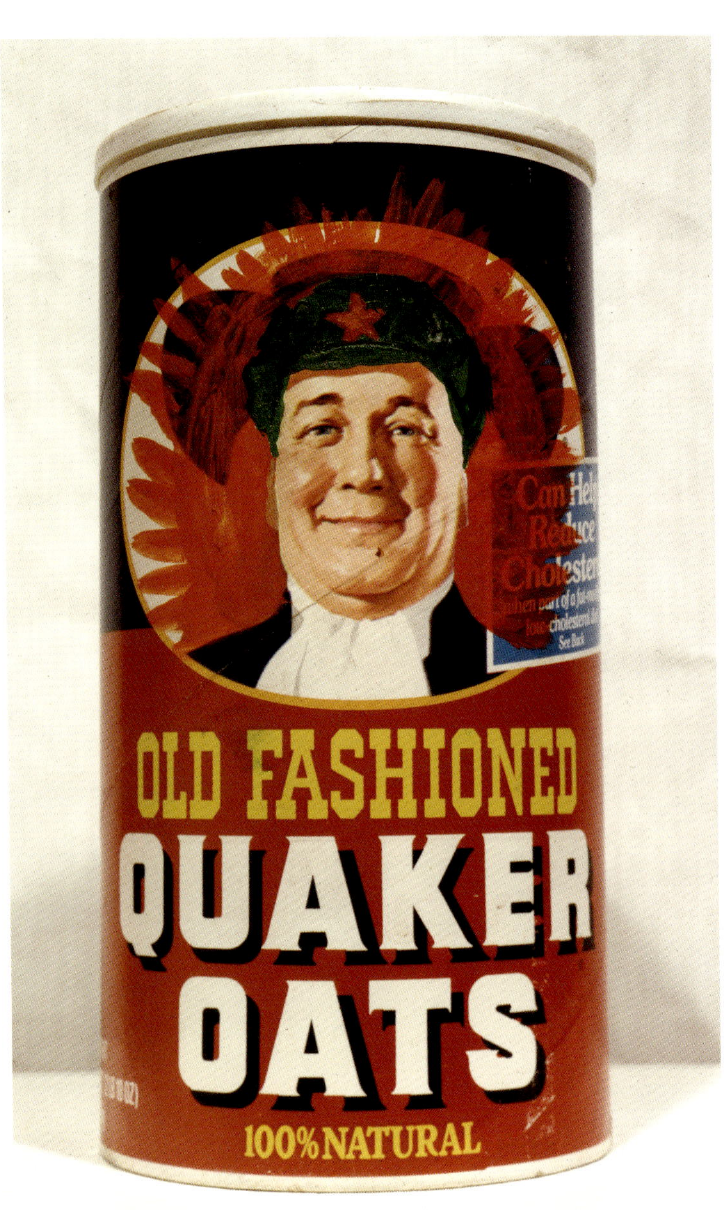

027

027
Quaker Oats Mao, 1987.
From the series "Long Live Chairman Mao,"
Acrylic on Quaker Oats box,
9 ¾ (H) x 5 (D) in.

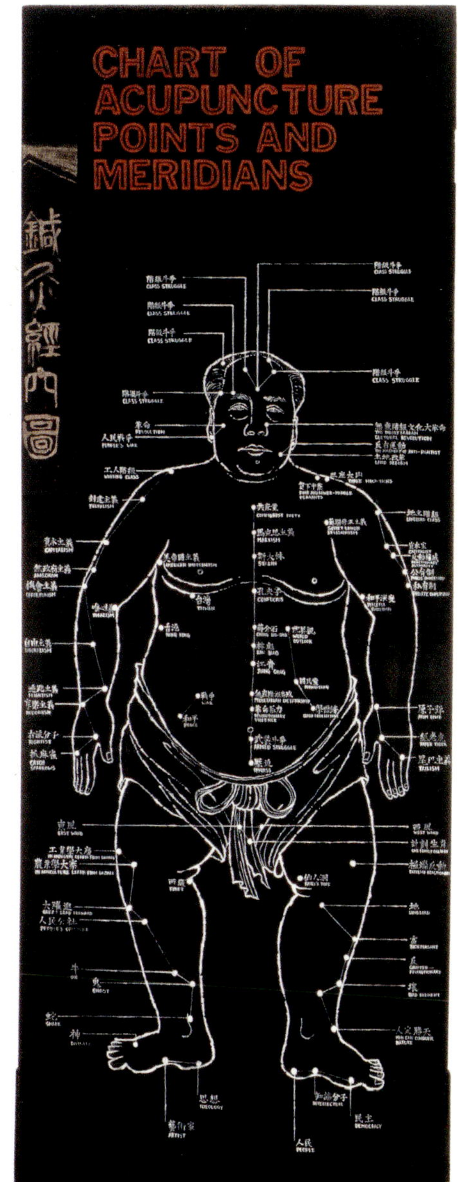

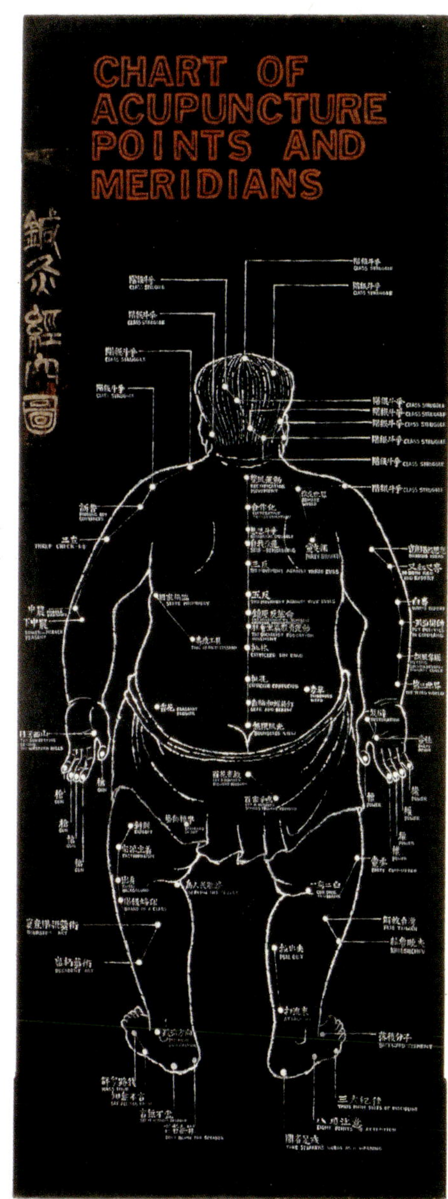

028
Bilingual Chart of Acupuncture Points and Meridians, 1990.
Acrylic and ink on panel (double sided,)
79 ¼ x 29 ¾ x 1 ¼ in.

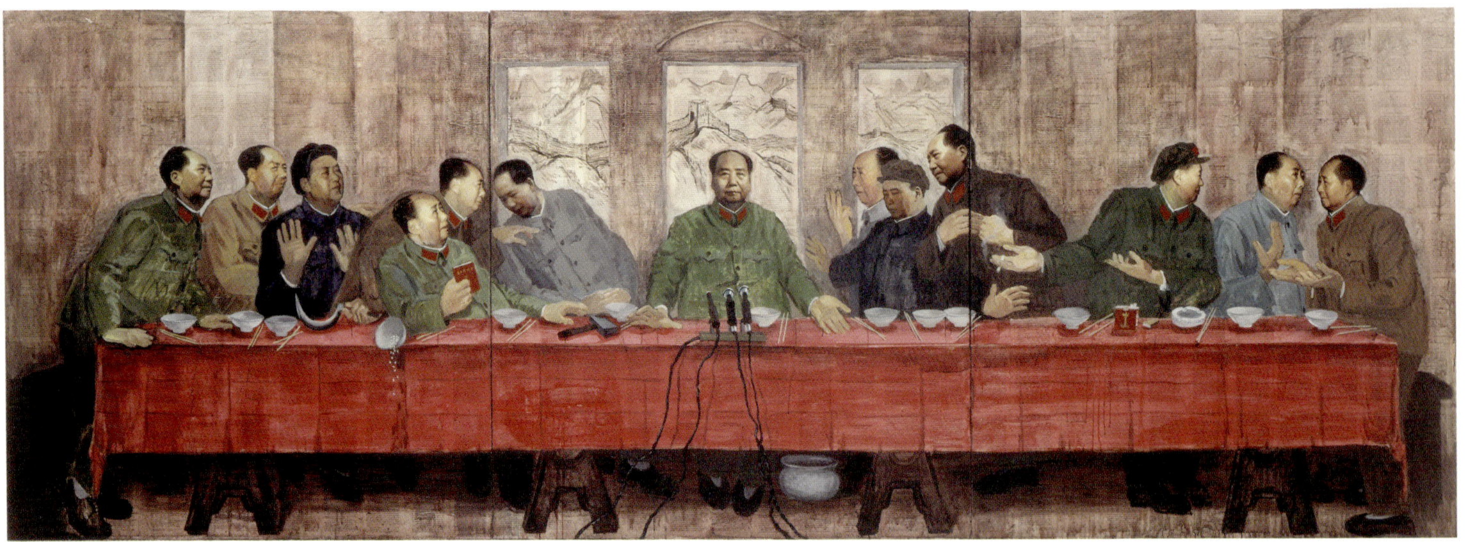

029

029
Last Banquet, 1989.
Laser prints, pages from the Little Red Book, and acrylic on canvas,
60 x 128 in.

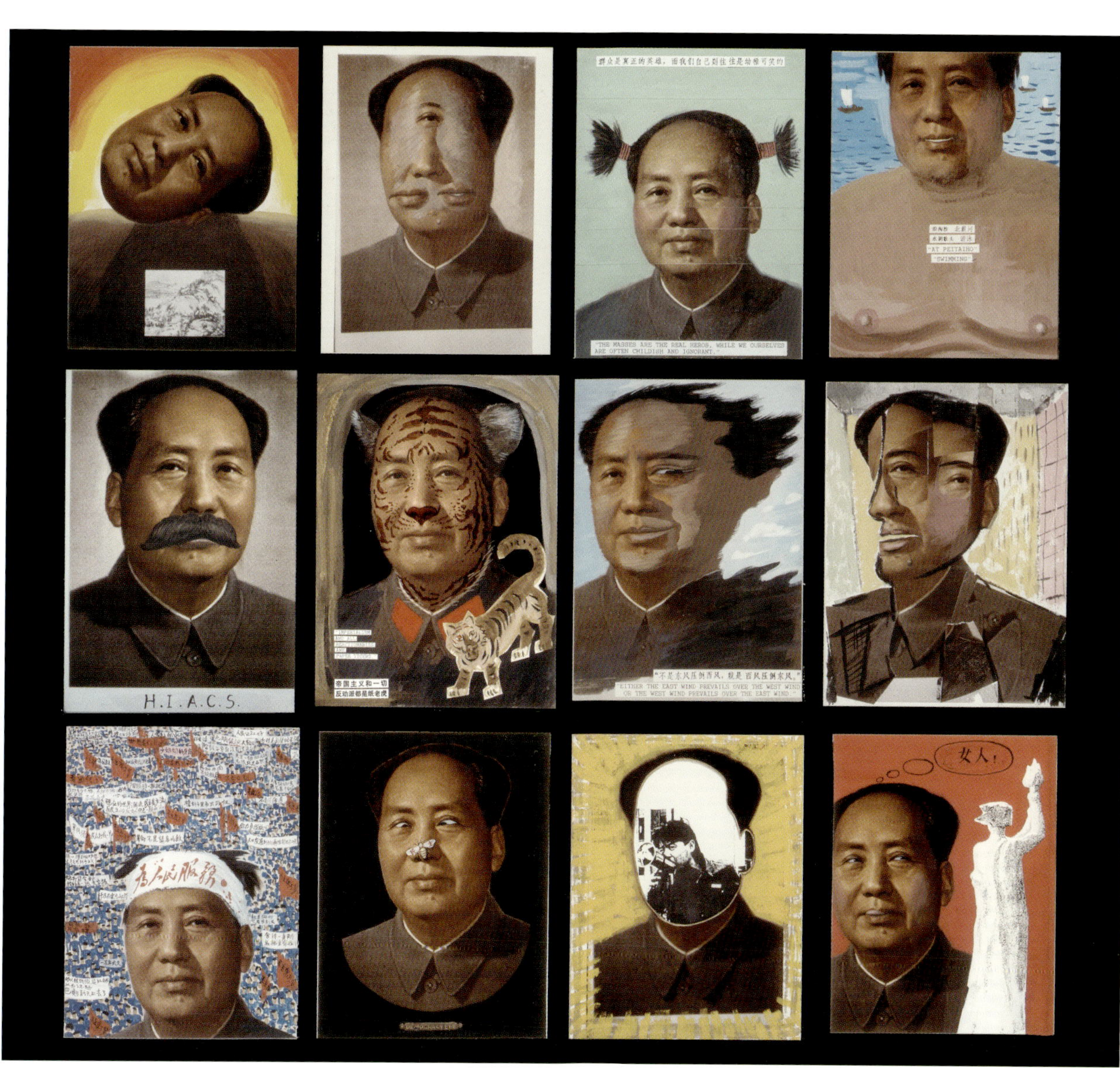

030
Chairmen Mao, 1989.
Photo collage and acrylic on paper,
11 x 8 ½ in. each.

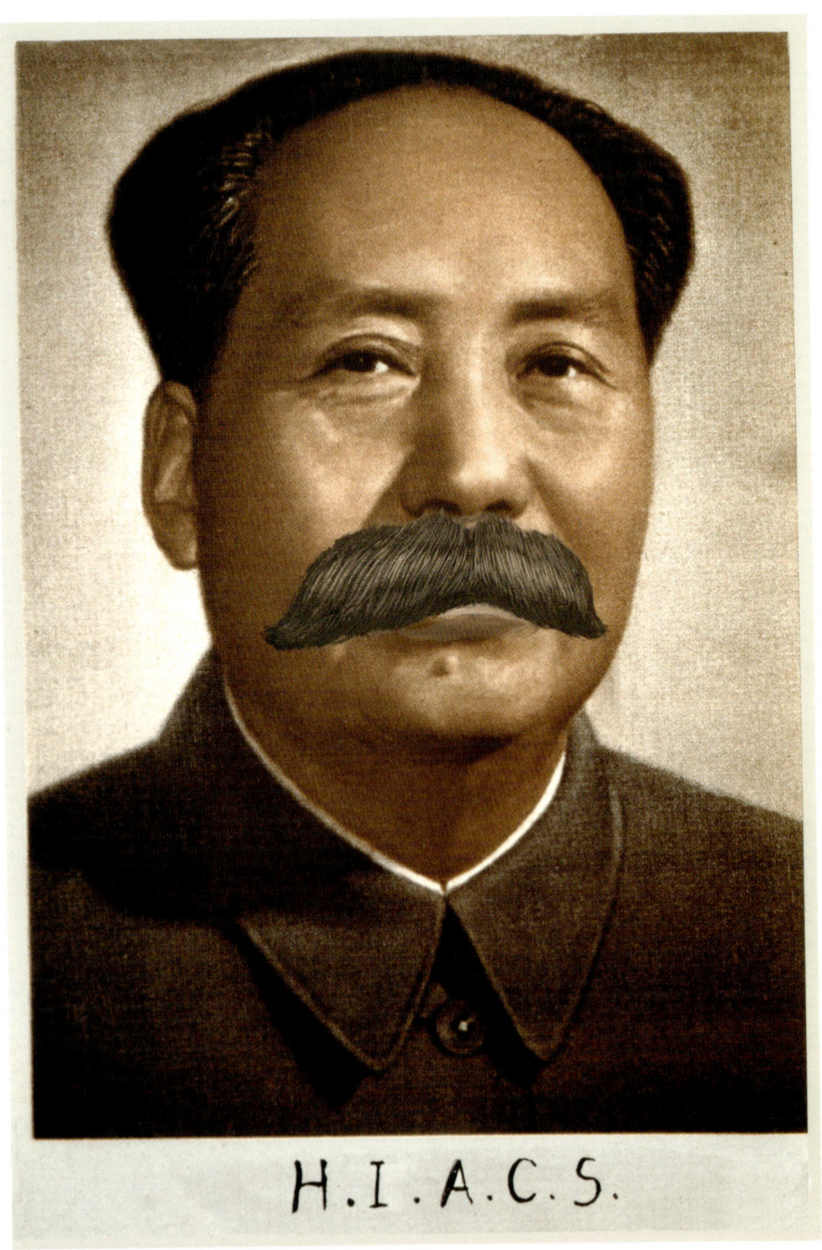

031

031

H. I. A. C. S. (He Is a Chinese Stalin) (detail from *Chairmen Mao*), 1989.

Photo collage and acrylic on paper,

11 x 8 ½ in.

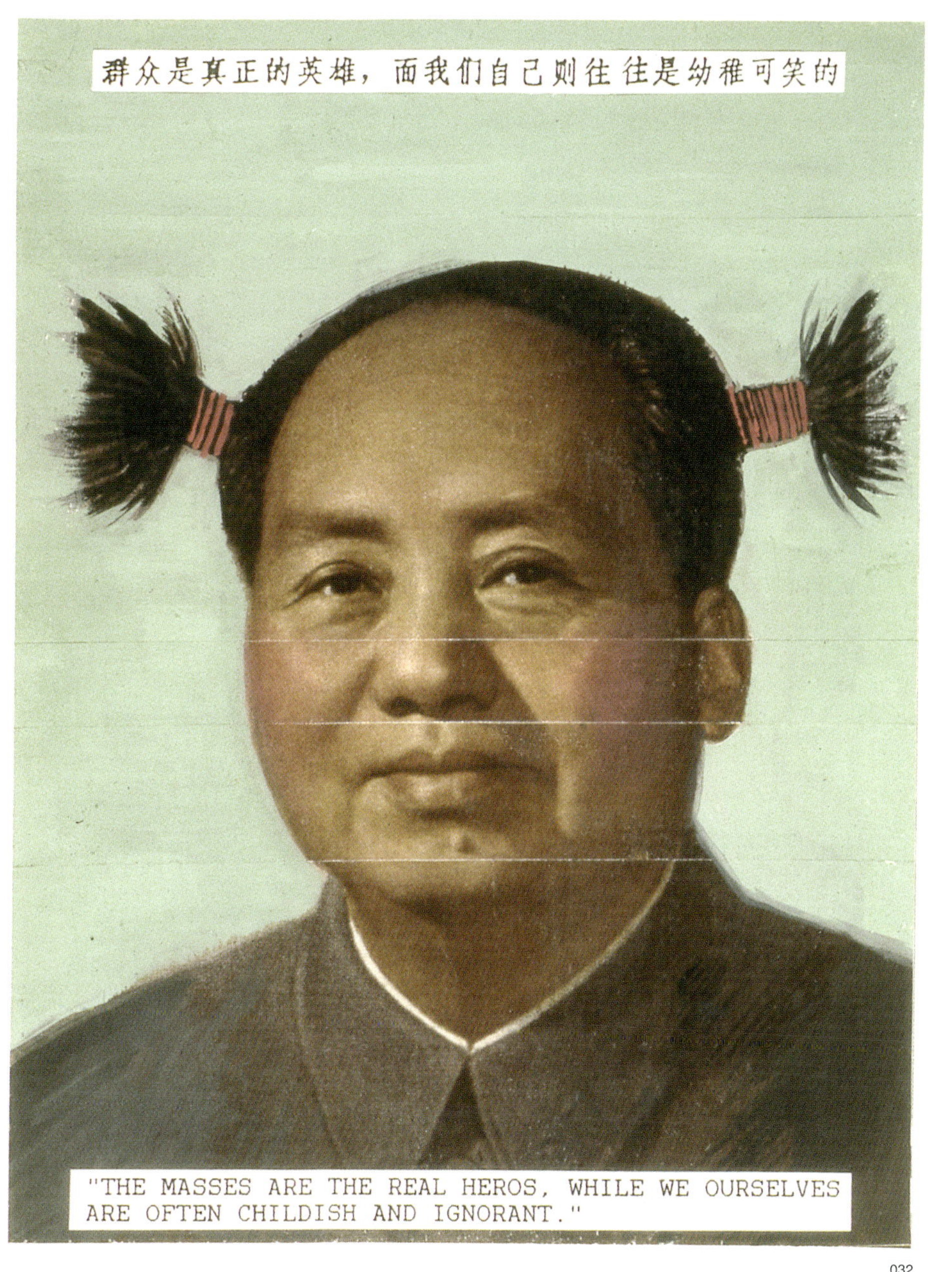

032

032
Mao with Pigtails (detail from *Chairmen Mao*), 1989.
Photo collage and acrylic on paper,
11 x 8 ½ in.

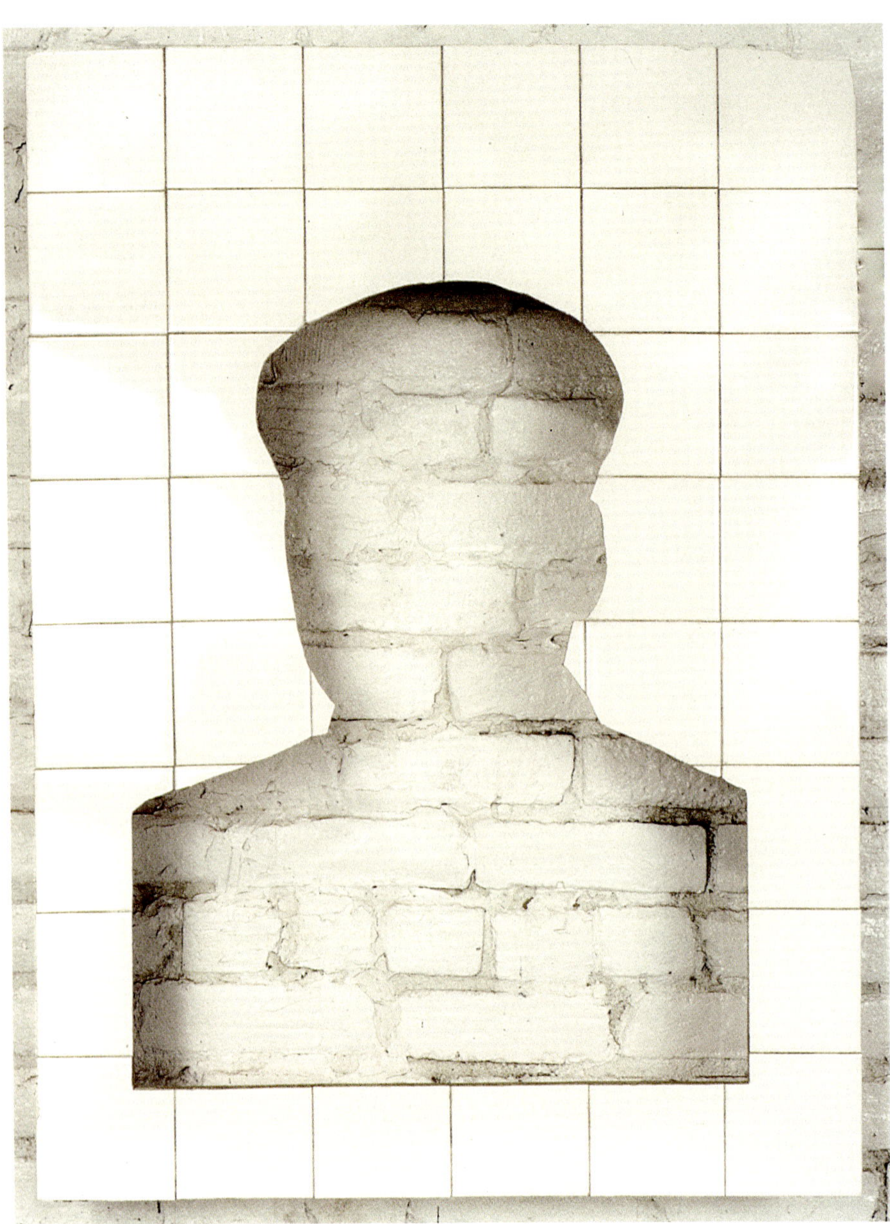

033

033
Tile Mao, 1992.
Tile and wood,
34 ½ x 26 in.

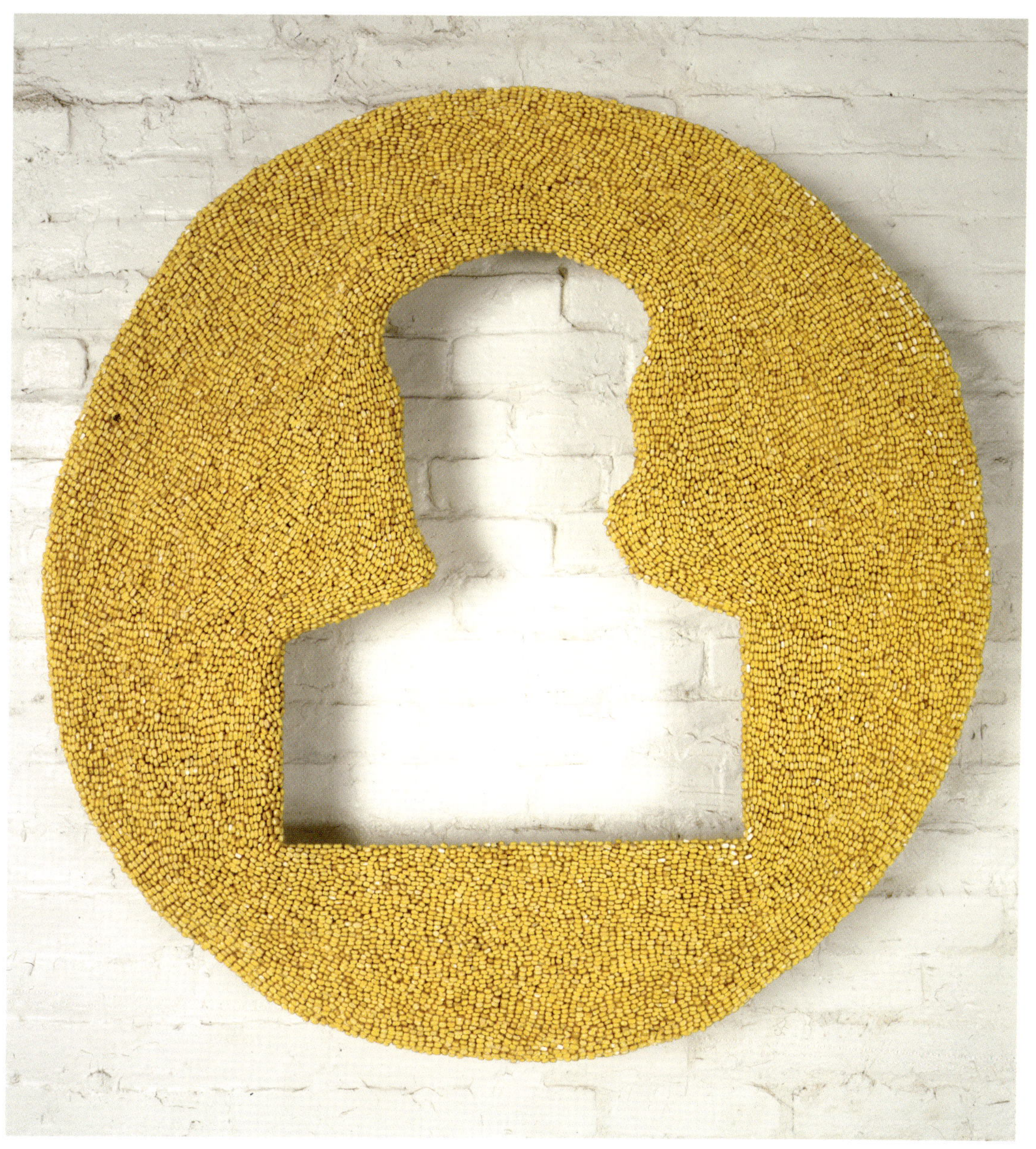

034
Corn Mao, 1992.
Corn on plywood,
39 in. diameter

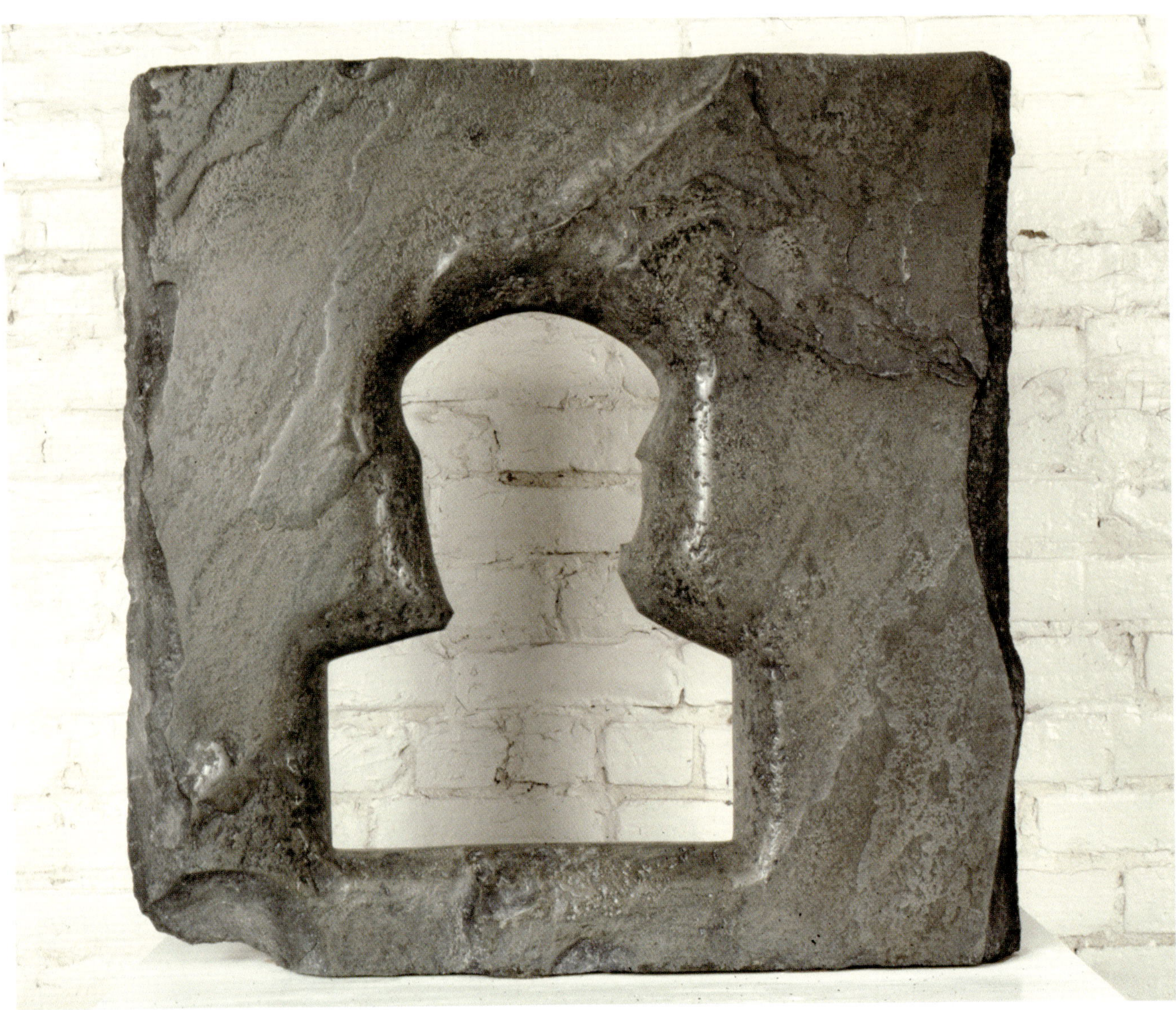

035
Stone Mao, 1992.
Stone,
25 ½ x 25 in.

035

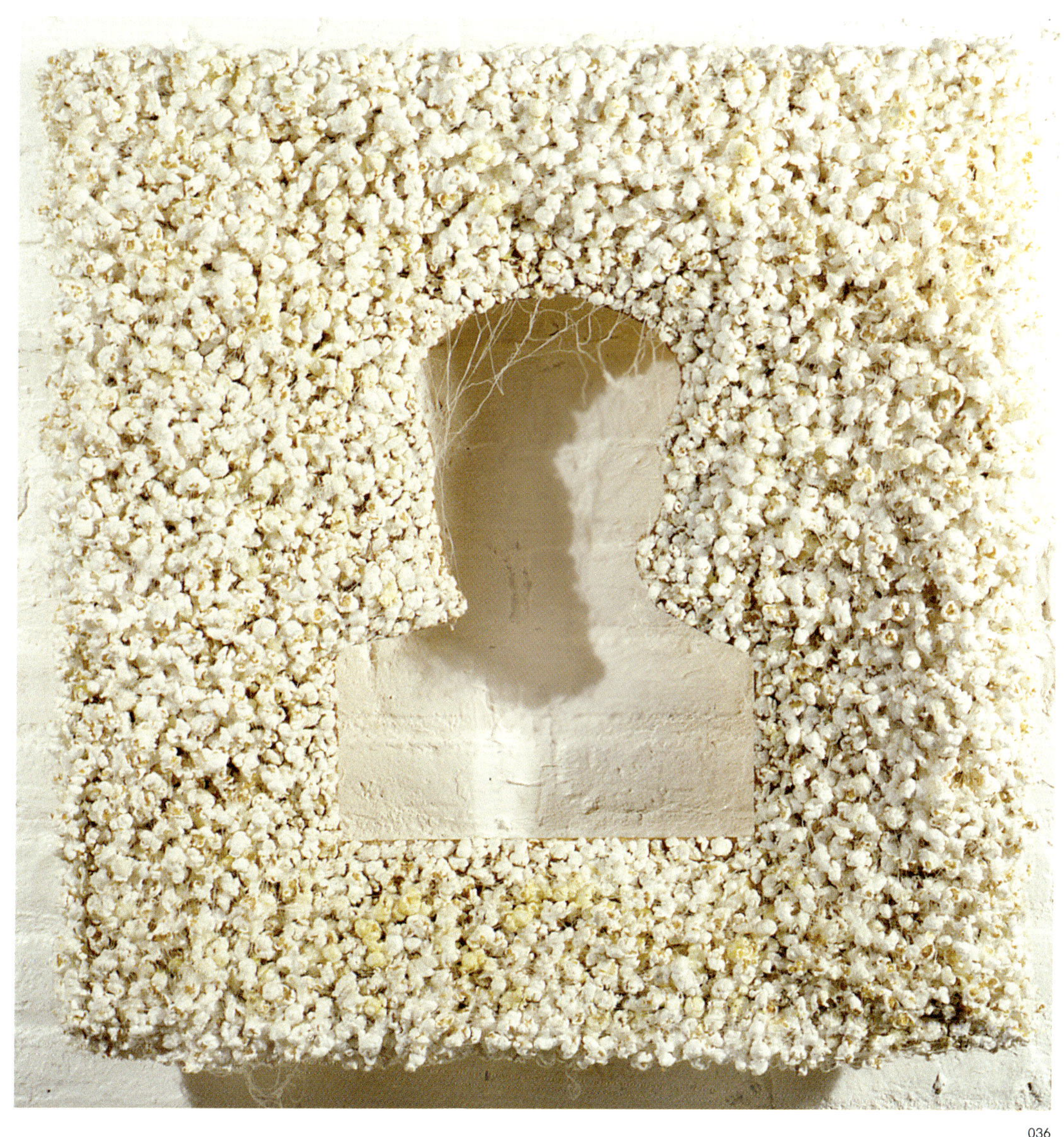

036
Popcorn Mao, 1995.
Popcorn on plywood,
28 x 28 in.

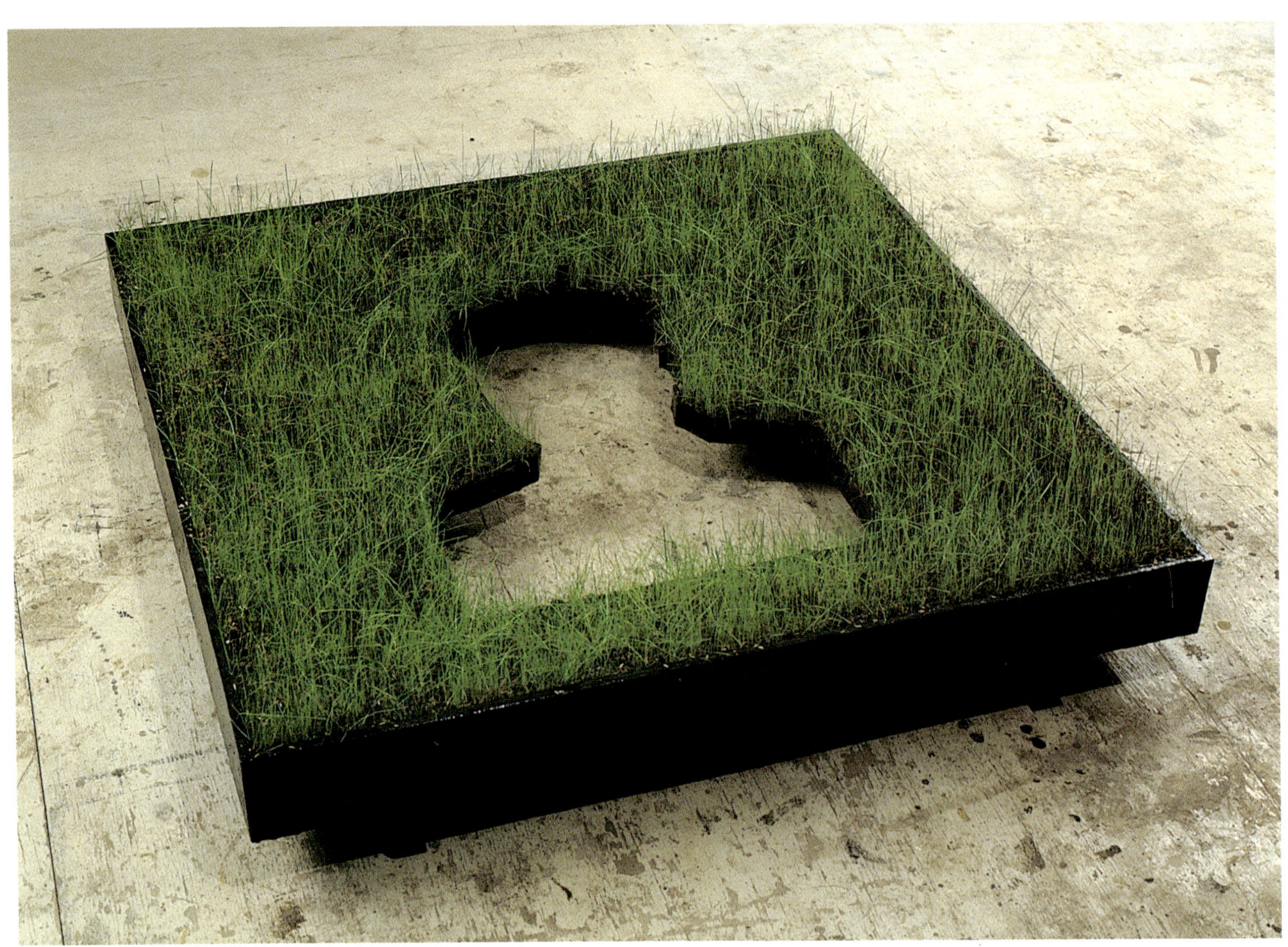

037

037
Grass Mao, 1992.
Grass, soil, and wood,
41 x 40 x 5 ½ in.

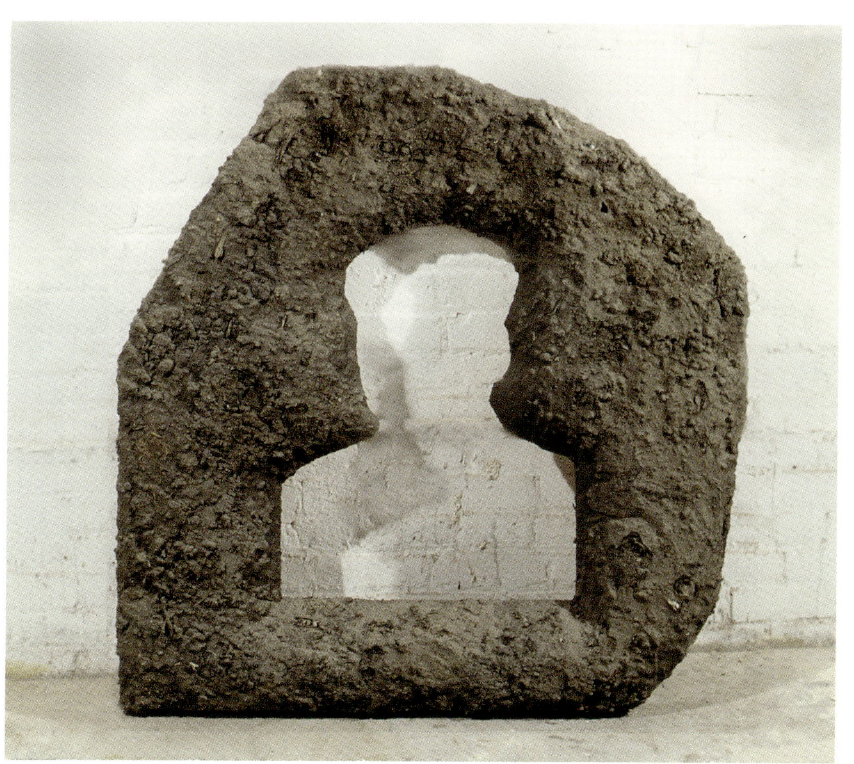

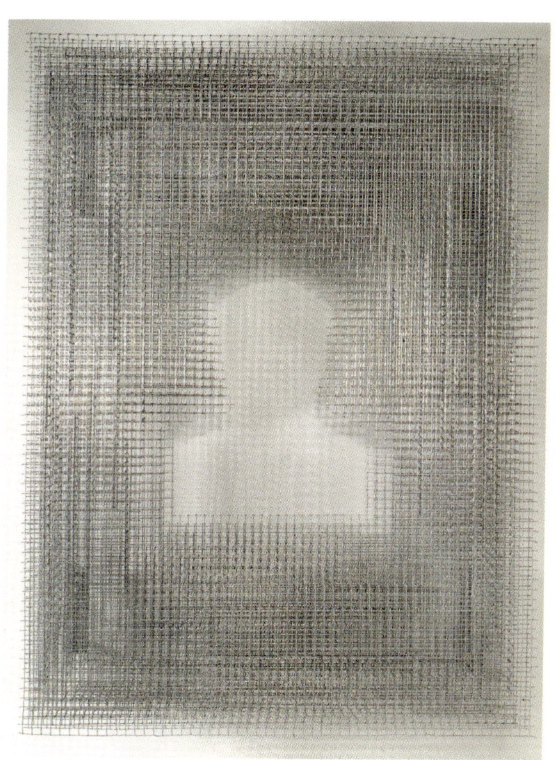

038-a

038-b

038-a
Dirt Mao, 1992.
dirt and wood
41.5 x 38 in.

038-b
Mesh Mao, 1992.
Wire mesh,
36 x 27 ½ x 8 ½ in.

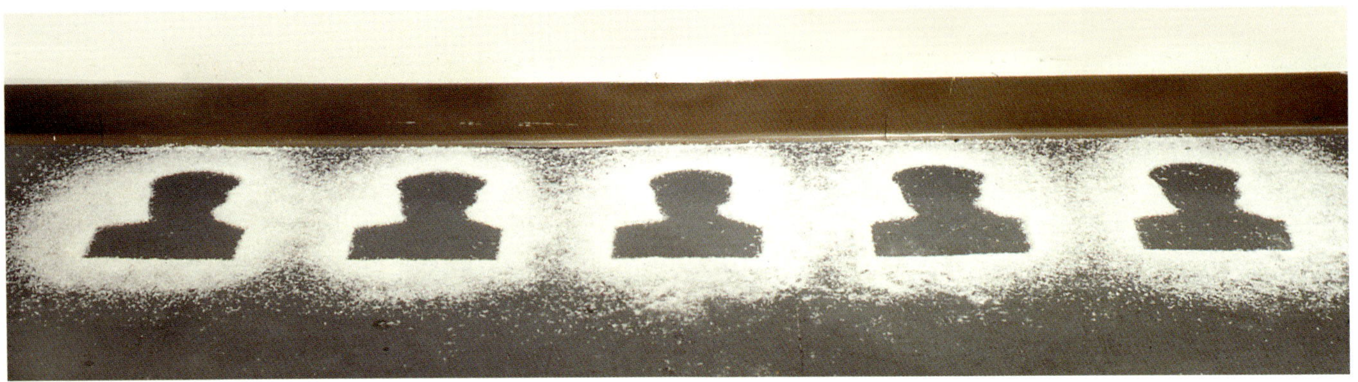

039
M.S.G. Mao, 1995.
Monosodium glutamate on floor,
Dimensions variable.

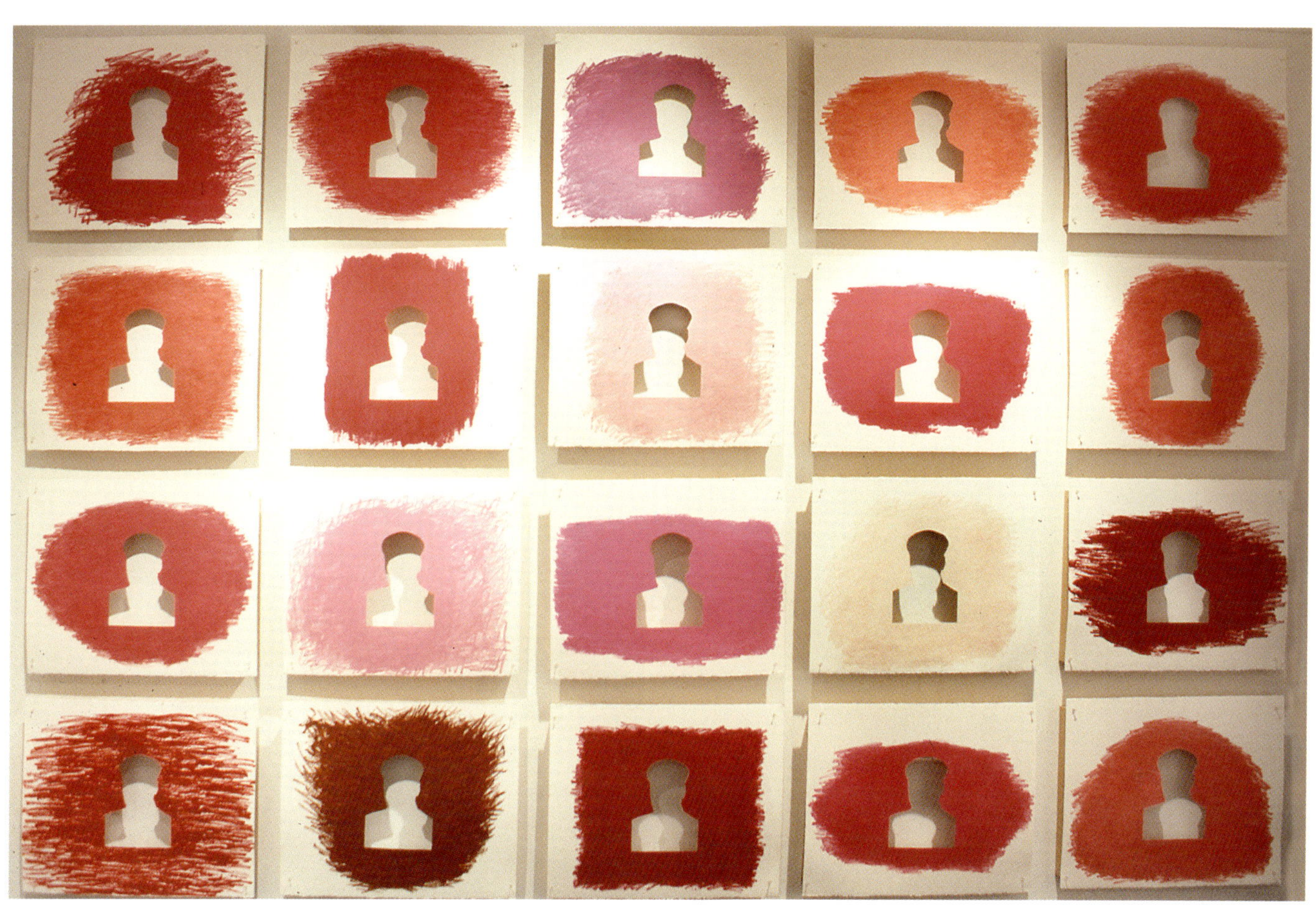

040
Lipstick Mao (20 pieces), 1992.
Lipstick on paper,
22 x 30 in. each.

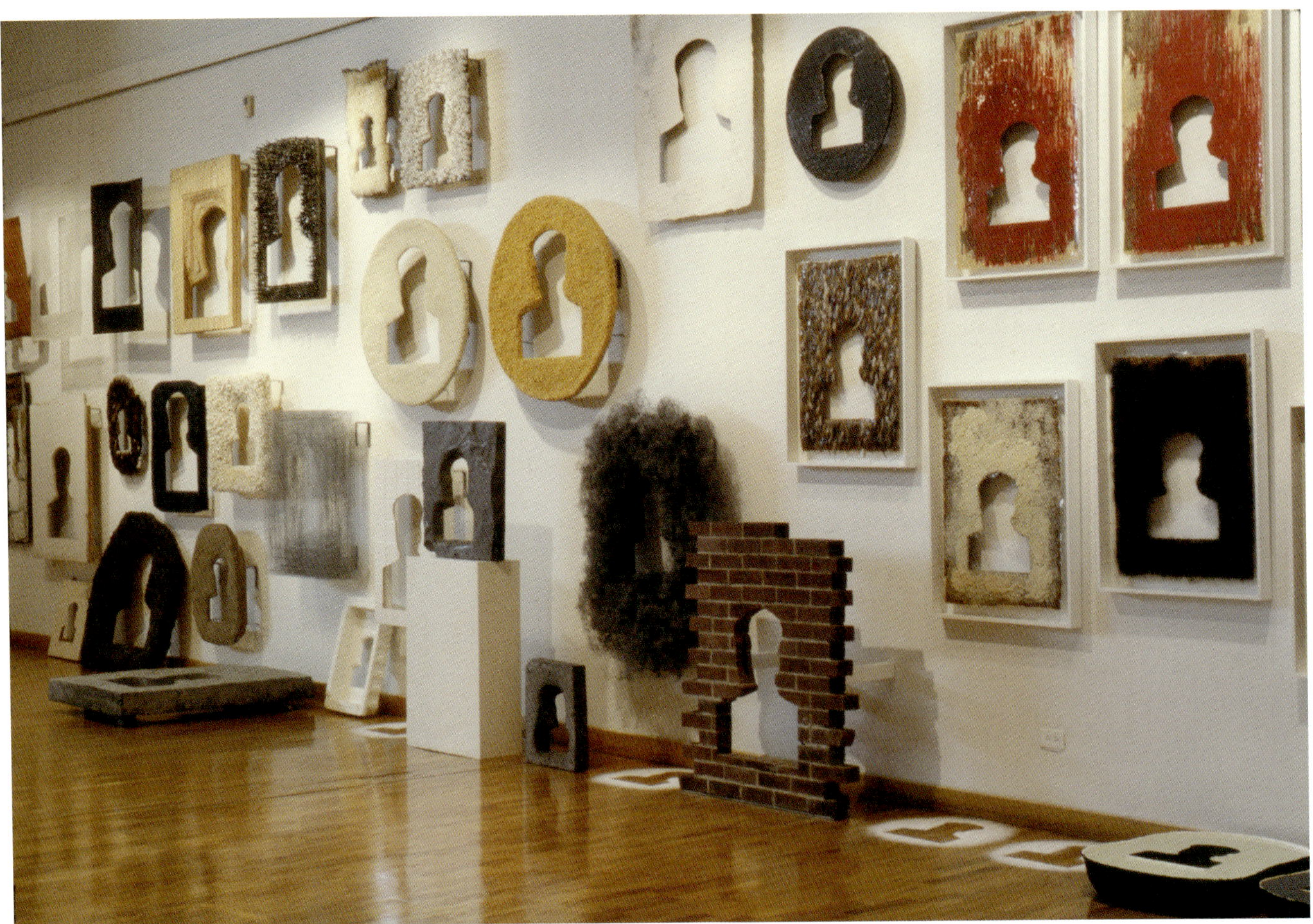

041

041
Installation view, "Material Mao," The Bronx Museum of Arts,
New York, 1995.

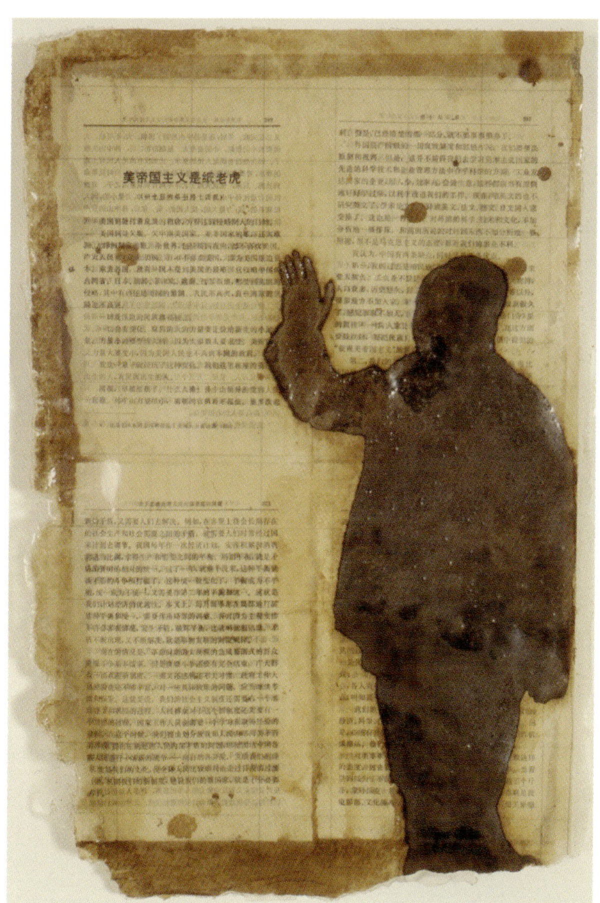

042-a

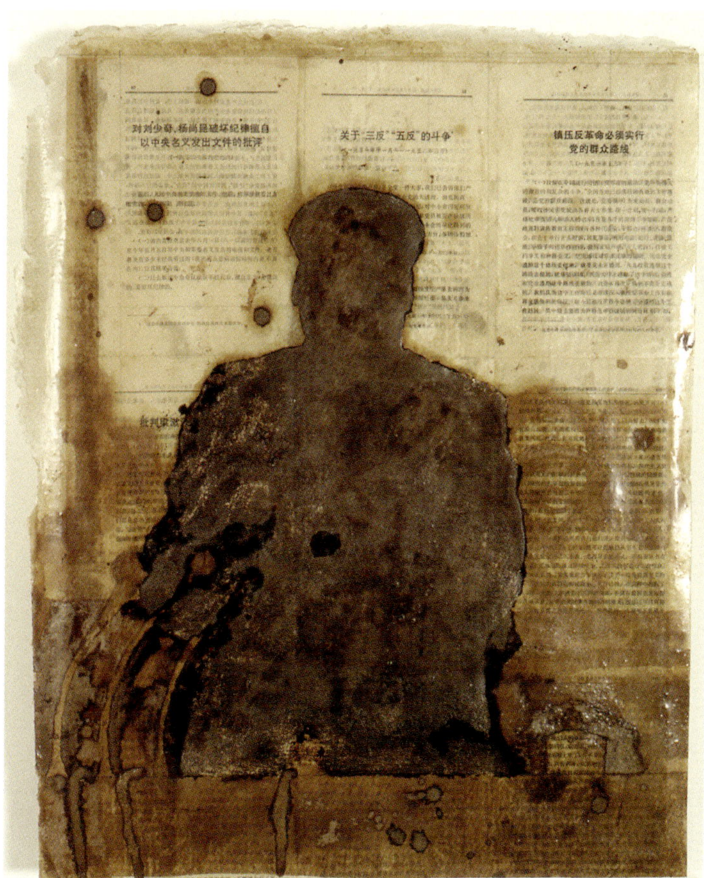

042-b

042-a and 042-b
Soy Sauce Mao, 1993.
Mixed media on paper,
17 x 13 ¾ in.; 19 x 12 in.

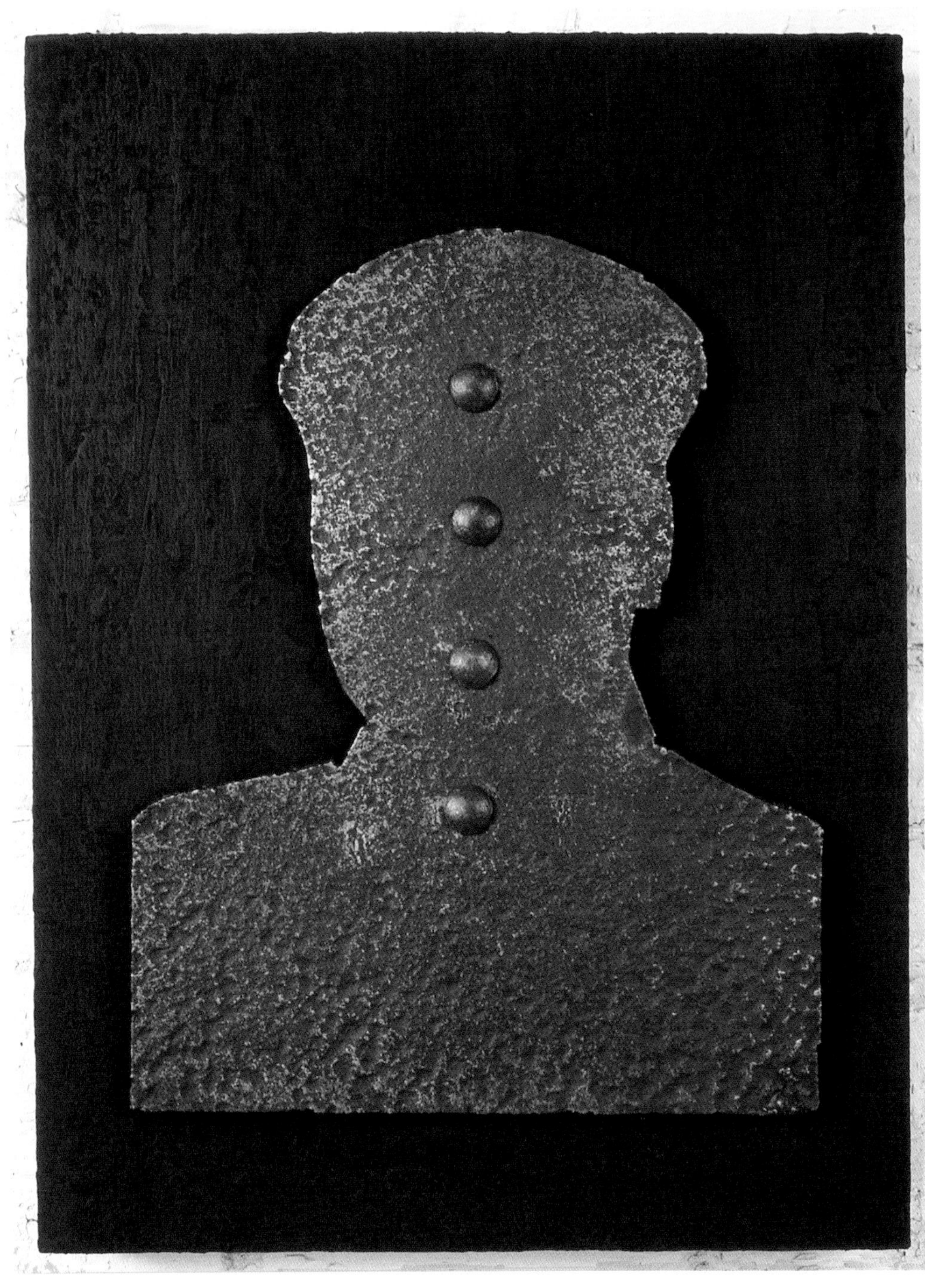

043
Mao Button, 1992.
Iron and acrylic on wood,
20 ¼ x 15 in.

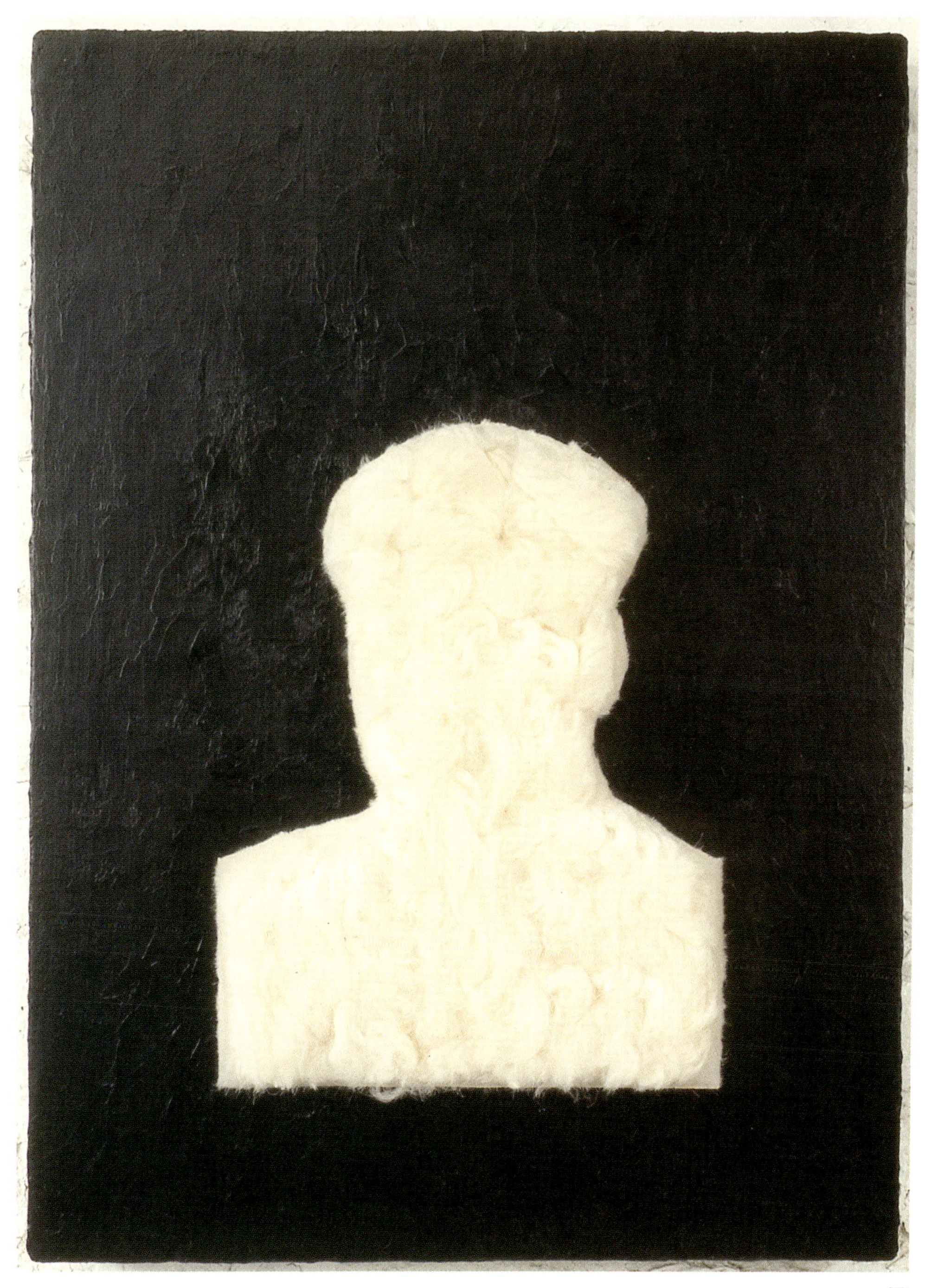

044

044
Mao Fur, 1992.
Fur and acrylic on wood,
20 ¼ x 15 in.

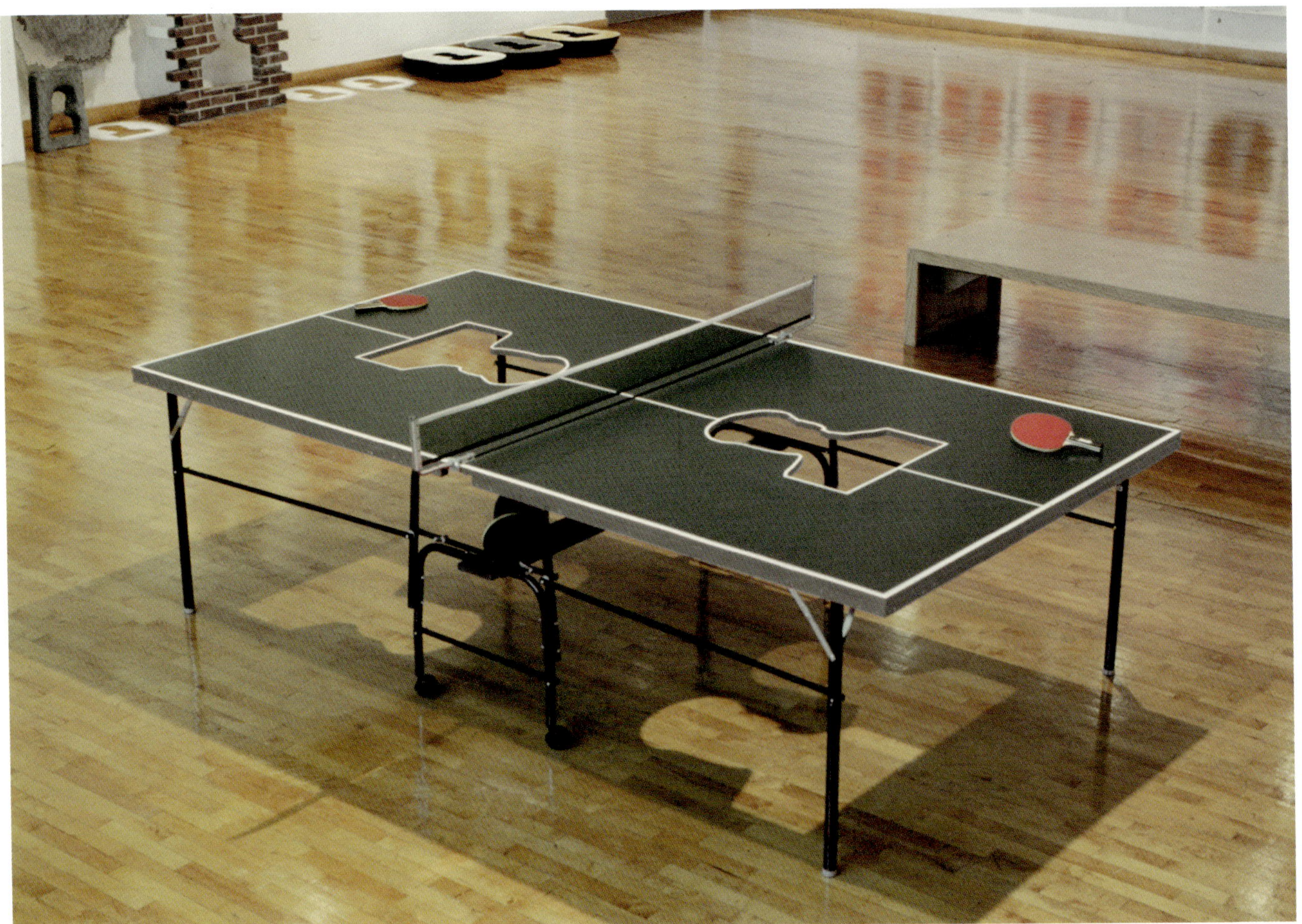

045
Ping-Pong Mao, 1995.
Mixed media installation,
30 x 60 x 108 in.

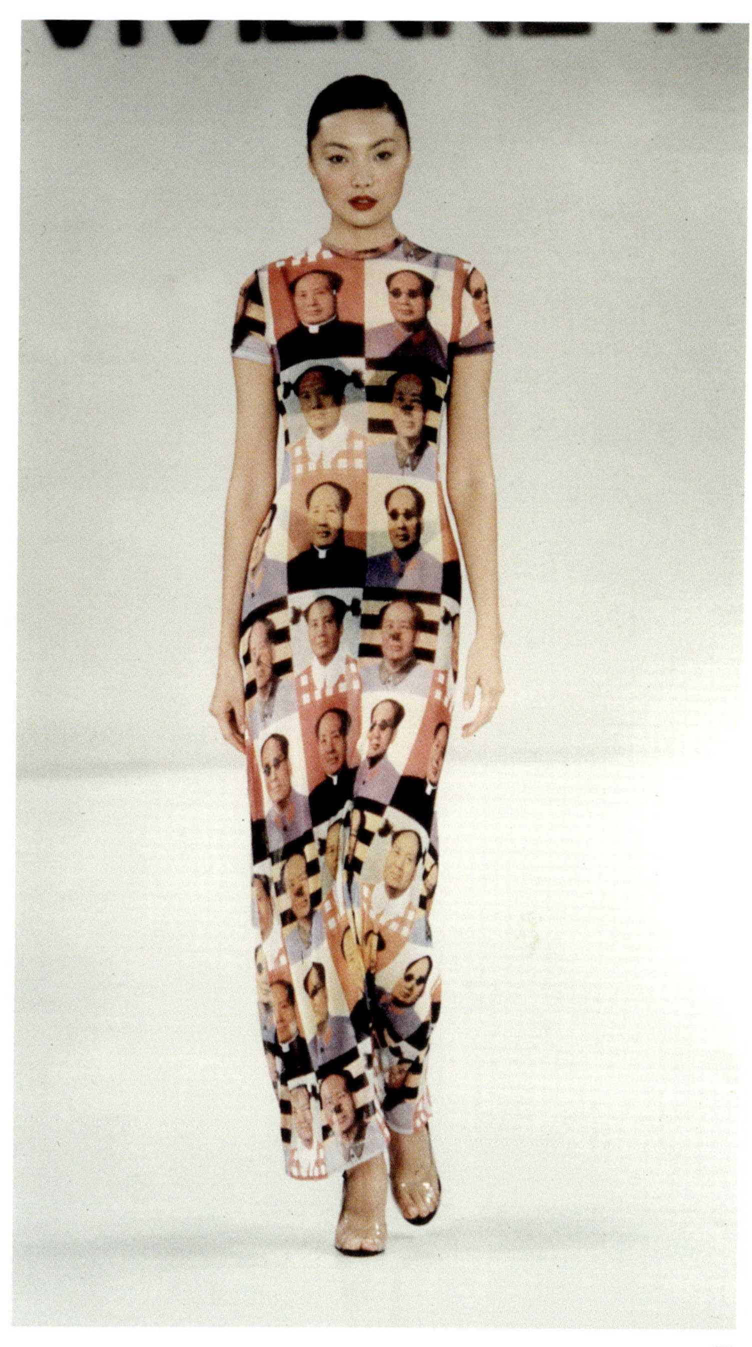

046

046
Collaboration between Zhang Hongtu and Vivienne Tam.
Fashion Mao, 1994, still from collaborative video.

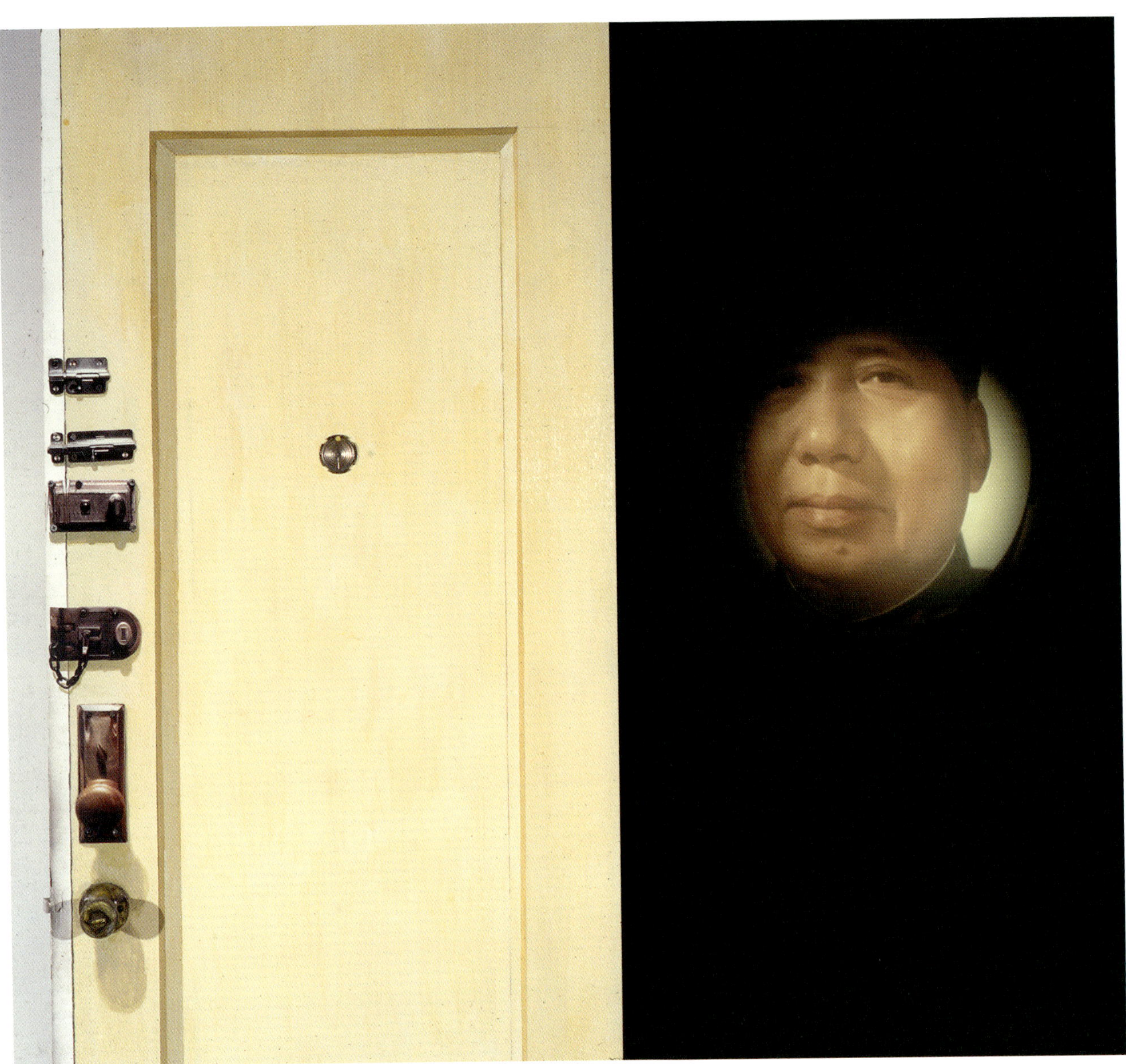

047

047
Front Door, 1995.
Mixed-media installation with audiotape,
84 x 32 in. Installation view and detail.

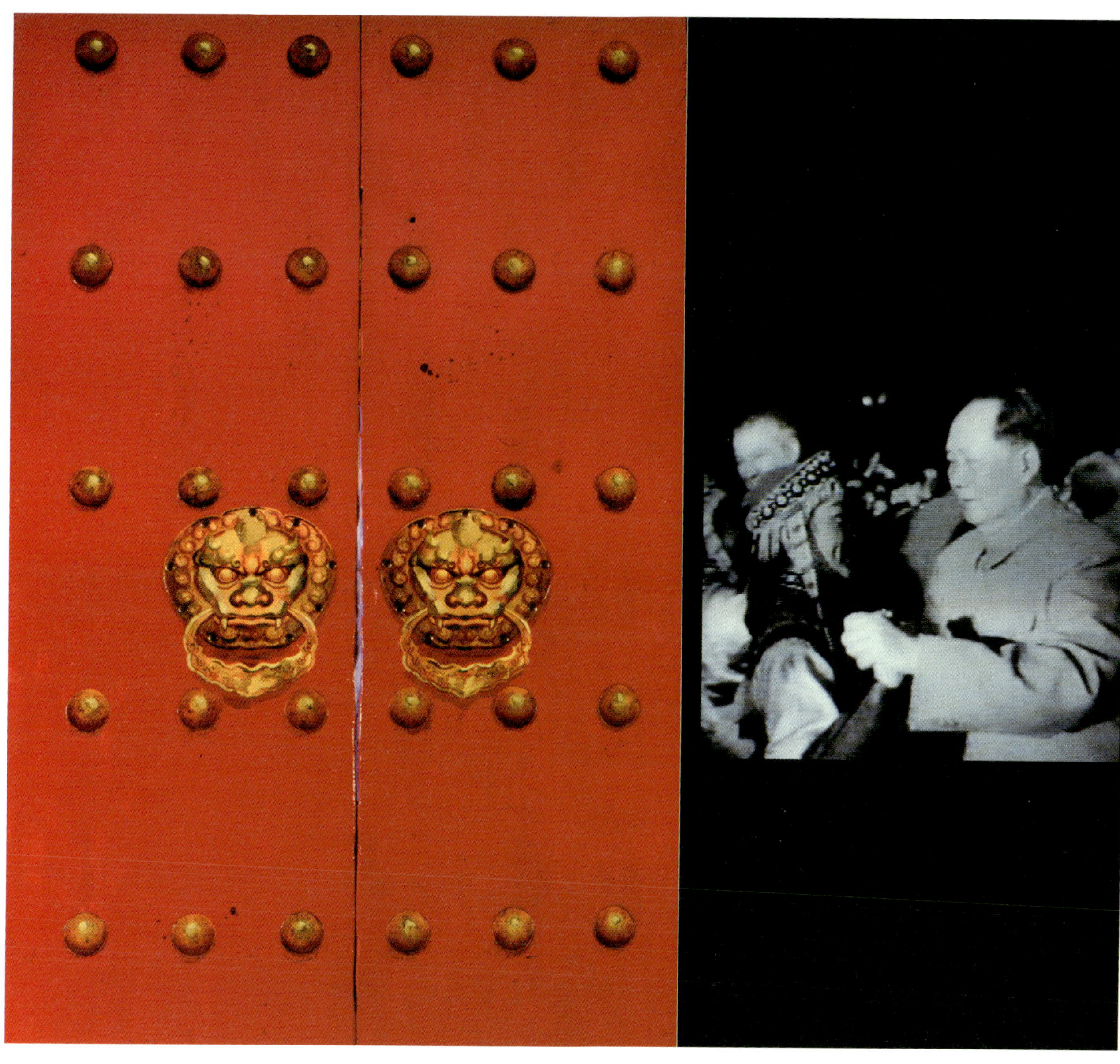

048
The Red Door, 1995.
Mixed-media installation with video,
84 x 32 in. Installation view and detail.

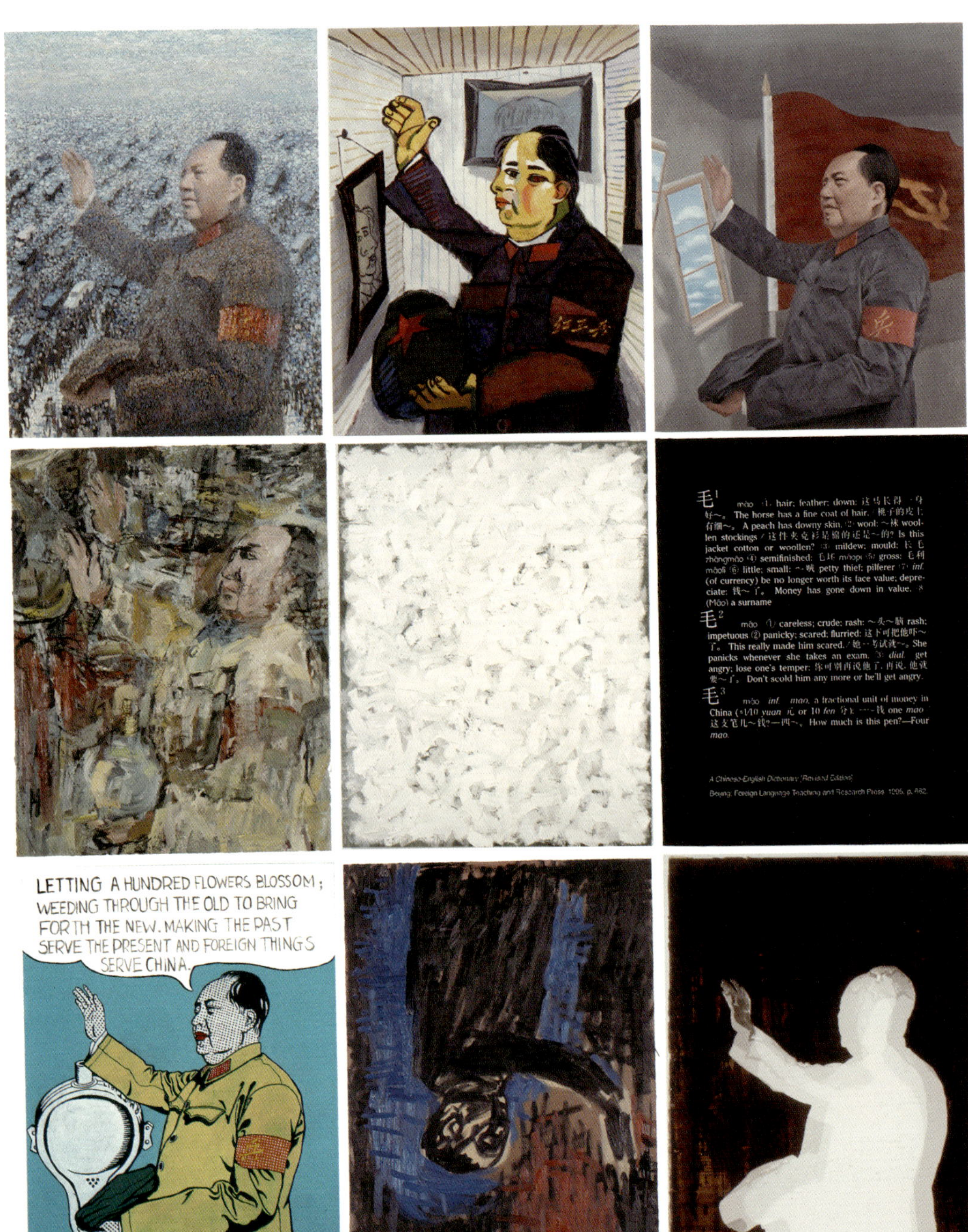

049

049
Unity and Discord, 1998.
Oil, acrylic, ink, and soy sauce on canvas board,
30 x 24 in. each.

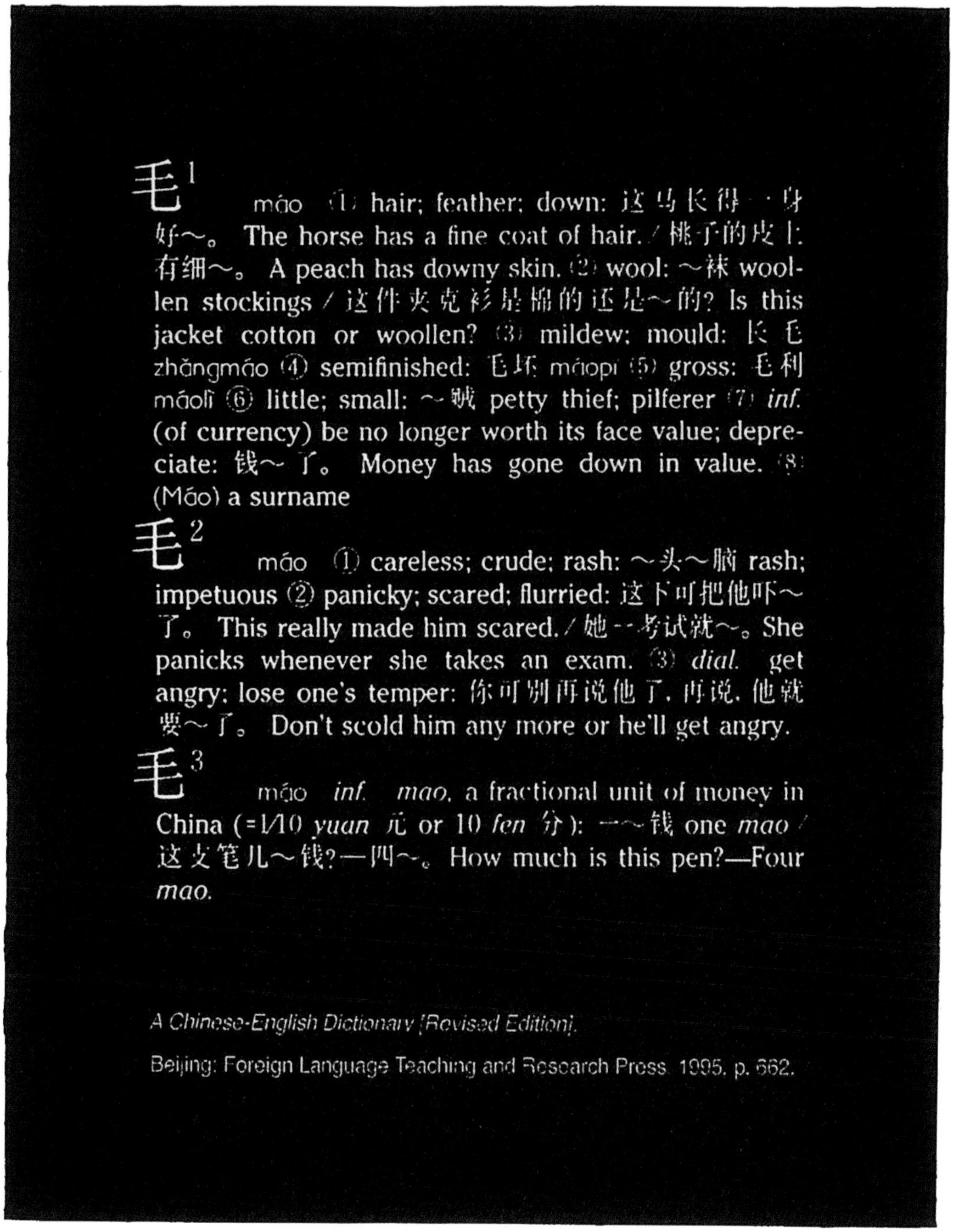

毛¹　　máo (1) hair; feather; down: 这马长得一身好～。 The horse has a fine coat of hair. / 桃子的皮上有细～。 A peach has downy skin. (2) wool: ～袜 woollen stockings / 这件夹克衫是棉的还是～的? Is this jacket cotton or woollen? (3) mildew; mould: 长毛 zhǎngmáo (4) semifinished: 毛坯 máopī (5) gross: 毛利 máolì (6) little; small: ～贼 petty thief; pilferer (7) inf. (of currency) be no longer worth its face value; depreciate: 钱～了。 Money has gone down in value. (8) (Máo) a surname

毛²　　máo (1) careless; crude; rash: ～头～脑 rash; impetuous (2) panicky; scared; flurried: 这下可把他吓～了。 This really made him scared. / 她一考试就～。 She panicks whenever she takes an exam. (3) dial. get angry: lose one's temper: 你可别再说他了, 再说, 他就要～了。 Don't scold him any more or he'll get angry.

毛³　　máo inf. mao, a fractional unit of money in China (=1/10 yuan 元 or 10 fen 分): 一～钱 one mao / 这支笔儿～钱?—四～。 How much is this pen?—Four mao.

A Chinese-English Dictionary [Revised Edition].

Beijing: Foreign Language Teaching and Research Press. 1995. p. 662.

050
After Joseph Kosuth (detail from *Unity and Discord*), 1998.
Oil, acrylic, ink, and soy sauce on canvas board,
30 x 24 in.

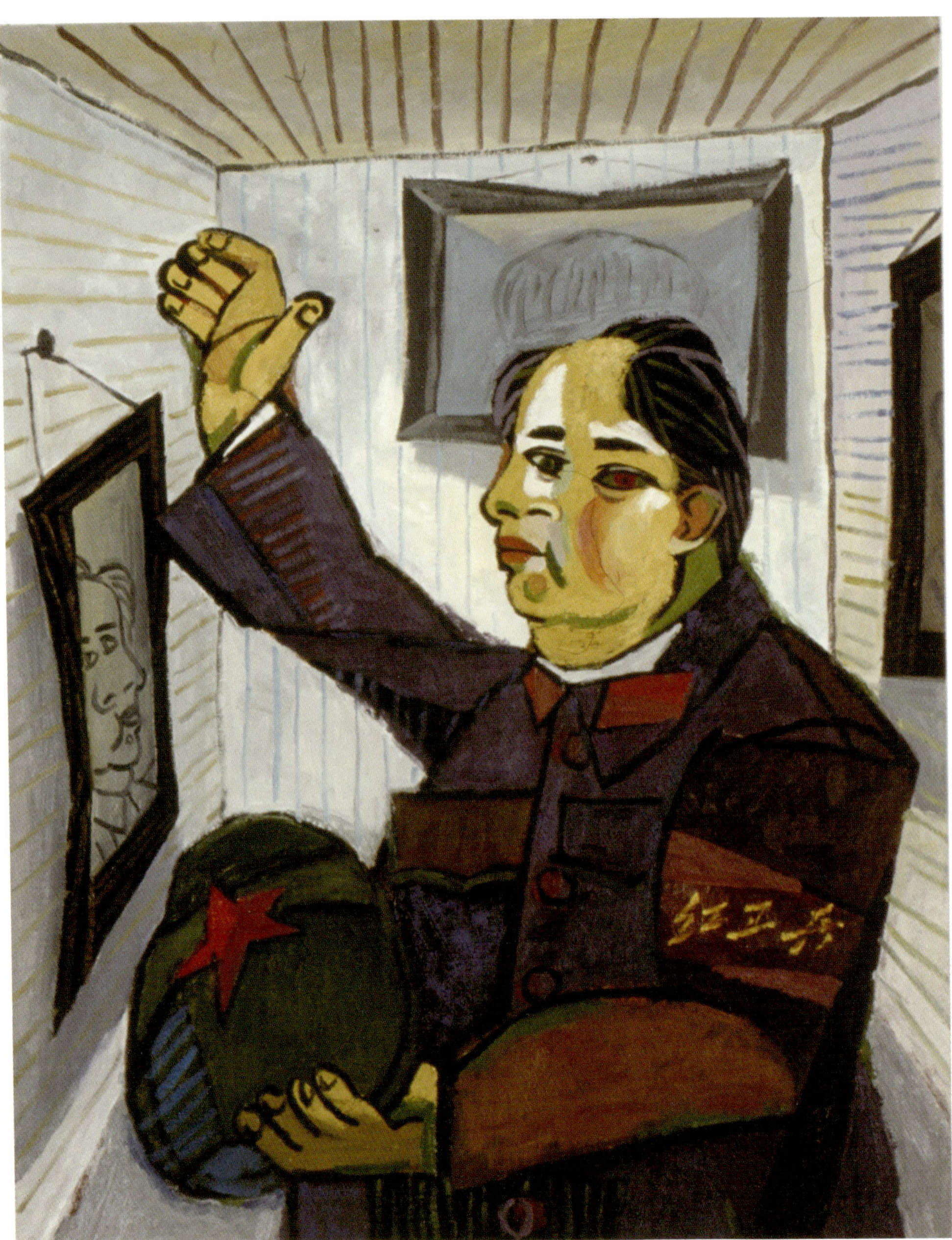

051

051
After Picasso (detail from *Unity and Discord*), 1998.
Oil, acrylic, ink, and soy sauce on canvas board,
30 x 24 in.

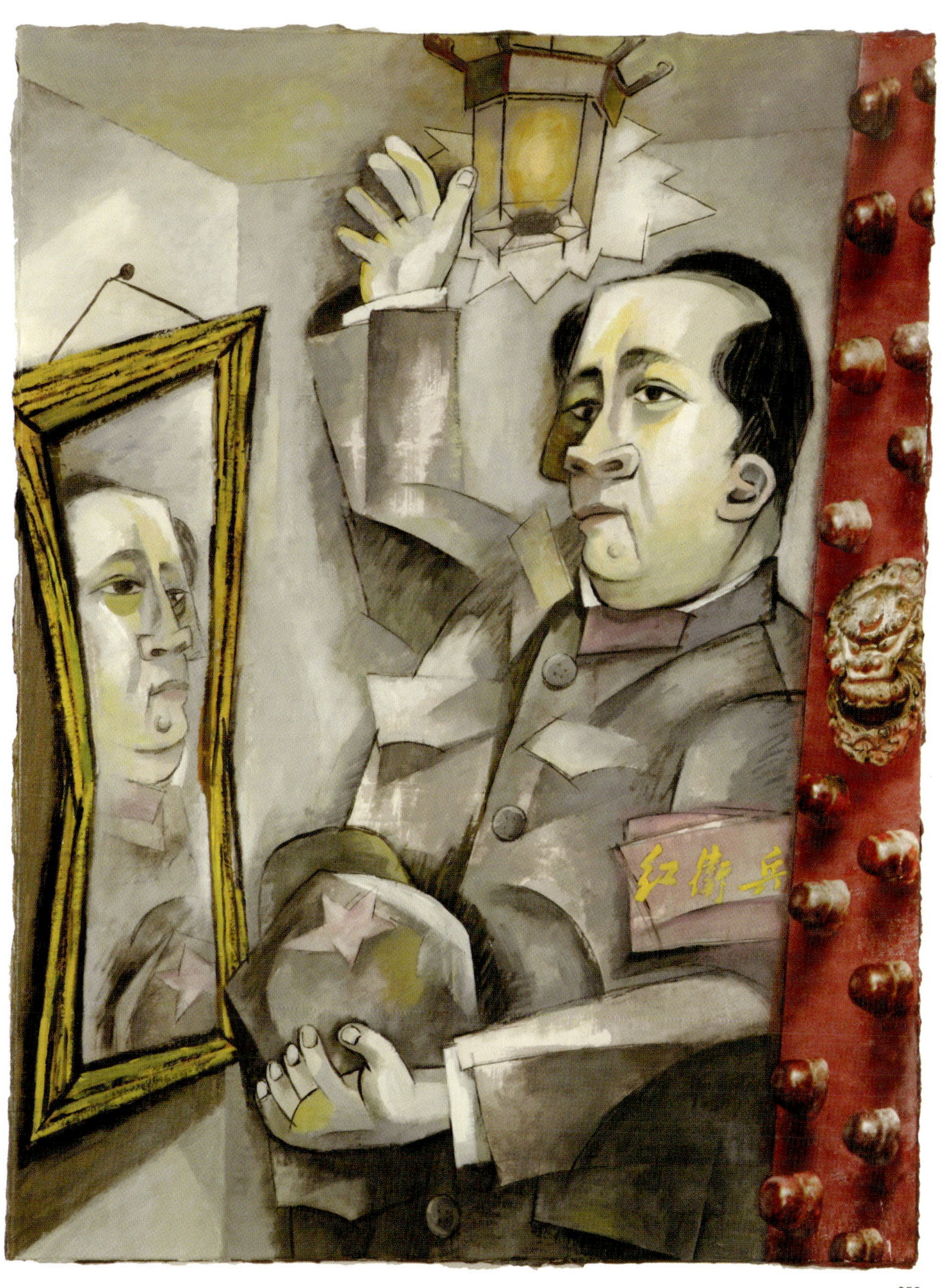

052

052
Mao, After Picasso, 2012.
Ink and oil on rice paper and photo collage mounted on canvas,
44 ½ x 34 ½ in.

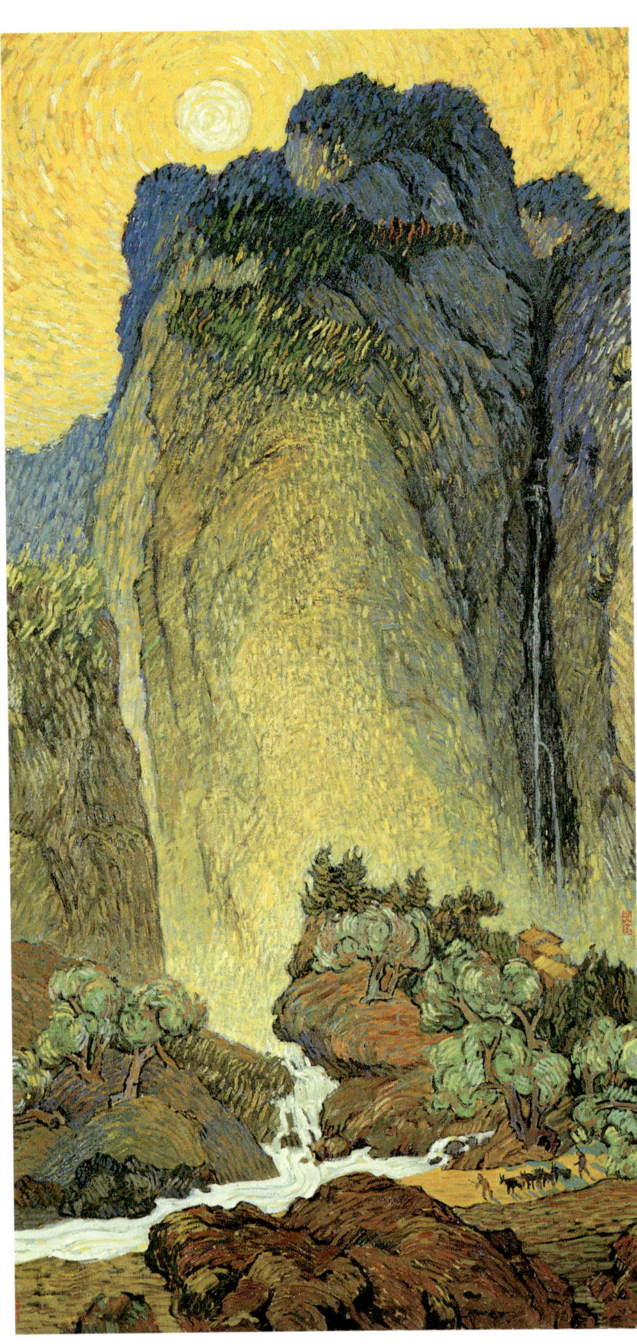

053

053
Fan Kuan—Van Gogh, 1998.
Oil on canvas,
64 x 32 in.

054
Dong Qichang—Cézanne #9, 2003.
Oil on canvas,
84 x 42 in.

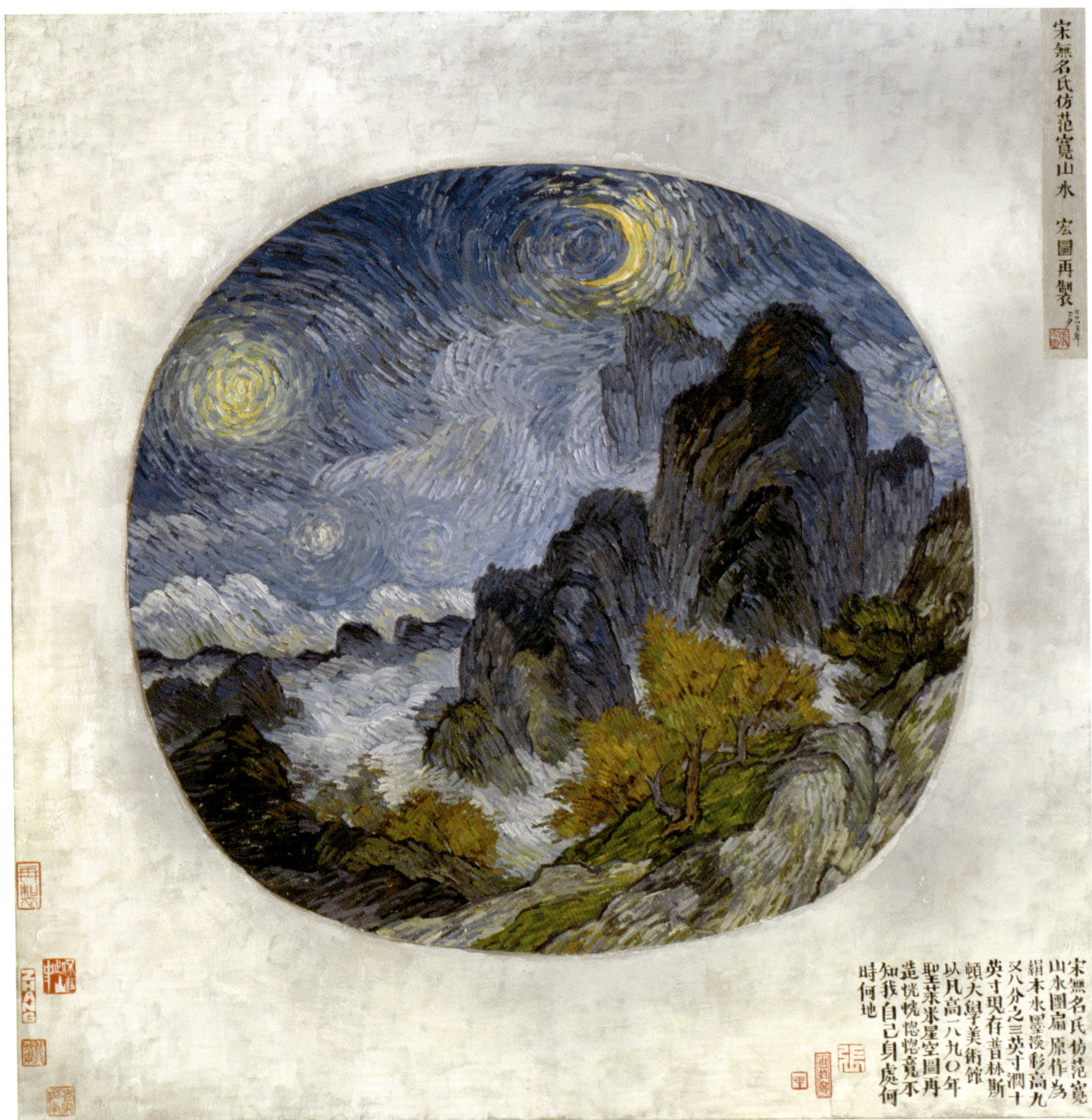

055

Anonymous (Song) – Van Gogh P, 2003.
Oil on canvas,
48 x 48 in.

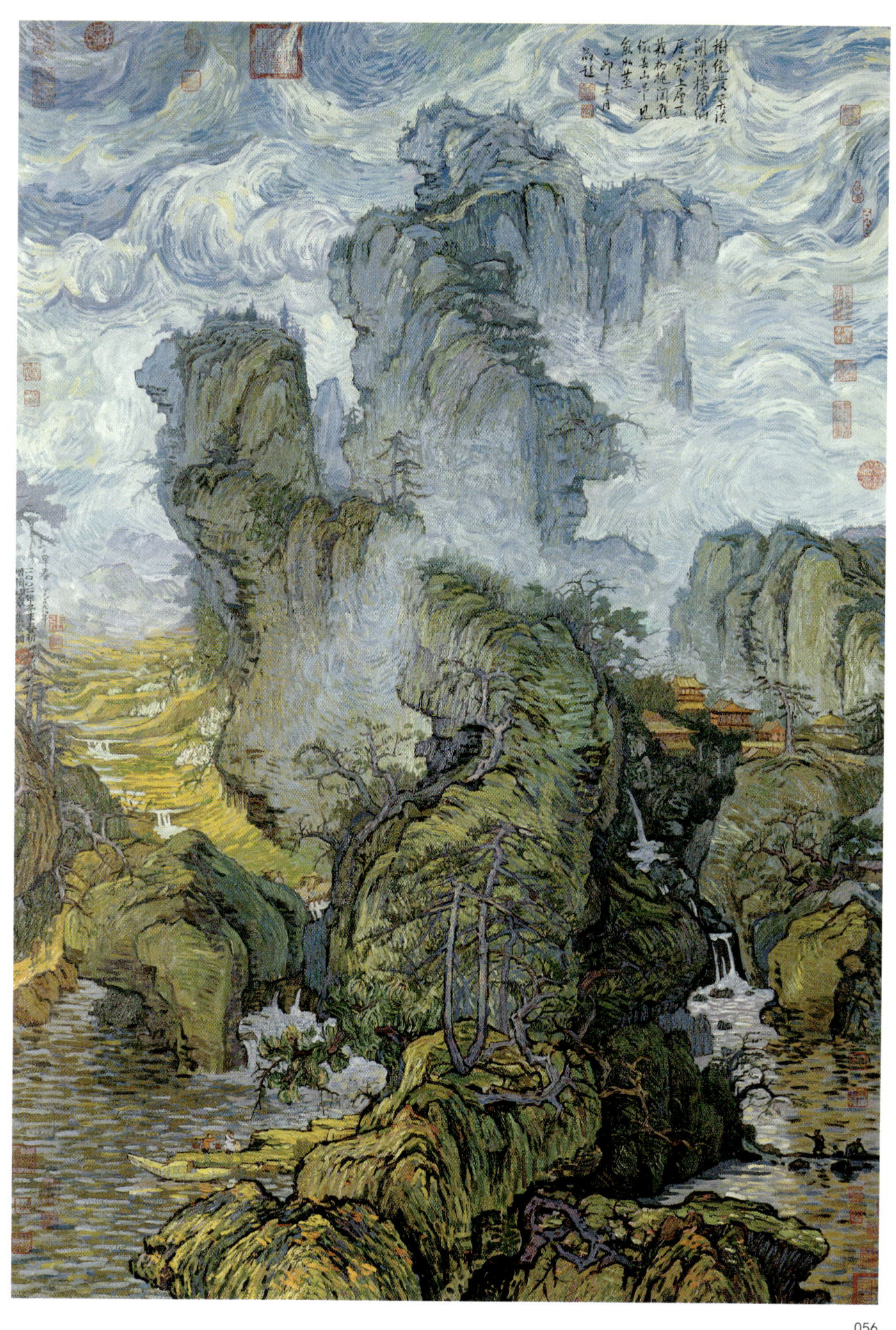

056
Guo Xi—Van Gogh, 1998.
Oil on canvas,
96 x 68 in.

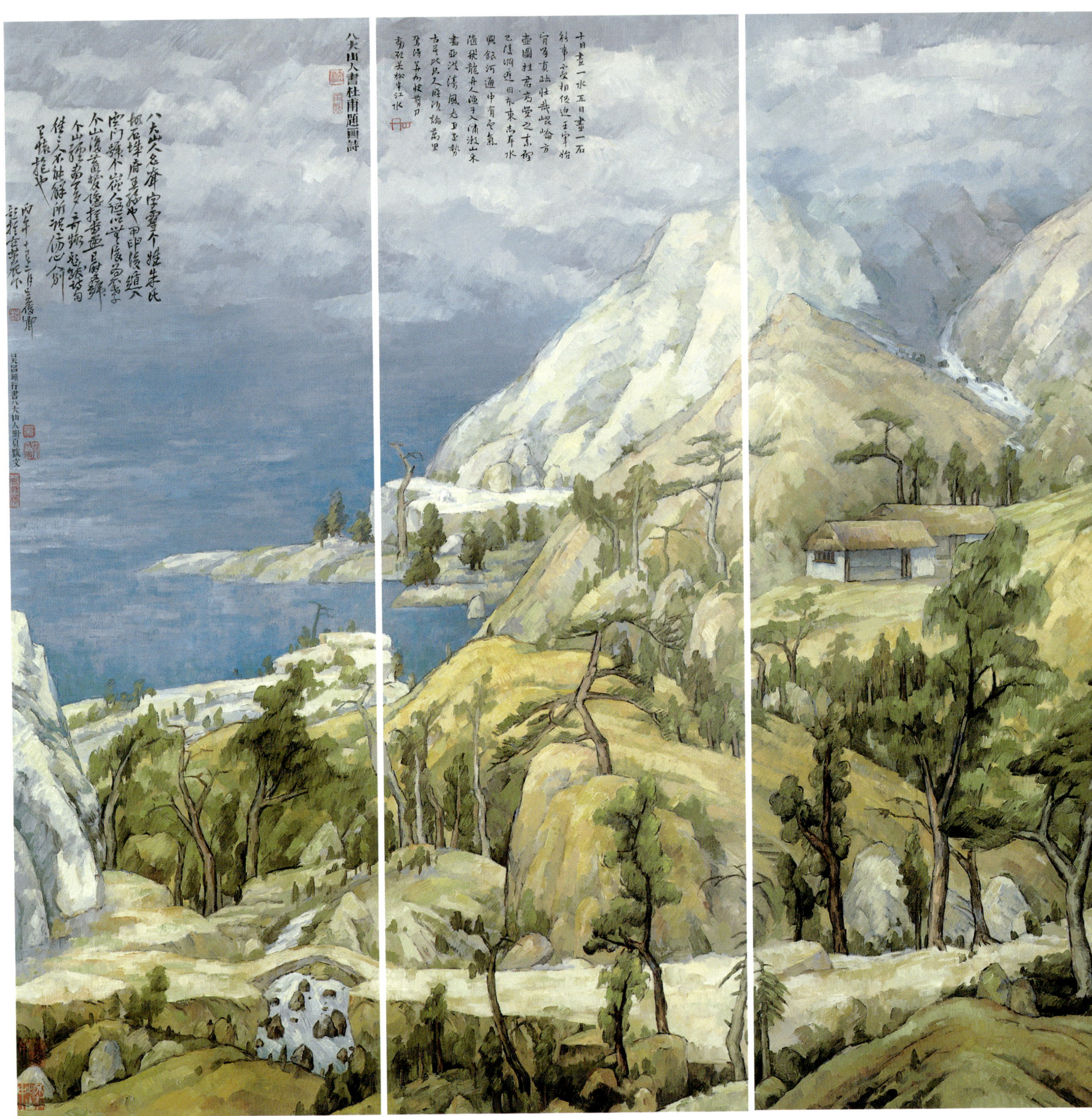

057

057

Bada (Six Panels)—Cézanne, 2006.

Oil on canvas,
82 ⅝ x 168 in.

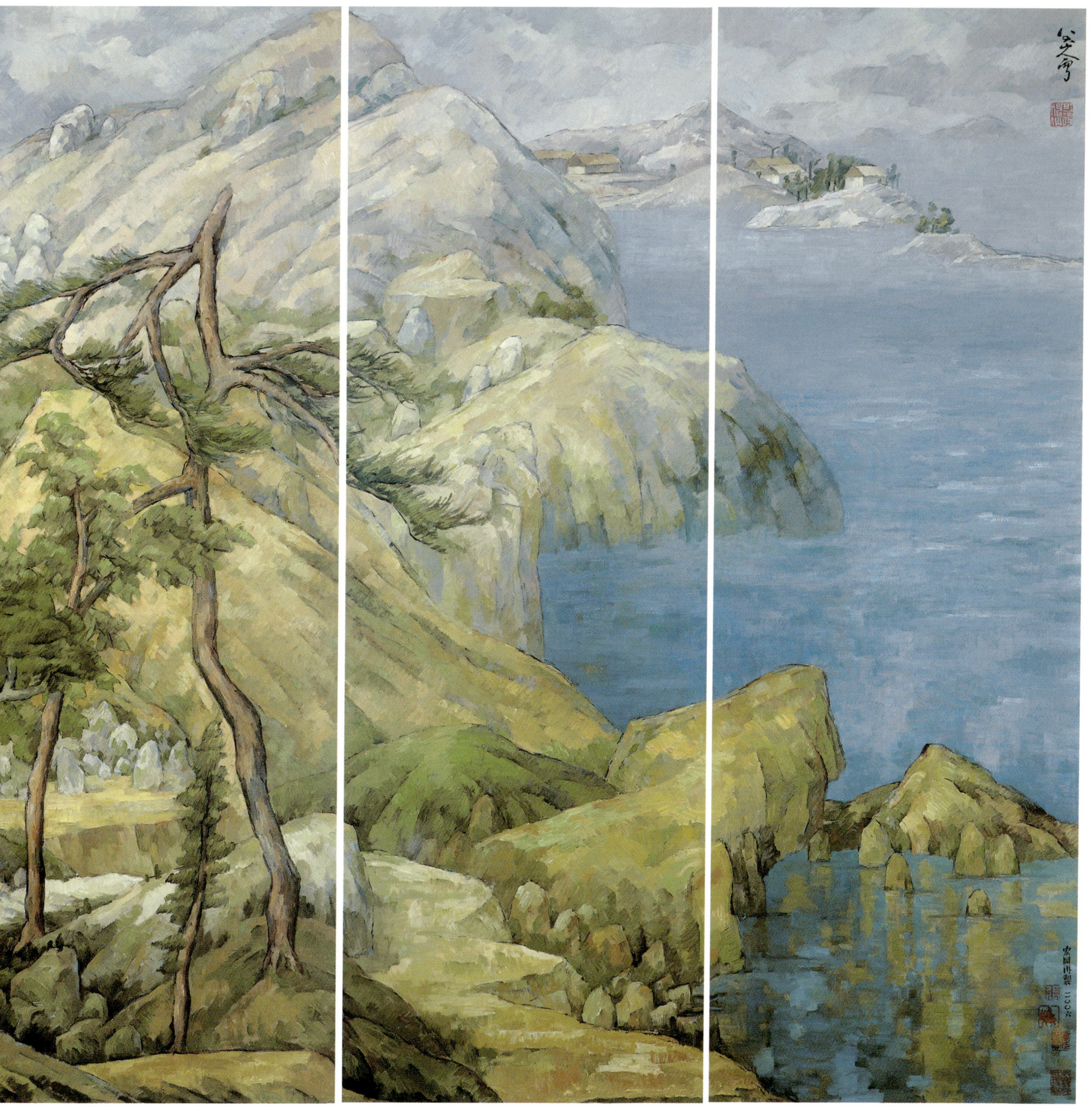

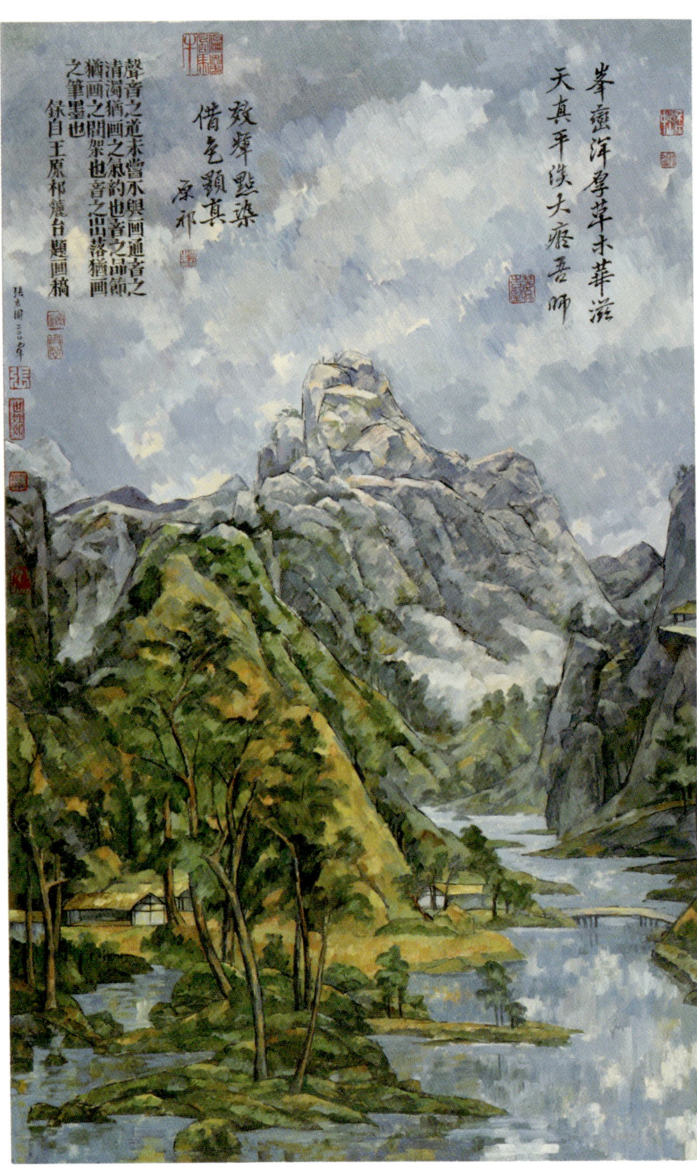

058

058
Wang Yuanqi—Cézanne #5, 2007.
Oil on canvas,
72 ½ x 45 in.

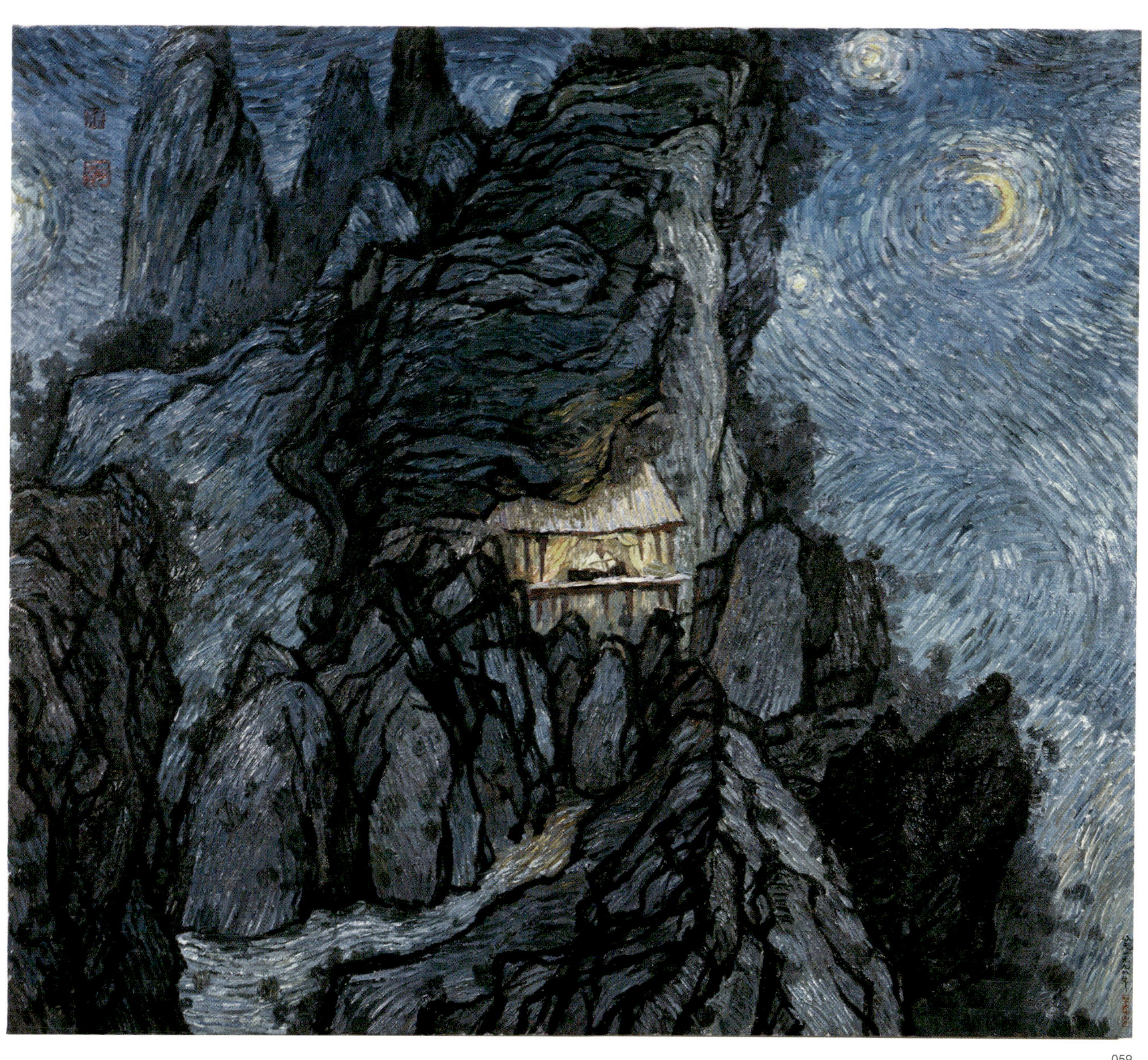

059

059
Shitao—Van Gogh, 1998.
Oil on canvas,
58 x 68 in.

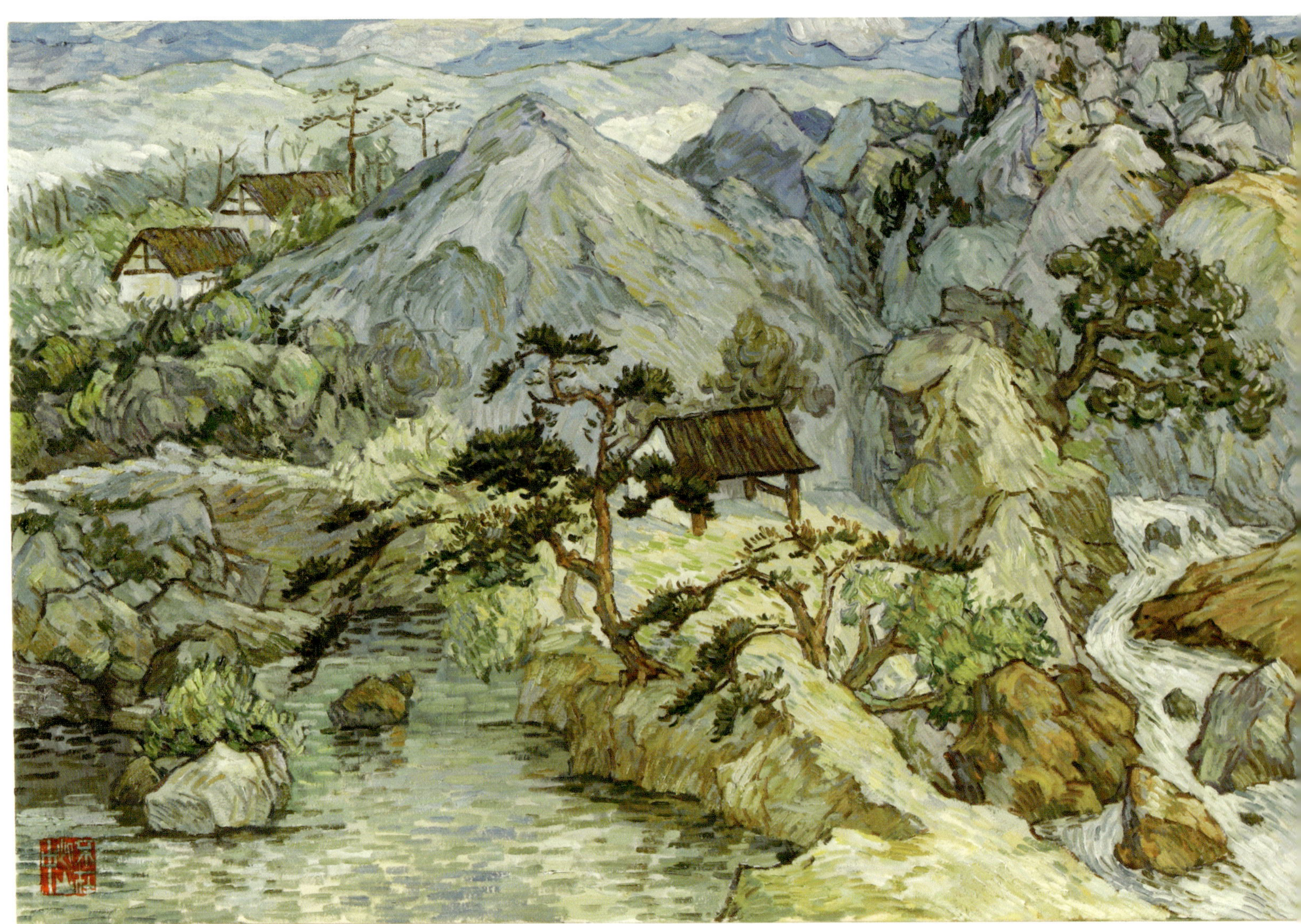

060-a

060-a
Shitao—Van Gogh M, 2008.
Oil on canvas,
32 x 78 in.

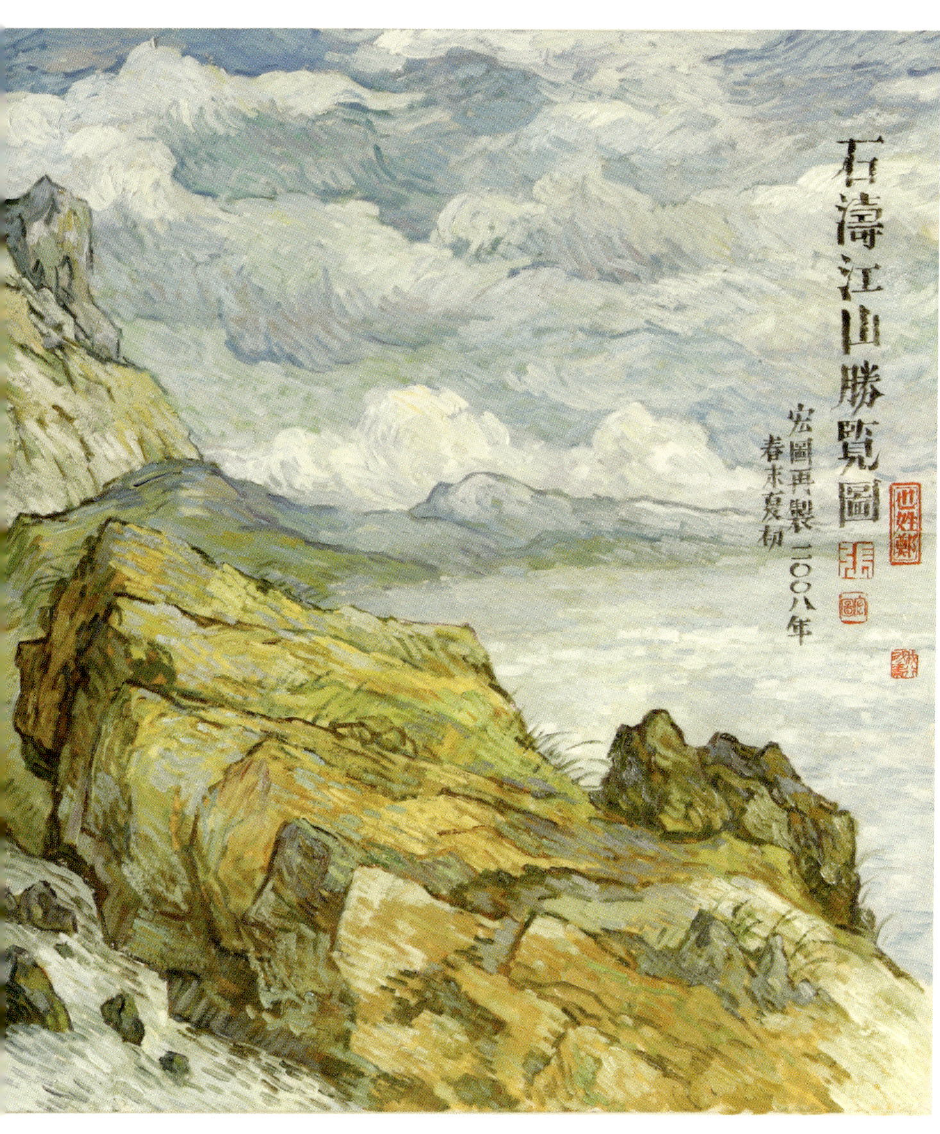

石濤江山勝覽圖
宏圖再製 二〇〇八年
春末夏初

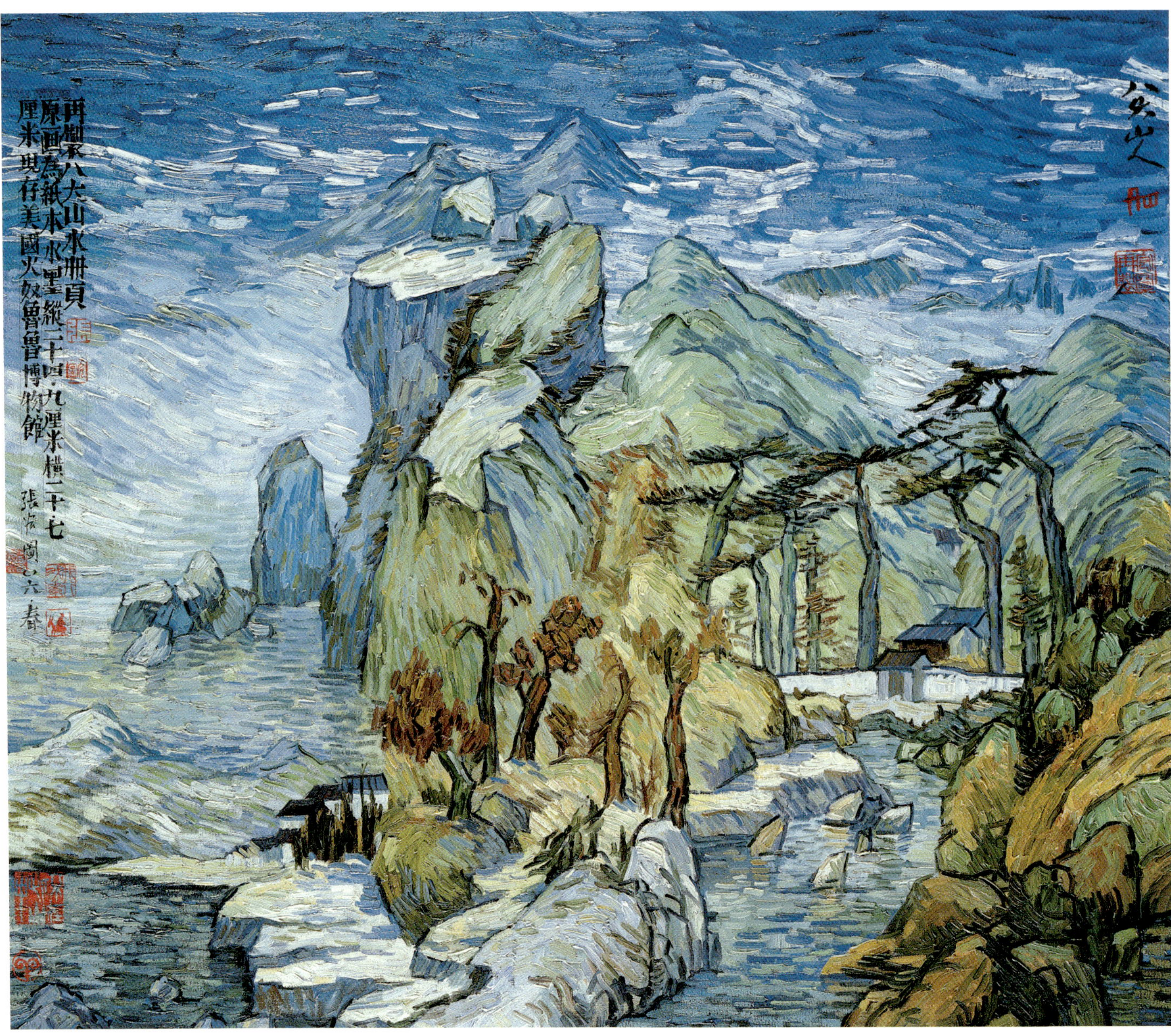

060-b

060-b
Bada—Van Gogh #6, 2006.
Oil on canvas,
44 x 52 in.

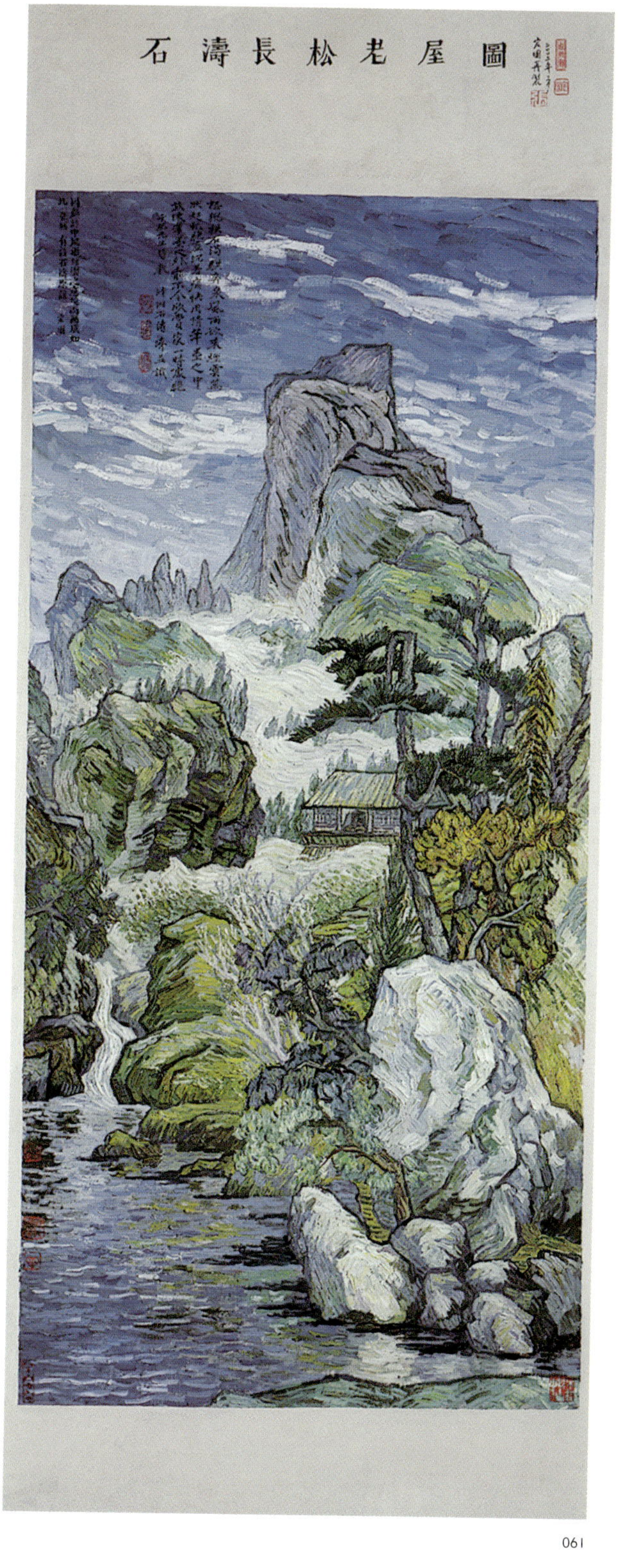

061
Shitao – Van Gogh P, 2002–3.
Oil on canvas,
94 x 37 in.

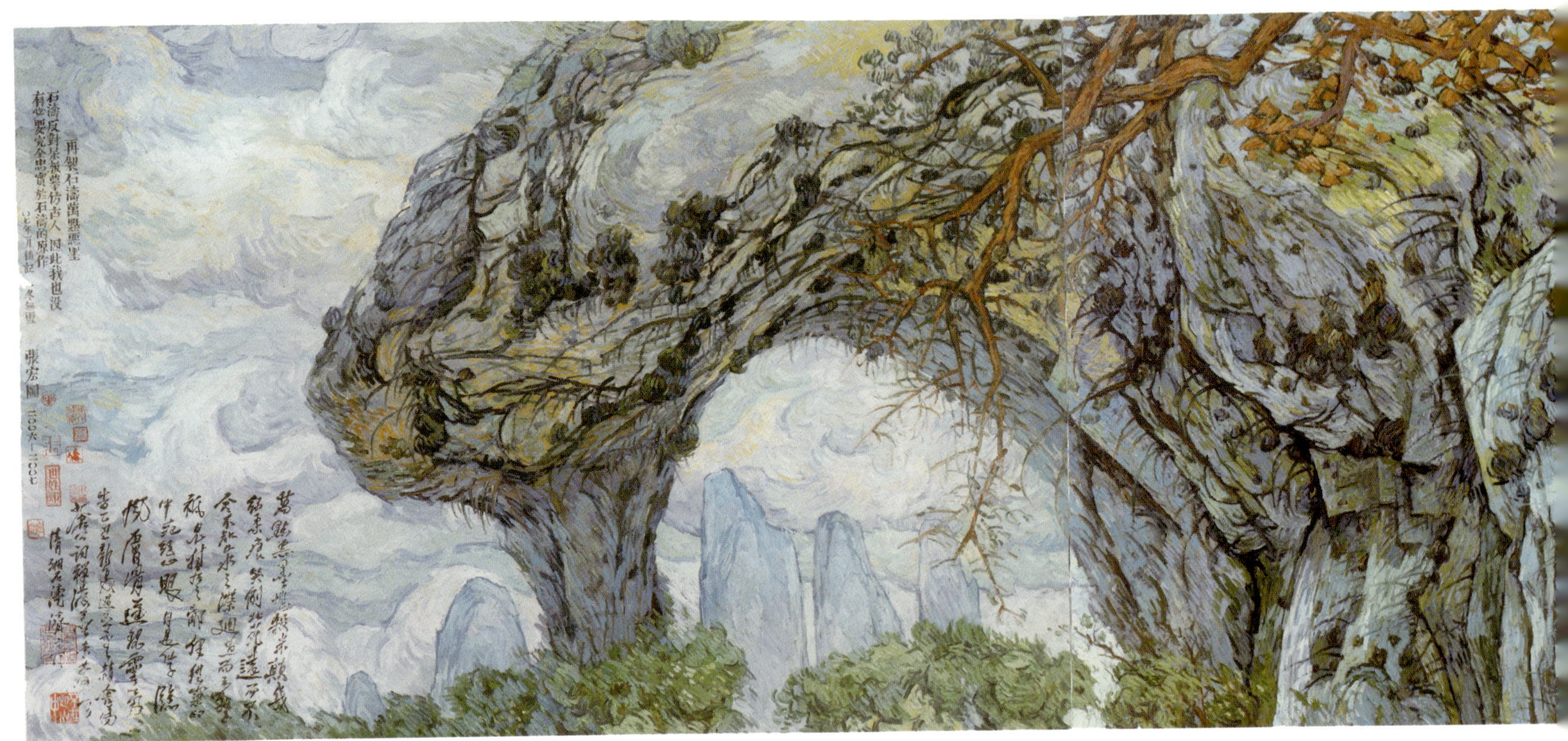

062
Shitao (Ten Thousand Ugly Inkblots Variation)—Van Gogh, 2007.
Oil on canvas,
53 x 240 in.

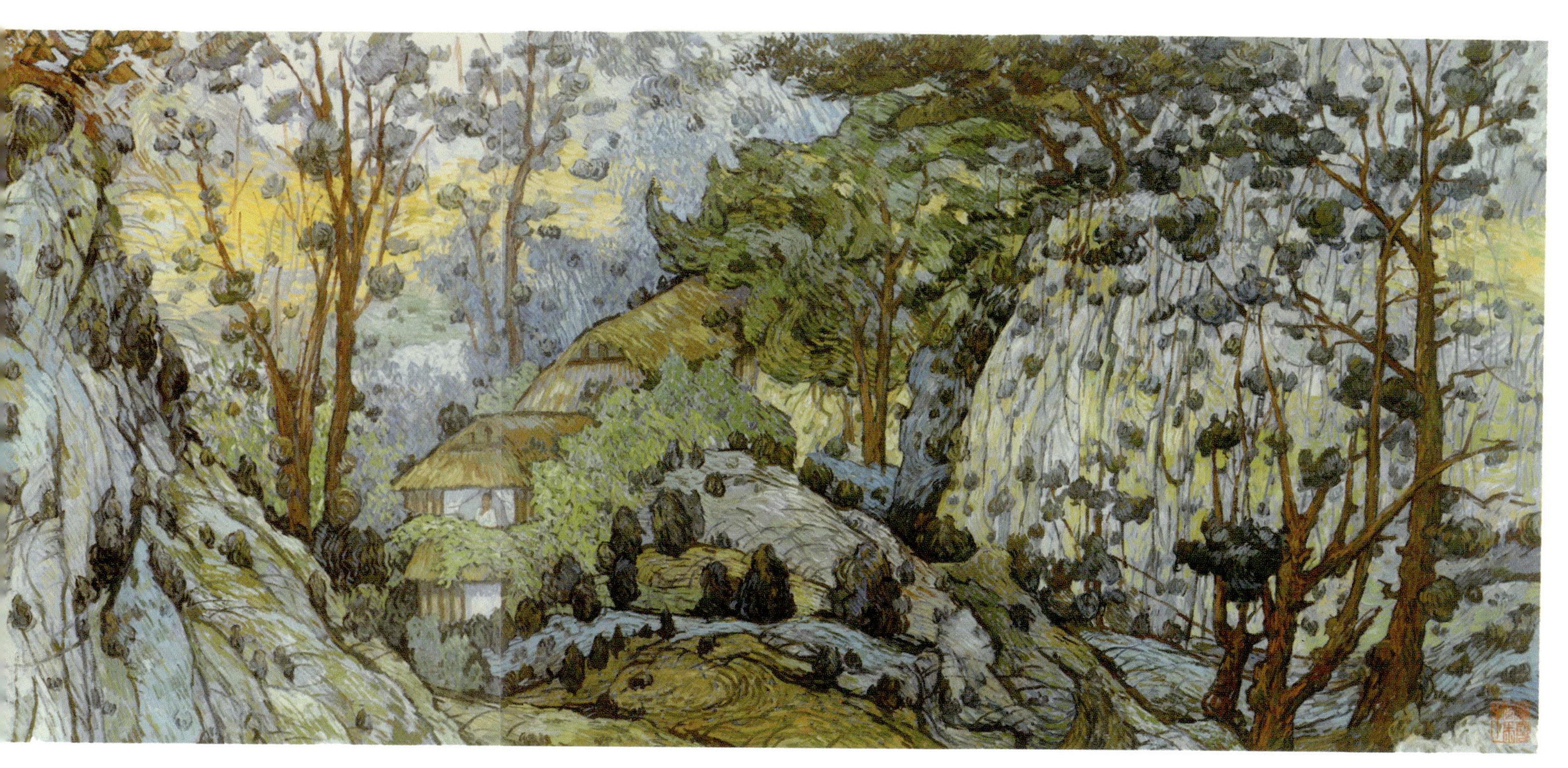

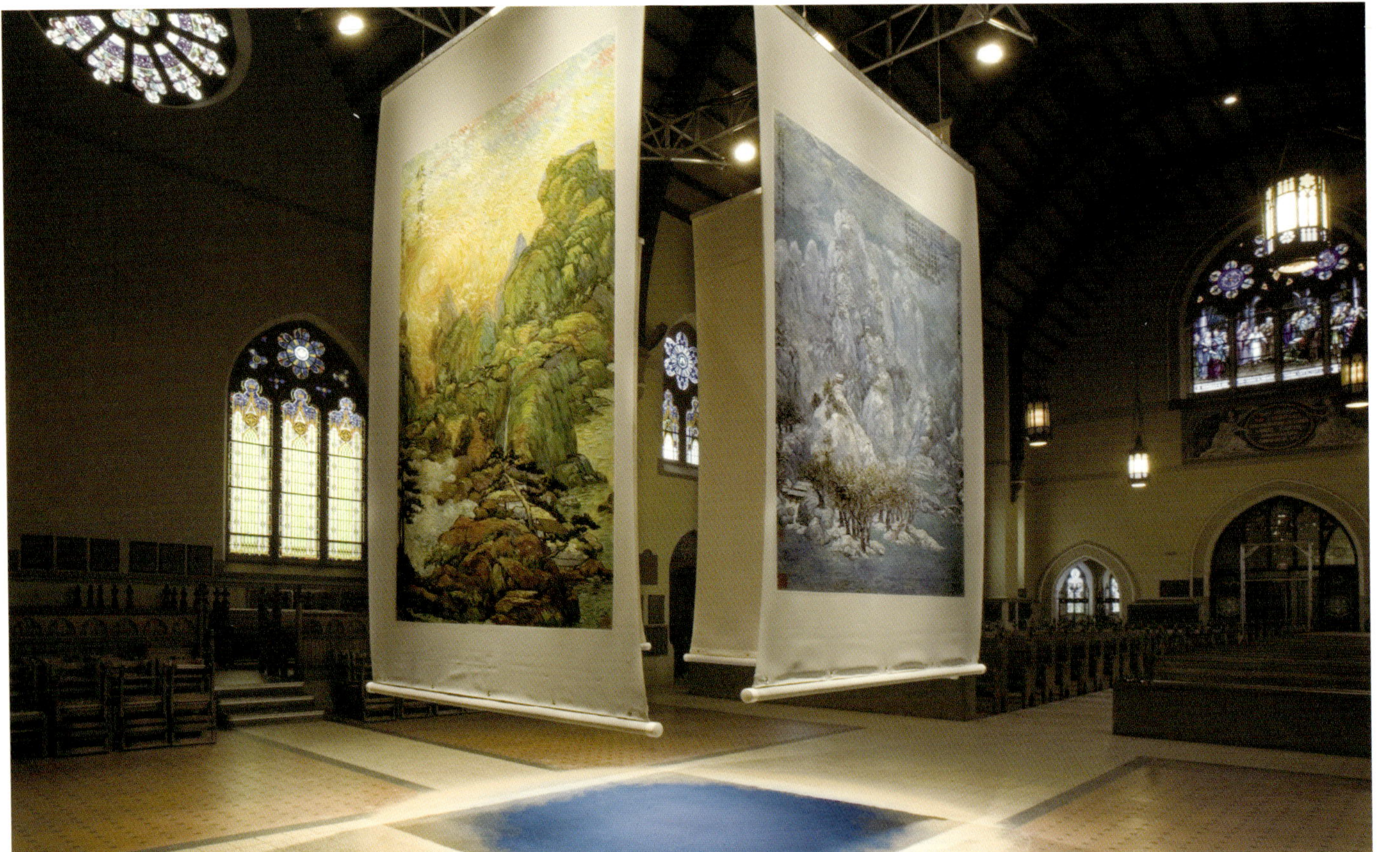

063
"Four Seasons—Earth Above and Heaven Below," Parker Chapel,
Lehigh University, Pennsylvania, 2006.

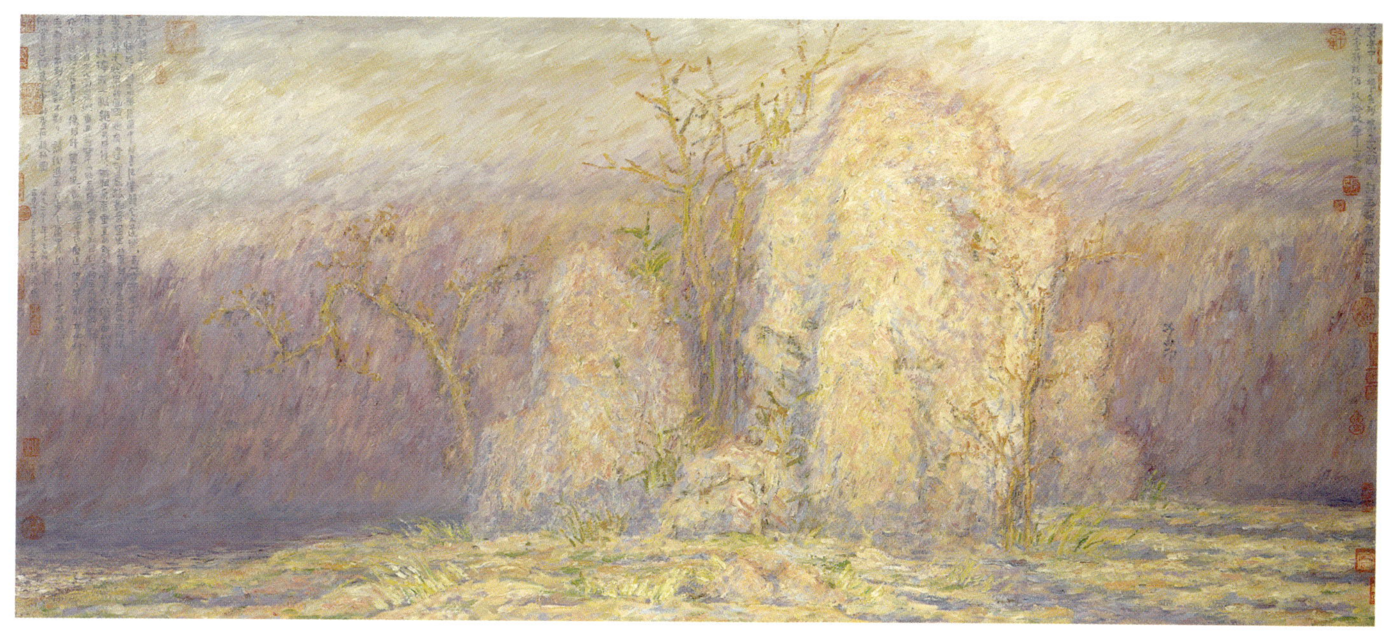

064

064
Zhao Mengfu—Monet (Morning), 1999.
Oil on canvas,
34 x 77 in.

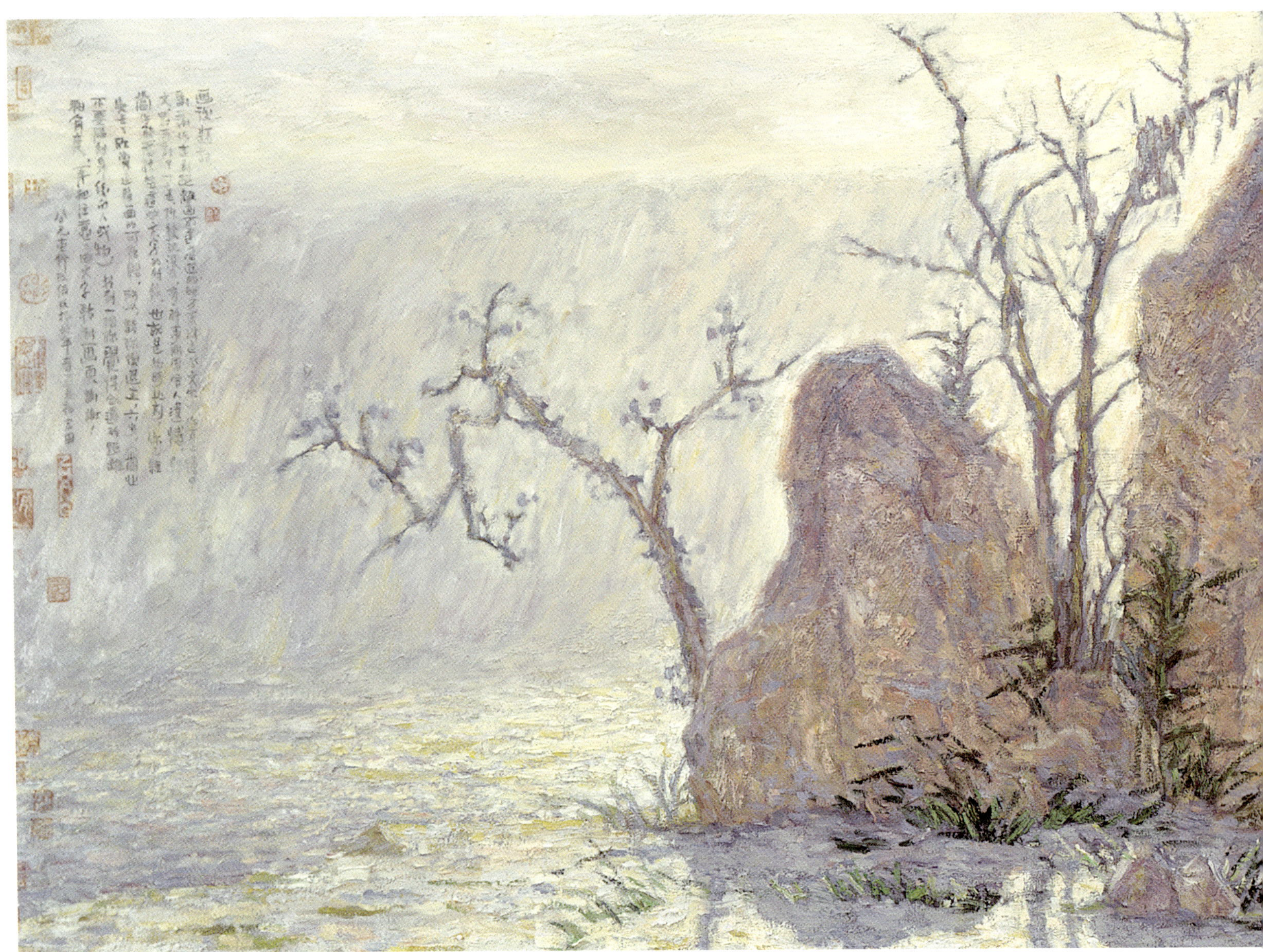

065

065

Zhao Mengfu—Monet (Noon), 1999.

Oil on canvas,
34 x 77 in.

"Thank you for coming so close in order to read this calligraphy. You must be able to understand Chinese, right? However, have you noticed something truly unfortunate has happened? When you come close enough to be able to read these words, which is to say just at this moment, you lose the possibility of enjoying the painting as a whole. So . . . please step back five or six steps (but be careful not to bump into anyone or anything behind you!). Find what you feel to be an appropriate distance and angle, and shift your attention from these words to the painting. Thank you for your attention."

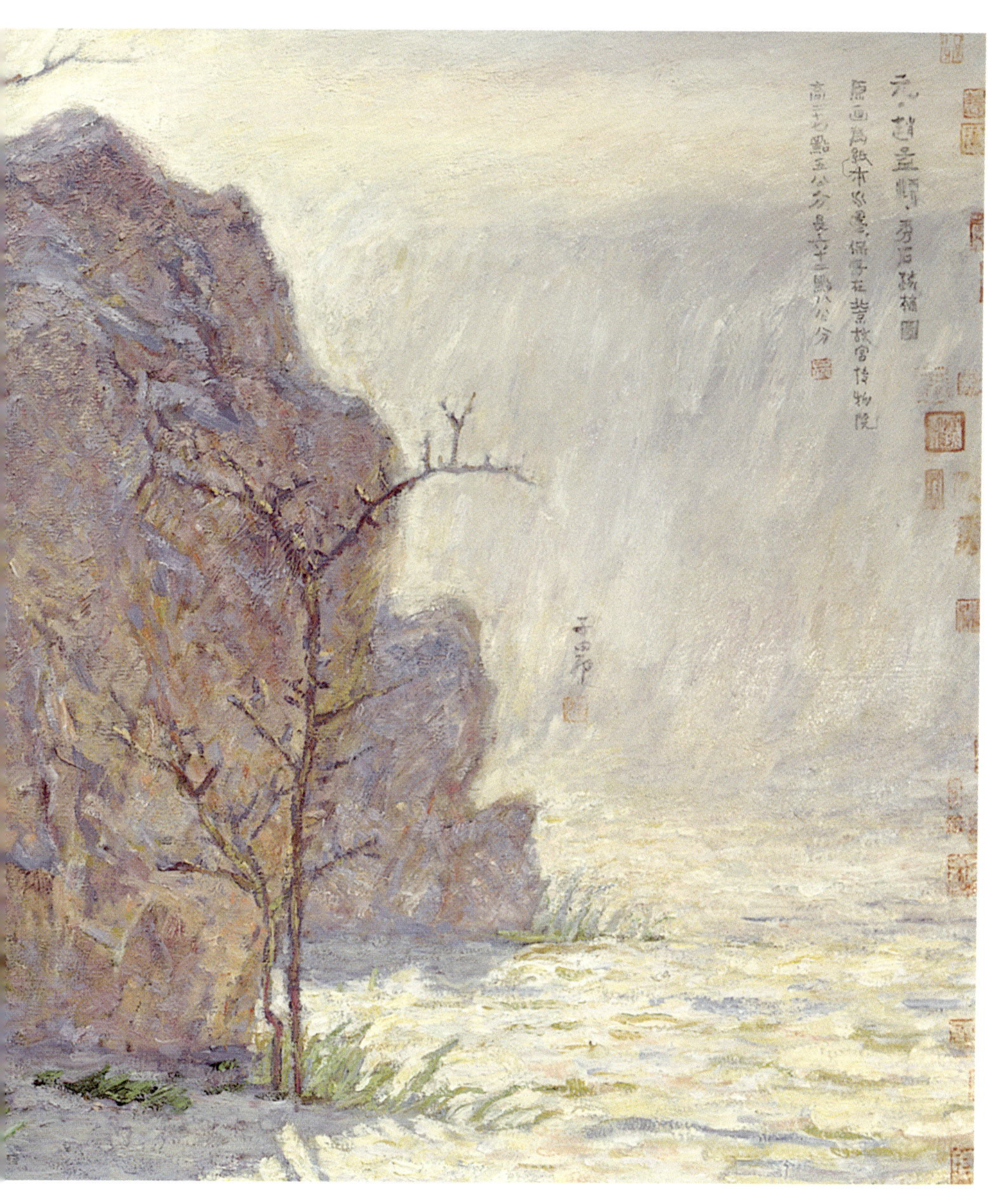

元‧趙孟頫‧秀石疏林圖
原畫為紙本水墨畫，保存在紫故宮博物院
高二七點五公分長六十二點八公分

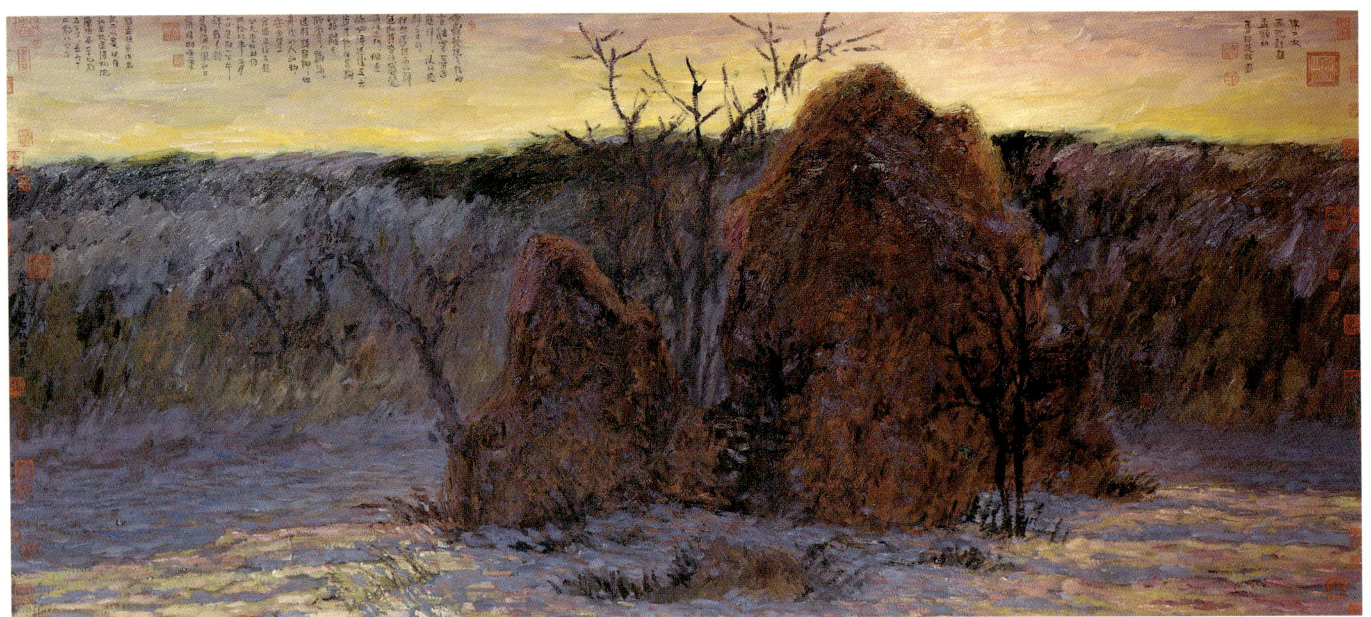

066

066
Zhao Mengfu—Monet (Evening), 1999.
Oil on canvas,
34 x 77 in.

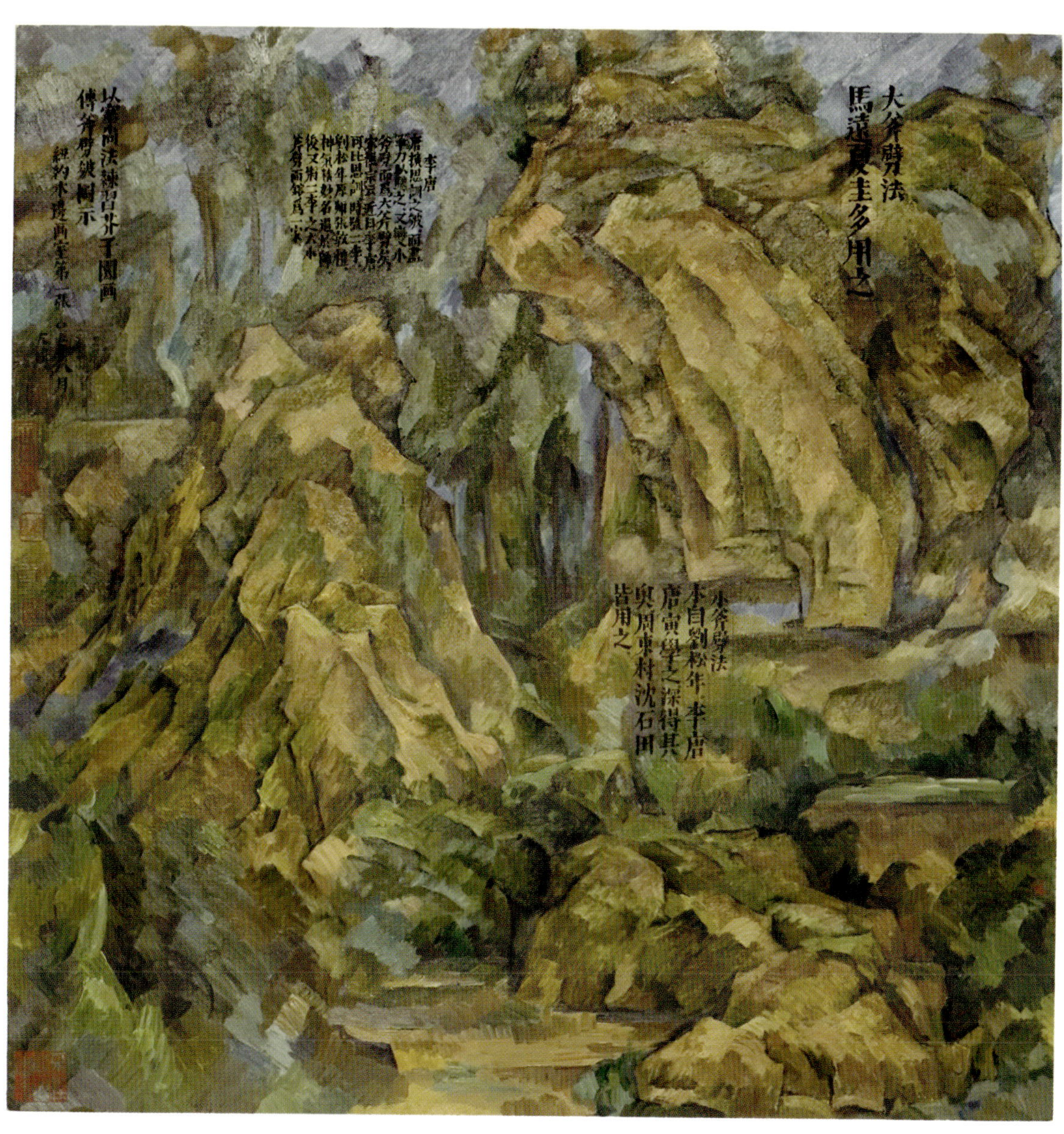

067
Cézanne, Study of axe ts'un, 2005.
Oil on canvas,
56 ½ x 56 ¼ in.

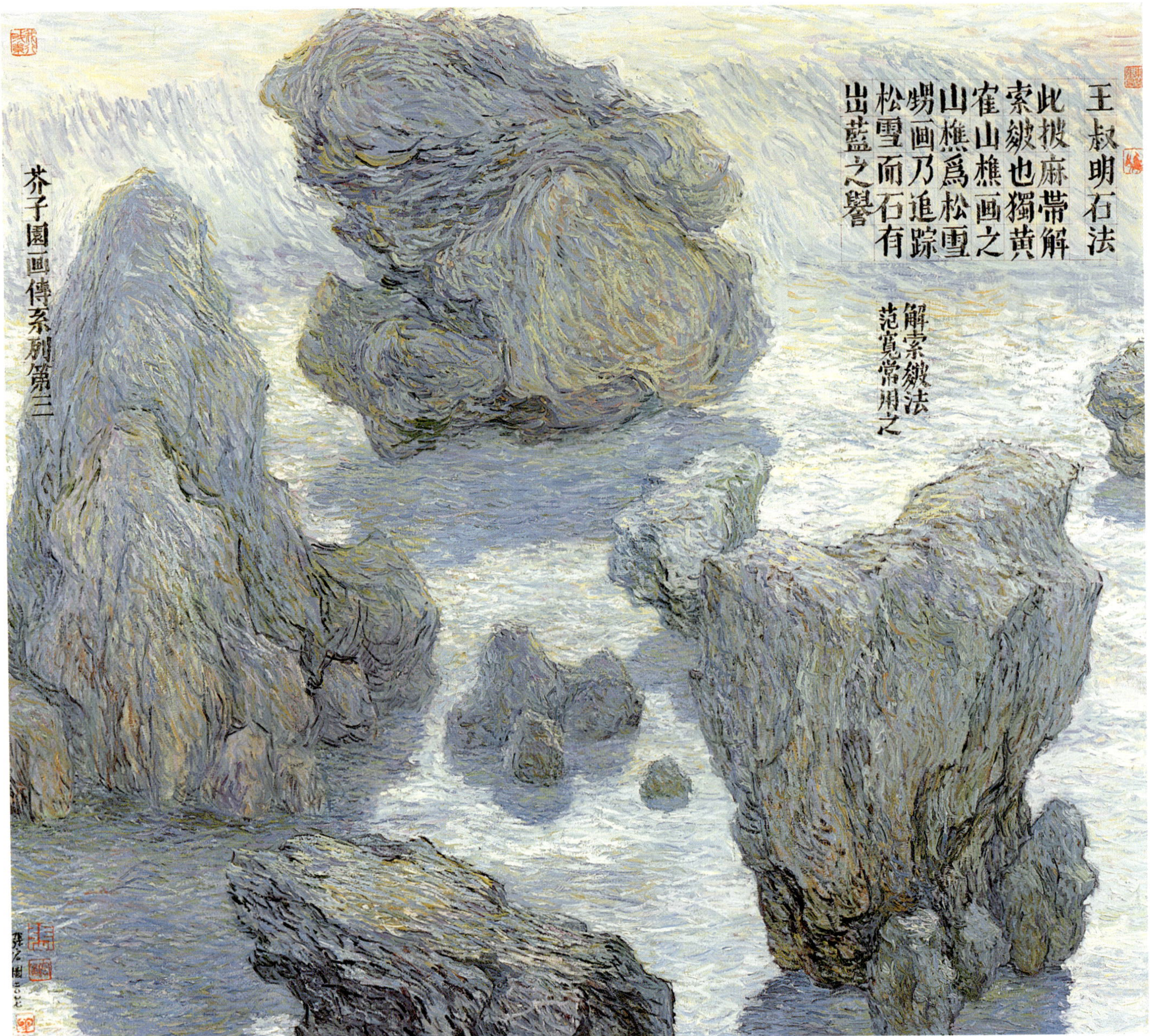

068
Monet, Study of Pi Ma Ts'un and Jie So Ts'un, 2007.
Oil on canvas,
57 ½ x 66 in.

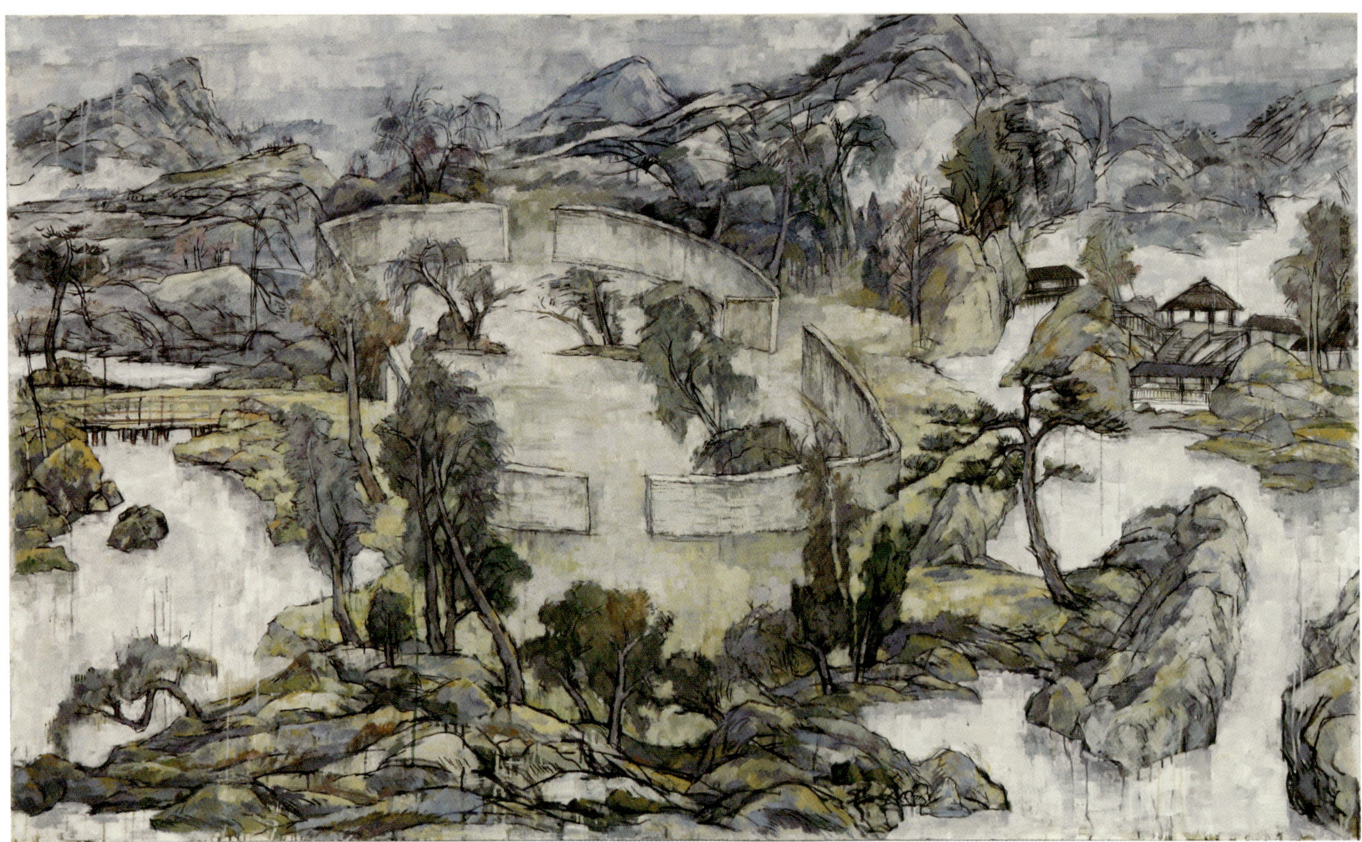

069

069
After Wang Yuanqi, 287 Years Later, 2008.
Oil on canvas,
64 x 108 in.

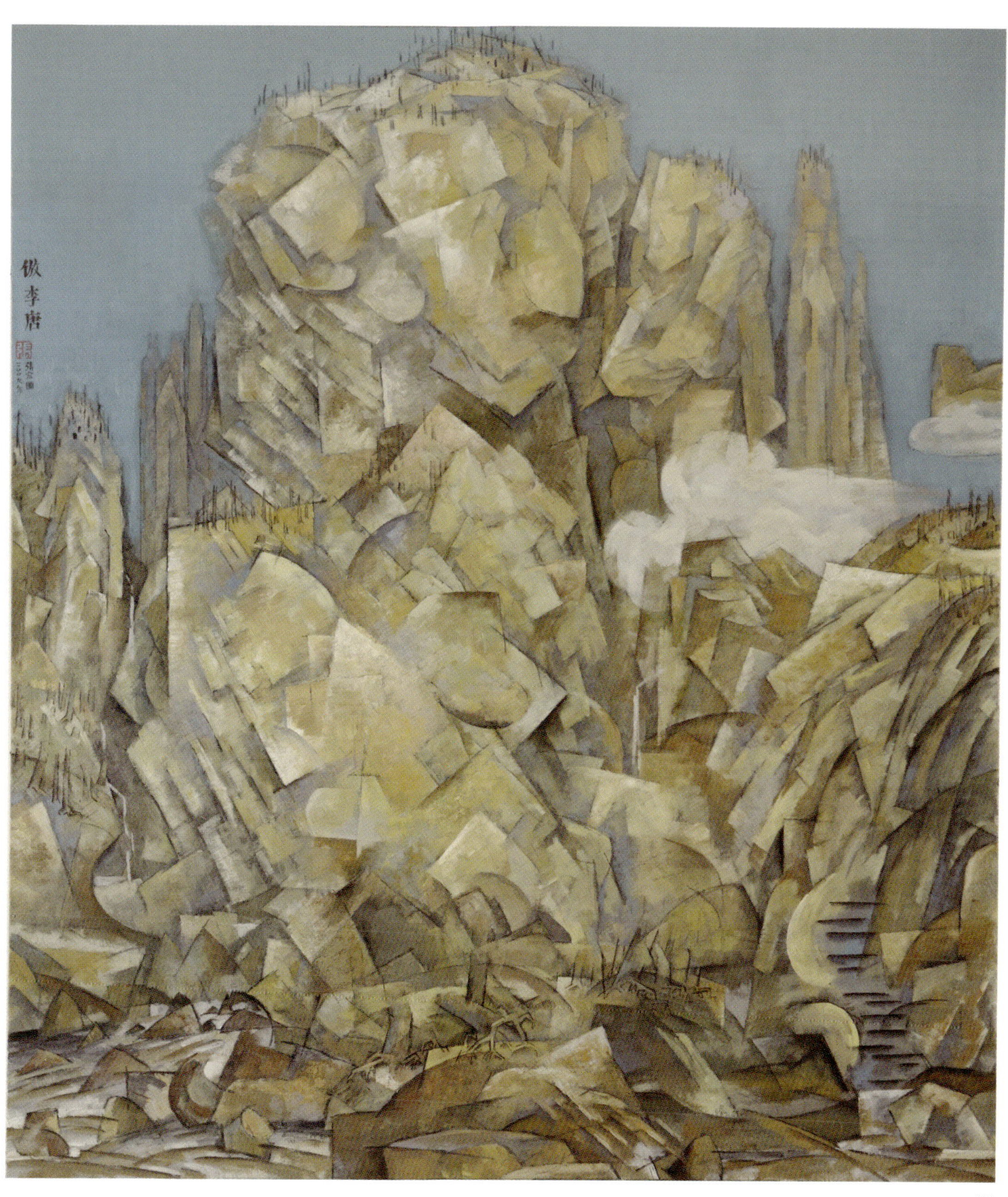

070

After Li Tang, 2009.
Oil on canvas,
76 x 67 in.

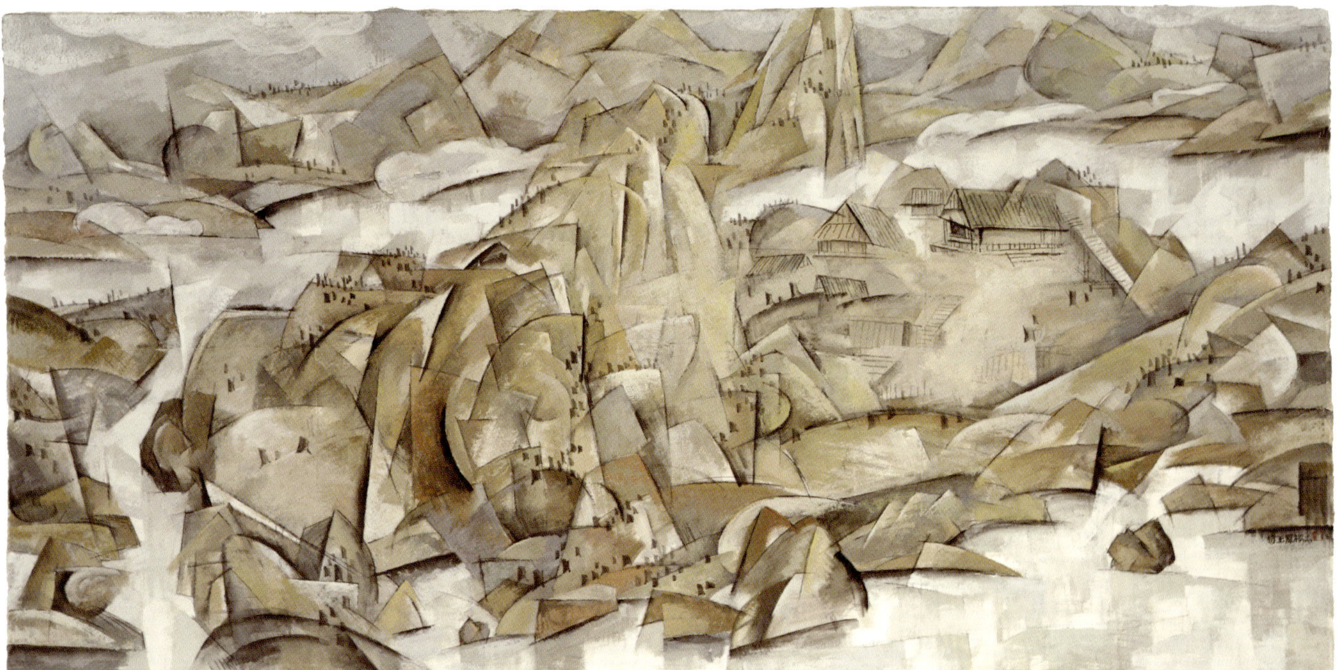

071

071

After Wang Yuanqi, 2009.

Ink and mixed media on rice paper mounted on canvas,
40 x 82 in.

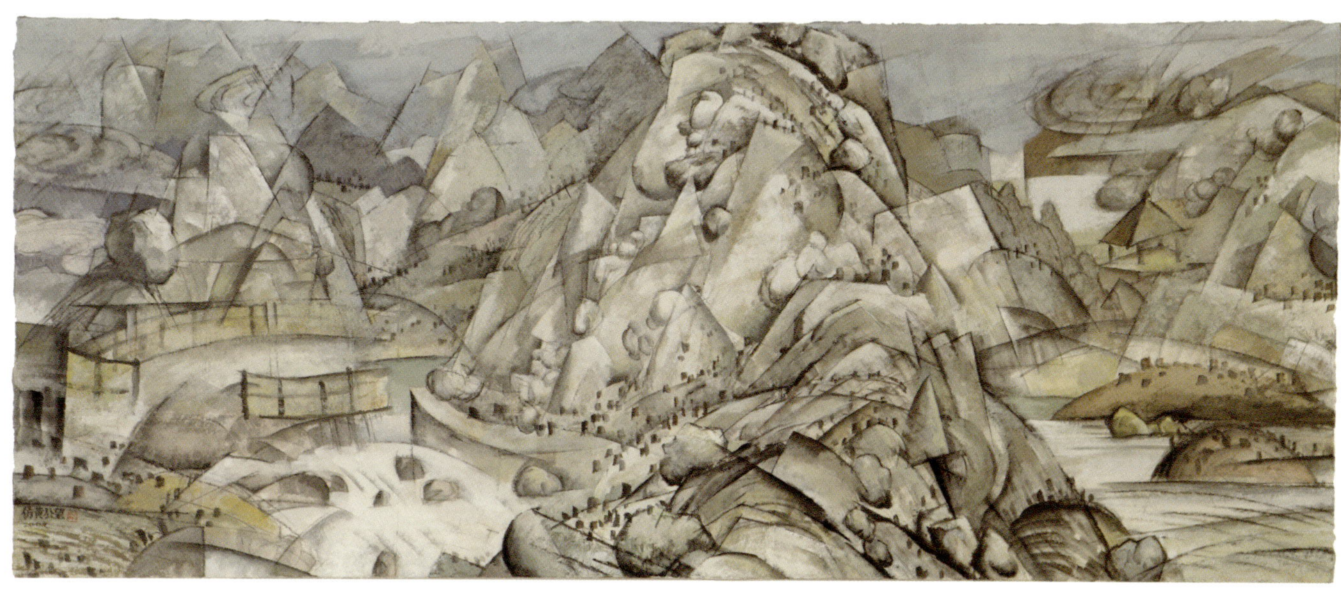

072
After Huang Gongwang, 2009.
Ink and mixed media on rice paper mounted on canvas,
32 x 78 in.

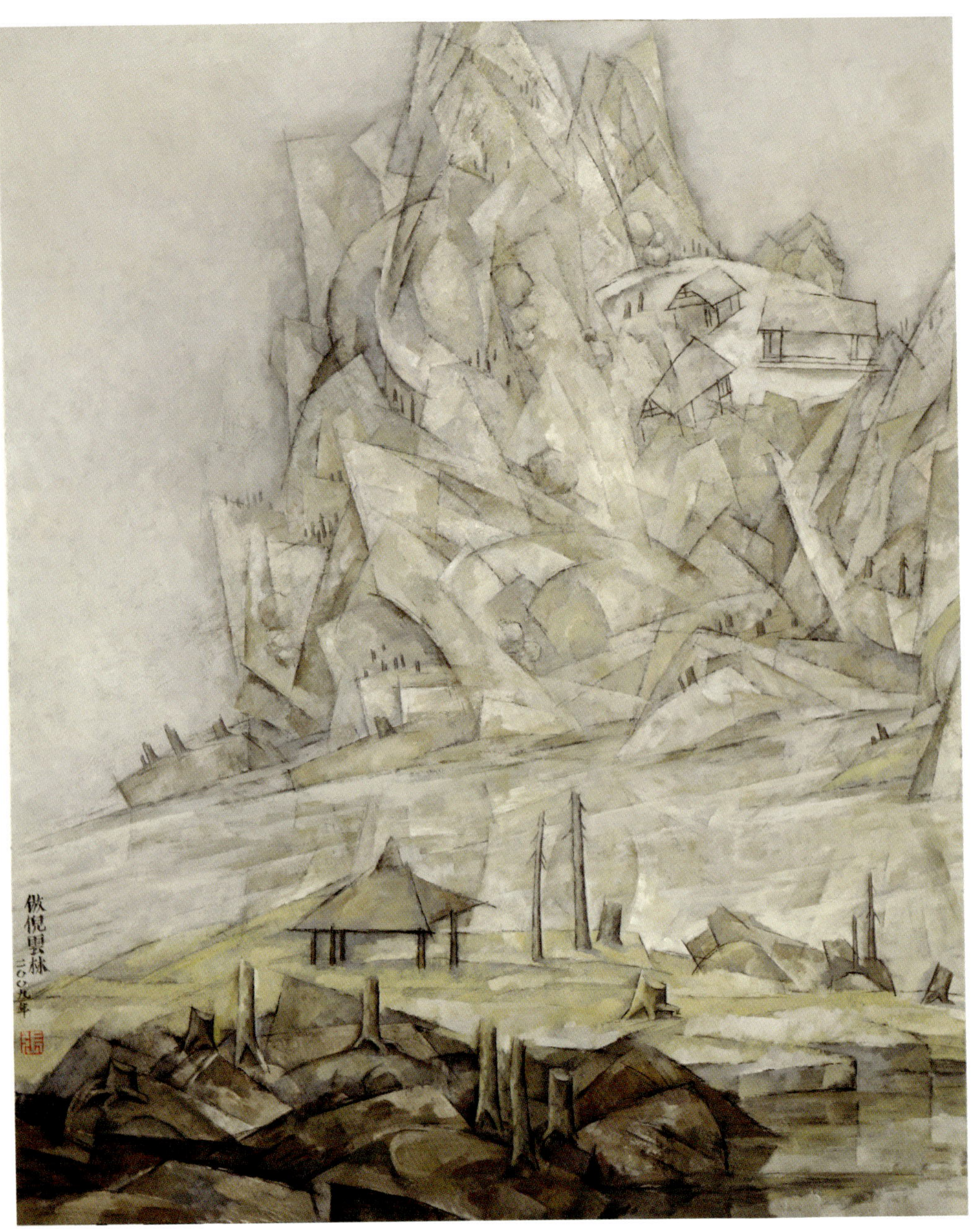

073

073
After Ni Zan, 2009.
Oil on canvas,
66 x 54 in.

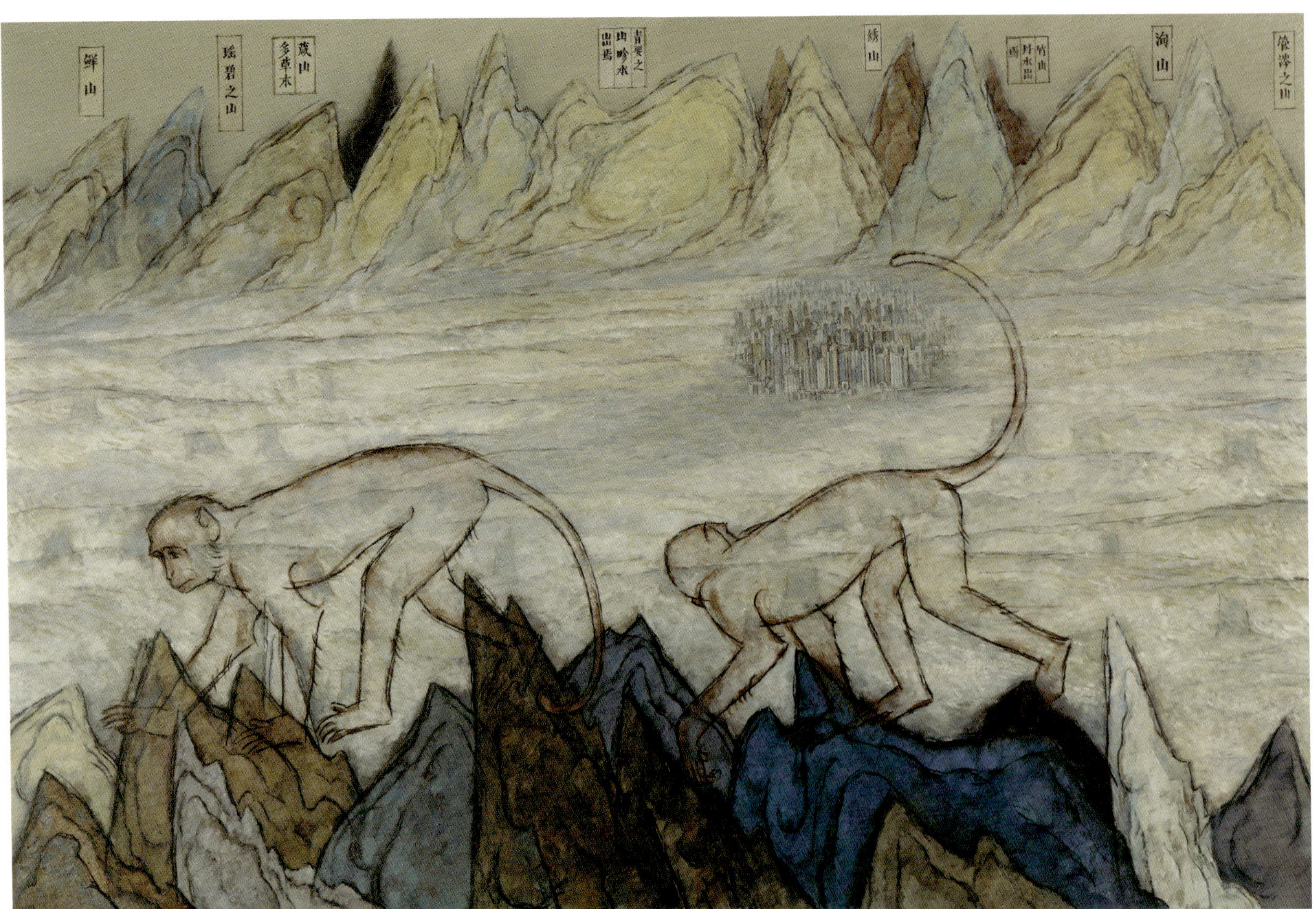

074

074
The Classic of Mountains and Seas (Two Monkeys), 2009–10.
Mixed media and oil on canvas,
64 x 96 in.

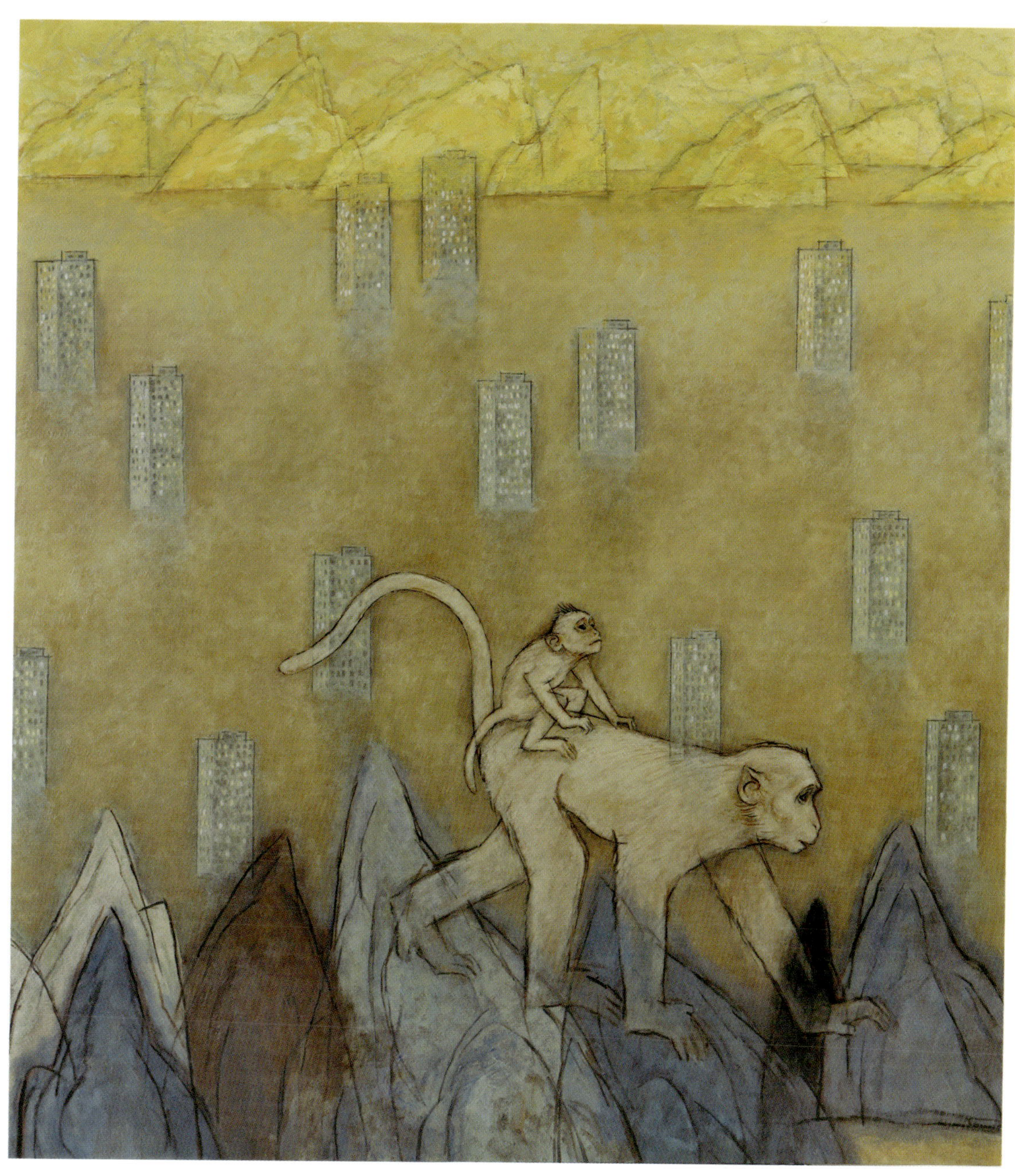

075
Untitled (Mother and Child), 2010.
Mixed media and oil on canvas,
74 x 67 in.

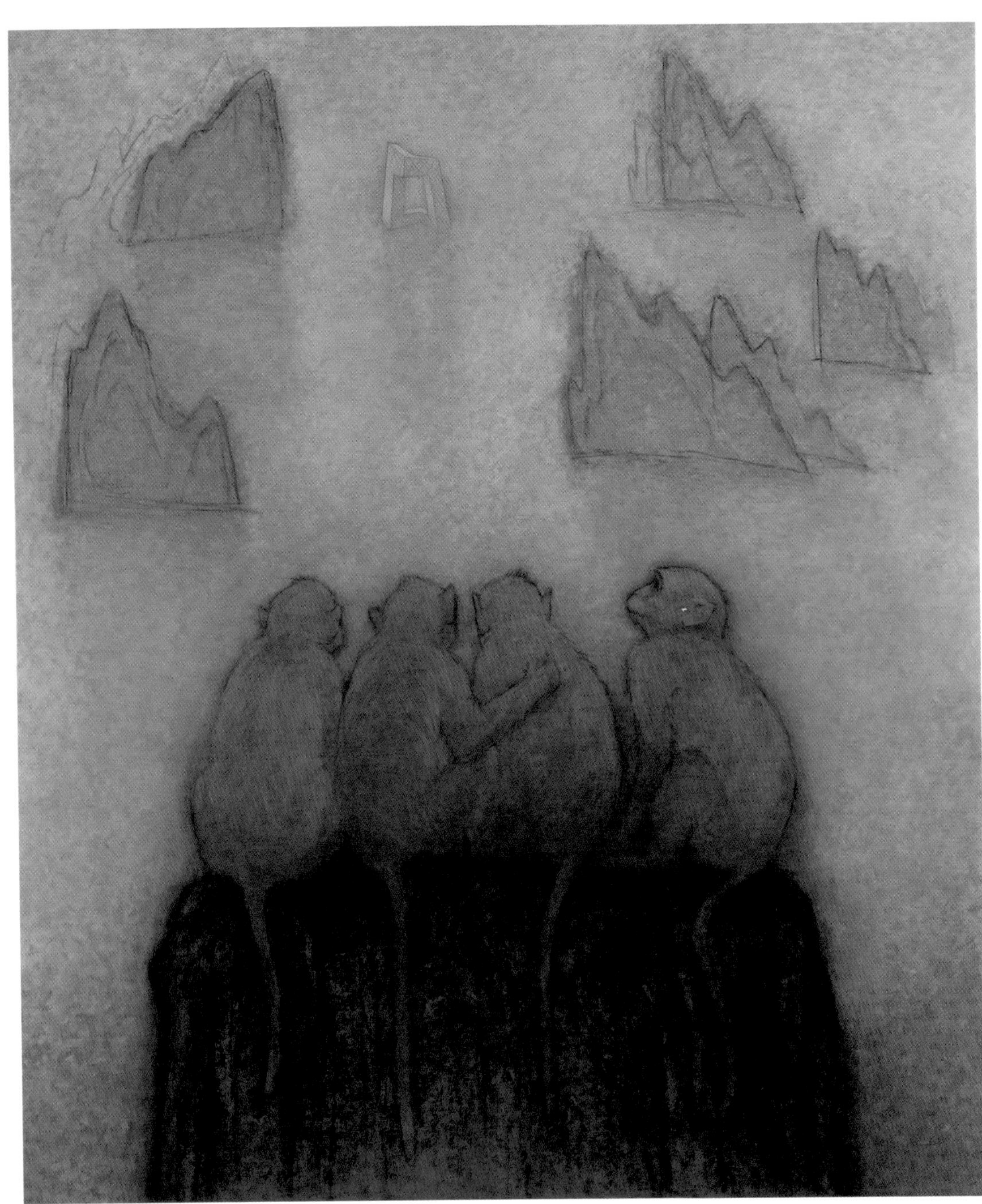

076

076
Untitled (Four Monkeys and CCTV), 2010.
Mixed media and oil on canvas,
74 ½ x 64 in.

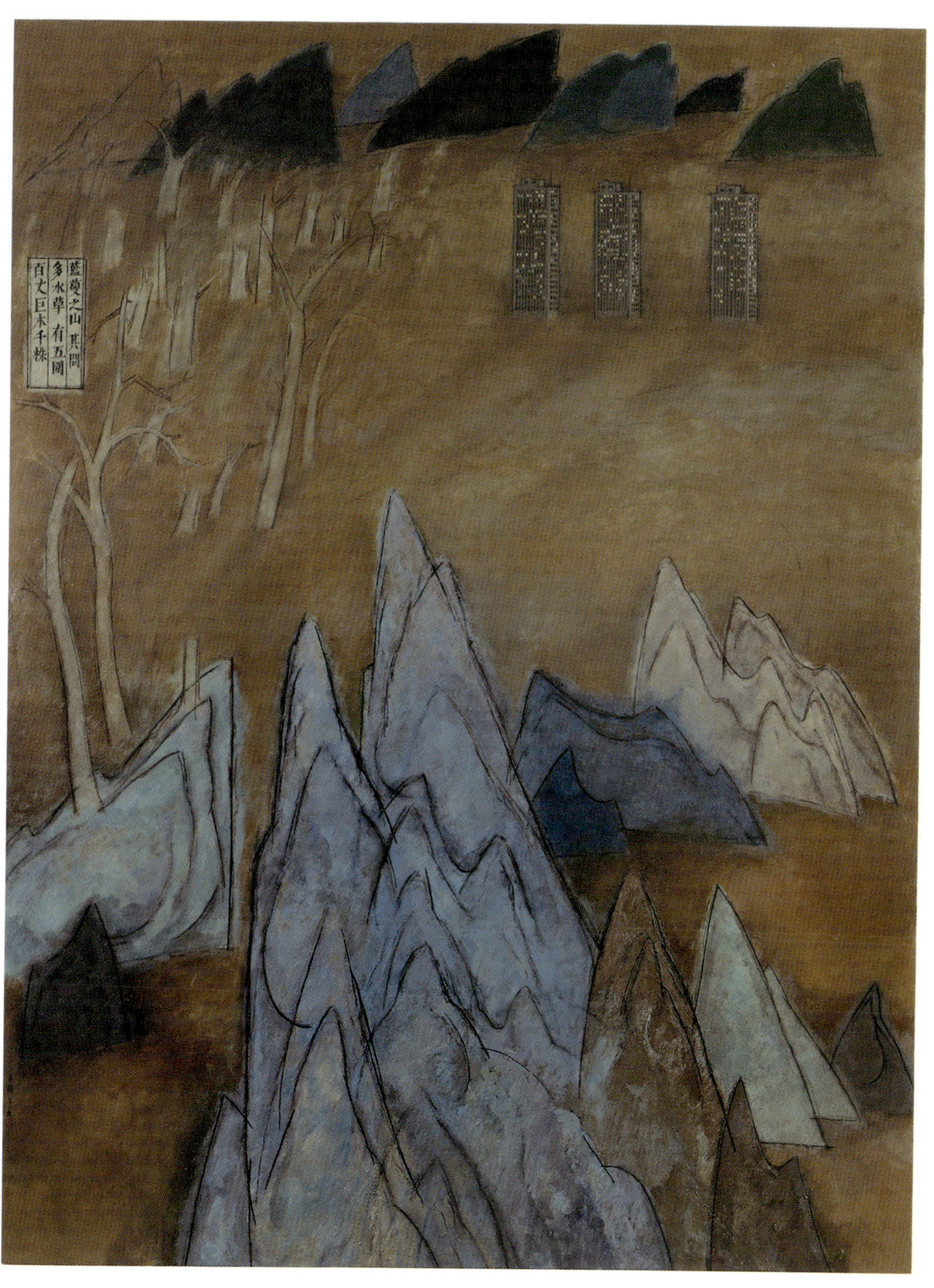

077

077
Homage to Ni Zan, 2010.
Mixed media and oil on canvas,
90 x 68 in.

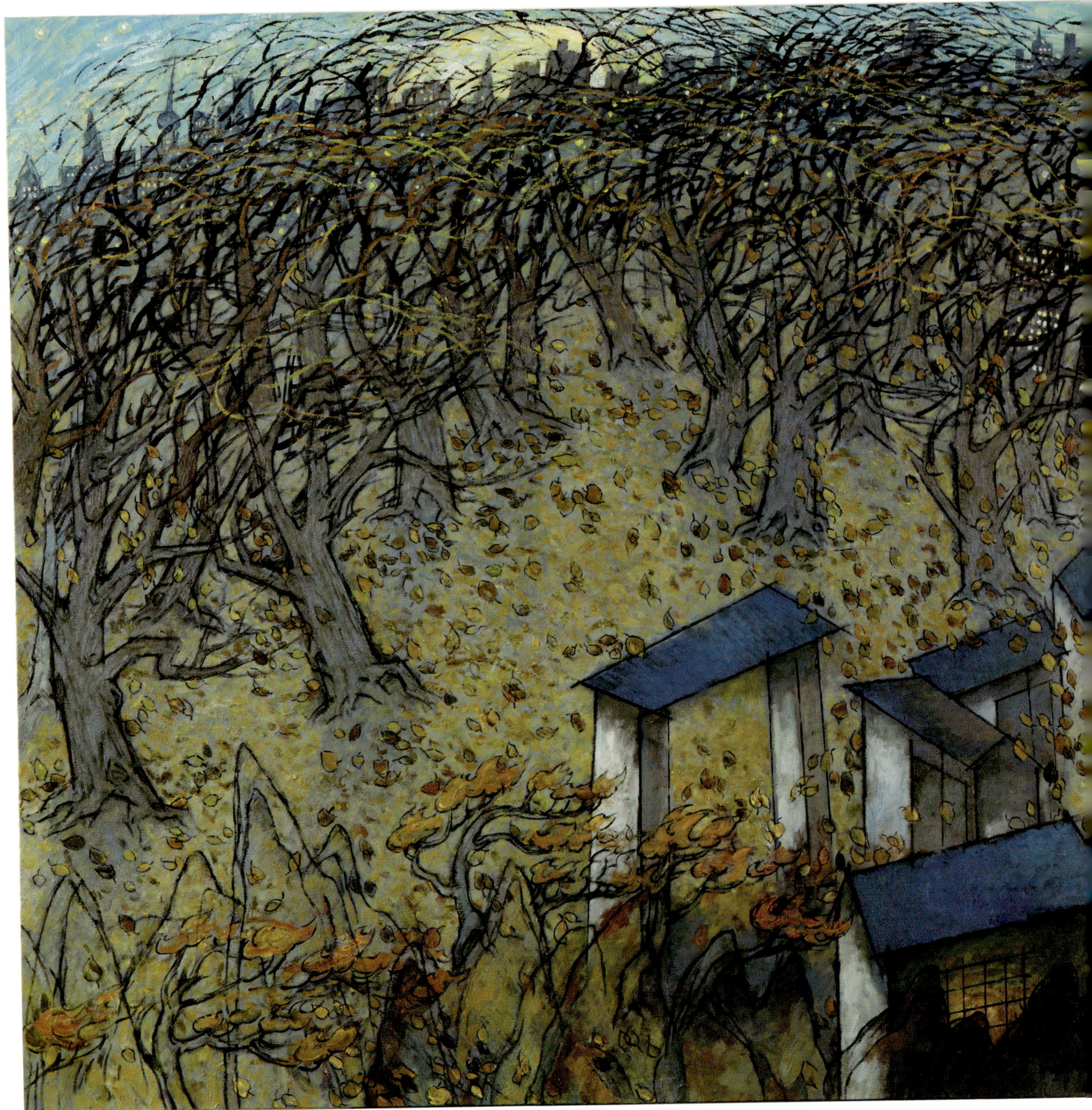
078

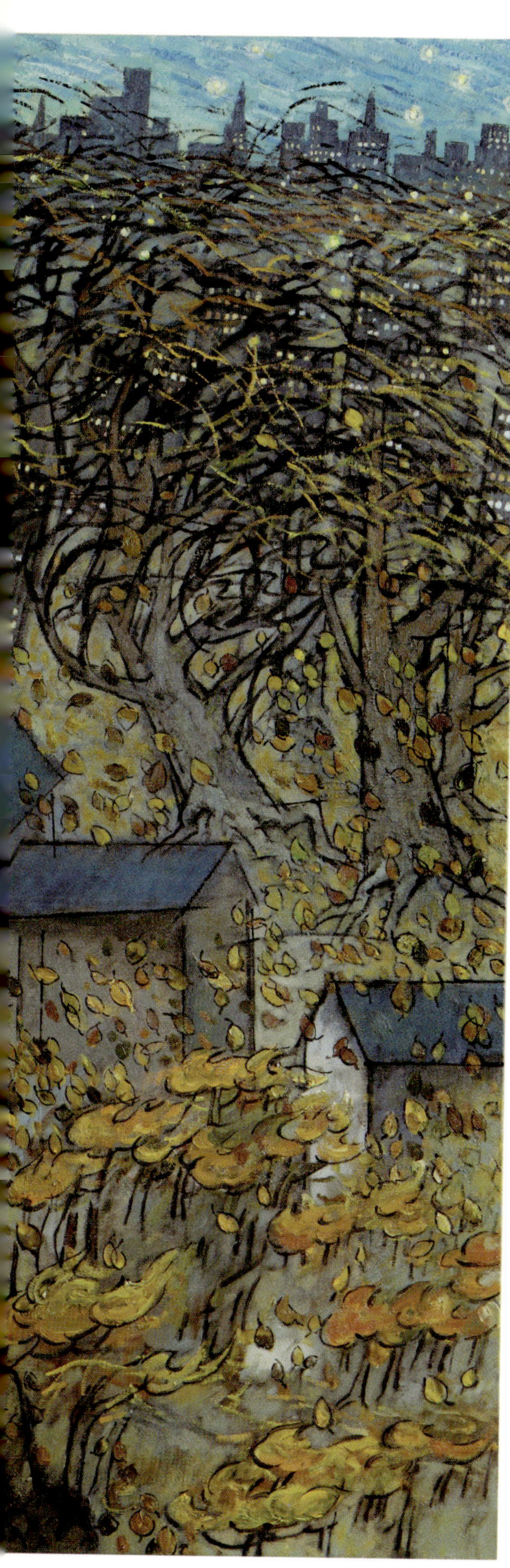

078
Ode to the Sound of Autumn, 2011.
Mixed media and oil on canvas,
64 ½ x 89 in.

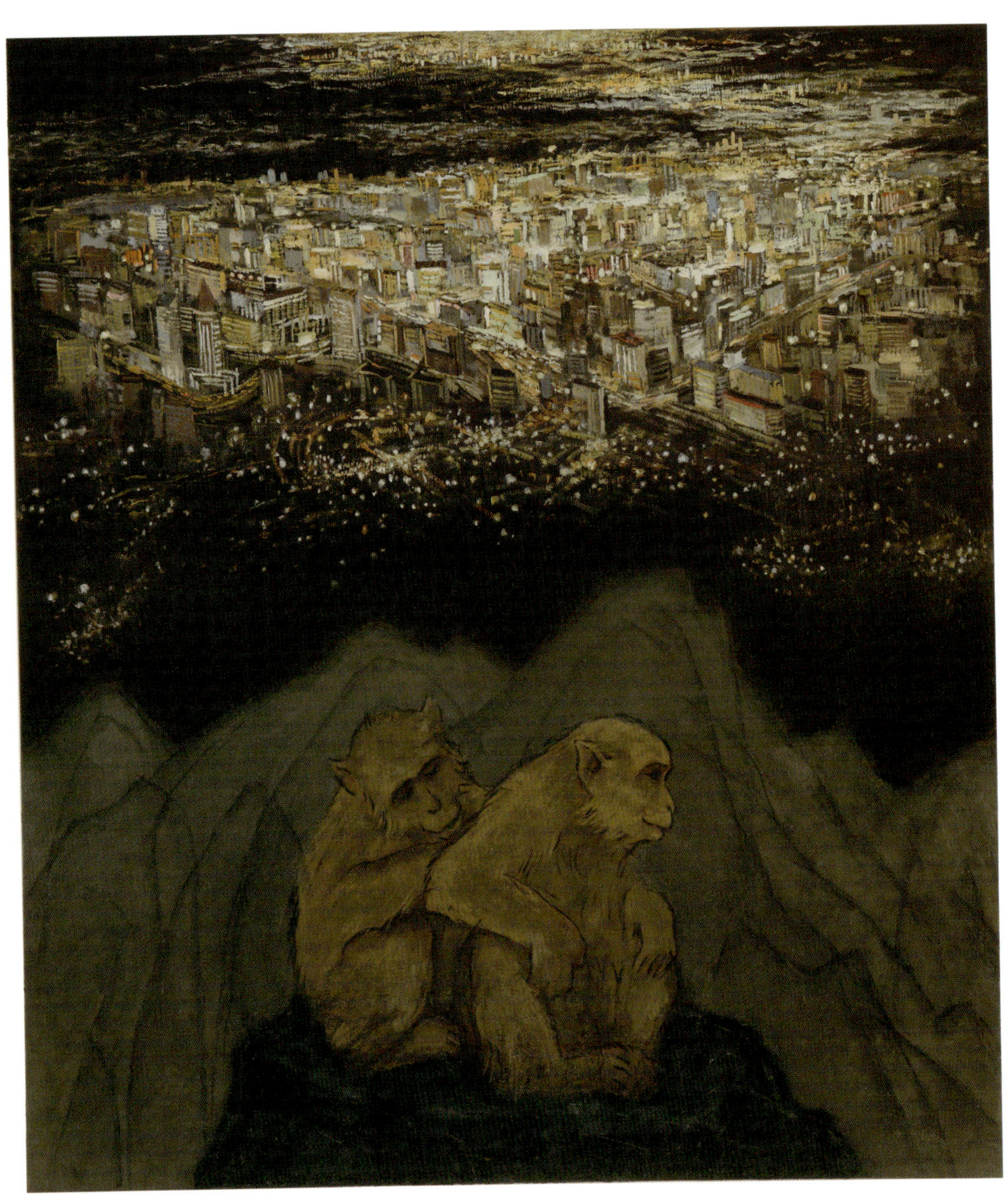

079

079
Untitled 10-L, 2010.
Mixed media and oil on canvas,
54 ½ x 48 in.

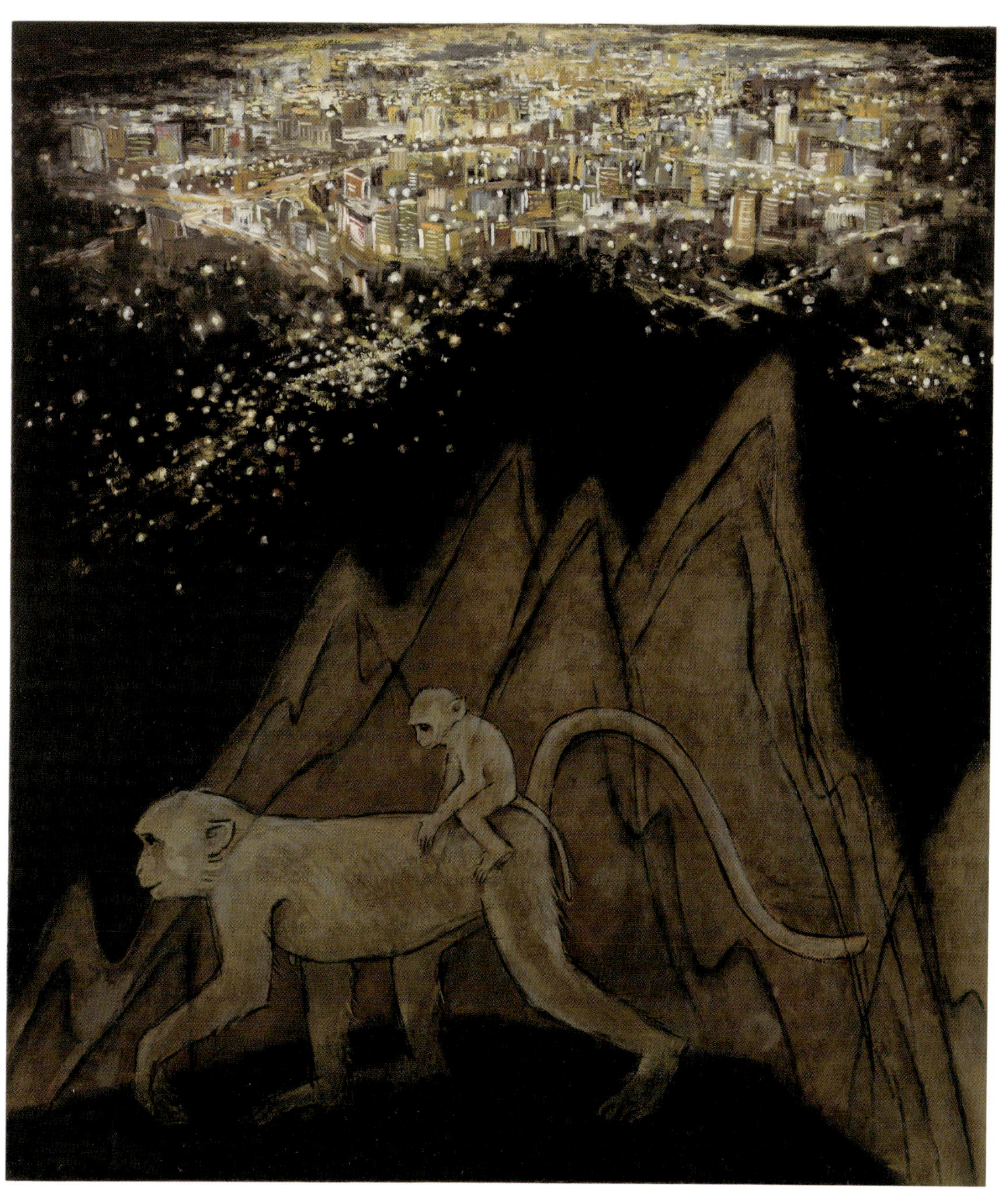

080

Untitled 10-M, 2010.
Mixed media and oil on canvas,
54 ½ x 48 in.

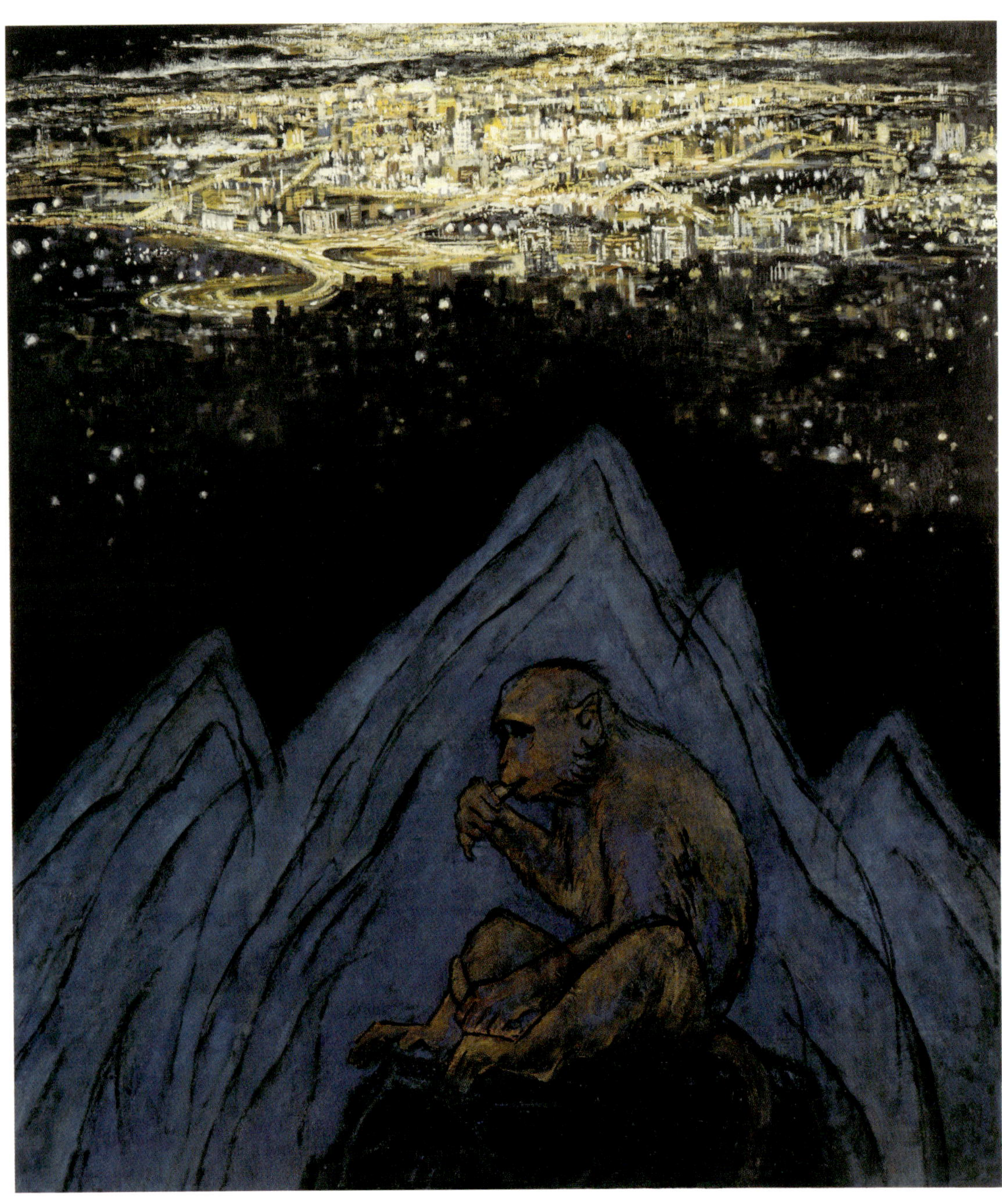

081

081
Untitled 10-B, 2010.
Mixed media and oil on canvas,
54 ½ x 48 in.

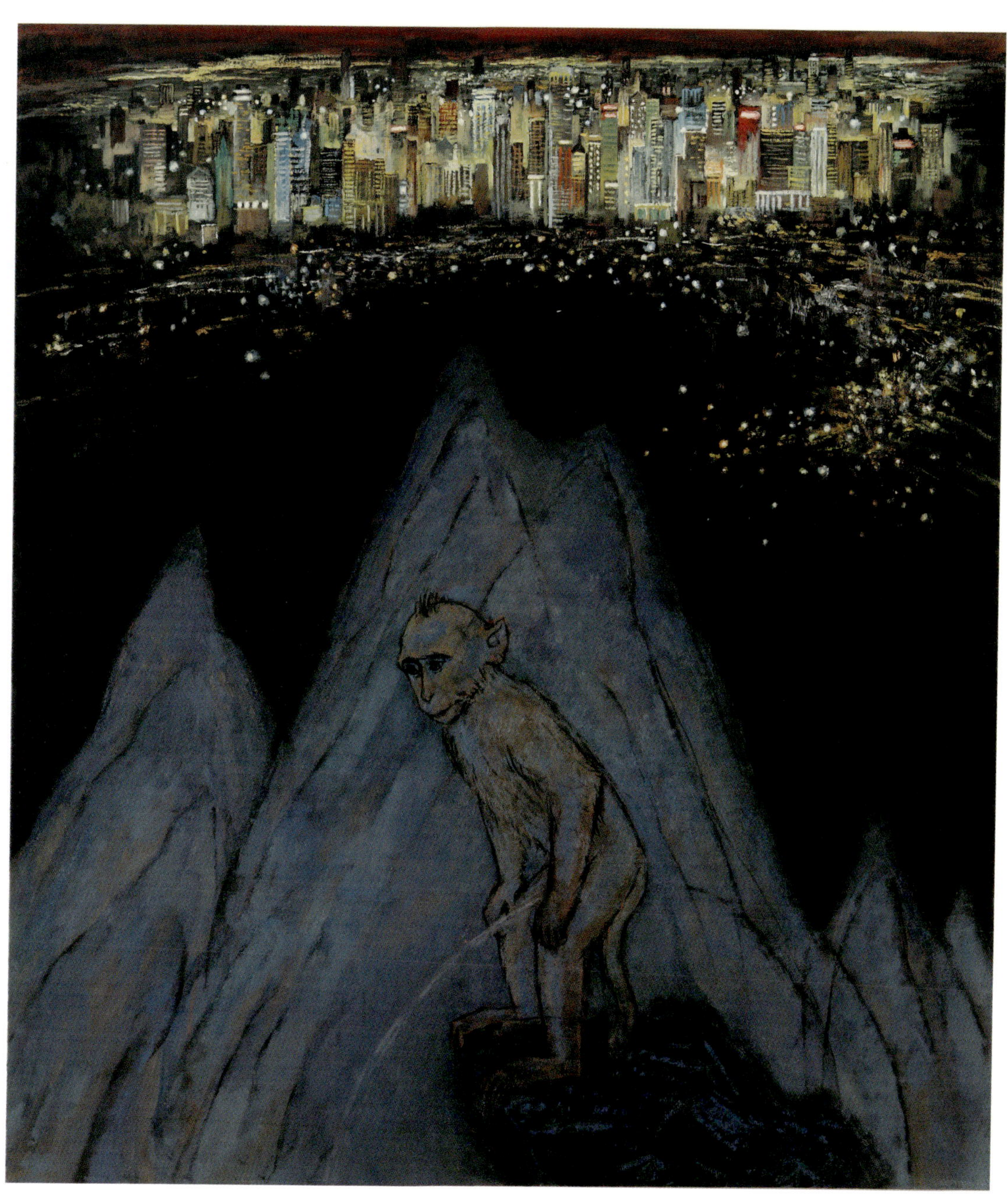

082
Untitled 10-P, 2010.
Mixed media and oil on canvas,
54 ½ x 48 in.

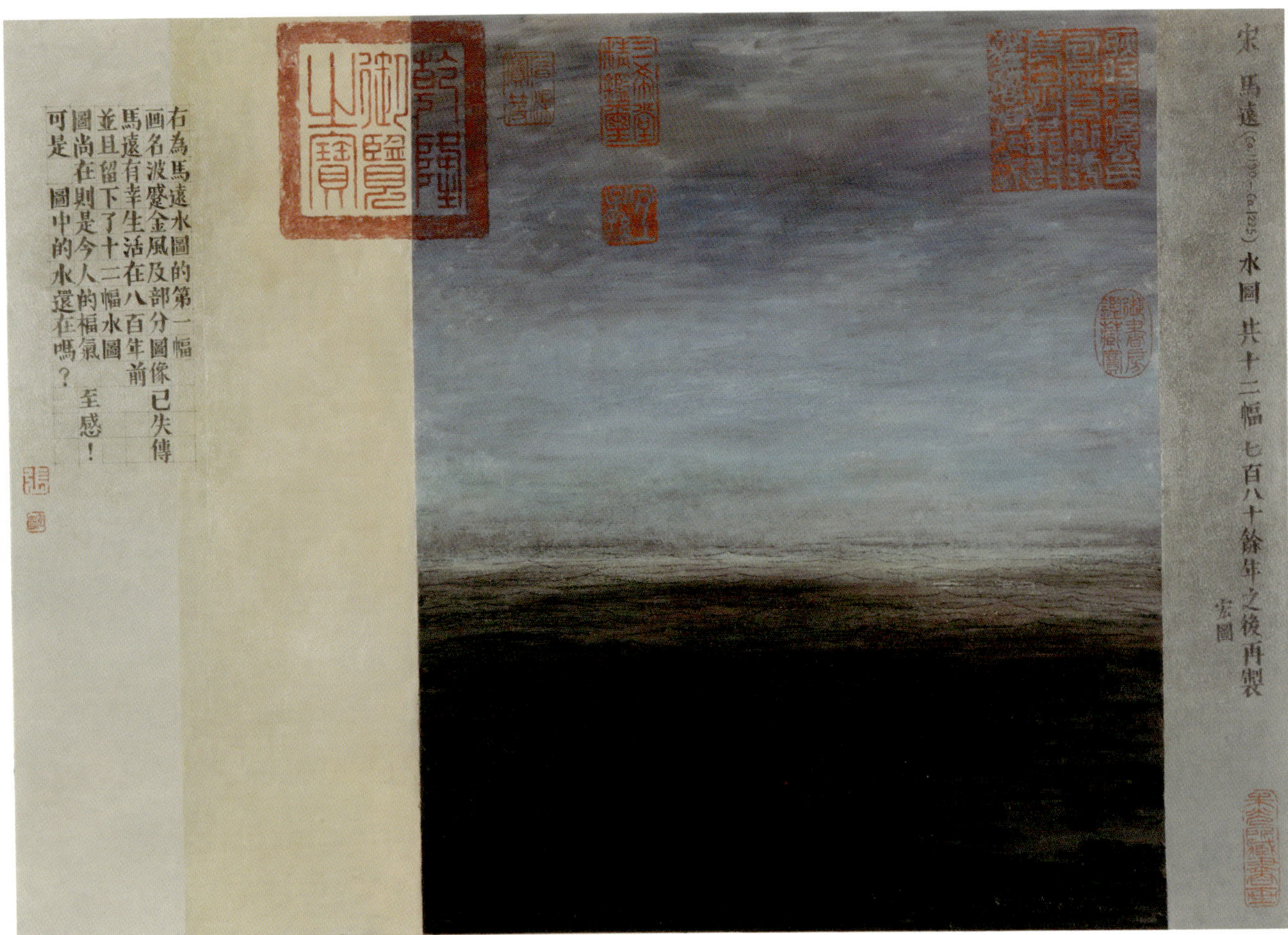

083

083
Re-Make of Ma Yuan's Water Album A (780 Years Later), 2008.
Oil on canvas,
50 x 72 in.

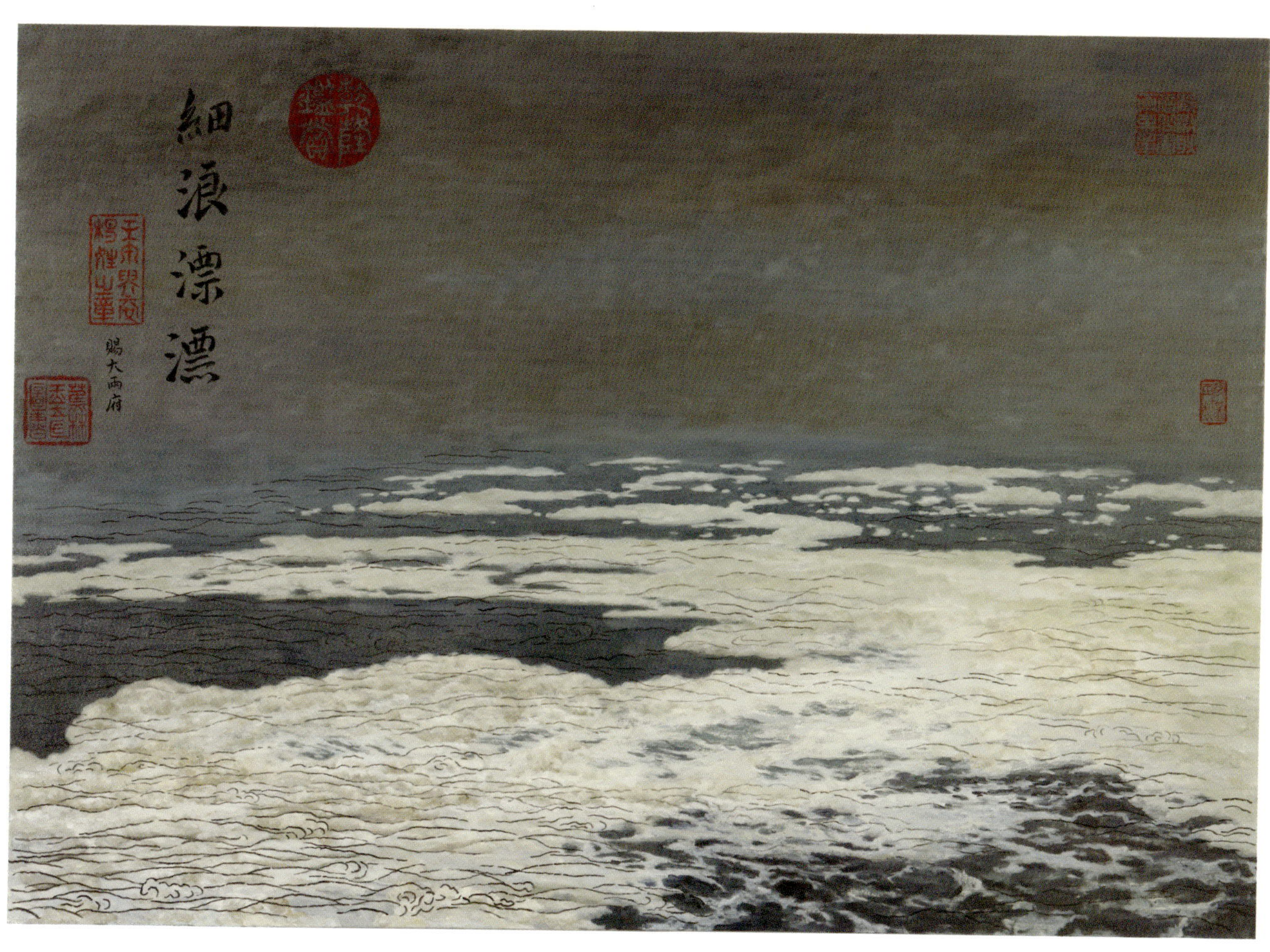

084

084

Re-Make of Ma Yuan's Water Album X (780 Years Later), 2008.
Oil on canvas,
50 x 72 in.

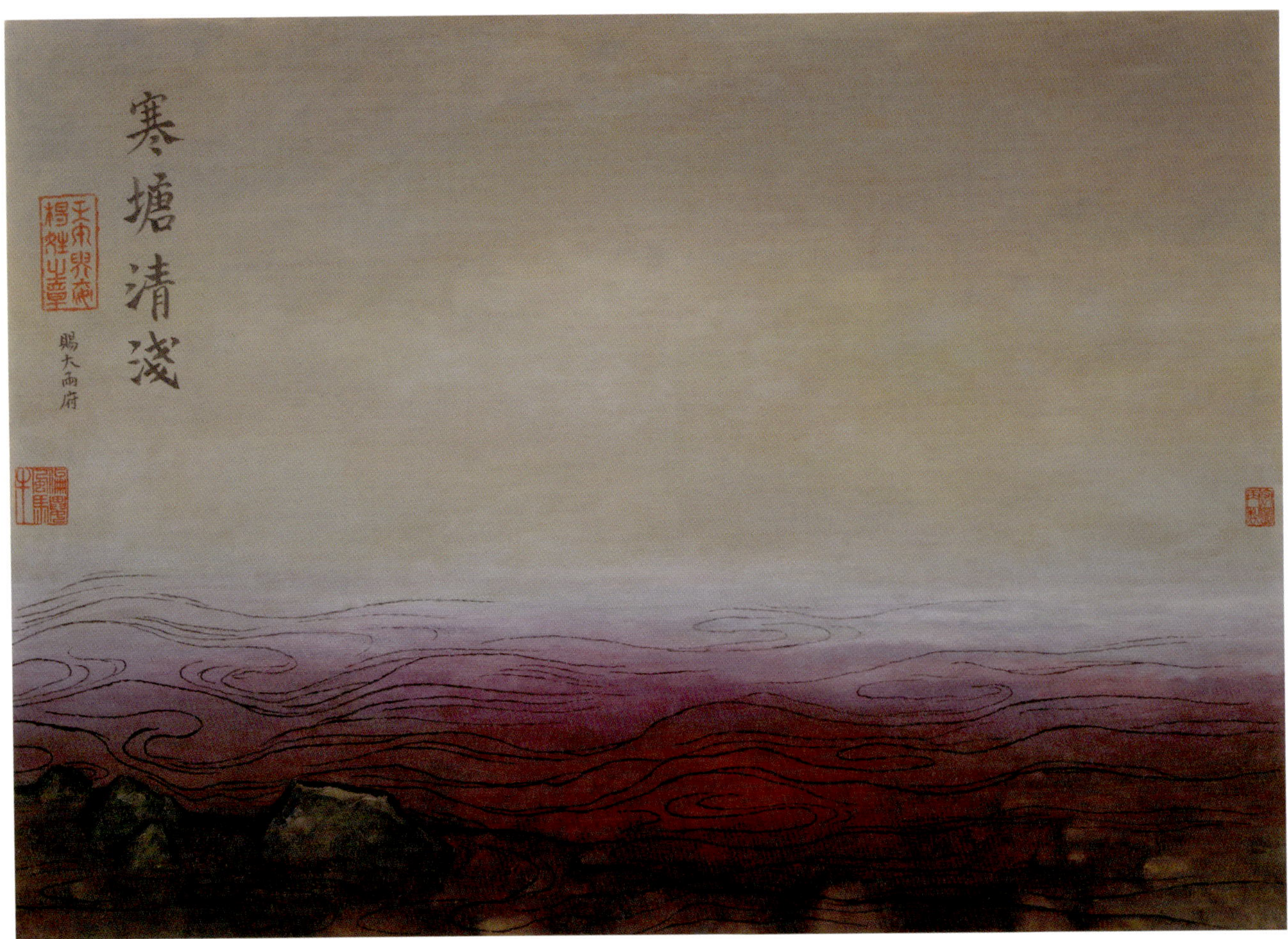

085

085

Re-Make of Ma Yuan's Water Album P (780 Years Later), 2008.
Oil on canvas,
50 x 72 in.

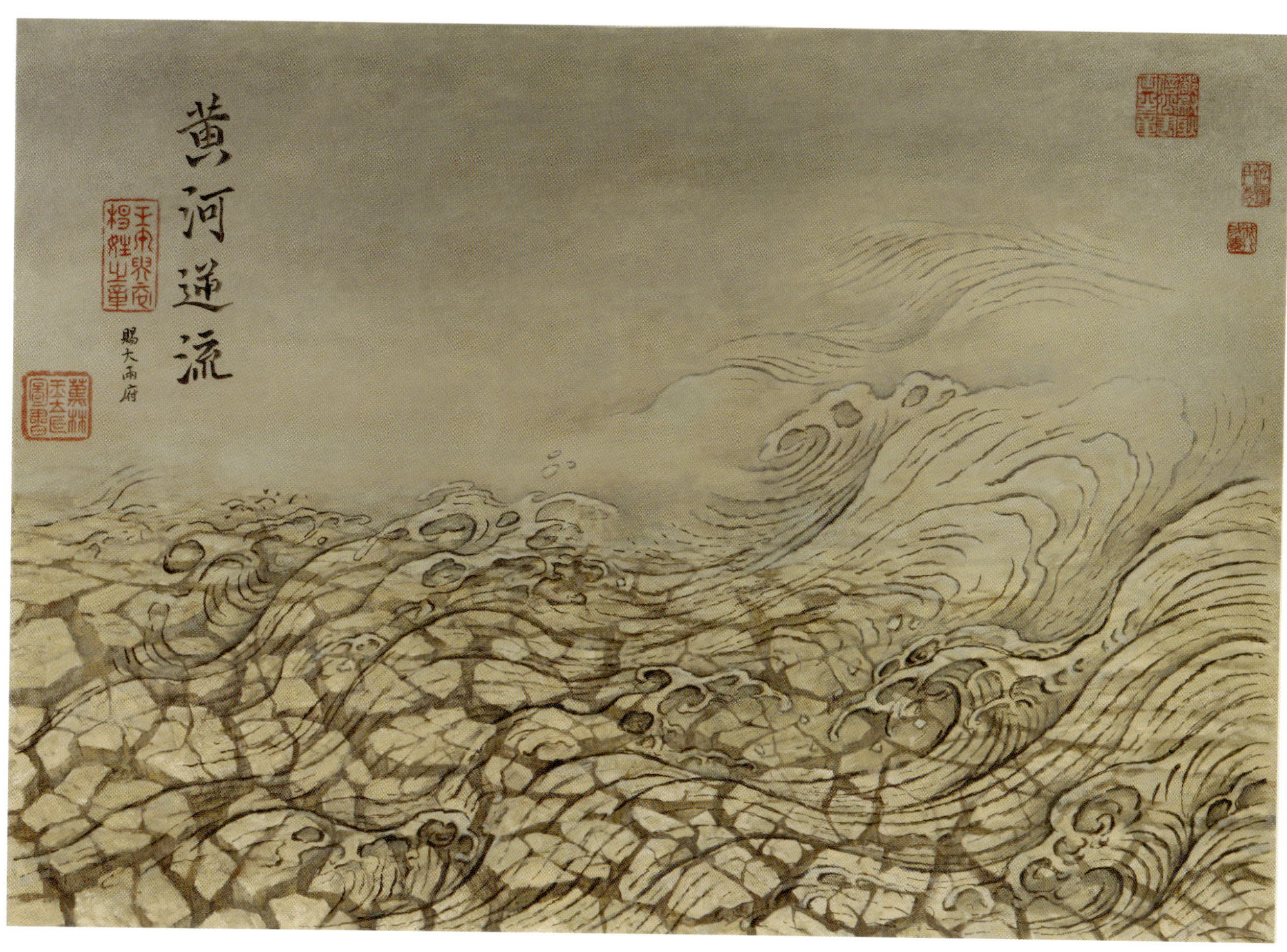

086
Re-Make of Ma Yuan's Water Album H (780 Years Later), 2008.
Oil on canvas,
50 x 72 in.

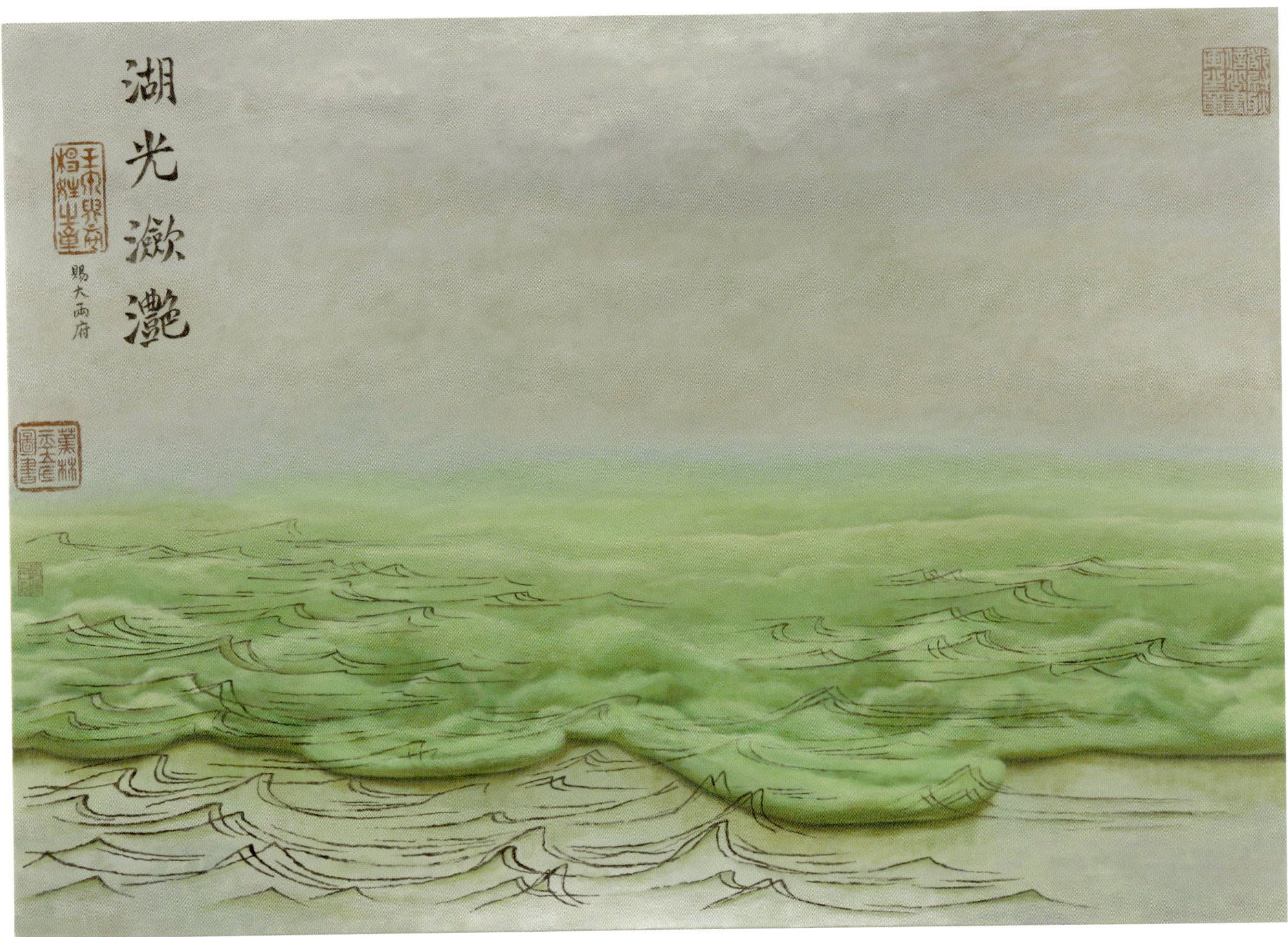

087

087
Re-Make of Ma Yuan's Water Album L (780 Years Later), 2008.
Oil on canvas,
50 x 72 in.

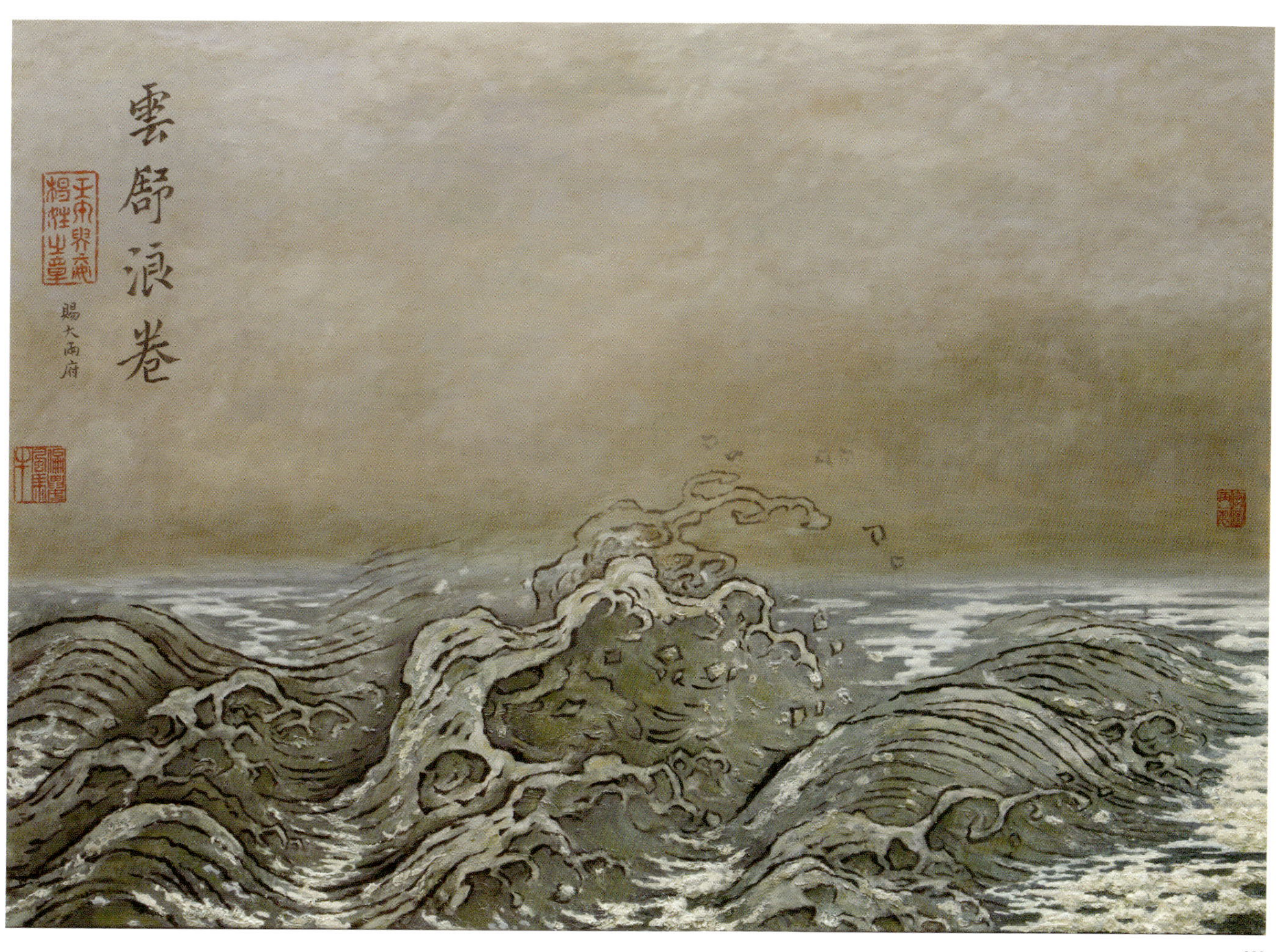

088
Re-Make of Ma Yuan's Water Album F (780 Years Later), 2008.
Oil on canvas,
50 x 72 in.

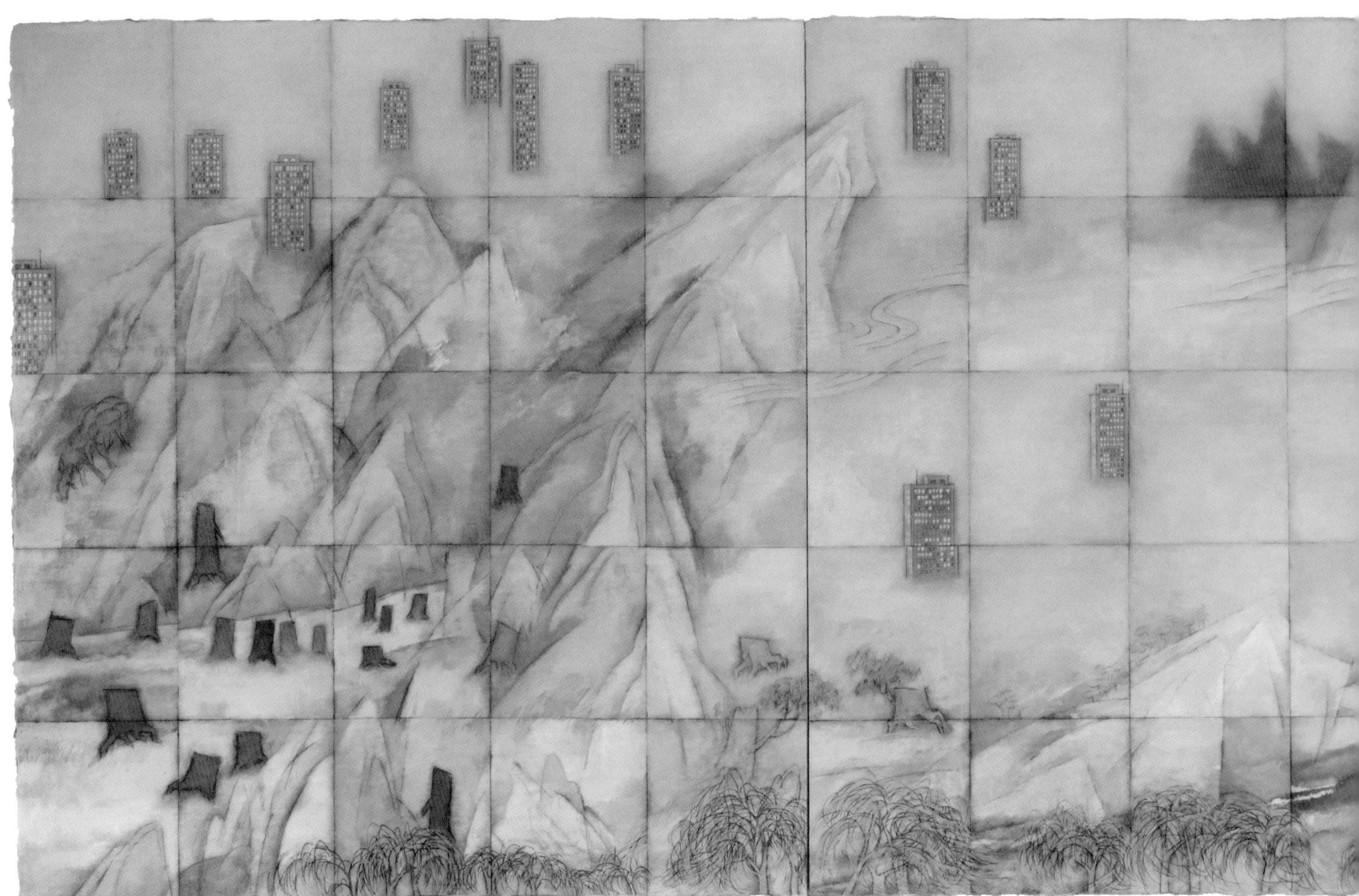

089
Shan Shui, Untitled, 2013.
Ink, oil, and mixed media on rice paper mounted on panels,
48 x 135 in.

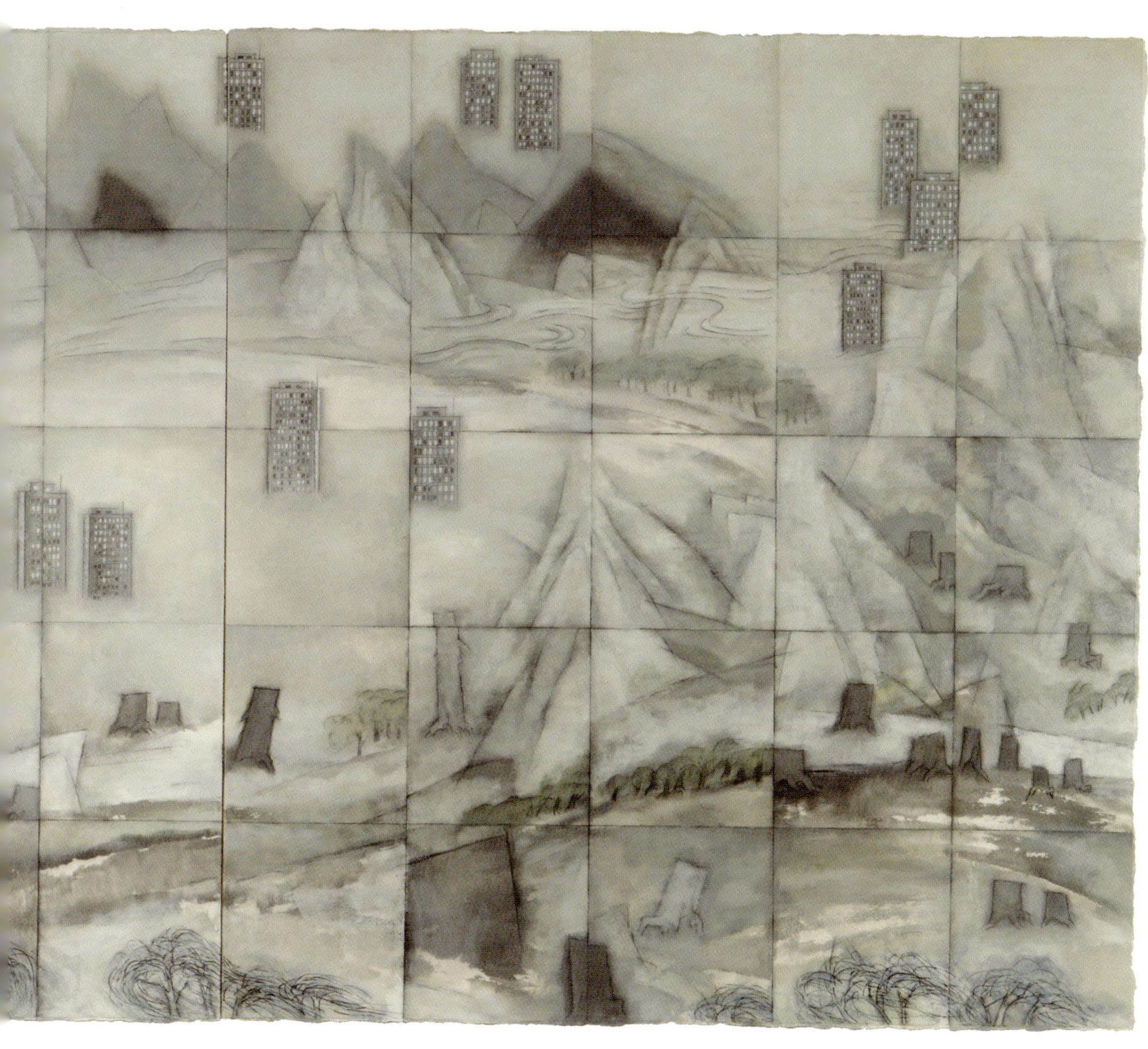

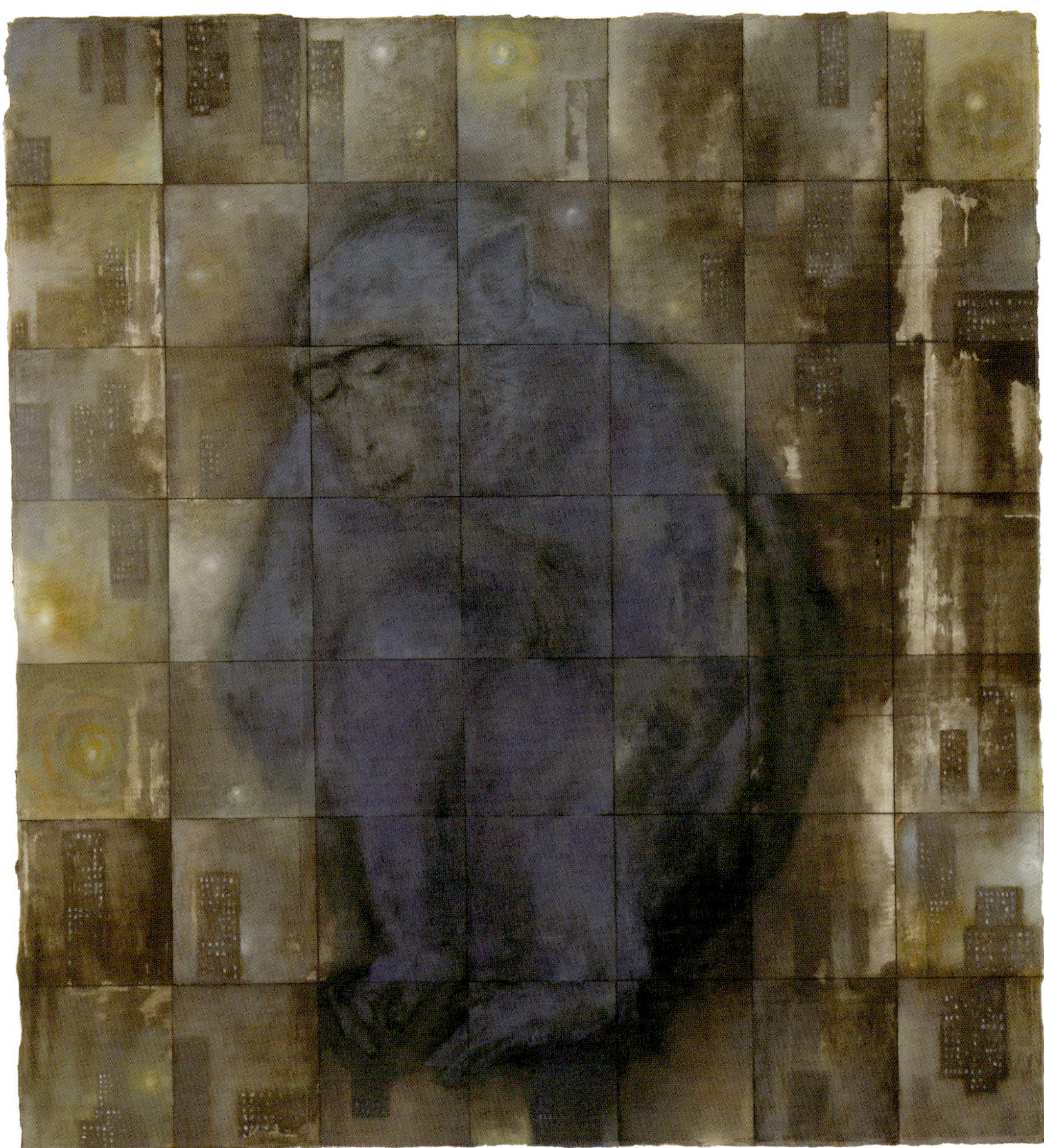

090

090
Sleeping Monkey, 2013.
Ink and oil on rice paper mounted on panel,
48 ½ x 46 in.

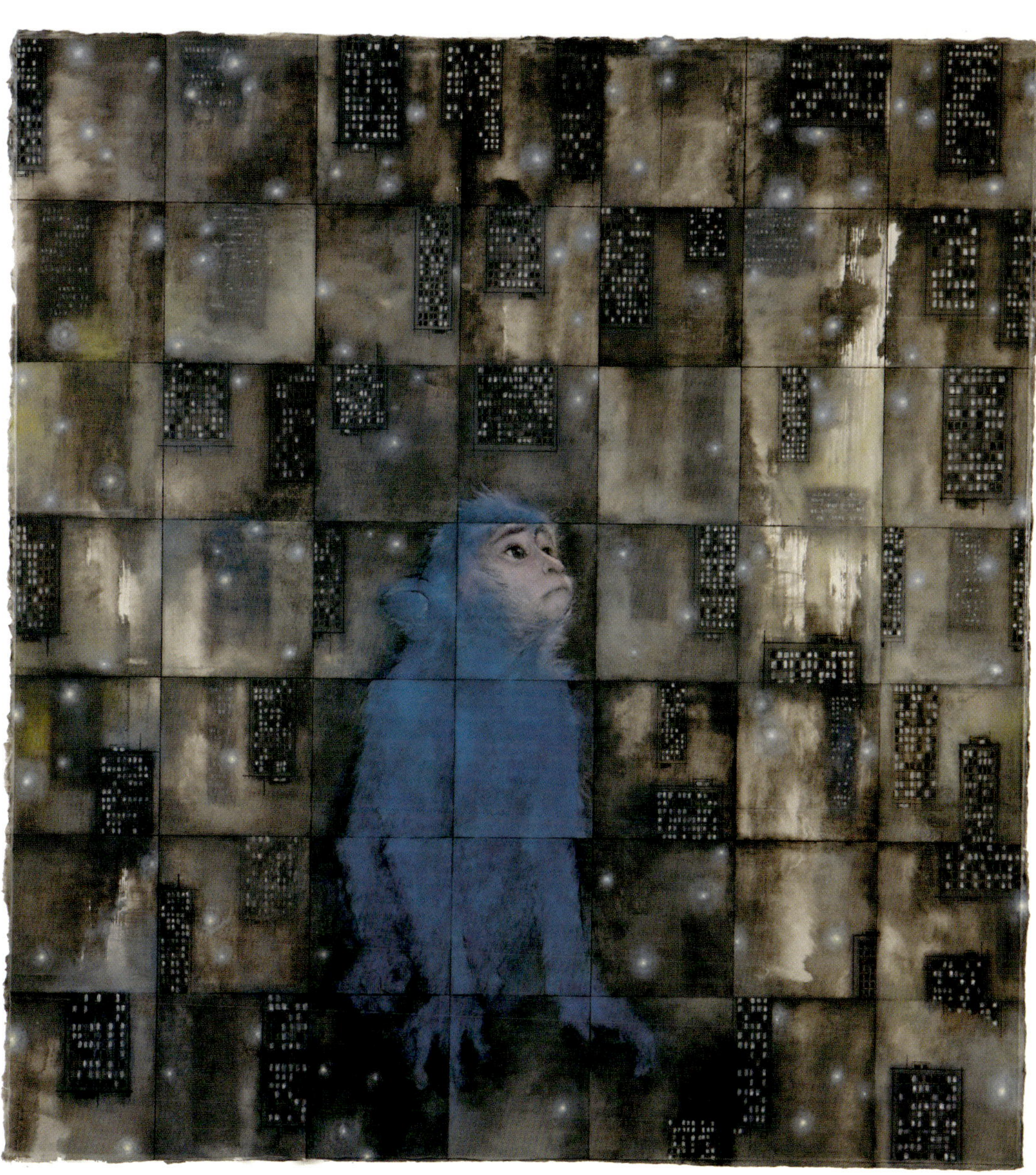

091

091
Little Monkey, 2013.
Ink and oil on rice paper mounted on panel,
48 ½ x 46 in.

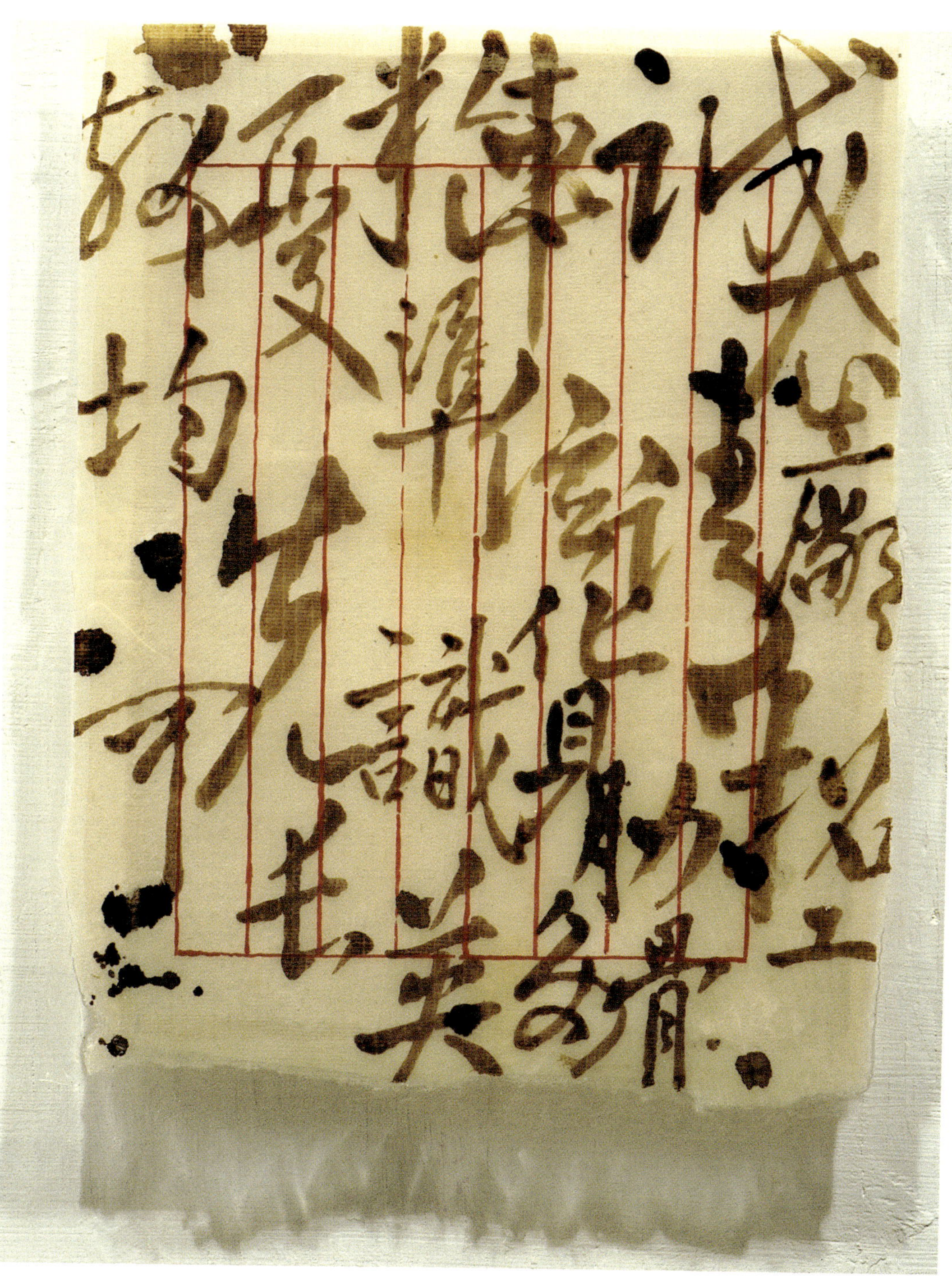

092
Chinatown Sweatshop Help Wanted Ad Wang Xizhi (303–361 A.D.) Style, 1996.
From the series "Soy Sauce Calligraphy,"
Soy sauce on rice paper, sealed in epoxy resin,
42 x 32 in.

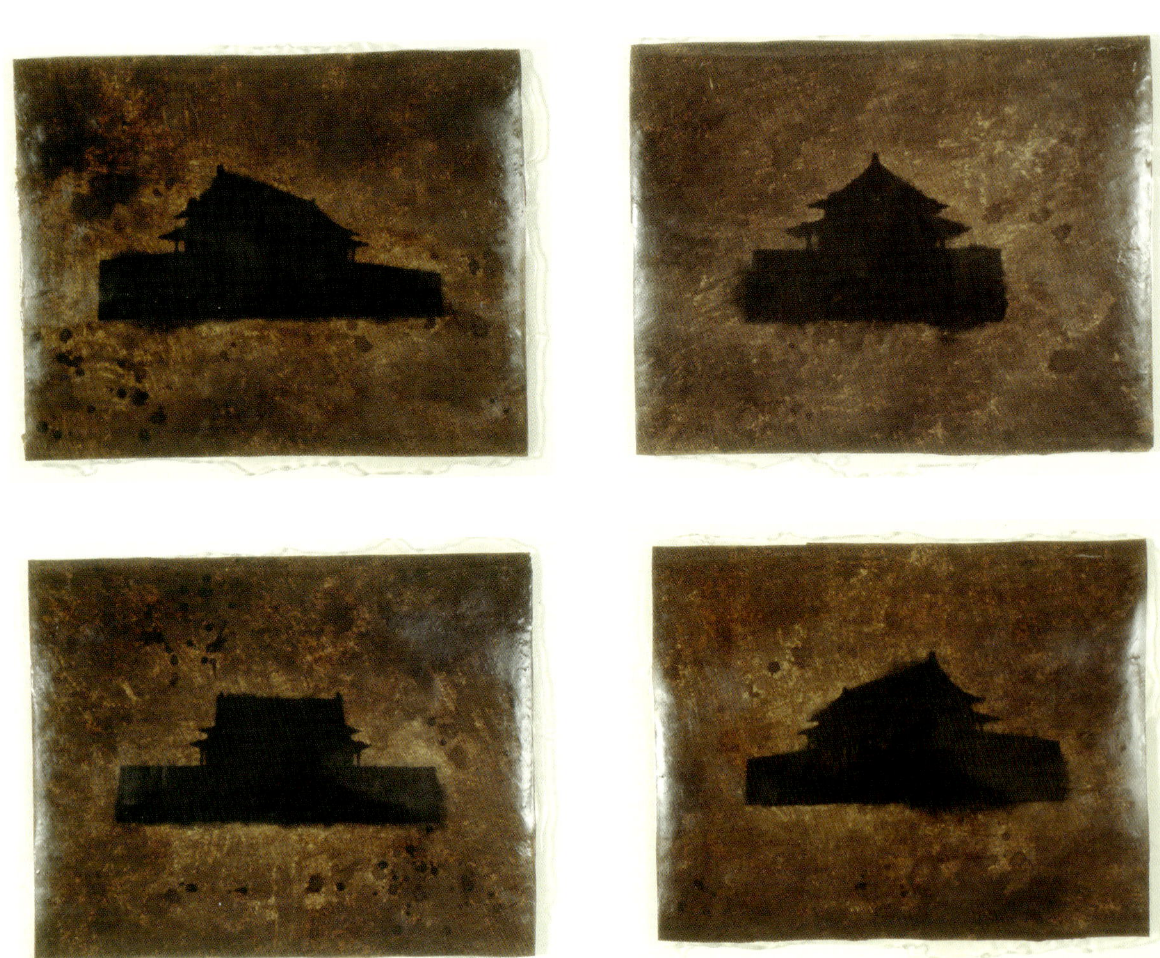

093

093
Soy Sauce Tiananmen, 2005.
Soy sauce and charcoal on rice paper,
56 x 70 in.

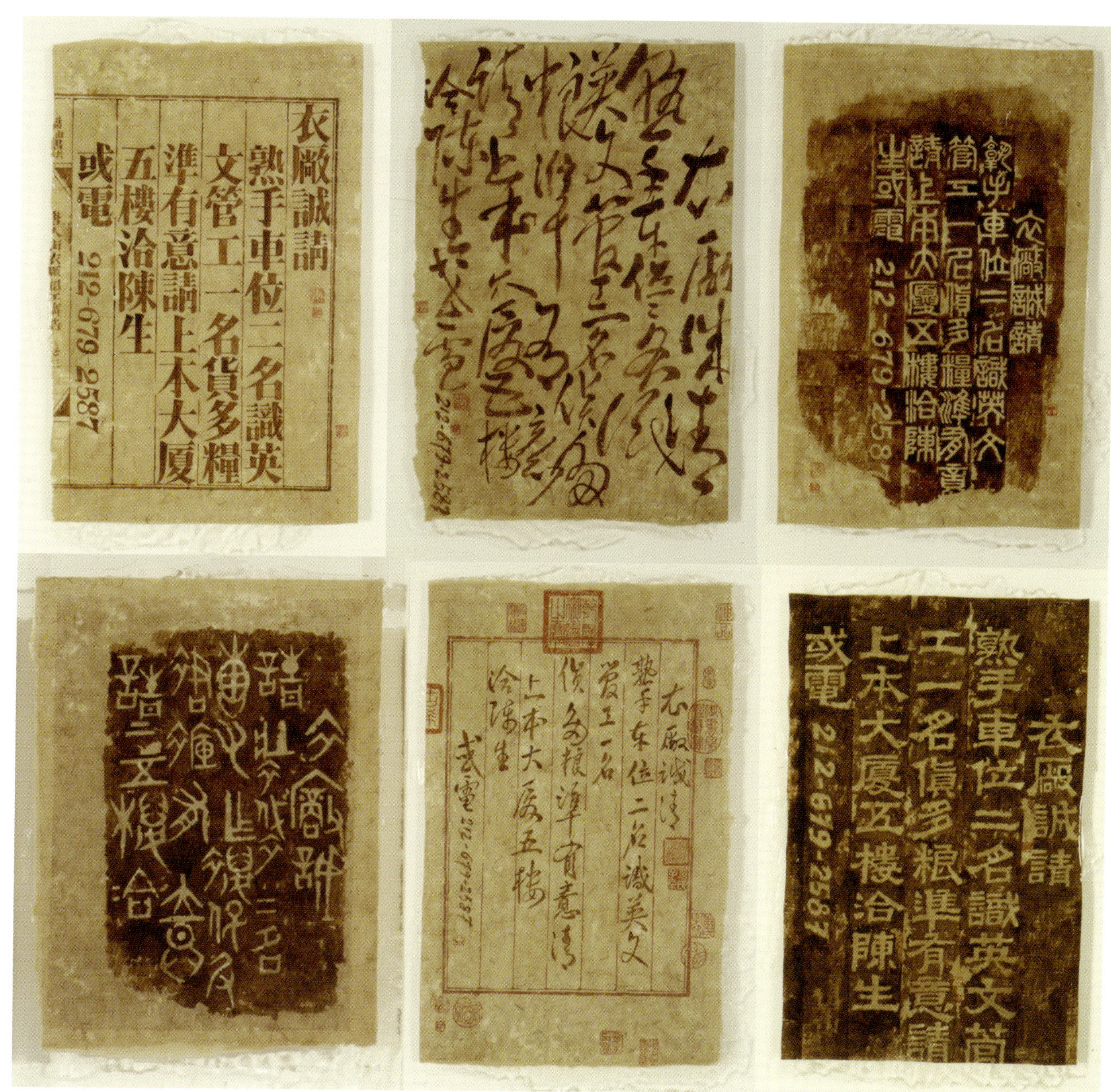

094

Chinatown Sweatshop Help Wanted Ad, 1995.
From the series "Soy Sauce Calligraphy,"
Soy sauce on rice paper, sealed in epoxy resin.
29 ½ x 19 in. each

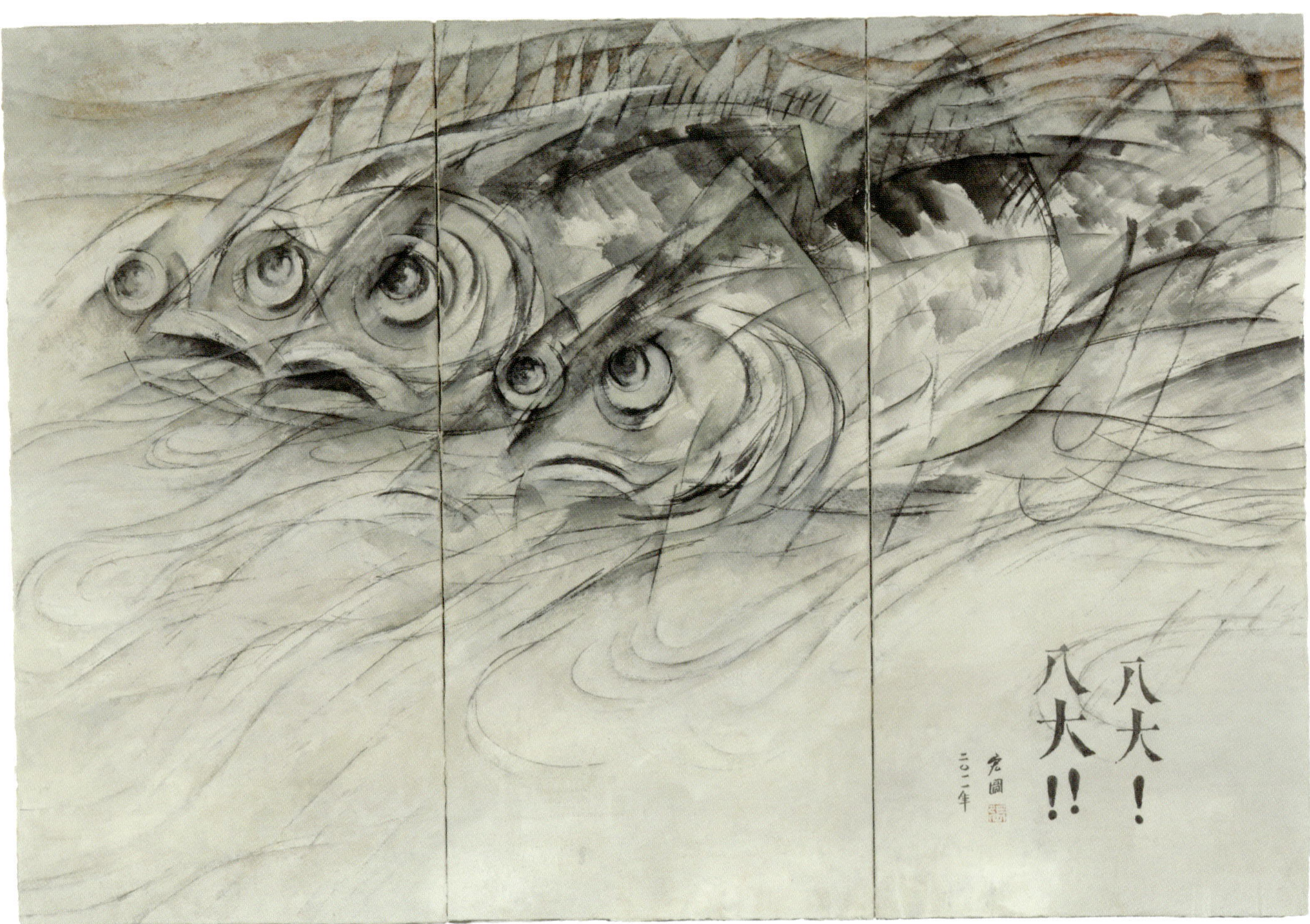

095

095
Bada! Bada!!, 2011.
Ink and mixed media on rice paper mounted on canvas,
48 x 72 in.

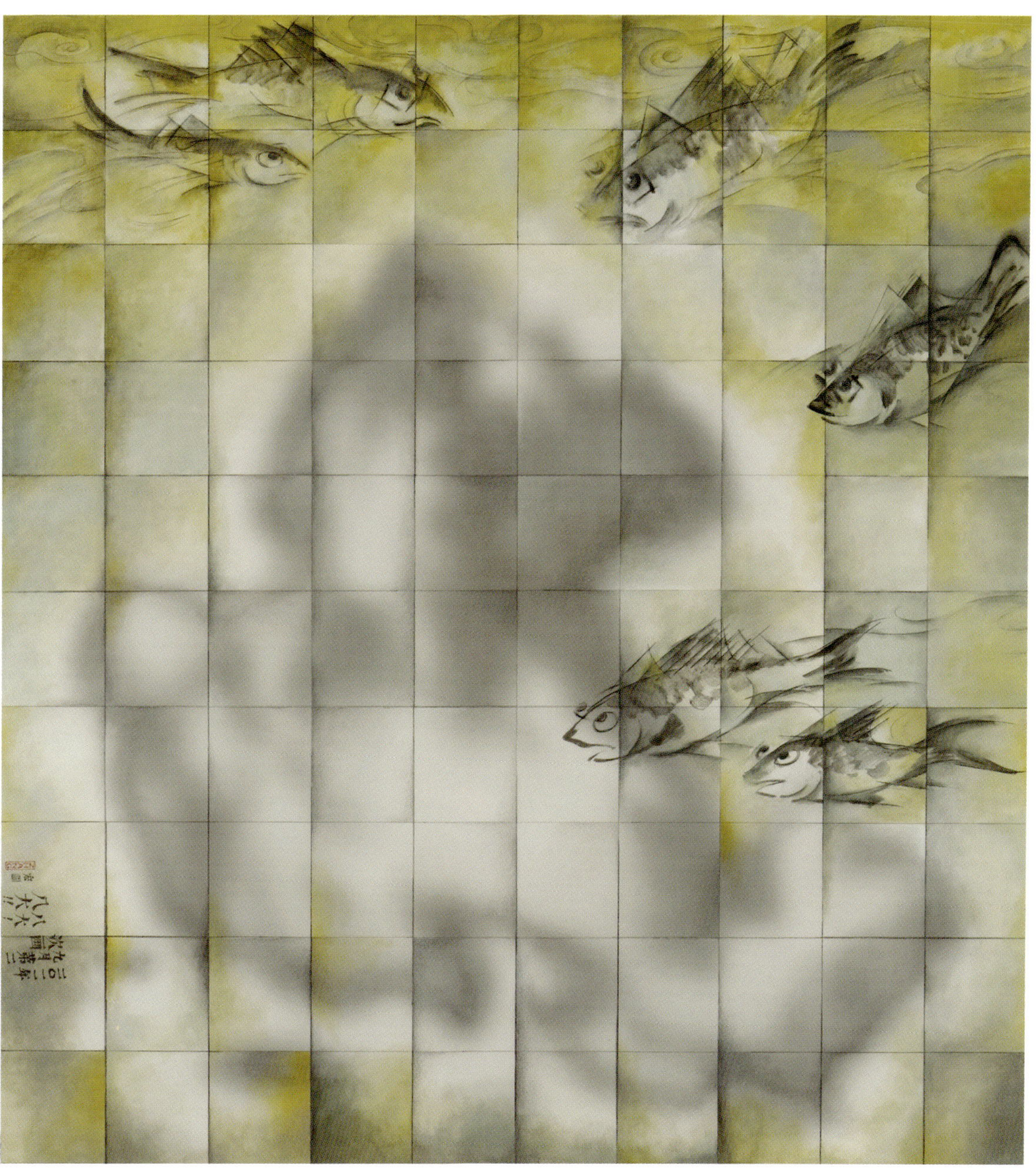

096

096
Bada! Bada!!—11 #2, 2011.
Oil and mixed media on paper mounted on panel,
74 x 68 in.

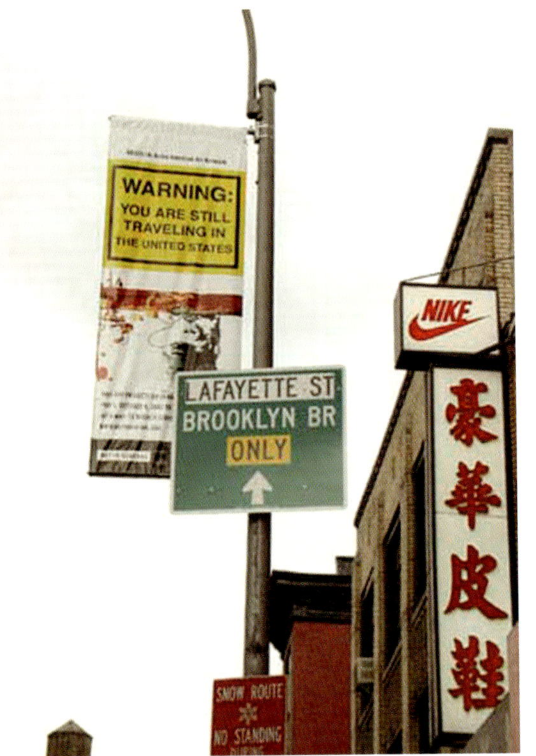

097

097
Warning Sign: Chinatown Canal Street Banner Project, 2001.
Computer printed image.

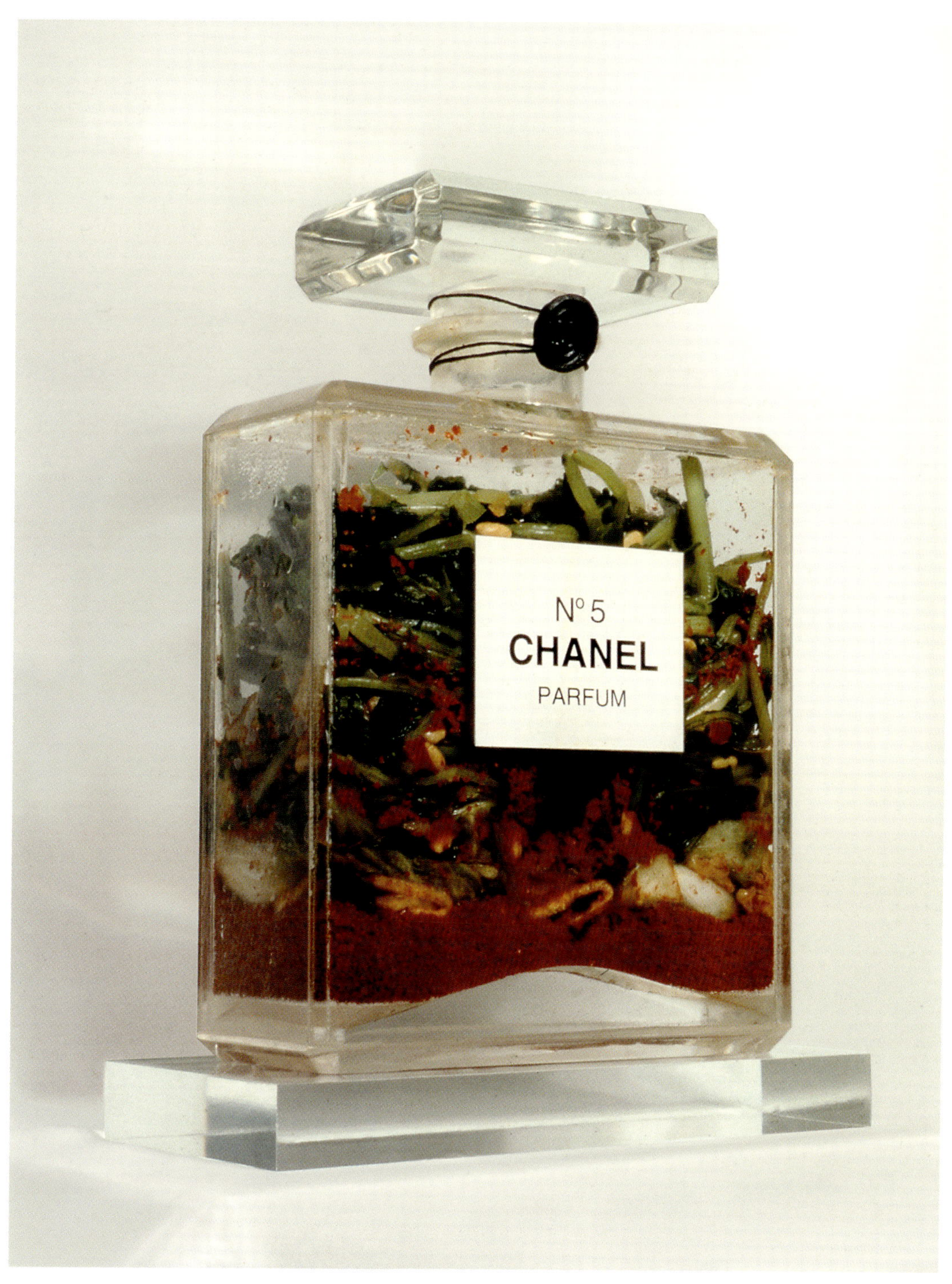

098

098
Kimchi—Chanel, 1997.
Plastic and kimchi,
11 ½ x 9 x 4 ¼ in.

099-a

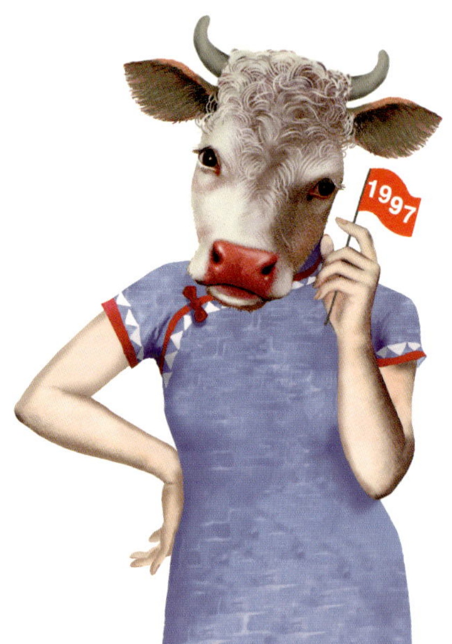

099-b

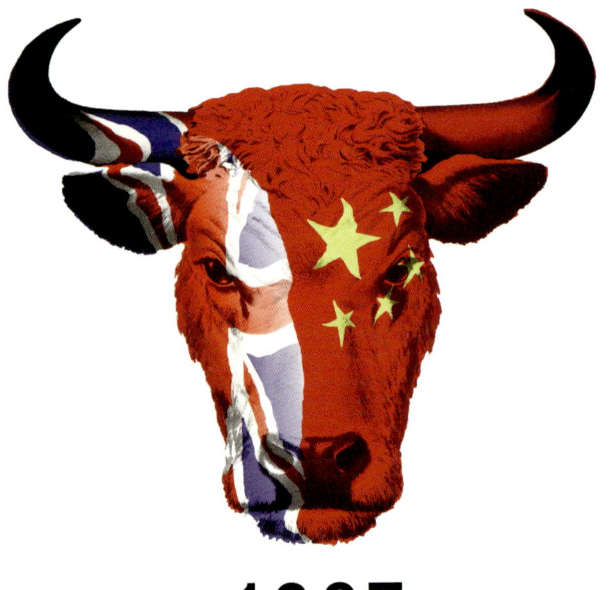

099-c

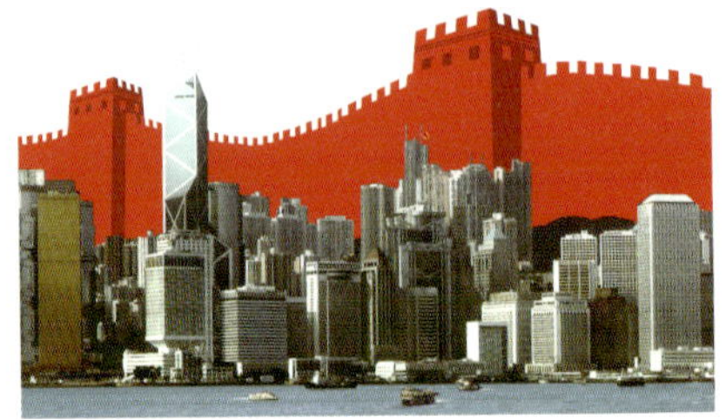

099-d

099 (a, b, c, d)
Designs from the "Hong Kong 1997" T-shirt series:

Transition/Translation.

Welcome!

Good Luck for the Year of the Ox.

Hong Kong 1997.

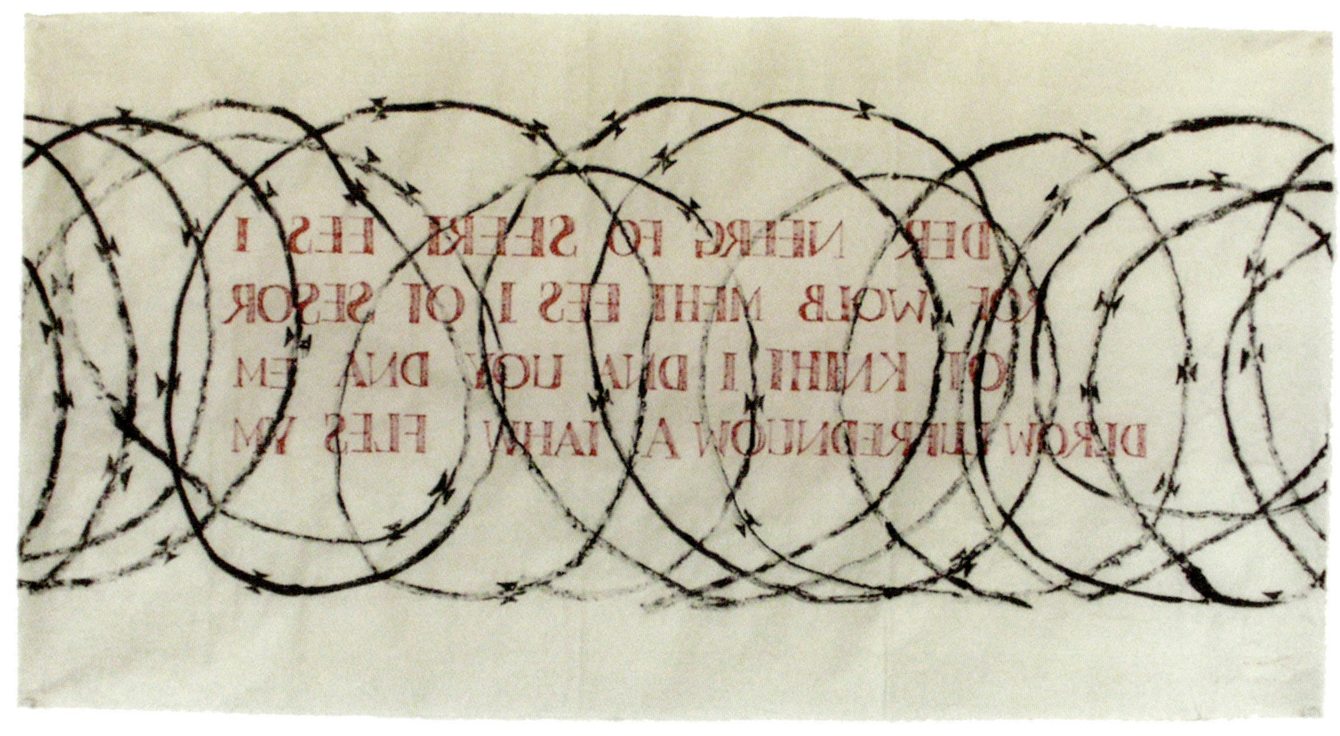

100
12.21.2000, Johannesburg (One Day One Picture Series): I was listening to Louis Armstrong's What a Wonderful World, 2000.
Ink on rice paper,
26 ½ x 52 ¼ in.

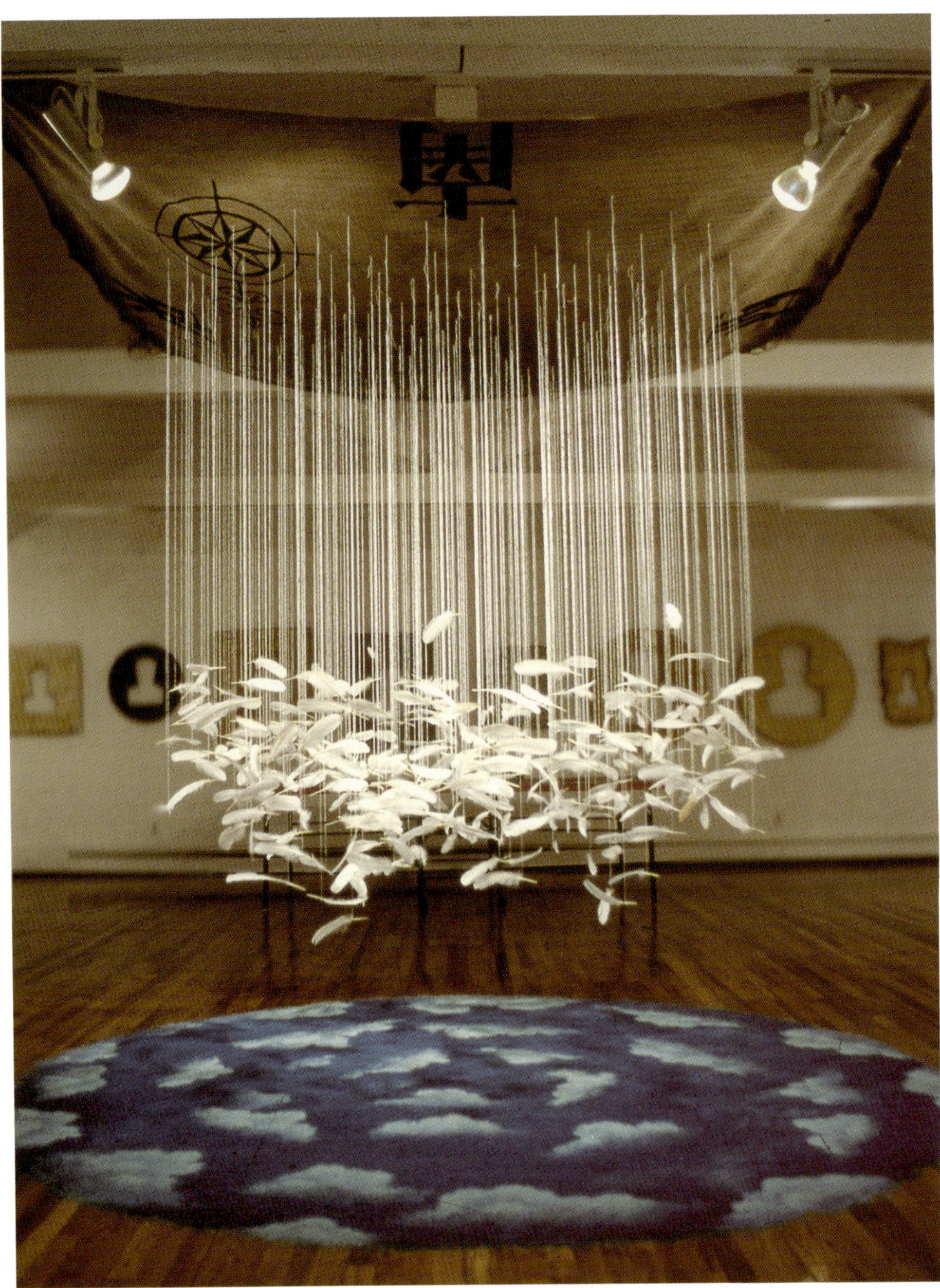

101
Flying Blues, 1996.
Sand, feather, and mixed-media installation,
96 x 96 x 118 in.

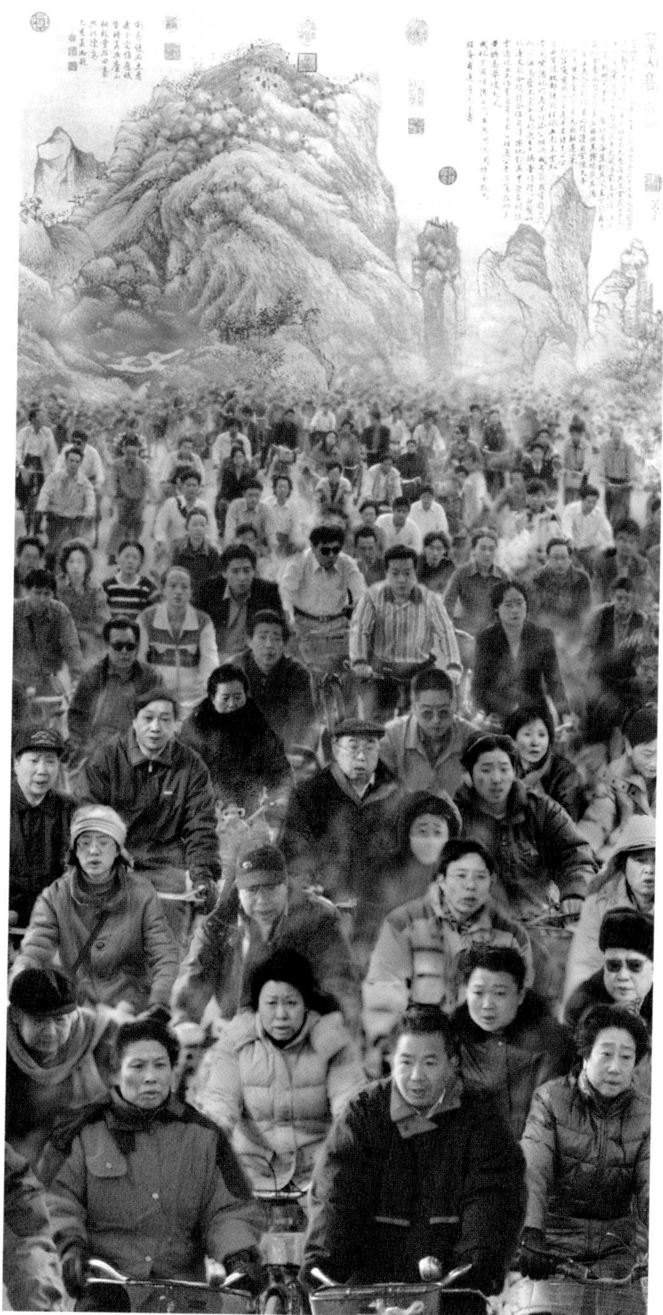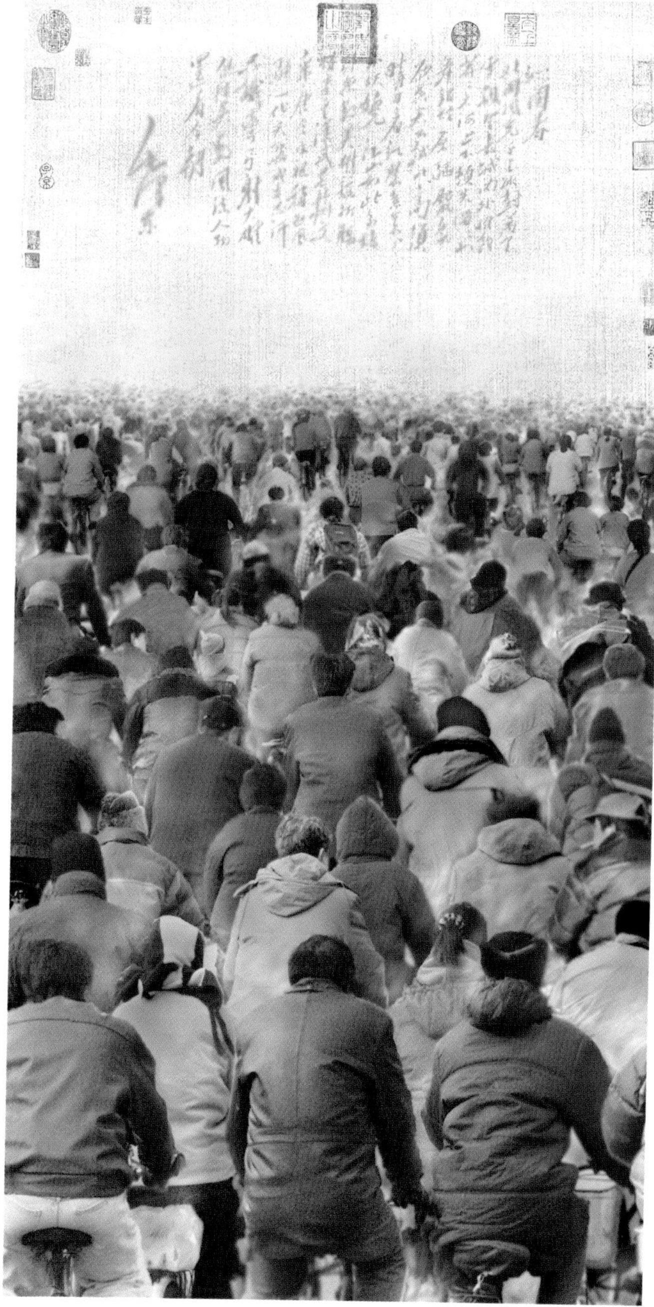

102

The Bikers, 2001.
Computer-generated image printed on canvas,
104 x 107 in.

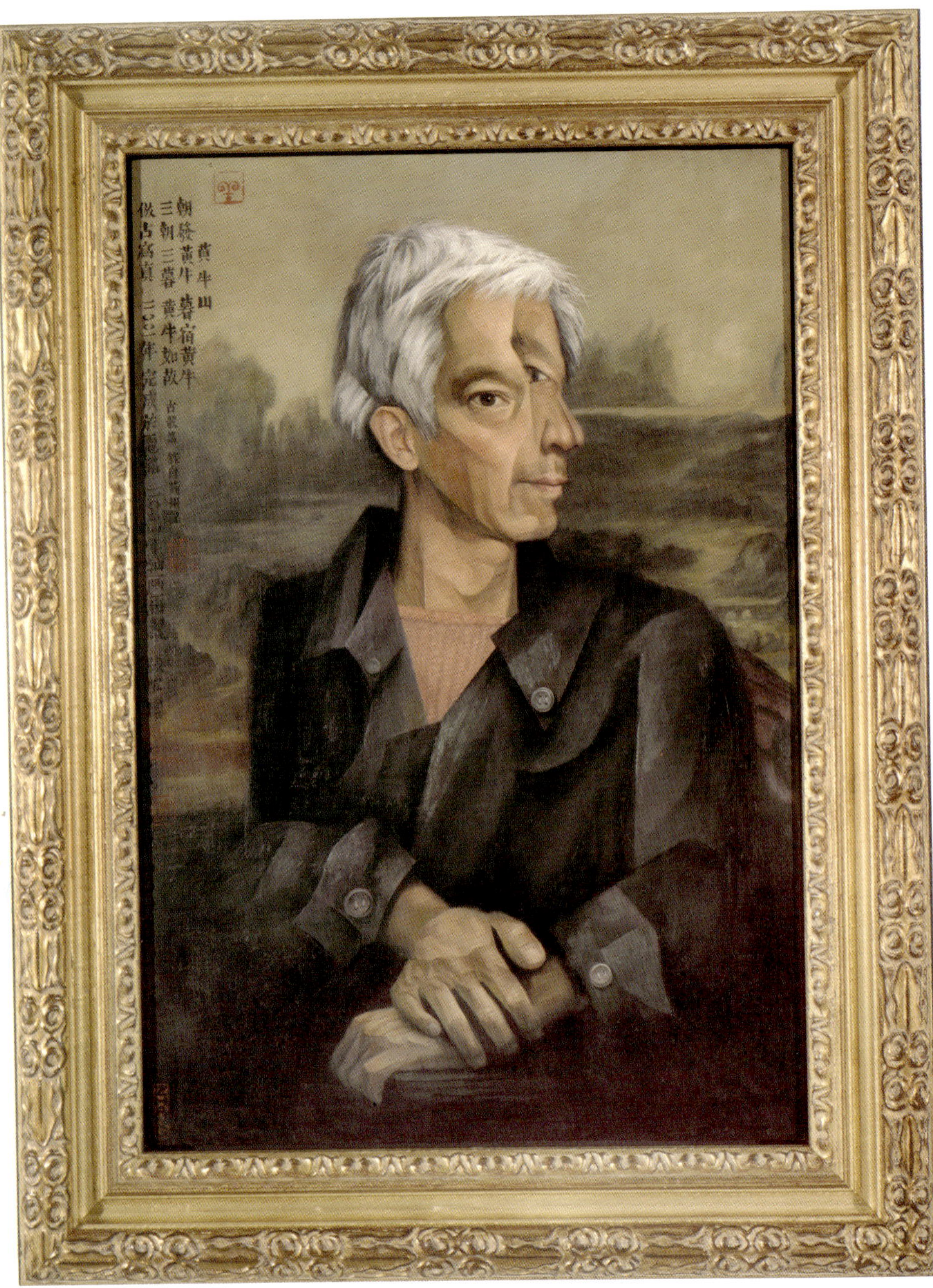

103

103
Self-Portrait in the Style of the Old Masters, 2004.
Oil on wood panel.
38 x 29 in.

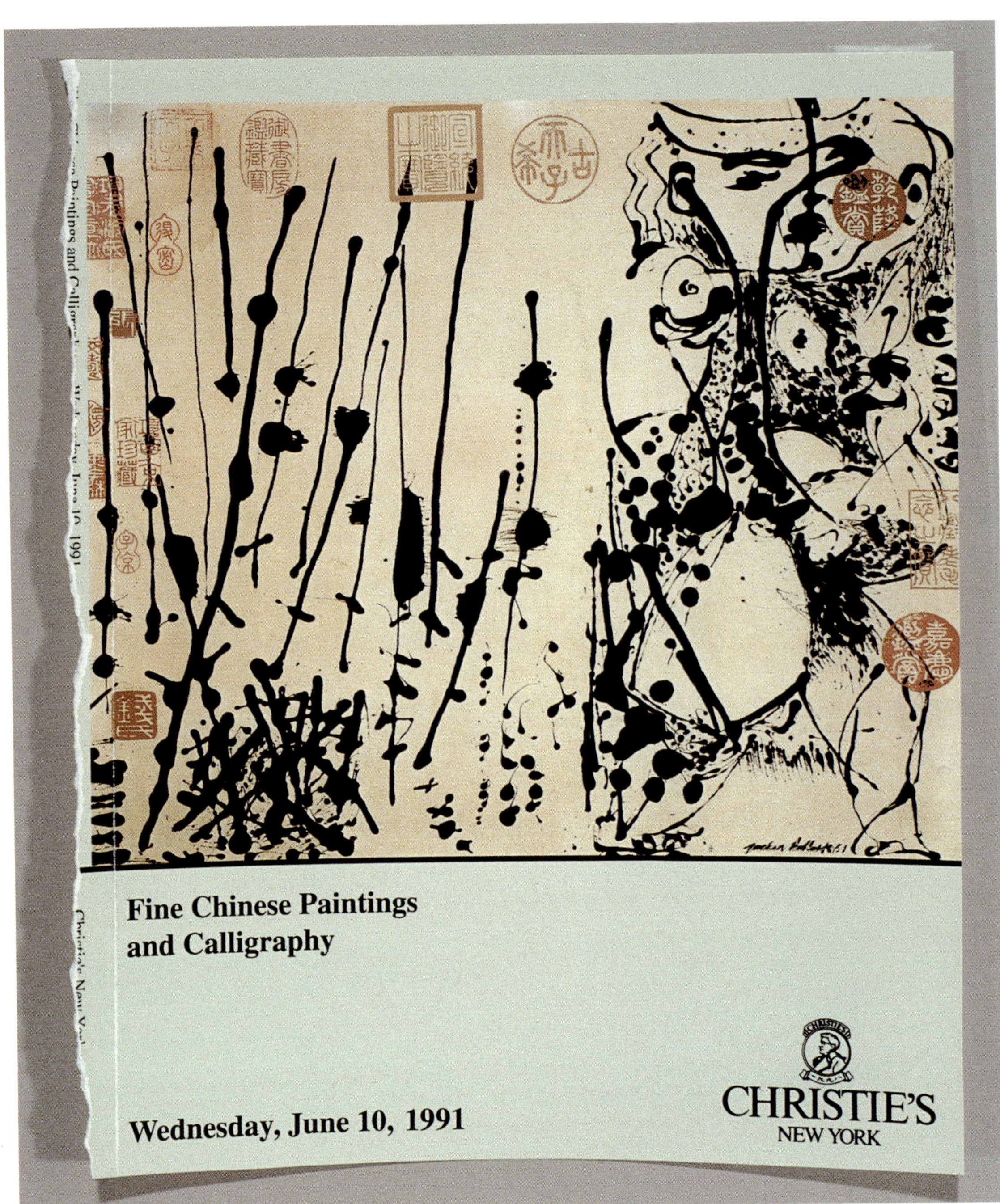

104

104
Christie's Catalog Project: The Cover, 1998.
Computer-generated image printed on paper,
10 x 8 in.

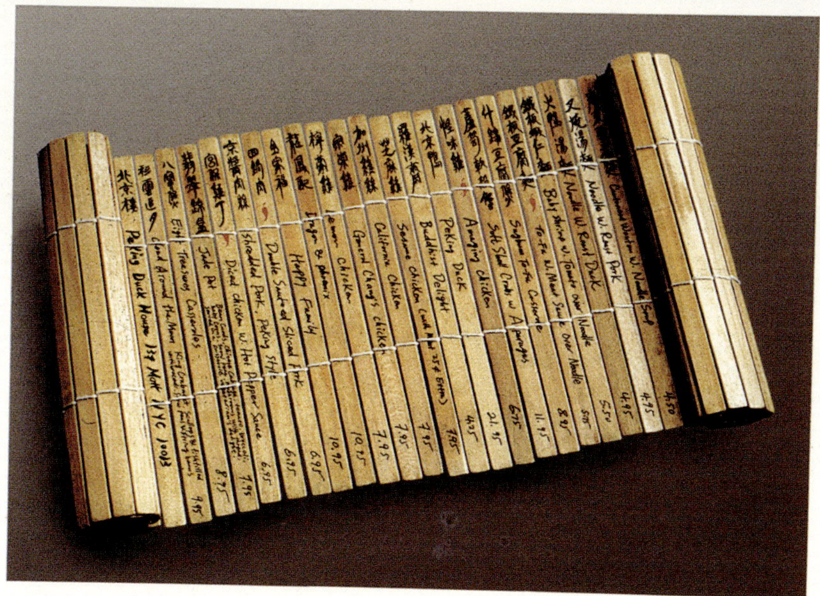

89

• 89   **BAMBOO SLIP**   (Han Dynasty, 206 B.C.- 220 A.D.)

Restaurant menu

Ink on bamboo slip, 23 x 75in. (58.5 x 187cm.)

$20,000 - 30,000

漢竹簡菜單

105
Christie's Catalog Project: Bamboo Slip, 1998.
Computer-generated image printed on paper,
10 x 8 in.

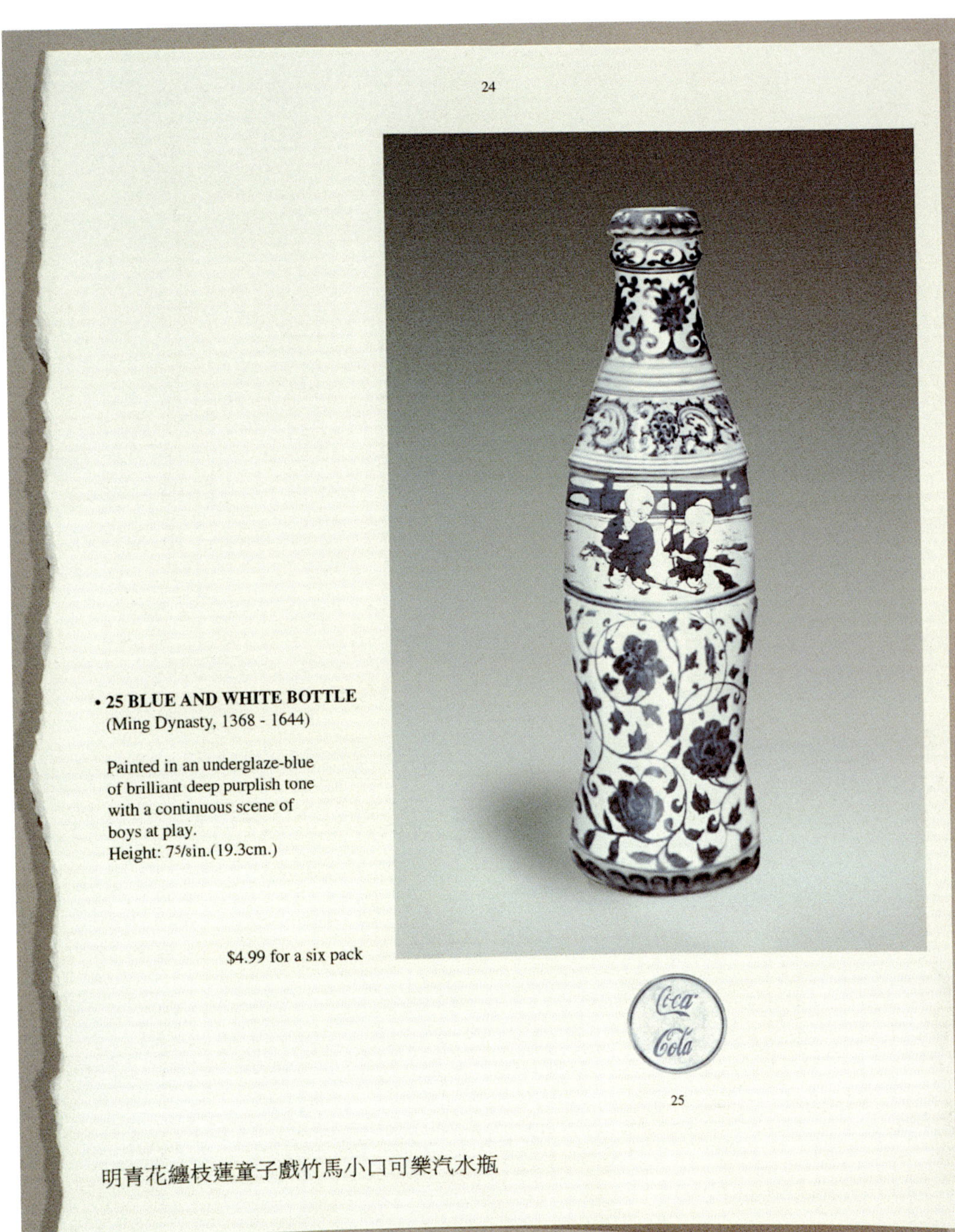

明青花纏枝蓮童子戲竹馬小口可樂汽水瓶

106
Christie's Catalog Project: Blue and White Bottle, 1998.
Computer-generated image printed on paper,
10 x 8 in.

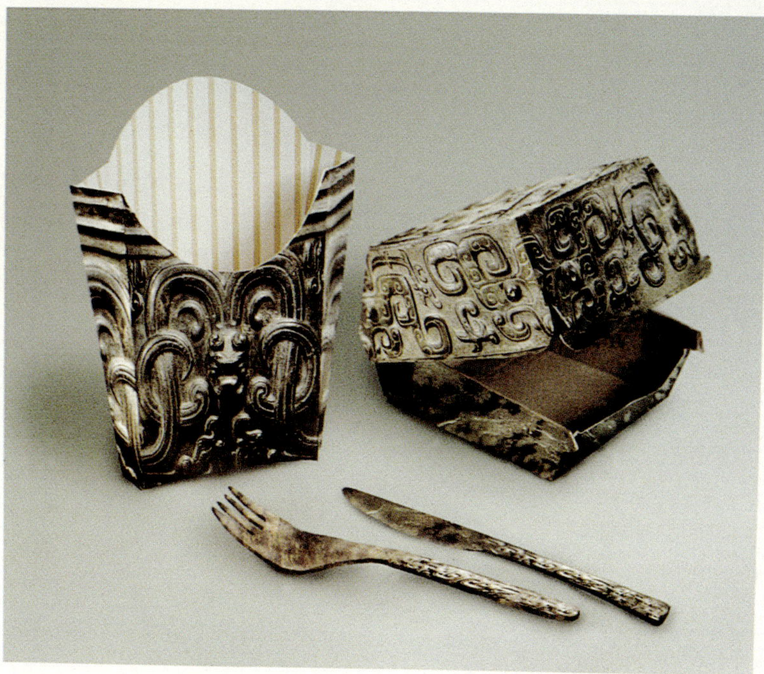

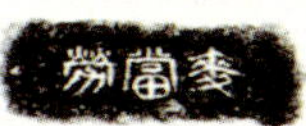

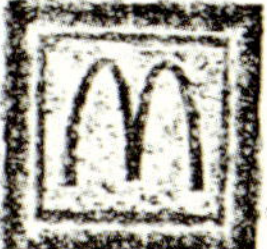

113

• **113   BRONZE TABLEWARE**   (Han Dynasty, 206 B.C. - 220 A.D.)

Two containers, one fork and one knife
Fries container: 6¼ x 4¼in. (15.8 x 11.4cm.)
Burger container: 3 x 4½ x 4½in. (7.6 x 11.4 x 11.4cm.)
Fork: 6 x ⅝in. (15.3 x 1.6cm.)
Knife: 6 x 1in. (15.3 x 2.5cm)

$3.99

漢青銅食具一組

Christie's Catalog Project: Bronze Tableware, 1998.
Computer-generated image printed on paper,
10 x 8 in.

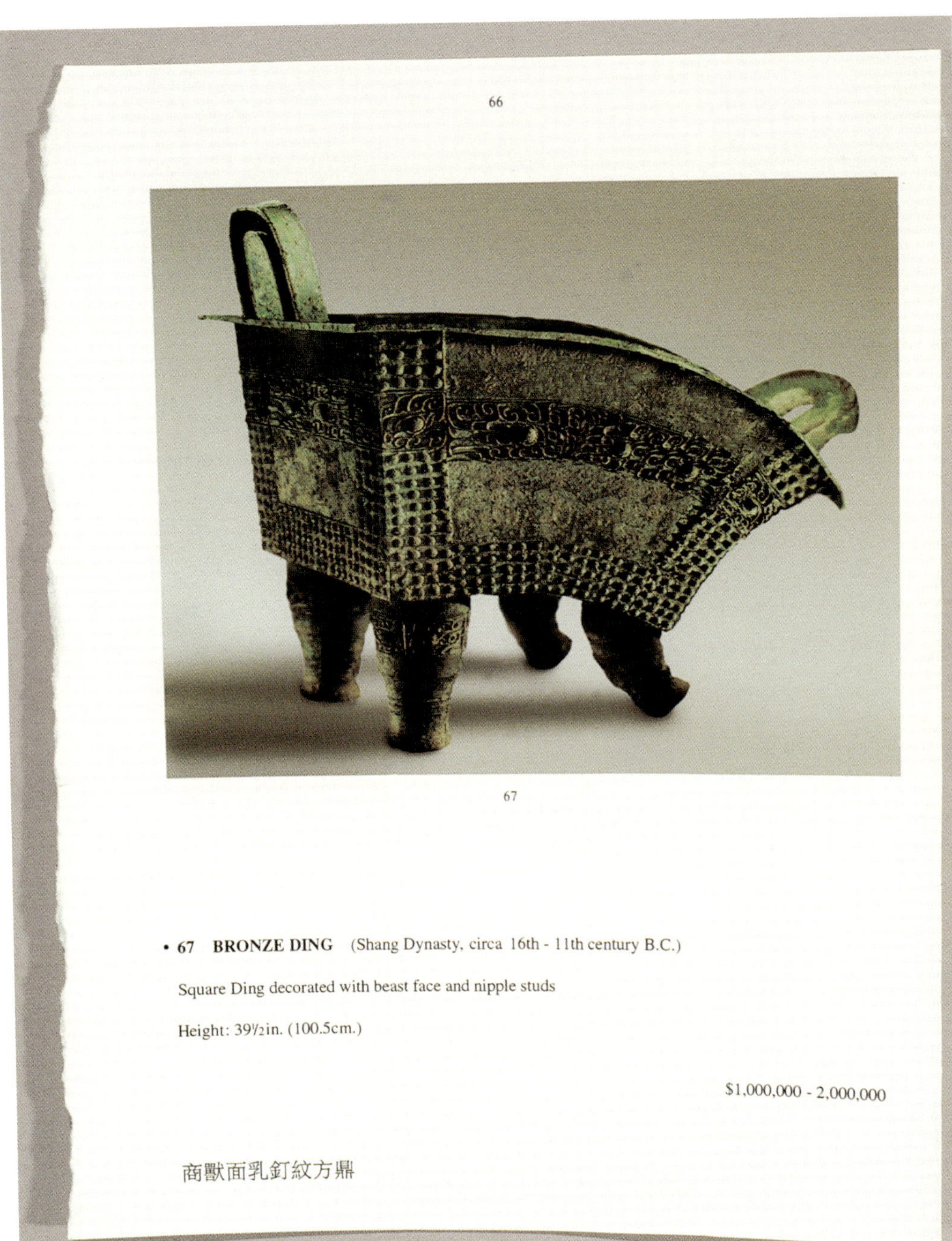

67

• 67 **BRONZE DING**   (Shang Dynasty, circa 16th - 11th century B.C.)

Square Ding decorated with beast face and nipple studs

Height: 39½in. (100.5cm.)

$1,000,000 - 2,000,000

商獸面乳釘紋方鼎

108

108
Christie's Catalog Project: Bronze Ding, 1998.
Computer-generated image printed on paper,
10 x 8 in.

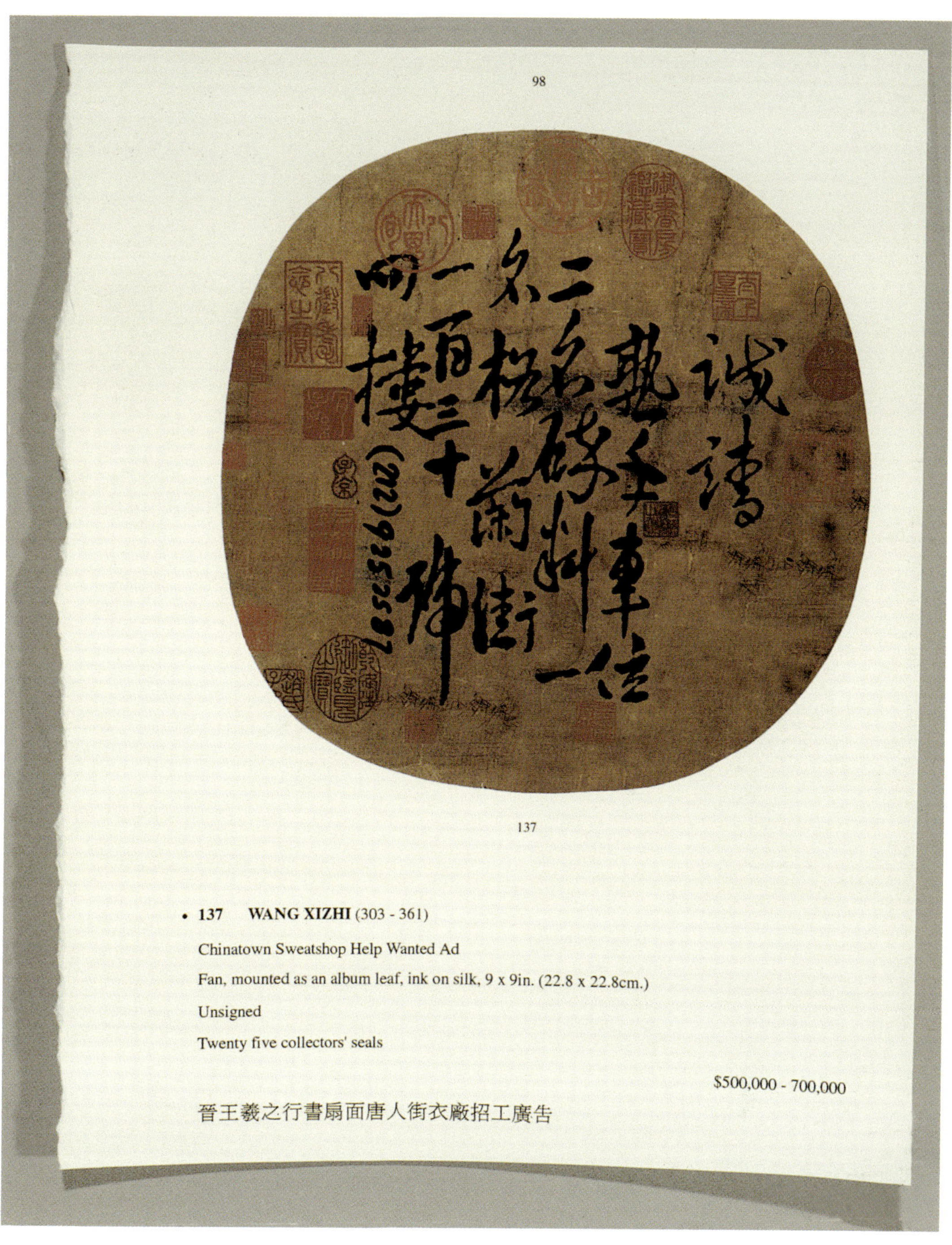

137

- **137**   **WANG XIZHI** (303 - 361)

Chinatown Sweatshop Help Wanted Ad

Fan, mounted as an album leaf, ink on silk, 9 x 9in. (22.8 x 22.8cm.)

Unsigned

Twenty five collectors' seals

$500,000 - 700,000

晉王羲之行書扇面唐人街衣廠招工廣告

109
Christie's Catalog Project: A Round Fan with Wang Xizhi Calligraphy, 1998.
Computer-generated image printed on paper,
10 x 8 in.

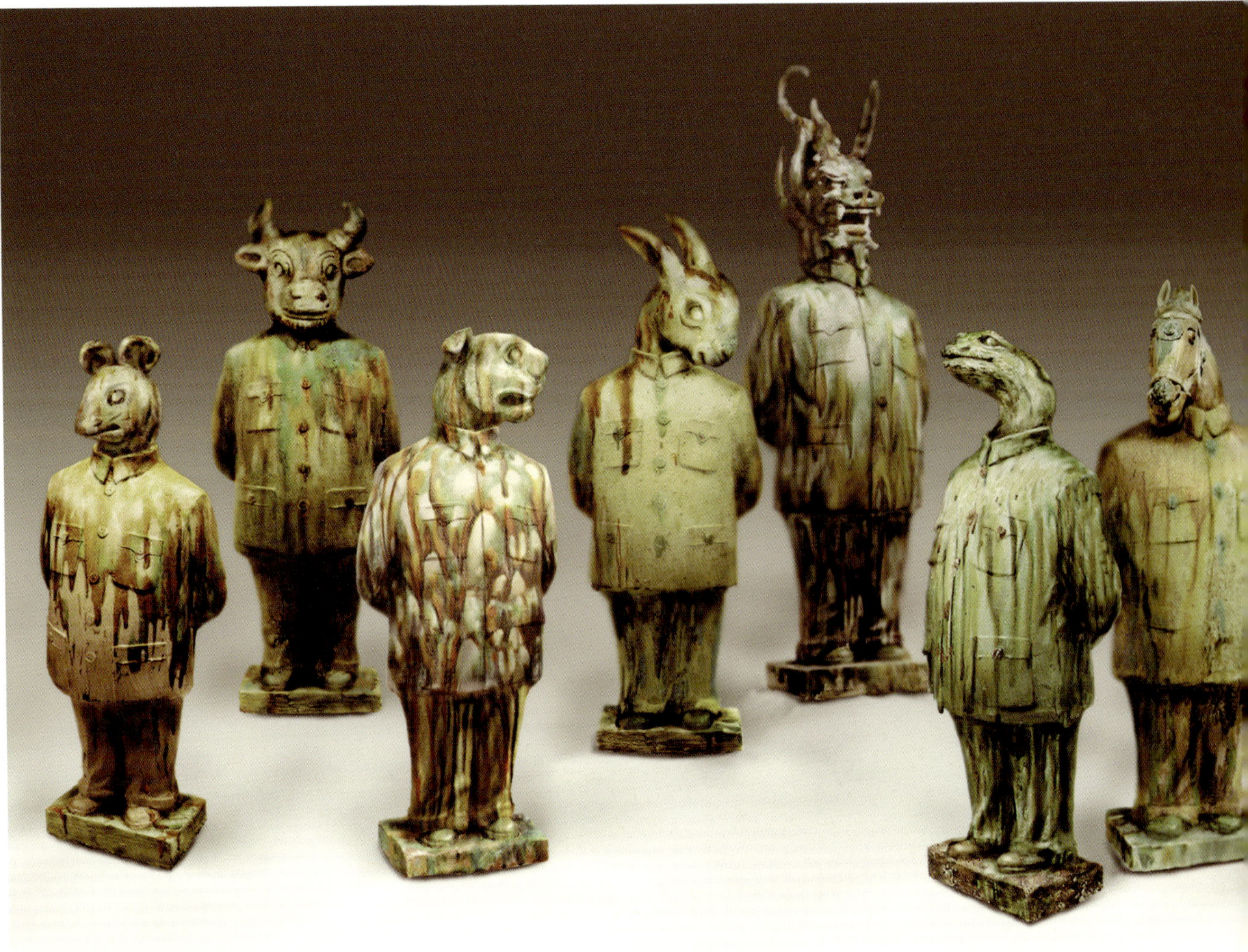

• **39 Very rare complete set of twelve zodiac figures**   (Tang Dynasty, 618 - 907)   39

全套唐三彩十二生肖 $1,200,000 - 2,000,000

110
Christie's Catalog Project: Twelve Zodiac Figures, 1998.
Computer-generated image printed on paper,
10 x 15 in.

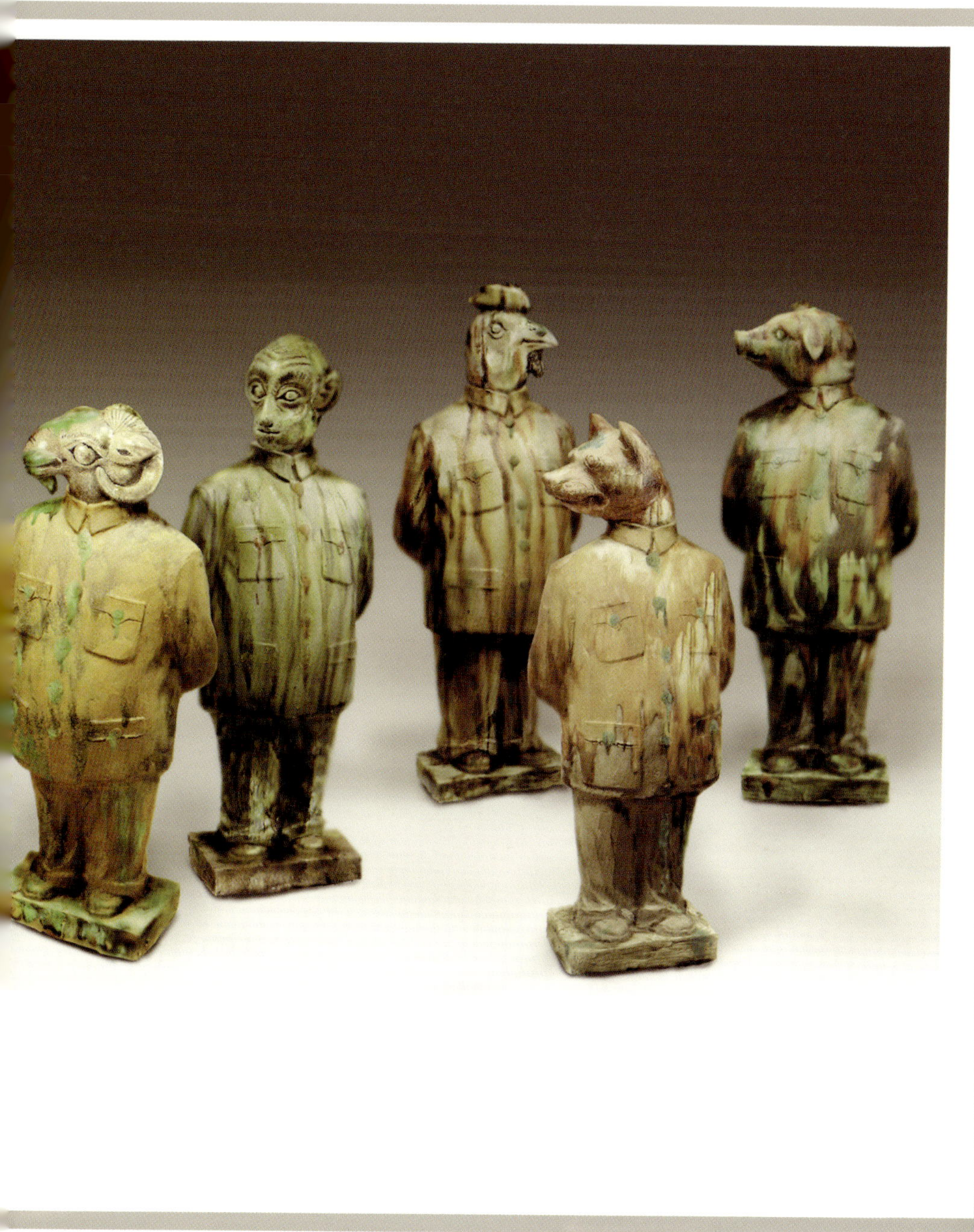

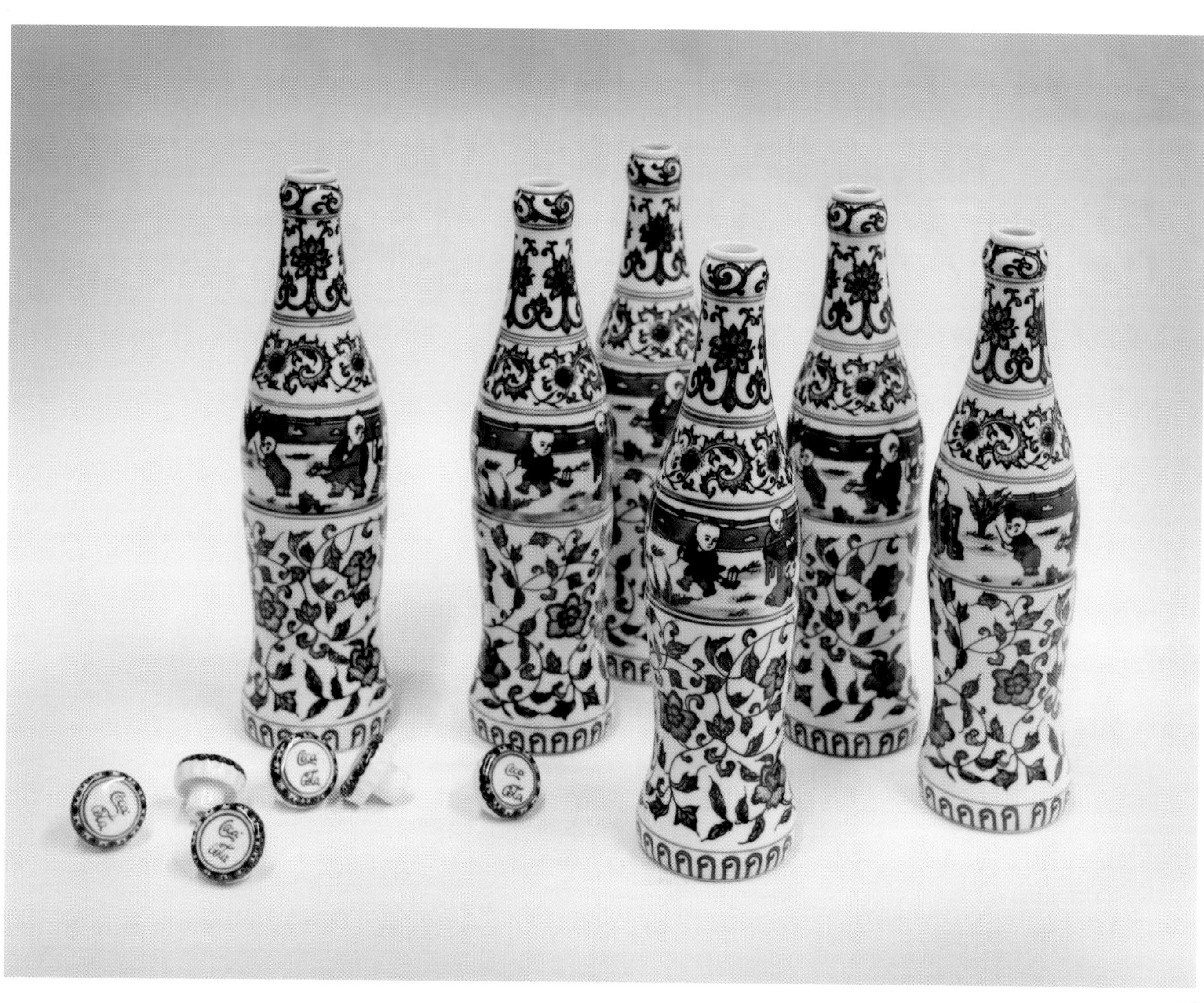

111
Kekou-Kele (Six Pack), 2002.
Porcelain, actual size.

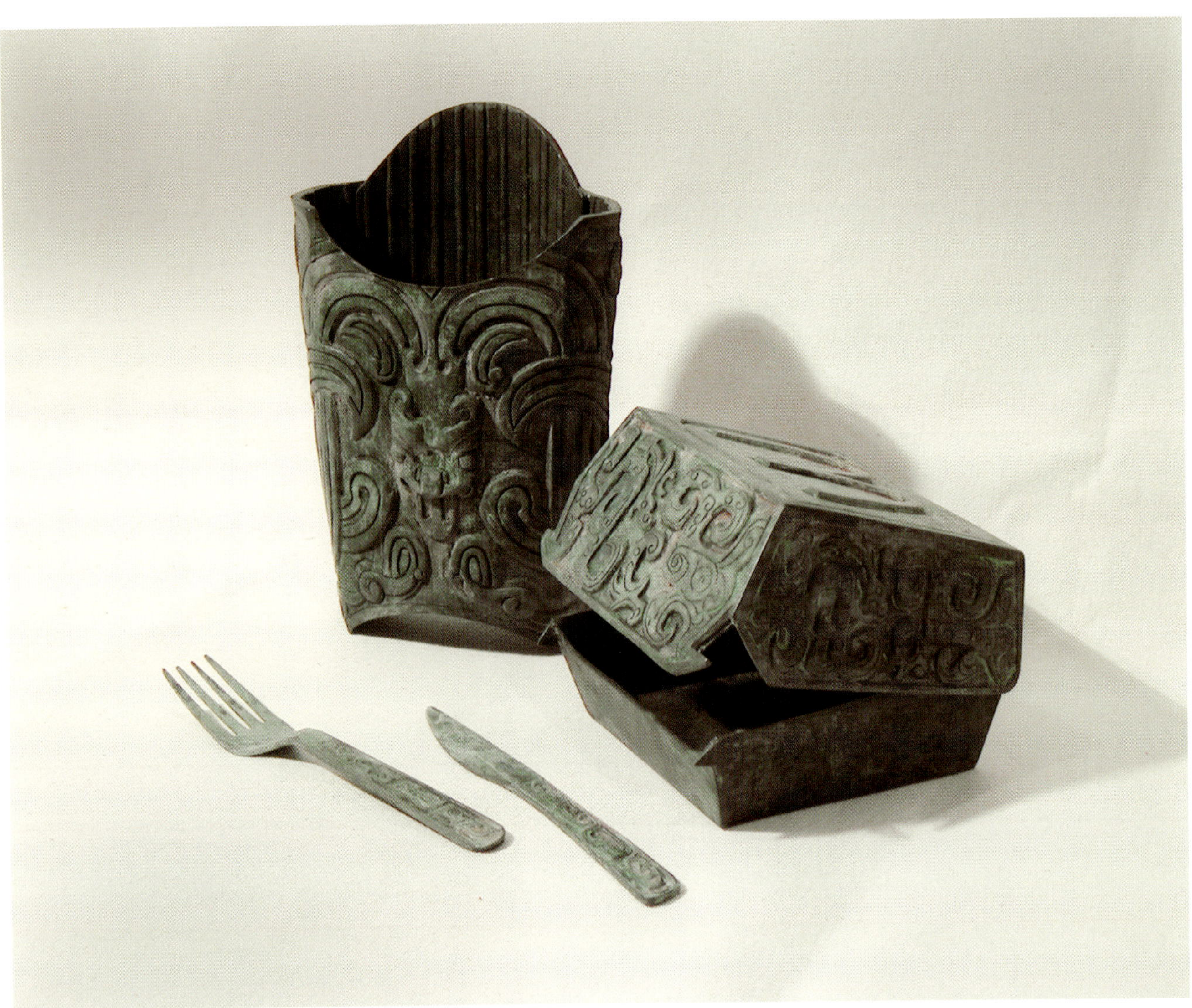

112
Mai Dang Lao, 2002.
Cast bronze, actual size.

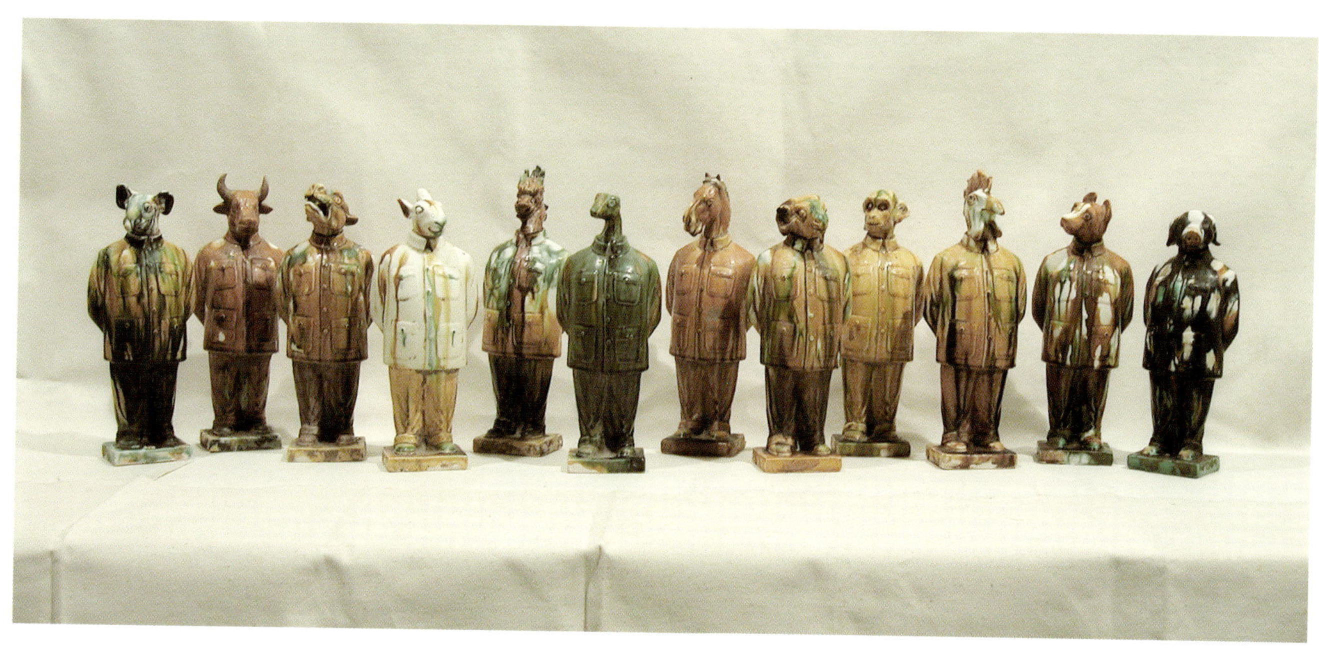

113
*A Complete Set of Chinese Zodiac Figures in Tang Dynasty Three Colors Glaze
Ceramic Style*, 2002
Dimensions variable.

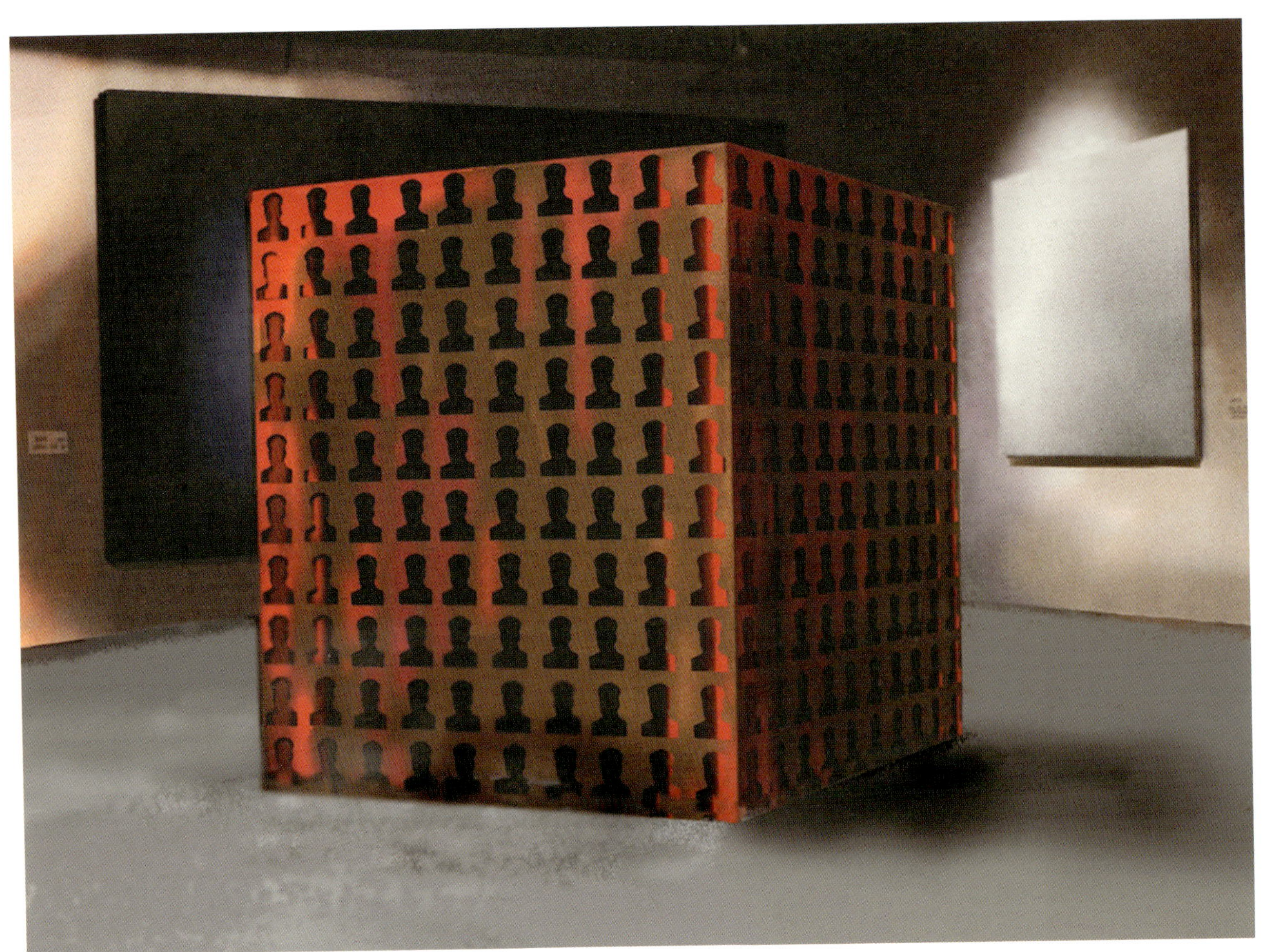

114

114
Big Cube, 1995.
Plywood, paper, paint, and sound installation,
96 x 96 x 96 in.

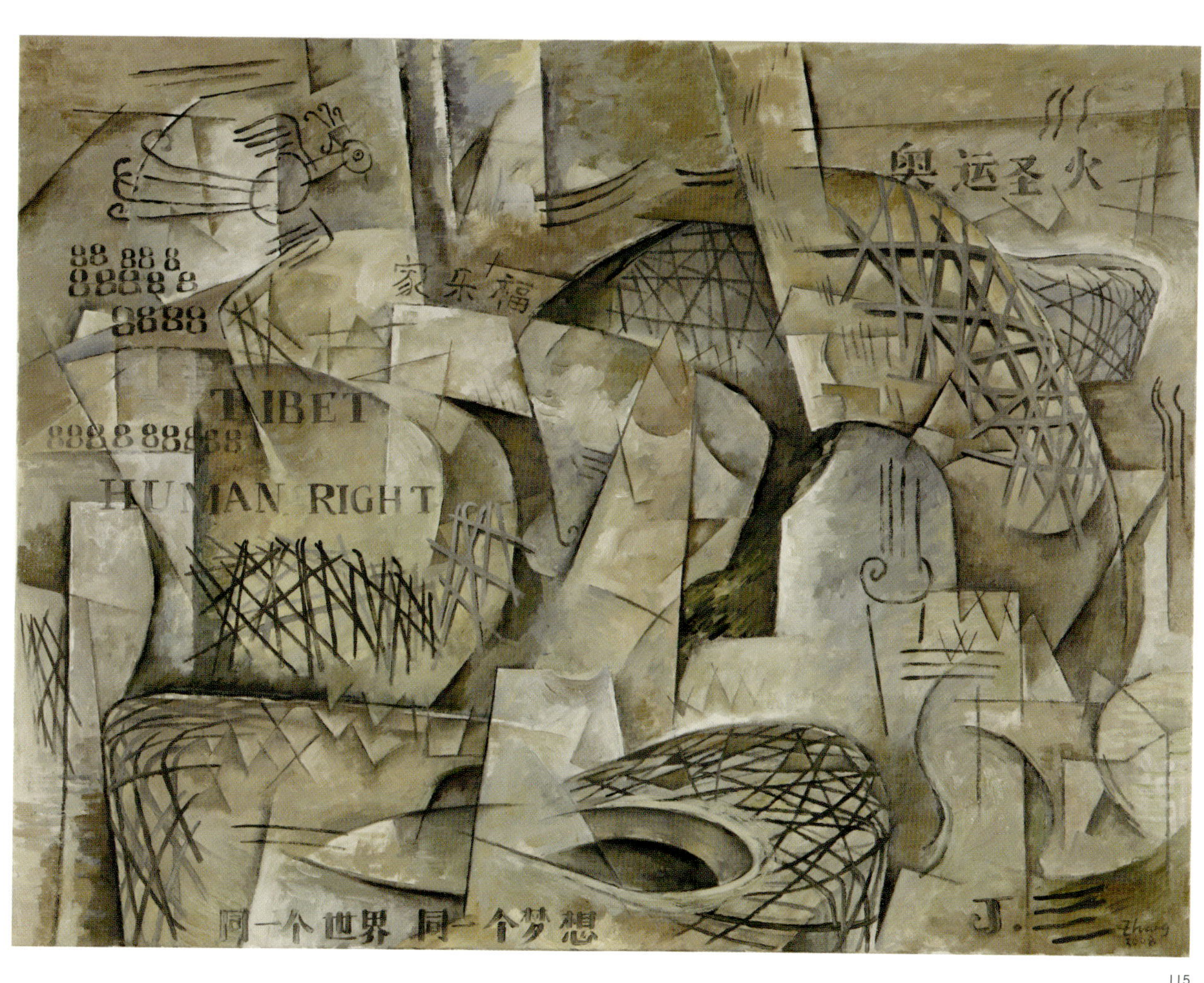

115
Bird's Nest in the Style of Cubism, 2008.
Oil on canvas,
36 x 48 in.

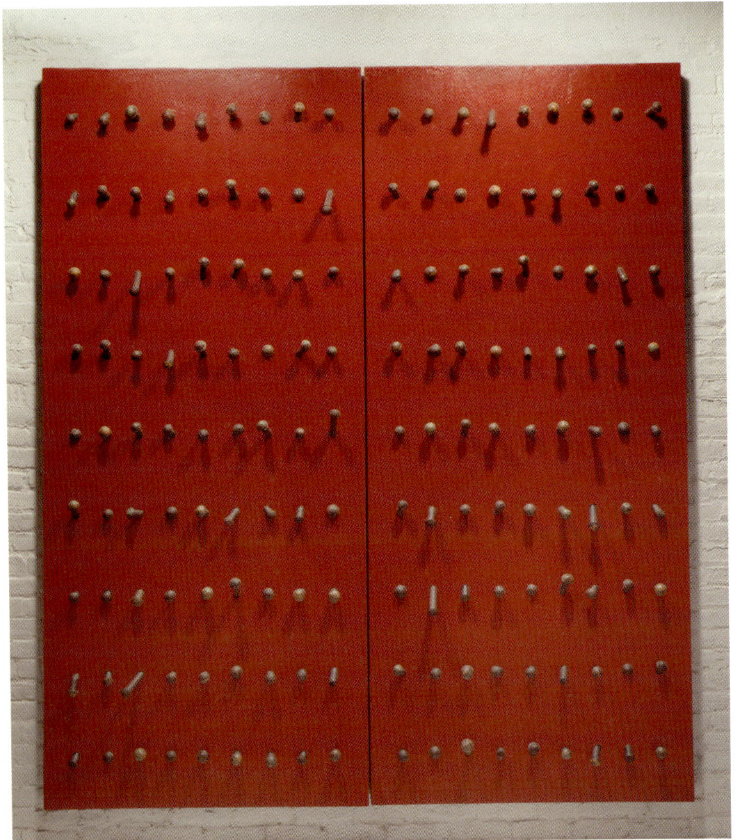 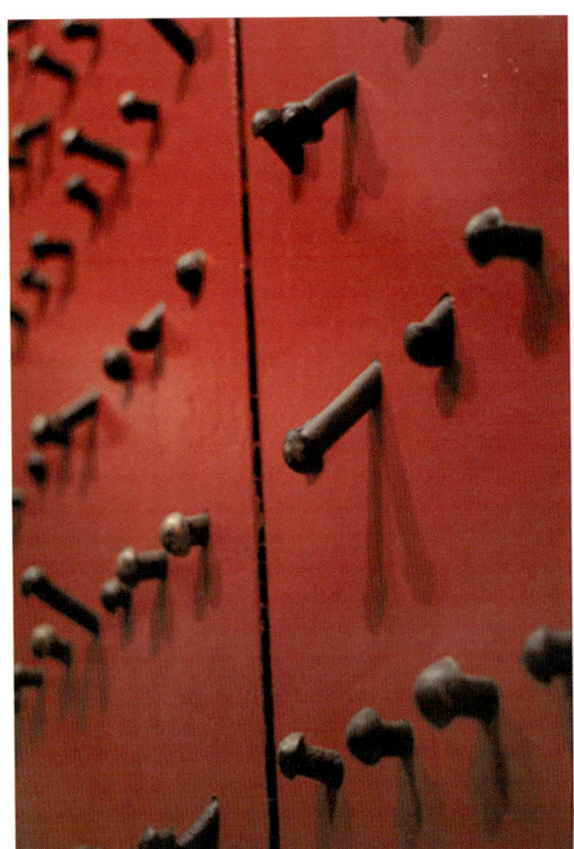

116

116
Studs 9 x 2 x 2, The Big Red Door, 1992.
Metal, wood, and paint
96 x 86 ½ x 6 in.

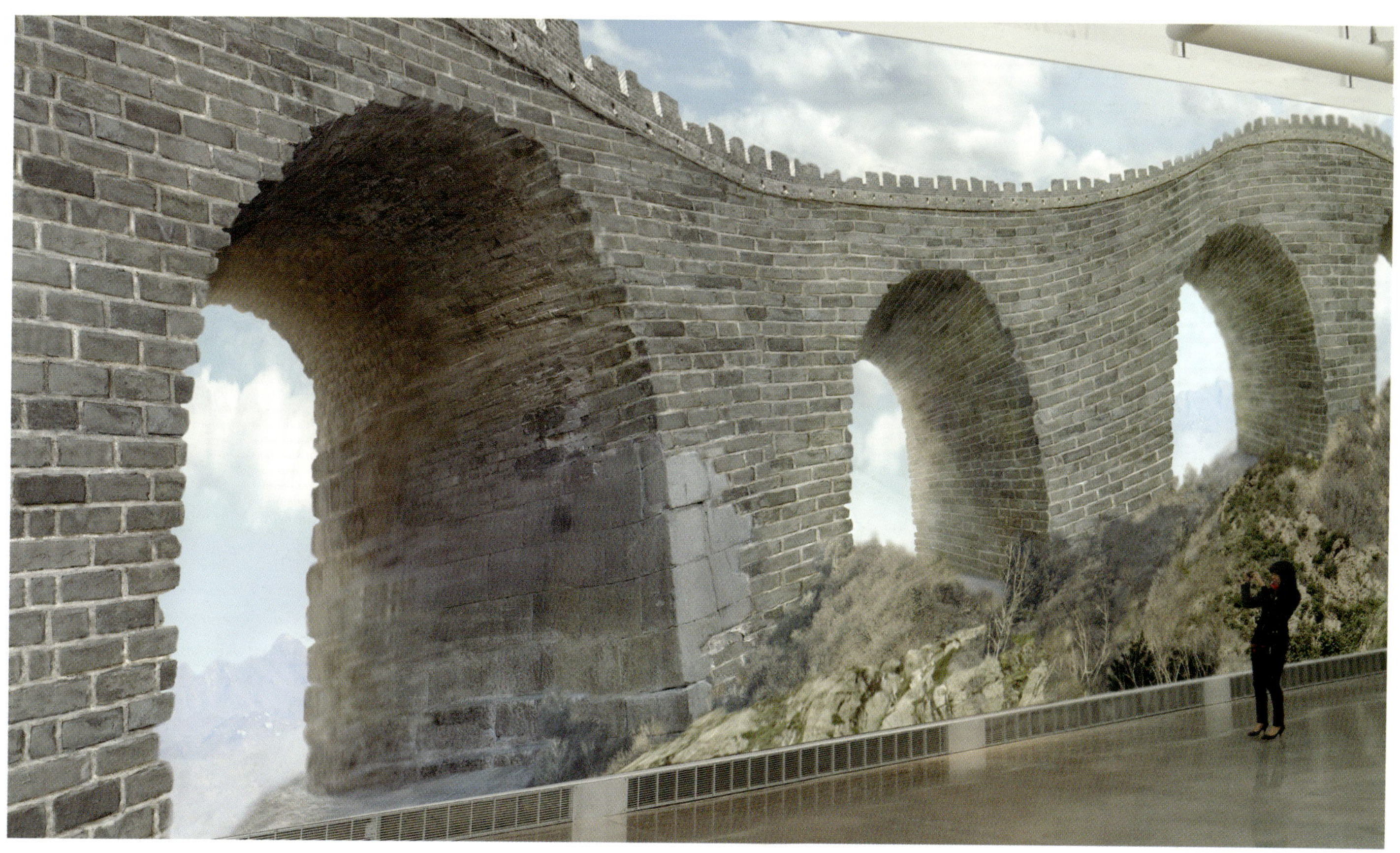

117
Great Wall with Gates II (detail), 2015.
Photographic wallpaper,
14 feet 9 inches x 98 feet.
Installation view, Queens Museum.

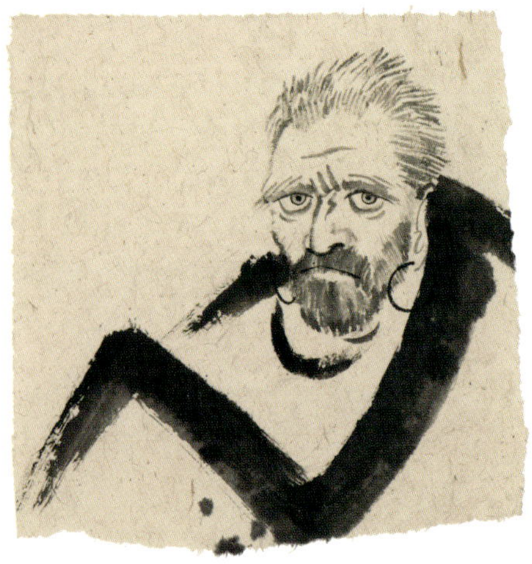

118-a

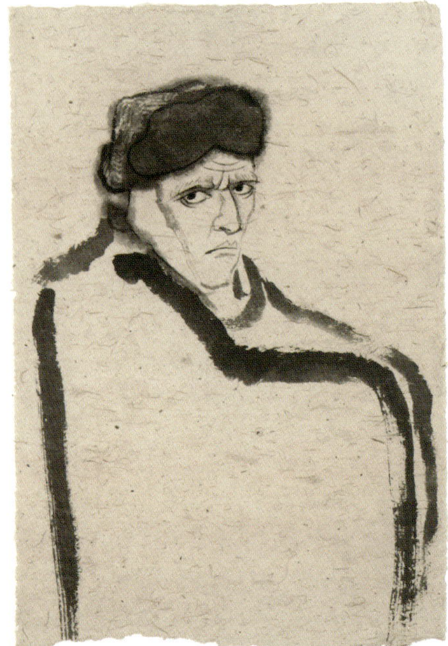

118-b

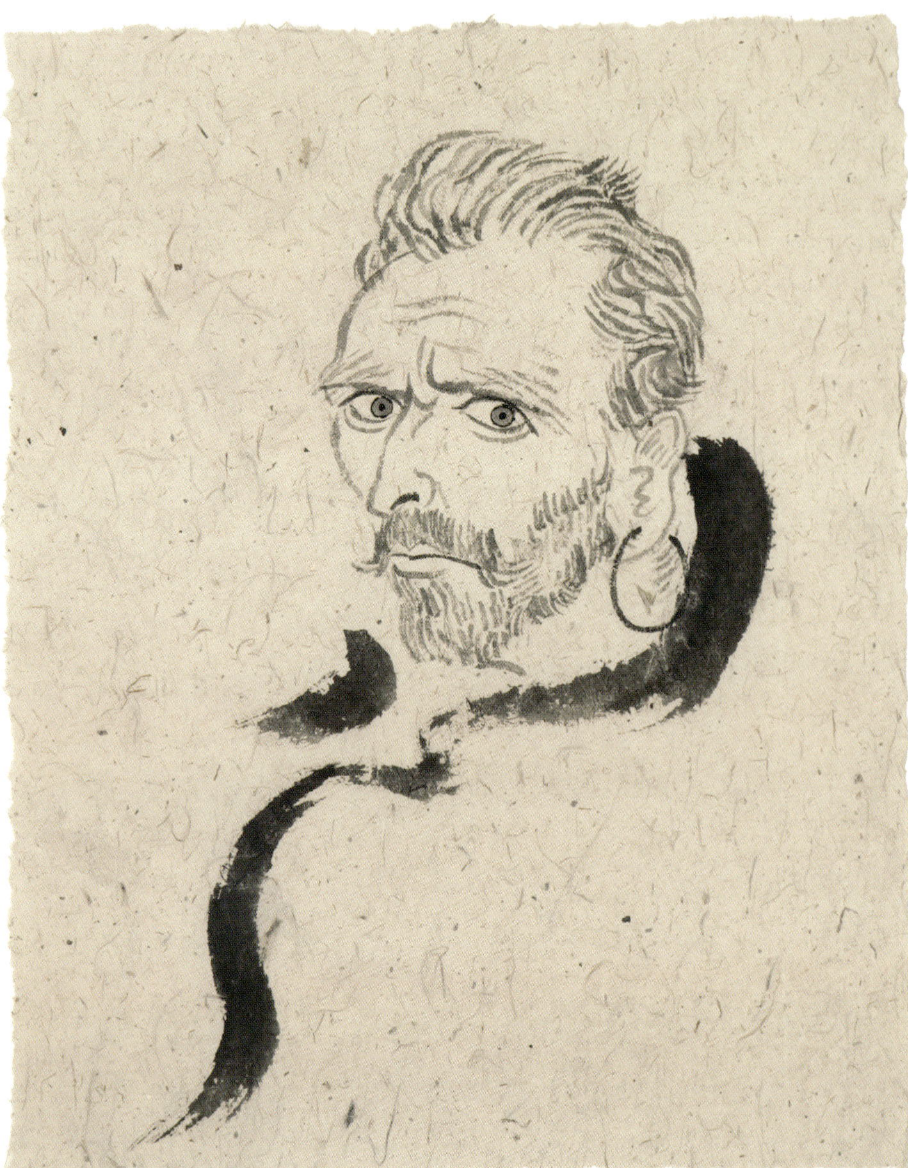

118-c

118
Van Gogh—Bodhidharma (6/39), 2014.
Ink on paper
Dimensions variable.

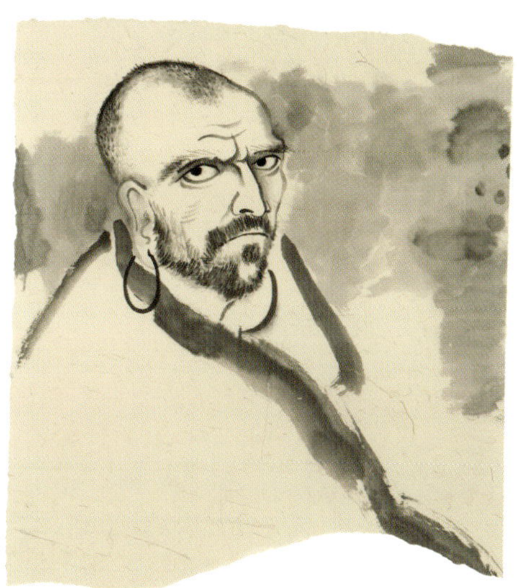

118-d

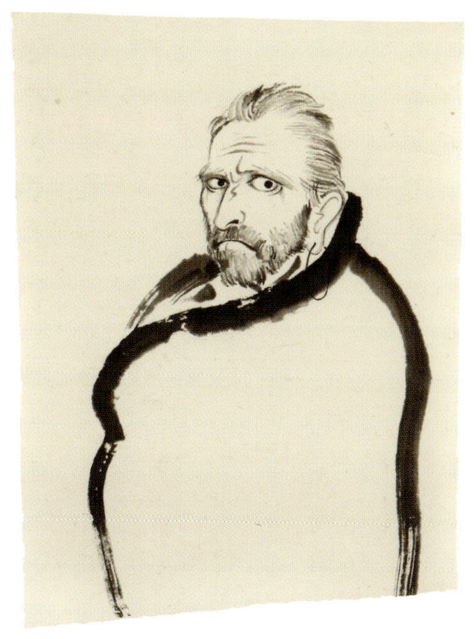

118-e

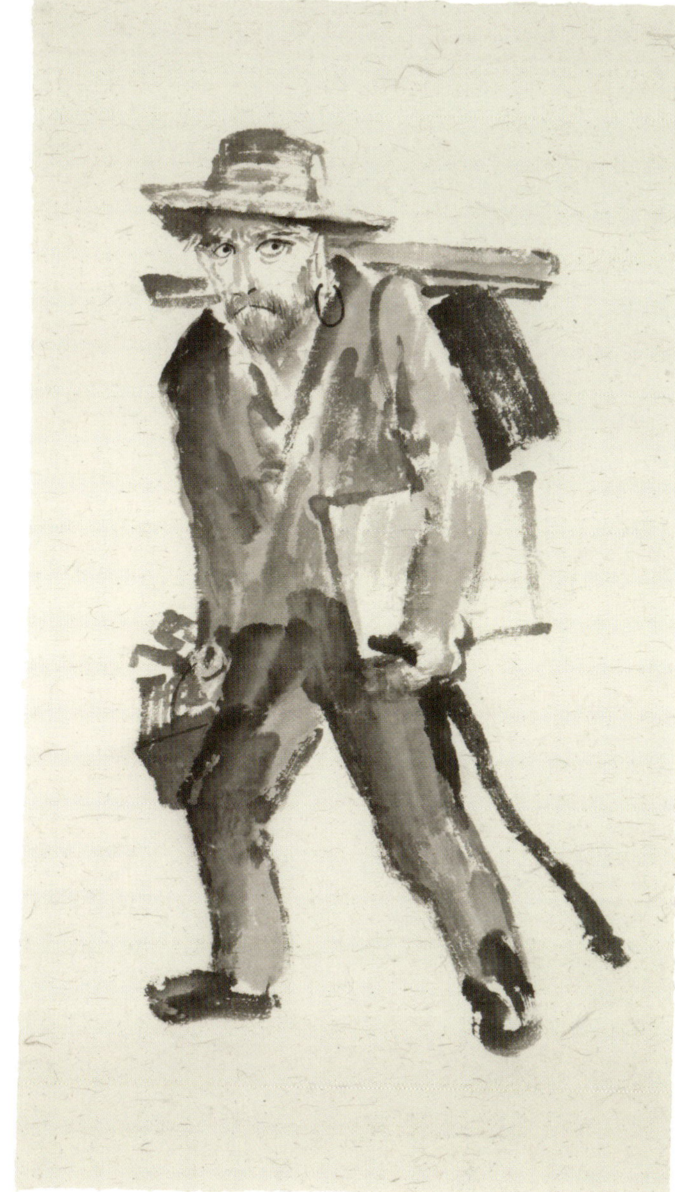

118-f

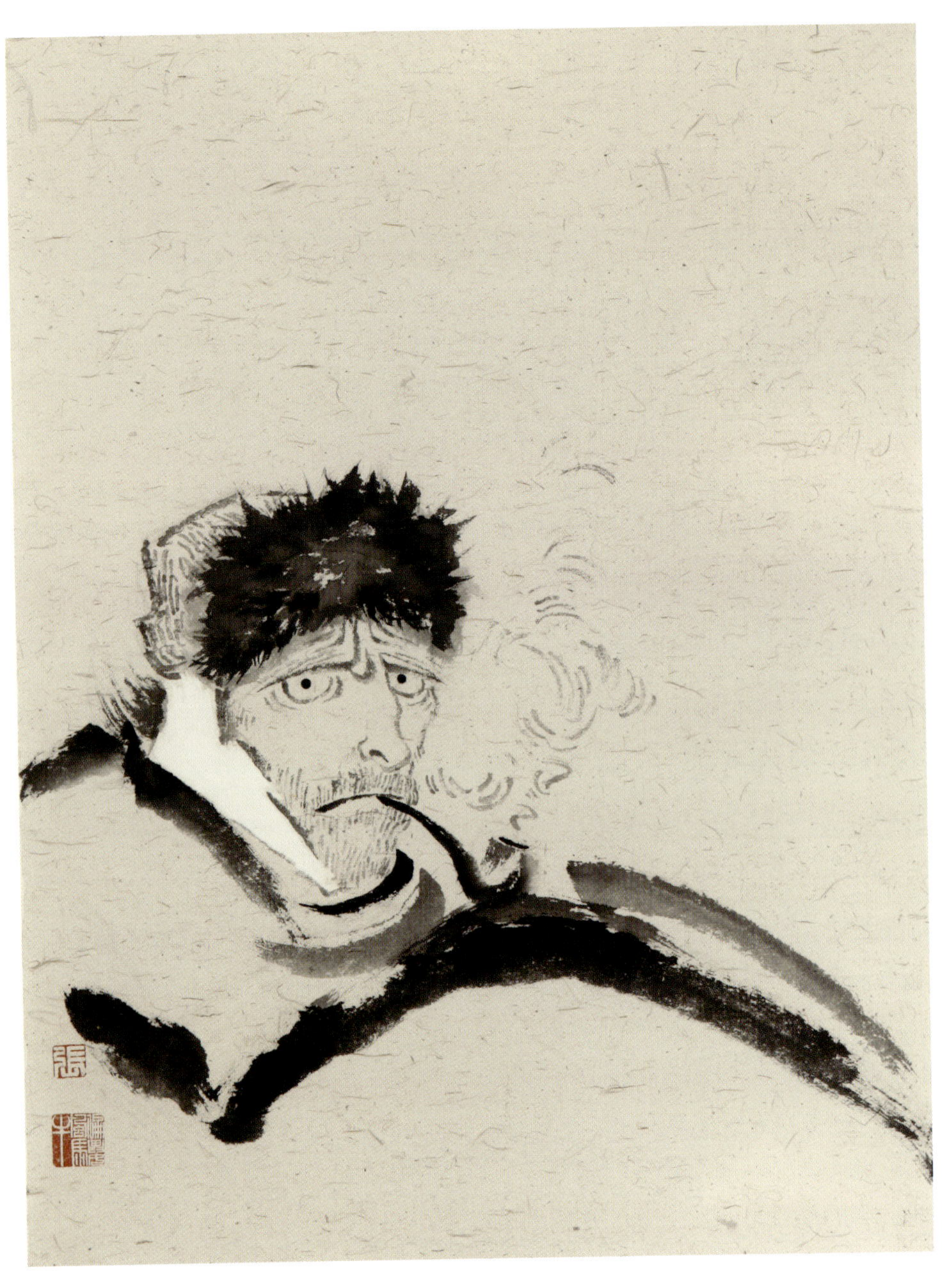

119

119
Van Gogh—Bodhidharma QM, 2015
Ink on paper
35 x 27 in.

Appendix

1943

The Year of the Goat. I was born into a traditional Muslim family in Pingliang, Gansu Province. The family ancestral home was Luoning, Henan Province.

1948

I left Pingliang with my parents for Shanghai via Xi'an. Later I lived in Nanjing, Suzhou, and Zhengzhou before finally ending up in Beijing in 1950.

1950

After settling in Beijing, my family moved frequently within the city and changed addresses no less than ten times. My six years of elementary education were completed in five different schools.

1957

My father was branded a Rightist. For the first time, I realized that other than schoolwork, drawing and painting pictures, and playing soccer, there was also this thing called politics in life; moreover, this thing was like your shadow, following you everywhere you go.

Entered Beijing 8th Middle School.

1960–64

Entered the high school attached to the Central Academy of Fine Arts. During my four years there, I learned some basic painting techniques including Western watercolors and drawing, Chinese calligraphy, and *shan shui*. But the basic teaching philosophy of the school was Socialist Realism imported from the Soviet Union. The purpose of studying art was so you could become a screw or gear inside the great revolutionary machine. (Even today I still have not figured out why a living person would want to become a screw or gear.) Art history taught at the school ended right before the French Impressionists. Impressionism and all Western art phenomena afterwards were condemned as "reactionary, decadent, and declining bourgeois arts." The four years of learning at the school were essentially a process of artistic foot-binding so that your natural creative instincts became deformed.

It was probably 1963 when students at the high school were organized to see an internal exhibit of the "negative examples of art" at the National Gallery of Art. On exhibit were print materials brought back to China by artists who studied in the West during the 1930s and 1940s. The exhibit was intended to teach the students what was bad art and what should not be emulated. It, however, afforded me the opportunity to see the paintings of Georges Rouault (1871–1958), which I have loved ever since.

After graduation from high school, I did not want to go to any college because the Central Academy of Fine Arts was not admitting new students. Instead, I dreamed about adventures in life and creating my own "masterpieces." As a result, the principal called me in and asked me to apply to the Central Academy of Arts and Crafts. He also added, "Whether you apply to the Central Academy of Arts and Crafts concerns whether you are a revolutionary or not!" So off to the academy I went. I chose the ceramics department, because Picasso also did ceramics.

I did not actually learn much about ceramics because two years later the Cultural Revolution broke out. Luckily, I met my future wife Huang Miaoling, who was a year ahead of me in the academy.

Another event worth mentioning was my stay, from fall of 1965 to spring of 1966, at Kunshan (outside Suzhou), as a member of the Central Academy of Arts and Crafts teacher and student team to conduct the so-called socialism education political campaign. During the first three months there, I could hardly communicate with the locals, and by the time I was able to understand half of their dialect, it was time to go back to Beijing. Although the eight months in Kunshan were pretty much wasted, afterwards whenever I saw the paintings of Mi Fu and his son or Huang Gongwang, depicting "the pastoral scenes south of the Yangtze" with their "plain ingenuous naturalness," I would always experience a feeling of closeness that's not entirely evoked by the color of ink and brushstrokes.

Mao launched the Great Proletariat Cultural Revolution. The idealism reflected in Mao's books on a Communist Utopia was the major motivating force for my eager participation in the campaign in 1966. Believing that "Children of the Rightists and the Five Black Types also have the rights to revolution," I was very active during the first three months, until one day, in a *hu-tong*, I saw a group of kids with the red armbands beating a middle-aged man to death with a leather belt that had a big copper buckle. These kids said, "This is a capitalist."

The most relaxing and happy period of time during the Cultural Revolution was during Dachuanlian, in which students could travel around the country for free. In the fall of 1966, I traveled by train to Urumqi, then went south to Guangzhou. After Dachuanlian had ended, several schoolmates of mine and I went on a "Long March": we walked three months from Guangzhou to Jinggang Mountain, then to Shaoshan, and afterwards took the train back to Beijing. By then it was already Spring 1967.

The entire Central Academy of Arts and Crafts was sent down to Huolu near the city of

Shijiazhuang, so the "May 16 counter-revolutionaries hidden among the faculty and students" could be discovered and caught under the watchful eyes of the military. We also worked in farm fields and learned how to plant rice.

If you sifted out the prisoner-like control of us by the PLA during the three years in the countryside, many wonderful memories would remain: the beautiful blue sky, the big white clouds, the horizon that was never obstructed by tall buildings, and the pleasant scents, at dusk, of horse and ox droppings and the farm fields permeating the air.

In 1972, our last year in Huolu, we were permitted to paint after farm work was done. I painted quite a few portraits of the old men and small kids there, as well as some country scenes.

1972

Married Huang Miaoling.

1973

Assigned to Beijing Jewelry Import-Export Co. In an era when wearing jewelry was condemned as "bourgeois lifestyle," I was sent to help factory designers design jewelry. What absurdity! In the nine years I worked for the company, there wasn't a single day when I didn't think about escaping it.

1976

Birth of my son Zhang Dasheng, who spent the very beginning of his life in an earthquake-proof shed.

1980

Formed the "Contemporaries" art group with friends from the high school attached to the Central Academy of Fine Arts, and held a joint exhibition at the National Gallery of Art. *Eternal Life*, one of my exhibited works, was collected by the gallery.

1981

Spent one month at Dunhuang studying the murals. For the first time I was awed by paintings outside the orthodox (court and scholar paintings). The fusion, in early Dunhuang murals, of traditional Chinese techniques and images with those from India and Central Asia influenced my later works. Equally unforgettable to me were the sand dunes around Dunhuang, the transparent nightly blue sky, and the moon and stars that you could almost touch with your hands.

On July 14, 1982, I flew from Beijing to New York via San Francisco. For four years beginning in the fall of that year, I took classes at the Art Students League in New York while working different jobs. One of my favorite teachers there was Richard Pousette-Dart (1916–1992). Although he would never tell you in class that you "should do this" or "should do that," neither would he tell you "Don't do this" or "Don't do that"!

"National art is bad; good art is national." This saying, which I saw in the fall of 1982 in a Guggenheim Museum exhibition catalogue, has had an everlasting influence on me. During these years, other than working, I experimented with this and that in order to shake off, as best as I could, the hold of the academic school and the so-called Socialist Realism on me. I finished a group of semi-abstract works on rice paper, a series of works painted on *New York Times* newspapers, a series of acrylic works influenced by the Neo-Expressionism in vogue in New York, as well as a "Back of the Head" series and an "Impression-Sunrise" series.

"In the Spirit of Dunhuang" was my first solo exhibition in New York City, held at the Asian Arts Institute. It later moved to the Adams House, Harvard University. In the same year, another solo exhibition of mine, "Zhang Hongtu: Recent New York Works," was presented at Hammerquist Gallery, New York.

During this period I also took part in group exhibitions in places such as the Alternative Museum, Henry Street Settlement, the Brooklyn Museum, and Yokohama, Japan.

In the fall of 1984, my wife and son came to America. The whole family was together again.

In 1986, I started working on *Quaker Oats Mao* and in 1987 made the initial ten pieces. In 1988, *Quaker Oats Mao* was shown to the public for the first time, at the Palladium night-club in New York.

In May–June 1989, the Chinese student democracy movement broke out in Tiananmen Square but was eventually crushed by the Chinese government's tanks and soldiers. The events prompted me to create, starting from August 1989, a group of works based on my own life experiences in China. These include *Last Banquet, Bilingual Chart of Acupuncture Points and Meridians, Chairmen Mao (12 units), Ping-Pong Mao*, and the "Material Mao" series.

In 1990, *Last Banquet* was banned from an exhibition held in Washington, DC. This unfortunate event, however, helped me. The media's extensive coverage of the ban allowed more people to see the painting.

In 1991, I received the Pollock-Krasner Foundation grant for painting, and afterwards moved into a studio located in Williamsburg, Brooklyn, sharing the space with two other painters.

The "Cut-out" series was also completed during this period of time. At the beginning, I used burlap, from which I cut out images of different cultural or religious icons. Starting from probably 1992, I concentrated on cutting out Mao images, but the materials I used went beyond burlap to include dirt, water, sand, rocks, rice, corn, etc.

In 1992, Webster Hall in New York presented a solo show of my work titled "The Angel's Ghost."

In 1994, the "Fashion Mao" series was completed in collaboration with fashion designer Vivienne Tam. These works gave me the feeling that they had entered an ever-moving museum without walls.

In 1995, I received the National Endowment for the Arts Visual Artists Fellowship.

Important group exhibitions I participated in during this period of time included "China June 4th 1989" at PS 1, New York; "The Decade Show" at the New Museum, New York; "Selection" at Artists Space, New York; and the Fifth Havana Biennial in Cuba.

From the fall of 1995 to the spring of 1996, a solo exhibition, "Zhang Hongtu: Material Mao" was held at The Bronx Museum of the Arts, New York. This exhibition included all my Mao works since *Quaker Oats Mao* of 1986.

While attending the high school attached to the Central Academy of Fine Arts in China, I ridiculed the colors in those European academic style paintings as "soy-sauce toned." However, in 1993, when I really applied soy sauce (mushroom soy sauce, to be exact) for the first time to rice paper, I was surprised by the beauty that could not be produced with oil and watercolor. Excited by the discovery, I did a series of Mao portraits using soy sauce. In 1995, after I decided to stop the Mao theme, I did several pieces of soy-sauce calligraphy.

1996–97

Flying Blues, a feather, sand, and mixed-media installation, was shown at the Anthony Giordano Gallery in 1996.

Also in 1996, a year before Hong Kong's return to China, I was invited by the Hong Kong University of Science and Technology to be an artist-in-residence. A solo exhibition, "Soy Sauce, Lipstick, Charcoal," was held there.

In 1997, I started a computer-generated work, *Christie's Catalog.* In the same year, I briefly revisited the Mao theme, completing "Unity and Discord" (nine works). Using eight different styles from modern Western art history and my own soy-sauce and cut-out styles, these works reproduced the photo of Mao waving to the Red Guards from Tiananmen in 1966. This series was the bridge connecting the Mao series and the "Repainted Shan Shui" series.

1998–2000

The "Repainted Shan Shui" series started with *Fan Kuan—Van Gogh* as the first painting. In the same year, a solo exhibition at the Cheryl McGinnis Gallery first showed some of my early works in the "Repainted Shan Shui" series to the public.

A solo exhibition of "Repainted Shan Shui" paintings was held at Yale-China Association, Yale University. During the same year, I participated in the group exhibition "TRANSIENCE: Chinese Experimental Art at the End of the Twentieth Century" at the Smart Museum of Art, University of Chicago.

A second solo exhibition was held at Cheryl McGinnis Gallery.

Took part in the "Word and Meaning" exhibition at the University of Buffalo Art Gallery, Buffalo, New York.

At the end of the year I was invited to Johannesburg, South Africa, and lived among local artists for a month. Every day I came into contact with many brilliant young Africans, and their natural talents in painting, music, and dance often made me feel inadequate. The experience also made me treasure my working and living conditions in New York more. Completed the "A Picture a Day" series.

2001

Although my works were shown in many exhibitions this year, two things worth writing here were not directly related to painting. First, in July, I visited the National Anthropology Museum in Mexico City. Second, in September, the World Trade Center in New York was attacked by terrorists, and 2,977 innocent people died that day. I am against terrorism; I am also against war, any war! No one has any excuse to start a war. If people in the twenty-first century still believe "My God is better than yours," the world will never be peaceful.

2002

Last Banquet was shown at the "Paris—Peking" exhibition in Paris.

Three "Repainted Shan Shui" works were shown at the Queens International exhibition at the Queens Museum of Art, New York.

Big Red Door was included in the Guangzhou Triennial held in Guangzhou, China.

In the summer, I traveled to Provence, France, and experienced the mountains, the waters, the wind, and the lights that Van Gogh and Cézanne experienced more than one hundred years ago.

Transformed these originally computer-generated virtual works into real sculptural objects: (1) bronze McDonald's packaging, (2) blue-and-white ceramic Coca-Cola bottles, and (3) the twelve Tang-style tri-color glazed Chinese zodiac ceramic animals.

2003

"Repainted Shan Shui" continued to be shown in many places, including the solo exhibition "Icon & Innovations: The Cross-Cultural Art of Zhang Hongtu" at the State University of New York at Potsdam, and a group exhibition at the Newark Museum, New Jersey.

In the spring, five of my oil *shan shui* works were included in the four-artist exhibition "Shuffling the Deck: The Collection Reconsidered" at Princeton University Art Museum. All five of these oil paintings are re-created ancient *shan shui* works found in the collections of the Princeton University Art Museum, and were shown alongside the original *shan shui* works by Ni Zan and Shitao, as well as the original oils of Monet and others.

2004

"Dialogue with the Taipei Palace Museum, Zhang Hongtu Solo Exhibition" was held at Lin & Keng Gallery, Taipei, Taiwan.

"Zhang Hongtu: Selected Works" was shown at Marlboro College, Vermont.

Took part in a group exhibitions held at University of Gettysburg and University of Pittsburgh in Pennsylvania.

In the same year, I found a studio in the Woodside neighborhood of Queens, New York, and moved in the next year. Finally, at the age of sixty-one, I had realized my dream of having my own studio, a dream that I had harbored since I was sixteen.

In July, my father passed away.

2005

A solo exhibition was held at Goedhuis Contemporary, New York.

Took part in the group exhibition "Trading Place" at the Museum of Contemporary Art, Taipei, Taiwan.

Participated in the group exhibition "On the Edge" at Stanford University, California.

Painted *Cézanne, Study of Axe Cut Ts'un*, the first painting in the currently ongoing "Mustard Seed Garden Manual of Painting" series.

2006

The exhibition "On the Edge: Contemporary Chinese Artists Encounter the West" traveled to the Davis Museum in Wellesley, Massachusetts, and the Indianapolis Museum of Art, Indiana.

At the beginning of the year, I participated in the "Dragon Veins" exhibition at the Contemporary Art Museum, University of South Florida.

In the spring, the solo painting installation "Four Seasons: Earth Above and Heaven Below" was shown at Lehigh University, Pennsylvania. The installation featured four of my re-created *shan shui* oils in the style of Van Gogh: *Spring, Summer, Fall,* and *Winter*, which hung, in the traditional Chinese hanging scroll style, from the highest point in the center of the university's Packer Memorial Chapel, amid the stained glass. The effect was that the paintings and the stained glass, with all their contradictions, merged into and became part of each other.

A documentary film, *Yellow Ox Mountain*, directed by Miao Wang, featuring my artistic pursuits and those of Zhang Jianjun, premiered in New York City.

2007

A second solo exhibition was held at the Lin & Keng Gallery, Taipei, Taiwan.

Participated in the grand opening exhibition at the Beijing Lin & Keng Galley.

Also was in a group show, "Made in China," at the Louisiana Museum of Modern Art, Denmark.

Shitao (Ten Thousand Ugly Inkblots Variation)—van Gogh was shown at the Third Chengdu Biennale, China.

Lin & Keng Gallery published *Zhang Hongtu: The Art of Straddling Boundaries*.

2008

Started a new series, "Shan Shui Today." Completed *Re-make of Ma Yuan's Water Album, 780 years later*. It is the first group painting in this series.

Bird's Nest in the Style of Cubism was seized by the Chinese authorities at customs. An article by David D'Arcy about this incident, "Artist's Pointed Critique Is Barred From Beijing," was published in the *Wall Street Journal*.

Took part in a group show at Asia Society Museum, New York.

Participated in a group show, "Reason's Clue," at Lin & Keng Gallery in Beijing and at the Queens Museum of Art in New York.

2009

Worked on the "Shan Shui Today" series.

Participated in the grand opening exhibition of Tina Keng Gallery, Taipei, Taiwan. Also took part in group shows at the National Arts Club in New York, Taipei Fine Arts Museum, Princeton University Art Museum, and 7th Floor Gallery, New York University, etc.

In October, my mother passed away.

2010

The influence of Cubism and the experience of studying the murals in Dunhuang twenty-nine years earlier can be perceived in the "Shan Shui Today" series. Although this series was inspired by my response to reality, I enjoyed the fun of dialoguing with ancient people in the process of making it.

Participated in group shows at The Bronx Museum of the Arts, New York; Museum of Chinese in America, New York; and several universities.

Christina Larson wrote an article on my work at the *Foreign Policy* website, introducing the Mao series and some recent works from the "Shan Shui Today" series.

2011

"Zhang Hongtu: Shan Shui Today" was held at Tina Keng Gallery, Taipei, Taiwan.

Worked on the "Bodhidharma—van Gogh" series, which had started in 2007.

2012

Completed thirty-nine re-made Van Gogh self-portraits in the style of Bodhidharma.

2013

A solo show of my work, "On the Road, Zhang Hongtu's Artistic Journey," was held at the Kaohsiung Museum of Fine Arts, Kaohsiung, Taiwan.

Participated in the exhibition "Inspiration from Dunhuang: Re-creations by Chinese Contemporary Artists" at China Institute Museum, New York.

Invited to give a lecture to students at the Yale University Pierson College. Numerous lectures and discussions in these years made me constantly organize my thoughts; I enjoyed exchanging opinions with the audience.

Seventieth birthday. Confucius said, "At seventy, I could follow what my heart desired, without transgressing what was right." I hope, from today, I can "follow what my heart desires," but keep my curiosity alive and "transgress what is right" sometimes.

2014

Participated in "Post-Picasso: Contemporary Reactions," at Museu Picasso, Barcelona, and "Oil and Water: Reinterpreting Ink," at Museum of Chinese in America, New York.

2015

Invited to participate in the Deichtorhallen's exhibition "Picasso in Contemporary Art," Hamburg; and the Israel Museum's exhibition "A Brief History of Humankind."

Also participated in a group show entitled "Wild Noise: Artwork from the Bronx Museum," at El Museo Nacional de Artes in Havana, Cuba.

Participated in "China: Through the Looking Glass," at The Metropolitan Museum of Art, New York.

In the fall, had a retrospective exhibition at the Queens Museum in New York. The exhibition was accompanied by a book entitled *Zhang Hongtu: Expanding Visions of a Shrinking World*, co-published by the Queens Museum and Duke University Press.

Selected Bibliography

compiled by Pei-Ching Norah Cheng, Samantha Yun Shao, and Hansi Liao

Books

On the Road: Zhang Hongtu's Artistic Journey. Kaohsiung: Kaohsiung Museum of Fine Arts, 2013.

Silbergeld, Jerome. *Zhang Hongtu: The Art Of Straddling Boundaries.* Taipei: Lin & Keng Gallery, Inc., 2007.

The Ten Ox-Herding Pictures: Chan Master Kuo-an Shih-yuan, Song Dynasty, Reproduced by Zhang Hongtu. Taipei: TKG Foundation for Arts & Culture, 2014.

Zhang, Hongtu, and Jerome Silbergeld. *Zhang Hongtu: An On-going Painting Project.* New York: On-going Publications, 2000.

Chapters or Sections of Books

Andrews, Julia F., and Kuiyi Shen. "No U-turn: Chinese Art after 1989." In *The Art Of Modern China*, 257–77. Los Angeles: The Regents of the University of California, 2012.

Barmé, Geremie R. *Shades of Mao: The Posthumous Cult of the Great Leader*, 46, 215. New York: M. E. Sharpe, Inc., 1996.

Barmé, Geremie R., and Linda Jaivin. Introduction to *New Ghosts, Old Dreams: Chinese Rebel Voices*, xxvi. New York: Times Books, 1992.

Callahan, William A. "Gender, Democracy and Representation: Asian Revolutionary Images." In *Gendering the International*, edited by Louiza Odysseos and Hakan Seckinelgin, 167–68. New York: Millennium, 2002.

Clarke, David. "Reframing Mao: Aspects of Recent Chinese Art, Popular Culture and Politics." In *Art & Place: Essays on Art from a Hong Kong Perspective*, 236–49. Hong Kong: Hong Kong University Press, 1996.

Chang, Alexandra. "Once More: Is There An Asian American Aesthetic?" In *Envisioning Diaspora: Asian American Visual Arts Collectives*, 98–109. Beijing: Timezone 8 Limited, 2009.

Chang, Arnold. "From Fengshui to Fractals: A User's Guide to Chinese Landscape Painting." In *ARTiculations: Undefining Chinese Contemporary Art*, edited by Jerome Silbergeld and Dora C. Y. Ching, 33–61. Princeton, NJ: Tang Center for East Asian Art and Princeton University Press, 2010.

Chiu, Melissa. "An Expanded Chinese Art History: Internationalization of the Chinese Art World." In *Asian Art History: In the Twenty-First Century*, edited by Vishakha N. Desai, 224. Williamstown: Sterling and Francine Clark Art Institute, 2007.

———. "Theories of Being Outside." In *Breakout: Chinese Art Outside China*, 8, 18, 39–72, 113, 212. Milan: Charta, 2006.

Clarke, David. "Revolutions in Vision: Chinese Art and the Experience of Modernity." In *The Cambridge Companion to Modern Chinese Culture*, 292–94. Cambridge: Cambridge University Press, 2008.

Cohen, Joan Lebold. "Groups: Contemporaries." In *The New Chinese Painting: 1949–1986*, 77. New York: Harry N. Abrams, 1987.

Delue, Rachael Z. "Neither Here Nor There: China, Global Culture, and the End of American Art." In *ARTiculations: Undefining Chinese Contemporary Art*, edited by Jerome Silbergeld and Dora C. Y. Ching, 250–71. Princeton, NJ: Tang Center for East Asian Art and Princeton University Press, 2010.

Dutton, Michael. *Streetlife China*, 162–63, 172, 174, 241, 262–65. Cambridge: Cambridge University Press, 1998.

Hallmark, Kara Kelly. "Zhang Hongtu." In *Encyclopedia of Asian American Artists: Artists of the American Mosaic*, 261–65. Westport: Greenwood Press, 2007.

Hay, Jonathan. "*Zhang Hongtu / Hongtu Zhang: An Interview*." In *Boundaries in China*, 280–98. London: Reaktion Books, 1994.

He, Xin. "Wheels: What's New?" In *New Ghosts, Old Dreams: Chinese Rebel Voices*, 409. New York: Times Books, 1992.

Huot, Claire. "China's Avant-Garde Art: Differences in the Family." In *China's New Cultural Scene: A Handbook of Changes*, 126–41. Durham: Duke University Press, 2000.

Kwon, Sowon. "Potatoes, Teddy Bears, Lipsticks, and Mao." In *Art in General Manual 1993–1994*. New York: Art In General, Inc., 1994.

Lao, She. "Wheels: A Big Confucius and Little Emiles." In *New Ghosts, Old Dreams: Chinese Rebel Voices*, 404. New York: Times Books, 1992.

Lim, Michelle. "Cultural Iconography as Style." In *Outside In: Chinese x American x Contemporary Art*, 270–81. Princeton, NJ: Princeton University Art Museum and Tang Center for East Asian Art, and New Haven: Yale University Press, 2009.

Lin, Xiaoping. "Globalism or Nationalism?" In *Children of Marx and Coca-Cola: Chinese Avant-Garde Art and Independent Cinema*, 72. Honolulu: University of Hawai'i Press, 2009.

———. "Globalism or Nationalism?" In *Global Visual Cultures: An Anthology*, 9–26. West Sussex: Wiley-Blackwell, 2011.

Liu, Changhan. *The Chinese Overseas Art Icons of The 100 Years*, 150–51. Taipei: Artist Publication, 2000.

Liu, Xiaobo. "Wheels: On Solitude." In *New Ghosts, Old Dreams: Chinese Rebel Voices*, 384. New York: Times Books, 1992.

McCausland, Shane. Introduction and Epilogue to *Zhao Mengfu: Calligraphy and Painting for Khubilai's China*, 3, 333–37. Hong Kong: Hong Kong University Press, 2011.

Mittler, Barbara. "Mao Wherever You Go: The Art of Repetition in Revolutionary China." In *A Continuous Revolution: Making Sense of Cultural Revolution Culture*, 298, 299, 300–1, 306, 311, 315, 326–27. Cambridge, MA, and London: Harvard University Asia Center, 2012.

Ngai, Jimmy S. Y. "The Cry: Tiananmen Days." In *New Ghosts, Old Dreams: Chinese Rebel Voices*, 76, 93. New York: Times Books, 1992.

Purtle, Jennifer. "Whose Hobbyhorse?: Loading the Deck." In *Chinese Landscape Painting as Western Art History*, 5–8. Hong Kong: Hong Kong University Press, 2010.

Schell, Orville. *Mandate of Heaven: A New Generation of Entrepreneurs, Dissidents, Bohemians, and Technocrats Lays Claim to China's Future*, 290–91. New York: Simon & Schuster, 1994.

Silbergeld, Jerome. "An Outsider's Outsider Comes In." In *Outside In: Chinese x American x Contemporary Art*, 257–69. Princeton, NJ: Princeton University Art Museum and Tang Center for East Asian Art, and New Haven: Yale University Press, 2009.

———. "Facades: The New Beijing and Unsettled Ecology of Jia Zhangke's *The World*." In *Chinese Ecocinema: In the Age of Environmental Challenge*, edited by Sheldon H. Lu and Jiayan Mi, 122. Hong Kong: Hong Kong University Press, 2009.

———. "The Space Between: Cross-Cultural Encounters in Contemporary Chinese Art." In *Meaning, Image, and Word: Resourcing "Word Play" in Chinese Cultural Discourse*, edited by Hsingyuan Tsao and Roger T. Ames, 177–98. Albany, NY: State University of New York Press, 2011.

Sullivan, Michael. *Art and Artists of Twentieth Century China*. Berkeley and Los Angeles: University of California Press, 1996.

Tam, Vivienne. "MAO ART: Interview with Zhang Hongtu." In *China Chic*, 92–4. New York: HarperCollins, 1999.

Tu, Thuy Linh Nguyen. "Material Mao: Fashion Histories Out of Icons." In *The Beautiful Generation: Asian Americans and the Cultural Economy of Fashion*, 145–48, 156–64. Durham: Duke University Press, 2011.

Valjakka, Minna. "Parodying Mao: Earliest Existing Caricatures of Mao." In *Many Faces of Mao Zedong*, 170. Helsinki: University of Helsinki, 2011.

Vine, Richard. *New China, New Art*. New York: Prestel, 2008.

Yang, Alice. "Review: A Group Show: We Are the Universe." In Alice Yang, *Why Asia?: Contemporary Asian and Asian American Art*. New York: New York University Press, 1998.

Zhang, Hongtu. "Blurring the Boundary Between Yesterday and Today, for Tomorrow." In *ARTiculations: Un-defining Chinese Contemporary Art*, edited by Jerome Silbergeld and Dora C. Y. Ching, 212–31. Princeton, NJ: Tang Center for East Asian Art and Princeton University Press, 2010.

———. "Live to Tell: I Don't Want to Do Anything Pure." In *Transculturalism: How the World Is Coming Together*, edited by Claude Grunitzky with Trace Magazine Contributors, 236–37. New York: True Agency, 2004.

Journal Articles

ART/LIFE vol. 22, No. 9, issue 241, 22-23. Ventura: ARTLIFE, 2002.

"The Black Hole Art of Zhang Hongtu." *Postcolonial Studies* 2, no. 2 (1999): 121, 165–69.

Bordeleau, Erik. "Le Political Pop: Un Art Profanatoire?" *Etc.: Revue de l'Art Actuel* 91 (2010–11): 21–25.

Boucher, Madeleine. "Beyond Pop: Imagery and Appropriation in Contemporary Chinese Art." *Columbia East Asia Review* vol. 2 (2009): 37–55.

Callahan, William A. "Vision of Gender and Democracy: Revolutionary Photo Albums in Asia." *Journal of International Studies*, vol. 27, no. 4 (1998): 1031–60.

Cline, Rob. "Mao Isn't Just for Breakfast Anymore." *Icon* (June 8, 2000).

Cohn, Don J. "Cultural Imports: Sotheby's Brings Chinese Contemporary Art to New York." *Art Asia Pacific* 48 (2006): 56–7.

Cornand, Brigitte. "Around the World." *Art Press International Edition* 185 (1993): 69.

Dal Lago, Francesca. "Personal Mao: Reshaping an Icon in Contemporary Chinese Art." *Art Journal* vol. 58, no. 2 (1999): 54.

Dudek, Ingrid. "Mao in Contemporary Chinese Art." *Andy Warhol's Mao*, auction catalog (New York: Christie's, 2006).

Erickson, Britta. "The Contemporary Artistic Deconstruction—and Reconstruction—of Brush and Ink Painting." *Yishu: Journal of Contemporary Chinese Art* vol. 2, no. 2 (2003): 82–9.

"Face of Protest." *US News & World Report* (September 18, 1989): 13.

Fang, Lizhi, and Richard Dicker. "Portraits of Oppression: A Leading Dissident Decries the Continued Atrocities in China." *The Sciences* vol. 32, 5 (1992): 16–21.

Goodman, Jonathan. "Exhibition Review: Zhang Hongtu at the Bronx Museum of the Arts." *Asia-Pacific Sculpture News* vol. 2, no. 2 (1996): 57–8.

———. "How Chinese Is It?" *Architrave: A Journal of the Arts* (1997): 43–6.

———. "Shuffling the Deck." *Art AsiaPacific* 38 (2003): 84–5.

———. "Zhang Hongtu." *Art AsiaPacific* 15 (1997): 91.

Hay, Jonathan. "Ambivalent Icons." *Orientations* (July 1992).

Hollow, Michele C. "Access to Art." *Summit Magazine* Holiday Issue (2006): 44–9.

Hunter, Felicia. "Exhibit Features Works of Chinese Artist Who Mixed Western and Eastern Styles and Symbols." *Yale Bulletin and Calendar* vol. 28, no. 7 (1999).

Jacoby, Russell. "Whither Marxism?" *Transition: An International Review* 69 (1996): 100–15.

Kaylan, Melik. "Dealer's Choice." *House and Garden* (April 1999): 92.

Kelley, Robin D. G., and Betsy Esch. "Black Like Mao: Red China and Black Revolution." *Souls: A Critical Journal of Black Politics, Culture, and Society* vol. 1, no. 4 (1999): 8–11.

Kumagai, Isako. "Chinese Artists in New York." *Bulletin of Museum of Contemporary Art, Tokyo* 9 (2003): 15–16.

———. "Zhang Hongtu and Ji Yunfei, Chinese Artists in New York City." *Saitama University Review* vol. 46 (2010): 79–88.

Lee, Robert. "Editorial." *Artspiral* vol. 6 (1992): 3.

Levin, Gail. "Changing Cultures: The Recent Immigration of Chinese Artists to the U.S." *Asian Art News* vol.

4, no. 5 (1994): 70–73.

———. "Immigrant Artists from China at Baruch College Gallery." *Art Times* (May 1991): 10–11.

Lin, Edward. "Censored!" *Transpacific* (June 1994): 58–61.

Marcus, David. "The Museum Takes on the Museum: Art Exhibition Offers New Perspectives on Familiar Works." *Princeton Alumni Weekly* (March 26, 2003).

Newman, Cathy. "Culture: Mao Now." *National Geographic* vol. 213, no. 5 (2008): 100–1.

Ng, Elaine W. "Artists on Spirituality." *Art Asia Pacific* 51 (2007): 91.

Pappas, Ben. "Boppa um Mao Mao." *Forbes* (January 26, 1998).

Pollack, Barbara. "China's Desert Treasure." *Art News* vol. 112, no. 11 (2013): 74–81.

Schell, Orville. "Once Again, Long Live Chairman Mao." *Atlantic* (December 1992).

Shen, Kuiyi. "Landscape as Cultural Consciousness in Contemporary Chinese Art." *Yishu: Journal of Contemporary Chinese Art* vol. 2, no. 4 (2003): 33–40.

"Shuffling the Deck: The Collection Reconsidered." *Asian Art: The Newspaper for Collectors, Dealers, Museums, and Galleries* (March 2003).

Snow, Crocker. "Graphic Expressions of Protest." *The World Paper* (October 1989).

Takahashi, Corey. "Art Imitates Queens Life—Museum Exhibit Mixes Global Spirit and Local Diversity." *Newsday* (September 20, 2002).

Tallmer, Jerry. "Chinese Works Bound & Unbound for Glory." *New York Post* (May 10, 1991).

Weyburn, Jennifer A. "Drawing on East and West." *The Yale-China Review* Centennial Issue, vol. 7, no. 3 (2002): 10–15.

Wojciechowski, Leigh Ann. "Chinese Artists: Reinventing Tradition." *Pitt Magazine* (Fall 2004): 3–4.

Wu, Hung. "Afterword: 'Hong Kong 1997'—T-shirt Designs by Zhang Hongtu." *Public Culture* vol. 9, no. 3 (1997): 417–25.

Yang, Alice. "Group Show at Haenah-Kent Gallery." *Asian Art News* vol. 4, no. 2 (1994): 94–5.

Zhu, Lillian. "Zhang Hongtu." *Asian Voices: Destiny* vol. 7 (1994): 26–30.

Newspaper Articles

Alonso, Nathalie. "Back to the Garden: Daily Life to Spiritual Vision." *Queens Chronicle*, April 17, 2008.

"Artist Famed for Mao's Image Visits Hong Kong." *Hong Kong Standard*, April 24, 1996.

Bischoff, Dan. "Making It Big: Summit Gallery Spotlights Massive Culture-Blending Creations by the China-born." *The Star-Ledger*, September 29, 2006.

"Bridging the Cultural Gap." *The Citizen*, January 15, 2001.

Cheung, Denise. "Art Meets Science in Bold Exhibition." *South China Morning Post*, May 9, 1996.

Cotter, Holland. "Art in Review." *New York Times*, June 22, 2001.

Cullinan, Helen. "A Great Wall of Protest: 'China 1989' Exhibit Speaks Tellingly on Human Rights." *The Plain Dealer*, August 27, 1992.

Dao, James. "From Shanghai to Soho: For Chinese Expatriates, It's Art for Heart's Sake." *Daily News*, October 29, 1989.

———. "Lady in Square Reborn: Student Symbol to Stand in N.Y." *Daily News*, June 8, 1989.

D'Arcy, David. "Artist's Pointed Critique Is Barred from Beijing." *Wall Street Journal*, August 21, 2008.

Dunning, Jennifer. "The Dance: 'Silk Road,' by Miss Yung." *New York Times*, April 8, 1984.

Fisher, Harry. "East Meets West in Color." *The Morning Call*, April 7, 2006.

Francia, Luis H. "Tiananmen Show Gutted." *Village Voice*, July 31, 1990.

Genocchio, Benjamin. "Sampling the Diverse Output of Artists from China: An Exhibition in Summit Touches on Issues of Identity and Culture Shock." *New York Times*, October 15, 2006.

Glueck, Grace. "Art in Review." *New York Times*, April 29, 2005.

Harrison, Helen A. "A Painter's Images of Mao as Reflected in a Changing China." *New York Times*, November 10, 1996.

———. " 'This Is Long Island,' Without Any Automobiles or People." *New York Times*, April 16, 1995.

Hernandez, Barbara. "East Meets West in Baruch Art Gallery." *Ticker Perspectives*, May 8, 1991.

Johnson, Ken. "A Pluralist Exhibition in the Plural Borough." *New York Times*, August 23, 2002.

Johnson, Patricia C. "The Station Offers 'Space' for Humanistic Self-Expression." *Houston Chronicle*, September 14, 2002.

Lee, Robert. "Zhang Hongtu." *Village Voice Art Issue*, Spring 1989.

Lovelace, Carey. "Memories of Mao: An Emigré Focuses on the Chairman." *Newsday*, November 8, 1996.

Mangaliman, Jessie. "Brushes Wielded Against Terror at Home." *New York Newsday*, June 23, 1989.

Mimoni, Victor G. "Flushing Art Show Makes Smiles Bloom." *Queens Courier*, March 13, 2008.

Morano, Marylou. "Chinese Artists Travel Between Cultures at VACNJ." *The Westfield Leader And The Scotch Plains—Fanwood TIMES*, October 5, 2006.

"Newton Display Driven by Notion of Art for All." *Sunday Independent*, January 21, 2001.

Parris, Sharon. "Changing Culture: Chinese Artists." *The Reporter*, May 1991.

Pellett, Gail. "Mao's Scorched Flowers Go West: Is There Art After Liberation?" *Village Voice*, May 13, 1986.

"Ping-Pong with Chairman Mao." *The Gazette*, May 5, 2000.

Raven, Arlene. "Days with Art." *Village Voice*, October 5, 1993.

Sand, Olivia. "Profile: Zhang Hongtu." *Asian Art: the Newspaper for Collectors, Dealers, Museums, and Galleries*, January 2011.

Schwendener, Martha. "Centuries Apart, Cultures Speak to Each Other." *New York Times*, August 12, 2012.

"Spirit of Tiananmen Square." *Akron Beacon Journal*, August 30, 1992.

Sugarman, Raphael. "Art Across Cultures." *Daily News*, April 4, 1994.

Vogel, Carol. "A New Art Capital, Finding Its Own Voice." *New York Times*, December 7, 2014.

Weiss, Birti. "Alle Eksisterer for Min Skyld." *Weekendavisen Boger*, June 17–23, 2005.

Zimmer, William. "Statement from the Chinese After Tiananmen Square." *New York Times*, November 6, 1994.

Exhibition Catalogues

Solo

Dialogue With the Taipei Palace Museum: Zhang Hongtu Solo Exhibition. Taipei: Lin & Keng Gallery, 2004.

Icons & Innovations: The Cross-Cultural Art of Zhang Hongtu. New York: The Gibson Gallery, 2003.

In the Spirit of Dunhuang: Studies by Zhang Hongtu. New York: Asian Arts Institute, 1984.

Recent Paintings by Zhang Hongtu. New York: Goedhuis Contemporary, 2005.

Zhang Hongtu: Material Mao. New York: The Bronx Museum of the Arts, 1996.

Zhang Hongtu: Recent Paintings. Taipei: Lin & Keng Gallery, 2007.

Zhang Hongtu: Shan Shui Today. Taipei: Tina Keng Gallery, 2011.

Group

AJITA. Houston: INERI Foundation, 2002.

Art and China's Revolution. New York: Asia Society, 2008.

The Art of Justice: Part II. White Plains: Krasdale Gallery, 1995.

Artists from China—New Expressions. New York: Sarah Lawrence College Art Gallery, 1987.

Back to the Garden: Daily Life to Spiritual Vision. New York: Crossing Art, 2008.

Beyond the Borders: Art by Recent Immigrants. New York: The Bronx Museum of the Arts, 1994.

Changing Cultures: Immigrant Artists from China. New York: Baruch College, City University of New York, 1992.

CHINA June 4, 1989: An Art Exhibition. Flint: Buckham Gallery, 1994.

China Onward: The Estella Collection—Chinese Contemporary Art, 1966–2006. Denmark: Louisiana Museum of Modern Art, 2007.

China Without Borders: An Exhibition of Chinese Contemporary Art. New York: Goedhuis Contemporary, 2001.

Chinese Painting Collection of Guy Ullens de Schooten. Beijing: The Palace Museum, 2002.

Collection Remix. New York: The Bronx Museum of the Arts, 2005.

Contemporary Art: Travel Diary. Montreal: Galerie Observatoire 4, 1998.

Contemporary Combustion: Chinese Artists in America. New Britain: New Britain Museum of American Art, 2007.

The Decade Show: Frameworks of Identity in the 1980s. New York: Museum of Contemporary Hispanic Art, The New Museum of Contemporary Art, and The Studio Museum in Harlem, 1990.

Dragon Veins. Tampa: Contemporary Art Museum at University of South Florida, 2006.

East/West: Visually Speaking. Lafayette: Paul and Lulu Hilliard University Art Museum, 2010.

Exhibition of Chinese American Artists. Taipei: American Institute in Taiwan, 2000.

Global Roots: Artists from China Working in New York. West Lafayette: Purdue University, 1998.

Godzilla: The Asian American Arts Network. New York: Artists Space, 1993.

Here + Now: Chinese Artists in New York. New York: Museum of Chinese in America, 2009.

Hypallage: The Post-Modern Mode of Chinese Contemporary Art. Shenzhen: OCT Art & Design Gallery, 2008.

In Memory—the Art of Afterward: An International Exhibition of Works Reflecting on Loss and Remembrance. New York: The Legacy Project, 2002.

Inspired by Dunhuang: Re-creation in Contemporary Chinese Art. New York: China Institute, 2013.

Inter Mediate: Selected Contemporary Chinese American Art. Ewing, NJ: The College of New Jersey Art Gallery, 2011.

Kimchi Xtravaganza!: A Multidisciplinary Showcase About Kimchi. Los Angeles: Korean American Museum, 1998.

Mythologies of Contemporary Art by Three Artists: Zhang Hongtu, Yang Maolin and Tu Weicheng. Taipei: Taipei Fine Arts Museum, 2009.

New Chinese Occidentalism: Chinese Contemporary Art in New York. New York: Ethan Cohen Fine Arts, 2005.

Oil & Water: Reinterpreting Ink. New York: Museum of Chinese in America, 2014.

On the Edge: Contemporary Art from Indonesia and China. Jakarta: The Pakubuwono Residence/Bank Mandiri PRIORITAS, 2004.

On the Edge: Contemporary Chinese Artists Encounter the West. Stanford: Iris & B. Gerald Cantor Center for Visual Arts, 2006.

Out of Time, Out of Place, Out of China: Reinventing Chinese Tradition in a New Century. Pittsburgh: The University Art Gallery, University of Pittsburgh, 2005.

Outside In: Chinese x American x Contemporary Art, edited by Jerome Silbergeld, Dora C. Y. Ching, and Cary Liu. Princeton, NJ: Princeton University Art Museum and Tang Center for East Asian Art, and New Haven: Yale University Press, 2009.

Paris-Pékin. Paris: Chinese Century, Ullens and Asiart Archive, 2002.

The Pavilion of Realism. Beijing: Other Gallery, 2010.

Post-Mao Dreaming: Chinese Contemporary Art. Massachusetts: Smith College Museum of Art, 2009.

Post-Picasso: Contemporary Reactions. Barcelona: Museu Picasso, 2014.

Reason's Clue. New York: Queens Museum of Art, 2008.

Reboot: The Third Chengdu Biennale. Chengdu: Chengdu Contemporary Art Museum, 2007.

Re-do China. New York: Ethan Cohen Fine Arts, 2003.

Reinventing Tradition in a New World: The Arts of Gu Wenda, Wang Mansheng, Xu Bing and Zhang Hongtu. Pennsylvania: Schmucker Art Gallery, 2004.

Revolution. New York: China Square Publishing Inc., 2007.

R/evolution. Taipei: Tina Keng Gallery, 2009.

The Revolution Continues: New Art from China. London: Saatchi Gallery, 2008.

Roots to Reality II: Alternative Visions. New York: Alliance for Asian American Arts and Culture, and Henry Street Settlement, 1986.

Selections: Aljira & Artists Space. New York: Artists Space, 1990.

Shuffling the Deck: The Collection Reconsidered. Princeton: Princeton University Art Museum, 2003.

Syncretism: The Art of the XXI Century. New York: Alternative Museum, 1991.

Tiananmen Memorial Art Exhibit. New York: Congressional Human Rights Foundation, 1990.

Trading Place: Contemporary Art Museum. Taipei: Museum of Contemporary Art, 2005.

Transcultural New Jersey: Diverse Artists Shaping Culture and Communities. New Brunswick, NJ: Jane Voorhees Zimmerli Art Museum, 2004.

Transience: Chinese Experimental Art at the End of the Twentieth Century. Chicago: The David and Alfred Smart Museum, 1999.

Travelers Between Cultures: Contemporary Chinese Artists in New York. Summit, NJ: Visual Art Center of New Jersey, 2006.

Unknown/Infinity: Culture and Identity in the Digital Age. New York: Taipei Gallery, 2001.

Urban Archives: Happy Together. New York: The Bronx Museum of the Arts, 2011.

Word and Meaning: Six Contemporary Chinese Artists. University at Buffalo Art Gallery, 2000.

Works by Zhang Hongtu. Hong Kong: The HKUST Center for the Arts, 1996.

Guide to Traditional and Simplified Chinese Characters

Chapter-page	Traditional Chinese	Simplified Chinese	Pronunciation
C1 – 14	大觀	大观	dà guān (da guan)
C1 – 14	孔子登東山而小魯，登泰山而小天下．故觀於海者難為水，遊於聖人之門者難為言．	孔子登东山而小鲁，登泰山而小天下．故观于海者难为水，游于圣人之门者难为言．	kǒngzǐ dēng dōngshān ér xiǎo lǔ, dēng tàishān ér xiǎo tiānxià. Gù guān yú hǎi zhě nánwéi shuǐ, yóu yú shèngrén zhī mén zhě nánwéi yán.
C1 – 17	掛羊頭賣狗肉	挂羊头卖狗肉	guà yángtóu mài gǒuròu (gua yang tou mai gou rou)
C1 – 19	逍遙派	逍遥派	xiāoyáo pài (Xiaoyao Pai)
C1 – 19	糞筐畫派	粪筐画派	fèn kuāng huà pài (Fen Kuang Huapai)
C1 – 20	同代人	同代人	tóng dài rén (Tong Dai Ren)
C1 – 20	星星畫派	星星画派	xīngxīng huà pài (Xingxing Hua Pai)
C1 – 27	風馬牛不相及	风马牛不相及	fēng mǎ niú bù xiāng jí (feng ma niu bu xiang ji)
C1 – 27	偏要風馬牛	偏要风马牛	piān yào fēng mǎ niú (pianyao feng ma niu)
C1 – 29	大成	大成	dà chéng (da cheng)
C4 – 76	王羲之	王羲之	wáng xīzhī (Wang Xizhi)

C4 – 78	山水	山水	shān shuǐ (shan shui)
C4 – 79	王原祁	王原祁	wáng yuánqí (Wang Yuanqi)
C5 – 86	隔靴搔癢	隔靴搔痒	gé xuē sāoyǎng (ge xue saoyang)
C5 – 89	天圓地方	天圆地方	tiānyuán dìfāng (tianyuan difang)
C5 – 95	文人	文人	wén rén (wenren)
C6 – 112	麥當勞	麦当劳	mài dāng láo (Mai Dang Lao)
C6 – 113	永樂宮	永乐宫	Yǒnglè gong (Yonglegong)
C6 – 113	國畫	国画	Guó huà (guo hua)
C11 – 163	殘山剩水	残山剩水	cán shān shèng shuǐ (Can shan sheng shui)
C11 – 172	波蹙金風、洞庭風細、層波疊浪、寒塘清淺、長江萬頃、黃河逆流、秋水回波、雲生滄海、湖光瀲灔、雲舒浪卷、曉日烘山、細浪漂漂	波蹙金风、洞庭风细、层波叠浪、寒塘清浅、长江万顷、黄河逆流、秋水回波、云生沧海、湖光瀲灔、云舒浪卷、晓日烘山、细浪漂漂	bō cù jīn fēng, dòngtíng fēng xì, céng bō dié làng, hán táng qīng qiǎn, chángjiāng wànqǐng, huánghé nìliú, qiūshuǐ huí bō, yún shēng cāng-hǎi, hú guāng liàn yàn, yún shū làng juǎn, xiǎo rì hōng shān, xì làng piào piào
C11 – 172	唐，杜甫《陪鄭廣文游何將軍山林》"剩水滄江破，殘山碣石開"	唐，杜甫《陪郑广文游何将军山林》"剩水沧江破，残山碣石开"	táng, dùfǔ "péi zhèng guǎngwén yóu hé jiāng-jūn shānlín""shèng shuǐ cāng jiāng pò, cán shān jiéshí kāi"

Credits:

Lenders to the exhibition:

Benito Sim, NY

Ethan Cohen Fine Arts, New York

Jeff Wimmer, New York

Leo Shih, Taichung, Taiwan

Lin & Lin Gallery, Taipei

Lybess Sweezey and Ken Miller, NY

Princeton University Art Museum, New Jersey

Private collection, courtesy Cheryl McGinnis Gallery, NY

Private collection, courtesy Christie's, London

Private collection, NY

Private collection

The Art Students League, New York

The Contemporary Chinese Art Fund, New York

Tina Keng Gallery, Taipei

Zhang Hongtu Studio, New York

Photographs:

Photographs of works of art reproduced in this volume have been provided in most cases by the owners or custodians of the works, identified in the captions. Individual works of art appearing herein may be protected by copyright in the United States of America or elsewhere, and may thus not be reproduced in any form without the permission of the copyright owners. The following credits appear at the request of the artist or the artist's representatives and/or the owners of the individual works.

© 2015 Artist's Right's Society (ARS), Scala/White Images / Art Resource, New York, page 140

Elizabeth G. DuHamel, page 121

Mia Huang, page 86

© Jeff Chien-Hsing Liao, page 156

© 2015 The Andy Warhol Museum, Pittsburgh; Founding Collection, Contribution Dia Center, page 146

© The Metropolitan Museum of Art, New York, page 65

Courtesy Pékin Fine Arts, Beijing, page 142

Wang Huaiqing, page 18

Courtesy Xu Bing Studio, New York, page 42

Zhang Honglu, page 15

Photography assistant Zhang Dazhi, page 52

© 2015 Zhang Xiaoli / China Foto Press, pages 164

Translators:

Rick Belsky

Louisa Chen

Hui Gao

Dasheng Zhang

Contributor List:

Julia F. Andrews, Ohio State University

Alexandra Chang, New York University

Tom Finkelpearl, Department of Cultural Affairs, City of New York

Michael FitzGerald, Trinity College - Hartford

Wu Hung, University of Chicago

Luchia Meihua Lee, Guest Curator, Queens Museum

Morgan Perkins, State University of New York

Kuiyi Shen, University of California, San Diego

Jerome Silbergeld, Princeton University

Eugenie Tsai, Curator, Brooklyn Museum

Thuy Linh Nguyen Tu, New York University

Lilly Wei, Independent Curator & Critic, New York City

This book is published on the occasion of the exhibition "Zhang Hongtu" at the Queens Museum, Queens, New York. Curated by Luchia Meihua Lee, October 18, 2015–February 28, 2016

The publication and exhibition are made possible by the generous support of the TKG Foundation for Arts & Culture, Taipei, Taiwan.

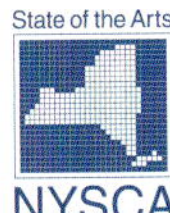

TKG FOUNDATION
FOR ARTS & CULTURE
財團法人耿藝術文化基金會

Queens Museum is supported in part by funds from the New York City Department of Cultural Affairs and New York State Council on the Arts with the support of Governor Andrew Cuomo and the New York State Legislature.

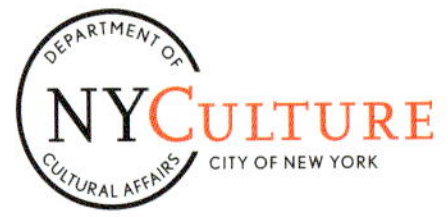

Co-published by
Queens Museum
New York City Building
Flushing Meadows Corona Park
Queens, New York 11368

and

Duke University Press
Durham, North Carolina, and London

Distributed by Duke University Press

ISBN 978-0-8223-6025-4 (cloth)
ISBN 978-0-8223-6042-1 (paperback)
Library of Congress Cataloging-in-Publication Data
Lee, Luchia Meihua and Silbergeld, Jerome
Zhang Hongtu: Expanding Visions of a Shrinking World/Luchia Meihua Lee and Jerome Silbergeld
With contributions by Jerome Silbergeld, Wu Hung, et alia

Includes bibliographical references and index.

Editors: Luchia Meihua Lee and Jerome Silbergeld
Copy editor: Nell McClister
Proofreaders: Nell McClister, Kenneth E. Howell
Publication Director: Shelly Wu
Production management: Catherine Y. Hsieh, TKG Foundation for Arts & Culture, Taipei, Taiwan
Design: Lin Xiao-Yi Design Studio
Printing: Shen's Art Printing Co., Ltd
Printed and bound in Taipei, Taiwan on acid-free paper